3,7
homework

PASCAL

PASCAL

Samuel L. Marateck

Courant Institute of Mathematical Sciences,
New York University

John Wiley & Sons, Inc.

New York   Chichester   Brisbane   Toronto   Singapore

To my mother, Rita
and the loving memory of my father Harold Marateck

Cover photo by George Cserna.

"Solving a Problem", problems 12, 18, 19 and project 5, from BASIC 3/E by Samuel Marateck copyright © 1986 by Harcourt, Brace, Jovanovich Inc., reprinted by permission of the publisher.

Recognizing the importance of preserving what has been written, it is a policy of John Wiley & Sons, Inc. to have books of enduring value published in the United States printed on acid-free paper, and we exert our best efforts to that end.

Library of Congress Cataloging in Publication Data: Marateck, Samuel L.

Marateck, Samuel L.
   Pascal / Samuel L. Marateck.
     p. cm.
   Includes bibliographical references.
   ISBN 0-471-60546-8
   1. Pascal (Computer program language) I. Title.
  QA76.73.P2M335 1991
  005.26'2—dc20   90-40175
                                   CIP

Printed in the United States of America

10 9 8 7 6 5 4 3 2 1

PREFACE

This book is an outgrowth of the notes I have used teaching an introduction to computer science course using Pascal—i.e., CS I. It is written for students who have no prior knowledge of computers or programming. The book comes in two versions, this volume discusses Standard Pascal, and a companion volume discusses Turbo Pascal.

The design of the book has special significance and deserves comment. The right-hand pages contain programming material (programs, output, and tables) which most students will readily understand; this is described in detail in "To The Reader." The left-hand pages contain explanatory text. Because of the length of the programs in the book, it has not always been possible to strictly adhere to this design, therefore, occasionally a self-test question will appear on a right-hand page. It has been my experience, with books on Fortran 77 and Basic I wrote and designed the same way, that students who have used a terminal without having previously gone to class and who have studied only the right-hand pages have been able to write and successfully run programs at their first session at the terminal. Of course, students should also read the text on the left-hand pages, to understand all facets of the programming technique described.

The easiest way for students to learn program design is to see as many examples as possible. With this in mind, we start presenting examples of programming design as early as Chapter 2. Moreover, as the text progresses, we present different programming planning techniques ranging from top-down design and stepwise refinement of pseudocode, to the bottom-up approach and including the divide and conquer, exhaustive search, induction and solution by analogy approaches. The tool box approach (in which general utility modules are developed; see Chapter 9) is also used to write some of the longer programs. For most of the longer programs, we use stepwise refinement not only of the pseudocode, but of the programs themselves. We used this approach with two things in mind: Just as it is easier to write a complicated program in stages, it is also easier to understand one written this way. Also, representing already written modules only by the procedure heading allowed us to fit most of the longer programs on one page. Thus, the student not only sees a pragmatic strategy for writing lengthy programs, but also has an easier time of assimilating the material. But isn't that one of the reasons for using procedures and functions in the first place?

An approach unique to this text is the discussion of the input buffer to explain the intricacies of input/output (see Chapter 4). This also allows us to take the mystery out of the workings of the eof and eoln functions (see Chapter 8). Another technique students find interesting is the reappearance of a given topic throughout the course of the book. With each subsequent appearance, a more sophisticated technique is used to write the program. One such topic that appears as a *leit motif* throughout the book is the writing of a calculator, starting in Chapter 7 with the appearance of a program that simply evaluates a three-character expression, and ending in Chapter 18 with a program that uses a tree to evaluate expressions that are fully parenthesized.

The programming part of the book starts in Chapter 2 with the introduction of pseudocode. We used this as an opportunity to introduce some of Pascal syntax so that the student early on becomes accustomed to where and why semicolons and the BEGIN and END delimiters are used. This also allows us to introduce procedures and top-down design at this early stage. It is an alternative approach to that of Richard Pattis in his book *Karel the Robot*.

Chapter 3 covers the basics of Pascal programming and applies the principles of the previous chapter to program design; Chapter 4 deals with input/output and concludes with a discussion of I/O using the buffer. Chapter 5 offers a consistent treatment of FOR loops for all types of variables so that the similarities in the different loops are revealed. We chose to discuss the FOR loop before the WHILE because of the inherent pitfalls in the latter due to infinite loops. Armed now with statements that allow us to write non-trivial programs, in Chapter 6 we give a detailed view of procedures and the implementation of top-down design. As we learn the different facets of the IF—THEN—ELSE and boolean operators in Chapter 6, we develop a word processing program and use stubs to design a program that converts strings of digits into integers. Chapter 7 rounds off our study of loops with a study of the WHILE and REPEAT—UNTIL loops. We use the bottom-up paradigm to design a two-dimensional random walk program. The chapter concludes with text files, so that from here on, we can write our data as files. Chapter 8, which describes functions, finishes our study of subprograms and concludes with the design and implementation of an elementary calculator. Chapter 9 formally introduces the concept of data structures in discussing arrays. We use the tool box approach here to design and implement a program that determines the frequency of letters in a sentence. The next logical step after learning arrays is to study an application of arrays—strings.

Chapter 10 begins by presenting the standard equivalents of the Turbo Pascal string functions and procedures and ends up by using them to design a global search and replace program. Chapter 11 uses one of the unique facets of Pascal—the user-defined type to write calendar programs and a program that generates Roman numerals—and concludes with the writing of a problem we first introduced in Chapter 2 and have intermittently discussed until now. Chapter 12 plans and implements a table look-up program. Chapter 13, on records, discusses many programs, one of which forms an index of words used in a paragraph. In writing this program we see that the bubble sort is stable, whereas the selection sort is not.

Chapter 14 reviews text files and covers binary files. It uses a binary file for a program that simulates a card-playing program. Chapter 15 gives a thorough introduction to recursion using a unique approach. Each time a subprogram is recursively activated, a copy of the subprogram and the stack is shown. These copies are connected so that you can trace the recursion. You will see the advantage of using this technique when you read the chapter.

The material in Chapters 17 and 18 deals with dynamic pointers. These chapters cover linked lists, stacks, trees, and queues as completely as they are treated in the CS II course.

It is a pleasure to thank Professor Max Goldstein for making available to me all the equipment of the Courant Institute Academic Computer Facility and, as always, to thank Professor Jacob T. Schwartz and Professor Goldstein for their friendship and constant support. I offer my thanks to my friends and colleagues, Professor Marsha Berger and Dr. David McQueen, for useful discussions, and a special thank you to Dr. Jeffery H. Gordon; to Professors Martin Davis, Ralph Grishman, and Olaf Widlund, on whose watch as chairmen I taught Pascal; to Professor Robert Dewar, for making available to me a copy of his screen editor DVED; to Gary Rosenblum, for his help in printing the manuscript in near camera-ready form in order to ease the reviewers' task; and to Lorenza Prignano, for taking notes on my original lectures.

Thanks go to my good friend Eugene Rodolphe for reviewing the original draft of the manuscript. I am also indebted to the following professors for reviewing either the Pascal or the Turbo Pascal manuscript: George Beekman and John Bertani, Oregon State University; C. Mark Bilodeau, United States Military Academy, West Point; Larry Crockett, Augsberg College; Amrik Dhillon, Borland International; Henry Etlinger, Rochester Institute of Technology; Charles E. Frank, Northern Kentucky University; Dale Grosvenor, Iowa State University; Taylor D. Hanna, Portland Area Community College; Herbert Koller, San Francisco University; Rose M. Laird, Northern Virginia Community College; Phyllis Lefton, Manhattanville College; Lewis Miller, Cañada College; Benedict Pollina, University of Hartford; Catherine Riccardo, Iona College; Robert G. Reynolds, Wayne State; Waldo Roth, Taylor University; Patricia Sterr, Joliet Junior College; and Delaine Timney, University of South Carolina. I am particularly indebted to Professors Bertani, Koller, Riccardo, and Sterr for invaluable phone conversations.

Samuel L. Marateck

TO THE READER

This book has been written on the premise that it is at times easier to learn a subject from pictorial representations supported by text than from text supported by pictorial representations. With this in mind, in Chapters 3–14 we have used a double-page format for our presentation. On the left-hand page (we call it the text page) appears the text, and on the right-hand page (we call it the picture page) appears the pictorial representation, consisting mostly of programs and tables.

Each picture page was written to be as self-contained as possible, so that readers (if they so desire) may read that page first and absorb the essence of the contents of the entire double page before going on to read the text. The text page consists of a very thorough discussion of the programming techniques presented on the picture page. It refers to parts of the programs and tables on the picture page; when reference is made on the text page to a given line of print on the picture page, that line—whenever it is feasible to do so—is reproduced in the text to promote readability. Students with a previous background in programming languages and others who understand the picture page completely may find that in some chapters they can skip the text (left-hand) pages and concentrate on the picture pages.

The following techniques are used as aids in making the picture page self-contained:

1. As many as possible of the ideas discussed in the text are illustrated in the programs and tables. The captions beneath these encapsulate much of what is said in the text.

2. Shaded words in the captions describe lines underlined in the figures. To illustrate this, a version of Figure 3.7a is reproduced below.

```
Salary 1: = 11.4;
Salary 2: = 20.2;
WriteIn (Salary1, Salary2)
```

FIGURE 3.7a.   In the program, the number 11.4 is assigned to the variable Salary 1 and 20.2 to Salary 2 in the assignment statement

The statements Salary 1: = 11.4; and Salary 2: = 20.2 are shaded to show that they are described by the words shaded in the caption. Thus they are both assignment statements.

3. To the right of most programs appears a table describing what effect certain statements in the program have on the computer's memory. For instance, the following table describes the effect that Salary1: = 11.4 has on the memory:

Description	Salary 1
Salary 1: = 11.4;	11.4

We see from the table that this statement caused the value 11.4 to be associated with Salary 1 in the computer's memory. The line-by-line analysis afforded by these tables should help the reader understand the program.

CONTENTS

3

AN INTRODUCTION TO PASCAL / 21

4

READING AND WRITING AND BUFFERING / 79

5

THE FOR–DO LOOP AND THE ORDINAL TYPES / 115

6

PROCEDURES AND TOP-DOWN DESIGN / 179

7

THE IF–THEN–ELSE AND CASE STATEMENTS; MORE ON PROGRAM DESIGN: PROGRAMMING BY STAGES AND TOP-DOWN TESTING / 225

8

THE WHILE AND REPEAT LOOPS, BOTTOM-UP DESIGN, THE
EOLN AND EOF FUNCTIONS, AND TEXT FILES / 287

9

FUNCTIONS / 357

10

ARRAYS; PROGRAMMING BY STAGES / 397

11

STRING PROCEDURES AND FUNCTIONS / 449

12

USER-ENUMERATED TYPES / 487

13

MULTIDIMENSIONAL ARRAYS / 513

14

RECORDS / 565

15

FILES AND SETS / 639

16

RECURSION / 681

17

POINTERS AND DYNAMIC STORAGE / 715

18

TREES AND QUEUES / 765

1

GETTING ACQUAINTED WITH COMPUTERS

CHAPTER OVERVIEW

Have you ever heard terms describing parts of a computer or operations that a computer performs and didn't know what they meant? This chapter gives an overview first of the computer's operations and then of its components.

1.1

GENERAL REMARKS

Those of you who have had little experience with computers may think of them as machines that produce your phone bills or predict the outcome of political elections. Certainly computers do this—and more. A computer is not a machine that does things of its own volition, however. At their present stage of development, computers can only follow sets of instructions that people give them. These sets of instructions are called *programs,* and the people who write them are called *programmers.*

The form that these instructions take depends on the programming language the programmer uses. The purpose of this book is to teach you

1.   How to formulate a problem so that it is amenable to computer solution.

2.   How to write programs in Pascal, one of the best languages for translating problems to the proper program form.

Pascal was devised by Niklaus Wirth in the early 1970s. He named it after the seventeenth-century French mathematician Blaise Pascal. The strength of the language is the ease with which the programmer can go from the correct formulation of a problem to writing the program that is the solution to the problem. Once you have set up the problem correctly and understand how to write programs in Pascal, you will be able to translate your problem to Pascal with relative ease. First, however, we'll make a few comments on computers and on programming languages in general.

One way of picturing a computer is as a vast collection of on–off electrical switches connected by wires. Thus, you might imagine a program as a series of on–off types of instructions. In fact, the first programs written were like this. The type of language that uses this form of instruction is called *machine language,* and it is still used today by certain programmers. In its most primitive form, a program written in machine language consists of strings of 0s and 1s, where a 0 represents an open switch and a 1 a closed switch, and is thus directly understandable by the computer. The 0s and 1s are called *binary digits,* abbreviated as *bits;* a group of eight bits is called a *byte.* When a number is represented with binary digits, it is called a *binary number.*

Writing programs in machine language can be very tedious. Therefore a language called *assembly language* was devised in which mnemonics for the different machine language instructions are used. For instance, SUB would be the assembly instruction for subtraction. Although writing programs in assembly language is easier than writing them in machine language, it is still difficult. Consequently, computer languages closer in form to English and algebra have been created. One of these languages is Pascal.

Computer languages that mirror the binary operations performed by the computer are called *low-level* languages. Machine language is an example of a low-level language. On the other hand, computer languages like Pascal that resemble the way we express ourselves are called *high-level* languages.

1.2

COMPILATION AND EXECUTION OF A PROGRAM

A program written in Pascal cannot be directly understood by the computer; it must first be translated into machine language. A program called a *compiler* does this. Since each make of computer requires a different machine language, Pascal compilers vary from one computer to another. However, the Pascal compilers on most larger computers accept programs written in accordance with the American National Standards Institute/Institute for Electrical and Electronics Engineers (ANSI/IEEE) standard. This book* describes the version of Pascal described by this standard.

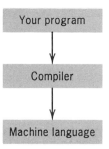

Pascal has grammatical rules that must be followed by the programmer. These rules, which we will learn in later chapters, are similar to the rules of English that govern word sequence, punctuation, and spelling. Before the compiler translates your program, it checks whether you have written your program instructions according to the grammatical rules used in Pascal. These rules are called the *syntax* of the language; thus grammatical errors are called *syntax errors.* If you make syntax errors, don't worry; the compiler will inform you where these errors are located in your program. You must correct the syntax errors and run the program through the compiler again so that it will translate the program.

Once you have successfully compiled your program, instruct the computer to follow the steps in your program. This process is called *running* or *executing* a program. The fact that your program has successfully compiled does not mean that it will run correctly (you may have made an error in the logical flow of the program). An error that occurs during execution is called an *execution* or *run-time* error.

*A companion volume describes Turbo Pascal, a version of Pascal written for desktop computers.

Some of your programs will require external information called *data.* For instance, if your program computes the average of all the grades in a class, you will have to supply all the grades as data to the program.

1.3

THE COMPUTER—MAINFRAMES AND MICROCOMPUTERS

BEFORE YOU BEGIN

> The following discussion is meant to familiarize you with the computer's components and operation. It is not essential that you master all the terms used and concepts explained here. However, you will encounter them later on in your computer career. So our advice is to read the rest of the material in this chapter as if you were reading a newspaper article. If you can't remember some of the definitions, don't worry.

The word *hardware* describes the physical components of the computer, whereas the word *software* describes the programs such as the compiler. Now let's take a more detailed look at the computer and its component hardware.

The computer consists of an *input unit,* a *memory unit,* an *arithmetic/logic unit (ALU),* an *output unit,* and a *control unit.* We communicate our program and data—the information the program processes—to the computer through the input unit. All the mathematics and decisions in the program are done in the ALU. The program and the information it uses are stored in the computer's memory, which consists of a multitude of memory locations. The computer communicates the results of our program to us through the output unit. Finally, the control unit directs the activities of the other units. The control unit and the ALU are referred to collectively as the *central processing unit (CPU).* This is the part of the computer that executes the program.

A device called a *bus* interconnects all the components of the computer, as shown in Figure 1.1. The bus serves the same purpose that the spinal cord does when it transmits neuron impulses: It passes electrical impulses from one part of the computer to another.

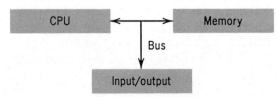

FIGURE 1.1　The bus connects all the components of the computer electrically.

FIGURE 1.2   The IBM PS/2 Model 30 microcomputer.

Medium-sized and large computers—the types that you would not want to pick up— are called *mainframes.* The smaller computers, the ones that fit on desktops, are appropriately called *desktop computers* or *microcomputers.*

Microcomputers

A microcomputer is a computer that uses a CPU miniaturized on a silicon chip called a *microprocessor.* A chip is typically a fraction of an inch long. For more information on the guts of the computer, see Appendix A.

One of the microcomputers manufactured by IBM is shown in Figure 1.2, and the Apple Macintosh is shown in Figure 1.3.

1.4

THE MEMORY

Since the memory is the part of the computer that stores information, let's investigate it. Each memory location is called a *word* and consists of a group of bits. The number of bits in a word depends on the computer you use. Some mainframes have 32 bits in a word, others have 64, and still others have another

Monitor

System unit

Disk drive

Keyboard

FIGURE 1.3   Photo of a Macintosh computer.

number, but the number of bits is always a multiple of 2. Microcomputers have either 8 or 16 bits in a word. When you run a program and instruct the computer to store a number in a location, it will set the bits so that they represent the number. If, later on in the program, you want to store a different number, the computer resets the bits so that they now represent the new number.

1.5

INPUT/OUTPUT DEVICES

Those of you who will be programming on a mainframe will be using a terminal as both an input and an output device. The most popular type of terminal is a television-like screen called a *monitor,* combined with a typewriter-like keyboard, as shown in Figure 1.4. The terminal is usually connected to the computer by an electrical cable. When you type a program on the terminal, the computer receives the program and is able to communicate the results on the terminal.

FIGURE 1.4   The IBM 3151 ASCII display station.

Although what you type appears on a line of the screen, the line is not sent to the computer until you hit the RETURN key. A spot on the screen called the *cursor* indicates where the next character typed will appear.

The Modem

Besides cable, another way of transmitting and receiving data and programs between a terminal and a mainframe, or between your microcomputer and the mainframe, or between two microcomputers is via a telephone line. A device called a *modem* converts the sending device's electrical impulses to a high-frequency sound wave (audio wave) that can be carried over the phone line; this process is called *modulating.* A modem at the other end of the line converts the sound wave to electrical impulses that can be understood by the receiving device; this process is called *demodulating.* The word *modem* derives from the fact that this device must transmit these impulses back and forth. It thus *mod*ulates and *dem*odulates.

If you connect a terminal in your home to a modem, once you call the phone number that will give you access to the computer's audio signal, you can communicate with the computer as if your terminal were connected to the computer with a cable.

The Line Printer

When you give the computer the proper instruction, the computer's output will be printed on a device called a *printer.* The part of the printer that touches the paper is called the *printing head.* A line printer is shown in Figure 1.5.

Secondary Storage Devices

There are devices that allow you to store information so that it is not erased when the computer is shut off. These are called *secondary storage devices.* One such device is called a *disk drive.* It contains a disk on which you can store information. A program or a set of data stored on the disk is called a *disk file.* You can both read information from and write information on a disk. When you shut off the computer, the information remains on the disk.

1.6

THE OPERATING SYSTEM

There is a master program called the *operating system* that manages the operation of all facets of the computer, including loading and running the programs, loading the compilers, and supervising the flow of data from the input devices to the CPU and from the CPU to the output devices. When you run your program, you will have to use a command dictated by the operating system in use. Since different types of computers use different operating systems, the command for executing a program will vary from computer to computer.

1.7

TIME SHARING AND BATCH MODE

On mainframes, a Pascal program can be run in what is called a *time-sharing* environment. As soon as the programmer compiles the program, the computer informs the programmer whether the program has compiled successfully. If there are syntax errors, the computer indicates what and where they are. Once the programmer corrects the syntax errors and runs the program, the computer produces the results immediately. Moreover, the programmer can write the program so that he or she can interact with the computer while the computer is running the program by entering values for the data required by the program.

The power of this system is that many programmers can communicate with the computer simultaneously and thus share a given amount of time on the computer—hence the term *time sharing.*

When programmers used cards on which they punched their programs, they submitted their programs as a batch of cards to be run by the computer operator. Hence this method of running programs was called *batch* mode.

FIGURE 1.5   The IBM 4245 line printer.

Today we use the term to describe the situation in which we submit our programs and data (usually to be run on a mainframe) and receive the output some time after the program has completely executed; the output usually appears on the printer.

NEW TERMS

arithmetic/logical unit (ALU)	compiler
assembly language	computer
batch	control unit
binary digit	cursor
bit	data
bus	desktop computer
byte	disk drive
central processing unit (CPU)	disk file

execute	modem
file	monitor
hardware	operating system
high-level language	output
input	printer
low-level language	program
machine language	secondary storage device
mainframe	software
memory unit	syntax
microcomputer	time sharing
microprocessor	word

2

PROGRAMMING PLANNING

CHAPTER OVERVIEW

Have you ever wondered whether there are alternatives to the haphazard way problems are usually solved in everyday life? Well, there are, and we'll show you one method of solving a problem step by step. In doing so, we'll write a description of the program that's the solution to the problem, using Pascal punctuation and grammar.

2.1

SOLVING A PROBLEM

The problem is to determine the regional distribution of people standing in line in a certain city. That is, we wish to determine how many people come from the north, south, east, and west sides of the city.

Let's begin by drawing on a piece of paper four boxes, which we label N, S, E, and W, as shown in Figure 2.1a. These letters represent north, south, east, and west, respectively. We shall keep a count in the appropriate box of the number of people in line from the different sections of the city.

The composition of the line is shown by the series of letters displayed across the top of each row of boxes in the figure. The fact that the first letter on the line is a W means that the first person on line comes from the west; the same type of correspondence applies to the rest of the line. The arrow indicates which person we are questioning. As we question each person and record his or her answer, the arrow will move one position to the right, indicating the next person to be questioned. Before reading the next paragraph, please study all of Figure 2.1.

To do the survey, first place a 0 in each of the four boxes, as shown in Figure 2.1a. This indicates that we have not yet begun questioning anyone. Next, ask the first person in line which part of the city he or she is from. Since the answer is "the west," record this by adding 1 to the 0 that is in the box marked W, obtaining 1. In order to record this result, erase the 0 that was originally in the box and replace it with 1. The box for the west now contains 1 and the rest of the boxes still contain 0, as shown in Figure 2.1b. Move the arrow to the second person and ask that person the same question. Since the answer is "the north," add 1 to the 0 in the box marked N, as shown in Figure 2.1c. When you advance the arrow and ask the third person the same question, the answer is "the west." Now add 1 to the 1 already in the box labeled W, obtaining 2. Erase the 1 already in the box and replace it with 2, as shown in Figure 2.1d. Continue this procedure until all the people on line have been questioned. The boxes then contain the numbers shown in Figure 2.1e.

BEFORE YOU BEGIN

Why have we chosen this problem to study instead of, for instance, a simple averaging problem or a set of instructions describing how to change tires on a car? The answer is that this survey problem teaches us some important yet easy-to-understand concepts about programming.

1. The function of the boxes—that is, to store the numbers—is performed by the computer's memory locations. Like the boxes, a memory location can store only one number at a time; moreover, when the computer places a new number in a memory location, it automatically erases the old number that was there.

2. The people standing on line correspond to the data for the program. We would type the data as the capital letters that comprise the line shown in Figure 2.1. This group of letters would be stored in a series of locations called the *input buffer*, where something like the arrow shown in the figure would indicate the next letter to be processed. As each letter is processed, the arrow moves to the next letter. We will see in later chapters that understanding the operation of the buffer will help us unravel some of the mysteries of Pascal.

Now let's see how we would plan the program to perform this survey.

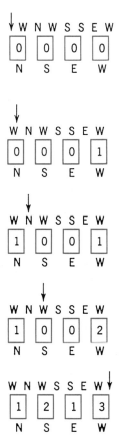

FIGURE 2.1*a*. The composition of the line and the contents of the boxes before questioning begins. The arrow is at the left of the line, indicating that the questioning has not begun.

FIGURE 2.1*b*. We add 1 to the box for west after questioning the first person.

FIGURE 2.1*c*. We add 1 to the box for north after questioning the second person.

FIGURE 2.1*d*. We add 1 to the box for west after questioning the third person. The box now contains 2.

FIGURE 2.1*e*. The contents of all the boxes after we have questioned everyone on line.

2.2

PSEUDOCODE

In order to show someone how to conduct the survey discussed in the previous section, you would have to write a set of instructions for him or her to follow. In computer science, a set of instructions written to solve a problem (in a finite number of steps) is called an *algorithm,* and in a programming language, each instruction is called a *statement.* Assuming that the boxes have already been drawn, a reasonable algorithm for performing the survey in which our line consists of, for instance, three people is:

> Tell people to stand in a line.
>
> Place a 0 in each box.
>
> Question the next person.
>
> Add 1 to the appropriate box.
>
> Question the next person.
>
> Add 1 to the appropriate box.
>
> Question the next person.
>
> Add 1 to the appropriate box.
>
> Print the contents of each box.

Since you'll be writing algorithms to help plan your Pascal programs, it is easier to write them using statements that are similar to their Pascal equivalents. When the algorithm is written this way, it is called *pseudocode.* However, when you write pseudocode, you can use any form for a statement; consequently, pseudocode is more flexible than programming code. For instance, one way of writing our algorithm is:

> PROGRAM *Survey;*
>
> BEGIN
>
>   *Tell people to stand in a line;*
>
>   *Place a 0 in each box;*
>
>   *Question the next person;*
>
>   *Add 1 to the appropriate box;*
>
>   *Question the next person;*
>
>   *Add 1 to the appropriate box;*
>
>   *Question the next person;*
>
>   *Add 1 to the appropriate box;*
>
>   *Print the contents of each box*
>
> END .

Since a statement in pseudocode could spill over to the next line, we'll begin the first word in every statement with a capital letter for the sake of clarity.

BEFORE YOU PROCEED

Since we're learning pseudocode, let's use it to learn some of the basics of Pascal syntax and program planning. Why? Because it will ease the transition to the writing of the actual Pascal program. Those words in pseudocode that are the same as the ones used in Pascal will be capitalized and set in computer type; those that are not will be set in italics. If you don't understand the syntax requirements we describe here, don't worry. We'll explain them again in subsequent chapters. **Remember the method described here is not the only way to write pseudocode; you can write it any way that is easiest for you.**

In Pascal a group of statements sandwiched between a BEGIN and an END is called a *compound statement.* For example, what follows PROGRAM *Survey;* in our pseudocode is a compound statement. Indent the statements in a compound statement to make them easier for the reader to spot.

The similarity between our pseudocode and a Pascal program is as follows:

1. As in Pascal, the pseudocode begins with the word PROGRAM, which is immediately followed by a program name, in our case *Survey.* The words PROGRAM *Survey* comprise the *program heading.* The program heading must end with a semicolon.

2. The compound statement that follows the programming heading is called the *statement part* of the program. As we just remarked, it begins with the word BEGIN and ends with the word END, which is followed by a period. BEGIN and END are not considered statements.

3. Each statement or compound statement is separated from the next statement or compound statement by a semicolon. Examples of statements we have used so far are *Question the next person, Add 1 to the appropriate box,* and *Print the contents of each box.* Since END is not considered a statement, the previous statement, *Print the results,* does not end with a semicolon.

2.3

TOP-DOWN DESIGN AND STEPWISE REFINEMENT

Stepwise Refinement

Although we have not stated it yet, we are designing our program as a series of stages of development of the pseudocode such that the more difficult aspects of the program are left for the later stages. For example, we have not specified how we will question the next person or how we will add 1 to the appropriate box. *Stepwise refinement* is the term for this technique. Using this technique makes it easier to write both the initial stages of the pseudocode and the ultimate program. Now that we have some sense of the syntax of the Pascal program that will eventually be derived from the pseudocode, let's backtrack for a moment and plan the problem from the beginning, using stepwise refinement.

We could have written the first version of the pseudocode for our problem as

Conduct the Survey

One of many possible next steps in the refinement of the pseudocode could have been to expand the pseudocode to

Tell people to stand in a line;

Place a zero in each box;

Question the three people on line and record the results;

Print the results.

For future reference, let's assign the following shorthand names to these four statements, respectively: *Prompt, ZeroBox, AskandRecord,* and *Print-Results.*

The next step would be to refine *Question the three people on line and record the results* to

Question the next person;

Add 1 to the appropriate box;

Question the next person;

Add 1 to the appropriate box;

Question the next person;

Add 1 to the appropriate box;

and refine *Print the results* to *Print the contents of each box.*

Assembling all of this, we get the pseudocode of the previous section:

PROGRAM *Survey;*

BEGIN

Tell people to stand in a line;

Place a 0 in each box;

Question the next person;

Add 1 to the appropriate box;

Question the next person;

Add 1 to the appropriate box;

Question the next person;

Add 1 to the appropriate box;

Print the contents of each box

END .

Again for future reference, we will assign the name *Question* to *Question the next person* and *Add* to *Add 1 to the appropriate box.*

Top-Down Design

Remember that the second stage in the development of the pseudocode was

> *Tell people to stand in a line;*
> *Place a zero in each box;*
> *Question the three people on line and record the results;*
> *Print the results.*

If we want to, we can use the shorthand names to rewrite this stage as follows:

> PROGRAM *Survey;*
> BEGIN
>   *Prompt;*
>   *ZeroBox;*
>   *AskandRecord;*
>   *PrintResults*
> END.

Another way of looking at this is diagrammatically:

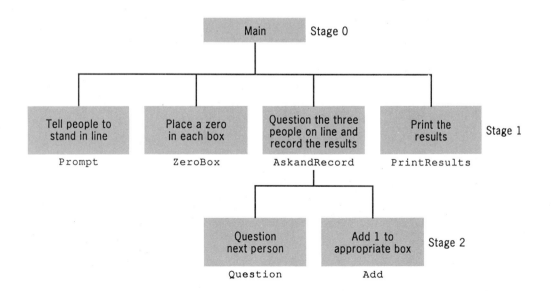

Here each rectangle contains a description of the task to be done and is labeled by the shorthand name we assigned these tasks. Since *Question* and *Add* are the tasks representing the refinement of *AskAndRecord*, we draw lines connecting them to *AskAndRecord* in the diagram. If a task described by a rectangle is repeated in the pseudocode (as *Question the next person* is), we do not repeat the rectangle in the diagram.

This diagram describes what is called *top-down* design, since the top of the diagram (stage 0) is the initial formulation of the problem and the lower line (or lines) represents successive refinements. The top-down approach facilitates division of the entire program into smaller do-able miniprograms called *subprograms;* here the subprogram names are *Prompt, ZeroBox, AskandRecord,* and *PrintResults.* Note that *stepwise refinement,* on the other hand, is the term used to describe the development of the different stages in the refinement of the pseudocode. Since the distinction between these two terms is a fine one, they are often used interchangeably.

The subprograms in a given stage of the diagram should be effectively independent of each other and should not refer to each other. For instance, *Prompt* performs one task and *PrintResults* performs another. The process of writing the subprograms in this way is called *modularization,* and the subprograms are called *modules.*

In a given stage, however, one module can depend on the action of other modules in the same stage. For instance, *PrintResults* can't be performed unless the other modules in the same stage are performed first.

2.4

COMMENTS

Someone reading your pseudocode or program can understand more easily what you have written if you insert comments in the code describing what's happening, and insert blank lines between the different parts of the program to underscore the fact that they are indeed different. Both comments and blank lines are ignored by the compiler.

Since in Pascal anything sandwiched between a "(*" and a "*)" is considered a comment, we will use these symbols to indicate comments in the pseudocode as well. Let's now add comments and blank lines to our pseudocode. We obtain

```
PROGRAM Survey;
(* Performs a survey and record the results. *)
BEGIN
    Tell people to stand in a line;

    Place a 0 in each box;

    (* Question everyone and record their answers *)
    Question the next person;
    Add 1 to the appropriate box;
    Question the next person;
    Add 1 to the appropriate box;
    Question the next person;
    Add 1 to the appropriate box;

    Print the contents of each box
END.
```

PROGRAMMING STYLE

Some programmers like to comment their program with the pseudocode they used to write it.

2.5

LOOPS

When a statement or a group of statements are repeated, for example, as in

> Question the next person;
> Add 1 to the appropriate box;
> Question the next person;
> Add 1 to the appropriate box;
> Question the next person;
> Add 1 to the appropriate box;

we can make the pseudocode (or program) more compact and the resulting program more efficient by using what is called a *loop*. When the computer executes the type of loop we describe now, it repeatedly executes the statements in the loop until some condition is satisfied. Thus in

REPEAT
>   *Question the next person;*
>   *Add 1 to the appropriate box*
UNTIL *everyone is questioned;*

Question the next person and *Add 1 to the appropriate box* are executed until everyone is questioned. Then the statement following UNTIL *everyone is questioned* is executed. As you might expect, this type of loop is called a REPEAT loop. The pseudocode for the entire program is now

PROGRAM *Survey;*
(* Perform a survey for an indefinite number of people *)
BEGIN
>   *Tell people to stand in a line;*

>   *Place a 0 in each box;*

>   *(* Question everyone and record their answers *)*
>   REPEAT
>   *Question the next person;*
>   *Add 1 to the appropriate box*
>   UNTIL *everyone is questioned;*

>   *Print the contents of each box*
END .

NEW TERMS

algorithm	prompt
comment	pseudocode
compound statement	statement
input buffer	statement part
loop	stepwise refinement
modularization	subprogram
modules	top-down design
program heading	

3
AN INTRODUCTION
TO PASCAL

CHAPTER OVERVIEW

Now that you have some idea of programming planning, you're ready for some of the basics of Pascal. Therefore we introduce the concepts of writing results on the printer or terminal screen; reading simple data sets from the keyboard; and performing mathematical operations on them.

3.1

THE SHORTEST PASCAL PROGRAM

Before you can apply the principles of programming planning presented in the last chapter, you have to learn the fundamentals of the Pascal language. Let's start by examining Figure 3.1, the shortest Pascal program that can be written. All Pascal programs must begin with what is called the *program heading.* This starts with the word *program* and is followed by one or more blanks and then by the program name, which is called the *program identifier.* Here the program identifier is *Null.* The program heading must end with a semicolon. Thus we write PROGRAM Null;.

The part of the program that performs different tasks is called the *statement part;* it begins with the word *begin* and ends with the word *end,* followed by a period. Since BEGIN and END define the extent of the statement part, they are called *delimiters.* Because our first program does not contain any tasks, it appears as shown in Figure 3.1. It makes no difference to the compiler whether or not uppercase* or lowercase letters are used in writing the program.

*We will explain why we write some words in uppercase later on in the chapter.

THE SHORTEST PROGRAM WE CAN WRITE

```
PROGRAM Null;
BEGIN
END.
```

FIGURE 3.1.   A program consists of *a program heading,* followed by a compound statement called the *statement part,* and ends with a period. This statement part contains no statements, just the delimiters BEGIN and END.

3.2

THE WRITE STATEMENT

BEFORE YOU BEGIN

At this point, you may wonder how the program communicates any results with the outside world. The write statement is one way it does this.

Figure 3.2*a* shows a program that will print some words on the terminal screen. Whenever a program produces output and/or requires input, an extra entry containing the word *input* and/or *output* must be made in the program heading. This entry is parenthesized and concludes the heading. Since our program produces output, we write

PROGRAM First(output);

where First is the program's name.
    The statement

write('This is our first example of output.')

appears in the statement part and instructs the computer to print what appears between the single quotation marks, here

This is our first example of output.

on the screen, as shown in Figure 3.2*b*, when the program is run. The instruction that does this is called the write statement. What appears between the single quotation marks (', the lower symbol on the " key) is called a *string constant.* On the other hand, comments to the reader are sandwiched between "(*" and "*)" and are ignored by the compiler.
    We've written the heading, the delimiters, and the statement, each on a separate line, and have indented the statement so that the program is easier to read. If you want, you could write the program on one line, as shown in Figure 3.2*c*:

PROGRAM First(output); BEGIN write('This is our first example of output.') End.

However, the program would have been much more difficult to read and understand.

USING THE WRITE STATEMENT

```
PROGRAM First(output);
(* Demonstrates the use of write statement *)
BEGIN
  write('This is our first example of output.')
END.
```

FIGURE 3.2a. We place a write statement in the statement part. The write statement copies a string constant to the monitor screen or printer.

```
This is our first example of output.
```

FIGURE 3.2b. Running the program of Figure 3.2a. Since we used a write, the cursor remains on the same line when the computer finishes printing.

A POOR WAY OF WRITING A PROGRAM

```
PROGRAM First(output); BEGIN write('This is our first example of output.')END.
```

FIGURE 3.2c. We can write the entire program on one line, but it is difficult to read.

Now, some more programming. The next program, shown in Figure 3.3*a*, contains two statements:

```
write('My name');
write('is Ivan')
```

After a write statement is executed, the cursor remains where it was when it printed the last character. Thus, after the computer executes write('My name'), the cursor is one column to the right of the *e*. When the computer executes the next output statement, write ('is Ivan'), it prints the string constant is Ivan on the same line where My name was printed, continuing from where it stopped. The result is

```
My nameis Ivan
```

as shown in Figure 3.3*b*, when the program is run.

In order to separate *name* and *is*, we have to start the string constant in the second write statement with a blank, that is, insert a blank after the first quotation mark, typing

```
write(' is Ivan')
```

Pascal grammar dictates that two statements must be separated by a semi-colon. Thus we conclude the first of the two write statements with a semicolon.

Transferring information from the program to the output device is an example of one of many complex processes done internally by the compiler in what is called a *predefined procedure* or *standard procedure*. A *procedure*, loosely defined, is a separate group of statements that does a specific task. The write is an example of a standard procedure. The word *standard* is used here because these procedures are specified in the Pascal Standard, the official document that describes the language.

A TWO-STATEMENT PROGRAM

```
PROGRAM OneLine(output);
BEGIN
  write('My name');
  write('is Ivan')
END.
```

FIGURE 3.3a.   Since the first statement is a write, the second write produces its output on the same line as the first write does.

```
My nameis Ivan
```

FIGURE 3.3b.   Running the program of Figure 3.3a. Because the last character in the first string is an e and the first character in the second string is an i, the two strings are printed contiguously.

3.3

THE WRITELN STATEMENT

After the computer executes a `writeln` statement, it prints what is indicated and then the cursor goes to the beginning of the next line.*

Thus, in Figure 3.4a, after the computer executes `writeln('My name')` and prints My name, the cursor (or printing head) proceeds to the next line, and when it executes

```
writeln('is Ivan')
```

it prints *is Ivan* on that line

```
My name
is Ivan
```

as shown in Figure 3.4b.

The next program, shown in Figure 3.5a, contains both `write` and `writeln` statements:

```
write('My country tis');
write(' of thee');
writeln(' Sweet land of liberty');
write('Of thee I sing.')
```

The computer prints the strings in the first three statements on the same line, producing "My country tis of thee Sweet land of liberty," as shown in Figure 3.5a. Since the last of these three statements is a `writeln`, the cursor goes to the beginning of the next line, and the string in the next `write` statement is printed on the next line, as shown in Figure 3.5b.

---

*A more technical explanation is that after the computer executes a `writeln` statement, it performs a carriage return (moves the cursor to the beginning of the line) and a line feed (moves up the information on the screen one line vertically).

USING THE WRITELN STATEMENT

```
PROGRAM TwoLines(output);
BEGIN
  writeln('My name');
  writeln('is Ivan')
END.
```

FIGURE 3.4*a*.   After a writeln is executed, the next write or writeln produces its output starting at the beginning of the next line.

```
My name
is Ivan
```

FIGURE 3.4*b*.   The string in writeln('is Ivan') is printed on the line after the string in writeln('My name') is printed.

AN EXAMPLE OF WRITE AND WRITELN

```
PROGRAM test(output);
BEGIN
  write('My country tis');
  write(' of thee');
  writeln(' Sweet land of liberty');
  write ('Of thee I sing.')
END.
```

FIGURE 3.5*a*.   The writeln and all the preceding writes produce their output on one line.

```
My country tis of thee Sweet land of liberty
Of thee I sing.
```

FIGURE 3.5*b*.   Running the program of Figure 3.5*a*. After a writeln is executed, the cursor is positioned at the left of the next line.

3.4

AN INTRODUCTION TO INTEGER VALUES

Before we write more complicated programs, we'll have to become a bit more technical by describing the different forms of items that can be stored in memory.

The contents of a memory location is called a *value*. The first type of value we describe is called an *integer value*. It consists of a number that does not contain a decimal point and may or may not be preceded by a + or a − sign. Examples of integer values are 4, 456, −543, 0, and −98, as shown in Table 3.1.

If an integer value contains one or more of the following characters, it is illegal:

1. A decimal point (e.g., 45.6).
2. A comma (e.g., 31,624).
3. A "+" or a "−" sign at the end of the value (e.g., 45+) (we have seen that an integer value can, however, start with a "+" or a "−").
4. Any other nonnumeric character (e.g., the "$" in $56).
5. A blank that follows one digit and precedes the next digit in the value (e.g., 45 67). A blank, such as the one appearing in this value, is called an *embedded blank*.

An illegal value will cause a syntax error during the program compilation. Examples of illegal integer values are 89−, 0.0, 12,345, and 345+. These illegal values and the reasons they are illegal are listed in Table 3.2.

Next, we'll see how to write a program that stores integers in memory.

TEST YOURSELF

QUESTION: What is produced by the following program?

```
PROGRAM Question1;
BEGIN
    write('One');
    write('Two');
    writeln('First');
    writeln('Second');
    writeln('Third');
END.
```

ANSWER:

```
OneTwoFirst
Second
Third
```

INTEGER VALUES

Examples of valid integer values

4	456	0
−543	−98	

TABLE 3.1. An integer value cannot contain a decimal point. It consists solely of digits (0, 1, 2, ... 9) and may be preceded by a minus or plus sign.

Examples of illegal integer values

Constant	Reason for illegality
89−	Ends with a minus sign
345+	Ends with a plus sign
2.34	Contains a decimal point
12,345	Contains a comma
12 345	Contains an embedded blank

TABLE 3.2. The appearance of the value 12,345 will cause an error.

3.5

USING VARIABLE IDENTIFIERS; THE ASSIGNMENT STATEMENT

Figure 3.6*a* demonstrates one way of storing integer values in memory locations. Before you store any values, you must list the names of the memory locations in what is called a VAR declaration. These names are called *variable identifiers* or simply *variables.* The VAR declaration precedes the statement part. In it you must declare what types of variables will be used. In

VAR Length, Width, Area: integer;

the variables are Length, Width, and Area. They form what is called a *list.* One or more blanks must separate VAR from the list. The list is followed by a colon and then by the type—here, integer—that describes the variables in the list. Since we are storing integer values, we store them in locations named by integer variables. The VAR declaration concludes with a semicolon. In contrast to other languages, since you must specify the type of each variable used in your program in Pascal, it is called a *strongly typed* language. In addition to the integer type, in this chapter we'll learn about the real, character, and boolean types.

Now let's see how to store the integer values. We do it in the statement part of the program, as shown in Figure 3.6*a*, by placing integer values in the locations named in the VAR statement. The statements that do this are called *assignment statements.* In the first assignment statement, the integer value 152 is placed in the integer location called Length

Length: = 152;

One way of describing this is by saying that Length gets 152. An assignment statement begins with a variable—here, the integer variable Length. This is followed by the symbol for gets, ": =", and then by what you want to place in the location named by the variable—here, 152. The other assignment statements used in the program are

Width: = 32;
Area: = Length * Width;

USING INTEGER VARIABLE IDENTIFIERS

```
PROGRAM Storing(output);
(* Demonstrates use of variables *)
VAR Length, Width, Area: integer;
BEGIN
  Length:= 152;
  Width:= 32;
  Area:= Length * Width;
  writeln('Length= ', Length, ' Width= ', Width, ' Area= ', Area)
END.
```

FIGURE 3.6a.   One way to store a value in a memory location is to use an assignment statement. The names of the locations (variables) must be declared in the VAR declaration.

How the assignments are made is shown in the table for Figure 3.6*a*. The first line

Statement	Length	Width	Area
Length: = 152	152	Undef	Undef

shows that although `Length` has been assigned a value, `Width` and `Area` have not been assigned values; they are thus undefined (we use the abbreviation *Undef* here). The second line shows that the computer remembers what has been stored in `Length` and that it stores 32 in `Width`:

Statement	Length	Width	Area
Width: = 32	152	32	Undef

The statement `Area: = Length * Width` uses the Pascal symbol for multiplication, "*". It instructs the computer to take the value stored in `Length`, multiply it by the value stored in `Width`, and assign the result to the location, `Area`, as shown in the third line of the table:

Statement	Length	Width	Area
Area: = Length * Width	152	32	4864

As usual, each statement is separated from the next one by a semicolon.

The statement part ends with a `writeln` statement that prints the values of the variables assigned in the program, as well as the strings that describe them.

```
writeln( 'Length= ', Length, ' Width= ', Width, ' Area= ', Area)
```

When the program is run, as shown in Figure 3.6*b*,

```
Length=      152 Width=      32 Area=      4864
```

the string constants (Length=, Width=, Area=) are printed exactly as they appear in the `writeln` statement. The computer, however, does not print the characters in the identifiers following the string constants, namely `Length`, `Width`, and `Area`, because they are variables, not strings; rather, the computer prints the values (152, 32, 4864, respectively) of the variables.

Note that all the variables used in the `writeln` statement were given values earlier in the program, as shown in the last line of the table. If a variable that has not been assigned a value is used in an output statement (e.g., if in this program, `Volume` had been declared and not assigned a value, and then we wrote `writeln( Volume ))` the computer will print an unexpected number as its value.

USING INTEGER VARIABLE IDENTIFIERS (Continued)

```
PROGRAM Storing(output);
(* Demonstrates use of variables *)
VAR Length, Width, Area: integer;
BEGIN
  Length:= 152;
  Width:= 32;
  Area:= Length * Width;
  writeln('Length= ', Length, ' Width= ', Width, ' Area= ', Area)
END.
```

FIGURE 3.6a.   (Repeated)

Statement	Length	Width	Area
Length:= 152	152	Undef	Undef
Width:= 32	152	32	Undef
Area:= Length * Width	152	32	4864
writeln	152	32	4864

TABLE FOR FIGURE 3.6a.   The contents of each location are given at each statement during the execution. Values must be stored in Length and Width before the computer can calculate the value to be stored in Area. Before a value is stored in a location, the location's contents is given as "Undef"ined.

Length=   152 Width=   32 Area=   4864

FIGURE 3.6b.   Running the program of Figure 3.6a. When a variable appears in a writeln or write, its value is printed.

Also note that if it were not for the blanks in the beginning of the strings, for instance before the W in ' Width= ', no spaces would appear in the output between the numerical values and the strings following them. It would have appeared as

```
    Length=      152Width=      32Area=      4864
```

and would have been difficult to read.

Identifier Names

In order for the compiler to distinguish identifiers from other items in the program, there are rules that must be followed in forming them. Here they are.

Identifiers must begin with a letter, and can contain letters as well as digits. If the Pascal compiler you are using can accommodate lowercase letters as well as uppercase ones, you may use both in identifier names. Thus the compiler considers LENGTH and Length the same identifier. It is tempting to use an embedded blank to distinguish two words comprising an identifier, for instance New length; however, it is illegal. You can overcome this limitation by eliminating the blank and capitalizing the L, thus writing NewLength. Using the rules for forming an identifier, we see that Length1 and Interest are legal, whereas le ngth and 2Length are not. Table 3.3 shows examples of legal identifier names and Table 3.4 examples of illegal ones. The identifiers we have encountered so far are variable and program identifiers.

Some compilers recognize only the first eight characters in the identifier and ignore the rest. Thus they would consider LENGTHSnew and LENGTHSold the same identifier. In order to distinguish identifiers that have similar names, use the distinguishing characters first. Here write the identifiers as NewLENGTHS and OldLENGTHS instead.

FORMING IDENTIFIERS
(so far, we have encountered program and variable identifiers)

Examples of valid identifier names

Length	WIDTH1

TABLE 3.3. An identifier must begin with a letter. The rest of the characters may be either letters or digits.

Examples of illegal identifiers

Variable	Reason for illegality
2Length	Begins with a digit
AB*3	Contains a "*", an illegal character
Len gth	Contains an embedded blank

TABLE 3.4. If an identifier begins with a digit, contains an embedded blank, or a character that is neither a letter or a digit, it is an illegal identifier and will cause a syntax error.

The reason the identifiers listed in the VAR declaration are called *variable identifiers* is that their values can be changed in the program. For instance,

```
Length:= 10;
Area:= Length * Width;
writeln( 'Length=', Length, ' Width= ', Width, ' Area=', Area)
```

can be placed after the first writeln, as shown in Figure 3.6c, thereby assigning new values to Length and Area, as shown in the table for Figure 3.6c. A memory location can store only one value at a time, the value represented by the binary number in the location. Thus, when we assign the new value 10 to Length, the binary number is changed from it what was when Length stored 152. The value 152 is now lost. The value Area, however, is not changed until Area:= Length * Width is executed again, as we see from the table:

Statement	Length	Width	Area
Length:= 10	10	32	4864
Area:= Length * Width	10	32	320

The results of running the program are shown in Figure 3.6d.

ASSIGNING NEW VALUES TO VARIABLES

```
PROGRAM Storing(output);
(* Assigns new values to variables *)
VAR Length, Width, Area: integer;
BEGIN
  Length:= 152;
  Width:= 32;
  Area:= Length * Width;
  writeln( 'Length= ', Length, ' Width= ', Width, ' Area= ',Area);
  Length:= 10;
  Area:= Length * Width;
  writeln( 'Length=', Length, ' Width= ', Width, ' Area= ', Area)
END.
```

FIGURE 3.6c.   In Length := 10 a new value is assigned to Length.

Statement	Length	Width	Area
Length:= 152	152	Undef	Undef
Width:= 32	152	32	Undef
Area:= Length * Width	152	32	4864
writeln	152	32	4864
Length:= 10	10	32	4864
Area:= Length * Width	10	32	320
writeln	10	32	320

THE TABLE FOR FIGURE 3.6c.   When we assign a new value to Length, the value of Area is not changed until Area := Length * Width is executed.

```
Length=       152 Width=       32 Area=       4864
Length=       10 Width=       32 Area=       320
```

FIGURE 3.6d.   Running the program of Figure 3.6c. The second line of output shows the effect of assigning a new value to Length.

3.6

AN INTRODUCTION TO REAL, BOOLEAN, AND CHARACTER VALUES

Real Values

Another type of value is called a *real* value. The form that you'll use most often is a number that contains a decimal point. The number can begin with a "+" or "−" sign. Examples of real values are 6.0, −89.34, and 0.786 (see Table 3.5). Real and integer values are called *numerical values.*

If a real value contains one or more of the following, it is illegal:

1. A comma (e.g., 14,265.36).
2. A "+" or a "−" sign at the end of the value (a real value can, however, start with a "+" or a "−").
3. A decimal point at the beginning of the value (thus .1 is an illegal value, whereas 0.1 is legal) or at the end of the value (34. is an illegal value, whereas 34.0 is legal).
4. An embedded blank.
5. Any other nonnumeric character.*

An illegal value will cause a syntax error during program compilation. Examples of illegal real values are 45,458.09, .34, $23.00, and 67.45−. These and other illegal values and the reasons they are illegal are listed in Table 3.6.

Character and Boolean Values

There are two types of nonnumeric values you can use. The first is called a *character value;* it consists of a 1-character string constant. For example, a, A, 2, and $ are all valid character values and are shown in Table 3.7. Any displayable character, including a blank, can be used as a character value.

Examples of illegal character values are as, ABX, and 123. These illegal values and the reason they are illegal (they all contain more than one character) are listed in Table 3.8.

---

*At the end of this chapter, we'll discuss a form of the real value that contains an exponential part. This part is written with an E. A real value containing any nonnumeric character except an E is illegal.

REAL VALUES

Examples of valid real values

6.0	−89.34	0.786

TABLE 3.5.   The most commonly used real values contain a decimal point.

Examples of illegal real values

Constant	Reason for illegality
89−	Ends with a minus sign
$23.00	Contains a non-digit ($)
.34	Starts with a decimal point
34.	Ends with a decimal point
67.45−	Ends with a minus sign
23 4.5	Contains an embedded blank

TABLE 3.6.   The appearance of the value 89. in a program will cause a syntax error; write it as 89.0 instead.

CHARACTER VALUES

Examples of valid character values

'a'	'A'	'2'	'$'
' '			

TABLE 3.7.   A character value can contain only one character. When it is written in the program it must appear in single quotation marks. Note that '2' is a character value, whereas 2 is an integer value; also ' ' represents a blank.

Examples of illegal character values

Constant	Reason for illegality
'as'	All these values
'ABX'	contain more than one
'123'	character

TABLE 3.8.   If a value contains more than one character, it is illegal and will cause a syntax error.

The second type of nonnumeric value is called a *boolean* value. It has two values: the identifier `true` and the identifier `false`. These two values can be written in uppercase, lowercase, or a mixture of both, as shown in Table 3.9. Why do we use boolean values? One reason is that they facilitate the writing of programming loops.

3.7

USING REAL VARIABLE IDENTIFIERS

The next program, shown in Figure 3.7*a*, uses three real variables to represent three different salaries:

```
VAR Salary1, Salary2, Total: real;
```

Since the list is followed by `real`, the type of the variables in the list is real. We subsequently store real values in them:

```
Salary1: = 345.23;
Salary2: = 543.45;
Total: = Salary1 + Salary2;
```

The last assignment statement uses the Pascal symbol for addition, "+." This statement instructs the computer to take the value stored in `Salary1`, add it to the value stored in `Salary2`, and assign the result to the location, `Total`, as shown in the third line of the table for Figure 3.7a.

The results are written as

```
writeln('Salary Week1= $', Salary1,' Salary Week2= $ ', Salary2,
   '  Total Salary= $', Total)
```

where we have included a "$" in the string constant so that the salaries will be preceded by dollar signs. As shown here, a statement can be continued on another line; note, however, that a string constant cannot be continued on another line. Thus

```
writeln(' Give me liberty or give
   me death')
```

would produce an error indicating that the string constant exceeds the line. The results of running the program are printed as

```
Salary Week1= $ 3.4523000000E+02   Salary Week2= $ 5.4345000000+02
Total Salary = $ 8.8868000000E+02
```

as shown in Figure 3.7*b*. Note two things here:

BOOLEAN VALUES

Examples of valid boolean values

true	false
TRUE	FAlse

TABLE 3.9. The boolean values TRUE and FALSE can be written in uppercase, lowercase, or a mixture of both.

USING REAL VARIABLE IDENTIFIERS

```
PROGRAM RealVariables(output);
(* Adds two salaries *)
VAR Salary1, Salary2, Total: real;
BEGIN
  Salary1:= 345.23;
  Salary2:= 543.45;
  Total:= Salary1 + Salary2;
  writeln('Salary Week1= $', Salary1, ' Salary Week2= $ ', Salary 2,
    '  Total Salary= $', Total)
END.
```

FIGURE 3.7a. The location names (variables) are declared to be real. We continue the writeln on the next line.

Statement	Salary1	Salary2	Total
Salary1:= 345.23	345.23	Undef	Undef
Salary2:= 543.45	345.23	543.45	Undef
Total:= Salary1 + Salary2	345.23	543.45	888.68
writeln	345.23	543.45	888.68

THE TABLE FOR FIGURE 3.7a. In the third line of the table, the sum of the two salaries is calculated and stored in Total. When the writeln is executed, the computer copies the values of the variables that appear in the writeln list onto the screen or printer page.

```
Salary Week1= $ 3.4523000000E+02 Salary Week2= $   5.4345000000E+
02   Total Salary= $ 8.8868000000E+02
```

FIGURE 3.7b. Running the program of Figure 3.7a. The computer continues to print on the next line output that does not fit on the first line.

1. On the monitor we used, when there is not enough room for the computer to print the results on one line, it automatically continues printing on the next line. In cases like this on other monitors, the material that does not fit on a line may be lost.

2. Real values are printed in exponential form. For instance, 345.23 is printed as $3.4523000000E+02$, that is, 3.4523×10^2. In the next chapter, we will see how to instruct the computer to print real values in regular (nonexponential) form.

3.8

REAL OPERATORS

The mathematical symbols used so far are the "+" and "*" signs. The term for these symbols is *operator,* and what they appear in is called an *expression.* For example, $2.3 + 4.2$ is an example of an expression using the "+" operator and $4.3 * 7.0$ is another example using the "*" operator. An expression, however, can also contain just a variable or a value. Thus 3 and Length are both valid expressions. In an assignment statement, a variable identifier gets the value of an expression; for example, in Wage := 4.50 * 40.0 the variable Wage gets the value of the expression $4.50 * 40.0$. What happens when the computer encounters more than one operator in an expression, for example, a "+" and a "*"? How does it know which operation to perform first? Thus, in $4.0 + 6.0 * 3.0$, is the + operation performed first, giving an intermediate result of 10.0, which is then multiplied by 3.0, giving 30.0? Or is the "*" operation performed first, giving an intermediate result of 18.0 and then adding 4.0 to this, producing 22.0? To permit the computer to evaluate expressions, a priority has been given to each of the operators. The real operators and their priorities are shown in Table 3.10. Let's see how the computer uses these priorities to evaluate the value of an expression.

TEST YOURSELF

QUESTION: What is wrong with the following program?

```
PROGRAM 2Quest(output);
VARTime, Velocity, Distance: real;
BEGIN
   Time:= .3;
   Veloc:= 24.;
   Distance:= Time * Veloc;
   writeln('Distance =', distance)
END.
```

ANSWER:

(1) The identifier 2Quest is illegal because it begins with a digit.
(2) The VAR declaration must contain a blank before the variable list (e.g., VAR Time, Velocity, Distance: real;).
(3) A numerical value can neither start nor end with a decimal point; thus .3 and 24. should be written as 0.3 and 24.0, respectively.
(4) The identifier Veloc is not declared in the VAR declaration.

THE PRIORITY OF REAL ARITHMETIC OPERATORS

Priority	Operation	Symbol
First	Division	/
	Multiplication	*
Second	Addition	+
	Subtraction	−

TABLE 3.10. The priority of real operations.

The computer reads the expression from left to right, first searching for multiplications and divisions and performing them as it encounters them, moving from left to right. It then returns to the left of the expression and searches for additions and subtractions, performing them, again, from left to right.

As an example of how a real expression is calculated in Pascal, let's evaluate the expression Y1 − Y2 / X1 − X2 * 3.0 + 4.1, which appears in

$$Y: = Y1 − Y2 / X1 − X2 * 3.0 + 4.1$$

in Figure 3.8a. The assignment of the variables is as follows Y1 : = 3.2, Y2 : = 2.3, X1= 4.2, and X2: = 1.5. Table 3.11 shows that the division and the multiplication have the highest priority. Since the division is the first of these operators, reading from left to right, Y2 / X1 is evaluated first, yielding the intermediate result 0.55 (to two significant digits), as shown in Table I for Figure 3.8a. Then X2 * 3.0 is evaluated, yielding 4.5 as the next intermediate result.

The computer next returns to the leftmost part of the expression (here, what is to the immediate right of the : =) and performs the additions and subtractions in the order that it encounters them, moving from left to right. Since a subtraction appears first, the computer evaluates Y1 − Y2 / X1 next and obtains 2.65 as an intermediate result. The second subtraction in Y1 −Y2 / X1 − X2 * 3.0 is done next, producing the result −1.85. Finally, the addition is performed and the computer obtains 2.25 as the final result, assigning it to Y, as shown in Figure 3.8b.

If part of an expression is parenthesized, the computer performs that part first and evaluates the operations in it according to the priorities given in Table 3.10. The computer evaluates the parenthesized parts in the order it encounters them, going from left to right. Thus, if we parenthesize Y1 − Y2 and in X2 − X1 in the expression, obtaining*

$$Y: = (Y1 − Y2) / (X1 − X2) * 3.0 + 4.1$$

the computer evaluates (Y1 − Y2) and then (X1 − X2), yielding 0.9 and 3.7, respectively. It then returns to the ":=" and evaluates the divisions and multiplications. The first operation done here is 0.9 / 2.7 giving 0.333. Next,

---

*This is the equation of a straight line where the slope is *(Y1− Y2)/(X1 −X2)*, the X-coordinate is 3.0 and the Y-intercept is 4.1.

USING THE REAL ARITHMETIC OPERATORS

```
PROGRAM RealCalc(output);
VAR Y, X1, X2, Y1, Y2: real;
BEGIN
  Y1:= 3.2;
  Y2:= 2.3;
  X1:= 4.2;
  X2:= 1.5;
  Y:= Y1 - Y2 / X1 - X2 * 3.0 + 4.1;
  writeln('Y = ', Y)
END.
```

FIGURE 3.8a. In evaluating Y, the computer scans the expression from the ": =" to the end, first for "*" and "/", doing the operations in the order it encounters them; then from the ": =" to the end for "+" and "−", again doing them as it encounters them.

$$Y = 2.252380952E+00$$

FIGURE 3.8b. Running the program of Figure 3.8a.

EVALUATING $Y := Y1 - Y2 / X1 - X2 * 3.0 + 4.1$
USING $Y1 := 3.2; Y2 := 2.3; X1 := 4.2; X2 := 1.5;$

Step	Part of expression evaluated	Value
1	Y2 / X1	0.55
2	X2 * 3.0	4.5
3	Y1 − Y2 / X1	2.65
4	Y1 − Y2 / X1 − X2 * 3.0	−1.85
5	Y1 − Y2 / X1 − X2 * 3.0 + 4.1	2.25

TABLE I FOR FIGURE 3.8a. At each step, the operation being performed is shaded.

0.33 * 3.0 is done, yielding 0.999. Finally, 4.1 is added to that result, giving 5.0990 (see Table II for Figure 3.8a).

Note that (Y1 − Y2) was divided by (X1 − X2) and not by (X1 − X2) * 3.0. To do the latter, parenthesize (X1 − X2) * 3.0 and write

$$Y := (Y1 − Y2) / ((X1 − X2) * 3.0) + 4.1$$

Also note that you can use an expression in a write or writeln statement. For instance, you can write writeln('One =', 1.0) or write(3.0 * Salary).

TEST YOURSELF

QUESTION: What are the values of the following expressions?

(a) 3.0 * 5.0 + 3.0 / 2.0 + 7.0
(b) 3.0 * (5.0 + 3.0) / 2.0 + 7.0
(c) 3.0 * 5.0 + (3.0 / 2.0) + 7.0
(d) 3.0 * (5.0 + 3.0 / 2.0) + 7.0

ANSWER:

(a) 23.500
(b) 19.000
(c) 23.500
(d) 26.500

3.9

INTEGER OPERATORS

The integer operators for addition, subtraction, and multiplication are the same as for reals. The operators used in integer division are, however, different from their real counterparts. The integer division operators are the MOD and the DIV. Before we define these operators, we remind you that in a division, the *dividend* is divided by the *divisor*. The number of times the divisor goes into the dividend is called the *quotient*. What is left over after the division is called the *remainder*.

The DIV operator produces the quotient and the MOD operator produces the remainder. For instance, 7 DIV 3 calculates 7 divided by 3, producing the quotient 2. On the other hand, 7 MOD 3 produces the remainder 1 for the same division. As another example, 3 DIV 4 is 0 because 4 goes into 3 zero times. The remainder is three; so 3 MOD 4 is 3. These and other examples of MOD and DIV are given in Table 3.11.

EVALUATING THE PARENTHESIZED EXPRESSION
```
Y: = (Y1 − Y2) / (X1 − X2) * 3.0 + 4.1
USING Y1: = 3.2; Y2: = 2.3; X1: = 4.2; X2: = 1.5;
```

Step	Part of expression evaluated	Value
1	(Y1 − Y2)	0.9
2	(X1 − X2)	2.7
3	(Y1 − Y2) / (X1 − X2)	0.333
4	(Y1 − Y2) / (X1 − X2) * 3.0	0.999
5	(Y1 − Y2) / (X1 − X2) * 3.0 + 4.1	5.0990

TABLE II FOR FIGURE 3.8a. At each step, the operation being performed is shaded. The computer first evaluates the parenthesized parts from left to right and then the operators in the usual order.

INTEGER DIVISION

7 DIV 3 →2	7 MOD 3 →1
11 DIV 4→2	11 MOD 4→3
12 DIV 4→3	12 MOD 4→0
3 DIV 4 →0	3 MOD 4 →3

TABLE 3.11. Examples of integer division.

The priority of the integer operations are shown in Table 3.12. As an example of how an integer expression is calculated in Pascal, let's evaluate the expression X MOD Y − U DIV V * 4 + 3 in

$$Z := X \text{ MOD } Y - U \text{ DIV } V * 4 + 3;$$

as shown in Figure 3.9a. The assignment of the variables is as follows: X := 3, Y := 2, U := 4, and V := 1. Note that the MOD, DIV, and multiplication have the highest priority. Since the MOD is the first of these operators, reading from left to right, X MOD Y is evaluated first yielding the intermediate result 1, as shown in the table for Figure 3.9a. Then U DIV V is evaluated, yielding 4 as the next intermediate result. Finally, U DIV V * 4 is evaluated, producing 16 as still another intermediate result.

The computer then returns to the ":=", and performs the additions and subtractions in the order that it encounters them. Since the subtraction appears to the left of the addition, X MOD Y − U DIV V * 4 is performed next, producing −15 as the next intermediate result. Finally, X MOD Y − U DIV V * 4 + 3 is performed, producing the final result, −12, as shown in Figure 3.9b.

If part of an expression is parenthesized, the computer performs that part first. Thus parenthesizing V * 4 in the expression

$$Z := X \text{ MOD } Y - U \text{ DIV } (V * 4) + 3;$$

changes the priority of the multiplication V * 4, since it is now done first. The computer evaluates 4 DIV 4 and obtains 3 as the value for Z.

USING THE INTEGER ARITHMETIC OPERATORS

Priority	Operation	Symbol
First	Integer division	MOD
	Remainder	DIV
	Multiplication	*
Second	Addition	+
	Subtraction	−

TABLE 3.1   The priority of integer operations.

```
PROGRAM IntegerPriority(output);
(* MOD, DIV, and * are done first, then + and − *)
VAR X, Y, Z, U, V: integer;
BEGIN
  X: = 3;
  Y: = 2;
  U: = 4;
  V: = 1;
  Z: = X MOD Y − U DIV V * 4 + 3;
  writeln('Z= ', Z)
END.
```

FIGURE 3.9a.   In evaluating Z, the computer scans the expression from the ": =" to the end, first for MOD, DIV, and *, then from the ": =" to the end for + or −. In a scan, it does the operations in the order in which it encounters them.

EVALUATING THE INTEGER EXPRESSION X MOD Y − U DIV V * 4 + 3
USING X: = 3; Y: = 2; U: = 4; V:= 1.

Step	Part of expression evaluated	Value
1	X MOD Y	1
2	U DIV V	4
3	U DIV V * 4	16
4	X MOD Y − U DIV V * 4	−15
5	X MOD Y − U DIV V * 4 + 3	−12

TABLE FOR FIGURE 3.9a.   At each step, the operation being performed is shaded.

$$Z= -12$$

FIGURE 3.9b.   Running the program of Figure 3.9a.

PITFALL

A division by zero will produce an execution error. Thus all of the following will produce errors:

1. 3.5 / 0.0
2. 4 MOD 0
3. 7 DIV 0
4. 8 / 0

In Standard Pascal you can't use a negative number as a divisor when you use the MOD. Thus both 8 MOD (−3) and 8 MOD −3 cause errors.

3.10

MIXED MODE

In general, the type of variable on the left-hand side of an assignment statement must be the same as the type of the expression on the right-hand side that is assigned to it. Thus, if Time is an integer variable, then Time : = 4 is a valid assignment; whereas Time : = 4.1 is not, since 4.1 is a real. Similarly, if Ch is a character variable, then Ch : = 'a' and Ch : = '6' are both valid, since both 'a' and '6' are characters; but Ch : = 4 is not valid because 4 is an integer value. However, you may assign either a real or an integer to a real. Thus, if Wage is a real variable, then both Wage : = 800.23 and Wage : = 800 are valid. What happens in the latter case is that the compiler converts 800 to the real value 800.0 and stores it in the location named Wage.

Although in general the type of variable on the left-hand side of an assignment statement determines the type of the expression that can occur on the right-hand side (as we have just seen), both reals and integers can appear simultaneously in an expression assigned to a real variable. When this occurs, the expression is said to be written in *mixed mode.* The computer evaluates these expressions by first converting the integers to reals. For instance, in

$$\text{Profit} := (3.0 * 4.0) / 2$$

where Profit is a real, the compiler converts the 2 to 2.0, views the statement as Profit : = (3.0 * 4.0) / 2.0, and assigns 6.0 to profit.

What happens when the computer evaluates writeln(2 / 4)? As we know, real division is not defined for integers, so the computer evaluates 2.0 / 4.0 and prints the result as the real 0.5 expressed as an exponential. Consequently, we see why Index : = 2 / 4, where Index is an integer, causes a compilation error; the computer tries to assign 0.5 to the integer Index. However, Cost : = 2 / 4 is allowed when Cost is a real.

You may use the MOD and the DIV in a real expression. Thus write(3.2 + 4 DIV 2) will produce 5.2000000000E+00 as output.

TEST YOURSELF

QUESTION: What are the values of the following expressions?

(a)   4 MOD 2 + 6 DIV (2 * 3)
(b)   4 MOD (2 + 6 DIV 2) * 3
(c)   (4 MOD 2 + 6) DIV 2 * 3
(d)   4 MOD 2 DIV 2 * 3

ANSWER:

(a)   1
(b)   12
(c)   9
(d)   0

TEST YOURSELF

QUESTION: What value will be stored in ANS?

$$Ans := 3 \,/\, (4 \text{ MOD } 3 + 4 \,/\, 8 * 5.5)$$

ANSWER: 0.8

3.11

THE READLN STATEMENT

BEFORE YOU BEGIN

Now that you've written a program that produces output, you may be wondering how to introduce data into the program while it's executing, as was done in the survey program of the previous chapter. Here's how.

The `readln` statement enables you to type data from the keyboard into memory locations specified in the program while the program is executing; it is also used to read data that have been stored on data files. The general process is called *reading data.* We'll discuss the use of this statement now only with respect to input from the keyboard. Note that the `readln` is another example of a standard procedure.

In the program in Figure 3.10*a*

```
readln(Length, Width, Price);
```

will read values for the two integer variables `Length` and `Width` and the real variable `Price` from the keyboard. Here the varaibles `Length`, `Width`, and `Price` form what is called the `readln` list.

When the computer executes a `readln` the computer pauses, waiting for you to type in data. Some compilers do not indicate that they require you to type in data. For that reason, precede the `readln` with a `writeln` statement that will indicate to the person running the program what to type:

```
writeln('Type in Length, Width and Price');
```

Since the first two variables in the list in `readln(Length, Width, Price)` are integer variables, you must type the first two items in the data as integers. If you type either one of them as a real, an execution error will occur. The third variable, `Price`, is a real, so just as in an assignment statement, you can type an integer or a real as the third piece of data. Thus, as shown in Figure 3.10*b*, we type the three pieces of data as

13   4   0.75

When you type numerical values for input, you must separate them by at least one blank. After you hit the carriage return, the computer transfers the values to the appropriate memory locations. Since 13 is the first value typed, the computer stores it in `Length`, the first variable in the read list. Since 4 is the second value, it is stored in `Width`, the second variable in the list. Finally, 0.75 is stored in `Price`. Beware: If you do not hit the carriage return after typing the last value in the line (here, 0.75), the computer will pause until you do. Running the program, as shown in Figure 3.10*c*, produces

THE READLN STATEMENT

```
PROGRAM Area(input, output);
(* Investigates reading *)
VAR Length, Width: integer;
  Cost, Price: real;
BEGIN
  writeln('Type in Length, Width and Price');
  readln(Length, Width, Price);
  writeln( 'Length= ', Length, ' Width= ', Width,
    ' Price = ', Price);
  Cost:= Length * Width * Price;
  writeln( 'Cost:= ', Cost)
END.
```

FIGURE 3.10a. When the readln is executed, the values we type at the keyboard are transmitted to the locations named by the variables in the readln after we hit the carriage return.

```
Type in Length, Width and Price
13   4   0.75
```

FIGURE 3.10b. Typing the data for the program of Figure 3.10a. We separate numerical values by one or more blanks and terminate the last value by hitting the carriage return.

```
Length=    13  Width=    4  Price=    7.5000000000E−01
Cost:=    3.9000000000E+01
```

FIGURE 3.10c. Running the program of Figure 3.10a.

```
Length= 13 Width= 4 Price= 7.5000000000E-01
Cost:= 3.9000000000E+01
```

3.12

CORRECTING SYNTAX ERRORS

If you've tried to type and run any program so far, you've probably incurred the wrath of the compiler by making some syntax errors. The following is an example of errors made in writing a program and how to correct them. The program of Figure 3.11a has several syntax errors that the compiler indicates after running the program. When the compiler prints the program for the syntax error analysis in Figure 3.11b, it lists each line with a number. The errors are as follows:

1. The omission of the final single quotation mark in writeln('Type in Length, Width and Price);
2. The omission of the variable Length in the VAR declaration.
3. The omission of the semicolon separating read(Price) and the writeln.
4. The omission of the closing parenthesis from writeln('Cost:=', Cost
5. The omission of the period at the end of the program.

The compiler doesn't always indicate the line in which the syntax error occurred. Thus

```
Line 10 : ';' expected.
Line 14 : ')' expected.
```

indicate the line after the error occurred. Also, if you make an error in one statement and its effect is felt in other statements, some compilers will indicate all those other statements. For instance, when we omitted Length from the VAR declaration, the compiler indicated that lines 7, 10, and 12 contained an error. When we insert Length in the VAR statement, those errors vanish.

After we correct all the errors and recompile the program, it compiles successfully.

QUESTION: If the input is 3 4 5, what are the values of the integer identifiers in the following:

(a) readln(Length, Width, Height)
(b) readln(Length, Width, Length)

ANSWER:

(a) Length is 3, Width is 4, and Height is 5
(b) Width is 4 and Length is 5, since the original value of 3 is replaced.

SYNTAX ERRORS

```
 1  PROGRAM Volume(input, output);
 2  (* Investigates reading *)
 3  VAR Width: integer;
 4     Cost, Price: real;
 5  BEGIN
 6     writeln('Type in Length, Width and Price);
 7     read(Length);
 8     read( Width);
 9     read( Price)
10     writeln( 'Length= ', Length, ' Width= ', Width,
11        ' Price= ', Price);
12     Cost:= Length * Width * Price;
13     writeln( 'Cost:=', Cost
14 END
```

FIGURE 3.11a.   A program with syntax errors.

Line 6: String constant exceeds line.
Line 7: Unknown identifier or syntax error.
Line 10: ; expected.
Line 10: Unknown identifier or syntax error.
Line 12: unknown identifier or syntax error.
Line 13:) expected.
Line 14: Unexpected end of source.

FIGURE 3.11b.   Running the program of Figure 3.11a. The line number refers to the line with the indicated syntax error.

3.13

THE CONST DEFINITION

It is sometimes advantageous to use identifiers whose values do not change during the program's execution. For instance, the value of π would not change. These identifiers are appropriately called *constant identifiers.* If you try to change the value of a constant identifier later in the program, a compilation error will occur. Constant identifiers must be defined in a CONST definition. Thus, in Figure 3.12*a*, Pi, Cost and H are defined as constants in

CONST Pi = 3.14159; Cost = 12.34E − 4; H = 6;

Note that the type of the constant identifier is determined by the values on the right of the "=" sign. Thus Pi and Cost are real constant identifiers, and H is an integer constant identifier. The CONST definition must precede the VAR declaration and must follow the program heading. The results of running the program are shown in Figure 3.12*b*.

In contrast to a character variable (to which you can assign only a 1-character string constant), when you use a constant identifier, you can assign to it as many characters as you can fit in a string constant that is constrained to fit on the rest of the line. Thus

CONST Noun = 'Ivan';

assigns the string constant 'Ivan' to the constant identifier Noun, as shown in Figure 3.13*a*.

writeln ('My name is ', Noun);
writeln ('My father is ', Noun);

The results of running the program are shown in Figure 3.13*b*.

The maximum value an integer can have is stored in a constant called maxint (it stands for *maximum integer*). Since maxint is a constant specified in the compiler, it is called a *predefined constant.* The value of an integer value you may use must be less than or equal to the value of maxint and greater than or equal to −maxint. On the version of Pascal used on the CYBER, the value of maxint is * 281474976710655; On the VAX version it is 2147483647. On microcomputers, the value is much smaller. For instance, on the IBM-PC and the Apple Macintosh, the value of maxint is 32767.

---

*This is $2^{48} - 1$, where there are 48 bits in an integer word.

CONSTANT IDENTIFIERS

```
PROGRAM Constant(input, output);
CONST Pi = 3.14159; H = 6;
VAR Volume, R: real;
BEGIN
  writeln('Type in the radius; you may use a real.');
  readln(R);
  Volume:= Pi * R * R * H;
  writeln('Volume = ', Volume:5:2)
END.
```

FIGURE 3.12a. In the CONST declaration, we associate values with identifiers. The identifier's type is determined by the value. Thus Pi is real and H is integer.

```
Type in the radius; you may use a real.

4.16
Volume = 3.2620259942E+02
```

FIGURE 3.12b. Running the program of Figure 3.12a.

```
PROGRAM CharConst(output);
CONST Noun= 'Ivan';
BEGIN
  writeln('My name is ', Noun);
  writeln ('My father is ',Noun);
END.
```

FIGURE 3.13a. In contrast to a character variable, you may assign a string constant of more than one character to a constant identifier.

```
My name is Ivan
My father is Ivan
```

FIGURE 3.13b. Running the program of Figure 3.13a.

The constant Maxint can be used in a program. For instance,

```
writeln('Maximum Integer is ', maxint)
```

prints the value of maxint, as shown in Figure 3.14a. The results of running the program are shown in Figure 3.14b. Beware: If maxint is declared as a variable or defined as another constant, it loses its value as a predefined constant.

Since a single quotation mark is the delimiter for a string, you can't use it in a string. For instance, John's would cause an error. The solution is to use two contiguous single quotation marks ('') to represent a single quotation mark. Thus, to assign a single quotation mark to a character identifier, for instance Quote, write Quote:= ''''. Similarly, the string John''s father represents John's father. A string that contains nothing, not even a blank, is called a *null string*. Unfortunately you can't use single quotation marks to represent a null string. Thus Null:= '' would cause an error.

3.14

AN AVERAGING PROBLEM

Now that we've gained some facility with Pascal, let's plan and write a program that separately averages two sets of four grades. The first version of our pseudocode is

> *Average the first set;*
> *Average the second set;*

Since the intent of the second line of the pseudocode is identical to that of the first, write the pseudocode as

> *Average a set of data;*
> *Average a set of data*

Refine the pseudocode on the first line to

> *Read four grades;*
> *Form a sum and compute the average;*
> *Print the average*

```
PROGRAM MaxInteger(output);
BEGIN
  writeln('Maximum Integer is ', maxint)
END.
```

FIGURE 3.14*a*. We print the value of the stored constant `maxint`.

```
Maximum Integer is 32767
```

FIGURE 3.14*b*. Running the program of Figure 3.14*a*.

The second line of the original pseudocode is refined just as the first one was, so the pseudocode for the entire program becomes

Read four grades;

Form a sum and compute the average;

Print the average

Read four grades;

Form a sum and compute the average;

Print the average

Since the averaging process is repeated, the rectangle representing it in the top-down diagram is not repeated.* It is thus written as

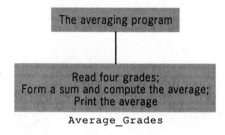

Average_Grades

CHOOSING THE APPROPRIATE TYPE

An important step in planning a program is to determine what types you'll choose for the identifiers. Since the four grades are whole numbers, declare them as integers. The average, however, will be a number like 87.5, so declare it a real.

The program appears in Figure 3.15*a*. The grades are averaged in

```
Average:= (Markl + Mark2 + Mark3 + Mark4) / NumberOfMarks;
```

Note that if parentheses had not been used in this expression, only Mark4 would have been divided by NumberOfMarks and the average would have been incorrect.

It is good programming practice to use constant identifiers instead of values in the program. Thus, in this statement, it is patently clear that the sum is divided by the number of marks. The results of running the program are shown in Figure 3.15*b*.

---

*The fact that it is not repeated means that we'll be able to write one subprogram to perform the average.

AN AVERAGING PROBLEM

```
PROGRAM SimpleAverage(input, output);
(* Averages two sets of marks *)
CONST NumberOfMarks = 4;
VAR   Mark1, Mark2, Mark3, Mark4:integer;
   Average:real;
BEGIN
   (* Compute average for first set of marks *)
   writeln('Type 4 marks on one line.');
   readln(Mark1, Mark2, Mark3, Mark4);
   Average:= (Mark1 + Mark2 + Mark3 + Mark4) / NumberOfMarks;
   writeln('Average of ', NumberOfMarks, ' marks is ', Average);
   writeln;

   (* Compute average for second set of marks *)
   writeln('Type 4 marks on one line.');
   readln(Mark1, Mark2, Mark3, Mark4);
   Average:= (Mark1 + Mark2 + Mark3 + Mark4) / NumberOfMarks;
   writeln('Average of ', NumberOfMarks, ' marks is ', Average);
END.
```

FIGURE 3.15a.   The program averages one set of data and then another set.

```
Type 4 marks on one line.
87 89 96 90
Average of 4 marks is   9.0500000000E + 01

Type 4 marks on one line.
98 86 67 75
Average of 4 marks is   8.1500000000E + 01
```

FIGURE 3.15b.   Running the program of Figure 3.15a.

3.15

SEPARATING THE DIGITS OF AN INTEGER

Let's tackle a slightly more difficult program. It should read a date as a six-digit or five-digit integer, for instance, 22387, and separate it into the month (here, 2), the day (here, 23), and the year (here, 87) by successively removing the left-hand digits from the integer. The pseudocode for this process is

Read the date;
Remove the month and store it;
Remove the day and store it;
Remove the year and store it;
Print the stored results.

The top-down diagram is

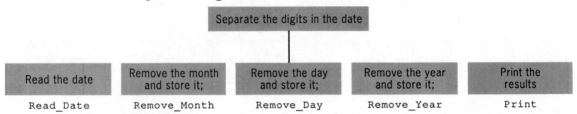

Before we show you how to remove digits from a number, you should be aware of the following: When you divide a number by a power of 10 (i.e., 10, 100, 1000, etc.), the quotient is the first few digits in the number and the remainder is the rest of the digits in the number. Thus 3675 DIV 100 is 36 (the first two digits) and the remainder, 3675 MOD 100, is what is left over, namely 75, the last two digits.

CHOOSING THE APPROPRIATE TYPE

> Since the integer operators MOD and DIV will be used to remove the day, month, and year from the date, declare these terms to be integers.

To determine how to remove the digits representing the month, rewrite the integer with a comma (22,387) so that you can see where the thousands digit is. We can now determine that by dividing (DIVing) the integer by 10,000, the quotient will be 2. Since Month represents the month, its value is obtained in

```
Month: = Date DIV 10000;
```

as shown in Figure 3.16a, where Date represents the date. The remainder of

SEPARATING THE DIGITS OF AN INTEGER

```pascal
PROGRAM DateDiv(input, output);
(* Separates a six-digit number into the month, day, and year *)
VAR   Date, Month, Day, Year: integer;
BEGIN
  writeln('Type the date');
  readln(Date);
  writeln('The numerical Date is: ', Date);
  Month:= Date DIV 10000;
  Date:= Date MOD 10000;
  Day:= Date DIV 100;
  Date:= Date MOD 100;
  Year:= Date;
  writeln('Month: ', Month, ' Day: ', Day, ' Year: ', Year)
END.
```

FIGURE 3.16a.   The program will successively remove the month, day, and year from an integer in which the first two digits are the month, the second two the day, and the third two the year.

this division is 2387 and is obtained by calculating `Date MOD 10000` in

```
Date: = Date MOD 10000;
```

Here we have assigned a new value to `Date`; it is no longer 22387 but is now 2387. So we have removed the digit representing the month from the date. (Note that if the date were a six-digit number, for instance 122,387, these two statements would produce 12 as the month, remove it from `Date`, and assign 2387 as the new value of the date.)

In

```
Day: = Date DIV 100;
Date: = Date MOD 100;
```

since the value of `Date` is 2387, we obtain the day (here, 23), and assign a new value (here, 87) to `Date`. Thus we have now also removed the digits representing the day from the date. In `Year: = Date`, we assign the value of the digits remaining in `Date` to `Year`. The table for Figure 3.16*a* shows how `Date` is assigned a new value each time it occurs in a calculation with the `MOD`. The data for the program are shown in Figure 3.16*b*, and the results of running the program are shown in Figure 3.16*c*.

Note that if you wanted to read the date 3/4/89 into the program as contiguous digits, you would have to type 30489.

Date	Month	Day	Year	Recalculating Date
22387	2	Undef	Undef	`Date:= Date MOD 10000;`
2387	2	23	Undef	`Date:= Date MOD 100;`
87	2	23	87	

TABLE FOR FIGURE 3.16a.   Shows how, by using the MOD, we recalculate the value of Date. The month, day, and year are consecutively assigned the leading digit(s).

```
            Type the Date
            22387
```

FIGURE 3.16b.   Typing the data for Figure 3.16a.

```
        The numerical Date is:   22387
        Month: 2   Day: 23   Year: 87
```

FIGURE 3.16c.   Running the program of Figure 3.16a. By using the DIV, we remove the first two digits. By using the MOD, we recalculate the value of Date.

PITFALL

> If you use an integer larger than `maxint` in a program, the program will produce an error message. On the compilers for many microcomputers, the value of `maxint` is 32767. Thus, if you input a date larger than this, for instance 122389, into the program of Figure 3.16a run on a microcomputer, the computer will produce an execution error.

3.16

RESERVED WORDS

There are certain words that have a special meaning reserved for the Turbo Pascal compiler; they are called *reserved words*. A reserved word cannot be used for an identifier, be it a variable identifier or another type of identifier. The reserved words are as follows:

and	array	BEGIN	case
CONST	DIV	do	downto
else	END	file	forward
for	function	goto	if
in	label	MOD	nil
not	of	or	packed
procedure	PROGRAM	record	repeat
set	then	type	to
until	VAR	while	with

We have capitalized those we have already encountered.

3.17

MORE ON REAL VALUES

Now that you're familiar with the numerical types, let's take an in-depth look at reals.

Another form that a real value can take is a number that contains a decimal point and is followed by an exponent, for instance, $24.2E+4$. It is equal to 24.2×10^4 and may be written without the "+" in the exponent, $24.2E4$. Similarly, $5.78E-4$ is equal to 5.78×10^{-4}. These examples are shown in Table 3.13. When describing reals written with exponentials, for instance, $24.2E+5$, we call the 24.2 the *number part* and the E+5 the *exponential part*. From our

TEST YOURSELF

QUESTION: Can you write the top-down diagram and the resulting program so that the removal of the first two leading digits is done in one rectangle? The first time the statements corresponding to the rectangle are executed, the month is removed; the second time, the day is removed; the third time, the year is removed.

ANSWER:

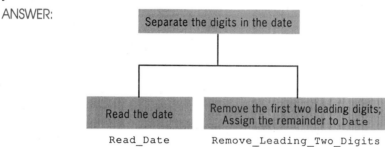

Read_Date   Remove_Leading_Two_Digits

The program is

```
PROGRAM DateSeparation;
(* Separates a 6-digit number into month, day and year *)
CONST Blank = ' ';
VAR Date, Digits, Divisor: integer;
BEGIN
  writeln('Type the date');
  readln(Date);
  writeln('The numerical Date is: ', Date);

  Divisor:= 10000;
  Digits:= Date DIV Divisor;
  Date:= Date MOD Divisor;
  write('Month: ', Digits, Blank);

  Divisor:= 100;
  Digits:= Date DIV Divisor;
  Date:= Date MOD Divisor;
  write('Day: ', Digits, Blank);

  Divisor:= 1;
  Digits:= Date DIV Divisor;
  Date:= Date MOD Divisor;
  write('Year: ', Digits);
END.
```

Here RemoveLeadingTwoDigits in the top-down diagram contains Digits:= Date DIV Divisor and Date:= Date MOD Divisor.

REAL VALUES WITH EXPONENTS

Examples of valid real values with exponents

242E+4	5.78E−05

TABLE 3.13.   A real value may contain an E and an exponent such as 242E+4 (i.e., 242×10^4) and 5.78E−05 (i.e., 5.78×10^{-5}). If it does not contain an exponential part, it must contain a decimal point.

knowledge of integer values, we see that the exponential part consists of E followed by an integer.

If a real value contains an exponential part, the number part does not have to contain a decimal point. Thus 35E+04 is a valid real. However, if a real value does not contain an exponential part, it must contain a decimal point, for example, 123.45.

Note that you can use the exponential notation to type real values either as data for a readln or in assignment statement. Thus you can type an input of 125000. as 12.5E+4.

Real values cannot always be stored exactly in the computer's memory. Thus, if you instruct the computer to store the real value 2.3 in its memory, it will store an approximation to the value, for instance, 2.29999999. This is called *roundoff error*. By contrast, integer values are stored exactly. Another difference between reals and integers is that the maximum value of a real is quite large. On the Cyber its limits are from 10^{-294} to 10^{322}, and on the VAX the limits are from 0.29×10^{-38} to 1.70×10^{38}; by contrast, the maximum value of an integer is maxint. Note, however, that the maximum value of the number part of a real is always less than the value of maxint.

Summary of Pascal Statements Covered

write/writeln   The form of the write statement is write(followed by one or more items that comprise a list. These items can be identifiers or expressions. If there are several items in the list, they must be separated by commas. The statement concludes with a ")". The same syntax applies to the writeln. Examples:

```
writeln('Salary =', 3 * 2);
write(Time, 'Strings', 4 + 5);
writeln(cost)
```

readln   The form of the readln statement is readln(followed by one or more variable identifiers. If there are several identifiers, they must be separated by commas. The statement concludes with a ")". You cannot use expressions in a readln. Each readln executed requires you to type your data on a new line. Examples:

```
readln(Cost, Area, Length);
readln(Flag, Name);
```

The Assignment Statement   The form of the assignment statement is an identifier, followed by := , followed by an identifier or expression. Examples of assignment statements we can write so far are:

```
Mortgage: = Loan;
Distance: = a * t * t / 2.0;
Time: = 4;
Answer: = 'Yes';
Sorted: = true
```

The CONST Definition   The form of the CONST definition is CONST followed by one or more blanks, followed by one or more constant definitions. A constant definition consists of an identifier, followed by an "=", followed by a number or boolean value or a string constant that is enclosed in single quotation marks and ending in a semicolon. If there are several constant definitions, they are separated by semicolons. Examples:

```
CONST Pi = 3.14159; OldCost = 12.34E - 4; H = 6; Valid = true;
```

The CONST definition follows the heading and must precede the VAR declaration.

The VAR Declaration   The form of the VAR declaration is VAR followed by one or more blanks, followed by one or more variable declarations. A variable declaration consists of a list of identifiers, followed by a ":", followed by a type and ending with a ";". The identifiers in the list must be separated from each other by commas. Examples of three different VAR declarations are:

```
VAR X, Y, Z, U, V: integer;
VAR M, X1, X2, Y1, Y2: real;
VAR Width: integer;
    Cost, Price: real;
    Flag: boolean;
    Character: char;
```

CHAPTER REVIEW

Identifiers

So far, we have encountered variable, constant, and program identifiers. The rules for forming variable, program and constant identifiers apply to all kinds of identifiers.

Reading

If you read a group of numerical values, you can separate them only with blanks. You must conclude each line of input by hitting the carriage return before the data are processed by the program.

Writing

After a write is executed, the cursor is placed one column to the right of the last character printed. After a writeln is executed, the cursor is placed at the beginning of the next line.

Embedded Blanks ·

The Pascal compiler does not allow you to place a blank within a value, identifier, reserved word, or multicharacter special symbol. The multicharacter special symbols we have encountered so far are the get sign (: =) and the comment delimiters "(*" and "*)". Thus Width : = 4 will produce a syntax error, and so will (* comments are free *   ).

Necessary Blanks

Reserved words and other identifiers must be separated from each other and from values by delimiters. If a comma, colon, parenthesis, or any other special symbol is prescribed by the syntax, it acts as the delimiter; otherwise, you must use a blank. Thus the following will cause syntax errors:

1. VARLength, Width:integer. It should be VAR Length, Width: integer.
2. 4MOD3. It should be 4 MOD 3.

Constant Identifiers

1. If a value or string constant appears more than once in the program, use a constant identifier in its place.
2. If a value is difficult to recognize, use a constant identifier in its place. For instance, the identifier Blank is easier to recognize than the string that contains one blank, ' '.

Standard Procedures

The standard procedures we have encountered so far are readln, write, and writeln.

PROGRAMMING STYLE

In order to make your programs easier to read, we recommend the following convention:

1. Write all reserved words in uppercase (e.g., BEGIN and END).
2. Write all identifiers that you define or declare in mixed case (e.g., Volume, Null, MaxLength, and Newvolume).
3. Write the identifiers that have special meaning to the compiler—for example, standard procedures and standard types (real, integer, char, and boolean)—in lowercase (e.g., read, write, maxint, input, and output).

4. Use blanks to separate identifiers from operators (e.g., type C : = A * B / C instead of C : = A*B/C).

5. Insert blanks between a comma and the next identifier in a list, and between the colon and the type in the VAR declaration (e.g., type VAR Length, Width, Area: integer; instead of VAR Length,Width,Area:integer;).

6. Place blank lines between parts of the program that perform different tasks.

PROGRAMMING PITFALL

You cannot use the same identifier in a VAR declaration that you do in a CONST definition. Thus

CONST Height = 4;

VAR Height: real;

will cause an error.

NEW TERMS

assignment statement	operator
boolean value	predefined constant
character value	procedure
constant identifiers	program
delimiter	program heading
embedded blank	program identifier
exponential part	reading data
expression	real value
integer value	reserved words
list	roundoff error
mixed mode	standard (predefined) procedure
null string	statement part
number part	string constant
numerical value	variable

EXERCISES

1. Write the output for each of the following statements:

$$writeln((5 - 8) + (4\ DIV\ 2)); \underline{\hspace{1.5cm}}$$
$$writeln(5 - (8 + 4)\ DIV\ 2); \underline{\hspace{1.5cm}}$$
$$writeln((5 - (8 + 4))\ DIV\ 2); \underline{\hspace{1.5cm}}$$
$$writeln((5 - 8 + 4)\ DIV\ 2); \underline{\hspace{1.5cm}}$$
$$writeln(5 - 8 + 4\ DIV\ 2); \underline{\hspace{1.5cm}}$$

2. State the type and value of each of the following expressions. If the expression will not compile, write *invalid* as the type and omit the value.

Expression	Type	Value
20 DIV 8 / 4	____	____
20 + 4 / 3 * 4	____	____
17 MOD 5 * 2 − 16 + 8 DIV 3	____	____

3. What are the syntax errors in the following program?

```
PROGRAM Type(output);
{program has an error that is very difficult to detect late at night}
VARIABLES Distance, Velocity, Time:integer;
BEGIN
   writeln('Type the velocity and time');
   Distance = Velco * Time;
   writeln('Distance = ', Distance);
END.
```

4. Write the Pascal equivalent of the following algebraic equations.

(a) $A = \dfrac{3 + B}{B + 2}$

(b) $R = \dfrac{3(A + B)^2 - R}{3}$

(c) $C2 = A^2 + B^2$

5. What is wrong with the following program?

```
PROGRAM Area(output);
VAR Length, Width: integer;
   Cost, Price: real;
BEGIN
   writeln('Type in Length, Width and Price');
   Cost:= Length * Width * Price;
   writeln( 'Cost:=', Cost)
END.
```

Will the program compile?

6. What is wrong with `writeln(' John's program')`?

7. What is the `writeln` statement that will produce `'Hi there'`?

8. Which of the following identifiers are illegal?

   Num#1   Probl.txt   Tim's   #One   tHINK

9. Give an example of valid input for `readln(Time, Wage)`, given

   VAR Time:integer; Wage:real;

10. What is wrong with `readln('Type the time', Time)`?

11. What will the following program produce if we type 300 400 as input?

```
PROGRAM Salaries(input, output);
VAR Salary1, Total: real;
BEGIN
   writeln('Type in your two weekly salaries');
   readln(Salary1, Salary1);
   Total:= Salary1 + Salary1;
   writeln( 'Total = ', Total)
END.
```

12. What is wrong with `VAR File, Record: integer`?

13. Is `VAR readln, write:integer` legal? What difficulties would it cause?

Programming Problems

14. Write a program to calculate the product of any five real numbers read. What difficulty would the program encounter if it calculated the product of five integers?

15. The formula for income tax is `Tax = (Income − Deductions) * TaxRate`. Write a program that calculates the tax for data read.

16. The Fibonacci sequence of numbers is defined such that each number in the sequence is the sum of the previous two numbers. Thus the first few numbers are 0, 1, 1, 2, 3, and 5. Write a program that reads any two consecutive numbers in the sequence and produces the next five. Thus, if the program reads 2 and 3, it would print 5, 8, 13, 21, and 34.

17. One can obtain the sum of the numbers from 1 to 10 by adding the sum of individual pairs of numbers. Thus we add 1 and 10 (their sum is 11), 2 and 9 (their sum is 11), 3 and 8 (their sum is 11), 4 and 7 (their sum is 11), and finally, 5 and 6 (their sum is also 11). Since each of the five individual sums is 11, the sum of the numbers from 1 to 10 is 5 times 11, or 55. In order to obtain a formula for the sum of the numbers from 1 to n, we represent 10 by n; consequently, 11 is $n + 1$ and 5 is $n / 2$. Thus the sum of the numbers from 1 to 11 expressed in terms of n becomes $(n + 1) \times n / 2$. Write a program that reads a value for n and then calculates the sum of the numbers from 1 to n.

18. Write a program to produce the following pattern:

```
      *
      **
      ***
      ****
      *****
      ******
      *******
```

19. It is obvious that the computer requires less memory to store one integer than it does to store three integers. Thus it takes three integers to store the month, day, and year (e.g., 12, 27, 90) but only one to store the integer formed when these three integers are contiguous (here, 122790). Write a program that performs this conversion.

20. Write a program to determine a worker's salary if it is based on the hourly rate times hours, for 40 hours or less, plus 1.5 times the hourly rate times hours worked in excess of 40 hours.

21. A salesperson's commissions for each of 8 weeks (rounded to the nearest dollar) are 485, 687, 234, 876, 456, 235, 1242, and 621. Write a program to determine the sum of the commissions and the average weekly commission. If you declare the commission to be integers and divide by 8 to obtain the average weekly commission, will the answer be as correct as if you had declared the commissions to be reals?

22. Do the previous problem so that weekly commissions are read by the program. If you type the commissions as they appear in the previous problem, can you read them as reals?

23. Given the following table for the ABC Rug Company's sales for a given hour, write a program that calculates, for each sale, the number of square yards of rug sold and the dollar amount of each sale. The price per yard is $16. Note that rug dimensions are given in feet.

Length	Width
12	12
10	18
12	18
12	20

24. Given the following as examples of salary information for workers on the day shift at Pro Tennis Balls, Inc., write a program that calculates each worker's gross salary (before taxes) and net salary (after taxes) and then prints all the information relating to the worker.

Worker number	Hourly wage	Hours	Tax rate
125	7.50	40	12%
304	11.80	40	15%
1204	9.60	40	14%

25. Given that

$$Y = 1 + X + X^2 + X^3 + X^4$$

write a program that calculates this sum for any value of X read.

26. The formula to convert from Celsius (C) to Fahrenheit (F) is

$$F = 9/5 \ C + 32$$

Write a program that reads Celsius temperatures and converts them to Fahrenheit. To test your program, read the freezing and boiling points of water (0° and 100°C, respectively). Their Fahrenheit equivalents are 32° and 212°F.

27. Solve the formula in the previous problem for Celsius in terms of Fahrenheit, and write a program that reads Celsius temperatures and converts them to Fahrenheit.

4

READING AND WRITING AND BUFFERING

4.1

FORMATTING INTEGER OUTPUT

BEFORE YOU BEGIN

Until now, you have had little control over the way your results were printed on the monitor or printer. We now show you how to instruct the computer to print the results in specific columns—this is called *formatting output*—so that the output is easier to read. The technique we have used until now produces what is called *unformatted output* (or *format-free output*).

Let's begin with two definitions:

1.   The group of columns in which results are printed is called a *field*.
2.   The number of columns in the field is called the *field width*.

The easiest way to learn formatting is to see as many examples as possible. In Figure 4.1*a*, the first `writeln` in the program, `writeln ('12345678 901234567890')`, prints the column numbers across the top of the screen, enabling us to see which columns are used for the various fields in our output. Next, `writeln( Sample)` instructs the computer to print the value of `Sample`, (i.e., 12365). Figure 4.1*b* shows that for the compiler on which the program was run the first value of `Sample` is printed in a field 16 columns wide so that the rightmost digit is printed in column 16. We say that the results are printed *right-justified*.

The field width of 16 columns is called the *default field width* because it is the field width used when you don't specify one. In `writeln(Sample:10)` the number that follows the colon indicates the field width, here 10, instructing the compiler to print the value of `Sample` in a field 10 columns wide:

12345678901234567890

12365

The value of `Sample` is printed in columns 6 to 10, right-justified. Similarly, `writeln( Sample:6);` instructs the compiler to print the value of `Sample` in a field six columns wide again, right-justified:

12345678901234567890

12365

What follows the colon (e.g., the 6 in `writeln(Sample:6)`) is called the *field specification*.

PRODUCING FORMATTED OUTPUT
INTEGERS

```
PROGRAM Field1(output);
(* Introduction to formatted output *)
VAR Sample, Test: integer;
BEGIN
  Sample:= 12365;
  Test:= 4444;
  writeln('12345678901234567890');
  writeln( Sample);
  writeln( Sample:10);
  writeln( Sample:6);
  writeln( Sample:3);
  writeln('12345678901234567890');
  writeln( Sample:10, Test:6)
END.
```

FIGURE 4.1a.   The space allocated to printed values is called a *field*. The integer after the colon specifies the field width for printing the preceding value.

```
12345678901234567890
                12365
        12365
      12365
12365
12345678901234567890
    12365   4444
```

FIGURE 4.1b.   Running the program of Figure 4.1a. The computer prints values *right-justified* (at the right of the field). When a field width is not specified, the computer substitutes its own—for this compiler, a width of 16. This is called the *default field width*.

Since in `writeln(Sample:3)` the field width, 3, is smaller than the number of digits in the integer, 12365, the compiler ignores the field width (3) and prints the entire integer, beginning with the leftmost column in the field:

```
12345678901234567890
12365
```

Finally, `writeln( Sample:10, Test:6)` instructs the compiler to print the value of `Test` (i.e., 4444), as well as the value of `Sample`. The field in which `Test` is printed is contiguous to the field in which `Sample` is printed:

```
12345678901234567890
    12365   4444
```

Thus the value of `Test` is printed in columns 13 to 16.

You must use an integer or integer expression to indicate the field width; you cannot use a real expression. Thus `writeln(Sample: 20 MOD 3)` is allowed, but `writeln(Sample:5.6)` is not.

4.2

FORMATTING REAL OUTPUT

Figure 4.2*a* shows how to format real value output. For purposes of comparison, let's begin the program by showing how a real value is printed without using a format. When `writeln(Sample)` is printed, the value of `Sample`, 123.65, is printed in exponential form in a field 18 columns wide on the compiler on which the program was run, as shown in Figure 4.2*b*. Thus, on this compiler, the default field width for reals is 18. Since the computer can't store

PRODUCING FORMATTED OUTPUT
REALS

```
PROGRAM Field2(output);
(* Introduction to formatted output *)
VAR Sample: real;
BEGIN
  Sample:= 123.65;
  writeln('12345678901234567890');
  writeln(Sample);
  writeln( Sample:10:3);
  writeln( Sample:10:2);
  writeln( Sample:10:1);
  writeln( Sample:12);
  writeln( Sample:2:1)
END.
```

FIGURE 4.2a.   When printing real values, after the second colon, specify how many digits should be printed to the right of the decimal point.

```
12345678901234567890
1.2365000000E+02
   123.650
   123.65
   123.7
1.236500E+02
124
```

FIGURE 4.2b.   Running the program of Figure 4.2a. When the number of digits to the right of the decimal point is greater than the digit d after the second colon, the computer rounds the result that appears to the right of the decimal point to d digits.

real values exactly, the value of Sample printed is just an approximation of 123.65. To print the value in nonexponential form, you have to specify not only the field width (as we did for integers), but also after a second colon, how many digits should be to the right of the decimal point. Thus

```
writeln( Sample:10:3);
```

specifies that the field width is 10 and that the number of digits to the right of the decimal point should be three. The result is printed as

```
12345678901234567890
123.650
```

Since 123.65 has only two digits to the right of the decimal point and the program specifies that the number printed should have three, the computer adds a zero in column 10 (at the end of the number). The 2 in writeln(Sample:10:2) specifies that the number of digits to the right of the decimal point should be two. The result is printed as

```
12345678901234567890
123.65
```

When the number of digits to the right of the decimal point is specified to be one in writeln(Sample:10:1), the compiler rounds 123.65 to 123.7. Note that the Pascal Standard does not allow a field width of 0 (e.g., writeln(X:0)) or zero digits to be printed after the decimal point (e.g., writeln(X:5:0)), although a specific implementation of Pascal may.

If only one colon is used in the specification, as in

```
writeln( Sample:12);
```

the compiler prints the result in exponential form, using a field width of 12 instead of 17. Finally, let's see what happens if the field width is too small, for instance, writeln(Sample:2:1). Here a field width of 2 is used to print 123.65, a number that requires a minimum field width of six (five for the digits and one for the decimal point). The compiler disregards the field width and prints the number as 124, the same way it would print an unformatted integer.

TEST YOURSELF

QUESTION: What does the following produce?

```
writeln(3:1);
writeln(3:2);
writeln(3:3);
writeln(3:4);
```

ANSWER:

```
3
 3
  3
   3
```

QUESTION: What does the following produce?

```
writeln(13.3567:10:3)?
```

ANSWER: 13.357

4.3

FORMATTING STRINGS AND BOOLEAN OUTPUT

Figure 4.3*a* shows how to format the printing of strings and character variables. Again, let's begin the program by showing how a string is printed without using a format. When `writeln('abcdefg')` is executed, `'abcdefg'` is printed with a field width equal to the number of characters in the string. Since this is the first thing printed, it is printed starting in column 1.

When the field width is specified, as in

```
writeln('abcdefg':10);
```

the string constant is printed right-justified, here in a field 10 columns wide, as shown in Figure 4.3*b*. When the field width is smaller than the number of characters in the string constant, as in

```
writeln('abcdefg':4)
```

the computer prints the first four characters in the string.

Next, let's see what happens when we print a character identifier using a field specification and without using one. The character value $ is assigned to Ch in `Ch:= '$'`. When the field width is specified, as in `writeln(ch:4)`, the character is printed right-justified in the field, here in column 4. When the field width is not specified, as in `'writeln(ch, ch)'`, the character is printed in a field one column wide.

PRODUCING FORMATTED OUTPUT
CHARACTERS AND STRINGS

```
PROGRAM Field3(output);
(* Introduction to formatted output *)
VAR Ch: char;
BEGIN
  writeln('1234567890');
  writeln('abcdefg');
  writeln('abcdefg':10);
  writeln('abcdefg':8);
  writeln('abcdefg':4);
  Ch:= '$';
  writeln(Ch:4);
  writeln(Ch,Ch)
END.
```

FIGURE 4.3a.   The same form of field width specifications is used for strings as for integers.

```
1234567890
abcdefg
   abcdefg
  abcdefg
abcd
   $
$$
```

FIGURE 4.3b.   Running the program of Figure 4.3a. If you don't specify a field width for a string, the computer uses the string width; otherwise, it prints the string right-justified in the specified field width.

Boolean Variables

Now let's investigate how boolean variables are printed, where the following assignments are made in Figure 4.4a:

First:= TRue;

Second:= FAlse;

As previously mentioned, the boolean values can be written in either uppercase or lowercase. Let's begin by printing the values of the variables without using field specifications, for example, writeln(First, Second, TRUE, FALSE). Figure 4.4b shows that the values are printed in uppercase without any intermcdiate spaces

TRUEFALSETRUEFALSE

Next, let's print the variables using a field width of 10 in writeln (First:10, Second:10). The values are printed right-justified. Finally, when a field width (here, 1) is specified that is smaller than the number of characters in the values (4 for true and 5 for false), the compiler prints the boolean values as it would print strings; it here prints the leftmost character, that is, T and F.

PRODUCING FORMATTED OUTPUT
BOOLEAN

```
PROGRAM Bool(output);
(* Investigates boolean output *)
VAR First, Second: boolean;
BEGIN
  writeln('12345678901234567890');
  First:= TRue;
  Second:= FAlse;
  writeln(First, Second, TRUE, FALSE);
  writeln(First:10, Second:10);
  writeln(First:1, Second:1)
END.
```

FIGURE 4.4*a*. The same form of field width specifications is used for boolean values as for strings.

```
12345678901234567890
TRUEFALSETRUEFALSE
          TRUE      FALSE
TF
```

FIGURE 4.4*b*. Running the program of Figure 4.4*a*. The boolean values are printed the same way as strings.

TEST YOURSELF

QUESTION: What does the following produce?

```
writeln('XXXXX':7)
writeln('XXXXX':6)
writeln('XXXXX':5)
writeln('XXXXX':4)
writeln('XXXXX':3)
writeln(TRUE:1)
```

ANSWER:

```
    XXXXX
    XXXXX
    XXXXX
    XXXX
    XXX
    T
```

Before leaving formatting, let's summarize what we've learned.

SPECIFYING FIELDS FOR INTEGER, CHARACTER, AND BOOLEAN VALUES

The field specification for integer, character, or boolean values consists of an integer expression that follows the colon (this specifies the field width). Examples are:

```
write(Time: 4);
write(Time: Width);
writeln(Time: X * X);
write(Name:8);
write(Flag: X)
```

where Time is an integer, Name is a character, and Flag is a boolean variable, and where Width and X are integer variables.

SPECIFYING FIELDS FOR REALS

The field specification for a real consists of an integer expression that follows the first colon (this specifies the field width) and another integer expression that follows the second colon (this specifies how many digits will be printed to the right of the decimal point). Examples for printing the value of the real variable Price are:

```
write(Price: 4: 2);
write(Price: Width: Digits);
write(Price: Width DIV Number: Digits * 2);
writeln(Price: Width)
```

where Width, Digits, and Number are integer variables. If only one colon is used, as in writeln(Price: Width), the value is printed in exponential form in a field that is Width columns wide.

4.4

READING NUMERICAL VALUES

BEFORE YOU BEGIN

As your programs become more sophisticated, they will require you to type data in ways not described in the previous chapter. Sections 4.4 to 4.6 will give you an understanding of how different types of data are transmitted from the keyboard to memory while the program is executing.

Readln

As opposed to the introductory information presented in Chapter 3, let's now explore the details of the reading operation. In Figure 4.5*a*,

```
readln(Length, Width, Price)
```

reads values for the two integer variables `Length` and `Width` and the real variable `Price` from the keyboard. We type the data as

```
13   4   0.75
```

as shown in Figure 4.5*b*.

When a program expects to read a group of numerical values, it skips any leading blanks until it encounters the first nonblank character; this must be a digit or a plus or minus sign. The numerical value starting with this digit and ending with a blank or carriage return will be the first value stored in memory. Thus, in our case, the program reads the 1, then the 3, and then the blank. It then knows that the first value is 13 and will assign it to `Length`. It then skips the blanks until it encounters the next digit, here the 4. Since the 4 is immediately followed by a blank, the computer assigns the 4 to `Width`. The computer then skips the blanks until it encounters the 0 in 0.75. Since `Price`, the next variable in the `read` list, was declared a real, the computer assigns the value starting with this 0 and ending with the carriage return, namely, 0.75, to `Price`. The results of running the program are shown in Figure 4.5*c*.

Since the blank and the carriage return are the symbols that indicate the end (or limit) of a real or integer value, they are called *delimiters*. What happens when the number of values on an input line exceeds the number of variables in the input list? For example, what would happen if the input statement was

```
readln(Length, Width)
```

and the input typed was as follows?

```
13   4   0.75.
```

THE readln STATEMENT

```
PROGRAM Area(input, output);
(* Investigates reading *)
VAR Length, Width: integer;
   Cost, Price: real;
BEGIN
   writeln('Type in Length, Width and Price');
   readln(Length, Width, Price);
   writeln( 'Length= ', Length: 2, 'Width= ':9 , Width:2,
   'Price= ':11, Price:5:2);
   Cost:= Length * Width * Price;
   writeln( 'Cost:=', Cost:5:2)
END.
```

FIGURE 4.5a.   When the readln is executed, the values typed at the keyboard are transmitted to the locations named by the variables in the readln after we hit the carriage return.

```
Type in Length, Width and Price
   13 4 0.75
```

FIGURE 4.5b.   Typing the data for the program of Figure 2.12a. Separate numerical values by one or more blanks and terminate the last value with the carriage return. Thus, when the program reads the 1, then the 3, and then the blank, it knows that the first value is 13. Since the blank and the carriage return define the limits of the numerical values, they are called *delimiters*.

```
Length= 13 Width= 4 Price= 0.75
Cost:= 39.00
```

FIGURE 4.5c.   Running the program of Figure 4.5a.

In our discussion, we will use a caret (∧) as a pointer to indicate what is to be read next. Once the variables in the list in a `readln` have been assigned values, the pointer is moved to the beginning of the next line of input so that the computer is prepared to read the next line of data to be typed. The values that remain on the previous line are discarded. Thus, in our present example, the value of 13 would be assigned to `Length` and the value of 4 to `Width`, and then the computer would proceed to the next line of data. The number 0.75 would be discarded. Even if a second `readln` were included, for example, `readln` (`Price`), the value of 0.75 would be inaccessible. See Table 4.1, Examples 1 and 2, where the next line is indicated by a ▬.

Read

There is a second type of input statement called the `read`. The difference between a `read` and a `readln` is that after a `read` is executed, the pointer remains on the same line of input, so that the next `read` or `readln` continues to read the remaining data on the line. Thus the problem just discussed (i.e., the 0.75 being inaccessible) would not have occurred if a `read` were used instead of the first `readln`, as for example, in

```
read(Length, Width);
read(Price);
```

The data that remain on the line, here 0.75, are now accessible and can be read by `read(Price)`, as shown in Table 4.1, Example 3.

Note that when the variables in the list in a `read` or `readln` have been assigned values, we say that the input list has been *satisfied*. As we have previously mentioned, when we type data, the computer pauses until the input list is satisfied.

If the data for a `read` or `readln` are typed on more than one line, as in

```
13   4
 0.75
```

the computer will continue to assign the data to the variables in the input statement until the input list is satisfied. Thus, if `readln(Length, Width, Price)` or `read(Length, Width, Price)` is used to read these data, after the computer reads 4 and assigns it to `Width`, it searches to the right of the 4 for more data. Since it encounters a carriage return, it moves to the next line of input to search for more data. It encounters the 0.75 and assigns this to `Price` (see Table 4.2, Example 1). Since the input list is now satisfied, when the computer encounters the next carriage return, it proceeds to execute the rest of the program.

The computer follows this same procedure if only the 13 appears on the first line and the 4 and 0.75 appear on the next line (see Table 4.2, Example 2)

```
13
4   0.75
```

or if a `read` is used instead of a `readln` (see Table 4.2, Example 3).

READING DATA—ALL THE DATA ARE ON ONE LINE

Example	Data	Input Statements	Length	Width	Price
1	13 4 0.75 ▄ ^	`readln(Length, Width);` `readln(Price)`	13 13	4 4	Undef Undef
2	13 4 0.75 ▄ ^	`readln(Length, Width);` `read(Price)`	13 13	4 4	Undef Undef
3	13 4 0.75 ^	`read(Length, Width);` `read(Price)`	13 13	4 4	Undef 0.75

TABLE 4.1. The caret indicates the next character to be read after the execution of the input statement in the first line of each set of two lines of code. In Examples 1 and 2, after the `readln` in the first line of code is executed, the caret is at the beginning of the next line of input. The " ▄ " indicates the next line of input. If the first line of code contains a `read`, however, the caret remains on the same line of input.

READING DATA—THE DATA ARE ON MORE THAN ONE LINE

Example	Data	Input Statements	Length	Width	Price
1	13 4 0.75	`readln(Length, Width, Price)`	13	4	0.75
2	13 4 0.75	`readln(Length, Width, Price)`	13	4	0.75
3	13 4 0.75	`read(Length, Width, Price)`	13	4	0.75

TABLE 4.2. If the data for a `read` or `readln` are typed on more than one line, the computer will continue to assign the data to the variables in the input statement until the input list is satisfied.

4.5

READING CHARACTERS

In the next program, Figure 4.6a, let's investigate how a read is used with character data. Each time one of the reads is executed, the character indicated by the pointer is assigned to the variable in the read and the pointer moves to the right, to the next column on the input line. Since only one character at a time can be read, there is no need for a delimiter. Therefore, the blank and the carriage return are not delimiters for the characters, but are read just as any other character is. For instance, if the input contains a blank, as does 1 3456 (see Figure 4.6b) when the second read, [read(B)], is executed, a blank is assigned to B. The results of running the program are shown in Figure 4.6c.

A= 1 B=   C= 3 D= 4 E= 5 F= 6

READING CHARACTERS

```
Program test(input, output);
(* Shows how READ works with char data *)
VAR A, B, C, D, E, F: char;
BEGIN
  writeln('Type 6 characters');
  read(A);
  read(B);
  read(C);
  read(D);
  read(E);
  read(F);
  writeln('A=', A, 'B=', B, 'C=', C, 'D=', D,
    'E=', E, 'F=', F)
END.
```

FIGURE 4.6a. The program reads six characters written on one line. Since a character location can store only one character, the program must read one character at a time.

RUNNING THE PROGRAM THE FIRST TIME

```
Type 6 characters
1 3456
```

FIGURE 4.6b. Typing the data for Figure 4.6a. Since the program reads one character at a time, there is no delimiter for characters. Thus the blank between the 1 and the 3 is assigned to B.

```
A=1 B=  C=3 D=4 E=5 F=6
```

FIGURE 4.6c. Running the program of Figure 4.6a.

What happens if instead you type as input three characters, press the carriage return, and then three more characters, as shown in Figure 4.6d?

123

456

The carriage return will be read as a character. It is read as a blank and is stored in D. Thus the 6, the last character, is not assigned to a variable. The results are shown in Figure 4.6e.

USING THE readln

As has just been shown, if the program reads the carriage return, it will produce erroneous output. In order to avoid reading it, place readln—without the parentheses and variables—after the appropriate read statement, here read(C):

```
read(A);
read(B);
read(C);
readln;
read(D);
read(E);
read(F);
```

The readln directs the program to skip the remaining data on the line, including the carriage return, and proceed to the next line. Thus, in read(D), the program reads as the value of D the first character typed on the next line, instead of the blank produced by the carriage return.

If a readln without parentheses occurs alone or precedes any reads in a program, the program will pause at the readln until you hit the carriage return.

RUNNING THE PROGRAM THE SECOND TIME

```
Type 6 characters
123
456
```

FIGURE 4.6d.   We type three characters, hit the carriage return, and then type three more characters.

```
A=1 B=2 C=3 D=   E=4 F=5
```

FIGURE 4.6e.   The carriage return is read as a blank and is stored in D. Thus the value of D is printed as a blank. The last character typed, 6, is not assigned to a variable.

TEST YOURSELF

QUESTION: What values will be stored in A, B, C, D, and E if

```
readln(A, B, C);
read(D, E)
```

is executed with

```
1  2
3  4  5
6  7  8
```

where all the variable identifiers are integers?

ANSWER: A contains 1, B contains 2, C contains 3, D contains 6, and E contains 7.

4.6

READING NUMERICAL AND
CHARACTER VALUES TOGETHER

The next program, Figure 4.7a, demonstrates how characters and digits are read on the same input line. The following declaration is used:

```
VAR A, B, C: char;
    Digit1, Digit2: integer;
```

The first readln statement reads two integers and then two character values:

```
readln(Digit1, Digit2, A, B);
```

We type 12 34 ab as input. Because the blank is one of the delimiters for numerical values, the first integer read is 12 and the second one is 34. The blank after 34 is not only a delimiter but also the first character value read. Thus the contents of A is a blank. The contents of B is a, as shown in Figure 4.7b.

READING INTEGERS AND CHARACTERS

```
PROGRAM mixed(input,output);
(* Shows how characters and digits are read on same input line *)
VAR A, B, C: char;
   Digit1, Digit2: integer;
BEGIN
   writeln('Type two integers and then two characters');
   readln(Digit1, Digit2, A, B);
   writeln('Digit1= ', Digit1:2, ' Digit2= ', Digit 2:2,
     ' A=', a, ' B=', B);
   writeln('Type two characters and then two integers ');
   readln(A, B, Digit1, Digit2);
   writeln(' A=', a, ' B=', B , 'Digit1=', Digit1:2, ' Digit2= ',
     Digit2:2)
END.
```

FIGURE 4.7*a*. The program reads two integers and then two characters. Next, it reads two characters and then two integers.

TYPING TWO INTEGERS FOLLOWED BY TWO CHARACTERS, CASE I

```
Type two integers and then two characters
12 34 ab←read by readln(Digit1, Digit2, A, B)
Digit1 = 12 Digit2 = 34 A=  B=a
```

FIGURE 4.7*b*.   The first integer is 12 and the second one is 34. The blank after 34 is not only a delimiter but also the first character value read. Thus the contents of A is a blank. The contents of B is a.

When a numerical constant is followed by a character constant, any nondigit character but the decimal point used in a real constant and an E being used to indicate the exponent in a real is also a delimiter. Thus, if we omit the second blank and type 12 34ab instead, the program reads 34 as the second integer and a as the first character, as shown in Figure 4.7c.

The second `readln` statement reads two character values and then two integers:

readln(A, B, Digitl, Digit2);

The input is 1234 56. Since character variables can store only one character, the first two characters read are 1 and 2. These are assigned to A and B, respectively. Since there is no delimiter for characters, the first integer read is 34. The second one read is 56. All of this is shown in Figure 4.7d.

TEST YOURSELF

QUESTION: What values will be stored in X, Operator, and Y if

read(X, Operator, Y)

is executed with the following declaration

VAR X, Y:integer;
Operator:char;

and with the following data?

1. 3 + 4
2. 3 +4
3. 3+4

The goal is to have X contain 3, Operator contain "+", and Y contain 4.

ANSWER:

1. X contains 3, Operator contains a blank, and Y contains a "+," which causes a run-time error.
2. X contains 3, Operator contains a blank, and Y contains + 4.
3. X contains 3, Operator contains a "+", and Y contains 4.

Reading Boolean Constants

You cannot read boolean values from the keyboard. They must be assigned in an assignment statement.

TYPING TWO INTEGERS FOLLOWED BY TWO CHARACTERS, CASE II

Type two integers and then two characters
12 34ab←*read by readln(Digit1, Digit2, A, B)*
Digit1= 12 Digit2= 34 A= a B=b

FIGURE 4.7c.   This shows what happens if we do not use a second blank in the input of Figure 4.7b. Since the a acts as a delimiter, the second integer read is 34 and the first character constant read is a.

TYPING TWO CHARACTERS FOLLOWED BY TWO INTEGERS

Type two characters and then two integers
1234 56 read by readln(A, B, Digit1, Digit2);
A=1 B=2 Digit1=34 Digit2=56

FIGURE 4.7d.   Since character variables can store only one character, the first two characters read are 1 and 2. Since there is no delimiter for characters, the first digit read is 34.

4.7

BUFFERED INPUT

BEFORE YOU BEGIN

Have you ever been on a checkout line in the supermarket and been told by the cashier that no one else should get on line? Then each person on line, from the first person to you, is taken in his or her order in the line. Similarly, on a computer system, the *buffer* is a holding area for data inputted to the computer until they are needed in a read or readln. When the carriage return is pressed, the data will be processed in the order in which they were typed. Remember how, in the survey problem, the arrow indicated the next person to be questioned? In the buffer, a *pointer* determines the next piece of data to be read. Understanding how the buffer works will give us insight into how the read and readln work.

The Effect of the Read on the Buffer

Whenever a read or readln is executed and you type a line of data terminated by hitting the carriage return, that line, along with a marker representing the end of the line, is stored in the buffer. When the computer reads data, it reads them from the buffer. The reading process discussed in the preceding sections of this chapter in fact describes how the computer reads data from the buffer.

The read and the readln have different effects on the buffer. First, let's see how the compiler treats a series of reads. For example, when the first read in the program of Figure 4.8a is executed,

```
read(A);
writeln('A= ', A:2);
read(B);
writeln('B= ', B:2);
read(C);
writeln('C= ', C:2)
```

if we type the values for the integer variables A, B, and C on one line, the computer stores all the values in the input buffer before it executes any of the other reads. When we hit the carriage return, the computer uses these values in the order in which they were stored in the buffer in executing the read statements until all the input lists have been satisfied.

Let's examine in detail what happens. When the program is run, as shown in Figure 4.8b, we type across the screen 23 45 67 and then hit the carriage return. These data are stored in the buffer character by character, ending with the end-of-line marker, as shown in the table for Figure 4.8b. We use "~" to represent this marker in our diagrams.

INTRODUCTION TO BUFFERS

```
PROGRAM IntroBuff;
{Shows how a buffer works}
VAR A, B, C:integer;
BEGIN
   writeln('Type 3 integers on a line, then hit CR');
   read(A);
   writeln('A= ', A:2);
   read(B);
   writeln('B= ', B:2);
   read(C);
   writeln('C= ', C:2)
END.
```

FIGURE 4.8a.   The values typed as input are stored in a temporary location called buffer and are not transferred to identifiers until the carriage return is hit.

```
Type 3 integers on a line, then hit CR
23 45 67
A= 23
B= 45
C= 67
```

FIGURE 4.8b.   The values typed on the line are stored as characters in the buffer.

```
23 45 67⌐
   ^
```

TABLE FOR FIGURE 4.8b.   This shows the input buffer for Figure 4.8b. Each time a read is executed, the value indicated by the pointer (shown as a caret) is assigned to the identifier in the read and the pointer is moved to the next value.

An indicator called the *pointer* originally points to the value in the first location in the buffer; we'll use a caret to show the pointer's position.

$$\boxed{23\ 45\ 67^\urcorner}$$
$$\wedge$$

When the carriage return is pressed, because the first input statement is read(A) and because A is an integer variable, the 23 in the buffer is copied to location A. The computer then moves the pointer to the next location in the buffer.

$$\boxed{23\ 45\ 67^\urcorner}$$
$$\wedge$$

The computer next executes writeln('A=', A:2), printing the value of A. When it executes read(B), it copies the 45 to location B and moves the pointer to the next location in the buffer. This process continues until each value in the buffer has been copied to the appropriate locations indicated in a read. At this point, the pointer is positioned at the end-of-line marker, "~". We will see in Chapter 8 that we can write a statement to test for this marker. If the program reads the end-of-line marker into a location and then prints the content of that location, it will be printed as a blank.

TEST YOURSELF

QUESTION: How is the following input stored in the buffer?

12 34.5 Ea12

ANSWER: All the characters typed, including the blanks, are stored in the buffer.

| 12 34.56 Ea12⁻ |

QUESTION: What will be stored in the various memory locations after the following program segment is executed, using the contents of the buffer?

```
VAR Int1, Int2:integer;
    Real1:real;
    Ch0, Ch1, Ch2:char;
BEGIN
    read(Int1, Real1);
    read(Ch0, Ch1, Ch2);
    read(Int2)
```

ANSWER: Int1 will contain 12, Real1 will contain 34.56, Ch0 will contain a blank, Ch1 will contain E, and Ch2 will contain a. Finally, Int2 will contain 12.

The Effect of the `readln` on the Buffer

Figure 4.9*a* shows a program in which a `readln` is followed by two `read` statements:

```
readln(A);
writeln('A= ', A:2);
read(B);
writeln('B= ', B:2);
read(C);
writeln('C= ', C:2)
```

When the `readln` is executed, we type three integers on one line, as shown in Figure 4.9*b*. These numbers are stored in the buffer, as shown in the table for Figure 4.9*b*. When we hit the carriage return, the first number in the buffer is copied into location A.

Because there are no more variables in the list, and because the input statement is a `readln` and not a `read`, the pointer is then reset to the beginning of the buffer and the buffer is cleared.

Thus the 34 and the 56 in the second and third locations of the buffer are lost. As a result, there are no numbers to copy into locations B and C in the next two `read`s.

This is exactly the situation we described previously in this chapter without the benefit of the buffer. The values remaining on the input line (here, 34 and 56) after the list in the `readln` has been satisfied are lost. In order to copy numbers into locations B and C, we must type two more values. We do, as shown in Figure 4.9*b*.

THE EFFECT OF THE `readln` ON THE BUFFER

```
PROGRAM IntroBuff;
{Shows how a buffer works with readnl}
VAR A, B, C:integer;
BEGIN
  writeln('Type 3 integers on a line, then hit CR');
  readln(A);
  writeln('A= ', A:2);
  read(B);
  writeln('B= ', B:2);
  read(C);
  writeln('C= ', C:2)
END.
```

FIGURE 4.9a.   The program has a `readln` followed by two reads.

```
Type 3 integers on a line, then hit CR
12 34 56
A= 12
78 90
B= 78
C= 90
```

FIGURE 4.9b.   After the `readln` is executed and 12 is copied to location A, the buffer is cleared. Thus more data have to be typed to satisfy `read(B)` and `read(C)`.

```
12 34 56⁻
```

TABLE FOR FIGURE 4.9b.   This shows the input buffer for Figure 4.9b. After the `readln` is executed, the buffer is cleared.

QUESTION: Using the program segment

```
VAR One, Two, Three:integer;
BEGIN
  read(One, Two, Three);
```

how are the following data processed?

12 34

56

ANSWER: The first line is stored in the buffer as

| 12 34~ |

Therefore, 12 is assigned to One and 34 to Two. After these assignments are made, the buffer is cleared because the carriage return is hit. The 56 is stored in the buffer. This is then assigned to Three.

| 56~ |

QUESTION: If read(A, B, C), where all the variables are character variables, reads the following data stored in the buffer

| 56~ |

how would write(A, B, C) print the results?

ANSWER: 56 and then a blank.

It is nice to use the capabilities of the buffer when you are typing data to be read by a read because you get an unobstructed view of the data. However, there are difficulties involved when you type more data than can fit on a line. You must be careful to place a blank between the last numerical value you type on a line and the first numerical value you type on the next line. If you don't, a run-time error will occur.

CHAPTER REVIEW

Reading

Character values are read one at a time. Thus there are no delimiters for characters. If the carriage return is read and then printed, it's printed as a blank. The delimiter for a numerical constant is any character that is not being used as part of a numerical constant (however, if you are reading a group of numerical constants, you can separate them only with blanks). For instance, if you are reading a real Re and a character Ch in read(Re, Ch) and you type 12.3E−4A as input, then 12.3×10^{-4} will be stored in Re and A will be stored in Ch. If you type 12.3E instead, the E is no longer part of the numerical constant but is now a delimiter. Thus 12.3 will be stored in Re and E will be stored in Ch.

The operation of the read in comparison to the readln is similar to the operation of the write in comparison to the writeln. After a read is executed, the computer reads the next item from the same line. After a readln is executed, a carriage return and a line feed are performed. Thus the next input statement reads the next item from the new line.

Buffers

Pascal uses a buffer to store information temporarily. Each line of input you type, terminated by hitting the carriage return, is stored in the buffer. The carriage return is stored as the end-of-line marker. Each time information from the buffer is read into memory, an indicator called a *pointer* is advanced to the next location in the buffer. After a readln is executed, the buffer is cleared. If the read or readln statement expects to read characters and reads an end-of-line marker (carriage return), this marker is printed as a blank.

NEW TERMS

buffer	field width
default field width	format
delimiter	formatting output
field	pointer
field specification	right-justified

EXERCISES

1. What is wrong with the following statements?
   a. `writeln(Time: 8/4)`
   b. `write(56:4:2)`
   c. `writeln(Quote:5:1)` where `Quote` is a character variable.

2. What will the following program produce?

```
PROGRAM Prob3 (output);
VAR Width:integer;
BEGIN
  Width:=6;
  writeln(37.5: Width DIV 3: Width DIV 2)
END.
```

3. If the value of `Salary` is 456.54, how is it printed when the following statements are executed?
   a. `writeln(Salary);`
   b. `writeln(Salary:4);`
   c. `writeln(Salary:4:2);`
   d. `writeln(Salary:4:4);`
   e. `writeln(Salary:10:2);`

4. What are the delimiters for the following?
   a. Real
   b. Integer
   c. Character
   d. Boolean

5. Write one input statement that would read the following:

```
12.3 14
13.56 12 67
12 16 43
```

6. What is assigned to the variables when the following is executed?

```
readln(One, Two, Three);
read(Four, Five);
read(Six)
```

with the following input:

```
12 13 14 15 16
17 18 19 20
```

where all the variables are integer type?

7. What is assigned to the variables when the following is executed:

```
readln(One, Two, Three);
read(Four, Five);
read(Six)
```

with the following input:

12 13 14 15 16
17 18 19 20

where all the variables are character type?

8. What is assigned to the variables when `read(One, Two, Three, Four, Five, Six)` is executed with the following input:

1 23
45 6

where all the variables are character type?

9. What is assigned to the variables when `read(Ch1, Ch2, Ch3, Num1, Num2, Num3)` is executed with the following input:

1 234 656 8

where Ch1, Ch2, and Ch3 are character type and Num1, Num2, and Num3 are of integer type?

10. Do Exercise 9 for `read(Num1, Num2, Num3, Ch1, Ch2, Ch3)`.

11. Show the contents of the buffer and the position of the pointer as the following is executed:

```
read(Four, Five);
read(Six)
```

with the following input:

12 13 14 15 16

where all the variables are integer type.

12. Show the contents of the buffer and the position of the pointer as the following is executed:

```
readln(One, Two, Three);
read(Four, Five);
read(Six)
```

with the following input:

```
12 13 14 15 16
17 18 19 20
```

where all the variables are integer type.

Programming Problems

13. Write a program that writes your name in block letters.

14. Write a program that calculates the volume of a cube from data read by the program and prints the results in a formatted form.

5

THE FOR–DO LOOP
AND THE ORDINAL TYPES

CHAPTER OVERVIEW

This chapter begins by showing that the integer type can be used to direct the computer to execute a statement or compound statement many times in what is called a FOR–DO loop. It then introduces the term *ordinal type* to describe the types other than integer whose values are discrete, that is, character and boolean, and it shows that these types can also be used to control FOR–DO loops.

5.1

INTRODUCTION TO THE FOR–DO LOOP

BEFORE YOU BEGIN

Have you ever wanted to perform a certain task repetitively, like printing a label with your name and address 100 times? The FOR–DO together with a few `writeln`s will enable you to do this.

Let's begin by recalling from Chapter 2 that a compound statement is a group of statements beginning with BEGIN and ending with END.

The FOR–DO instructs the computer how many times to perform the next statement or compound statement. To do this, insert between the FOR and the DO the first and last value that should be assigned to a variable, called the *control variable*. Thus

```
FOR Index:= 1 TO 5 DO
    writeln('My name is Ivan')
```

by indicating that the control variable (the integer variable Index) should get the integer values from 1 to 5, instructs the computer to execute `writeln('My name is Ivan')` for the value of Index equal to 1, 2, 3, 4, and 5, that is, five times.

After the action of the FOR on the statement or compound statement following the FOR has been completed, the computer executes the next statement in the program. Since in the program of Figure 5.1a no statement follows `writeln('My name is Ivan')`, the program terminates. The results of running the program are shown in Figure 5.1b.

A statement or group of statements that the program repeatedly executes is called a *loop*. Therefore it is appropriate that the group of statements beginning with the FOR–DO we have just discussed is called a FOR–DO *loop*. We have indented the statement following the FOR–DO so that anyone reading the program can immediately see what statement is executed in the loop. The indentation has absolutely no meaning to the compiler.

THE FOR–DO LOOP

```
PROGRAM Intro(output);
(* Prints a string five times *)
VAR Index: integer;
BEGIN
   FOR Index:= 1 TO 5 DO
      writeln('My name is Ivan')
END.
```

FIGURE 5.1*a*. The statement following the FOR–DO is executed for each value of the control variable (here, from 1 to 5).

```
My name is Ivan
My name is Ivan
My name is Ivan
My name is Ivan
My name is Ivan
```

FIGURE 5.1*b*.   Running the program of Figure 5.1*a*.

PROGRAMMING PITFALL

We've learned that each statement must be separated from the next statement or compound statement by a semicolon. However, the FOR–DO is not a complete statement; therefore, don't end it with a semicolon. What happens if you do? For instance, if you write

```
FOR Index:= 1 TO 5 DO;
   writeln('My name is Ivan')
```

the computer considers what separates the DO and the "; " an empty or *null* statement; consequently, when it executes this statement five times, it accomplishes nothing. It then goes on to execute writeln('My name is Ivan') once.

If you're wondering how to print an address label many times, here's how. In the program of Figure 5.2*a*, place the compound statement

```
BEGIN
   writeln('Jon Mackle');
   writeln('1075 Nelson Ave');
   writeln('New York, NY 10454');
   writeln('--------------------------')
END {FOR}
```

immediately after FOR Index := 1 TO NumberTimes DO. Since the value of the constant NumberTimes is 3, the compound statement is executed three times and produces the output shown in Figure 5.2*b*.

A COMPOUND STATEMENT IN THE FOR–DO LOOP

```
PROGRAM Block(output);
CONST NumberTimes = 3;
(* Prints an address NumberTimes times *)
VAR Index: integer;
BEGIN
  FOR Index:= 1 TO NumberTimes DO
    BEGIN
      writeln('Jon Mackle');
      writeln('1075 Nelson Ave');
      writeln('New York, NY 10454');
      writeln('-------------------------')
    END (* FOR *)
END.
```

FIGURE 5.2a.   The compound statement following the FOR–DO is executed for each value of the control variable (here, from 1 to 3).

```
Jon Mackle
1075 Nelson Ave
New York, NY 10454

-------------------------

Jon Mackle
1075 Nelson Ave
New York, NY 10454

-------------------------

Jon Mackle
1075 Nelson Ave
New York, NY 10454

-------------------------
```

FIGURE 5.2b.   Running the program of Figure 5.2a.

What happens if you forget to sandwich the `writeln`s between BEGIN and END, as shown in Figure 5.2c?

```
FOR Index:= 1 TO NumberTimes DO
    writeln('Jon Mackle');
    writeln('1075 Nelson Ave');
    writeln('New York, NY 10454');
    writeln('-------------------------')
```

The computer will execute `writeln('Jon Mackle')` three times and the other `writeln`s only once, as shown in Figure 5.2d. The fact that the other `writeln`s are indented has no meaning to the compiler, so it doesn't consider those `writeln`s part of the loop.

INDENTATION DOES NOT AFFECT THE SCOPE OF THE FOR–DO LOOP

```
PROGRAM Block(output);
CONST NumberTimes = 3;
(* Prints an address Number_times times *)
VAR Index: integer;
BEGIN
  FOR Index:= 1 TO NumberTimes DO
    writeln('Jon Mackle');
    writeln('1075 Nelson Ave');
    writeln('New York, NY 10454');
writeln('-------------------------')
END.
```

FIGURE 5.2c. The FOR–DO affects only the next statement or compound statement. The indentation of the second statement has no effect on the FOR–DO.

```
Jon Mackle
Jon Mackle
Jon Mackle
1075 Nelson Ave
New York, NY 10454

-------------------------
```

FIGURE 5.2d. Running the program of Figure 5.2c. The first statement is executed three times and the second one only once.

5.2

USING VARIABLE LIMITS FOR THE CONTROL VARIABLE

In `FOR Index:= 1 TO 5 DO`, the integer 1 is the initial value of the control variable, and 5 is its final value. Since `Index` is an integer, its initial and final values must also be integers. However, they do not have to be constant values. They can be variable or constant identifiers, or any valid integer expression as well. Thus in Figure 5.3*a* we can write

```
FOR I:= 1 TO Number DO
    write('x');
```

where `Number` is an integer variable whose value was read into the program. When you run the program, type 8 as Number's value. The computer now interprets the `FOR–DO` as `FOR I:= 1 TO 8 DO`. The results of running the program are shown in Figure 5.3*b*. Since the `write` does not produce a carriage return and line feed, all the X's are printed on one line.

What happens if a `writeln` is substituted for the `write` in the loop, as shown in Figure 5.3*c*?

```
FOR I:= 1 TO Number DO
    writeln('x')
```

Since the `writeln` includes an implied carriage return and line feed, each x is printed on a separate line, as shown in Figure 5.3*d*.

Note that if the final value of the control variable is less than the initial value, as in `FOR I: = 3 TO 1 DO`, the loop is not executed.

USING A VARIABLE AS THE UPPER LIMIT OF THE FOR–DO LOOP

```
PROGRAM Pattern(input, output);
(* Prints a horizontal line of Xs *)
VAR I, Number: integer;
BEGIN
  writeln('Type how many Xs do you want printed.');
  readln(Number);
  FOR I:= 1 TO Number DO
    write('x');
END.
```

FIGURE 5.3a.   The value of Number read from the keyboard is now the upper limit of the FOR–DO loop.

```
Type how many Xs do you want printed?
8
XXXXXXXX
```

FIGURE 5.3b.   Running the program of Figure 5.3a.

EACH WRITELN PRODUCES ITS OUTPUT ON A NEW LINE

```
PROGRAM Pattern2(input, output);
(* Prints a vertical line of Xs *)
VAR I, Number: integer;
BEGIN
  writeln('Type how many Xs do you want printed.');
  readln(Number);
  FOR I:= 1 TO Number DO
    writeln('x')
END.
```

FIGURE 5.3c.   Each time the writeln is executed, the computer performs a carriage return and line feed.

```
Type how many Xs do you want printed.
3
X
X
X
```

FIGURE 5.3d.   Running the program of Figure 5.3c.

5.3

USING THE CONTROL VARIABLE IN THE LOOP

The control variable can be used in a statement in the loop, as shown in Figure 5.4a, which produces a diagonal line. In

```
FOR J : = 1 TO 8 DO
    writeln( 'x' :J)
```

the control variable J is used to indicate the field width for x in the writeln statement. Thus, when the value of J is 1, the computer interprets the writeln as writeln('x' : 1) and prints an x in a field one column wide. When the value of J is 2, the computer interprets the writeln as writeln('x' : 2) and prints an x in a field two columns wide on the next line. As the value of J increases, the x is printed one column to the right on the next line, as shown in Figure 5.4b.

BEFORE YOU BEGIN

> The output of this program is of interest because we will use it to label the output of word processing programs that we will write in future chapters.

Now let's solve a more challenging problem, namely, labeling columns 1 through 79 on the monitor screen or printer page. Since only one digit can be printed in a column, we use two rows to label each column—the first row for the tens digit and the second row for the units digit. Thus the first 30 columns would look like this:

```
000000000111111111122222222223
123456789012345678901234567890
```

so column 14 would be labeled as $\frac{1}{4}$. The first version of the pseudocode for the program is

Print the tens digits on the first line;
Print the units digits on the second line;

USING THE CONTROL VARIABLE AS THE FIELD WIDTH

```
PROGRAM Diagonal(output);
(* Prints a diagonal consisting of Xs *)
VAR J: integer;
BEGIN
  FOR J:= 1 TO 8 DO
    writeln( 'x' : J)
END.
```

FIGURE 5.4a.   Each time the writeln is executed, the field width is increased by 1.

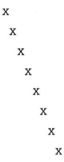

FIGURE 5.4b.   Running the program of Figure 5.4a.

We refine this to

> *Print nine 0s, ten 1s, ten 2s, etc. on the first line*
> *Print 0...9 eight times on the second line.*

and translate this to the program shown in Figure 5.5*a*.

The following loop produces the required results for the first line of pseudocode:

```
FOR I: = 1 TO NumCol DO
    write(I DIV 10:1);
```

as shown in the table for Figure 5.5*a*; the value of NumCol is defined in the CONST definition. We have used a field width of 1 in write(I DIV 10:1) so that one digit is printed per column.

In order to print the second line of results, follow this write with a statement that does not print any information, but only supplies a carriage return and a line feed. Just typing writeln does this.* To get the repetitions of the digits 0 to 9 on the second line, use

```
FOR J: = 1 TO NumCol DO
    write(J MOD 10:1)
```

Again, the table shows that this produces the required results. The results of running the program are shown in Figure 5.5*b*. We could have used I as the control variable for the second FOR–DO, but we used J instead to simplify our exposition.

TEST YOURSELF

QUESTION: Write the program segment to produce

```
            x
          x
        x
      x
```

ANSWER:

```
FOR J: = 1 TO 5 DO
    writeln('x':10 – J)
```

*If you run this program with NumCol equal to 80, you do not need the writeln. The reason is that after the monitor displays the 80 characters on the first line, since the screen width is 80, the monitor automatically displays the next set of characters on the next line. This feature is called *wrap around*.

LABELING THE COLUMNS

```
PROGRAM LabelColumns(output);
(* Labels the columns on a page *)
VAR I, J:integer;
CONST NumCol = 79;
BEGIN
  (* Print tens digit *)
  FOR I: = 1 TO NumCol DO
    write(I DIV 10:1);
  writeln;
  (* Print units digit *)
  FOR J: = 1 TO NumCol DO
    write(J MOD 10:1)
END.
```

FIGURE 5.5a.   By using the MOD and the DIV, we can select the first and second digits of the value stored in the control variable.

I	I DIV 10	J	J MOD 10
1	0	1	1
9	0	9	9
10	1	10	0
11	1	11	1
20	2	20	0

TABLE FOR FIGURE 5.5a.   Shows how the digits on the first and second lines are produced.

```
0000000001111111111222222222233333333334444444444555555555566666666667777777777
1234567890123456789012345678901234567890123456789012345678901234567890123456789
```

FIGURE 5.5b.   Running the program of Figure 5.5a. A digit on the first line of the output represents the first digit of the column number. The corresponding digit on the second line represents the second digit.

5.4

AVERAGING NUMBERS

Were you dissatisfied with the first version of the averaging program (Chapter 3), which averaged only a fixed number of values? A more flexible program would average a variable number of grades. The first version of the pseudocode for this program is as follows:

> *Read the number of grades to be averaged;*
> *Sum all the grades to be averaged;*
> *Compute and print the average.*

To sum the grades, use a location—let's call it *Sum*—to which you add the value of the grade just read. This means that you must originally set *Sum* to zero. This leads to our refining the pseudocode to:

Read the number of grades to be averaged;
Set Sum to zero;
FOR *GradeNumber:= 1* TO *number of grades to be averaged* DO BEGIN
  Read grade;
  Add grade to sum;
END (*FOR*);
Compute average;
Print the sum and average.

The meaning of *Add grade to sum* is "Add the value in *grade* to the value in *sum* and store the result in *sum*." Thus write it as Sum: = Sum + Grade.

The program is shown in Figure 5.6*a* and the data for the program, in Figure 5.6*b*. Since 5 is read as the value of the number of grades, the program executes

PERFORMING AN AVERAGE

```
PROGRAM AverageGrade(input,output);
(* Averages grades read *)
VAR Number, GradeNumber, Sum, Grade: integer;
  Average: real;
BEGIN
  writeln('Type in number of grades to be read.');
  readln( Number);
  Sum := 0;
  writeln('Type each grade on a new line.');

  FOR GradeNumber:= 1 TO Number DO BEGIN
    readln(Grade);
    Sum:= Sum + Grade;
  END (* FOR *);

  writeln;
  Average:= Sum / Number;
  writeln('The sum of ', Number:2, ' marks is ', Sum);
  writeln('The average of ', Number:2, ' marks is ', Average:5:1)
END.
```

FIGURE 5.6a. Each time Sum:= Sum + Grade is executed, the value of Grade is added to the value of Sum and the result is stored in Sum.

```
Type in number of grades to be read.
5
Type each grade on a new line.
97
89
76
93
81
The sum of 5 marks is 436
The average of 5 marks is 87.2
```

FIGURE 5.6b. Running the program of Figure 5.6a. We print both the sum and the average to check whether there is an error.

the loop five times. Thus five grades will be summed and then averaged. The table for Figure 5.6a shows how the summing works. Looking at two consecutive lines of the output, for instance,

Grade	Sum
97	97
89	186

we see that the value of Sum for the second line (186) equals the value of Grade for that line (89) plus the value of Sum for the preceding line (97). This is the meaning of Sum: = Sum + Grade; that is, after this statement is executed, the value of Sum equals the present value of Grade added to the previous value of Sum. A variable, such as Sum, whose value is increased in this way is called an *accumulator*.

Why did we set Sum to zero before the loop? We wanted the initial value of Sum to be zero the first time Sum: = Sum + Grade is executed. Giving an accumulator, such as Sum here, its first value is called *initializing* it.

TEST YOURSELF

QUESTION: What is wrong with placing Sum : = 0 in the loop in Figure 5.6a?

```
FOR GradeNumber: = 1 TO Number DO BEGIN
    Sum : = 0;
    readln(Grade);
    Sum: = Sum + Grade;
END {FOR};
```

ANSWER: Each time the loop is executed, the value of Sum would be set to zero before Grade is added to it. The final value of Sum would be the last value of Grade read; consequently the average would be wrong. The correct thing to do is to initialize Sum to zero before the loop.

The average is calculated in Average: = Sum / Number. Calculating it using the loop control variable GradeNumber, as in

$$Average: = Sum / GradeNumber$$

would cause an error because the loop control variable is undefined after the loop is executed.

We print both the sum and the average in the output to enable us to check our results. For instance, if the average did not agree with a hand calculation, but the sum did, we would know that we divided by the wrong value.

Grade	Sum
97	97
89	186
76	262
93	355
81	436

TABLE FOR FIGURE 5.6a. The value of sum for a given line is the sum of the value of Grade for that line and that of Sum for the previous line. This is the meaning of Sum: = Sum + Grade.

Now let's examine a problem that at first seems unrelated to any other problem we've done. The problem is to generate the monthly bank statement you receive for your checking account. The pseudocode for a first attempt at a solution is as follows:

Enter the starting balance;
Subtract from the balance the sum of the checks;
Add to the balance the sum of the deposits;
Print the results.

This suggests the following top-down diagram:

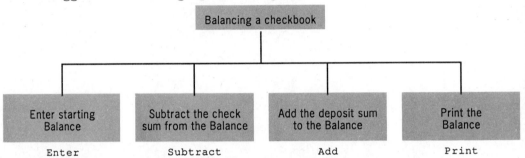

This would mean forming two separate sums—one for the deposits and one for the checks. However, we've just done a problem that involves just one sum (the averaging program in Figure 5.6a), which, with a little alteration, becomes the solution to our present problem. If you look at your checking account statement, you'll see that the amounts on the checks are subtracted from the balance and the deposits are added to the balance as these transactions are made. So if Sum from the last problem becomes Balance in this problem, and Grade becomes Transaction, then with the following provisos, the present problem is solved:

1. The initial value of Balance is set to the starting balance and not to zero.

2. The amounts on the checks are entered as negative numbers into location Transaction.

3. Deposits are entered as positive numbers into location Transaction.

The resulting top-down diagram is shown in the table for Figure 5.6c.

BALANCING A CHECKBOOK

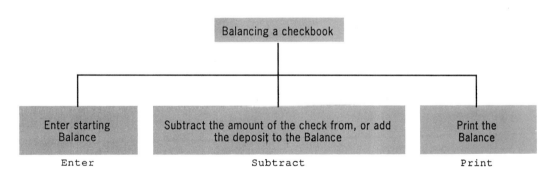

TABLE FOR FIGURE 5.6c.   The pseudocode indicates one sum for both the deposits and checks.

This produces the program shown in Figure 5.6c.

PROGRAMMING STYLE

In order to be able to fit as much of the program as possible on one page, we have placed the BEGIN for a compound statement on the same line as the FOR–DO statement, as shown, for example, in

```
FOR GradeNumber : = 1 TO Number DO BEGIN
```

BALANCING A CHECKBOOK (CONTINUED)

```
PROGRAM BalancingCheckbook(input,output);
(* Balances a checkbook *)
USES Crt, Printer;
VAR Number, Entry, CheckNo: integer;
  AccountNumber:longint;
  Transaction, Balance: real;
  Date, Name:string[20];
BEGIN
  writeln('Type in account number.');
  readln( AccountNumber);
  writeln('Type in number of transactions to be read and starting balance.');
  readln( Number, Balance);

  writeln('Account number is: ', AccountNumber);
  writeln('Starting balance is: ', Balance:10:2);
  writeln;
  writeln('Type each check number and transaction on a new line ');
  writeln;
  writeln('Number':22, 'Transaction':20, 'Balance':20);

  FOR Entry:= 1 TO Number DO BEGIN
    readln(CheckNo, Transaction);
    Balance:= Balance + Transaction;
    writeln(CheckNo:22, Transaction:20:2, Balance:20:2)
  END (* FOR *);

  writeln('The Balance after ', Number:2, ' transactions is ',
    Balance:20:2)
END.
```

FIGURE 5.6c. By subtracting the amount of a check from the sum and adding the amount of the deposit to the sum, the final sum is the correct balance.

Since checking account statements have the number for each check, we have entered the check numbers with the other data for the checks and 0 for the check number entry with the other data for deposits. The running of the program is shown in Figure 5.6*d*. Printing the results to the right of the screen enables us to see the results so that they are not obstructed by the input (which appears to the left of the screen).

BALANCING A CHECKBOOK (CONTINUED)

```
Type in account number.
12004
Type in number of transactions to be read and starting balance.
5 1265.41
Account number is: 12004
Starting balance is: 1265.41


Type each check number and transaction on a new line
```

	Number	Transaction	Balance
1004 −54.00			
	1004	−54.00	1211.41
1003 −100.00			
	1003	−100.00	1111.41
0 300			
	0	300.00	1411.41
1005 −201.45			
	1005	−201.45	1209.96
1007 −125.00			
	1007	−125.00	1084.96

```
The balance after 5 transactions is     1084.96
```

FIGURE 5.6d. Running the program of Figure 5.6c. Printing the results to the right of the screen enables us to see the results so that they are not obstructed by the input (which appears to the left of the screen).

5.5

ORDINAL TYPES

The *ordinal numbers* indicate position in a sequence. Thus *first, second,* and *third* are ordinal numbers. You can assign ordinal numbers to the integers. For instance, if you call 0 the first integer in a sequence, then 1 will be the second and 2 will be the third. You cannot, however, make a similar assignment to the reals. For example, if you call 0.0 the first real, what is the second? You cannot call it 0.0001 because there is an infinite number of reals between these two numbers. However, you can give ordinal values to characters and to the boolean values. Thus integer, character, and boolean types are called the *ordinal types.*

BEFORE YOU BEGIN

Why is the concept of ordinal types introduced here? Because the FOR–DO loop control variable must be an ordinal type. By using ordinal types other than the integer type as control variables, you can write more powerful programs. Before we study FOR–DO loops that have character control variables, let's explore the properties of the character type.

The Pascal compiler contains a table that associates an integer—called the *ordinal position*—with each character available. The table may differ from compiler to compiler. Besides containing displayable characters, this table contains operations such as the carriage return and line feed. One table in common use is the ASCII (American Standard Code for Information Interchange). It is shown in Table 5.1. In all of the tables, each successive digit has been assigned a higher number than the preceding digit so that these numbers are contiguous, and each successive letter of the alphabet has been assigned a higher number than the preceding letter. The term given to the order of the characters in the table is the *collating sequence.*

In order to obtain the ordinal position for a given character, type the character in quotation marks between the parentheses in ord( ). Thus, if you wanted to assign the ordinal position for B to the integer variable Code, you would type

$$Code := ord('B')$$

If the value B had been assigned to the character variable Letter, you could type Code := ord(Letter) instead. In the ASCII table, the ordinal position of B is 66.

The appearance of ord( ) in a program activates a program segment referred to as the ord *function.* Since it is specified in the Pascal Standard and is thus contained in the Pascal compiler, ord is an example of a *standard function.* What appears between the parentheses is called the *argument* of the function. As you may have guessed, ord is an abbreviation of *ordinal.*

ASCII Code	Character	ASCII Code	Character
0	NULL	76	L
7	BELL	77	M
8	BACKSPACE	78	N
9	HORIZONTAL TAB	79	O
10	LINE FEED	80	P
11	VERTICAL TAB	81	Q
12	FORM FEED	82	R
13	CARRIAGE RETURN	83	S
32	SPACE	84	T
33	!	85	U
34	"	86	V
35	#	87	W
36	$	88	X
37	%	89	Y
38	&	90	Z
39	'	91	[
40	(	92	\
41	)	93	]
42	*	94	^
43	+	95	_
44	,	96	`
45	-	97	a
46	.	98	b
47	/	99	c
48	0	100	d
49	1	101	e
50	2	102	f
51	3	103	g
52	4	104	h
53	5	105	i
54	6	106	j
55	7	107	k
56	8	108	l
57	9	109	m
58	:	110	n
59	;	111	o
60	<	112	p
61	=	113	q
62	>	114	r
63	?	115	s
64	@	116	t
65	A	117	u
66	B	118	v
67	C	119	w
68	D	120	x
69	E	121	y
70	F	122	z
71	G	123	{
72	H	124		
73	I	125	}
74	J	126	~
75	K	127	DEL

TABLE 5.1.   The ASCII table. This is an example of a collating sequence, since it places the available characters and operations in a sequence. The column labeled ASCII CODE contains the ordinal values, and the column labeled CHAR contains the character corresponding to the ordinal value.

The ord function can be used with integer and boolean expressions as well, as shown in Figure 5.7a. For the boolean constants, the value of ord(true) is 1 and that of ord(false) is 0. The value of the ord of an integer is the integer itself. Thus the value of ord(8) is 8 and that of ord(−8) is −8, as shown in Figure 5.7b. It is important to realize the difference between the integer 8 and the character 8. The explicit representation of the character 8 in a program is '8', and its ordinal position in, for instance, the ASCII table is 56. However, the explicit representation of the integer 8 in a program is simply 8 and its ordinal position in the integer sequence, as we have just seen, is also 8. Except for integers, the ordinal position of an ordinal type begins with 0 and not 1. For example, the value of ord(false) is zero. Similarly, the first entry in the collating sequence has an ordinal position of zero.

It is appropriate that the argument of the ord function can only be an ordinal type; the argument cannot be a real. Thus ord(1.2) would produce an error.

THE ORDINAL FUNCTIONS

```
PROGRAM Ordinal(input,output);
(* Shows how different ordinal functions work *)
VAR ch: char;
    int: integer;
    bool: boolean;
BEGIN
    writeln('Type a character');
    readln(ch);
    writeln('Character is ', ch, '. Ordinal value is ', ord(ch):3,
       '. Successor is ', succ(ch), '. Predecessor is ', pred(ch) );
    writeln('Type an integer');
    readln(int);
    writeln('Integer is ', int:2, '. Ordinal value is ', ord(int):3,
       '. Successor is ', succ(int):2, '. Predecessor is ', pred(int):2 );
    bool:= true;
    writeln('Constant is ', bool, '. Ordinal value is ', ord(bool):1,
       '. Successor is ', succ(bool), '. Predecessor is ', pred(bool) )
END.
```

FIGURE 5.7a. The characters have been placed in an order in a table in the compiler. The ord function determines the ordinal position of the character between the parentheses.

```
Type a character
R
Character is R. Ordinal value is 82. Successor is S. Predecessor is Q
Type an integer
34
Integer is 34. Ordinal value is 34. Successor is 35. Predecessor is 33
Constant is TRUE. Ordinal value is 1. Successor is TRUE. Predecessor is
FALSE
```

FIGURE 5.7b. Running the program of Figure 5.7a. The ordinal position for an integer is the integer itself. The ordinal value of FALSE is 0.

The arguments of the standard functions succ and pred are ordinal types. The standard function succ gives the next value (i.e., the successor) and pred gives the preceding value, (i.e., the predecessor) of the ordinal type used as the argument. Thus the value of succ('L') is 'M' and that of pred('L') is 'K'. Other examples of using the functions are given in Table 5.2. Since the value of ord(TRUE) is 1 and there is no boolean constant that follows TRUE, the value of succ(TRUE) does not exist, as shown in the table. If you try to print a value of the succ or pred function that does not exist, such as succ(TRUE), you will obtain an execution error.

To obtain the character that corresponds to a given ordinal position, use the standard function chr. For instance, the value of chr(66) for a compiler using the ASCII table is B, and the value of chr(56) is 8. Figure 5.7c shows how the chr function is used in a statement, and Figure 5.7d shows the results of the program. If you use an argument for which a value of the chr function does not exist, an execution error will occur. Thus chr(−4) will produce an error.

On a compiler using the ASCII table, if we enter into the program an ASCII code that corresponds to an operation, that operation will be performed. Thus, in Figure 5.7e, we enter the code 10. (This corresponds to a line feed, that is, moving the cursor vertically one line.) When the program is run, the string that follows chr(10) in the writeln is printed on the next line

```
CHR(10) is
            End of program.
```

directly below where it was in Figure 5.7d.

TEST YOURSELF

QUESTION: What are the values of the following expressions?

a. succ(pred('R'))   **b.** pred(succ('R'))
c. ord(chr(45))   **d.** chr(ord('A'))

ANSWER: **a.** R, **b.** R, **c.** 45, **d.** A.

Argument	Type	Succ	Pred
'D'	CHAR	'E'	'C'
'5'	CHAR	'6'	'4'
FALSE	Boolean	TRUE	Does not exist
TRUE	Boolean	Does not exist	FALSE
3	Integer	4	2
−11	Integer	−10	−12

TABLE 5.2   Examples of the Succ and Pred functions.

USING THE CHR FUNCTION

```
PROGRAM IntroChar(output);
(* Prints CHR of inputted number *)
VAR ordin:integer;
BEGIN
  writeln('Type an ordinal number');
  readln(ordin);
  writeln('CHR(', ordin:1, ') is ', chr(ordin), ' End of program.')
END.
```

FIGURE 5.7c.   The CHR function determines the character in the collating table corresponding to an ordinal position.

```
Type an ordinal number
56
CHR(56) is 8 End of program.
```

FIGURE 5.7d.   Running the program of Figure 5.7c. Note that the 8 printed here is the character 8 and not the digit 8.

```
Type an ordinal number
10
CHR(10) is
                End of program.
```

FIGURE 5.7e.   Running the program of Figure 5.7c. The ordinal value of the line feed operation is 10.

5.6

USING A CHARACTER VARIABLE AS THE CONTROL VARIABLE

One of the strengths of Pascal is that it offers the programmer many types from which to choose. One must learn to use the type of variable appropriate for the problem's solution. For instance, what type of variable would you choose as a loop control variable to print the characters in the collating sequence between A and Z inclusive? As shown in Figure 5.8a, the most elegant approach uses a character variable. The heart of the program is

```
FOR Letter:= 'A' to 'Z' DO
    write(Letter)
```

The reason A and Z are in quotation marks is that, for instance, A without quotation marks indicates the variable A as opposed to the value A. The results of running the program are shown in Figure 5.8b.

Some students find it difficult to understand how the computer can perform a loop from 'A' to 'Z', two noninteger values. What the compiler does, in effect, is to find the ordinal positions of A and Z in the collating sequence (in the ASCII table, they are 65 and 90, respectively) and performs the loop between these two limits. On a compiler using the ASCII table, the equivalent loop would be

```
FOR Number:= 65 TO 90 DO
    write(chr(Number))
```

as shown in Figure 5.9a. (See Figure 5.9b for the results of running the program.) We could have solved the original problem this way, but I am sure (or at least hope) that the reader would agree that this would be an awkward solution. For starters, the programmer would have to know the ordinal positions of A and Z. Even writing FOR Number:= ord ('A') TO ord ('Z') DO write(chr(Number)) is awkward.

Depending on the compiler used, this last approach and the method used in Figure 5.8a may or may not produce just the letters of the alphabet. Some compilers, notably the ones* implemented on IBM mainframes, use a collating sequence in which the letters of the alphabet are not contiguous.

---

*Compilers on IBM mainframes use the EBCDIC character set, where EBCDIC is an abbreviation for Expanded Binary Coded Decimal Interchange Code and is pronounced *ebb-sa-dik*. There, the letters from *A* to *I* are contiguous, but *I* and *J* are not. Similarly, the letters from *J* to *R* are contiguous, but *R* and *S* are not. Finally, the letters from *S* to *Z* are contiguous. The same type of correspondence holds for the lowercase letters in the EBCDIC set.

USING A char VARIABLE AS THE LOOP CONTROL VARIABLE

```
PROGRAM Alphabet;
(* Prints the characters from A to Z *)
VAR Letter: char;
BEGIN
  FOR Letter:= 'A' TO 'Z' DO
    writeln(Letter)
END.
```

FIGURE 5.8a. We use a char as the control variable. Thus the loop is executed for the ordinal position of A to that of Z in the collating table.

ABCDEFGHIJKLMNOPQRSTUVWXYZ

FIGURE 5.8b. Running the program of Figure 5.8a.

AN AWKWARD APPROACH

```
PROGRAM Alphabet(output);
(* Prints the characters from A to Z using integers *)
VAR Number: integer;
BEGIN
  FOR Number:= 65 TO 90 DO
    write(chr(Number))
END.
```

FIGURE 5.9a.   We can obtain the same results as in the previous program by using the ordinal values of A and Z.

ABCDEFGHIJKLMNOPQRSTUVWXYZ

FIGURE 5.9b. Running the program of Figure 5.9a.

Have you ever wondered what the position of the letter *M* (or any other letter) is in the alphabet? Let's find the answer to this question. We'll write a program that counts and prints the characters in the alphabet from *A* to a letter read by the program. The first version of the pseudocode is

> *Read required-letter;*
> *Print and count the characters in the collating sequence*
> *from A to a letter read by the program.*

To count the characters, you must use a location—let's call it *Count*—to which you will add 1 for every character encountered. But this means that *Count* must have an original or initial value equal to zero. We thus refine our pseudocode to

> *Set Count to zero;*
> *Read required-letter;*
> FOR *symbol gets 'A' TO required-letter* DO
>   BEGIN
>   *Add 1 to Count;*
>   *Write the symbol*
>   END;
> writeln;
> writeln(Count).

The meaning of *add 1 to Count* is "Add 1 to the number in *Count* and store the result in *Count*." This becomes Count : = Count + 1. A variable like Count used to count is appropriately called a *counter*. A writeln appears immediately after the loop, so that writeln(Count) prints the value of Count on a new line and not at the end of the list of characters.

The resulting program is shown in Figure 5.10*a*. The reading of the *required-letter* and the loop take the following form:

> readln(Letter);
> FOR Let : = 'A' TO Letter DO
>   BEGIN
>   Count : = Count + 1;
>   write(Let)
>   END {FOR};

where Let has been declared a character variable. If L is the input, the computer stores L in the location Letter and interprets the FOR–DO as FOR Let : = 'A' TO 'L' DO, producing the results shown in Figure 5.10*b*:

USING A COUNTER

```
PROGRAM FindLetter(input,output);
(* Determines the position of a letter in the alphabet. *)
VAR Let, Letter: char;
  Count: integer;
BEGIN
  Count:= 0;
  writeln('Type an uppercase letter');
  readln( Letter);

  (* Find the position of a letter in the collating sequence *)
  writeln('The characters from A to ', Letter, ' are:');
  FOR Let:='A' to Letter DO
    BEGIN
      Count:= Count + 1;
      write(Let)
    END (* FOR Let *);

  writeln;
  writeln(Letter, ' is letter #', Count:2, ' in the alphabet.')
END.
```

FIGURE 5.10a.   Each time Count:= Count + 1 is executed, the value 1 is added to the contents of the counter and the result is stored in the counter.

```
Type an uppercase letter
L
The characters from A TO L are:
ABCDEFGHIJKL
L is letter #12 in the alphabet.
```

FIGURE 5.10b.   Running the program of Figure 5.10a. The counter must be zeroed before the loop.

```
The characters from A to L are:
ABCDEFGHIJKL
L is symbol #12 from A.
```

Note that when you type the data, type L without single quotation marks because the single quotation mark is itself a character.

We must initialize Count before the loop. Had we placed Count : = 0 in the loop, the value of Count would always be 1 after the loop. Similarly, had we placed

```
writeln(Letter, 'is symbol #', Count:2, ' from A.')
```

in the loop, the program would have printed the position of each character in the collating sequence from A up to and including Letter.

TEST YOURSELF

QUESTION: Write a program that uses the `succ` function to print the first 10 letters of the alphabet.

ANSWER:

```
PROGRAM Prob2;
VAR Ch:char;
   Digit:integer;
BEGIN
   Ch:= pred('A');
   FOR Digit:= 1 TO 10 DO BEGIN
      Ch:= succ(Ch);
      write(Ch:3)
   END {FOR}
END.
```

The statement `Ch:= succ(Ch)` is similar to the counter in Figure 5.10a. Just as we had to give the counter an initial value before the loop, we set the initial value of Ch to the predecessor of A. Thus the first time `Ch := succ(Ch)` is executed, the value of Ch is A.

5.7

USING THE DOWNTO

The next program, shown in Figure 5.11*a*, determines how far from *Z* a given letter is and prints the letters from *Z* back to the letter typed as input. This program is the same as the preceding one, except that now the loop is executed backward, that is, from 'Z' to a given letter. If we wrote the FOR–DO as FOR Let:= 'Z' TO Letter DO and the value of Letter was, for instance, L, the statement would be interpreted as FOR Let:= 'Z' TO 'L' DO. If the final value of the control variable is less than the initial value when the TO form of the FOR–DO is used (as it is here), the loop is not executed. To instruct the computer to decrease the control variable each time the loop is executed, use DOWNTO in the FOR–DO. We thus write

FOR Let:='Z' DOWNTO Letter DO

Using L as input, as shown in Figure 5.11*b*, we obtain

The characters from Z down to L are:
ZYXWVUTSRQPONML
L is 15 symbols from alphabet end.

If you want an integer control variable I to go from 3 to 1, write FOR I:= 3 DOWNTO 1 DO.

If the final value of the control variable is greater than the initial value in a FOR–DO containing a DOWNTO, as in FOR Let:='A' DOWNTO 'L' DO or FOR I:= 1 DOWNTO 3 DO, the loop is not executed.

TEST YOURSELF

QUESTION: How many times would the FOR–DO loop beginning with the following statements be executed?

a. FOR J:= 1 TO 5 DO   **b.** FOR J:= 5 DOWNTO 1 DO
c. FOR J:= 4 TO 4 DO   **d.** FOR J:= 1 DOWNTO 1 DO
e. FOR J:= 4 TO 3 DO   **f.** FOR J:= −2 DOWNTO 1 DO
g. FOR Ch:= '1' TO '5' DO   **h.** FOR Ch:= 'A' TO 'F' DO

ANSWER: **a.** Five times, **b.** five times, **c.** once, **d.** once, **e.** zero times, **f.** zero times, **g.** five times, **h.** compiler dependent, but normally six times.

USING THE DOWNTO

```
PROGRAM FindLet2(input,output);
(* Determines how far from Z a letter is *)
VAR Let, Letter: char;
    Count:integer;
BEGIN
  Count:=0;
  writeln('Type an uppercase letter');
  readln( Letter);

  (* Find the position of a letter in the collating sequence *)
  writeln('The characters from Z down to ', Letter, ' are:');
  FOR Let:='Z' DOWNTO Letter DO
    BEGIN
      Count:= Count + 1;
      write(Let)
    END (* FOR Let *);

  writeln;
  writeln(Letter, ' is ', Count:2, ' letters from alphabet end.')
END.
```

FIGURE 5.11a. If the initial value of the control value is greater than the final value, you must use the DOWNTO instead of the TO.

```
Type an uppercase letter
L
The characters from Z down TO L are:
ZYXWVUTSRQPONML
L is 15 letters from alphabet end.
```

FIGURE 5.11b. Running the program of Figure 5.11a. The letters are printed in reverse order.

5.8

BUFFERED INPUT WITH THE FOR–DO LOOP

You can use a read in a FOR–DO loop to read data stored in the buffer. Let's examine the FOR–DO in Figure 5.12a:

```
FOR K: = 1 TO NumChar DO
    BEGIN
        read(Letter);
        write( Letter)
    END {FOR K}
```

where Letter is a character variable and the value of NumChar, 5, is defined in the CONST definition. The computer waits for all the values of Letter to be typed on a line, storing these values in the input buffer, as shown in the table for Figure 5.12a:

abcde~

After the carriage return is pressed, the computer copies these values in the order they were stored, to location Letter each time it executes read(Letter). Thus, first the computer stores a in Letter and then prints it. Then it stores b in Letter and then prints it. So when the program is run, as shown in Figure 5.12b, the data appear across the screen and then are printed on the next line using write(Letter).

USING THE BUFFER

```
PROGRAM Buffer(input,output);
(* Shows how data are stored in the buffer *)
CONST NumInt = 5;
VAR K:integer;
  Letter:char;
BEGIN
  writeln('Type ', NumInt:2, ' characters on one line');
  FOR K:= 1 TO NumInt DO
    BEGIN
      read(Letter);
      write( Letter)
    END (* FOR K *)
END.
```

FIGURE 5.12a.   The data we type on one line are stored in the buffer. After we hit the carriage, each character, in turn, is copied to the location Letter.

```
abcde⁻
```

TABLE FOR FIGURE 5.12a. The input buffer for Figure 5.12a.

```
Type 5 characters on one line
abcde
abcde
```

FIGURE 5.12b.   Running the program of Figure 5.12a. The input appears on a different line from the output because nothing is transferred from the buffer until we hit the carriage return.

5.9

AVERAGING NUMBERS READ AS CHARACTER TYPE

Let's use the properties of the buffer to write a program that calculates the average of five quiz marks that range from 0 to 9 and, for convenience, are typed as five contiguous digits. Thus, if the quiz marks are 7, 5, 8, 9, and 9, they are typed as 75899. The easiest way to do the problem is to assume that the five contiguous digits are read as five characters. We leave it as an exercise for you to do the problem, reading the five digits as one integer. The pseudocode and the ensuing program assume that *digit* is a character:

> *Sum:= 0;*
> FOR *Index:= 1 TO 5* DO BEGIN
>   read(digit);
>   *Convert digit to the integer, Mark;*
>   *Add Mark to Sum*
> END; {FOR}
> *calculate average;*
> writeln(average).

Once *digit* is read, it must be converted to a digit. It's done in Figure 5.13*a* in Mark:= ord(digit) − ord('0') and is explained in the table for Figure 5.13*a* which assumes that your compiler uses the ASCII table. The first line of this table shows how the first character read, 3, is converted:

Digit	ord(Digit)	ord('0')	Mark
3	51	48	3

This method will work no matter which conversion table your compiler uses because, for instance, the value of ord(3) is always three higher than the value of ord('0').

READING DIGITS AS CHARACTERS

```
PROGRAM ExamAverage2(input,output);
(* Average five quiz marks using the character approach *)
CONST NumQuiz = 5;
VAR Sum, Mark, Index : integer;
  Average: real;
  Digit:char;
BEGIN
  writeln('Type ', NumQuiz:2, ' contiguous digits for quiz marks');
  Sum:= 0;
  (* Now print the digits vertically *)

  FOR Index:= 1 TO NumQuiz DO
    BEGIN
      read(Digit);
      writeln('Mark ', Index:2, ' is', Digit:2);
      Mark:=ord(Digit) − ord('0');
    Sum:= Sum + Mark;
    END;

  Average:= Sum / NumQuiz;
  writeln('Quiz average is', Average:4:1)
END.
```

FIGURE 5.13a.   By declaring Digit to be a character, we read one digit at a time from the buffer.

Digit	ord(Digit)	ord('0')	Mark
3	51	48	3
1	49	48	1
9	57	48	9
7	55	48	7
8	56	48	8

TABLE FOR FIGURE 5.13a.   Shows how Mark:−ord(Digit)−ord('0') works. The value of Mark is compiler independent because the digits are consecutive entries in the collating sequence.

Each time the read is executed, the program reads the next character to the right in the buffer. The data are typed without quotation marks. When the average is calculated in average:= Sum / NumQuiz, the denominator is NumQuiz and not Index. As you remember, the reason is that after the loop is completely executed, the value of the control variable is undefined; it could be any value. The data read by the program and the results of running the program are shown in Figure 5.13b.

TEST YOURSELF

QUESTION: What would happen in the previous program if you tried to read each of the digits in the number 75899 using an integer variable, for instance, Mark? Note that this number ends with a carriage return and that the key statements in the program would now appear as

```
VAR Sum, Mark, Index : integer;
BEGIN
   Sum:= 0;
   FOR Index:= 1 TO 5 DO
      BEGIN
         read(Mark);
         Sum:= Sum + Mark;
      END;
```

ANSWER: Remember that the delimiter for an integer is a carriage return or a blank. Therefore, since Mark is an integer variable, its first value would be 75899. The program would then stop, since it requires four more integers.

```
Type 5 contiguous digits for quiz marks
75899
Mark 1 is 7
Mark 2 is 5
Mark 3 is 8
Mark 4 is 9
Mark 5 is 9
Quiz average is 7.6
```

FIGURE 5.13*b*.   Running the program of Figure 5.13*a*. Since each digit is read separately, it can be added to the sum.

How the Computer Interprets Characters
Typed in Response to a READ or READLN Statement

You may have asked yourself how we can read numerical input into the program as integers and reals on the one hand, or as characters on the other (as was done in this program), simply by declaring the variable's type. The answer is that all data typed at the keyboard are read into the program as characters. For instance, when we type 34 at the keyboard, a code—let's say the ASCII code—for the character 3 followed by the code for the character 4 is sent to the screen. As a result, pictures of the numbers 3 and 4 are displayed there, as shown in Figure 5.14. At the same time, these codes are transmitted to the input buffer, and the internal representations for the characters 3 and 4 are stored there:

Input buffer

If you type these two digits in response to read(Number) and then hit the carriage return, the following will happen. If Number has been declared an integer variable, the standard procedure read will convert the symbols 3 and 4 to the number 34 and will store it in Number. On the other hand, if Number has been declared a character variable, the character 3 is stored in Number and 4 remains in the buffer, waiting to be read by the next input statement.

HOW DIGITS ARE READ FROM THE KEYBOARD

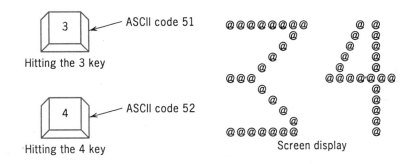

Input buffer

FIGURE 5.14.   When you type 34, a picture of the same number is displayed on the screen. Then, depending on how the variable in the `read` is declared, 34 will be stored either as the number 34 or as the characters 3 and 4.

5.10

NESTED LOOPS

Remember the multiplication tables you used in grade school? Here's a program that produces a multiplication table in which each of the numbers from 2 to 4 are multiplied by each of the numbers from 5 to 7. The pseudocode is:

```
FOR Outer:= 5 TO 7 DO BEGIN
    Multiply each value of Outer by values of Inner from 2 to 4;
    writeln
END {FOR Outer}
```

In Figure 5.15a we translate *Multiply each value . . .* into

```
FOR Inner:= 2 TO 4 DO
    write (Inner, '*', Outer, '=', Inner * Outer, ' ')
```

where Inner, '*', Outer, '=' labels the results. This loop is called the *inner loop.* The loop in which it is placed is called the *outer loop;* here it begins with FOR Outer:= 5 TO 7 DO. We say that the inner loop is *nested* in the outer one.

The results, given in Figure 5.15b, show that the inner loop is executed completely for each value of the outer loop. Thus, when the value of Outer is 5, the value of Inner varies from 2 to 4; when the value of Outer is 6, the value of Inner again varies from 2 to 4; this happens again when the value of Outer is 7. We describe this by saying that the outer control variable varies more slowly than the inner one.

Note that if writeln had been omitted, all the results would have been printed on one line.

The wallpaper in your kitchen has repeating patterns. Let's write a program that will produce a repeating pattern on a smaller scale. It will repeat the pattern xxxx---- on three lines, once per line. The pseudocode is

```
FOR Outer:= 1 TO 3 DO BEGIN
    Print pattern;
    writeln
END {FOR Outer}
```

The pseudocode *Print pattern* translates into

```
FOR Inner:= 1 TO InnerLimit DO
    write ('x');
FOR Inner := 1 TO InnerLimit DO
    write('-');
```

NESTED LOOPS
PRODUCING A MULTIPLICATION TABLE

```
PROGRAM Nested(output);
(* Produces a multiplication table *)
VAR Inner, Outer: integer;
BEGIN
FOR Outer:= 5 TO 7 DO
    BEGIN
        FOR Inner := 2 TO 4 DO
            write (Inner, '*', Outer, '=', Inner * Outer:3, ' ');
        writeln;
    END
END.
```

FIGURE 5.15a. Because the inner loop is executed for each value of the control variable for the outer loop, we say that the inner loop executes more rapidly than the outer loop does.

```
2*5= 10 3*5= 15 4*5= 20
2*6= 12 3*6= 18 4*6= 24
2*7= 14 3*7= 21 4*7= 28
```

FIGURE 5.15b. Running the program of Figure 5.15a.

where the value of InnerLimit is defined as 4 in the CONST statement. Now instead of one inner loop, there are two. Of course, the loop in which these loops are nested is the outer loop. When the original pseudocode is translated to Pascal, we obtain the program of Figure 5.16a. The results of running the program are shown in Figure 5.16b. Note that if writeln had been omitted, all the results would have been printed on one line.

For each value of Outer, the two inner loops are executed completely. Thus, when the value of Outer is 1, the value of Inner varies from 1 to 4 for the first inner loop, and then for the second one; when the value of Outer is 2, the value of Inner varies from 1 to 4 for both loops. This happens once more when the value of Outer is 3. The two inner loop control variables can be the same, as shown here. However, the outer control variable must be different from any inner loop index; otherwise, a syntax error will occur.

TEST YOURSELF

QUESTION: Write the program to produce

                    a
                    ab
                    abc
                    abcd
                    abcde

until the complete alphabet is printed.

ANSWER:

```
PROGRAM Alphabet;
VAR Ch:char;
    Digit, Number:integer;
BEGIN
  FOR Number:= 1 to 26 DO BEGIN
    Ch:= pred('A');
    FOR Digit:= 1 TO Number DO BEGIN
      Ch:= succ(Ch);
      write(Ch)
    END (* FOR Digit *);
    writeln
  END (* FOR Number *)
END.
```

NESTED LOOPS
PRODUCING A MULTIPLICATION TABLE (CONTINUED)

```
PROGRAM Nest(output);
(* Produces a repeating pattern *)
CONST InnerLimit = 4;
   OuterLimit = 3;
VAR Inner, Outer: integer;
BEGIN
   FOR Outer := 1 TO OuterLimit DO
     BEGIN
       FOR Inner:= 1 TO InnerLimit DO
         write ('x');
       FOR Inner := 1 TO InnerLimit DO
         write('-');
       writeln
     END
   END.
```

FIGURE 5.16a.   For each value of Outer, the inner loops are completely executed. The inner loops are said to be *nested* in the outer loop.

```
XXXX----
XXXX----
XXXX----
```

FIGURE 5.16b.   Running the program of Figure 5.16a. You cannot use the same variable for the nested loop control variable that you use for the outer loop control variable.

5.11

DEBUGGING A PROGRAM

Figure 5.17*a* shows a program that is the same as the one in Figure 5.13*a* (it calculates the average of five quiz marks), except that the present version contains an error. The simplest way to test the program is to input marks that will yield an obviously correct answer if the program is correct and an obviously wrong one if the program is incorrect. Let's input five identical marks—five 7s—since the average should be the same as each of the marks, that is, 7. In Figure 5.17*b*, we see that it is not.

A PROGRAM THAT PRODUCES AN EXECUTION ERROR

```
PROGRAM ExamAverage2(input,output);
(* Average five quiz marks using the character approach *)
CONST NumQuiz = 5;
VAR Sum, Mark, Index : integer;
   Average: real;
   Digit:char;
BEGIN
   writeln('Type ', NumQuiz:2, ' contiguous digits for quiz marks');
   Sum:= 0;

   (* now print the digits vertically *)
   FOR Index:= 1 TO NumQuiz DO
     BEGIN
       read(Digit);
       writeln('Mark ', Index:2, ' is', Digit:2);
       Mark:=ord(Digit) − ord(0);
       Sum:= Sum + Mark;
     END;

   Average:= Sum / NumQuiz;
   writeln('Quiz average is', average:4:1)
END.
```

FIGURE 5.17a. This program is the same as the one in Figure 5.12a, except that it contains an error.

```
          Type 5 contiguous digits for quiz marks
          77777
          Mark 1 is 7
          Mark 2 is 7
          Mark 3 is 7
          Mark 4 is 7
          Mark 5 is 7
          Quiz average is 55.0
```

FIGURE 5.17b. Running the program of Figure 5.17a. We test the program by inputting five identical marks. We know immediately that the average should be 7, the same as each of the marks. We see that it is not.

In order to debug the program, insert statements that print the intermediate results—the values of Mark and Sum, as shown in Figure 5.17c. When we run the program, as shown in Figure 5.17d, we see that the numerical mark obtained from the digit read is incorrect. Consequently, the expression for Mark

$$\texttt{Mark:=ord(Digit)} - \texttt{ord(0);}$$

is incorrect. If we do not realize that ord(0) is the culprit—it should be written as ord('0')—the next step in debugging the program would be to print the values of the two terms that constitute the expression for Mark, namely, ord(Digit) and ord(0).

Here is where we can make a mistake that will make the problem seem unsolvable. We might insert ord('0') in the debugging writeln statement instead of ord(0), that is, type

```
writeln('Values contributing to Mark are ', ord(Digit), ' and ', ord('0'))
```

Thus the debugging statement would print the correct value, but the incorrect value would still be used in the calculation of Mark. The only way to solve this problem is either by careful inspection or by asking someone else to look at your debugging program.

DEBUGGING HINT

If you still cannot debug your program after following our suggestions, try the following: If an expression consists of several terms, assign each term to a separate variable. For instance, in this problem, write Term1:= ord(Digit) and Term2:= ord('0'). Finally, write Mark:= Term1 − Term2 and then print all of these values.

DEBUGGING A PROGRAM THAT PRODUCES EXECUTION ERRORS

```
PROGRAM ExamAverage2 (input, output);
(* Average 5 quiz marks using character approach *)
(* Program has an error. *)
CONST NumQuiz = 5;

VAR Sum, Mark, Index : integer;
    Average: real;
    Digit:char;
BEGIN
    writeln('Type ', NumQuiz:2, ' contiguous digits for quiz marks');
    Sum:= 0;

    (* now print the digits vertically *)
    FOR Index:= 1 TO NumQuiz DO
      BEGIN
        read(Digit);
        write('Mark ', Index:2, ' is', Digit:2);
        Mark:=ord(Digit) - ord(0);
        write(' ; Numerical mark is ', Mark:3);
        Sum:= Sum + Mark;
        writeln('; Sum is ', Sum:4)
      END;

    Average:= Sum / NumQuiz;
    writeln('Quiz average is', average:6:1)
END.
```

FIGURE 5.17c. In order to debug the program, we insert statements to print the intermediate results—the values of Mark and Sum.

```
Type 5 contiguous digits for quiz marks
77777
Mark 1 is 7 ; Numerical mark is 55; Sum is  55
Mark 2 is 7 ; Numerical mark is 55; Sum is 110
Mark 3 is 7 ; Numerical mark is 55; Sum is 165
Mark 4 is 7 ; Numerical mark is 55; Sum is 220
Mark 5 is 7 ; Numerical mark is 55; Sum is 275
Quiz average is 55.0
```

FIGURE 5.17d. Running the program of Figure 5.17c. We see that the numerical mark obtained from the digit read is incorrect. Thus the expression for Mark is incorrect. If we do not realize that ord(0) is the culprit, the next step would be to print ord(Digit) and ord(0).

5.12

THE OTHER STANDARD FUNCTIONS

The standard functions we have studied so far are the ord, chr, succ, and pred functions. They determine the characteristics of the ordinal types. However, there are arithmetic, transfer, and boolean functions as well (the transfer functions convert real values to integer values). We now list the rest of the functions.

The Arithmetic Functions

Function	Use	Argument type	Function type
sqr(x)	Squares x	Real or integer	Same as argument
sqrt(x)	Positive square root of x where $x >= 0$	Real or integer	Real
abs(x)	Absolute value of x	Real or integer	Same as argument
exp(x)	Raises e to the x power	Real or integer	Real
ln(x)	Log of x to the base e where $x > 0$	Real or integer	Real
cos(x)	Cosine of x, x in radians	Real or integer	Real
sin(x)	Since of x, x in radians	Real or integer	Real
arctan(x)	Arctangent of x	Real or integer	Real

Note that sqr(10) is 100 and sqrt(100) is 10; the square root of a negative number will produce a run-time error. The value of abs(8) is 8, and the value of abs(−8) is also 8. Finally, in order to calculate A^X, write exp(X * ln(A)).

An example using these functions is writing the Gaussian distribution

$$H = \frac{e^{-Z^2/2}}{\sqrt{2\pi}}$$

as H: = exp(− sqr(Z)/2) / sqrt(2 * 3.1459).

The Transfer Functions

Function	Use	Argument type	Function type
round(x)	Rounds off x to the closest integer	Real	integer
trunc(x)	Truncates (lops off) part of x to the right of the decimal point	Real	integer

Note that round(4.8) is 5 and trunc(4.8) is 4.

The Boolean Functions

Function	Use	Argument type	Function type
odd(x)	Determines whether x is odd	Integer	Boolean

Note that odd(3) is true and odd(4) is false.*
For the sake of completeness, we list the ordinal functions again.

The Ordinal Functions

Function	Use	Argument type	Function type
ord(x)	Ordinal value of x	Ordinal	Integer
succ(x)	Successor of x	Ordinal	Same as argument
pred(x)	Predecessor of x	Ordinal	Same as argument
chr(x)	Character or operation in the ASCII table corresponding to x	Integer	Character (for nonoperations)

TEST YOURSELF

QUESTION: How would you rewrite the following program segment, which calculates the commission on sales, so that it is more efficient? The commission is given by Percent * Sale.

```
Commission := 0.0;
FOR J := 1 TO NumberOfSales DO BEGIN
   read(Sale);
   Commission := Commission + Percent * Sale
END {FOR};
```

ANSWER: Multiplying by Percent should be done only once, at the end of the loop. The segment should be:

```
Sum := 0.0;
FOR J := 1 TO NumberOfSales DO BEGIN
   read(Sale);
   Sum := Sum + Sale
END {FOR};
Commission := Percent * Sum
```

*There are two other boolean functions, namely, eoln, and eof which we'll learn about in Chapter 8.

PROGRAM PITFALLS

1. The assignment of new values to the initial and final values of the control variable in a FOR–DO loop does not affect the function of the loop. Thus in

```
Initial:= 1;
Final:= 3;
FOR Control:= Initial TO Final DO
   BEGIN
      write(Control:2);
      Final:= 5
   END
```

the fact that we include Final:= 5 in the loop does not affect its operation. The output it produces is still 1 2 3. However, it is bad programming practice to place these variables in the loop.

2. Placing the control variables in a FOR–DO loop may affect the function of the loop. For instance, if by mistake you place Control:= Control + 1 in the loop, as in

```
Initial:= 1;
Final:= 3;
FOR Control:= Initial TO Final DO
   BEGIN
      write(Control:2);
      Control:= Control + 1;
   END
```

the loop will not stop executing.*

3. In Mark:=ord(Digit) − ord('0') the character value stored in Digit is converted to its corresponding integer value, Mark. If we forget to place the 0 in quotation marks and write Mark:= ord(Digit) − ord(0) instead, we'll get the wrong answer, as was shown in Figure 3.17*b*. For instance, when you convert a value of Digit equal to '8' on a compiler that uses the ASCII table, the value of ord(Digit) is 56. Since ord(0) is always 0, the value of Mark will be 56 instead of 8.

---

*The value of Control will be 1, 3, 5,...,maxint. It will then go back to 1 through the negative numbers in steps of −2, and then back to maxint, and so on.

CHAPTER REVIEW

Ordinal Types and the FOR–DO Loop

In this chapter we categorize the integer, boolean, and character types as being ordinal types; that is, a variable of any of these types can assume a finite number of values. A variable that is real, on the other hand, can assume an infinite number of values. Only an ordinal type variable can be used as the control variable for FOR–DO loops.

The FOR–DO Loop

1. If the values of the FOR–DO loop control variable have a negative increment, the reserved word DOWNTO must be used in place of TO.

2. If the value of the control variable or its initial or final values are redefined within the loop, the loop still uses the original values specified in the FOR–DO statement.

3. The value of the loop control variable is undefined after the loop is executed. Thus in

                FOR J:= 1 TO 5 DO write(J); writeln(J),

   the writeln will produce unexpected results.

4. Finally, if the initial value of the control variable is larger than the final value, as in FOR I:= 3 TO 1 DO, the loop is not executed. Similarly, if the initial value of the control variable is smaller than the final value in a DOWNTO loop, as in FOR I:= 1 DOWNTO 3 DO, the loop is not executed.

Nested Loops

One FOR–DO loop can be placed within another. The inner loop is completely executed for each value of the control variable of the outer loop. The control variables for the inner and outer loops must be different; otherwise, a compilation error will occur.

FOR–DO

The form of the FOR–DO is FOR, followed by an ordinal type variable, followed by ":=", followed by an identifier indicating the initial value of the control variable, followed by TO or DOWNTO, followed by an identifier indicating the final value. This is followed by DO. One or more blanks must follow FOR, and both precede and follow TO or DOWNTO. If the value of the control variable is being increased, TO is used; if it is being decreased, DOWNTO is used. Examples:

```
        FOR Character:= 'A' TO 'Z' DO
        FOR Character:= Lower TO Upper DO
        FOR Time:= 10 DOWNTO 1 DO
```

NEW TERMS

accumulator	loop
argument	nested loop
ASCII table	ord function
collating sequence	ordinal numbers
control variable	ordinal position
FOR–DO loop	ordinal types
function	standard function
initializing	wrap around

EXERCISES

1. State the type and value of each of the following expressions. If the expression will not compile, write "invalid" as the type and leave the "Value" column blank.

Expression	Type	Value
succ('5')	_____	_____
ord('3') – ord('0')	_____	_____
odd(pred(8))	_____	_____
ord(chr('4'))	_____	_____
chr(ord('3'))	_____	_____
trunc(19.8)	_____	_____
round(19.8)	_____	_____
abs(3 + 6 MOD round(4.5) + 2)	_____	_____

2. What is the output of the following program?

```
PROGRAM One(input,output);
VAR Index, First, Second:integer
BEGIN
   First:= 200;
   Second:= 200;
   FOR Index:= 1 TO 5 DO BEGIN
      First:= 50 – First;
      Second:= 50 + First;
      writeln(Index:4, First:6, Second:6)
   END (* FOR *);
END.
```

3. What is the output of the following code segment?

```
FOR I:= 1 TO 5 DO
    write('X');
    writeln('-')
```

4. What does the following program produce?

```
PROGRAM Prob4(input,output);
VAR I, J, K:integer;
BEGIN
  FOR I:= 1 TO 3 DO
    FOR K:= 1 TO I DO
      FOR J:= I TO K DO
        writeln((I, J:3, K:3)
END.
```

5. What is the final value of Count?

```
Count:= 0;
FOR M:= 5 DOWNTO 2 DO
    FOR N:= 1 TO 3 DO
        Count:= Count + 1
```

Programming Problems

6. Write a program to produce a pattern such that the Nth line contains N asterisks, such as the following:

```
*
**
***
****
*****
******
*******
```

7. Write a program to produce a pattern such that the Nth line contains $2N - 1$ asterisks, such as the following:

8. Write a program that takes a date (such as 12 08 89) written as one integer (here, 120889) and resolves it into the month, day, and year.

9. Write a program that converts three integers representing the month, day, and year (for instance, 12, 27, 90) into one integer (here, 122790).

10. Write a program that uses a FOR–DO loop to generate the first N Fibonacci numbers for $N \geqslant 3$ (see exercise 16 in Chapter 2). Hint: Start by defining First as 0 and Second as 1. In a loop, set Third to the sum of First plus Second, and then redefine First and Second.

12. Write a program to produce the following pattern, where the number of Xs and dashes should be variables:

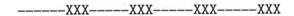

13. Write a program to produce the following pattern, where the number of Xs and dashes should be variables:

14. Write a program that prints the numbers from 1 to 19 using a write statement in a FOR–DO loop such that each number will be preceded by one space.

15. Write a program that sums the integers from the initial to the final value read into the program.

16a. Write a program that reads a social security number written as contiguous digits (for instance, 509435456) and then prints each digit on a separate line, followed by a colon and the digit printed the number of times equal to its value. Thus the output for 509435456 would be

```
5:55555
0:
9:999999999
4:4444
3:333
5:55555
4:4444
5:55555
6:666666
```

Hint: Use a character variable (e.g., `Index`) for the inner loop control variable and write the inner loop FOR as `FOR Index := '1' TO Digit DO`, where `Digit` is the character variable used to read each digit.

b. Write the program so that `Index` is an integer variable. This means that you will have to convert the character assigned to `Digit` to an integer.

17. Write a program that calculates

$$Y = \sum_{N = 0}^{N = 4} X^N$$

that is, $Y = 1 + X + X^2 + X^3 + X^4$. The symbol Σ stands for the sum of the expression to its right, where N assumes the values of all the integers from, in this case, 0 to 4. The value of X is 3 and is read from a DATA statement. Hint: Place $Y := Y + X$; $X := X * X$ in a FOR–DO loop.

18. Write a program that calculates

$$Y = \sum_{N = 0}^{M} X^N$$

That is, $Y = 1 + X + X^2 + X^3 + \cdots + X^m$. The values of M and X should be read.

19. The statistic χ^2 enables us to test a theoretical model by comparing it with experimental data. χ^2 is approximated by

$$\chi^2 = Y = \sum_{i}^{N} \frac{(observed_i - expected_i)^2}{expected_i}$$

where *observed$_i$* and *expected$_i$* are the experimental and theoretical quantities, respectively, in the ith interval and N is the number of intervals. In this problem we will use χ^2 to test whether a die is fair (not loaded). Since a die has six faces, we will be placing the observations into six different intervals (i.e., the value of N equals 6). The number of observations per face (i.e., per interval) should be typed on a different line of data. If the die is tossed 60 times, a possible set of data for the observations per face would be 12, 8, 13, 11, 9, 7, and the expected number per interval would be 60/6 or 10. Then χ^2 would be $(23 - 10)^2/10 + (8 - 10)^2/10 + (13 - 10)^2/10 + (11 - 10)^2/10 + (9 - 10)^2/10 + (7 - 10)^2/10$. Note that the sum of the data must equal 60. If the value of χ^2 exceeds 11.07, the probability that the die is fair (our model) is less than 5%. Write a program that calculates χ^2 for any number of tosses of a die. Note that in order for the χ^2 formula we present here to apply, the expected number per interval must exceed 10.

20. The geometric mean of a group of N numbers is the Nth root of the product of the N numbers. Thus the geometric mean of 3, 5, 4, and 9 is the fourth root of 3 * 5 * 4 * 9. Write a program that determines the geometric mean of N numbers read by your program. Your program must, of course, first read the value of N.

21. Write a program that produces all three-letter combinations that have *a* as the second letter. Most of these combinations will not be words.

22. Rewrite the program of Figure 4.13*a* so that the data are read as an integer instead of a series of characters.

23. Write a program that prints the first 10 letters of the alphabet using FOR Digit: = 1 TO 10 DO BEGIN and the chr and ord functions.

The following exercises are a series of programs that use loop control variables that are changed by nonunit increments. They culminate in one that determines the area under the curve.

24. Write a program that converts the even-numbered temperatures from 20° to 40° C to Fahrenheit.

25. Write a program that converts every N degrees of temperature from 20° to 40° C to Fahrenheit. Thus, if N was 5° C, the program would convert 20° C, 25° C, 30° C, 35° C, and 40° C.

26. Write a program that sums the real numbers 1.0, 1.1, 1.2, 1.3, . . ., 2.0. Hint: Multiply these numbers by 10 so that the loop control variable goes from 10 to 20. To compensate for this, divide by 10 within the loop.

27. The height, y, of the normal curve in terms of z is given as

$$Y = \frac{e^{-z^2}}{\sqrt{2\pi}}$$

where e is 2.71828 and π is 3.14159. Write a program that evaluates y for z varying from -4.0 to 4.0 in intervals of 0.25.

28.   In order to determine the area under the curve shown in the diagram, we partition the area under the curve into rectangles. The height of any rectangle is determined by the y value of the curve; its width is given by dz. Thus the area of a given rectangle is ydz and the area of all the rectangles is $y_1dz + y_2dz + \ldots y_Ldz$, where yL is the height of the last rectangle. The smaller dz is, the more closely the area of the rectangles approximates the area under the curve. Write a program that approximates the area under the normal curve from $z = -4$ to $z = 4$, with $dz = 0.001$. Note that the area of the rectangles can be expressed by $dz(y_1 + y_2 + \ldots + y_L)$ or dz times the sum of the y's.

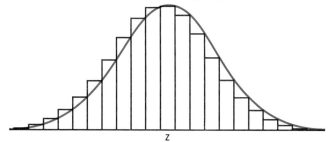

z

6

PROCEDURES AND TOP-DOWN DESIGN

CHAPTER OVERVIEW

This chapter introduces the following concepts:

1. A subprogram is part of a program that has all the elements of the program itself.
2. The identifiers that have a value throughout the entire program are called *global identifiers*, and those that have a value only in the subprogram are called *local identifiers*.
3. The identifiers whose values can be passed to a subprogram but not passed back are called *value parameters*, and those whose values can be passed to a subprogram and passed back are called *variable parameters*.

BEFORE YOU BEGIN

A necessary tool in program design is the ability to group statements into miniprograms called *subprograms,* to separate the subprograms from the statement part of the program, and to refer to these subprograms subsequently by name in the statement part. Subprograms facilitate the translation of the top-down diagram into the final program because they allow us to concentrate on one task at a time. When we discuss subprograms, we will call the part of the program that is not a subprogram the *main program.* The type of subprogram discussed in this chapter is called a *procedure.*

6.1

AN INTRODUCTION TO PROCEDURES

Let's start by writing the pseudocode for a program that draws a rectangle:

> *Draw a horizontal line 20 units long;*
> FOR K: = 1 TO 6 DO
>   *Print two "x"s 18 spaces apart;*
> *Draw a horizontal line 20 units long;*

This overall description of the program will become the main program. The top-down diagram for the program is shown in Figure 6.1*a,* where Horizontal and Vertical are the two procedures used in the main program. Although Horizontal is used twice in the main program and Vertical six times, the rectangles describing them appear only once in the top-down diagram. The reason is that these rectangles indicate the procedures to be written, not the number of times they will be used. The main program written in terms of these procedures is:

> Horizontal;
> FOR K: = 1 to 6 DO
>   Vertical;
> Horizontal

USING PROCEDURES

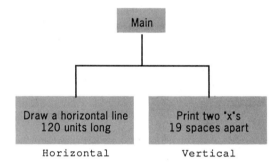

FIGURE 6.1a.   The top-down diagram for a program that draws a rectangle. Although `Horizontal` is used twice in the main program and `Vertical` is used six times, the rectangles describing them appear only once in the top-down diagram because these rectangles indicate the procedures to be written, not the number of times they will be used.

as shown in Figure 6.1*b*. When a procedure is referred to in the program, we say that it has been *activated*. The main program activates a procedure when we include a statement consisting of the procedure name (here, Horizontal and Vertical). Let's take a detailed look at these procedures.

The procedure for Horizontal is

```
PROCEDURE Horizontal;
(* produces a horizontal line *)
VAR J: integer;
BEGIN
   FOR J: = 1 to 20 DO
      write('x');
   writeln
END (* Horizontal *);
```

and that for Vertical is

```
PROCEDURE Vertical;
(* Produces entries in two vertical lines *)
BEGIN
   writeln('x', 'x':19)
END (* Vertical *);
```

Note that a procedure is similar in construction to a program. It contains its own VAR declaration (and can contain a CONST definition), and it has its own statement part that's sandwiched between a BEGIN and an END. The differences are as follows:

1. The reserved word PROCEDURE replaces the reserved word PROGRAM.
2. The final END in the procedure is followed by a semicolon, not a period.

Procedures must precede the statement part and must follow the VAR declaration in the main program, as in Figure 6.1*b*. After a procedure has been activated and executed, program control returns to the statement after the one that activated the procedure. Thus, after Horizontal is activated and the computer draws a horizontal line, the main program executes FOR K: = 1 to 6 DO Vertical.

The advantages of using procedures are as follows:

1. You can write the main program as a sequence of tasks and describe the details in the procedures. The main program is now easier to read and write.
2. If you write a segment of the program that is repeated as a procedure, just repeat the procedure name each time you want the segment

USING PROCEDURES (CONTINUED)

```
PROGRAM Box(output);
(* Produces a rectangle *)
VAR K: integer;

PROCEDURE Horizontal;
(* produces a horizontal line *)
VAR J: integer;
BEGIN
  FOR J: = 1 to 20 DO
    write('x');
  writeln
END (* Horizontal *);

PROCEDURE Vertical;
(* Produces entries in two vertical lines *)
BEGIN
  writeln('x', 'x':19)
END (* Vertical *);

BEGIN (* main program *)
  Horizontal;
  FOR K: = 1 to 6 DO
    Vertical;
  Horizontal
END.
```

FIGURE 6.1*b*. The program uses two procedures, Horizontal and Vertical. Each time the procedure is activated (its name used) in the main program, the program executes the statements in the procedure and then returns to the main program.

repeated instead of repeating the segment, as shown in the main program, where Horizontal is activated twice

```
Horizontal;
FOR K:= 1 to 6 DO
    Vertical;
Horizontal
```

and Vertical is activated six times.

In the simplest version of the top-down design of a program, you follow the steps indicated by the top-down diagram by writing first the main program and then the procedures. The running of the program is shown in Figure 6.1c.

TEST YOURSELF

QUESTION: Write a program that averages two sets of marks, where each set consists of four marks (see Figure 3.15a).

ANSWER:

```
PROGRAM SimpleAverage(input,output);
(* Averages two sets of marks *)

PROCEDURE AverageMarks;
(* Averages four marks *)
VAR Mark1, Mark2, Mark3, Mark4:integer;
   Average:real;
BEGIN
   writeln('Type 4 marks on one line.');
   readln(Mark1, Mark2, Mark3, Mark4);
   Average:= (Mark1+Mark2+Mark3+Mark4)/4;
   writeln('Average of 4 marks is ', Average:10:2);
   writeln
END (* AverageMarks *);

BEGIN
   (* Compute average for first set of marks *)
   AverageMarks;
   (* Compute average for second set of marks *)
   AverageMarks
END.
```

```
XXXXXXXXXXXXXXXXXXXX
X                  X
X                  X
X                  X
X                  X
X                  X
X                  X
XXXXXXXXXXXXXXXXXXXX
```

FIGURE 6.1c.   Running the program of Figure 6.1b. The horizontal lines are produced by Horizontal and the vertical lines by successive activation of Vertical. In the top-down design of a program, you follow the steps indicated by the top-down diagram by first writing the main program and then the procedures.

6.2

GLOBAL AND LOCAL IDENTIFIERS

Just as the main program can activate a procedure, a procedure can activate another procedure.* Let's begin by discussing main programs and the procedures they activate, and leave the discussion of procedures that activate other procedures to later in the chapter.

There are two categories of identifiers in a program that has procedures. The identifiers in the main program are called *global* identifiers, and those declared in the procedures are called *local* identifiers. Thus, in the program of Figure 6.2*a* (a slightly altered version of the previous program), K, since it is declared in the main program, is a global variable and J, since it is declared in the procedure, is a local variable. The fact that K is global means that it can be used in the main program and in the procedures it activates, here Horizontal and Vertical, as well. You may think of a global identifier as being like a federal law, the main program as being like the federal government, a local identifier as being like a state law, and the procedures as being like one of the 50 states. The federal law applies to the federal government and to each of the 50 states as well. Thus the global variable K can be used in procedure Vertical, as is done in writeln('x', 'x':19, ' K=',K). However, you cannot use a local identifier in the main program, just as a state law does not apply to the federal government. (Another way of looking at this is to say that local variables are hidden from the main program.) Thus, using the local variable J in the main program, for instance writing writeln('J=', J), would produce a syntax error. For that reason, we wrote this statement as a comment. The running of the program is shown in Figure 6.2*b*. In Standard Pascal, a loop control variable must be declared as a local variable.

DISCLAIMER

Global variables are discussed here so that the student will appreciate why it is not a good programming practice to use them. We discourage their use.

---

*We shall see in Chapter 16 that a subprogram can even activate itself.

GLOBAL AND LOCAL VARIABLES I

```
PROGRAM Box(output);
VAR K: integer;

PROCEDURE Horizontal;
(* produces a horizontal line *)
VAR J: integer;
BEGIN
  FOR J:= 1 to 20 DO
    write('x');
  writeln
END (* Horizontal *);

PROCEDURE Vertical;
(* Produces entries in two vertical lines *)
BEGIN
  writeln('x', 'x':19, ' K=',K)
END (* Vertical *);

BEGIN (* MAIN PROGRAM *)
  Horizontal;
  FOR K:= 1 to 6 DO
    Vertical;
  Horizontal;
  (* Print Local variable *)
  (* writeln('J=', J) *)
END.
```

FIGURE 6.2*a*.   Variables declared in the main program are called *global* and can be used in the procedure. Any variable declared in a procedure is called *local* and can't be used in the main program. Thus `writeln('J=', J)` would produce an error if used in the main program. The loop control variable in a procedure must be a local variable.

```
xxxxxxxxxxxxxxxxxxxx
x                  x K = 1
x                  x K = 2
x                  x K = 3
x                  x K = 4
x                  x K = 5
x                  x K = 6
xxxxxxxxxxxxxxxxxxxx
```

FIGURE 6.2*b*.   Running the program of Figure 6.2*a*. Since K is a global variable, it can be used in the procedure.

When the same identifier is used as both a global and a local identifier, two locations are established—one for the local identifier and one for the global identifier. The local one takes precedence within the procedure in which it is used. For example, in Figure 6.3a the variable One is declared in the main program (and is thus global), and is also declared in procedure Deep (and is thus local there). When One is used in procedure Deep in

```
writeln('Deep global One= ', One)
```

the value of the local variable is used. Since we are using One before we assign a value to it, the program prints the unexpected results −3514 (as it does when no value has been assigned to an identifier) and not the global value of One. Once a local value has been assigned to One in One := 3, the program prints the local value, as shown in Figure 6.3b. When the computer returns to the main program and executes writeln ('Main value of One = ', One), the value of One used is the global value.

Next, let's explain how the computer allocates memory to local and global identifiers. As we've said, when the same identifier is used both as a global and as a local one (as is the case for One), the compiler establishes two separate locations, one in the main program (its global) and one in the procedure (its local). For example, see the table for Figure 6.3a. Therefore a change in one does not affect the contents of the other.

Main program   [1]
                One

Procedure deep [3]
                One

GLOBAL AND LOCAL VARIABLES II

```
PROGRAM Test(output);
(* Shows local & global use of variables *)
VAR One: integer;

PROCEDURE Deep;
VAR One: integer;
BEGIN
  writeln('Deep global One= ', One);
  One:= 3;
  writeln('Deep local One= ', One)
END (* Deep *);

BEGIN (* MAIN *)
  One:= 1;
  Deep;
  writeln('Main value of One= ', One)
END.
```

FIGURE 6.3a. If the same variable (One) is declared in the main program and also in a procedure, the one declared in the procedure takes precedence. Thus the first time One is used in Deep, it is undefined.

```
Deep global One= −3514
Deep local One= 3
Main value of One= 1
```

FIGURE 6.3b. Running the program of Figure 6.3a. When the computer returns from the procedure to the main program, the value of One is the global value.

Main program One [1]

Procedure Deep One [3]

TABLE FOR FIGURE 6.3a. Since One is declared in procedure Deep as well as in the main program, two separate locations are established. Each one stores a separate value.

Next, let's see what happens when a new value is assigned to a global variable in a procedure. Thus in Figure 6.4*a*, One is global both in the main program and in procedure Deep; it is not a local variable there because it is not declared in the VAR declaration in Deep. Consequently, there is only one location called One. In the main program, the variable One is originally assigned the value 1. However, when

$$One := 3$$

is executed in procedure Deep, since One is global, the contents of One in the main program is changed to 3. Thus after Deep is executed and the computer returns to the main program and executes

```
writeln('Main value of One= ', One)
```

the program does not print the value assigned to One in the main program, 1, but prints the value assigned to it in procedure Deep, 3, as we see in Figure 6.4*b*.

By now, your instructor has probably told you that it is bad programming practice to use global variables. Let's see why. If you use a global variable in a procedure, as shown in Figure 6.4*a*, you may unwittingly assign a new value to it there. When execution is returned to the main program and this global variable is used in a calculation or an output statement, an unexpected result will occur there. This phenomenon is called a *side effect.*

You don't have to worry that a local variable will produce a side effect because, as we have seen, you can't use a local variable in the main program.

GLOBAL VERSUS LOCAL IDENTIFIERS

A scratch sheet on which you jot down intermediate results in a calculation is like the local variables used in a procedure. Once you no longer need the intermediate results, you throw the sheet away. Similarly, once the program leaves a procedure, the local variables are lost. If you use global variables in a procedure, it's like using a scratch sheet for your final as well as intermediate results. Results that were meant to be discarded suddenly appear in the final answer.

SIDE EFFECTS

```
PROGRAM Test(output);
(* Demonstrates side effects *)
VAR One: integer;

PROCEDURE Deep;
BEGIN
  One:= 3;
END (* Deep *);

BEGIN (* MAIN *)
  One:= 1;
  Deep;
  writeln('Main value of One= ', One)
END.
```

FIGURE 6.4a.   **If you assign a value to a global variable in a procedure, that value will** be the one used in the main program.

```
Main value of One= 3
```

FIGURE 6.4b.   Running the program of Figure 6.4a. We see that the value printed in the main program is not the one that was assigned there, but is the one assigned in the procedure. This is called a *side effect*.

TEST YOURSELF

QUESTION: The following program shows the danger of using global variables in procedures. If the input is 20 5, what is the value of VFinal (the final velocity) printed in the main program?

```
PROGRAM Travel(input,output);
VAR VFinal, g, Time: real;

PROCEDURE Calculate;
VAR Distance, Velocity :real;
BEGIN
  writeln('Type velocity and time');
  readln(Velocity, Time);
  Distance:= Velocity * Time
  writeln('Distance =', Distance:8:1)
END (* Calculate *);

BEGIN (* MAIN PROGRAM *)
  g:= 32.0;
  Time:= 4.0;
  Calculate;
  VFinal:= g * Time;
  writeln('Final velocity = ', VFinal:8:1)
END.
```

ANSWER: The value of Time becomes 5.0 in Calculate. Since it is global, it becomes 5.0 in the main program as well. The value of the final velocity is therefore incorrectly calculated as 160 instead of 128.

6.3

VALUE PARAMETERS

Is there a way of passing information to procedures without using global variables, thus avoiding the possibility of side effects? Figure 6.5a shows how. The program produces repetitions of the line of characters xxxxx------, where the numbers of X's, dashes, and repetitions of the pattern are stored in the variables NumX, NumDash, and NumLine, respectively. The pseudocode for the main program is

Read # of Xs, # of -s, # of repetitions;
FOR K:= 1 TO # of repetitions DO
      Draw pattern.

INTRODUCTION TO VALUE PARAMETERS

```
PROGRAM IntroProc(input, output);
(* Produces a pattern *)
VAR Outer, NumX, NumDash, NumLine: integer;

PROCEDURE Pattern(LimitX, LimitD: integer);
(* Produces a line consisting of Xs and dashes *)
VAR Xindex, Dindex: integer;
BEGIN
  FOR Xindex:= 1 to LimitX DO
    write ('x');
  FOR Dindex := 1 to LimitD DO
    write('-');
  writeln
END(* Pattern *);

BEGIN
  writeln('Type # of Xs, # of Dashes, & Number of lines');
  readln(NumX, NumDash, NumLine);
  FOR Outer := 1 to NumLine DO
    Pattern(NumX, NumDash)
END.
```

FIGURE 6.5a.   **The values of NumX and NumDash** are passed to procedure Pattern. They are called *value parameters.*

and thus the top-down diagram becomes:

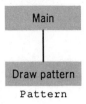

Pattern

Let's refine *Draw pattern* to

```
FOR J : = 1 TO # of Xs DO
    write('x');
FOR J : = 1 TO # of -s DO
    write('-')
writeln
```

This will be translated into the code for procedure Pattern.

In order to pass the values of NumX and NumDash to the procedure so that you don't have to use the global properties of these variables in the procedure, do the following: Write the procedure identifier Pattern in the main program, but now follow Pattern with the list of the variables whose values you wish to send to the procedure. Enclose these variables in parentheses:

Pattern(NumX, NumDash);

The variables NumX and NumDash are called the *actual parameters* of procedure Pattern. Now when you write the procedure heading, you must include a list of the local variables that correspond to the actual parameters used in the activating statement. These local variables are called the *formal parameters* or *dummy parameters.* We will use LimitX and LimitD as the formal parameters corresponding to NumX and NumD, respectively. The parameter LimitX must be the same type as NumX, and LimitD must be the same type as NumDash. In our program, the type of both formal parameters is integer. When listing the formal parameters in the procedure heading, follow the list with a colon and the type of the parameters, just as in a VAR declaration. Thus write

PROCEDURE Pattern(LimitX, LimitD: integer)

When Pattern(NumX, NumDash) is executed, the computer copies the contents of NumX into LimitX and the contents of NumDash into LimitD. If we assign any values to the formal parameters in the procedure, these values never get back to the activating procedure or main program; this type of one-way parameter is called a *value parameter.* Thus if the value of NumX is 4 in the main program, the value of LimitX will be 4 when the procedure is activated. If we assign 2 to LimitX in the procedure, the value of NumX will not be affected; it will remain 4. Thus, although NumX is global and its contents are copied to LimX, the identifier LimX is local. The results of running the program are shown in Figure 6.5*b*.

```
Type # of Xs, # of Dashes, & Number of lines
3 4 5
xxx----
xxx----
xxx----
xxx----
xxx----
```

FIGURE 6.5b. Running the program of Figure 6.5a. The variable used in the main program when activating the procedure is called the *actual parameter* and the one used in the procedure heading is called the *formal parameter*.

The compiler establishes one memory location for each actual parameter and another location for the corresponding formal parameter, as shown in the table for Figure 6.5a.

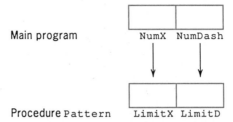

Main program   NumX NumDash

Procedure Pattern   LimitX LimitD

Hence the number of actual and formal parameters must be the same; and as we have seen, the type of the formal and corresponding actual parameters must agree. You can't also list a formal parameter in the VAR declaration of the procedure in which it is used. Thus it would be a mistake, for instance, to also declare LimitX in VAR Xindex, Dindex: integer.

TEST YOURSELF

QUESTION: What would happen if the procedure heading was

        PROCEDURE Pattern(LimitD, LimitX: integer);

if the activating statement remained Pattern(NumX, NumDash)?

ANSWER: Since LimitD and LimitX are in the wrong relative order in the procedure heading, the number of X's printed would be the number of dashes we wanted printed, and vice versa. Thus, although the computer would not print any syntax or execution errors, it would produce incorrect results.

Let's rewrite the program, using constant identifiers instead of variables as the final limits of the FOR–DO loops (see Figure 6.5c). This program shows how to define constants in a procedure. Since LimitX and LimitD are the limits of the loops in the procedure, for the sake of clarity we place CONST LimitX = 3; LimitD = 4 within the procedure. Since a procedure has the same structure as the program, you must place this CONST definition between the procedure heading and the VAR declaration. We could have defined LimitX and LimitD in a CONST definition in the main program instead; however, this would have made the program harder to read.

Note that since the numbers of X's and dashes are no longer read into the program but are defined as constants, the present program does not have the flexibility of the previous one. Each time it is run, it produces the same result. Also, information is no longer passed to the procedure, so parameters are no longer used.

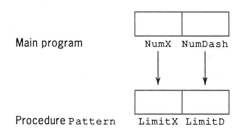

Main program   NumX   NumDash

Procedure Pattern   LimitX   LimitD

TABLE FOR FIGURE 6.5a.   Each value parameter has two locations, one in the main program and one in the procedure. The names of these locations are the ones used in the main program and in the procedure heading. If something is assigned to a value parameter in the procedure, it is not transmitted to the main program. Thus there are no side effects.

USING THE CONST DEFINITION IN A PROCEDURE

```
PROGRAM IntroProc(output);
(* Produces a pattern using constant identifiers *)
CONST NumLine = 5;
VAR Outer: integer;

PROCEDURE Pattern;
(* Produces a line consisting of Xs and dashes *)
CONST LimitX = 3; LimitD = 4;
VAR Xindex, Dindex: integer;
BEGIN
  FOR Xindex:= 1 to LimitX DO
    write ('x');
  FOR Dindex := 1 to LimitD DO
    write('-');
  writeln
END(* Pattern *);

BEGIN
  FOR Outer := 1 to NumLine DO
    Pattern
END.
```

FIGURE 6.5c.   We write the previous program using a CONST definition in the procedure.

Planning Procedures

The next program reads NumData pairs of data, consisting of a person's ID and income, and makes a histogram (a bar graph) of the income using bars of X's such that one X represents $1000. The pseudocode for the main program is:

> FOR J := 1 to NumData DO BEGIN
>   *Read the ID and Income;*
>   *Plot income*
> END (* FOR–J *)

Plot income becomes the procedure Plot. Thus the top-down diagram is

Plot

It is often easier to use the following approach to write procedures:

1. Incorporate the statements that will eventually be a procedure into a separate program.
2. Once you test this program, convert the appropriate statements into a procedure and test it from an appropriately written main program.
3. Alter the main program so that it will use the procedure as your goal dictates.

Step I: Forming the Program

Let's take this approach in writing the present program by first writing a program (see Figure 6.6a) that will do what will eventually be done by procedure Plot—drawing one bar of a histogram. Since the program will read only one pair of data, we set NumData to 1 in the CONST definition. In the statement part we divide Income by 1000 and assign the result to RndIncome, using it to produce that number of X's in

> FOR K := 1 to RndIncome DO
>   write ('x')

Because of the writeln following read(ID, Income), the computer will display the first line of results on the line following the one on which the data were typed. Use a write next, that is,

> write('ID=', ID:4, ' Income=', Income:6:0, Blank)

so that the row of X's produced by the FOR loop will continue on the same line as the information produced by this write. The results of running this program are shown in Figure 6.6b. Our final program will draw the bars sideways because this is the best we can do at this point.

STEP I: PLANNING A PROCEDURE

```
PROGRAM Graph(input, output);
(* Makes a histogram of people's incomes *)
CONST NumData =1; Blank = ' ';
VAR
  Income: real;
  RndIncome, K, ID : integer;
BEGIN
  writeln('Type ', NumData, ' sets of: ID# followed by Income');
  read(ID, Income);
  writeln;
  write('ID=', ID:4, ' Income=',Income:6:0, Blank);
  RndIncome : = round(Income) DIV 1000;

  FOR K: = 1 TO RndIncome DO
    write ( 'x' );

  writeln;
  writeln('------------------------');
  writeln('Each X represents $1000')
END.
```

FIGURE 6.6a.   The first step is to write the procedure as a program. Since the resulting procedure plots only one salary, so does this stage of the program.

```
Type 1 sets of: ID# followed by Income
1001 23451
ID= 1001 Income= 23451 xxxxxxxxxxxxxxxxxxxxxxx
------------------------
Each X represents $1000
```

FIGURE 6.6b.   Running the program of Figure 6.6a.

Step II: Forming the Procedure
Take the statements

```
write('ID=', ID:4, ' Income=',Income:6:0, Blank);
RndIncome := round(Income) DIV 1000;
FOR K:= 1 TO RndIncome DO
   write ( 'x' )
```

from the preceding program and incorporate them into a procedure. This means that you have to pass ID and Income as parameters to the procedure. Since the formal parameters ID and Income are not the same type, list these parameters in the procedure heading as you'd list them in a VAR statement, that is, separate ID: integer from Income: real with a semicolon:

PROCEDURE Plot(ID: integer; Income: real)

You must also declare RndIncome and K as local variables in Plot, so remove them from the VAR declaration in the main program, as shown in Figure 6.6c. Of course, you must activate Plot in the main program.

When you run the program with the same set of data used for Figure 6.6a, you get the same results (see Figure 6.6d), so you can be confident that our procedure works.

The same pair of variables, ID and Income, have been used for the actual and formal parameters, as shown in Figure 6.6c. The compiler sets aside two separate locations called Income and two separate locations called ID, one for use in the main program and one for use in procedure Plot.

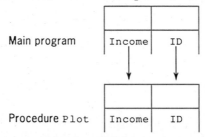

When the procedure is activated, the contents of the locations ID and Income in the main program are copied to the locations ID and Income, respectively, in the procedure. However, if a new value were assigned to either ID or Income in the procedure, this value would not be passed back to the corresponding location in the main program.

STEP II: TESTING THE PROCEDURE

```
PROGRAM Graph(input, output);
(* Makes a histogram of people's incomes *)
CONST NumData = 1; Blank = ' ';
VAR
  Income: real;
  J, ID : integer;

PROCEDURE Plot(ID: integer; Income: real);
(* Produces a histogram of incomes *)
VAR RndIncome, K:integer;
BEGIN
  write('ID=', ID:4, ' Income=',Income:6:0, Blank);
  RndIncome := round(Income) DIV 1000;
  FOR K:= 1 TO RndIncome DO
    write ( 'x' )
END(* Plot *);

BEGIN
  writeln('Type ', NumData, ' sets of: ID# followed by Income');
  read(ID, Income);
  writeln;
  Plot(ID, Income);
  writeln;
  writeln('------------------------');
  writeln('Each X represents $1000')
END.
```

FIGURE 6.6c. The plotting part of the previous program is now made into a procedure. When we use different types in the procedure heading, we must separate the declarations with a semicolon.

```
Type 1 sets of: ID# followed by Income
1001 23451
ID= 1001 Income= 23451 xxxxxxxxxxxxxxxxxxxxxxx
------------------------
Each X represents $1000
```

FIGURE 6.6d.   Since this output is identical to that shown in Figure 6.6b, we see that the procedure is written correctly.

Step III: Altering the Main Program

Since we want to process many pairs of data, let's alter the main program so that it now includes

```
FOR J := 1 TO NumData DO
    BEGIN
        read(ID, Income);
        writeln;
        Plot(ID, Income);
    END (* FOR J *);
```

as shown in Figure 6.6*e*.

The results of running the program are shown in Figure 6.6*f*. Since the information is read using a read in the loop, type all the pairs of data at one time so that they will all be transferred to the buffer. Only after you finish typing all the data should you hit the carriage return.

TEST YOURSELF

QUESTION: What would happen if we wrote the procedure heading as

```
PROCEDURE Plot(Income: real; ID: integer);
```

if the activating statement remained Plot(ID, Income)?

ANSWER: The compiler would print a syntax error, since the types of the corresponding actual and formal parameters do not match.

STEP III: USING THE TESTED PROCEDURE IN THE ACTUAL MAIN PROGRAM

```pascal
PROGRAM Graph(input, output);
(* Makes a histogram of people's incomes *)
CONST NumData =3; Blank = ' ';
VAR
  Income: real;
  J, ID : integer;

PROCEDURE Plot(ID: integer; Income: real);
(* Produces a histogram of incomes *)
VAR RndIncome, K:integer;
BEGIN
  write('ID=', ID:4, ' Income=',Income:6:0, Blank);
  RndIncome := round(Income) DIV 1000;
  FOR K:= 1 TO RndIncome DO
    write ( 'x' )
END(* Plot *);


BEGIN
  writeln('Type ', NumData, ' sets of: ID# followed by Income');
  FOR J:= 1 TO NumData DO
    BEGIN
      read(ID, Income);
      writeln;
      Plot(ID, Income);
    END (* FOR J *);
    writeln;
    writeln('------------------------');
    writeln('Each X represents $1000')
END.
```

FIGURE 6.6e.   We alter the program of Figure 6.6c so that it processes many salaries.

```
Type 3 sets of: ID# followed by Income
1001 23456 1003 18976 1009 12345
ID=1001 Income= 23456 xxxxxxxxxxxxxxxxxxxxxxx
ID=1003 Income= 18976 xxxxxxxxxxxxxxxxxxx
ID=1009 Income= 12345 xxxxxxxxxxxx
------------------------
Each X represents $1000
```

FIGURE 6.6f.   Running the program of Figure 6.6e.

The next program makes a histogram from five contiguous digits, like 38698, representing the quiz marks a student received on five different exams. The number of *x*'s on a given line of the histogram is determined by the mark for that line; the marks vary between 0 and 9. To simplify matters, we'll read each mark as a character. The pseudocode for the main program is

```
FOR index:= 1 To NumMarks DO BEGIN
    Read mark;
    Graph mark
FOR (* FOR *)
```

where NumMark represents the number of quizzes the student took, here five. Since Mark is a character variable, each digit in the group of five contiguous digits is read separately. We translate this into the main program, as shown in Figure 6.7*a* and *Graph mark* into procedure Graph, also as shown in Figure 6.7*a*:

```
PROCEDURE Graph( Digit:char);
VAR K: char;
BEGIN
  FOR K:= '1' to Digit DO
      write('x')
END(* Graph *);
```

The formal parameter Digit corresponds to the actual parameter Mark. Both are of character type. Thus the FOR–DO is written as FOR K:= '1' to Digit DO, where K is a character variable. Note that it would be a mistake to type the 1 without the quotation marks, that is, FOR K:= 1 to Digit DO, because 1 is an integer, whereas '1' is a character value.

Note the importance of using the most convenient type to solve a problem. This FOR–DO could have been written using an integer control variable, but this would require us first to convert the character variable Digit to an integer and thus would have been an awkward approach.

The writeln in the loop in the main program makes each line of results appear on a new line, as shown in Figure 6.7*b*, when the program is run. Also note that if one of the grades is zero, the computer interprets FOR K:= '1' to Digit DO as FOR K:= '1' to '0' DO and prints no digits for that grade.

PRODUCING A HISTOGRAM FROM CONTIGUOUS QUIZ MARKS

```
PROGRAM Graph(input, output);
(* Produces histogram of five quiz marks *)
CONST Blank = ' ';
   NumMarks = 5;
VAR Index: integer;
   Mark: char;

PROCEDURE Graph( Digit:char );
VAR K: char;
BEGIN
   FOR K:= '1' to Digit DO
      write('x')
END(* Graph *);

BEGIN(* MAIN *)
   writeln('Type ', NumMarks:3, ' quiz marks');
   FOR Index:= 1 to NumMarks DO
   (* Read marks as characters *)
      BEGIN
         read(Mark);
         writeln;
         write('Exam #', Index:2, ' Mark=', Mark:2, Blank);
         Graph(Mark)
      END (* FOR Index *)
END.
```

FIGURE 6.7a. Since each grade is read as a character, we write the limits of the FOR as characters so that we don't have to convert to integers.

```
Type 5 quiz marks 38698
Exam # 1 Mark= 3 xxx
Exam # 2 Mark= 8 xxxxxxxx
Exam # 3 Mark= 6 xxxxxx
Exam # 4 Mark= 9 xxxxxxxxx
Exam # 5 Mark= 8 xxxxxxxx
```

FIGURE 6.7b. Running the program of Figure 6.7a.

6.4

VARIABLE PARAMETERS

BEFORE YOU BEGIN

Sometimes it's necessary to pass information from a procedure to the main program. A variable parameter allows us to do this.

Let's examine a program that averages five quiz marks, read as five contiguous digits, to see how values are passed back to the main program. The digits are read as one integer and stored in the location number. The pseudocode for the main program is

> *Read number;*
> *Sum:= 0;*
> FOR index: = 1 To 5 DO BEGIN
>   *Remove leftmost digit;*
>   *Sum:= Sum + digit*
> END; (* FOR *)
> *Calculate average;*
> *writeln(average).*

In order to translate *Remove leftmost digit* to Pascal, we remind the reader of the method used in the program of Figure 3.16a. Before the FOR–DO loop, we calculate a value for the variable Power that is equal to 10 * 10 * 10 * 10, that is, 10,000. By DIVing, for instance, 23145 by Power, we get the leftmost digit, 2, and assign this to Mark. The remainder, which becomes the new value of Number, is 3145 and is obtained by using the MOD. Thus the leftmost digit of 23145—namely, the 2—has been removed. To remove the leftmost digit of each new value of Number, divide Power by 10 each time the loop is executed.

The leftmost digit of Number is removed when Remove(Mark, Number, Power) is executed. We want the main program to be able to both send information (the values of Number and Power) to procedure Remove and obtain information (the value of Mark and the altered values of Number and Power) from it. Since value parameters only allow us to send information to procedures, we now introduce parameters that allow us to both pass information to and receive information from a procedure. This type of parameter is called a *variable parameter.* An example is given in Figure 6.8a.

INTRODUCTION TO VARIABLE PARAMETERS

```
PROGRAM ExamAverage(input, output);
(* Average 5 quiz marks *)
VAR Sum, Mark, Index, Power: integer;
  Number:longint;
  Average: real;

PROCEDURE Remove(VAR Grade, Power,Number:integer);
(* Removes leading digit *)
BEGIN
  Grade:= Number DIV Power;
  writeln('Mark is', Grade:2);
  Number:= Number MOD Power;
  Power:= Power DIV 10
End (* Remove *);

BEGIN
  writeln('Type 5 contiguous digits FOR quiz marks');
  readln(Number);
  (* First calculate 10 ** 4 *)
  Power:=10 * 10 * 10 * 10;
  Sum:= 0;
  (* Now remove the leading digit and add TO sum *)

  FOR Index:= 1 TO 5 DO BEGIN
    Remove(Mark, Power, Number);
    Sum:= Sum + Mark;
  END (* FOR Index *);

  Average:= Sum / 5;
  writeln('Quiz average is', Average:4:1)
END.
```

FIGURE 6.8a. All the quiz grades are read as one integer and thus must be separated. In order to pass information back from the procedure, we must use variable parameters.

```
PROCEDURE Remove(VAR Grade, Power, Number: integer);
(* Removes leading digit *)
BEGIN
    Grade:= Number DIV Power;
    writeln('Mark ', index:2, ' is', Grade:2);
    Number:= Number MOD Power;
    Power:= Power DIV 10
END(* Remove *);
```

The VAR in the procedure header instructs the compiler to set up one memory location for each pair of actual and corresponding formal parameters instead of the two locations established for a value parameter. If Number were a different type of variable from Grade and Power, you would have to repeat* VAR. The table for Figure 6.8a shows how the locations are set up.

Main program	Mark	Number	Power
Remove	Grade	Number	Power

The actual parameter Mark and the formal parameter Grade label the same memory location; Mark is its name in the main program and Grade is its name in procedure Remove. Because there is only one location for each pair of actual and formal parameters, whenever a value is placed in the procedure in a location labeled by a variable parameter, it can be used in the main program when control is returned there. Thus when Sum:= Sum + Mark is executed in the main program, since Mark is the name used there for the location labeled by Grade in the procedure, the computer can calculate the sum of the grades and their average, as shown in Figure 6.8b.

Note that if Number and Power were value parameters instead of variable parameters, their new values calculated in the procedure would not be passed back to the main program. Thus each time the procedure was activated by the main program, the original values of Number (23798) and Power (10 * 10 * 10 * 10) would be passed to the procedure. Therefore, the value of Grade would always be the first digit of the original value of Number, here, 2. However, since Number and Grade are variable parameters, the new values calculated in Remove are passed back to the main program, and these values are used the next time the procedure is activated.

Both value and variable parameters can be passed to a procedure. For example, you can write as a procedure heading

```
PROCEDURE Example(VAR One, Two :integer; Three, Four:integer);
```

where One and Two are integer variable parameters and Three and Four are integer value parameters.

*For example, you would write PROCEDURE Remove(VAR Grade, Power:integer; VAR Number:Real);

main program Remove	Mark Grade	Number Number	Power Power

TABLE FOR FIGURE 6.8a. For a variable parameter, one location is used per parameter both in the main program and in the procedure. Thus anything stored in the location in the procedure is passed back to the main program, and vice versa.

```
Type 5 contiguous digits for quiz marks
23798
Mark is 2
Mark is 3
Mark is 7
Mark is 9
Mark is 8
Quiz average is 5.8
```

FIGURE 6.8b.   Running the program of Figure 6.8a.

6.5

VARIABLE PARAMETERS VERSUS VALUE PARAMETERS

If One and Two are corresponding value parameters, where One is the actual and Two is the dummy parameter, they label two separate locations as shown in Table 6.1. The value stored in One is copied into Two; however, any change in the contents of Two does not affect the contents of One.

If One and Two are corresponding variable parameters, however, they label the same location as shown in Table 6.2. Thus any change in the contents of the main program or activating procedure is reflected in the activated procedure, and vice versa. Variable parameters are like global variables. The difference is that you, the programmer, are immediately aware that a variable is a variable parameter when you scan the procedure heading.

Another difference between the two types of parameters is that you can use an expression as an actual value parameter but not as an actual variable parameter. Thus if a procedure heading is

PROCEDURE Remove(VAR grade: integer);

you cannot* write Remove(22) or Remove(22 + A). However, if a procedure heading is PROCEDURE Plot(grade:integer), that is, if grade is a value parameter, you can write Plot(22) or Plot(22 + A). You can never, however, use an expression as a formal parameter, whether it be a variable or a value parameter. Thus PROCEDURE Plot(5:integer) will cause an error.

In order to avoid side effects, use a variable parameter only when you want the value of the formal parameter passed back to the activating program; otherwise, use a value parameter.

Another term for passing variable parameters is passing values *by reference* or *by address*, because the computer passes the address of the variable parameter to the procedure. Thus when the computer activates procedure Remove, it passes the address of Grade to the procedure. We note that passing value parameters is also called passing *by value*.

---

*If you could, then if you assign the value of 3 to Grade in procedure Remove, the computer will store the value 3 in the location reserved for 22 when control of execution is transferred to the main program. This means that each time 22 is used subsequently in the main program, its value will be 3. For instance, 22 + 5 will be evaluated as 8.

QUESTION: What is the value of Y printed by the following program?

```
PROGRAM Test(output);
VAR X, Y:integer;

PROCEDURE Add(VAR Sum:integer);
BEGIN
  Sum:= Sum + 1
END (* Add *);

BEGIN (* Test *);
  X:= 1;
  Add(X);
  Add(Y);
  writeln('The value of Y = ', Y)
END.
```

ANSWER: The value of Y is unpredictable for the following reason: Since X is a variable parameter, it and Sum label the same location.

2

Main program   X
Procedure Add   Sum

However, when the program exits a procedure, all the locations used in the procedure (here, Sum) become unaccessible. Thus, although Y and Sum label the same location the second time Add is activated, it is not the same location that X labels.

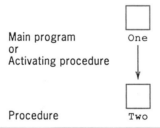

Main program
or
Activating procedure   One

Procedure   Two

TABLE 6.1

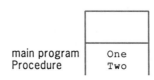

main program Procedure	One Two

TABLE 6.2

6.6

NESTING PROCEDURES AND THE SCOPE OF IDENTIFIERS

Since procedures appear in the main program between the VAR declaration and the statement part, we say that the procedures are *nested* in the main program. Just as all procedures are nested in the main program, a procedure may be nested within another procedure, as shown in Figure 6.9a:

```
PROCEDURE Deep;
VAR Two: integer;

  PROCEDURE Deeper;
  VAR Three :integer;
  BEGIN
    Three:= 3;
    writeln('Deeper local Three= ', Three);
    writeln('Deeper Global Two= ', Two);
    writeln('Deeper Global One= ', One)
  END(* Deeper *);

BEGIN (* Deep *)
  Two:= 2;
  writeln('Deep local Two= ', Two);
  writeln('Deep global One= ', One);
  Deeper
END (* Deep *);
```

The procedure that is nested must appear between the VAR declaration and the statement part of the procedure in which it is nested. Thus we see that Deeper is nested within Deep. All procedures that are nested within a procedure plus the procedure itself (from its VAR declaration down to the end of the procedure) form the *block* of the procedure. Thus Deeper is nested within the block of Deep, and both Deep and Deeper are nested within the main program block.

Any identifier declared in the main program is global for any procedure in the main program block. For instance, in Figure 6.9a we see that One is global in any procedure used in the program. On the other hand, Two is local in procedure Deep; however, it can be used in any procedure in the block of Deep, i.e., Deeper (see Figure 6.9b). Thus it is relatively global there; if its value is

THE SCOPE OF A VARIABLE

```
PROGRAM Test(output);
(* Shows scope of variables *)
VAR One: integer;

PROCEDURE Deep;
VAR Two: integer;

  PROCEDURE Deeper;
  VAR Three :integer;
  BEGIN
    Three:= 3;
    writeln('Deeper local Three= ', Three);
    writeln('Deeper Global Two= ', Two);
    writeln('Deeper Global One= ', One)
    END(* Deeper *);

BEGIN (* Deep *)
  Two:= 2;
  writeln('Deep local Two= ', Two);
  writeln('Deep global One= ', One);
  Deeper
END (* Deep *);

BEGIN (* MAIN *)
  One:= 1;
  Deep;
  writeln('Main value of One= ', One)
END.
```

FIGURE 6.9a. The block of a procedure consists of all the subprograms nested in it plus the procedure itself from the VAR declaration to the end of the procedure. The scope of an identifier is the block in which the identifier is declared. The scope of TWO is shaded.

```
Deep local Two= 2
Deep global One= 1
Deeper local Three= 3
Deeper Global Two= 2
Deeper Global One= 1
Main value of One= 1
```

FIGURE 6.9b. Running the program of Figure 6.9a. Since Two is declared in the block of Deep, its scope includes Deeper.

changed in one of the procedures in the block, its global value is changed throughout the block. If Deeper contained any procedures within its block, then Two could be used in these procedures as well, and in any procedures appearing in their blocks *ad infinitum.*

The *scope* of an identifier is the set of procedures in which the identifier can be used; it is the block in which the identifier is first declared. Thus the scope of Two is Deep and Deeper.

As we have said, using global variables in procedures can cause side effects. Similarly, using variables in procedures in their scope can cause side effects; for instance, using Two in procedure Deeper, where it is relatively global, can cause side effects in procedure Deep. Then why does Pascal support global and relative global identifiers? One reason is that it enables you to use constants defined at the beginning of a block throughout the block. Since you cannot change a value of a constant once it has been defined, there is no danger of side effects.

Since Deep activates Deeper, the top-down diagram for this program is

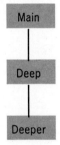

Since the rectangle for procedure Deep in the top-down diagram descends directly from the main program, it is activated there. Since the rectangle for procedure Deeper descends directly from Deep, it is activated there and not in the main program.

Figure 6.9c also shows the use of an identifier outside its scope. Here Deeper is not nested in Deep. When we use Two, an identifier declared in Deep, in Deeper (a procedure outside its scope), we get a syntax error, as shown in Figure 6.9d:

Line 9: Unknown identifier or syntax error.

When a procedure activates another procedure not nested in it (just as Deep activates Deeper in Figure 6.9c), the activated procedure, here Deeper, must precede the activating procedure, here Deep.

USING AN IDENTIFIER OUTSIDE ITS SCOPE

```
1    PROGRAM Test(output);
2    (* Shows use of identifier outside scope *)
3    VAR One: integer;

4    PROCEDURE Deeper;
5    VAR Three :integer;
6    BEGIN
7      Three:= 3;
8      writeln('Deeper local Three= ', Three);
9      writeln('Deeper Global Two= ', Two);
10     writeln('Deeper Global One= ', One)
11   END(* Deeper *);

12   PROCEDURE Deep;
13   VAR Two: integer;
14   BEGIN
15     Two:= 2;
16     writeln('Deep local Two= ', Two);
17     writeln('Deep global One= ', One);
18     Deeper
10   END (* Deep *);

20   BEGIN (* MAIN *)
21     One:= 1;
22     Deep;
23     writeln('Main value of One= ', One)
24   END.
```

FIGURE 6.9c. Since Deeper is no longer within the block of Deep, the identifier Two cannot be used there.

```
Line 9: unknown identifier or syntax error.
```

FIGURE 6.9d. Running the program of Figure 6.9c. The compiler indicates the line on which the error occurred.

6.7

THE READLN, READ, WRITELN, AND WRITE STANDARD PROCEDURES

An examination of the syntax of read, readln, write, and writeln shows that these statements are similar to the ones that activate procedures. For example, in readln(Length, Width, Cost), the identifiers that form the list are enclosed in parentheses and are separated from each other by commas, just as the actual parameters of a procedure are. In fact, read, readln, write, and writeln are procedures that are incorporated into the Pascal compiler. As mentioned in Chapter 3, they are called *standard procedures.* The actual parameters of the readln (here, Length, Width, and Cost) and read correspond to variable parameters in the standard procedure (since the data read are being passed back through them), whereas the actual parameters of the write and writeln correspond to value parameters in the standard procedure (since the information to be printed is being passed to the standard procedure and nothing is returned). The important difference between using procedures that you write and using these standard procedures is that in your own procedures the number of actual parameters must equal and agree in type with the formal parameters, whereas for the standard procedures these restrictions do not apply.

6.8

WHY WE USE SUBPROGRAMS

Using subprograms makes both the planning of the program and the reading of the resulting program easier, since we write the main program as a sequence of tasks and describe their details in the subprograms. However, there are other reasons for using subprograms.

When you have to write a difficult program, it may be almost impossible to write the entire program at once. Your first step should be to write a program that is a simplification of the program that is your goal and get that simplified version to execute properly. Then incorporate the procedures you used for this version into a more sophisticated version. Continue to do this until you have written the intended program.

We will use this technique in the next chapter to write a group of programs that determine the average number of letters per word in a sentence typed as input.

PROGRAMMING PITFALLS

1. A common error is assuming that since we have indicated that the parameters of the first type listed in a procedure heading are variable parameters, the parameters of the subsequent types are automatically variable parameters as well. For example, in

    ```
    PROCEDURE Example(VAR One, Two:integer; Three,
                      Four:real);
    ```

    the parameters Three and Four are value and not variable parameters. The statement written correctly is

    ```
    PROCEDURE Example(VAR One, Two:integer; VAR Three,
                      Four:real);
    ```

2. Another error is not declaring variables that are used as actual parameters. Thus if in a PROCEDURE called Process, we use the actual parameter Data, as, for example, in

    ```
    ReadIt(Data);
    Print(Data)
    ```

    then Data must either be declared in the VAR declaration or listed as a formal parameter in the procedure heading of Process.

3. A third error is not using a local variable as a FOR–DO loop control variable in a procedure. This is an error only in Standard Pascal.

PROGRAMMING STYLE

1. A procedure should be able to fit on your terminal screen without having to scroll to see all of it. If your original plan for a procedure produces one that is too long, break it up into smaller constituents.

2. A procedure should perform a complete operation. Thus don't write a procedure that reads data and performs part of a calculation, and a second one that performs the second part of the calculation and then prints the results. Instead write one procedure to read data, another one to perform the calculation, and a third one to print the results.

CHAPTER REVIEW

Global Variables

Variables that are declared in the main program are called *global parameters*. At this stage of your development, don't use them! We note, however, that objects that are used throughout a program (for instance, a tax table in an accounting program) are often declared as global variables. This means that when you write procedures for the program, you can assume that the object (in this case, a table) is accessible; thus you do not have to encumber the parameter list with these global objects.

Local Variables

Variables that are declared in a subprogram or that are formal value parameters are considered local.

Formal Parameters

The parameters appearing in the procedure heading are called *formal parameters*. They are also called *dummy parameters*. A formal parameter cannot be a constant or an expression.

Actual Parameters

The identifiers used when a procedure is activated are called *actual parameters*. Formal and actual parameters can be but need not be identical.

Value Parameters

A parameter not described by VAR in the subprogram heading is called a *value parameter*. The values from the main program or activating subprogram are passed to the locations described by value parameters in the activated subprogram but cannot be passed back to the main program or activating procedure. Thus there cannot be side effects. An actual value parameter can be a constant value or a calculation.

Variable Parameters

A parameter described by VAR in the subprogram heading is called a *variable parameter*. The values from the main program or activating subprogram are passed to the locations described by variable parameters in the activated subprogram and are passed back. An actual variable parameter cannot be a constant value or a calculation.

Procedures Activating Other Procedures

A procedure can only activate:

1. Another procedure that precedes it.
2. Another procedure nested in it.

We will see in Chapter 16 that a procedure can also activate itself.

NEW TERMS

activate

actual parameter

block

directory

dummy parameter

formal parameter

global identifiers

local identifiers

main program

nesting

passing by address

passing by reference

passing by value

procedure

scope

side effect

subprogram

value parameter

variable parameter

EXERCISES

1. What does the following program produce for the input 5 4 3 2 1?

```
PROGRAM Prob1(input, output);
CONST NumberOf = 5;
VAR Factor, Product:real;
PROCEDURE Multiply(VAR Product:real; Factor:real);
VAR K:integer;
BEGIN
  writeln('Type your ', NumberOF, ' factors');
  Product:= 1;
  FOR K:= 1 TO NumberOf DO BEGIN
    read(Factor);
    Product:= Product * Factor
  END (* WHILE *)
END (* Multiply *);
BEGIN (* Main *)
  Factor:= 1;
  Multiply(Product, Factor);
  writeln(Product:10:2, Factor:10:2)
END.
```

Product	Factor
5	1
20	4
60	3
120	2
120	1

2. What does the following program produce?

```
PROGRAM Prob2(input, output);
VAR A, B, C:integer;
PROCEDURE Shift(VAR A, D:integer; B:integer);
VAR C:integer;
BEGIN
  C:= D;
  A:= succ(A);
  B:= D + 2;
  writeln('Results of procedure');
  writeln('B= ',B, ' C= ', C, ' D= ', D)
END (* Shift *);
```

```
BEGIN (* Main *)
  A: = 3;
  B: = 4;
  C: = 6;
  Shift(C, B, A);
  writeln('Results of main program');
  writeln('A= ', A, ' B= ', B)
END.
```

3. What does the following program produce?

```
PROGRAM Prob3(input, output);
VAR X, Y, Z:integer;
PROCEDURE Change(X:integer; VAR Y:integer);
BEGIN
  X: = X + 1;
  Y: = Y + 1;
  Z: = Z + Y;
  writeln('Change values: X= ', X, ' Y= ', Y, ' Z= ', Z)
END (* Change *);
BEGIN
  X: = 1;
  Y: = 0;
  Z: = 0;
  Change(Y, Z);
  writeln('Main values: X= ', X, ' Y= ', Y, ' Z= ', Z)
END.
```

4. What is wrong with the following program if it is run on a Standard Pascal system?

```
PROGRAM Prob4(input, output);
CONST NumberOf = 5;
VAR Factor, Product:real;
    K:integer;
PROCEDURE Multiply(VAR Product:real; Factor:real);
BEGIN
  writeln('Type your ', NumberOF, ' factors');
  Product: = 1;
  FOR K: = 1 TO NumberOf DO BEGIN
    read(Factor);
    Product: = Product * Factor
  END (* FOR K *)
END (* Multiply *);
BEGIN (* Main *)
  Multiply(Product, Factor);
  writeln(Product:10:2, Factor:10:2)
END.
```

5. What is wrong with the following program that multiplies all the numbers read?

```
PROGRAM Prob1(input, output);
CONST NumberOf = 5;
VAR Factor, Product:real;
PROCEDURE Multiply(VAR Product:real; Factor:real);
BEGIN
  writeln('Type your ', NumberOF, ' factors');
  Product:= 1;
  Fact(Product, Factor);
END (* Multiply *);
PROCEDURE Fact(VAR Product:real; Factor:real);
VAR K:integer;
BEGIN
  FOR K:= 1 TO NumberOf DO BEGIN
    read(Factor);
    Product:= Product * Factor
  END (* FOR *)
END (* Fact *);
BEGIN (* Main *)
  Multiply(Product, Factor);
  writeln(Product:10:2, Factor:10:2)
END.
```

6. What is wrong with the following program?

```
PROGRAM Prob1(input, output);
CONST NumberOf = 5;
VAR Factor, Product:real;
PROCEDURE Factor(VAR Product:real; Factor:real);
VAR K:integer;
BEGIN
  writeln('Type your ', NumberOF, ' factors');
  Product:= 1;
  FOR K:= 1 TO NumberOf DO BEGIN
    read(Factor);
    Product:= Product * Factor
  END (* FOR K *)
END (* Factor *);
BEGIN (* Main *)
  Factor(Product, Factor);
  writeln(Product:10:2, Factor:10:2)
END.
```

7. Why does the following program produce 1 as the product, independently of what the program reads?

```
PROGRAM Prob7(input, output);
CONST NumberOf = 5;
VAR Product:real;
PROCEDURE Multiply(VAR Product:real);
VAR Factor:real;
PROCEDURE Fact(Product:real);
VAR K:integer;
```

```
BEGIN
  FOR K:= 1 TO NumberOf DO BEGIN
    read(Factor);
    Product:= Product * Factor
  END (* FOR *)
END (* Fact *);
BEGIN (* Multiply *)
  writeln('Type your ', NumberOF, ' factors');
  Product:= 1;
  Fact(Product);
END (* Multiply *);
BEGIN (* Main *)
  Multiply(Product);
  writeln(Product:10:2)
END.
```

What is the block of `Multiply` and the scope of `Factor`? What is the scope of `Product`?

8. Given

    PROCEDURE Factor(VAR Product:real; Factor:real);

would the main program statement `Factor(Product)` produce an error?

Programming Problems

9. Write a procedure that raises X to the Nth power. Hint: Use exercise 1 as a guide.

10. In Chapter 4 we learned that the argument of the trigonometric functions must be an angle in radians. Write a procedure that takes an angle measured in angles as a parameter and returns the sine of the angle. Note that there are 2π radians in 360 degrees.

11. Write a procedure that interchanges the values of two memory locations. Thus if `One` contains 7 and `Two` contains 55 before execution, then `Two` will contain 7 and `One` will contain 55 after execution. Hint: Use a temporary location `Temp` to store `One`. Next, store `Two` in `One`. Finally, store `Temp` in `Two`.

12. Write a program that uses a procedure to determine the original price of an item if the discounted price and the discount are given. For instance, if the discounted price is $80 and the discount is 20%, then the original price is $100. Use the formula

    Original:= DiscountPrice / (1 − Discount/100)

where the discount is given in percent. For example, if the discount were 20%, then the value of `Discount` would be 20.

13. At each weekly auction of U.S. Treasury bills, the prices of 90-day and 180-day bills are given as a number less than or equal to 100. For instance, one week the price of the 180-day bill was 96.628. That means that for each $100 worth of bills you buy, you pay $96.628. The

yield (interest rate) is obtained by subtracting the price from 100 (here, 100 − 96.628 or 3.372), then dividing the difference by the price (here, 3.372 / 96.628 or 0.0349), and finally, multiplying by 365/180 and obtaining 0.0349 * 365 / 180 or 7.08% as the yield. Write a procedure to which is passed the price and the term (number of days) and that passes back the yield via a var parameter.

14. Wallis's formula for π/2 is given by the infinite product

$$\frac{2^2}{1*3} \quad \frac{4^2}{3*5} \quad \frac{6^2}{5*7}$$

where the Nth term is given by

$$\frac{(2N)^2}{(2N-1)(2N+1)}$$

Write a procedure that calculates the product of the first N terms. Why should N be a real? If that is the case, why is maxint the maximum value of N? Sample values of π versus N are:

N	π
200	3.1376779002
500	3.1400238167
1000	3.1408077422
5000	3.1414355743
32767	3.1415685578

15. Write a program that produces all three-letter combinations in which the second letter is a vowel. In order to do this, use a procedure in which the parameter is the second letter.

16. Do the date program of Chapter 3 using a procedure and a FOR–DO loop, that is, type the date as six contiguous digits and remove the leading digits two at a time.

17. Write a procedure that produces the following pattern, where the number of "#"s is a parameter:

18. Write a procedure that produces a parabola for

$$y = ax^2$$

where "a" is a parameter:

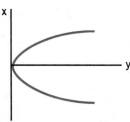

19. Write a procedure that produces a sine curve for an angle varying from 0 to 360 degrees in steps of 10 degrees. To convert from angles to radians, multiply the angle by 3.14159 / 180. The *x*-axis should be at column 40 and the amplitude of the sine should be 25. Hint: Use a variable field width to print the string "*". The step in which the angle is incremented is a parameter:

20. Write a procedure that produces a sine curve in which the halves are filled with *s. Hint: Use a nested loop to produce the *s. From 0 to 180 degrees, use write(' ':40). From 190 to 360 degrees, use write(' ':40 − abs(round(25 * sin(Radians)))). The step in which the angle is incremented is a parameter:

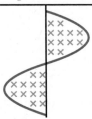

21. Write a program that uses a procedure that reads two times and calculates the difference between them in minutes. The times read should be military times, that is, 12:45 A.M. is 045 and 1:35 P.M. is 1335.

22. Rewrite the program of exercise 21 so that the difference is calculated in hours and minutes.

23. Write a procedure that converts a lowercase letter to an uppercase letter. Note that in the ASCII table the ordinal position of a given uppercase letter is 32 lower than that of the corresponding uppercase letter. Hint: Use the pred function.

24. Write a procedure that converts an uppercase letter to a lowercase letter.

7

THE IF-THEN-ELSE
AND CASE STATEMENTS;
MORE ON PROGRAM DESIGN:
PROGRAMMING BY STAGES
AND TOP-DOWN TESTING

CHAPTER OVERVIEW

There are two types of statements that enable the program to make decisions: IF-THEN-ELSE and CASE. The IF-THEN-ELSE requires a boolean expression. The boolean operators AND, OR, and NOT and sets make the evaluation of boolean expressions more versatile. As we learn about these devices, we use them to write a word processing program in stages.

7.1

THE IF–THEN STATEMENT

One way of performing an action only if something is true is to use the IF–THEN statement. For instance, to add 1 to Count only if the value of Code is 30 and then print the value of Code, regardless of its value, you would write

```
IF Code = 30 THEN
    Count: = Count + 1;
writeln('Code=', Code)
```

What is sandwiched between the IF and the THEN (here, Code = 30) is called a *boolean expression* or a *condition*. The value of Code = 30 is true if the value of Code is 30; otherwise, it's false. If the boolean expression is true, then the statement immediately following the THEN is executed (here, Count : = Count + 1). On the other hand, if the boolean expression is false, the statement following the THEN is skipped. In either case, at this point the next statement executed is the one following the IF–THEN statement, here writeln ('Code=', Code).

ANALOGY

> The IF–THEN is like a one-way switch. Either the program executes the statement following the THEN or it doesn't.

The symbols (here, the "=" in IF code = 30 THEN) used to compare the values of identifiers are called *comparison operators.* They are shown in Table 7.1. These operators can be used with any type of variable or constant identifier, provided that the same type of identifier appears on both sides of the operator. The exception is that a real value can be compared with an integer. Thus if Three is a character variable, then IF Three > 2 THEN would be illegal, since 2 is an integer. However, IF Three > '2' THEN would be valid since '2' is a character value. Finally, IF 4 >= 2.0 THEN is legal, since an integer is compared with a real.

The meaning of 4 >= 2.0 is "4 greater than 2.0 or 4 equal to 2.0." It is true, since the "4 greater than 2.0" part is true. Similarly, 6 <= 6 is true, since the 6 = 6 part is true. The comparison operations are performed after the mathematical ones. Thus in 5 > 2 + 1, the addition is performed before the ">" is, so the computer views the expession as 5 > 3 and evaluates it as true.

Comparison Operators	Meaning
=	Equal to
<>	Not equal to
<	Less than
>	Greater than
>=	Greater than or equal to
<=	Less than or equal to

TABLE 7.1. The operators used in boolean expressions. For example, the expression $8 > 9$ is false.

7.2

AN INTRODUCTION TO WORD PROCESSING

BEFORE YOU BEGIN

Have you ever wanted to know the number of words in a paragraph you wrote or the average number of letters per word in a sentence? The following is the first step in a series of programs that answers these questions.

One way of solving a difficult problem is to write the program that solves it in stages. Let's use this technique to determine the average number of letters per word in a sentence.

1. Let's start by writing a program that determines the number of words in a sentence in which only one blank can separate words. Only letters and blanks appear in the sentence.
2. We'll alter the program so that it calculates the average number of letters per word in a sentence.
3. Then, after we've learned some more Pascal syntax, we'll alter the program further so that it calculates the average number of letters per word in a sentence that can contain any type of punctuation and that can have one or more blanks separating words.

Here we present a simplified version of a technique used in some word processors to count the number of words in a sentence. If only one blank separates two words, the number of words in the sentence equals the number of blanks plus 1. For instance, "How are you?" contains two blanks and three words.

The initial pseudocode is

>   *Prompt the user to type # of characters in sentence;*
>   *Label the columns;*
>   *Count the number of blanks in the sentence;*
>   *Print the results*

In LabelColumns, shown in the top-down diagram (Figure 7.1*a*), we'll number the columns of the monitor screen so that we can see how many characters constitute our sentence.

PITFALLS USING THE IF

1. You cannot use the ":=" instead of the "=" in a boolean expression. Thus IF Code:= 3 THEN is incorrect. Note that "=" tests for equality in a boolean expression, whereas ":=" is used to assign a value to an identifier in an assignment statement.

2. You cannot write "=<" instead of "<=" or "=>" instead of ">=", that is, the equals sign must follow the other symbol.

3. You cannot place an embedded blank between the ">" and "="; between the "<" and "="; or between the "<" and ">". Doing so will cause a syntax error.

4. Note that the "=" operator should not be used with real values in a boolean expression, since, as we saw in Chapter 3, real values, because of roundoff error, are not exact. For example, even though you may expect that the computer will evaluate the value of Cost as 3.00, the computer may actually stored it as 2.99999999. Therefore a boolean expression like Cost = 3.00, where Cost is a real, may never be true.

TEST YOURSELF

QUESTION: What is the value of the following boolean expressions?

a. 4 + 3 >= 7   **b.** 8 MOD 4 = 0

c. 6 <= 3 + 3   **d.** A = 3.00, where the value of A is

e. 3.0 > 2   previously printed as 3.00.

ANSWER: (a), (b), (c), and (e) are all true, whereas (d) may be false because of roundoff error.

USING THE IF STATEMENT

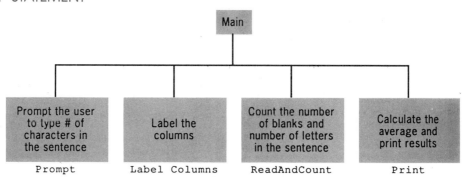

FIGURE 7.1a. The top-down diagram for a program that counts the number of words in a sentence.

In order to plan procedure ReadAndCount, we refine *Count the number of blanks . . .* to

```
BlankCount := 0;
FOR each character in the sentence DO
    IF character = Blank THEN
        BlankCount := BlankCount + 1
```

where BlankCount represents the number of blanks in the sentence.

In procedure PROMPT, shown in Figure 7.1b(I), the computer reads into the program the number of characters in the sentence, stores it in Length, and then passes its value to the main program. This value is passed, in turn, to ReadAndCount. The Pascal equivalent of the pseudocode for ReadAndCount is

```
BlankCount := 0;
FOR J := 1 TO Length DO
    BEGIN
        read(Character);
        IF Character = Blank THEN
            BlankCount := BlankCount + 1
    END (*FOR J*);
```

as shown in Figure 7.1b(II), where Blank is defined as a blank in the CONST definition. Using the constant identifier Blank makes the program easier to read than if IF Character = ' ' THEN is used.

The table for Figure 7.1b shows how the IF–THEN works for the first four characters of the sentence "How are you." When the contents of Character is not a blank

J	Character	Character = Blank	Next statement
1	H	False	Beginning of loop

the boolean expression Character = Blank is false and control is transferred to the beginning of the loop. Then the next character is read. On the other hand, when the contents of Character is a blank, BlankCount := BlankCount + 1 is executed next and then control is transferred to the beginning of the loop. After the last character is processed, since the number of words in the sentence is 1 plus the final value of BlankCount, we write WordCount := BlankCount + 1 and pass this value to the main program. Finally, procedure Print prints the results.

```
PROCEDURE Prompt(VAR Length:integer);
(* Types prompt messages *)
BEGIN
  writeln('Type # of columns in sentence');
  readln(Length);
  writeln('Type your sentence')
END (* prompt *);
```

FIGURE 7.1b(I). Reads the number of characters in a sentence.

```
CONST Blank = ' ';
PROCEDURE ReadAndCount(Var WordCount:integer; Length: integer);
(* Reads sentence & counts words *)
VAR Character: char;
    BlankCount, J: integer;
BEGIN
  BlankCount:= 0;
  FOR J:= 1 TO Length DO
    BEGIN
      read(Character);
      IF Character = Blank THEN
        BlankCount:= BlankCount + 1
    END (* FOR J *);
  WordCount:= BlankCount + 1
END(* ReadAndCount *);
```

FIGURE 7.1b(II). By adding 1 to the number of blanks counted in a sentence, we obtain the number of words. The CONST definition from the main program appears above the procedure.

J	Character	Character = Blank	Next statement
1	h	False	Beginning of loop
2	o	False	Beginning of loop
3	w	False	Beginning of loop
4	Blank	True	BlankCount:= BlankCount + 1

TABLE FOR FIGURE 7.1b. Shows how IF Character = Blank THEN BlankCount:= BlankCount + 1 works for the first four characters of the sentence "How are you?"

Procedure LabelColumns is shown in Figure 7.1*b*(III) and Print is shown in Figure 7.1*b*(IV). Since the user doesn't know how many characters there are in a sentence, we write the main program (Figure 7.1*c*) so that it asks the user to type the sentence twice

```
Prompt(Length);
LabelColumns(Length);
ReadAndCount( LetCount, WordCount, Length);
Prompt(Length);
ReadAndCount( LetCount, WordCount, Length);
Print( LetCount, WordCount)
```

the first time so that the user can determine how many columns the sentence occupies, and the second time so that the program can determine how many words there are in the sentence. Here's how it's done.

```
PROCEDURE LabelColumns(Length: integer);
(* Numbers the columns *)
VAR I, J:integer;
BEGIN
  (* Prints units digit *)
  FOR I:= 1 TO Length DO
    write(I MOD 10:1);
  writeln;
  FOR J:= 1 TO Length DO
    write('-');
  writeln
END; (* LabelColumns *)
```

FIGURE 7.1b(III). The procedure labels the columns.

```
PROCEDURE Print ( WordCount: integer);
(* Prints the results *)
BEGIN
  writeln('There are ', WordCount, ' words in the sentence.')
END(* Print *);
```

FIGURE 7.1b(IV). The procedure prints the results.

```
PROGRAM Word1(input, output);
(* Determines # of words in a line *)
(* Assume words are separated by one blank *)

CONST Blank = ' ';
VAR Length, WordCount: integer;

PROCEDURE Prompt(VAR Length:integer);                            {See page 231}
PROCEDURE LabelColumns(Length: integer);                        {On this page}
PROCEDURE ReadAndCount(VAR WordCount:integer; Length: integer);{See page 231}
PROCEDURE Print ( WordCount: integer);                          {On this page}

BEGIN (* MAIN *)
  (* Determines the number of characters in the sentence *)
  Prompt(Length);
  LabelColumns(Length);
  ReadAndCount( WordCount, Length);

  (* Determines average word length *)
  Prompt(Length);
  ReadAndCount( WordCount, Length);
  Print( WordCount)
END.
```

FIGURE 7.1c. The main program and the headings for the procedures used. If you run the program, you must also include the procedures themselves.

Procedure `Prompt` asks for the number of columns in the sentence:

```
Type # of columns in sentence
30
Type your sentence
123456789012345678901234567890
------------------------------
How are you
```

and `LabelColumns` labels the columns as shown in Figure 7.1*d*. Since you don't know this number, type a large number (here, 30). When the program activates `ReadAndCount`, since the Read will be executed 30 times, type the sentence and then blanks from the end of the sentence to column 30 (don't worry if you pass column 30.) Then hit the carriage return. When the program next asks for the column count, by seeing in which column the last character in the sentence was printed, you can type the correct number (here, 11) when you are again prompted.

```
Type # of columns in sentence
11
Type your sentence
How are you
There are 3 words in the sentence.
```

Then retype the sentence, and the computer prints the number of words in it. We realize that the method used to determine the number of characters in the sentence is awkward; however, it does the job until we learn how the computer can do it without our intervention.

```
Type # of columns in sentence
30
Type your sentence
1234567890 1234567890 1234567890
------------------------------
How are you
Type # of columns in sentence
11
Type your sentence
How are you
There are 3 words in the sentence.
```

FIGURE 7.1d.   Since you don't know how many characters are in the sentence, type a large number (here, 30). Since the read will be executed 30 times, type blanks from the sentence's end to column 30 and then hit the carriage return. When the program next asks for the column count, type the correct number.

Before going on to the next stage of the program, let's learn some more about the syntax of the IF statement.

7.3

THE IF–THEN–ELSE STATEMENT

Another form of the IF–THEN statement is IF–THEN–ELSE. Let's look at the following example, which adds a surcharge to the tax if the price of the item is greater than 10000.0:

```
IF Price > 10000.0 THEN
   Tax: = 0.08 * Price + Surcharge
ELSE
   Tax: = 0.08 * Price;
writeln('Tax = ', Tax)
```

If the boolean expression sandwiched between the IF and the THEN (here, Price > 10000.0) is true, then the statement immediately following the THEN is executed (here, Tax: = 0.08 * Price + Surcharge). On the other hand, if the boolean expression is false, the statement following the THEN is skipped and the statement following the ELSE is executed (here, Tax: = 0.08 * Price). In either case, at this point, the next statement executed is the one following the IF–THEN–ELSE statement (here, writeln('Tax = ', Tax)). Now let's return to our word processing program.

TEST YOURSELF

QUESTION: Write a procedure that determines the regional distribution of people living in a city (we discussed this in Chapter 2). There are 10 people in line. An example of data for the procedure is NNSEWESSNW, where N represents north, S represents south, and so on. The four counters are zeroed and then passed to the procedure, as shown in the heading:

```
PROCEDURE Calculate (Var NorthCount, SouthCount, EastCount,
WestCount:integer);
```

ANSWER:

```
PROCEDURE Calculate(VAR NorthCount, SouthCount, EastCount,
WestCount:integer);
VAR Region:char;
BEGIN
  writeln('Type the regions for 10 people standing in line');
  FOR J:= 1 TO 10 DO BEGIN
    read(Region);
    IF Region = 'N' THEN NorthCount:= NorthCount + 1;
    IF Region = 'S' THEN SouthCount:= SouthCount + 1;
    IF Region = 'E' THEN EastCount:= EastCount + 1;
    IF Region = 'W' THEN WestCount:= WestCount + 1
  END (* FOR *)
END (* Calculate *);
```

7.4

CALCULATING THE AVERAGE WORD LENGTH

Let's alter the program of Figure 7.1*b* so that

1. When the line is calibrated, a dash is printed in every 10th column. This makes it easier to determine which column a character is in.
2. The program calculates the average word length.

The top-down diagram is

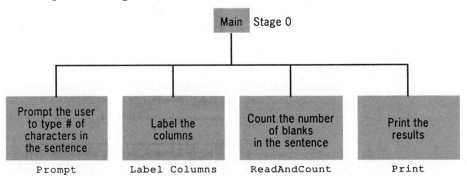

where procedure Prompt is the same as the one used in Figure 7.1*a*.
Now we translate *Label the columns* into

```
FOR I: = 1 TO Length DO
    IF I MOD 10 = 0 THEN
        write('-')
    ELSE
        write(I MOD 10:1);
    writeln;
```

as shown in Figure 7.2*a*(I). Since I MOD 10 = 0 is true for the values of I equal to 10, 20, 30, and so on, the program prints a dash in these columns; otherwise, it prints the appropriate digit. The reason a BEGIN and an END are not needed with this FOR–DO is that the latter applies to only one stateme:.t, the IF–THEN–ELSE.

As was done previously, 1 is added to the counter for the blanks, Blank–Count, every time a blank is encountered in order to determine the number of words. Otherwise, 1 is added to the letter counter, LetterCount, every time a letter (i.e., a nonblank character) is encountered. This is done in procedure ReadAndCount (Figure 7.2*a*[II]):

USING THE IF–THEN–ELSE STATEMENT

```
PROCEDURE LabelColumns(Length: integer);
(* Numbers the columns *)
VAR I, J:integer;
BEGIN
  (* Print units digit *)
  FOR I: = 1 TO Length DO
    IF I MOD 10 = 0 THEN
      write('-')
    ELSE
      write(I MOD 10:1);
  writeln;
  FOR J: = 1 TO Length DO
    write('-');
  writeln
END; (* LabelColumns *)
```

FIGURE 7.2a(I). This version of the procedure prints a dash every 10th column.

```
PROCEDURE ReadAndCount(VAR LetterCount, WordCount:integer; Length:
integer);
(* Reads sentence & counts letters and words *)
VAR Character: char;
  BlankCount, J: integer;
BEGIN
  BlankCount: = 0;
  LetterCount: = 0;
  FOR J: = 1 TO Length DO
    BEGIN
      read(Character);
      IF Character = Blank THEN
        BlankCount: = BlankCount + 1
      ELSE
        LetterCount: = LetterCount + 1
    END (* FOR J*);
  WordCount: = BlankCount + 1
END(* ReadAndCount *);
```

FIGURE 7.2a(II). We assume that if a character is not a blank, it is a letter. The number of blanks are counted in the THEN part of the IF.

```
IF Character = Blank THEN
    BlankCount := BlankCount + 1
ELSE
    LetterCount := LetterCount + 1
```

Thus it not only computes the numbers of words but also calculates the average word length. The former is done in `WordCount := BlankCount + 1`, and then this information is passed to the main program. Procedure `Print` (Figure 7.2*a*[III]) calculates the average word length:

```
Average := LetterCount / WordCount;
```

The main program and the headings for the procedures used are shown in Figure 7.2*b*. We assume that the sentence does not contain any nonletters such

```
PROCEDURE Print( LetterCount, WordCount: integer);
(* Calculates average and prints the results *)
VAR Average:real;
BEGIN
  writeln('There are ', WordCount, ' words in the sentence.');
  Average:= LetterCount / WordCount;
  writeln('Total # of nonblanks: ', LetterCount:2);
  Writeln('The average word length is: ', Average:5:1)
END(* Print *);
```

FIGURE 7.2a(III).   Calculates the average and prints the results.

```
PROGRAM Word2(input, output);
(* Determines # of words in a line *)
(* Assumes words are separated by one blank *)
(* Calculates average word length *)

CONST Blank = ' ';
VAR Length, LetterCount, WordCount: integer;

PROCEDURE Prompt(VAR Length:integer);                {See page 231}
PROCEDURE LabelColumns(Length: integer);             {See page 239}
PROCEDURE ReadAndCount(VAR LetterCount, WordCount:integer;
                       Length: integer);             {See page 239}
PROCEDURE Print( LetterCount, WordCount: integer);  {On this page}

BEGIN (* MAIN *)
  (* Determines the number of characters in the sentence *)
  Prompt(Length);
  LabelColumns(Length);
  ReadAndCount( LetCount, WordCount, Length);
  writeln;

  (* Determines average word length *)
  Prompt(Length);
  ReadAndCount( LetCount, WordCount, Length);
  Print( LetCount, WordCount)
END.
```

FIGURE 7.2b.   The main program and the headings for the procedures used. If you run the program you must also include the procedures themselves.

as commas and a period; otherwise, the value of LetterCount would be too large. The running of the program is shown in Figure 7.2c. In the third stage of our word processing program, we'll see how to eliminate nonletters from the value of LetterCount. But first, we must learn some more Pascal syntax.

```
Type # of columns in sentence
40
type your sentence
123456789-123456789-123456789-123456789-
------------------------------------------
My country tis of thee
Type # of columns in sentence
22
Type your sentence
My country tis of thee
There are 5 words in the sentence.
Total # of nonblanks: 18
The average word length is: 3.6
```

FIGURE 7.2c.   Running the program of Figure 7.2b. Both the number of words and the total number of nonblanks are printed so that one can check whether the average is correct. Punctuation marks are not included in the sentence, since they would increase the letter counter.

7.5

THE BOOLEAN OPERATORS: AND, OR, AND NOT

The AND

The boolean operators AND, OR, and NOT simplify the writing of complex IF–THEN–ELSE statements. The program of Figure 7.3*a* shows how the AND works in

```
IF (K >= 2) AND (K <= 4) THEN
    writeln( 'K= ', K:1)
```

The AND is sandwiched between two boolean expressions, forming a compound boolean expression, here (K >= 2) AND (K <= 4). The AND operator has a higher priority than the comparison operators, so you must parenthesize both K >= 2 and K <= 4. If you don't, and write K >= 2 AND K <= 4 THEN instead, the computer will try to evaluate 2 AND K. Since neither 2 nor K is a boolean expression, a syntax error will occur.

The rules that the compiler uses to evaluate such compound boolean expressions are summarized in the table for Figure 7.3*a*. This type of table is called a *truth table*, because it determines whether or not an expression like A AND B is true. Read it as you would a multiplication table. For instance, to determine the value of TRUE AND FALSE, look at the intersection of the row (horizontal line) marked TRUE and the column (vertical line) marked FALSE, and you will see the entry FALSE. Applying this to our program we see that:

1. Both of the boolean expressions must be true in order for the compound expression to be true. In

   ```
   IF (K >= 2) AND (K <= 4) THEN
   ```

   both K >= 2 and K <= 4 must be true in order for (K >= 2) AND (K <= 4) to be true. Since for the values of K equaling 2, 3, and 4 both K >= 2 and K <= 4 are true, these values are printed in writeln('K= ', K:1), as we see in Figure 7.3*b*.

2. If either of the boolean expressions is false, the entire expression is false and nothing is printed. Since for the value of K equal to 1 the expression K >= 2 is false, even though K <= 4 is true, the entire compound boolean expression is false. Thus nothing is printed for this value of K.

3. If both boolean expressions are false, the entire expression is false and nothing is printed.

USING THE AND OPERATOR

```
PROGRAM IntroAnd(output);
(* Shows how to use AND *)
VAR K: integer;
BEGIN
  For K:= 1 TO 5 DO
    IF (K >= 2) AND (K <= 4) THEN
      writeln( 'K= ', K:1)
END.
```

FIGURE 7.3a.   Both boolean expressions must be true in order for the entire expression to be true.

	FALSE	TRUE
FALSE	FALSE	FALSE
TRUE	FALSE	TRUE

TABLE FOR FIGURE 7.3a.   Shows the value of A AND B for values of A and B. Read this table like a multiplication table. Thus FALSE AND TRUE is false.

```
K= 2
K= 3
K= 4
```

FIGURE 7.3b.   Running the program of Figure 7.3a.

The OR

Next, let's discuss the boolean operator OR. The program of Figure 7.4*a* shows how it works by generating the truth table for the OR. It does this by evaluating the nested loop:

```
FOR Horizontal:= False TO True DO BEGIN
   write(Horizontal:9, '|');
   FOR Vertical:= False TO True DO
     write( Horizontal OR Vertical:10);
   writeln
END (*FOR Horizontal*)
```

The results are shown in Figure 7.4*b*. The table shows that

1.   If either of the boolean expressions is true, the compound expression is true.
2.   If both boolean expressions are true, the entire expression is true.
3.   If both boolean expressions are false, the entire expression is false.

To summarize: In an expression using an AND, both parts of the expression must be true for the entire expression to be true. In one using an OR, either part must be true for the entire expression to be true.

USING THE OR OPERATOR

```
PROGRAM Table(output);
(* Produces a boolean truth table *)
CONST Blank= ' ';
VAR Horizontal, Vertical:Boolean;
BEGIN
  writeln(Blank:10, 'FALSE':10, 'TRUE':10);
  writeln(Blank:10, '-------------------');
  FOR Horizontal:= False TO True DO BEGIN
    write(Horizontal:9, '|');
    FOR Vertical:= False TO True DO
      write( Horizontal OR Vertical:10);
    writeln
  END (* FOR Horizontal *)
END.
```

FIGURE 7.4a. Either of the boolean expressions (here, just boolean identifiers) must be true in order for the entire expression to be true.

```
                    FALSE          TRUE
         ----------------------------------
FALSE |             FALSE          TRUE
 TRUE |             TRUE           TRUE
```

FIGURE 7.4b. Running the program of Figure 7.4a. TRUE OR FALSE is true.

The NOT

The program of Figure 7.5*a* is the same as the one in Figure 7.3*a*, except that now a NOT precedes the boolean expression:

$$\text{IF NOT } (K >= 2) \text{ AND } (K <= 4) \text{ THEN}$$

The effect of the NOT is to reverse the boolean value of the boolean expression that appears immediately to its right. The NOT is executed before the AND and the AND before the OR. Thus here the NOT operates only on $(K >= 2)$ and not on $(K >= 2)$ AND $(K <= 4)$. Thus the equivalent boolean expression is

$$(K < 2) \text{ AND } (K <= 4)$$

But this is equivalent to $K < 2$, so only the value of K equal to 1 is printed, as shown in Figure 7.5*b* and the table for Figure 7.5*a*. We have just seen an example where, with a little forethought, we could have greatly simplified the program; we should have written

$$\text{IF } K < 2 \text{ THEN}$$

in the original program.

Although Figure 7.5*a* had boolean expressions containing the comparison operators ($<$, $>$, $=$, etc.) and mathematical expressions, the NOT can be used with boolean identifiers as well. Thus if Valid, Found, and Flag are boolean identifiers, then the following are all boolean expressions:

1. NOT Valid AND Found,
2. NOT (Valid AND Found),
3. Flag or (NOT Valid AND Found),

where the parenthesized parts of the expressions are evaluated first.

USING THE NOT OPERATOR

```
PROGRAM IntroNot(output);
(* Shows how to use NOT *)
VAR K: integer;
BEGIN
   FOR K:= 1 TO 5 DO
      IF NOT (K >= 2) AND (K <= 4) THEN
         writeln( 'K= ', K:1)
END.
```

FIGURE 7.5a.   The NOT operates only on the boolean expression that immediately follows it (here (K >= 2).

$$K= 1$$

FIGURE 7.5b.   Running the program of Figure 7.5a.

K	(K >= 2)	NOT (K >= 2)	NOT (K >= 2) AND (K <= 4)
1	False	True	True
2	True	False	False
3	True	False	False
4	True	False	False
5	True	False	False

TABLE FOR FIGURE 7.5a.   Shows how the NOT works. In order to have NOT operate on the entire expression, you must parenthesize it: NOT ((K >= 2) AND (K <= 4)).

TEST YOURSELF

QUESTION: What is the value of the following boolean expressions?

a. $(4 + 3 >= 7)$ AND $(8 \text{ MOD } 3 = 0)$
b. $(6 <= 3 + 3)$ OR NOT $(7 > 2)$
c. $(3.0 > 2)$ AND $(4 \text{ MOD } 2 = 0)$ or $('3' = '3')$

ANSWER:

a. Since $(8 \text{ MOD } 3 = 0)$ is false, the entire expression is false.
b. Since $(6 <= 3 + 3)$ is true, the entire expression is true.
c. Since $(3.0 > 2)$ AND $(4 \text{ MOD } 2 = 0)$ is evaluated first and is true, and the rest of the expression involves an OR, the entire expression is true.

Figure 7.5c sums the even numbers from 0 to 10. To do this, we use the NOT to reverse the value of the odd function. Thus NOT odd(Number) is true when the value of Number is an even number:

```
FOR Number : = 0 TO Limit DO
    IF NOT odd(Number) THEN
        SumEven: = SumEven + Number;
```

The results are shown in Figure 7.5d.

CREATING AN EVEN FUNCTION

```
PROGRAM OddEven(output);
(* Sums the even numbers *)
CONST Limit = 10;
VAR Number, SumEven: integer;
BEGIN
   SumEven:= 0;
   FOR Number := 0 TO Limit DO
     IF NOT odd(Number) THEN
        SumEven:= SumEven + Number;
   writeln(' The sum of the even #s from 0 to ', Limit:2, ' is ', SumEven:2)
END.
```

FIGURE 7.5c. `NOT odd(Number)` is the equivalent of a function that determines whether a number is even. Remember that `odd(Number)` is true if the value of `Number` is odd and false if it's even.

```
The sum of the even #s from 0 to 10 is 30
```

FIGURE 7.5.d. Running the program of Figure 7.5c.

7.6

INTRODUCTION TO SOME SET OPERATIONS

In Pascal the programmer has the ability to refer to collections of items of any ordinal type. Such a collection is called a *set*, and the items in the set are called the *elements of the set*. The elements are enclosed in brackets and separated by commas; for instance, the set of integers from 1 to 5 can be written as [1, 2, 3, 4, 5]. However, if the elements can be arranged such that one is the successor of the next, as is the case of integers or consecutive characters in a range of characters in the ASCII table or collating sequence, then the set can be written as follows: First, type the element having the lowest ordinal value in the set, then two periods, and then the element having the highest ordinal value. Thus the set of numbers from 1 to 5 can be written as [1..5], the set of characters from 'A' to 'L' can be written as ['A'..'L']. and True and False can be written as [False..True].

At this point, we'll use sets in boolean expressions only to test whether an item is in the set; we use the operator IN for this test. For instance, the program of Figure 7.6a prints the digits in the set [5..8]. In the following loop, the boolean expression Digit IN [5..8] tests whether the integer Digit is in the set:

```
FOR Digit:= 0 TO 9 DO
   IF Digit IN [5..8] THEN
      write(Digit:2);
```

Similarly, the following loop prints the consonants in the alphabet:

```
FOR Letter:= 'A' TO 'Z' DO
   IF NOT (Letter IN ['A', 'E', 'I', 'O', 'U']) THEN
      write(Letter);
```

The results of the program are shown in Figure 7.6b.

In order to understand the last IF, let's compare the IN and NOT operators. The IN is a binary operator, that is, it is sandwiched between two operands, as in Digit IN [5..8]. The NOT, on the other hand, is a unary operator; it operates on only one operand. The NOT has the highest priority, as we see in Table 7.2. The IN, on the other hand, has the lowest priority; it has the same priority as the relational operators. Why did we parenthesize Letter IN ['A', 'E', 'I', 'O', 'U']? Because we wanted the IN to operate before the NOT did. Bearing all this in mind, let's answer the following question.

USING SETS IN A BOOLEAN EXPRESSION

```
PROGRAM IntroSet(input, output);
(* Introduction to sets *)
VAR Digit:integer;
  Letter: char;
BEGIN
  FOR Digit:= 0 TO 9 DO
    IF Digit IN [5..8] THEN
      write(Digit:2);
  writeln;

  (* print vowels *)
  FOR Letter:= 'A' TO 'Z' DO
    IF NOT (Letter IN ['A', 'E', 'I', 'O', 'U']) THEN
      write(Letter:2);
  writeln
END.
```

FIGURE 7.6a.   [5..8] is the equivalent of [5, 6, 7, 8]. The IN tests membership in a set.

```
5 6 7 8
B C D F G H J K L M N P Q R S T V W X Y Z
```

FIGURE 7.6b.   Running the program of Figure 7.6a.

Priority	Operator
1st	NOT
2nd	AND, *, /, MOD, DIV
3rd	OR, +, −
4th	=, <>, >, <, >=, <=, IN

TABLE 7.2.   Shows the priority of the nonarithmetic operators. Since NOT precedes AND and OR, if you want to change the value of a boolean expression containing an AND or an OR, for example, $(x > 3)$ OR $(y < 2)$, you must parenthesize the compound expression; thus NOT ($(x > 3)$ OR $(y < 2)$). The arithmetic operators (*, /, etc.) have higher priorities than the relational operators (=, >, etc.) do.

7.7

OUR WORD PROCESSOR REVISITED

Now that we've learned more about the capabilities of Pascal, let's write the third version of our word processing program. This time we calculate the average word length for sentences that may contain any type of punctuation, may start with one or more blanks, and may have more than one blank separating the words. However, there may be no blanks at the end of a sentence. Since the number of blanks in the sentence can no longer be correlated with the number of words, the approach is different from the one used in the programs of Figures 7.2 and 7.3. How do we now count the number of words in a sentence? Let's look at the sample sentence "How are   you?"

A word is terminated when the current character is a blank and the previous character is not. The first version of the pseudocode for counting the words is therefore

```
IF current character is a blank and the previous one is not THEN
    WordCount: = WordCount + 1
```

Since the current character will be called the *previous character* in the next execution of the loop, expand the pseudocode to

```
FOR J: = 1 TO Length DO BEGIN
    read(Current);
    IF (Current = Blank) AND (Previous <> Blank) THEN
        WordCount: = WordCount + 1
    save Current in Previous
END (* FOR *)
```

For J equal to 1, however, the value of Previous is undefined. You must therefore precede the loop with an assignment to Previous. The only choice that works for all cases is assigning it a blank. The Pascal code thus far becomes

```
Previous: = Blank;
FOR J: = 1 TO Length DO BEGIN
    read(Current);
    IF (Current = Blank) AND (Previous <> Blank) THEN
        WordCount: = WordCount + 1;
    Previous: = Current
END (* FOR *)
```

TEST YOURSELF

QUESTION: Why are the following wrong?

   a.   IF NOT Letter IN ['A', 'E', 'I', 'O', 'U'] THEN
   b.   IF Letter NOT IN ['A', 'E', 'I', 'O', 'U'] THEN

ANSWER:

   a.   Because there are no parentheses, the NOT operates on Letter, which is a character, not a boolean variable.
   b.   The NOT operates on IN ['A', 'E', 'I', 'O', 'U'], which has no type.

as shown in the program of Figure 7.7*a*. This loop is not complete, since we must include another IF to count only the letters in the sentence:

```
IF (Current In ['a'..'z']) OR (Current IN ['A'..'Z']) THEN
    LetterCount: = LetterCount + 1; (*count letters*)
```

As in the previous programs, all this is placed in ReadAndCount. Note that IF (Current IN ['a'..'z']) OR (Current IN ['A'..'Z']) THEN can be written more simply as

```
IF Current IN ['a'..'z', 'A'..'Z'] THEN
```

Since procedures Prompt, LabelColumns, and Print are the same as they were in Figure 7.2*a*, we omit them here.

OUR WORD PROCESSOR REVISITED

```
PROGRAM Word3(input, output);
(* Determines number of words in a line *)
(* Words are separated by one or more blanks *)
(* Calculates average word length *)
CONST Blank = ' ';
VAR Length, LetterCount, WordCount: integer;

PROCEDURE Prompt(VAR Length:integer);                    {See page 231}
PROCEDURE LabelColumns(Length: integer);                 {See page 239}
PROCEDURE Print ( LetterCount, WordCount: integer);      {See page 241}

PROCEDURE ReadAndCount(VAR LetterCount, WordCount:integer; Length:
integer);
(* Reads sentence & counts letters and words *)
VAR Previous, Current: char;
  J: integer;
BEGIN
  WordCount: = 0;
  LetterCount: = 0;
  Previous: = Blank;
  FOR J: = 1 TO Length DO
    BEGIN
      read(Current);
      IF (Current IN ['a'..'z']) OR (Current IN ['A'..'Z']) THEN
        LetterCount: = LetterCount + 1; (* count letters *)
      IF (Current = Blank) AND (Previous <> Blank) THEN
        WordCount: = WordCount + 1; (* count words *)
      Previous: = Current
    END (* FOR J*);
  WordCount: = WordCount + 1
END(* ReadAndCount *);
BEGIN (* MAIN *)
  (* Determines the number of characters in the sentence *)
  Prompt(Length);
  LabelColumns(Length);
  ReadAndCount( LetCount, Words, Length);
  writeln;

  (* Determines average word length *)
  Prompt(Length);
  ReadAndCount( LetCount, Words, Length);
  Print( LetCount, Words)
END.
```

FIGURE 7.7a. By using (Current = Blank) AND (Previous <> Blank) in ReadAndCount, you are able to test for the end of a word even if more than one blank separates two words. The headings for the other procedures are also included. If you run the program, you must also include the other procedures.

The input for the program and the results are shown in Figure 7.7*b*. The first character read is a blank. Since we assigned a blank to `Previous` before the loop, the compound expression `(Current = Blank) AND (Previous <> Blank)` is false, and therefore the word counter is not incremented (see the table for Figure 7.7*a*). Had we assigned any other character to `Previous` before the loop, the compound expression would be true for the first character read (a blank), and we would have counted a word where there is none!

PROGRAMMING HINTS

If you are faced with writing a difficult program, such as the present one, write a simplified version first; we started with the program of Figure 7.1*a*. Gradually alter this version until you finally have the desired program. The preliminary versions may indicate heretofore unseen difficulties involved in writing the final program. It is not uncommon for a programmer to find it impossible to write the final version of the program without first writing the preliminary one.

7.8
ADDING TWO NUMBERS CONTAINING A $ AND A COMMA: TOP-DOWN TESTING

BEFORE YOU BEGIN

From previous chapters, we know that all data—numerical as well as character—are read into the program as characters. If the variable in the `read` or `readln` [e.g., `Number` in `read(Number)`] is declared as a real or integer, Pascal converts the characters into numerical values. In order to have a nonsuperficial understanding of Pascal, it is helpful to understand how this is done. The following program shows the method used.

The next program adds two numbers. We'll restrict ourselves to four-digit numbers that contain a "$" and a comma. The program first strips the $ and the comma from the numbers and then adds the numbers. For instance, it adds $1,234 and $4,321 and obtains 5555. If $1,234 and $4,321 were read as integers or reals, a run-time error would result, since they contain the nonnumeric characters "$" and ",". The input must therefore be read as characters and converted, digit by digit, into integers. The pseudocode for the main program is

Read and convert first line of characters to the integer, Number1;

Read and convert second line of characters to the integer, Number2;

Set the sum of Number1 plus Number2 to Sum;

Print Sum.

where *Read and convert* is translated into procedure `Convert`.

J	Current	Previous	(Current = Blank) AND (Previous <> Blank)	Next statement
1	Blank	Blank	False	Previous: = Current
2	M	Blank	False	Previous: = Current
3	y	M	False	Previous: = Current
4	Blank	y	True	WordCount: = WordCount + 1
5	Blank	Blank	False	Previous: = Current

TABLE FOR FIGURE 7.7a. How IF (Current = Blank) AND (Previous <> Blank) THEN works for the first five characters of Figure 7.7b. When the computer encounters the blank after the *y* in *My*, it adds 1 to the word counter.

```
Type # of columns in sentence
50
Type your sentence
123456789-123456789-123456789-123456789-123456789-
--------------------------------------------------
 My   country tis of thee, Sweet land of liberty.
Type # of columns in sentence
48
Type your sentence
 My   country tis of thee, Sweet land of liberty.
There are 9 words in the sentence.
Total # of letters: 36
The average word length is: 4.0
```

FIGURE 7.7b. Running the program of Figure 7.7a.

The top-down diagram is

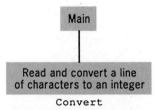

Convert

This program will be written using top-down testing. In this approach, dummy procedures called *stubs* are substituted for the eventual actual procedures, and the entire program is tested as shown in Figure 7.8*a*. The main program is

```
Convert (Number1);
Convert(Number2);
Sum:= Number1 + Number2;
writeln('Sum=', Sum)
```

The values of Number1 and Number2 are calculated in Convert and passed to the main program. In order to test the main program and whether the correct values of Number1 and Number2 are being passed to it, write procedure Convert as a stub; that is, just read an integer and pass its value to the main program:

```
PROCEDURE Convert (VAR Number: integer);
(* Stub for testing passing of parameter*)
BEGIN
  writeln('Type a 4–digit.');
  readln(Number);
  writeln('Converted number=', Number);
END (* Convert *);
```

The running of the program is shown in Figure 7.8*b*. If there were more procedures, they would all be written as stubs. Each time an actual procedure is substituted for one of the stubs, the whole program is tested. Thus we would program a little and test a little.

SUMMING TWO NUMBERS THAT CONTAIN A $ AND A COMMA
STEP I

```
Program Addition;
(* Adds two numbers that contain nonnumeric characters *)
VAR Number1, Number2, Sum: integer;
PROCEDURE Convert (VAR Number: integer);
(* Stub for testing passing of parameter *)
BEGIN
  writeln('Type a 4-digit.');
  readln(Number);
  writeln('Converted number=', Number)
END (* Convert *);
BEGIN (* main *)
  Convert (Number1);
  Convert(Number2);
  Sum: = Number1 + Number2;
  writeln('Sum=', Sum)
END.
```

FIGURE 7.8a.   In the first step in summing two numbers, write a dummy procedure that just tests that values are correctly passed to the main program from the procedure. This procedure is called a *stub*.

```
Type a 4-digit.
1234
Converted number=1234
Type a 4-digit.
4321
Converted number=4321
Sum=5555
```

FIGURE 7.8b.   Running the program of Figure 7.8a.

The next step in the present program is to substitute the actual procedure for the stub. The pseudocode for the procedure is

```
FOR J := 1 TO 6 DO BEGIN
    read(character);
    IF character equals a digit THEN
        Form number from character
    ELSE
        Print the character
END (* FOR *)
```

Let's refine *Form number from character* so that it will produce a four-digit number that will be stored in the variable Number. To do this, write

$$Number := Number * 10 + digit$$

where *Number* is set to zero before the loop. Since *digit* is obtained from ord(Ch) − ord('0'), where Ch corresponds to *character*, the Pascal code is written as

```
Number := Number * 10 + ord(Ch) − ord('0')
```

as shown in Figure 7.8c. This statement is an example of programming "lore." You are not expected to devise this solution on your own, but once you've seen it, you'll probably be able to apply it to other situations.

The table for Figure 7.8c shows how this statement works. Note that in the table, "Number before" is the value of Number before the statement is executed and "Number after" is its value afterward. The first two lines of the table show that the first time the loop is executed

Ch	Number before	Number * 10 before	Number after
'8'	0	0	8
'7'	8	80	87

the first value of Number after the statement is executed is 8. The second time the loop is executed, the value of Number is multiplied by 10, giving 80. Then the second digit read, '7', is added to this, giving 87. This process continues until all the digits are read. Thus it doesn't depend on how many digits are read, and it can be used if you wish to generalize this technique to any number of digits.

SUMMING TWO NUMBERS THAT CONTAIN A $ AND A COMMA
STEP II

```
PROCEDURE Convert (VAR Number: integer);
(* Stores the digits in "Number" *)
CONST Quote = '"';
VAR Ch: char;
   J: integer;
BEGIN
  Number:= 0;
  writeln('Type a 4-digit number with $ and , ');
  FOR J:= 1 TO 6 DO BEGIN
    read(Ch);
    IF Ch IN ['0'..'9'] THEN
      Number:= Number * 10 + ord(Ch) - ord('0')
    ELSE
      write(Quote, Ch, Quote, ' encountered. ');
  END (* FOR-J *);
  writeln;
  writeln('Converted number=', Number);
  readln
END (* convert *);
```

FIGURE 7.8c.   This is the actual procedure that converts a string of digits read as characters into an integer.

Ch	Number before	Number * 10 before	Number after
'8'	0	0	8
'7'	8	80	87
'6'	87	870	876
'5'	876	8760	8765

TABLE FOR FIGURE 7.8c.   Shows how Number:= Number * 10 + ord(Ch) − ord('0') works for an input of $8,765. "Number before" is the value of Number before the statement is executed and "Number after" is its value afterward.

Since Ch is a character, test whether it is a digit by writing

```
IF Ch in ['0'..'9'] THEN
   Number:= Number * 10 + ord(Ch) − ord('0')
ELSE
   write(Quote, Ch, Quote, ' encountered. ')
```

Using [0..9] here instead would produce a compilation error, since Ch is a character.

Note that if the program encounters any character that is not a digit, that character is not converted to an integer but is printed in the encountered message. We'll presently see (in the next "Programming Hints") why it is important to do this. The results of running the program are shown in Figure 7.8d.

PROGRAMMING HINTS

In the question on the opposite page, if we had printed those characters that aren't digits, we would have had some indication of why the addition was done incorrectly. It would have been better yet had we printed the ordinal value of the nondigit characters, that is, had written the IF as

```
IF Ch IN ['0'..'9'] THEN
   Number:= Number * 10 + ord(Ch) − ord('0')
ELSE
   write(ord(Ch), ' encountered. ');
```

The reason is that the carriage return is printed as a blank, so we can't see what has been printed; but ord of a carriage return is a digit—on an ASCII system, it's 10.

PROGRAMMING INSIGHTS

How would you write a program that simulates the process that Pascal uses to convert six contiguous characters read as an integer into a six-digit number? To solve this problem, don't try to reinvent the wheel. We have already solved it in Figure 7.8c. If the program reads only digits, it uses all six of them to contribute to the sum stored in Number. The only difficulty that may arise may occur if the six-digit number is greater than the value of maxint.

In the exercise, you are asked to write a program that converts a binary number (e.g., 10011) into its decimal equivalent. The solution is surprisingly simple if you realize that, for instance, a decimal number is the sum of each of its digits multiplied by the appropriate power of 10. For example 435 is the sum of $4 \times 100 + 3 \times 10 + 5 \times 1$. We used this fact when we wrote Number:= Number * 10 + digit. By analogy, the binary conversion problem can be solved in a similar manner.

```
Type a 4-digit number with $ and ,
$8,765
"$" encountered. "," encountered.
Converted number=8765
Type a 4-digit number with $ and ,
$5,678
"$" encountered. "," encountered.
Converted number=5678
Sum=14443
```

FIGURE 7.8d.   Running the program of Figure 7.8a, with the procedure in Figure 7.8c taking the place of stub shown in Figure 7.8a.

TEST YOURSELF

QUESTION: Why does the following version of procedure `Convert` contribute to the wrong result for the sum of the two numbers read?

```
PROCEDURE Convert (VAR Number: integer);
VAR Ch: char;
    J: integer;
BEGIN
  Number:= 0;
  writeln('Type a 4-digit number with $ and ,');
  FOR J:= 1 TO 6 DO BEGIN
    read(Ch);
    IF Ch in ['0'..'9'] THEN
    Number:= Number * 10 + ord(Ch) - ord('0')
  END (* FOR-J *);
END (* Convert *);
```

The result obtained is

```
Type a 4-digit number with $ and ,
$1,234
Type a 4-digit number with $ and ,
$4,321
Sum=1666
```

The sum should be 5555.

ANSWER: Because we have omitted the `readln`, the computer reads the carriage return following $1234 as the first character of the second number. It then reads the first four characters of $4321, namely, $432 and converts them to 432. Finally, it adds 432 to 1234, obtaining 1666.

7.9

NESTING IF STATEMENTS

In the following IF–THEN–ELSE statement (shown in Figure 7.9*a*), is writeln('second') executed if A > B is false or if C > D is false? In other words, is the ELSE matched with the first IF or the second IF?

```
IF A > B THEN
  IF C > D THEN
    writeln('first')
  ELSE
    writeln('second');
writeln('third')
```

First, note that IF C > D THEN can be executed only if A > B is true. The ELSE is matched with the IF to which it is closest, namely, IF C > D THEN. Thus if C > D is false, writeln('second') is executed; then writeln('third') is executed, as shown in Figure 7.9*b*. If C > D is true, first writeln('first') is executed and then writeln('third') is executed, as shown in Figure 7.9*c*. If A > B is false, writeln('third') is executed next, as shown in Figure 7.9*d*.

NESTING IF STATEMENTS

```
PROGRAM Nested(input, output);
(* Shows that ELSE is matched with nearest preceding IF *)
VAR A, B, C, D: integer;
BEGIN
  writeln('Type in four integer values');
  readln(A, B, C, D);
  writeln('A= ', A:1, ' B= ', B:1, ' C= ', C:1, ' D= ', D:1);
  IF A > B THEN
    IF C > D THEN
      writeln('first')
    ELSE
      writeln('second');
  writeln('third')
END.
```

FIGURE 7.9a. The ELSE is matched with the IF that immediately precedes it (here, IF C > D THEN).

```
Type in four integer values
2 1 3 4
A= 2 B= 1 C= 3 D= 4
second
third
```

FIGURE 7.9b. Running the program of Figure 7.9a for A > B true and C > D false.

```
Type in four integer values
2 1 4 3
A= 2 B= 1 C= 4 D= 3
first
third
```

FIGURE 7.9c. Running the program of Figure 7.9a for A > B true and C > D true.

```
Type in four integer values
1 2 3 4
A= 1 D= 2 C- 3 D= 4
third
```

FIGURE 7.9d. Running the program of Figure 7.9a for A > B false. Since the IF–THEN–ELSE is not executed, the only statement that is executed is the last one.

7.10

THE MULTIPLE ALTERNATIVE IF—THEN—ELSE

ANALOGY

> The multiple IF—THEN—ELSE is a multiway switch that allows you to choose only one of many options. An example follows.

The tax rate schedule for Schedule X from IRS Form 1040 is given for taxable incomes below $10,800:

Over	But not Over	Tax		of the amount over
$0	$2,300	-0-		
2,300	3,400	......	14%	$2,300
3,400	4,400	$154 +	16%	3,400
4,400	6,500	314 +	18%	4,400
6,500	8,500	692 +	19%	6,500
8,500	10,800	1,072 +	21%	8,500

Thus the tax for a taxable income of $8700 is 1,072 + 0.21(8700 − 8500), or $1114. This represents 12.8% of the taxable income. Using this table, let's write a program that calculates the tax and the percentage the tax represents of the taxable income. The percentage is 100 times the ratio of tax to income. The pseudocode is

read income;
IF income <= 2300 THEN
    Tax is 0 ; ratio is 0
ELSE IF income <= 3400 THEN
    Tax is 0.14 * income; ratio is .14
ELSE IF income <= 4400 THEN
    Tax is 0.16 * difference + 154; ratio is Tax / income
ELSE IF income <= 6500 THEN
    Tax is 0.18 * difference + 314; ratio is Tax / income
ELSE IF income <= 8500 THEN
    Tax is 0.19 * difference + 692; ratio is Tax / income
ELSE IF income <= 10800 THEN
    Tax is 0.21 * difference + 1072; ratio is Tax / income
ELSE
    writeln('Sorry your income is too large for present program')

TEST YOURSELF

QUESTION: Write the previous IF–THEN–ELSE so that the ELSE is matched with IF A > B THEN.

ANSWER: As it is written now, the ELSE is matched with IF C > D THEN. To achieve the desired result, make IF C > D THEN writeln('first') a complete statement by sandwiching it between a BEGIN and an END:

```
IF A > B THEN
   BEGIN
      IF C > D THEN
         writeln('first')
   END
   ELSE
      writeln('second');
```

QUESTION: Which IF is the second ELSE matched within the following?

```
IF A > B THEN
   IF C > D THEN
      writeln('first')
   ELSE
      writeln('second');
ELSE
   writeln('third')
```

ANSWER: It is matched with the closest IF that hasn't been matched with another ELSE. Thus it is matched with IF A > B THEN.

where the tax table dictates that the value of *difference* is the amount following the "<=" in the previous *if* subtracted from *income*. Thus the value of the first *difference* is *income* − *3400*, the second is *income* − *4400*, the third is *income* − *6500*, and so on. We translate this into the program of Figure 7.10*a*. Since this type of IF–THEN–ELSE contains many decisions, it is called the *multiple alternative* IF–THEN–ELSE.

Since each ELSE is matched with the preceding IF, if any of the boolean expressions is true, the computer executes the next statement or compound statement and then quits the multiple alternative IF–THEN–ELSE. Thus here it would next execute the Percent: = Ratio * 100. As an example, if the value of income is 8500, the program executes

```
ELSE IF Income <= 8500 THEN BEGIN
    Tax := 0.19 * (Income − 6500) + 692;
    Ratio := Tax / Income
END
```

because the boolean expressions in all the preceding IFs were false. It thus executes Tax : = 0.19 * (Income − 6500) + 692, calculates the ratio, and then executes the Percent: = Ratio * 100.

If all the compound statements in the IF THEN ELSE contain the same statement, you can remove that statement and place it at the end of the multiple alternative IF–THEN–ELSE. For instance, if the statement were

```
IF Income <= 4400 THEN BEGIN
    Tax := 0.16 * (Income − 3400) + 154;
    Ratio := Tax / Income
END
ELSE IF Income <= 6500 THEN BEGIN
    Tax := 0.18 * (Income − 4400) + 314;
    Ratio := Tax / Income
END
```

and thus each compound statement contained Ratio : = Tax / Income, you could rewrite the multiple alternative statement as

```
IF Income <= 4400 THEN
    Tax := 0.16 * (Income − 3400) + 154;
ELSE IF Income <= 6500 THEN
    Tax := 0.18 * (Income − 4400) + 314;
    Ratio := Tax / Income
```

The results of running the program are shown in Figure 7.10*b*. Note that in this program if all the boolean statements are false, the computer executes the compound statement following the last ELSE:

```
Tax:=−1;
Ratio:=−1;
writeln('Sorry your income is too large for present program')
```

THE MULTIPLE IF—THEN—ELSE

```
PROGRAM IncomeTax(input, output);
VAR Tax, Ratio, percent: real;
  Income: integer;
BEGIN
  writeln('Type your taxable income');
  readln(Income);
  IF Income <= 2300 THEN BEGIN
      Tax := 0 ;
      Ratio := 0
    END
  ELSE IF Income <= 3400 THEN BEGIN
      Tax := 0.14 * Income;
      Ratio := 0.14
    END
  ELSE IF Income <= 4400 THEN BEGIN
      Tax := 0.16 * (Income - 3400) + 154;
      Ratio:= Tax / Income
    END
  ELSE IF Income <= 6500 THEN BEGIN
      Tax := 0.18 * (Income - 4400) + 314;
      Ratio := Tax / Income
    END
  ELSE IF Income <= 8500 THEN BEGIN
      Tax := 0.19 * (Income - 6500) + 692;
      Ratio := Tax / Income
    END
  ELSE IF Income <= 10800 THEN BEGIN
      Tax := 0.21 * (Income - 8500) + 1072;
      Ratio := Tax / Income
    END
  ELSE BEGIN
      Tax:=-1;
      Ratio:=-1;
      writeln('Sorry your income is too large for present program')
    END;
    percent:= Ratio * 100;
  writeln('Income= ', Income: 5, ' Tax= ', Tax:6:2, ' percent= ',
          percent:4:1)
END.
```

FIGURE 7.10a.   If one of the IFs is executed, the boolean expressions in all of the preceding IFs are false. The computer then leaves the multiple IF—THEN—ELSE.

```
Type your taxable income
8700
Income= 8700 Tax= 1114.00 percent= 12.8
```

FIGURE 7.10b.   Running the program of Figure 7.10a.

7.11

THE CASE STATEMENT

The CASE statement is a construction that enables the computer to decide which of many statements to execute, depending on the value of an ordinal variable. For instance, in Figure 7.11*a*

```
FOR X: = 1 TO 4 DO
    CASE X OF
        1: writeln('one');
        2: ;
        3, 4: writeln('three or four')
    END (* CASE *)
```

X, the ordinal variable, is in this case an integer variable. If the value of X is 1, the computer executes the statement or compound statement to the right of 1: , here writeln('one'). It then executes the statement after the CASE, here executing the loop for the next value of X.

If the value of X is 2, the computer executes the statement or compound statement to the right of 2: , here the empty statement. It then executes the statement after the CASE.

If the value of X is 3 or 4, the computer executes the statement or compound statement to the right of 3, 4: , here writeln('three or four'). It then executes the statement after the CASE. The results of running the program are shown in Figure 7.11*b*. The set of values of the ordinal value is called the CASE *constant list;* here, it consists of 1, 2, 3, and 4.

Note that the CASE statement doesn't have a BEGIN at the beginning, but it has an END at the end.

If the value of the ordinal variable doesn't correspond to one of the constants in the form of the CASE statement, an error occurs. Thus, always protect the CASE statement from faulty values of the ordinal variable by preceding the CASE with an IF that tests for these faulty values.

TEST YOURSELF

QUESTION: The CASE statement can simplify the translation of pseudocode to Pascal by avoiding using many IF–THENs. Rewrite the CASE statement of the previous program using IF statements so that you can appreciate this simplification.

ANSWER:

```
IF X = 1 THEN writeln('one');
IF X = 2 THEN;
IF (X = 3) OR (X = 4) THEN writeln('three or four')
```

THE CASE STATEMENT

```
PROGRAM Intro(output);
(* Introduction to CASE statement *)
VAR X: integer;
BEGIN
  FOR X:= 1 TO 4 DO
    CASE X OF
      1: writeln('one');
      2: ;
      3, 4: writeln('three OR four')
    END (* CASE *)
END.
```

FIGURE 7.11a. The expression appearing between CASE and OF must be of ordinal type. The statement following CASE, having a label corresponding to the value of the expression, is the one executed.

```
one
three OR four
three OR four
```

FIGURE 7.11b. Running the program of Figure 7.11a.

7.12

CASE STATEMENTS THAT COVER RANGES OF VALUES

Figure 7.12*a* shows a program that uses the CASE statement to determine a letter grade from a numerical mark. An *A* is given for marks ranging from 90 to 100, a *B* for marks from 80 to 89, a *C* for marks from 70 to 79, and a *D* for marks from 60 to 69. If the mark falls between 0 and 59, the student must retake the exam. In addition, if the marks falls outside of the range from 0 to 100, the CASE statement is skipped. The pseudocode is

> read(grade)
> IF 0 ≤ grade ≤ 100 THEN
>   *assign a letter or comment to the grade*
> ELSE writeln(' Out of range.')

In order to use the CASE statement to print the letter grade, you must first associate an integer (let's call it Index) with each range of marks. This suggests the following top-down diagram:

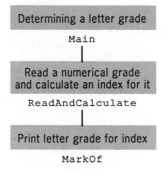

The reason the MarkOf rectangle descends from the ReadAndCalculate rectangle is that procedure ReadAndCalculate activates MarkOf.

An integer is associated with each range of marks as follows: The grades from 80 to 89 should correspond to 8; from 70 to 79 should correspond to 7, and so on. DIVing the grade by 10 will do this, so we write

$$Index := grade \ DIV \ 10;$$

in procedure ReadAndCalc. Because of IF (grade >= 0) and (grade <= 100) THEN, the only grade that a value of Index equaling 10 will correspond to will be 100. Moreover, the IF insures that an out of range value of grade will not cause an error in the CASE statement. Index is passed to procedure MarkOf, which will determine the letter grade.

USING A CASE FOR A RANGE OF VALUES

```
PROGRAM ConverToLetter(output);
(* Converts numerical grade to letter grade *)
CONST NumStudent = 4;

PROCEDURE MarkOf(Index: integer);
(* Prints grade for index *)
BEGIN
     CASE Index OF
        9, 10: writeln( 'A');
        8: writeln( 'B');
        7: writeln( 'C');
        6: writeln( 'D');
  0, 1, 2, 3, 4, 5: writeln( 'Retake Exam')
     END (* CASE *)
END(* mark *);

PROCEDURE ReadAndCalc;
(* Reads grade and converts it to Index *)
VAR grade, ID, Index, J: integer;
BEGIN
  FOR J:= 1 TO NumStudent DO BEGIN
      read(ID, grade);
      write('ID= ', ID, ' grade= ', grade:4 );
      IF (grade >= 0) AND (grade <= 100) THEN BEGIN
        Index:= grade DIV 10;
        write ( ' Mark= ');
        MarkOf(Index)
      END (* IF *)
    ELSE
        writeln( ' Mark out of Range.')
  END (* FOR J *)
END (* ReadAndCalc *);

BEGIN (* MAIN *)
  writeln('Type ', NumStudent, ' pairs of IDs and grades on one line')
  ReadAndCalc
END.
```

FIGURE 7.12a. By using `Index:= grade DIV 10`, we convert a range of values into an index so that we can use the CASE statement. The `IF` statement insures that an out of range value of `Grade` will not cause an error in the CASE.

Since the values of Index equaling 9 and 10 should correspond to an *A*, we write in procedure MarkOf

```
CASE Index OF
      9, 10: writeln( 'A' );
      8: writeln( 'B' );
      7: writeln( 'C' );
      6: writeln( 'D' );
      0, 1, 2, 3, 4, 5: writeln( 'Retake Exam' )
END (* Case *)
```

The results of running the program are shown in Figure 7.12*b*. Since read(ID, grade) is used in the J loop, we can type all the data on one line:

```
Type 4 pairs of IDs and grades on one line
1001 34 1002 99 1003 85 1004 106
```

as done here (it makes the results easier to read), or each pair of ID and grade can be typed on a separate line.

7.13

AN ELEMENTARY CALCULATOR

BEFORE YOU BEGIN

When 3 × 5 is written on a sheet of paper, it has no intrinsic value. We must perform the calculation in our head in order to obtain the result. Similarly, when the computer encounters a numerical expression such as 3 * 5 (e.g., in Area: = 3 * 5), it reads it as characters. The computer must then evaluate the expression. In order to appreciate how this is done, let's investigate the following program.

The next program evaluates mathematical expressions consisting of three characters, for example, 4 * 3. Such a program is called a *calculator*, one of the basic programming tools used in computer science. First, we give some definitions.

As you know, the real mathematical operators are "+", "−", "*", and "/". The variables and constants used with operators are called *operands*. Thus in 2+6 both 2 and 6 are operands. Our calculator will work only for operands that are digits. Thus an input of 10+3 will cause an error, since the first operand, 10, is not a digit. The pseudocode is

```
Type 4 pairs of IDs and grades on one line
1001 34   1002 99   1003 85   1004 106
ID= 1001 grade=    34 Mark= Retake Exam
ID= 1002 grade=    99 Mark= A
ID= 1003 grade=    85 Mark= B
ID= 1004 grade=   106 Mark out of Range.
```

FIGURE 7.12b. Running the program of Figure 7.12a.

TESTING PROGRAMS

After you finish writing a program you should run it with sets of data that test whether the boolean expressions in the IFs and the constant list in the CASEs are performing correctly. For instance in Figure 7.12b, the data set 1004 106 tests whether (grade >= 0) AND (grade <= 100) in the IF in Figure 7.12a eliminates data that is out of range; whereas the other data sets in Figure 7.12b test whether the CASE is performing correctly.

Readln(operandl, operator, operand2);

Convert operand1 to a digit;

Convert operand2 to a digit;

CASE *operator* OF

plus sign: perform addition;

minus sign: perform subtraction;

multiplication sign: perform multiplication;

Division sign: perform division

END (* CASE *)

Write results.

The CASE statement translates to

CASE Operator OF

'+': Term: = Digitl + Digit 2;

'−': Term: = Digitl − Digit 2;

'*': Term: = Digitl * Digit 2;

'/': Term: = Digitl / Digit 2;

END (* CASE *);

as shown in Figure 7.13*a*, where Term is the result of the calculation.

The operators (+, −, /, and *) must appear in the constant list in single quotation marks, since they are characters. When they appear in the calculation (e.g., Term: = Digitl + Digit2), they occur, of course, without quotation marks. Procedure Convert converts the input digits (they are read as characters*) to integers. The results of running the program are shown in Figure 7.13*b*.

TEST YOURSELF

QUESTION: Why does the computer know the meaning of the "+" in the statement Term: = Digitl + Digit2 but not in the input 3+5?

ANSWER: The "+" is just a symbol. When the computer sees the "+" in the statement Term: = Digitl + Digit2, it performs an addition in machine language and stores the result in the location labeled by Term. When it sees the "+" in the data, it reads it as a character. You must instruct the computer how to process it.

---

*This will be helpful in later versions of the program that tests for valid input.

WRITING A SIMPLE CALCULATOR

```
PROGRAM CALCUL(input, output);
(* Evaluates an expression that has one operator *)
VAR Operandl, Operand2, Operator: char;
   Term: real;
   Digitl, Digit2, j: integer;

PROCEDURE Convert( Oper:char; VAR Digit:integer);
(* Converts character Digit to integer *)
BEGIN
   Digit:=ord(Oper)-ord('0')
END (* Convert *);

BEGIN (* MAIN *)
   writeln('Type your 3 character expression');
   readln(Operandl, Operator, Operand2);
   Convert(Operandl, Digitl);
   Convert(Operand2, Digit2);
   IF Operator IN ['*', '/', '+', '-'] THEN
     CASE Operator OF
       '+': Term:= Digitl + Digit2;
       '-': Term:= Digitl - Digit2;
       '*': Term:= Digitl * Digit2;
       '/': Term:= Digitl / Digit2;
     END (* CASE *);
   ELSE BEGIN
     Writeln (Operator, ' is an illegal operator');
     Term := 0.0 .
   END (* ELSE *);
   writeln( 'Value of ', Digitl, Operator, Digit2, ' is ', Term :3:1);
END.
```

FIGURE 7.13a.   **The program takes character input consisting of a digit followed by an operator followed by another digit and evaluates the expression formed. This type of program is called a** *calculator.* **The IF statement insures that a faulty operator will not cause an error in the CASE statement.**

```
Type your 3 character expression
4*8
Value of 4*8 is 32.0
```

FIGURE 7.13b.   Running the program of Figure 7.13a. If the value of an operand is not valid, an error will occur. Future versions of the program will test for such errors.

Summary of the Pascal Statements Studied

The CASE Statement   The form of the CASE statement is CASE followed by an ordinal expression followed by OF. This is followed by one or more lines, each of which has the following format: a list of ordinal values of the same type as the identifier that followed CASE, followed by ":", followed by a statement or compound statement. If there is more than one such line, all but the last must end with a "; ". The last of these lines is followed by an END. For example:

```
CASE Operator OF
    '+': Term: = Digitl + Digit 2;
    '-': Term: = Digitl - Digit 2;
    '*': Term: = Digitl * Digit 2;
    '/': Term: = Digitl / Digit 2;
    '&', '#', ": Error (Operator);
    '^': BEGIN
        Term: =1;
        FOR J: = 1 TO Digit2 DO
            Term: = Term * Digit
        END (*^BEGIN *)
END (* CASE *);
```

Note that Error(Operator) activates procedure Error.

The IF Statement   The form of the IF statement is IF followed by a boolean expression followed by a statement or compound statement. If there is an ELSE part, the ELSE follows the previous statement or compound statement. Another statement or compound statement follows the ELSE. For example:

```
IF Income <= 2300 THEN BEGIN
        Tax : = 0 ;
        Ratio : = 0
    END
ELSE
    BEGIN
        Tax : = 0.14 * Income;
        Ratio : = 0.14
    END
```

PROGRAMMING PITFALLS

1. A common mistake is to translate the mathematical inequality $A < B < C$ to what seems to be the mathematical equivalent in Pascal, namely, B > A AND < C, instead of the correct boolean expression (B > A) AND (B < C).

2. Some compilers translate expressions containing boolean operators such that the entire expression is evaluated, even though the first part is false. This is called *full boolean evaluation.** For instance, in

```
IF (X >= 0) AND (sqrt(X) > 4 ) THEN
    writeln(X)
```

even if the value of X is negative and thus (X >= 0) is false, the computer will evaluate sqrt(X) and a run-time error will occur because it cannot evaluate the square root of a negative number. To avoid this error, write the program such that (X > 0) is evaluated in a separate IF–THEN:

```
IF (X >= 0) THEN
    IF sqrt(X) > 4 THEN
        writeln(X)
```

3. A common error is to terminate the statement preceding an ELSE with a semicolon:

```
IF Income <= 2300 THEN BEGIN
    Tax := 0 ;
ELSE
    Tax := 0.14 * Income
```

This produces a syntax error that can be difficult to locate.

4. Another common mistake is to place a semicolon after the ELSE. This produces an empty statement following the ELSE.

5. Omitting the parentheses in a boolean expression using the NOT and the IN, such as NOT LETTER IN ['a'..'z'] instead of NOT (Letter IN ['a'..'z']), will cause a type incompatibility error. The reason is that in NOT Letter IN ['a'..'z'], the NOT operates on Letter, a char variable. It can only operate on a boolean value.

6. Using 3 dots instead of 2 dots in the set notation (i.e., writing ['a'...'z'] instead of ['a'..'z']) will cause an error.

*When a boolean expression is not evaluated when the first part is false, we call this process *short-circuit boolean evaluation.* For example, if (X >= 0) is false, then on a compiler that short-circuits, boolean expression (X >= 0) AND (sqrt(X) > 4) would not be evaluated.

TEST YOURSELF

QUESTION: How would you rewrite the following if you wanted the computer to print Negative X for negative values of X and Small value of X for positive values of X for which sqrt(X) > 4 is false.

```
IF X >= 0 THEN
    IF sqrt(X) > 4 THEN
        writeln(X)
```

ANSWER:

```
IF X >= 0 THEN
    IF sqrt(X) > 4 THEN
        writeln(X)
    ELSE
        writeln('Small value of X')
ELSE
        writeln('Negative X')
```

CHAPTER REVIEW

IF–THEN–ELSE

An ELSE is matched with the immediately preceding IF that has not already been matched with an ELSE. An ELSE can never have a semicolon immediately preceding it. For instance,

```
If sqrt(X) > 4 THEN
    writeln(X);
ELSE
    writeln('Small value of X')
```

would cause a syntax error. However, a semicolon following an ELSE will not cause a syntax error but will produce a run-time error. For example, in

```
If sqrt(X) > 4 THEN
    writeln(X)
ELSE;
    writeln('Small value of X')
```

an empty statement follows the ELSE. Thus the writeln statement is executed whether or not sqrt(X) > 4 is true.

CASE

Only an ordinal type variable can be used with a CASE statement. If the value of the ordinal variable does not correspond to one of the constants in the CASE statement, the computer executes the next statement.

NEW TERMS

boolean expression	multiple alternative IF–THEN–ELSE
calculator	operands
CASE constant list	set
comparison operators	short-circuit boolean evaluation
condition	stub
elements of a set	truth table
full boolean evaluation	

EXERCISES

1. Can the following be written without parentheses, and if so, why?

$$IF\ 3 + A > B - 5\ THEN$$

Can the following be written without parentheses, if not, why not?

$$IF\ 3 + R > B\ AND\ Valid\ THEN$$

2. Evaluate the following:
   a. $(3 > 7)$ AND NOT $(5 = 2)$ **b.** NOT $(5 > 4)$ OR $(3 < 2)$
   c. NOT $((5 > 4)$ OR $(3 < 2))$ **d.** NOT $(6 < 8)$ OR $(3 > 5)$ AND
                                             $(8 = 8)$

3. Is the following correct? If not, how would you correct it?

$$NOT\ NOT\ NOT\ (3 = 2)$$

4. What is the output of the following program if the input is 8 3 2 5 7?

```
PROGRAM Prob1(input, output);
VAR Number, I, K: integer;
BEGIN
  read(Number);
  FOR K:= 4 DOWNTO 1 DO BEGIN
    write(Number);
    FOR I:= 1 TO 5 DO
      IF odd(I) AND NOT odd(Number) THEN
        write(I * Number)
      ELSE write(I + Number);
      writeln;
      read(Number)
  END (* FOR K *)
END.
```

5. What is the output of the following program?

```pascal
PROGRAM Prob2(input, output);
CONST Dash = '-';
VAR X, Y :integer;
BEGIN
  FOR Y:= 1 TO 5 DO BEGIN
    FOR X:= 1 TO 5 DO
      IF( abs(X - 3) > 1) AND (abs(Y - 3) > 1) OR ((X = 3)
        AND (Y = 3))
        THEN write ('*')
      ELSE write(Dash);
    writeln
  END (* FOR Y *)
END.
```

6. What does the following program produce?

```pascal
PROGRAM Prob3(input,output);
VAR A, B: integer;
BEGIN
  FOR A:= 3 TO 5 DO BEGIN
    FOR B:= A DOWNTO 1 DO
      IF odd(B) OR (A = 3) THEN
        write(A + B:3);
    writeln
  END (* FOR A *)
END.
```

7. Indicate whether each of the following is valid or not. If not, explain why not.

a. IF 1 < Mark 6 THEN writeln(Mark);

b. Value:= (X = Y) AND Q;

c. 1 AND 7

d. CASE Number OF
```
        1: writeln('One');
        2: writeln('Two');
        3: writeln('Three')
```

e. Value:= One AND Two AND Three;

d. NOT odd(7)

Programming Problems

8. Write a program that determines how many odd and even numbers there are in a group of 20 numbers.

9. Write a program that finds the lowest grade in a group of N grades. Hint: Assign 100 to LowGrade before the loop. Assign each subsequent grade read that is lower than LowGrade to LowGrade. The value of LowGrade at the end of the program is the lowest grade.

10. Write a program that determines the average of the four highest grades a student got in a course where five exams were given. Hint: Find the lowest grade and subtract it from the sum.

11. Write a program that converts a four-digit binary number (e.g., 1001) into its decimal equivalent. The solution is surprisingly simple if you realize that, for instance, a decimal number is the sum of each of its digits multiplied by the appropriate power of 10. For example, 435 is the sum of $4 \times 100 + 3 \times 10 + 5 \times 1$. We used this fact when we wrote `Number := Number * 10 + digit`. The sum is equivalent to $4 \times 10 + 3 \times 10 + 5 \times 10$. By analogy, the binary conversion problem can be solved in a similar manner. A binary number is the sum of each of its digits multiplied by the appropriate power of 2. For example, 1011 is the sum of $1 \times 2^3 + 0 \times 2^2 + 1 \times 2^1 + 1 \times 2^0$.

12. Write a program that converts a four-digit hexadecimal number to its decimal equivalent. The digits for a hexadecimal number are {0, 1, 2, 3, 4, 5, 6, 7, 8, 9, A, B, C, D, E, and F}, where A to F correspond to 10 to 15, respectively. A hexadecimal number is the sum of each of its digits multiplied by the appropriate power of 16. For example, A83B is the sum of $10 \times 16^3 + 8 \times 16^2 + 3 \times 16^1 + 11 \times 16^0$.

13. Write a program that finds the geographic distribution for the people standing on line in the survey problem discussed in Chapter 2. The input should be the number of people standing on line followed by a string consisting of the characters N, S, E, and W. For example,

8

NSEEWWSS

14. Write a program that produces the following, where every fifth x is replaced by an I.

```
x
xxxx
xxxxIxxxx
xxxxIxxxxIxxxxIx
xxxxIxxxxIxxxxIxxxxIxxxxI
```

15. Write a program that reads the month, day, and year on which a person was born and the current date, and then calculates the person's age in years.

16. Write a program that reads 50 numbers and computes the average of the negative numbers and that of the positive numbers.

17. A branch bank has 100 depositors. Write a program that determines the average balance and how many depositors have balances greater than $100,000.

18. Write a program that prints the prime numbers between 2 and 100. If a number N is divisible by any number between 2 and `sqrt(N)`, it is not a prime. Hint: Use the MOD function.

19. Write a program that finds the divisors of a number.

20. Write a program that converts seven letters to a phone number. Look at your phone to see the correspondence between the numbers and the letters.

21. Before the 1970s, the first two characters in a phone number representes the first two letters in an exchange. For instance, 588-3496 was written as LU8-3496, where *LU* were the first two letters in the Ludlow exchange. Similarly, *LA* represented Lackawanna; *LE*, Lehigh; *LI*, Ligget; and *LO*, Lorraine. Write a program that reads seven contiguous digits as characters and, if the first digit is a 5, prints the phone number in the pre-1970 mode with the proper exchange.

22. Write a program that encodes a string such that each letter is transformed into the letter that follows it in the alphabet. Thus *a* becomes *b*, and so on, but *z* should become *a*.

23. Write a program that uses loops to produce the following:

```
|1111111111|222222222|333333333|444444444|555555555|666666666|
123456789|123456789|123456789|123456789|123456789|123456789|123456789|
```

24. Write a program that produces all three-letter combinations in which the second letter is a vowel. In order to do this, use a procedure in which the parameter is the second letter. Activate this procedure in a FOR loop.

25. A multiple-choice examination is scored by subtracting the number of incorrect answers from the number of correct ones and then dividing by the number of questions, in this case, 50. A grade ranging from 50% to 100% is an *A*; 0% to 49% a *B*; −50% to −1% a *C*; and −100% to −50% a *D*. Write a program that reads the number of correct answers and then prints the letter grade.

26. Write a program that makes change for a given sum of money such that the number of coins is a minimum. Thus it converts $1.44 into two 50-cent pieces, one quarter, one dime, one nickel, and four pennies.

27. Write a program that plots the sin and cos on one display. Hint: See Chapter 6, exercise 19.

8

THE WHILE AND REPEAT LOOPS, BOTTOM-UP DESIGN, THE EOLN AND EOF FUNCTIONS, AND TEXT FILES

CHAPTER OVERVIEW

Introduced in this chapter are loops that are executed only while a boolean expression in the statement that starts the loop is true (the WHILE loop) or until a boolean expression in a statement that concludes the loop is true (the REPEAT UNTIL loop). To test for end of data, the end-of-line (eoln) and end-of-file (eof) functions are presented. The chapter concludes with an introduction to external files.

8.1

THE WHILE STATEMENT

The programs we've discussed so far that use a FOR–DO loop to process a given amount of data (e.g., averaging five marks, conducting a survey of 10 people, or summing two 4-digit numbers containing a $ and a comma) all have a major flaw: Before you run the program, you must count the number of items to be processed. If you count incorrectly, you encounter difficulties when running the program. Sometimes it's impossible to count by hand the number of items in a set of data. For instance, if you wrote a program to calculate the average height of the students in a particular college, you wouldn't want to count the number of students beforehand. At other times, the purpose of the program is to count the items in a group—for instance, the number of characters in a word. How can we do this? The answer to our problem is the WHILE loop.

A WHILE loop consists of a WHILE–DO and the statement or compound statement following it. An example of a WHILE loop that counts the number of characters in a sentence that ends with a period is

```
WHILE Ch<> Period DO
  BEGIN
    Count: = Count + 1;
    read(Ch)
  END (* WHILE *);
```

where WHILE Ch <> Period DO is the WHILE–DO and the value of Period is '.'. As long as the boolean expression in the WHILE–DO (here, Ch <> Period) is true, the program repeats the execution of the statement or compound statement following the WHILE, in our case,

```
  BEGIN
    Count: = Count + 1;
    read(Ch)
  END (* WHILE *);
```

When the expression becomes false, the computer skips to the statement following the loop.

In the first program, let's determine how many characters (including blanks but excluding the period) there are in a sentence. The pseudocode is shown in Figure 8.1a.

USING THE WHILE LOOP
COUNTING THE NUMBER OF CHARACTERS IN A SENTENCE

Set the character counter to 0;
Read a character;
As long as the character read is not a period, execute the
following compound statement again and again:
  BEGIN
    Add 1 to the character counter;
    Read the next character
  END;
Print the value of the character counter.

FIGURE 8.1a. The pseudocode for determining how many characters are in a sentence.

This is translated into the program in Figure 8.1*b*:

```
Count:= 0;
read(Ch);
WHILE Ch <> Period DO
  BEGIN
    Count:= Count + 1;
    read(Ch)
  END (* WHILE *);
writeln('The number of characters including blanks is ', Count:2)
```

The identifiers in the boolean expression in the WHILE must all be defined. Since the expression is Ch <> Period, we preceded the WHILE with read(Ch). This is called *priming* the WHILE. Moreover, at least one of the statements in the loop—here, read(Ch)—must change the value of the boolean expression in the WHILE. Otherwise, the loop would execute forever. Such a loop is called an *infinite loop.* For example, WHILE Ch <> Period DO Count:= Count + 1 will go on forever if the value of Ch before the loop is not a period, because the value of Ch is never changed. The screen will freeze, and nothing you type will appear on it.

MANUALLY TERMINATING A PROGRAM

Sometimes it's necessary to stop the execution of a program, as in the case of the infinite loop just described. On most systems, when you hit Ctrl-Break, your program will terminate.

In Figure 8.1*a*, the statement Count:= Count + 1 counts the characters. The first time it's executed, it counts the character read in the read before the loop. The second time, it counts the character read in the first execution of the loop. From then on, it always counts the character read in the previous execution of the loop. When the period is read, Ch <> Period becomes false and the program quits the loop. Thus the period is not counted, as shown in the table for Figure 8.1*b*:

CHECKING WHILE LOOPS

It is a good idea to check that your program processes data correctly when the WHILE loop is executed only once and when it is executed for a normal data set. We have already done the latter; let's check the former. When the input is only a period, the value of Count printed is 0 (the correct result).

The input for the program and the results are shown in Figure 8.1*c*.

```
PROGRAM LetterCount(input, output);
(* Program counts the number of characters in a sentence *)
CONST Period = '.';
VAR Count: integer;
  Ch: char;
BEGIN
  Count:= 0;
  writeln('Write a sentence and end it with a period.');
  read(Ch);
  WHILE Ch <> Period DO
  BEGIN
    Count:= Count + 1;
    read(Ch)
  END (* WHILE *);
  writeln('The number of characters including blanks is ', Count:2)
END.
```

FIGURE 8.1b. The value of Ch must be defined before the WHILE statement. Also, if the value of Ch is not altered in the loop, an infinite loop will result.

Ch	Ch <> Period	Next statement	Count
i	True	Count:=Count + 1	22
s	True	Count:=Count + 1	23
.	False	writeln	23

TABLE FOR FIGURE 8.1b. Shows how the last three characters in the sentence of Figure 8.1b are treated.

```
Write a sentence and end it with a period.
What a great life it is.
The number of characters including blanks is 23
```

FIGURE 8.1c. Running the program of Figure 8.1b. We type a sentence as input.

BEFORE YOU BEGIN

Remember that in the word-counting programs in Chapter 7, we had to input the number of characters in a sentence before the program processed the data further. This made the program impractical. By using a WHILE loop, we can eliminate this requirement.

The next program is a more sophisticated version of the previous one. It counts the number of words in a sentence in which more than one blank can separate words. Unlike the previous word-counting programs we've written, we relax the requirements on the inputted sentence somewhat by allowing one or more blanks to immediately precede the period. For instance, "My name is John   ." is now a valid input. The end of a word is indicated by the fact that the present character is either a blank or a period, and that the previous character is not a blank. The pseudocode is

> *Set Previous and Present characters to blank;*
> *Set Word counter to zero;*
> WHILE Present <> Period DO BEGIN
>   *Read Present character;*
>   IF *(Present is a Blank or Period)* AND *(Previous <> Blank)*
>   THEN *Add 1 to Word counter;*
>   *Enable next letter to be compared with this one, so:*
>   *Set Previous character to Present one*
> END (* WHILE *);

Why were *Previous* and *Present* initialized as they were?

1. It is more elegant for the read to appear only in the loop rather than both in the loop and before it. Therefore, since the WHILE is WHILE *Present <> Period* DO, any character but a period must be assigned to *Present* before the loop; so we set it equal to a blank.

2. Since the first character read may be a blank, *Previous* is set to a blank before the loop. Consequently, the boolean expression in

    IF *(Present is a Blank or Period)* AND *(Previous <> Blank)* THEN

    which determines whether 1 is added to the word counter, must be false when the first character is read. The reason is that *Previous <> blank* is false.

The pseudocode becomes the program shown in Figure 8.1d. The statement

    IF *(Present is a Blank or Period)* AND *(Previous <> Blank)* THEN

COUNTING THE NUMBER OF WORDS IN A SENTENCE

```
PROGRAM WordCounter(input, output);
(* Counts the number of words in a sentence *)
CONST Period = '.';
   Blank = ' ';
VAR WordCount: integer;
   Present, Previous: char;
BEGIN
   WordCount:= 0;
   writeln('Write a sentence and end it with a period.');
   Previous:= Blank;
   Present:= Blank;
   WHILE Present <> Period DO BEGIN
      read(Present);
      (* Test for end of word *)
      IF (Present IN [Blank, Period]) AND (Previous <> Blank) THEN
         WordCount:= WordCount + 1;
      (* Enables next letter to be compared with this one *)
      Previous:= Present
   END (* WHILE *);
   writeln;
   writeln('The number of words in the sentence is ', WordCount:2)
END.
```

FIGURE 8.1d. A word ends when a nonblank is followed by a blank or a period.

becomes

```
IF (Present IN [Blank, Period]) AND (Previous <> Blank) THEN
```

The results shown in Figure 8.1*e* are for standard input and in Figure 8.1*f* are for nonstandard input, that is, input that starts with a blank, has more than one blank separating words, and has a blank immediately preceding the period.

8.2

WHILE LOOP PITFALLS

1. As in the case of the FOR statement, omitting the BEGIN and the END in the compound statement that follows the WHILE, for instance, writing the WHILE loop of Figure 8.1*a* as

```
WHILE Ch <> Period DO
    Count: = Count + 1;
    read(Ch)
```

instructs the WHILE to act only on Count : = Count + 1. If the sentence used as data does not begin with a period, the expression Ch <> Period will always be true, resulting in an infinite loop.

2. A similar situation occurs when a WHILE–DO terminates with a semicolon, that is,

```
WHILE Ch <> Period DO;
```

The computer will act on the empty statement following the DO an infinite number times because the boolean expression Ch <> Period will always be true. Consequently, it will never perform the statements in the compound statement that follows.

STANDARD INPUT

```
        Write a sentence and end it with a period.
        My country tis of thee, sweet land of liberty.
        The number of words in the sentence is 9
```

FIGURE 8.1e.   The input begins with a letter, and the character immediately preceding the period is a nonblank.

NONSTANDARD INPUT

```
        Write a sentence and end it with a period.
        My country tis of thee, Sweet   land of   liberty   .
        The number of words in the sentence is 9
```

FIGURE 8.1f.   The input begins with blanks, has more than one blank between some words, and has blanks immediately preceding the period. The program computes the same answer as for the input in Figure 8.1e.

8.3

USING SENTINELS

A *sentinel* is a piece of data that ends a set of data but isn't a possible value of the data. Thus, it is not included in the calculation. For instance, in Figure 8.1*a*, a period was used as a sentinel to indicate the last character in a sentence; however, the program didn't count it as one of the characters in the sentence.

BEFORE YOU BEGIN

In the previous averaging program, we had to know the number of items that were to be averaged. Most of the time, we don't know this number. Now by using a WHILE loop, we calculate the average of a set of an arbitrary number of grades simply by following the last grade in the set by a sentinel, here −999. The sentinel must be outside the range of the actual data and is not included in the average. Since grades can range from 0 to 100, the sentinel −999 is certainly outside the range of the grades.

The next program, Figure 8.2*a*, calculates the average of the set of grades. In Figure 8.2*b* the numbers are typed on one line, since it is easier to distinguish the input from the output that way; however, the program would work just as well if each number was typed on a different line and −999 was typed on the last line.

8.4

AN APPLICATION OF TOP-DOWN DESIGN

Let's use top-down design to write a program that does the following:

1. Reads a student's ID and his or her grades on two homework assignments, two tests, and a final exam.

2. Calculates the cumulative grade based on the following data: The maximum grade on either a homework assignment or a test is 50 and the maximum final test grade is 100. The cumulative grade is obtained by taking 30% of the sum of the homework grades, plus 30% of the sum of the test grades, plus 40% of the final grade. An *A* is given for a cumulative grade in the range 90 to 100; a *B* for the range 80 to 89; a *C* for the range 70 to 79; and a *D* for the range 60 to 69. A student who scores below 60 must retake the course.

3. Finds the class average.

PERFORMING AN AVERAGE

```
PROGRAM IntroSen(input, output);
(* Calculates the grade average *)
CONST Sentinel = -999;
VAR Count, Grade: integer;
  Sum, average : real;
BEGIN
  Count:= 0;
  Sum:= 0.0;
  writeln('Type your grades on one line, -999 terminates.');
  read(Grade);
  writeln;
  WHILE Grade <> Sentinel DO
    BEGIN
      Count:= Count + 1;
      Sum:= Sum + Grade;
      writeln('For grade # ', Count:2, ', running sum is ', sum:4:0);
      read(Grade)
    END (* WHILE *);
  writeln;
  average:= Sum / Count;
  writeln('average = ', average: 3:1)
END
```

FIGURE 8.2a.   When −999 is read, the averaging stops. Here −999 acts as a sentinel. The sentinel should be chosen so that it cannot be a possible value of any of the input.

```
Type your grades on one line, -999 terminates.
89 99 78 68 95 99 -999
For grade # 1, running sum is  89
For grade # 2, running sum is 188
For grade # 3, running sum is 266
For grade # 4, running sum is 334
For grade # 5, running sum is 429
For grade # 6, running sum is 528
average = 88.0
```

FIGURE 8.2b.   Running the program of Figure 8.2a.

The top-down diagram for the program is shown in Figure 8.3*a*.

In Level 1:

1. `Initialize` initializes the counter and sum for the class average.
2. `Prompt` tells the user what data are required.
3. `ReadAndCalculate` reads the data and calculates a student's cumulative numerical grade and the corresponding letter grade. It also counts the number of students and sums the cumulative numerical grades in order to obtain the class average.
4. `ConvertToLetterGrade` converts a numerical grade, here the class average, to an index that will enable the program in `PrintLetterGrade` to print the corresponding letter grade.

In Level 2:

1. `NumericalGrade` calculates a student's cumulative numerical grade.
2. `ConvertToLetterGrade` converts a numerical grade, now a student's cumulative grade, to an index.
3. `PrintLetterGrade` prints the letter grade (for the class average) corresponding to a given index.

In Level 3:

`PrintLetterGrade` prints the letter grade for a given student.

Procedure `ReadAndCalculate`, shown in Figure 8.3*b*(I), is written so that only the value of ID is read before the WHILE loop:

```
read(ID);
WHILE ID <> sentinel DO
   BEGIN
      read( HW1, HW2, Test1, Test2, Final);
      Count:= Count + 1;
      NumericalGrade(Grade, ID, HW1, HW2, Test1, Test2, Final);
      write('ID= ', ID, ': grade= ', Grade, ', mark= ');
      ConvertToLetterGrade(Grade);
      Sum:= Sum + Grade;
      read(ID)
END (* WHILE *);
```

DETERMINING A CLASS AVERAGE

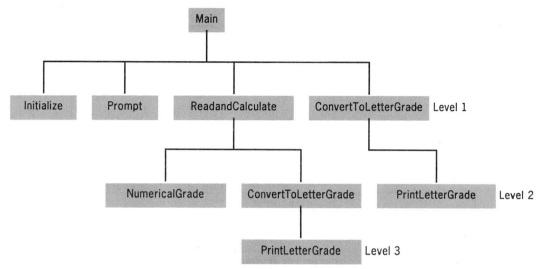

FIGURE 8.3a. The top-down diagram for a class average program. In Level I `ConvertToLetterGrade` converts the class average to a letter grade. In Level II, it converts the student average to a letter grade.

```
PROCEDURE ReadAndCalculate(VAR Sum:real; VAR Count: integer);
(* Reads and calculates the grade *)
VAR Grade:real;
   ID, HW1, HW2, Test1, Test2, Final: integer;
BEGIN
   read(ID);
   WHILE ID <> Sentinel DO
     BEGIN
       read( HW1, IIW2, Test1, Test2, Final);
       Count:= Count + 1;
       NumericalGrade(Grade, ID, HW1, HW2, Test1, Test2, Final);
       write('ID= ', ID, ': grade= ', round(Grade):4, ', mark= ');
       ConvertToLetterGrade(Grade);
       Sum:= Sum + Grade;
       read(ID)
     END (* WHILE *);
   writeln
END (* ReadAndCalculate *)
```

FIGURE 8.3b(I). Reads a set of a student's marks and activates procedures to get the cumulative numerical grade and equivalent letter grade. Also calculates the class total.

This allows the program to read separately in the loop all of the grades in read(HW1, HW2, Test1, Test2, Final) and, at the end of the loop, to read separately the value of ID. To terminate the program, you need only type the value of the sentinel, −999, as the value of the ID. If the ID had not been read separately but had been placed in read(ID, HW1, HW2, Test1, Test2, Final) both before and in the loop, you would have had to type −999 0 0 0 0 0 to end the program. The cumulative numerical grade for a student is calculated in procedure NumericalGrade, shown in Figure 8.3*b*(II).

In procedure ConvertToLetterGrade, shown in Figure 8.3*b*(III), the calculated cumulative grade, which varies from 0 to 100, is converted to an integer Index, whose value varies from 0 to 10:

$$\text{Index}: = \text{trunc}(\text{Grade} / 10 + 0.0001);$$

The value of Index is then passed to procedure PrintLetterGrade, shown in Figure 8.3*b*(IV), where the appropriate letter grade is printed. The reason for adding 0.0001 is to correct for roundoff error. For instance, if the value of Grade is 90, the value of Grade / 10 should be 9; however, because of roundoff error, it may be 8.9999999. When 0.0001 is added and the result is then truncated, the proper value for Index and consequently the proper letter grade, *A*, are obtained. Had we not corrected for roundoff error, the letter grade would have been improperly calculated as a *B*.*

---

*We chose 0.0001 instead of 0.1 for the following reason: If the grade average is 89.1, then Grade / 10 is 8.91 but Grade / 10 + 0.1 would be truncated to 9. The student would then get an *A* instead of the *B* that the grade merits.

```
PROCEDURE NumericalGrade (VAR Grade:real; ID,HW1,HW2, Test1,
        Test2, Final:integer);
(* Calculates the total numerical grade *)
BEGIN
  Grade:= 0.3 * (HW1 + HW2) + 0.3 * (Test1 + Test2) + 0.4 * Final;
END (* NumericalGrade *);
```

FIGURE 8.3*b*(II).   Calculates the cumulative numerical grade for a student.

```
PROCEDURE ConvertToLetterGrade(Grade: real);
(* Converts the numerical grade to an index *)
VAR Index: integer;
BEGIN
  Index:= trunc( Grade / 10 + 0.0001 );
  IF Index IN [0..10] THEN
    PrintLetterGrade(Index)
  ELSE
    writeln(' Out of Range')
END (* ConvertToLetterGrade *);
```

FIGURE 8.3*b*(III).   Converts a range of numerical grades to an index. The amount 0.0001 is added to compensate for roundoff error.

```
PROCEDURE PrintLetterGrade(Index: integer);
(* Prints the grade for Index *)
BEGIN
  CASE Index of
    9, 10: writeln( 'A');
    8: writeln( 'B');
    7: writeln( 'C');
    6: writeln( 'D');
    0, 1, 2, 3, 4, 5: writeln( 'Retake course')
    END (* Case *)
END (* mark *);
```

FIGURE 8.3*b*(IV).   Converts the index to a printed letter grade.

Using level 1 in the top-down diagram, we write the main program as shown in Figure 8.3c:

```
Initialize(Count, Sum);
Prompt;
ReadAndCalculate( Sum, Count);
average:= Sum / Count;
write('Class average: grade= ', round(average):4, ', mark= ');
ConvertToLetterGrade(average)
```

This figure also includes the procedure that prompts the user to type the data, and the procedure that initializes the counter and the sum. In order to test

```pascal
PROGRAM ClassAver(input, output);
(* Calculates the grade average *)
CONST sentinel = -999;
VAR Count:integer;
  Sum, average:real;

PROCEDURE Initialize(VAR Count: integer; VAR Sum: real);
BEGIN
  Count:= 0;
  Sum:= 0.0
END (* Initialize *);

PROCEDURE Prompt;
BEGIN
  writeln('Type ID, HW1, HW2, Test1, Test2, Final.')
END (* Prompt *);
PROCEDURE PrintLetterGrade(Index: integer);                {See page 301}
PROCEDURE ConvertToLetterGrade(Grade: real);               {See page 301}
PROCEDURE NumericalGrade (VAR Grade:real;ID,HW1,HW2, Test1,
        Test2, Final:integer);                             {See page 301}
PROCEDURE ReadAndCalculate(VAR Sum:real; VAR Count: integer);
                                                           {See page 299}

BEGIN (* MAIN *)
  Initialize(Count, Sum);
  Prompt;
  ReadAndCalculate( Sum, Count);
  average:= Sum / Count;
  write('Class average: grade= ', round(average):4, ', mark= ');
  ConvertToLetterGrade(average)
END.
```

FIGURE 8.3c. The main program and two simple procedures. The headings for the other procedures used are also included. If you run the program, you must include the entire procedures.

the program, we type a set of data consisting of a student's ID followed by the maximum scores, 108 50 50 50 50 100, as shown in Figure 8.3*d*, where 108 is the student's ID. As we expect, the computed grade is 100 and the letter grade is *A*. Similarly, we see that a data set for a student who only did the homework assignments, 109 50 50 0 0 0, yields a total grade of 30 (in other words, 30% of the total possible grade).

One of the pitfalls of typing the data across the monitor screen, as done here

101 34 35 36 37 83　　102 45 45 50 50 89　　103 48 49 50 50 70　　108 50 50 50 50 100
109 50 50 0 0 0　　−999

is that at least one blank must be inserted between the last constant typed on a line (here, 100) and the first constant typed on the next line (here, 109). If this is not done, both constants will be read as one (here, 100109) and an error will occur. Because of the possibility of pitfalls, it is safer to type the set of data for each student on a separate line.

8.5

THE REPEAT LOOP

There is an alternative to using the WHILE loop. It is called the REPEAT loop. An example that determines how many digits are in an integer is

```
REPEAT
    Number := Number DIV 10;
    Count := Count + 1
UNTIL Number = 0;
```

The statements sandwiched between the REPEAT and the UNTIL are repeatedly executed until the boolean expression in the UNTIL statement, here Number = 0, is true. When this happens, the statement following the UNTIL is executed. Note that the BEGIN and END delimiters are not required here. We will see later that the effect of the WHILE and the REPEAT can be different.

```
Type ID, HW1, HW2, Test1, Test2, Final.
101 34 35 36 37 83   102 45 45 50 50 89   103 48 49 50 50 70   108 50 50 50 50 100
109 50 50 0 0 0   −999
ID= 101: grade=  75, mark= C
ID= 102: grade=  92, mark= A
ID= 103: grade=  87, mark= B
ID= 108: grade= 100, mark= A
ID= 109: grade=  30, mark= Retake course
Class average: grade= 77, mark= C
```

FIGURE 8.3*d*.   Running the program of Figure 8.3c. The data includes two sets that test the program. The first has the maximum scores; the second includes the maximum scores for the homework but zeroes for the exams.

The following program determines how many digits an integer, Number, has. An application of this program is the determination of the field width with which we print the value of Number. If the number of digits is stored in count, then we could write writeln('Number =', Number:Count + 1). If we did not use a variable field width here, the results might be printed as Number =   7621, as opposed to the one obtained using a field width of 5, Number = 7621.

The first version of the pseudocode to determine how many digits an integer has is

> *Remove the digits from* Number *(simultaneously counting them) until there are none left.*

One way of doing this is to use the approach of Figure 6.8a, where both the MOD and the DIV were used; however, there is a more elegant approach. Whenever you divide a number by 10, you move the decimal point one place to the left. For instance, 7621.0 / 10 is 762.1 and 762.1 / 10 is 76.21. Therefore, if we repeatedly divide the integer Number by 10 and store the result in Number, the final result will be zero. Using this procedure, let's refine the original pseudocode to

> REPEAT
>> *Divide* Number *by 10 and assign the results to* Number;
>> *Add 1 to Count*
> UNTIL *Number is zero*

This is translated into the program in Figure 8.4a. Each time the REPEAT loop is executed, because of Number := Number DIV 10, the integer has one less digit and the value of Count is increased by 1, as shown in the table for Figure 8.4a. Thus, since the value of Number is 3145 before the computer enters the loop

Number	Number DIV 10	Count	Number = 0
3145	314	1	False

USING THE REPEAT

```
PROGRAM Count(input, output);
(* Introduction to the REPEAT *)
(* Determines how many digits there are in an integer *)
VAR number, StoreNum, Count: integer;
BEGIN
  writeln('Type an integer');
  readln(number);
  StoreNum:= number;
  Count:= 0;
  REPEAT
    number:= number DIV 10;
    Count:= Count + 1
  UNTIL number = 0;
  writeln(StoreNum, ' has ', Count:2, ' digits')
END.
```

FIGURE 8.4a. Unlike the WHILE loop, the REPEAT loop is executed at least once.

number	number DIV 10	Count	number = 0
3145	314	1	False
314	31	2	False
31	3	3	False
3	0	4	True

TABLE FOR FIGURE 8.4a. Each time the loop is executed, the number of digits in Number is decreased by 1 and the value of Count is increased by 1.

its value is 314 at the end of the first execution of the loop. Thus Number = 0 is false and the loop is executed again. This continues until Number = 0 is true. The value of Count is now the number of digits in Number. Since the value of Number changes for each execution of the loop, let's store its value in StoreNum before the loop. This enables the original value to be printed at the end of the execution

```
StoreNum: = Number;
Count: = 0;
REPEAT
  Number: = Number DIV 10;
  Count: = Count + 1
UNTIL Number = 0;
writeln(StoreNum: Count + 1, ' has ', Count:2, ' digits')
```

as shown in Figure 8.4b.

Note that if the value read for Number is 0, the loop is executed once and the value of Count is 1, as it should be (indicating that 0 has one digit). However, if the WHILE loop had been used instead

```
WHILE Number <> 0 DO BEGIN
  Number: = Number DIV 10;
  Count: = Count + 1
END (* WHILE *)
```

the loop would not be executed at all if the value of Number were zero, and the value of Count would be 0 at the program's end. This, of course, would be an error.

Type an integer
3145
3145 has 4 digits

FIGURE 8.4b. Running the program of Figure 8.4a.

TEST YOURSELF

QUESTION: How would you write a procedure that not only determines how many digits there are in the original number but adds the digits as well?

ANSWER:

```
PROCEDURE DigitCount(Number:integer; VAR Count: integer; VAR
Sum:real);
(* Determines the number of digits in an integer *)
BEGIN
  Count:= 0;
  Sum:= 0.0;
  REPEAT
    Sum:= Sum + Number MOD 10;
    Number:= Number DIV 10;
    Count:= Count + 1
  UNTIL Number = 0;
END (* DigitCount *);
```

THE DIFFERENCE IN THE EXECUTION OF A WHILE AND A REPEAT LOOP

In order to explain the differences between the WHILE and the REPEAT, let's examine the program segment of Figure 8.1a—which counted the number of characters in a sentence—written with a WHILE and a REPEAT:

```
Count:= 0;                          Count:= -1;
read(Ch);                           REPEAT
WHILE Ch <> Period DO BEGIN           Count:= Count + 1;
  Count:= Count + 1;                  read(Ch)
  read(Ch)                          UNTIL Ch = Period
END (* WHILE *)
```

The fundamental difference is that the program evaluates the boolean expression in the WHILE before it executes the loop, whereas it evaluates the one in the UNTIL after it has entered the loop. Further analysis reveals the following:

1. Each of the identifiers in the WHILE statement must be assigned values in statements preceding the WHILE (e.g., read(Ch) precedes the WHILE), whereas the identifiers in the UNTIL may be assigned values in the REPEAT loop.

2. A REPEAT loop is executed at least once, whereas a WHILE need not be executed at all. Thus, if our input consists only of a period, the WHILE will not be executed, but the REPEAT will be executed once. That's why the initial value of Count is −1.

3. The boolean expression in the WHILE statement should have the opposite value from the one in the UNTIL statement for the same values of the identifiers, as shown in Table 8.1.

4. Compared to the WHILE loop, if there is more than one statement to be executed in the REPEAT loop, you don't have to use a BEGIN and an END as delimiters; the REPEAT and the UNTIL also serve that purpose.

Relational operator used in WHILE	Relational operator used in UNTIL
>	<=
>=	<
<	>=
<=	>
=	<>
<>	=

TABLE 8.1. If the operator in the first column is used in a boolean expression and is replaced by the operator in the same line in the second column, the value of the boolean expression will be reversed. For instance, if A > B is true, then A <= B will be false.

TEST YOURSELF

QUESTION: If you use a sentinel to terminate your data, should you use a REPEAT or a WHILE to process the data?

ANSWER: Always use a WHILE with a sentinel. If you use a REPEAT, you'll have to compensate for the reading of the sentinel, as we did in the previous box when we initialized Count to −1.

QUESTION:

   1. What type of loop would you characterize as "test and execute"?
   2. What type of loop would you characterize as "execute and test"?

ANSWER:

   1. WHILE
   2. REPEAT

Construction of a Program

The construction of a program depends on the following:

1. The sequence of statements. For instance, in the last program, if you set `Count` to 0 in the loop rather than before the loop, you'd get a different—and incorrect—answer. On the other hand, you can interchange `Number : = Number DIV 10` and `Count : = Count + 1` because the variables in one statement are independent of those in the other.

2. Repetition (either a `WHILE`, a `REPEAT`, or a `FOR–DO` loop).

3. Decision (`IF–THEN–ELSE` or `CASE` statement).

8.6

BOTTOM-UP DESIGN

BEFORE YOU BEGIN

> At times, it is easier to solve a complex program by first writing the subprograms at the bottom of the top-down diagram as complete programs and then testing them. Next, incorporate them into the subprograms on the next level and test those subprograms as separate programs. We thus work our way up the top-down diagram until the main program is completely tested. This technique is called *bottom-up* design.

Given the top-down diagram shown in Table 8.2, one way of solving the program using the bottom-up technique is to write E as a separate program and test it. Then convert E to a procedure and have C activate it in a separate program. Then write C as a procedure. Next, write D as a program and test it, and then make it a procedure. Write B as a separate program and have it activate C and D. As the next to the last step, test A as a separate program and then write it as a procedure. Finally, write the main program and have it activate A and B.

Recall that in the top-down approach, you write the activating procedures and use stubs (dummies) in place of the fundamental procedures. Test the activating procedures before you convert the stubs to procedures. Each time you replace a stub with an actual procedure, test the entire program. Continue to do this, working your way from the top of the top-down diagram to the bottom, until all the stubs have been replaced.

Both of these techniques are rather formal. Most programmers use a variation of one or the other. The one we adopt for the more difficult programs is the modified bottom-up approach used in Chapter 7 to write the word processing programming: Write a simplified version first and build on it until you reach the desired program. Let's use this technique to solve what is called the *two-dimensional random walk problem.* To underscore this method, we will guide the student through this technique in a series of exercises at the end of this and later chapters, displayed in the "Bottom-Up Approach" box.

BOTTOM-UP DESIGN

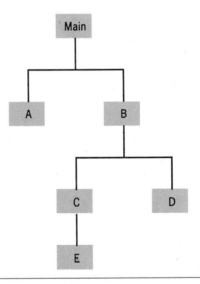

TABLE 8.2. In bottom-up design, we write the subprogram at the bottom of the diagram first as separate programs. We then rewrite them as procedures and use them in the procedures (written as stand-alone programs) on the next level. We continue, converting programs to procedures, until we reach the top of the diagram.

A Monte Carlo Method: Random Walk

Random numbers are useful for simulating phenomena that are random, for instance, the toss of a die or the decay of subnuclear particles. Although the Pascal standard doesn't specify a random number generator, most compilers include one. A random number generator that is on some compilers (e.g., on Turbo Pascal) is called `random`. It generates the same set of pseudorandom numbers* each time you use it. For instance,

FOR I: = 1 TO 10 DO writeln(random)

will generate the same set of 10 random numbers each time the program is run. However, if you precede the loop with `randomize`, for example,

randomize;

FOR I: = 1 TO 10 DO writeln(random)

the loop will produce a different set of random numbers each time the program is executed. The random numbers in both cases will be real numbers greater than or equal to 0 but less than 1. On the other hand, `random(10)` will produce random integers between 0 and 9. The following table summarizes this information.

Function	Use	Argument type	Function type
random	Generates a random number $0 < \text{random} <= 1$	No argument	Real
random(N)	Generates a random integer $0 < \text{random} <= N - 1$	Integer	Integer

The Monte Carlo method uses random numbers to simulate actual events, for instance, nuclear decay or the card game black jack. We describe the process called *random walk*. In the one-dimensional model, a man who has temporarily lost his memory is constrained to walk on a line. At any point, he may take one step in either direction. He cannot remember which direction he chose for any of his previous steps, so it can be assumed that he chooses a direction at random. If he starts at the origin $(X = 0)$ and can move one unit in either direction, an example of his X-values after 10 steps might be 1, 2, 1, 0, -1, 0, -1, -2, -1, -2.

Let's use a modified bottom-up approach to solve the two-dimensional random walk problem. In the two-dimensional model, the man can walk on the X-Y coordinate system. At any point, there is an equal probability that he can walk north, south, east, or west. In order to solve the two-dimensional problem, let's solve the one-dimensional one first, because it's easier.

The program will determine how many steps it takes the man to reach $X = 6$ or -6. The top-down diagram is shown in Figure 8.5a.

*Since if we know the algorithm for producing random numbers we can predict their values, the numbers the function generates are not truly random. Therefore they are called *pseudorandom* numbers.

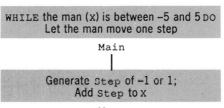

FIGURE 8.5a.   The top-down diagram for a one-dimensional random walk.

Step I: The Man Takes 10 Steps

First, let's write a program to move the man 10 steps by randomly adding 1 or -1 to his present X-position. The statement that produces 1 or -1 randomly is

$$\text{Step} := 1 - 2 * \text{round}(\text{random})$$

(see Figure 8.5b) where, as we've just learned, random produces a number between 0 and 1. The table for Figure 8.5b show how this works for two values of random, and Figure 8.5c shows the results of running the program. Since the random numbers are uniformly distributed between 0 and 1, half the time Step will be 1, and half the time, -1.

AN APPLICATION OF BOTTOM-UP DESIGN: RANDOM WALK
STEP I: ONE-DIMENSIONAL RANDOM WALK

```
PROGRAM RandomWalk2(output);
(* Random walk in one dimension *)
VAR X, Step, Count, Index:integer;
BEGIN
  randomize;
  Count:=0;
  X:=0;
  (* Takes 10 random steps *)
  writeln('The X values are:');
  FOR Index:= 1 TO 10 DO BEGIN
    Step:= 1 − 2 * round(random);
    X:= X + Step;
    write(X:3)
  END (* FOR *);
END.
```

FIGURE 8.5*b*.   We test the procedures (here, Move) at the bottom of the top-down diagram as a separate program. It determines the distance a man goes after 10 random steps.

random	round(random)	Step
0.25	0	1
0.75	1	−1

TABLE FOR FIGURE 8.5*b*. Shows how Step:= 1 − 2 * round(random) works.

```
The X values are:
−1  0  1  2  3  2  3  2  3  4
```

FIGURE 8.5*c*.   Running the program of Figure 8.5*b*.

Step II: Making Part of the Previous Program a Procedure

Let's make the statements that generated the man's position on the X-axis

```
Step:= 1 - 2 * round(random);
X:= X + Step
```

a procedure and alter the previous program so that it activates it, as shown in Figure 8.5d. To check the program, run it (Figure 8.5e).

STEP II: MAKING PART OF THE PREVIOUS PROGRAM A PROCEDURE

```
PROGRAM RandomWalk2(output);
(* Random walk in one dimension *)
VAR X, Step, Count, Index:integer;

PROCEDURE Move(VAR X:integer);
(* Produces the position on the grid *)
VAR Step:integer;
BEGIN
  Step:= 1 - 2 * round(random);
  X:= X + Step
END (* Move *);

BEGIN (* RandomWalk2 *)
  randomize;
  Count:=0;
  X:=0;
  (* Take 10 random steps *)
  writeln('The X values are:');
  FOR Index:= 1 TO 10 DO BEGIN
    Move(X);
    write(X:3)
  END (* FOR *);
END.
```

FIGURE 8.5d. We write part of the previous program as procedure Move and activate it in the main program.

```
The X values are:
 1  2  1  0  1  0  -1  -2  -1  0
```

FIGURE 8.5e. Running the program of Figure 8.5d.

Step III: Using the Procedure of the Previous Program for One-Dimensional Random Walk

Let's alter the previous program so that it determines how many steps are required to reach either $X = 6$ or -6 by placing the activation of Move in the following loop

```
WHILE abs(X) <= 5 DO Begin
  Move(X);
  write(X:2);
  Count: = Count + 1;
END (* WHILE *);
```

as shown in Figure 8.5*f*. Here we have implemented the bottom-up design, since we have included in our program the pretested procedure Move. The results of running the program are shown in Figure 8.5*g*.

STEP III: USING THE PROCEDURE OF THE PREVIOUS PROGRAM FOR ONE-DIMENSIONAL RANDOM WALK

```
PROGRAM RandomWalk(output)
VAR X, Index, Count:integer;

PROCEDURE MOVE(VAR X:integer);          {See page 319}

BEGIN (* RandomWalk *)
  randomize;
  Count:=0;
  X:=0;
  writeln('The X values are:');
  WHILE abs(X) <= 5 DO Begin
    Move(X);
    write(X:2);
    Count:= Count + 1;
  END (* WHILE *);
  writeln;
  writeln('# of steps is: ', Count)
END.
```

FIGURE 8.5f. We use Move in a program that determines how many steps it takes the man to reach $X = 6$ or -6. The heading for the procedure is also shown. If you run the program you must include the entire procedure.

```
The X values are:
1 2 3 2 1 2 1 0 −1 −2 −3 −2 −3 −2 −3 −2 −3 −4 −5 −4 −5 −6
# of steps is: 22
```

FIGURE 8.5g. Running the program of Figure 8.5f.

Step IV: Two-Dimensional Random Walk

Let's convert the previous program into one that does a two-dimensional walk by including in the present program another random number, Switch. This number determines whether the man will walk in the Y or the X direction. Since this decision is like flipping a coin, write Switch:= round(random). Half the time its value will be 0, the other half 1. In the CASE statement, Switch determines whether Move(X) or Move(Y) is activated, as shown in Figure 8.5*h*.

```
WHILE (abs(X) <= 5) AND (abs(Y) <= 5) DO Begin
   Switch:= round(random);
   (* Switch determines whether X or Y is incremented *)
   CASE Switch OF
      0: Move(X);
      1: Move(Y)
   END (* CASE *);
   write( '(', X, ',', Y, ')');
   Count:= Count + 1;
END (* WHILE *);
```

The results of running the program are shown in Figure 8.5*i*.

STEP IV: TWO-DIMENSIONAL RANDOM WALK

```
PROGRAM RandomWalk3(output);
(* Two-dimensional random walk *)
VAR X, Y, Switch, Count:integer;

PROCEDURE Move(VAR X:integer);                    {See page 319}

BEGIN (* RandomWalk *)
  randomize;
  Count:=0;
  X:=0;
  Y:=0;
  (* Generate steps until wall is crossed *)
  writeln('The (X, Y) values are:');
  WHILE (abs(X) <= 5) AND (abs(Y) <= 5) DO BEGIN
    Switch:= round(random);
    (* Switch determines whether X or Y is incremented *)
    CASE Switch OF
      0: Move(X);
      1: Move(Y)
    END (* CASE *);
    write( '(', X, ',', Y, ')');
    Count:= Count + 1;
  END (* WHILE *);
    writeln;
    writeln('# of steps is: ', Count)
  END.
```

FIGURE 8.5h. By including a second random number, Switch, the program randomly chooses the direction in which the man should move. The heading for the procedure is also shown.

```
The (X, Y) values are:
(1,0)(2,0)(3,0),(3,-1),(3,0),(3,1),(3,0),(3,1)(2,1)(3,1)(2,1)(2,2)
(2,3)(1,3)(2,3)(3,3 )(2,3)(1,3)(0,3)(-1,3)(0,3)(-1,3)(0,3)(-1,3)(0,3)
(-1,3)(0,3)(0,4)(1,4)(0,4)(-1,4 )(-1,3)(-1,4)(-1,5)(0,5)(0,6)
# of steps is: 36
```

FIGURE 8.5i. Running the program of Figure 8.5h.

8.7

THE EOLN FUNCTION

We've seen that as you type data into a program, they are stored in a series of locations collectively called the *input buffer*, and when you hit the carriage return, the end-of-line mark is stored in the next location in the buffer. For instance, if you type qwerty and then hit the carriage return, the input buffer appears as

qwerty~

where "~" represents the location occupied by the end-of-line mark. Then the data are transferred to the locations indicated in the read or readln statement as these statements are executed. By using the eoln function—it stands for *end of line* and is a standard function—the computer can determine whether the next item in the buffer is the end-of-line mark. If it is, the eoln function returns true; otherwise, false. This function enables us to use the WHILE loop without priming it. Although we will first use the eoln function with keyboard input, its major use is with files saved on a disk.

BEFORE YOU BEGIN

If we did not know about the buffer, we might think that the eoln function had the magical power of predicting whether or not the next item to be read is the end-of-line mark.

Figure 8.6*a* uses the eoln function to determine how many characters there are in a word terminated by a carriage return:

```
WHILE NOT eoln DO BEGIN
    read(Ch);
    Count:= Count + 1;
    writeln('character ', Count:2, ' is ', Ch)
END (* WHILE *);
```

COUNTING THE NUMBER OF CHARACTERS IN A WORD

```
Program LetterCount(input, output);
(* Program counts the number of characters in a word *)
VAR Count: integer;
   Ch: char;
BEGIN
  Count:= 0;
  writeln('Print a word and then hit the carriage return.');
  WHILE NOT eoln DO BEGIN
    read(Ch);
    Count:= Count + 1;
    writeln('character ', Count:2, ' is ', Ch);
  END (* WHILE *);
  writeln;
  writeln('The number of characters in the word is ', Count)
END.
```

FIGURE 8.6a.   The word we type and the end-of-line mark are stored in the buffer. Each time the WHILE is executed, the computer looks at the next character in the buffer. If it is the end-of-line mark, the value of eoln is true.

Because the eoln function looks ahead in the buffer, we do not precede the WHILE with read(Ch). How the WHILE NOT eoln works is shown in the table for Figure 8.6a for the input qwerty shown in Figure 8.6b. After qwerty is typed, the buffer looks like this:

qwerty~

Let's look at the last three lines of the table:

Ch	Count	Next character in buffer	eoln
r	4	t	False
t	5	y	False
y	6	~	True

While the next item in the buffer is not the end-of-line mark (the "~") the value of eoln is false, so the loop is executed again. However, when the "y" is read, the next item in the buffer is the "~". Thus when the WHILE phrase is executed the next time, NOT eoln is false and the program quits the loop. The results of running the program are shown in Figure 8.6b. Since the readln clears the buffer, when you read data in a loop using the eoln function, you must use the read and not the readln.

This program may be used to determine how many digits there are in an integer as well, as shown in Figure 8.6c.

Ch	Count	Next character in buffer	eoln on next loop execution
q	1	w	False
w	2	e	False
e	3	r	False
r	4	t	False
t	5	y	False
y	6	~	True

TABLE FOR FIGURE 8.6a.   When the next item in the buffer is the end-of-line mark (shown here by a "~"), the loop is skipped.

```
Print a word and then hit return.
qwerty
character 1 is q
character 2 is w
character 3 is e
character 4 is r
character 5 is t
character 6 is y
The number of characters in the word is 6
```

FIGURE 8.6b.   Running the program of Figure 8.6a. When you use eoln, you must use the read and not the readln to read data.

```
Print a word and then hit the carriage return.
65432
character 1 is 6
character 2 is 5
character 3 1s 4
character 4 is 3
character 5 is 2
The number of characters in the word is 5
```

FIGURE 8.6c.   Running the program of Figure 8.6b so that it determines the number of digits in an integer.

In Figure 8.7*a*, the `eoln` function is used to determine the average of an arbitrary number of integers typed on a line. The principle involved here is the same as that of the previous program, but now the program reads integers instead of characters. This means that the blank is no longer read as a character, but as a delimiter. For this reason, after you type the last integer, you must immediately hit the carriage return, as shown in Figure 8.7*b*. If you don't, and type blanks before hitting the carriage return, as shown in Figure 8.7*c*, the computer thinks that there are more integers to follow. It treats the "˜" as a blank and therefore goes past the "˜" in the buffer. Since it finds nothing to read there, the program halts, waiting for more data to be typed.

The previous example underlines the fact that all data are read as characters; otherwise, the computer could not both read the integers and check for the end-of-line mark, a character. As noted in Chapter 5, Pascal reads integers as characters and then transforms them into numerical values.

AVERAGING THE INTEGERS TYPED ON A LINE

```
Program NumberCount(input, output);
(* Program averages integers typed on a line *)
VAR number, Count: integer;
  Sum, average: real;
BEGIN
  Count: = 0;
  Sum: = 0.0;
  writeln('Type a line of integers and then hit the carriage return.');
  WHILE NOT eoln DO
  BEGIN
    read(number);
    Count: = Count + 1;
    Sum: = Sum + number;
    writeln('Number ', Count:2, ' is ', number:4);
  END (* WHILE *);
  writeln;
  average: = Sum / Count;
  writeln('The number of digits read is ', Count:2);
  writeln('Their average is ', average:3:1)
        xin   END.
```

FIGURE 8.7a. The program sums and counts the integers written on a line until the end-of-line mark is encountered. It then skips the WHILE and calculates the average.

THE LAST NUMBER TYPED MUST BE FOLLOWED IMMEDIATELY BY A CARRIAGE RETURN

```
Type a line of integers and then hit the carriage return.
12 23 43 23 45 56 23~
number 1 is 12, number 2 is 23, number 3 is 43, number 4 is 23,
number 5 is 45,
number 6 is 56, number 7 is 23,
The number of digits read is 7
Their average is 32.1
```

FIGURE 8.7b. A carriage return (marked by the "~") must immediately follow the last integer typed. The "~" indicates where a carriage return appears, the "~" is not typed.

ONE OR MORE BLANKS SEPARATES THE LAST INTEGER FROM THE CARRIAGE RETURN

```
Type a line of integers and then hit the carriage return.
12 34 56  ~
number 1 is 12, number 2 is 34, number 3 is 36,
```

FIGURE 8.7c. If one or more blanks precede the carriage return, the compiler thinks that there are more integers to follow and reads the "~" as a blank. The program then halts, waiting for more data.

8.8

THE EOF FUNCTION

The computer interprets a group of lines of data (each, of course, ending with a carriage return) concluding with a line containing only a carriage return as a file called the *input file* (similarly, it treats everything written by the program as a file called the *output file*). It interprets the last carriage return as the end-of-line mark followed by an end-of-file mark. The eof function looks at the next data item in the buffer. If it is an end-of-file mark, the value of eof is true; otherwise, it is false. Like the eoln function, the eof function enables you to use a WHILE loop without priming it; its major use is with disk files. The difference is that the eoln determines the end of a line, whereas the eof determines the end of a series of lines.

The program of Figure 8.8a calculates the average of numbers read on separate lines. Each time you hit the carriage return, the previous item in the buffer is transferred to the location referred to in the read or readln, here Number. When the end-of-file mark is in the next location in the buffer, the value of eof is true and therefore NOT eof is false. Consequently, the program quits the loop and calculates the average, as shown in Figure 8.8b.

Note that on some systems you must hit the Z key while the Ctrl key is depressed in order to transmit the end-of-file mark to the computer.

USING THE EOF FUNCTION

```
Program NumberCount(input, output);
(* Program averages integers typed on a line *)
VAR number, Count: integer;
   Sum, average: real;
BEGIN
   Count:= 0;
   Sum:= 0.0;
   writenl(' After each integer typed, hit the carriage return. ');
   WHILE NOT eof DO
   BEGIN
      read(number);
      Count:= Count + 1;
      Sum:= Sum + number;
   END (* WHILE *);
   writeln;
   average:= Sum / Count;
   writeln('The number of digits read is ', Count:2);
   writeln('Their average is ', average:3:1)
END.
```

FIGURE 8.8a.   The WHILE loop executes until an end-of-file mark is encountered. On some computers you must hit the Z key while depressing the Ctrl key in order to send an end-of-file mark to the buffer.

```
After each integer typed, hit the carriage return.
12
23
34
45
~
The number of digits read is 4
Their average is 28.5
```

FIGURE 8.8b.   Running the program of Figure 8.8a. We type a carriage return after each integer and terminate the data by typing nothing on the last line except a carriage return (indicated here by a "~").

8.9

READING A PARAGRAPH

The program of Figure 8.9a reads the lines of a paragraph. Remember that in Figure 8.6a the program segment

```
WHILE NOT eoln DO
    BEGIN
        read(Ch);
        write(Ch);
END (* WHILE NOT eoln *);
```

reads a line of characters until the next the symbol in the buffer is the end-of-line mark and then prints the line just read. Because of WHILE NOT eoln DO, the last character read is the last character on the line. The next item to be read is the next one in the buffer, the end-of-line mark. In order to read a paragraph, we want the program to read the next line, and since it serves no purpose for the program to read the end-of-line mark, we follow this WHILE loop with a readln. Since the next line of output should start on a new line, we include a writeln here as well. The results of running the program are shown in Figure 8.9b.

TEST YOURSELF

QUESTION: The following does not include a readln. What output does it produce? The input is My country tis of thee, followed by a carriage return.

```
WHILE NOT eof DO BEGIN
    WHILE NOT eoln DO BEGIN
        read(Ch);
        write(Ch);
    END (* WHILE NOT eoln *);
    write('X')
END (* WHILE NOT eof *);
```

ANSWER: If we do not include the readln in the program, the pointer remains at the end-of-line mark in the buffer after the computer reads the first line of input. Thus the value of eoln remains true and that of NOT eoln remains false, so the computer skips read(Ch); write(Ch). Since no statement changes the position of the pointer, it never reaches the eof mark. Thus the program enters an infinite loop. It prints

READING AND PRINTING A PARAGRAPH

```
PROGRAM TextPrint(input, output);
(* Program prints a paragraph read in *)
VAR Ch:char
BEGIN
  writeln('Print your paragraph');
  WHILE NOT eof DO BEGIN
    WHILE NOT eoln DO BEGIN
        read(Ch);
        write(Ch);
    END (* WHILE NOT eoln *);
    readln;
    writeln
  END (* WHILE NOT eof *);
  writeln('Thats all folks')
END.
```

FIGURE 8.9a.   The WHILE NOT eoln DO loop executes until an end-of-line mark is encountered.

```
Print your paragraph
My country tis of thee,
My country tis of thee,
Sweet land of liberty,
Sweet land of liberty,
Of thee I sing.
Of thee I sing.
Thats all folks
```

FIGURE 8.9b.   Running the program of Figure 8.9a. Every line we type is repeated by the program.

```
My country tis of theeXXXXXXXXXXXXXXXXXXXXXXXXXXXXXXXXXXXXXXXXX
XXXXXXXXXXXXXXXXXXXXXXXXXXXXXXXXXXXXXXXXXXXXXXXXXXXXXXXXXXXXXXX
XXXXXXXXX....
```

The program never gets the chance to read the next line of input.

QUESTION: What will the following produce upon reading a paragraph? This is the same set of statements appearing in Figure 7.9*a*, except that we have replaced readln with readln(Ch).

```
WHILE NOT eof DO BEGIN
    WHILE NOT eoln DO BEGIN
        read(Ch);
        write(Ch);
    END (* WHILE NOT eoln *);
    readln(Ch);
    writeln
END (* WHILE NOT eof *);
```

ANSWER: The output is the paragraph inputted, just as in Figure 7.9*b*. The statement readln(Ch) reads the end-of-line mark.

Note that if we read the end-of-line mark and print it, it will be printed as a blank. However, if we read the end-of-file mark, an execution error will result. Finally, it is an error to activate the eoln when eof is true.

8.10
USING A COUNTER TO TERMINATE A WHILE LOOP: OFF BY ONE ERRORS

Let's alter the program of Figure 8.10*a* so that it counts only the characters that appear in one line (up to 80 characters). If we type more than 80 characters, the program should count only the first 80. We do this by including a test for the counter Count in the WHILE statement (see Figure 8.10*a*):

```
WHILE (Ch <> Period) AND (Count <= LineLength) DO
```

When we run the program, we type input that overflows the line. The result for the number of characters read (Figure 8.10*b*) is 81 instead of the correct result, 80. This is appropriately called an *off by one error.* The result is one more than it should be because after the program reads the 80th character, the expression (Count <= LineLength) is still true. Consequently, it executes the loop one more time, increasing the count to 81. We correct this error by changing the "<=" to a "<" in the WHILE, so that it is now WHILE (Ch <> Period) AND (Count < BufferLength) DO.

USING A COUNTER TO TERMINATE A WHILE LOOP: OFF BY ONE ERRORS

```
Program LetterCount(input, output);
(* Program counts the number of characters in a sentence *)
CONST Period = '.';
  LineLength = 80;
VAR Count: integer;
  Ch: char;
BEGIN
  Count:= 0;
  writeln('Write a sentence and end it with a period.');
  read(Ch);
  WHILE (Ch <> Period) AND (Count <= LineLength) DO BEGIN
    Count:= Count + 1;
    read(Ch)
  END (* WHILE *);
  writeln('The number of characters including blanks is ', Count:2)
END.
```

FIGURE 8.10a.   We use a counter to terminate a WHILE loop. The program counts the characters inputted only until they fill one line on the screen.

```
Write a sentence and end it with a period.
aaaaaaaaaaaaaaaaaaaaaaaaaaaaaaaaaaaaaaaaaaaaaaaaaaaaaaaaaaaaaaaaaaaaaaaaa
aaaaaaaaaaaa
The number of characters including blanks is 81
```

FIGURE 8.10b.   Running the program of Figure 8.10a. Because of the "=" in Count <= LineLength, the final value of the counter is one more than it should be. We correct this error by using a "<" only, thus writing WHILE (Ch <> Period) AND (Count <= LineLength) DO BEGIN.

We have now presented the three ways of terminating a WHILE loop:

1. Using a sentinel.
2. Using an eof, or eoln.
3. Using a counter, e.g., count <= LineLength

We defer the discussion of the fourth way—using a boolean variable in the WHILE, e.g., WHILE Sorted DO—until we have a cogent reason to use this technique.

8.11

USING THE DEFAULT FILES IN THE STANDARD INPUT/OUTPUT SUBPROGRAMS

Information you've typed at the keyboard as input to your programs comprises what is known as the *standard input file*. This file is designated as input. The *standard output file* is the output displayed on the monitor screen when you run your program and is designated as output.

If you wish, you can place input as the first parameter in the input standard procedures read and readln. You can, for instance, write read(input, Ch) instead of read(Ch); readln(input, Ch) instead of readln(Ch), and readln(input) instead of readln. Similarly, you can use input as the parameter of the eoln and eof functions and thus write eof(input) and eoln(input). All of this would explicitly state that you're reading data from the standard input file input. If you don't use input as a parameter in these standard subprograms, the compiler assumes that input is a parameter. For this reason, the input file is called the *default input file*.

Similarly, output is called the *default output file*. If you wished, you could write write(output, Ch) instead of write(Ch) and writeln(output, Ch) instead of writeln(Ch). All of this is shown in Table 8.3. The next section discusses how the program communicates with nondefault files.

USING THE DEFAULT FILES

With default file	Without default file
read(input,Ch)	read(Ch)
readln(input,Ch)	readln(Ch)
readln(input)	readln
eoln(input)	eoln
eof(input)	eof
write(output,Ch)	write(Ch)
writeln(output,Ch)	writeln(Ch)
writeln(output)	writeln

TABLE 8.3. You may use input as the first parameter of an input statement, and output as the first parameter of an output statement. If you don't, the compiler assumes that they are the first parameter. For this reason, input is called the "default input file" and output the "default output file."

8.12

USING TEXT FILES: AN INTRODUCTION TO DATA FILES

In the course of writing programs, you'll find it necessary to use the same set of data many times. For instance:

1. You may write several versions of a program that will use the same data, or

2. You'll compile a program many times as you debug it and each time require the same data set, or

3. You may write different programs that require the same data.

Because of situations like these, it is convenient to save data for a program permanently on a disk in what is called a *data file*. A data file can either be input to or output from a program. The size of the saved file is limited only by the storage capacity of the disk. Files that exist external to the computer's memory—for example, data files or the input or output files—are called *external files*. Files saved in the computer's memory are called *internal files*. Data files can be permanently saved on a disk.

In this chapter, we discuss a type of data file called a *text file*. Text files derive their name from the fact that they consist of characters, just as a literary text does. A text file can store both numerical and char information and is structured as lines of data. Each line ends with an end-of-line marker, and the entire file ends with an end-of-file marker. The input and output default files, although not data files, are also text files. Other types of files consist of binary information.

The program, shown in Figure 8.11a, is similar to the one in Figure 8.9a. It too reads a paragraph from the standard input file; but instead of copying the paragraph to the standard output file, it copies it onto the text file Parag. For that reason, we add Parag to the program heading, PROGRAM Paragraph (input, output, Parag). We can also write the heading as PROGRAM Paragraph(Parag, input, output); the order in which we place the files in the program heading is immaterial. Any file name that appears in the program heading is an external file. Thus, input, output, and Parag, the files we have used in the program heading so far, are all considered external files. The nondefault external files, here Parag, can be saved at the end of the program's execution, so that they can be used at some later date as input. Note that any file except input and output can be used as either an input or an output file. The input file can only be used for input, and the output file can only be used for output.

We declare Parag to be a text file in

```
Parag:text;
```

where text is a predefined type. Any file that is declared in the VAR declaration but does not appear in the program heading is an internal file and will be erased

COPYING A PARAGRAPH TO A TEXT FILE

```
PROGRAM Paragraph(input, output, Parag);
(* Copies a paragraph to a file *)
VAR Ch :Char;
    Parag:text;
BEGIN
  writeln('Please type your paragraph');
  rewrite(Parag);
  WHILE NOT eof DO BEGIN
    WHILE NOT eoln DO BEGIN
      read(Ch)
      write(Parag,Ch)
    END (* WHILE NOT eoln *);
    readln;
    writeln(Parag)
  END (* WHILE NOT eof *)
END.
```

FIGURE 8.11a.   The same as the previous program, but now the output is written to data file. Both write(Parag, Ch) and writeln(Parag) write their output to file Parag, the latter producing an end-of-line mark on the file.

at the end of the program's execution. Thus if we wrote VAR Parag, Temp: text in the program of Figure 8.11a, the file Temp would be an internal file. We could use it to both read and write data.

A data file has a buffer associated with it, and of course, this buffer has a pointer that indicates where the next item is to be read or written. Before a program can write any information to a data file, you must position the pointer at the beginning of the file. The standard procedure rewrite does this for the file used as its parameter. Thus rewrite(Parag) repositions the pointer at the beginning of the file Parag. The rewrite procedure also erases any information previously written on the file. You must place rewrite(Parag) in the program before the appearance of a write or writeln that refers to the file Parag.

When you write on a data file that is a text file, you can use either a write or a writeln; however, you must include the file variable as the first parameter. We thus use write(Parag, Ch) to write the characters and writeln(Parag) to start a new line. How information is written on the file is shown in the table for Figure 8.11a.

When the program is run, the only information that appears on the screen is the prompt Please type your paragraph and the paragraph typed, as shown in Figure 8.11b. You don't see the information after it is typed on the file. In

My country tis of thee~ ^

TABLE FOR FIGURE 8.11a.   When `writeln(Parag)` is executed, the computer—since it has written the first line of output—places an End-of-line mark ("~") on file `Parag` and advances the pointer (indicated by a "^") on the file.

```
Please type your paragraph
my country tis of thee
sweet land of liberty
of thee i sing
```

FIGURE 8.11b.   Running the program of Figure 8.11a. We type a paragraph to be copied onto the file. File `Parag` must appear in the programming heading. The statement `rewrite(Parag)` erases the file and sets the pointer at the beginning of the file.

order to see it, let's write a program that reads information from the file, as shown in Figure 8.12a.

This program is similar to the one in Figure 8.9a. It too copies a paragraph to the standard output file, but instead of reading the paragraph from the standard input file, it reads it from the text file Parag. We thus change the program heading to PROGRAM Paragraph1(Parag, output).

Before a program can read any information from a data file, the pointer must be positioned at the beginning of the file. The standard procedure reset does this for the file used as its parameter. Thus reset(Parag) does this for Parag; unlike rewrite, procedure reset does not erase the file. You must place reset(Parag) in the program before the appearance of any statement that refers to file Parag.

Since you'll be testing for the end-of-file for Parag, you must use eof‾(Parag). Similarly, since you'll be reading information from Parag, you must use read(Parag, Ch) and readln(Parag). When readln(Parag) is executed, the computer skips the end-of-line mark ("‾"), and advances the pointer to what is, in effect, the beginning of the next line in the file, as shown in the table for Figure 8.12a.

When the program is run, as shown in Figure 8.12b, the paragraph copied to Parag in the previous program reappears.

Reading Characters and Numbers from Text Files

The default files input and output are automatically declared as text files. We've seen that we can read both numeric and character data from the default file input, depending on how we declare the locations into which the data will be read. This is true for any text file. For instance, if 12 appears in the text file Parag, the two characters in 12 can be read into the two character locations One and Two if we use read(One, Two) to read them. Alternatively, 12 can be read into the integer location Number if we use read(Number) to read the characters. This is because the read automatically converts these characters to their numerical equivalents.

TEST YOURSELF

QUESTION: What is wrong with the following program fragment that should sum the numbers read from a file?

```
Sum: = 0;
read(File1, Number);
WHILE NOT eoln(File1) DO BEGIN
   Sum: = Sum + Number;
   read(File1, Number)
END (* WHILE *);
writenl('The sum = ', sum:4)
```

COPYING A PARAGRAPH FROM A TEXT FILE

```
PROGRAM Paragraphl( Parag, output);
(* Reads a paragraph from a file *)
VAR Ch :char;
   Parag:text;
BEGIN
   reset(Parag);
   WHILE NOT eof(Parag) DO BEGIN
     WHILE NOT eoln(Parag) DO BEGIN
        read(Parag,Ch);
        write( Ch);
     END (* WHILE NOT eoln *);
     readln(Parag);
     writeln
   END (* WHILE NOT eof *)
END.
```

FIGURE 8.12a.   This is the same as the previous program, except that characters are read from file Parag. The statement reset(Parag) sets the pointer at the beginning of the file but does not erase it.

```
My country tis of thee~Sweet
                          ^
```

TABLE FOR FIGURE 8.12a.   When readln(Parag) is executed, the computer—since it has read the first line on the file—skips the end-of-line mark ("~") on file Parag and advances the pointer on the file.

```
my country tis of thee
sweet land of liberty
of thee i sing
```

FIGURE 8.12b.   Running the program of Figure 8.12a.

The numbers on the file appear as

$$\text{File1}\quad\boxed{\texttt{12 43 522 61}^{\sim}}$$

ANSWER: When the number being read is 61, the end-of-line mark is in the buffer; thus eoln(File1) is true. This means that the computer will not execute the loop again, but it also means that 61 will not be added to the sum. To correct this, delete the read that precedes the loop, and change the order of the statements in the loop.

Summary of Pascal File Functions Covered

The eoln Function　The value of the eoln function is true if the file or buffer pointer is at the end-of-line mark or if the value of eof is true; otherwise, it is false. The eoln function cannot be used with a binary file.

The eof Function　The value of the eof function is true if the file or buffer pointer is at the end-of-file mark.

Facts About Files　Some facts to remember about files are as follows:

1. A file can be passed to a subprogram only as a variable parameter.
2. You cannot assign one file to another. Thus, if Parag and Temp are two text files, Parag: = Temp is illegal.
3. The input file is automatically reset and the output file is automatically rewritten at the beginning of a program.
4. The eoln function can be used only with text files.
5. Once a text file has been opened for writing (with a rewrite), you can't read from it in the same program unless you open it for reading by using a reset at a later point in the program.
6. Once a text file has been opened for reading (with a reset), you can't write on it in the same program unless you open it for writing by using a rewrite at a later point in the program.

TEST YOURSELF

QUESTION (a):　Write a program that copies numbers to a file.
ANSWER:

```
PROGRAM Question4a(input, output, Data);
VAR Data:text;
   Number:real;
BEGIN
   rewrite(Data);
   writeln('Type your data');
```

```
        WHILE NOT eoln DO BEGIN
           read(Number);
           write(Data, Number);
        END (* WHILE *);
     END.
```

Since the data 12 34 1 41 9 will be typed on one line (followed by the carriage return), use the read and eoln here. Because we use write(Data, Number) and not writeln to write on the file, the file will consist of one line.

QUESTION (b):   Write a program that will average the numbers read from the file Data.

ANSWER:

```
        PROGRAM Question4b(input, output, Data);
        VAR Data:text;
           Number, Sum, Average:real;
           Count:integer;
        BEGIN
           reset(Data);
           Sum:=0.0;
           Count:=0;
           WHILE NOT eoln(Data) DO BEGIN
              read(Data, Number);
              Sum:= Sum + Number;
              Count:= Count + 1
           END (* WHILE *);
           Average:= Sum / Count;
           writeln('Sum = ', Sum:10:1, ' Count= ',
              Count:4, ' Average = ', Average);
        END.
```

Since the file consists of one line, use read(Data, Number) and eoln here instead of a readln and eof. What happens if you do use readln(Data, Number) and eof(Data)? The computer assigns 12 to Number and then skips to the end-of-line mark. Since there are no more data, eof is true. Thus only one number would be read, and the average would be the value of that number.

QUESTION (c):   What would be the consequence of using an eof in QUESTION (a)?

ANSWER: In order to avoid errors, you'd have to use `readln` and `writeln` throughout. Thus the loop in (a) would become:

```
WHILE NOT eof DO BEGIN
    readln(Number);
    writeln(Data, Number);
END (* WHILE *);
```

and the beginning of the loop in (b) would become

```
WHILE NOT eof(Data) DO BEGIN
    readln(Data, Number);
```

PROGRAMMING PITFALLS

1. If you write integer or real numbers on a text file, you must make sure that the last number on a line is immediately followed by a carriage return without any intervening blanks. If this is not done, an error will occur when you read the numbers from the file using a `read` and the `eoln` function.

2. Although a text file is a file of characters, it is not equivalent to FILE OF char on all implementations of Pascal. Thus, given the following declaration

```
VAR FileA:FILE OF char;
    Number:integer;
```

on some implementations of Pascal, the statement `write(FileA, Number)` will cause a compiler error indicating a type mismatch because `Number` is an integer. Had we declared `FileA:text`, we could have written an integer on the file on all implementations.

CHAPTER REVIEW

The WHILE and REPEAT Loops

Both WHILE and REPEAT loops must include a statement that changes the boolean expression that determines whether or not the execution of the loop should terminate. A REPEAT loop is executed at least once, whereas a WHILE loop does not have to be executed at all.

The EOLN and EOF Functions

The eoln and eof functions determine whether the next item to be read is the end-of-line or end-of-file mark, respectively. The program should not read the end-of-line mark, but if it does, an error will not occur; however, reading the end-of-file mark will produce an error.

Summary of the Pascal Statements Presented in This Chapter

The WHILE Statement   The form of the WHILE statement is WHILE followed by one or more blanks, followed by a boolean expression, followed by one or more blanks, followed by DO. Examples:

```
WHILE NOT eoln DO
WHILE A > B DO
WHILE Sorted DO
```

The REPEAT Loop   The form of the REPEAT loop is REPEAT followed by one or more statements, followed by UNTIL, followed by one or more blanks, followed by a boolean expression. Example:

```
REPEAT
   read(X);
   Count: = Count + 1
UNTIL Count = 100
```

NEW TERMS

bottom-up design	output file
data file	priming the WHILE
default input file	random walk
default output file	REPEAT loop
external file	sentinel
infinite loop	standard input file
input file	standard output file
internal file	text file
off by one error	WHILE loop

EXERCISES

1. Give sample input for the following program. What is the output?

```
PROGRAM Prob1(input, output);
VAR Variable1, Variable2:real;
  Operator:char;
BEGIN
  read(Variable1);
  read(Operator);
  WHILE Operator <> '=' DO BEGIN
    read(Variable2);
    CASE Operator OF
      '+': Variable1:= Variable1 + Variable2;
      '-': Variable1:= Variable1 - Variable2;
      '*': Variable1:= Variable1 * Variable2;
      '/': Variable1:= Variable1 / Variable2;
    END (* CASE *);
    read(Operator)
  END (* WHILE *);
  writeln(Variable1)
END.
```

2. What does the following program do? Which standard function does it resemble? How does it differ? Test it with the following input: 4 9 25.

```
PROGRAM Prob2(input, output);
VAR Number, Answer, Counter:integer;
BEGIN
  writeln('Type your number');
  WHILE NOT eoln DO BEGIN
    read(Number);
    writeln('For input ', Number);
    Answer:= 0;
    Counter:= 0;
    WHILE Number > Counter DO BEGIN
      Answer:= Answer + 1;
      Number:= Number - Counter;
      Counter:= Counter + 2
    END (* WHILE *);
```

```
          writeln(' Result is ', Answer);
          writeln('Type your number');
      END (* WHILE NOT eoln *)
    END.
```

3. What does the following program do? Test it with the input 1342 and then with 42613.

```
PROGRAM Prob3(input, output);
VAR Number, Digit:integer;
BEGIN
   writeln('Type a number');
   read(Number);
   writeln;
   REPEAT
     Digit:= Number MOD 10;
     Number:= Number DIV 10;
     write(Digit:1)
   UNTIL Number = 0
END.
```

4. What does the following program do? Test it with the input 24532 and then with 45.

```
PROGRAM Prob4(input, output);
VAR Original, Number, Counter:integer;
BEGIN
   Counter:= 0;
   writeln('Type an integer');
   read(Number);
   Original:= Number;
   REPEAT
     Number:=trunc(Number / 10);
     Counter:= Counter + 1
   UNTIL Number = 0;
   writeln('For ', Original, ' we have ', Counter)
END.
```

5. What is the output of the following program?

```
PROGRAM Problem5(input, output);
VAR Index, Variable1, Variable2:integer;
BEGIN
  Variable1:= 300;
  Variable2:= 300;
  FOR Index:= 1 TO 6 DO BEGIN
    Variable1:= 100 − Variable1;
    Variable2:= 100 + Variable1;
    writeln(Index:4, Variable1:6, Variable2:6)
  END (* Index *)
END.
```

Rewrite it, using a WHILE loop instead. Rewrite it, using a REPEAT loop instead.

6. What is the output of the following program, given the input 5 10 15 10 5 5 0 10 7 5?

```
PROGRAM Prob6(input, output);
CONST Limit = 8;
VAR Counter, Sum, InputValue:integer;
  Test:boolean;
BEGIN
  Sum:= 10;
  Counter:= 1;
  Test:= false;
  writeln('Type your integers on one line');
  WHILE (Counter < Limit) AND NOT Test DO BEGIN
    read(InputValue);
    IF InputValue > 10 THEN
      Sum:= Sum + InputValue
    ELSE IF InputValue = 0 THEN
      Test:= True;
    Counter:= Counter + 1
  END (* WHILE *);
  writeln('Sum = ', Sum, ' InputValue = ', InputValue)
END.
```

7. Indicate whether the following statements are valid or invalid.
   a. WHILE X < Y
       X: = X + Y
   b. writeln(eoln);
   c. WHILE Z <> Y DO BEGIN Z: =U + 1 END (* WHILE *);
   d. REPEAT EachOf; TheQuestions UNTIL Finished;
   e. WHILE Ch <> Final DO Ch: = succ(Ch)
   f. REPEAT BEGIN read(Ch); N: = N + 1 END;

8. Why would the following program not print the prompt message
   properly?

```
Program NumberCount;
(* Program averages integers typed on a line *)
VAR Number, Count: integer;
   Sum, Average: real;
BEGIN
   Count: = 0;
   Sum: = 0.0;
   WHILE NOT eof DO BEGIN
      writeln('After each integer typed, hit the carriage
      return. ');
      read(Number);
      Count: = Count + 1;
      Sum: = Sum + Number;
   END (* WHILE *);
   writeln;
   Average: = Sum / Count;
   writeln('The Number of digits read is ', Count:2);
   writeln('Their Average is ', Average:3:1 )
END.
```

9. Why does the program of Figure 8.1a count the characters read in the
   previous execution of the loop? Would it make any difference if we
   interchanged Count : = Count + 1 and read(Ch) as follows?

```
Count: = 0;
read(Ch);
WHILE Ch <> Period DO BEGIN
   read(Ch);
   Count: = Count + 1
END (* WHILE *);
```

10. What is the criterion for interchanging the order of two statements?

11. In the two programs displayed in the last QUESTION in the text, the following loops were used, respectively:

```
WHILE NOT eoln DO BEGIN
    read(Number);
    write(Data, Number)
END {WHILE};

WHILE NOT eoln(Data) DO BEGIN
    read(Data, Number);
    Sum: = Sum + Number;
    Count: = Count + 1
END {WHILE};
```

Would it make a difference
a. if `writeln(Data, Number)` was used to write the data to the file?
b. if `writeln(Data, Number)` was used to write the data and `readln(Data, Number)` was used to read them?
c. if `write(Data, Number)` was used to write the data and `readln-(Data, Number)` was used to read them?

Programming Problems

12. Alter the program of Figure 8.1*a* so that it determines the number of letters in the sentence.

13. Alter the program of Figure 8.1*a* so that it includes only one `read` statement.

14. Write a program that reads a number and then stores it with the digits reversed in another variable. Hint: See exercise 3.

15. Write a program that reads an integer and then prints it with commas in the proper places. Thus 123456 would be printed as 123,456.

16. Write a program that reads an integer and then stores it with commas in the proper places in a variable. Thus 123456 would be stored as 123,456. In order to store the commas and the digits, store the `ord` values of the characters read.

17. Write a program that reads a number and then prints it in a field one greater than the number of digits in the number. Thus 2342 would be printed in a field five columns wide.

18. Write a program that reads a real number and then determines how many digits precede and follow the decimal point. Hint: Read the number as characters. This and the next two exercises will be useful in doing the exercises in Chapter 9 that consider significant digits in multiplying two numbers.

19. The following program was written to determine the digits after the decimal point in a real number (e.g., in 12.345, the 345). Why does it not produce the proper result?

```
PROGRAM Prob16(input, output);
VAR Difference, Number:real;
   TruncValue:integer;
BEGIN
   writeln('Type a real number with a decimal point');
   read(Number);
   TruncValue:= trunc(Number);
   Difference:= Number − TruncValue;
   writeln('Difference ', Difference)
END.
```

20. Write a program that stores the digits that follow the decimal point in a separate variable from the one in which it stores all the digits. Thus in 23.45, the 45 would be stored separately from the 2345.

21. Write a program that reads a real number, Amount, and prints the results using `writeln( ' Amount is $', Amount:Width:2)`, where the value of `Width` is 3 plus the number of digits to the left of the decimal point.

A Bottom-Up Approach Stock prices are given in terms of an integer followed by a blank and then a fraction—for instance, 20 1/8. Problems 22 to 26 walk you through a bottom-up approach to writing a program that finds the average of a group of stock prices. Note that if there is no fraction following the integer, you should type the fraction with 0 as the numerator (e.g., 20 0/8).

22. Write a program that reads a stock price and converts it to its decimal equivalent (e.g., it should convert 20 1/4 to 20.25).

23. Write a program that reads a stock price given in terms of an integer followed by one or more blanks followed by a fraction and converts it to a its decimal equivalent (e.g., it should convert 20bbb 1/4 to 20.25). (We use bs to represent blanks here for clarity; however, you should hit the space bar to type a blank.)

24. Write a program that reads a stock price typed so that the integer can be preceded by one or more blanks (e.g., bbbb20bbbb1/4) and converts it to a its decimal equivalent.

25. Convert the previous program into a procedure and activate it from the main program.

26. Using the procedure of the previous program, write a program that calculates the average of a series of stock prices typed on one line such

that each price is typed according to the specifications of the previous exercise and one or more blanks separates each price. Note that in exercise 31, after some preparatory exercises, we will present the last one in this series.

In the following programs, you may find it convenient to use a data file for input.

27. In Central City, the temperature was read many times on each of several days in July. Calculate the average temperature for each day and the average for all the days on which readings were made. Use the following test data, where the first integer on each line is the date and the remaining data are the readings. Your program should accommodate any number of readings per day for any number of days.

```
1 100 0 0
2 90 89 67
3 88 78 69 90
5 99 77 56 33
12 89 97 102
17 98 88 77
```

28. Write a program that calculates the class average, where each student's average is obtained from his or her three highest marks on four exams. Use the following data to test your program, where the first item on each line is the student's ID and the other four integers are the student's grades. The grades must vary between 0 and 100. Your program must accommodate any number of students.

```
1009 100 100 100 100
1006 87 100 100 100
1001 78 98 67 99
1003 45 78 65 45
1008 120 34 89 88
1010 123 125 125 123.
```

29. Write a program that calculates the average highest temperature from data for several cities, where the temperature was read on 3 days. In the following test data, the first integer on a line is the city number and the remaining three are the temperature readings on three separate days. Thus, here, the average highest temperature is $(90 + 78 + 105 + 100) / 4$. Your program must accommodate any number of cities.

1 89 90 78
2 78 56 67
3 87 104 105
4 0 100 0

30. Write a program that calculates the average highest weekly salaries for several salespersons at Central Tennis Apparel who work a variable number of weeks per month. The following are test data:

1001 345 239 578
1002 100 0 0
1003 0
1008 567 897 876 456
1004 456

31. The prices that Acme Tennis Balls, Inc., trades on the International Stock Exchange on 1 week were:

Monday 20 1/8 23 3/4 18 7/8 15 0/8
Tuesday 15 1/8 22 3/8 21 1/2 16 1/4
Wednesday 20 3/8 22 3/4
Thursday 19 1/4 20 3/4 21 5/8
Friday 20 0/8

Each price consists of an integer and a fraction. Write a program that determines the highest and lowest selling prices on a given day and the average highest and lowest prices for any week. The previous data (excluding the day) should be used to test your program. Use the results of exercise 23.

32. Write a program that makes a histogram of a set of incomes read by the program such that one X represents $1000.

33. Write a program that reads a name but prints it using all the consonants but only the first vowel. Thus *Charles* is printed as *Charls.*

9 |
FUNCTIONS |

9.1

SUBPROGRAM FUNCTIONS

Since mathematical functions are similar to programming functions, let's begin with a brief explanation of the former. In the following mathematical function

$$S(X) = X + X^2 + 3$$

S is called the *function name*, X is called the *argument*, and $X + X^2 + 3$ is called the *function*. If the argument in the function name is replaced with another argument, the argument is changed in the function as well. For instance, $S(4)$ is given by

$$S(4) = 4 + 4^2 + 3$$

Similarly, $S(Y)$ is given by

$$S(Y) = Y + Y^2 + 3$$

Functions can be used in expressions as well. Thus the meaning of

$$T = 3 * S(X)$$

is $T = 3 * (X + X^2 + 3)$. When we discuss functions, we will use the terms *argument* and *actual parameter* interchangeably.

Subprogram functions are like subprogram procedures in that they are miniprograms that are activated by statements in the activating program. The principles of local and global identifiers, block, and scope apply to functions, just as they do to procedures. Moreover, a Pascal function heading is the same as a procedure heading, except that since the function identifier is used in

expressions just as variable and constant identifiers are, we must declare the function's type. We must also replace the reserved word PROCEDURE with FUNCTION. For example, the heading of function CentsFrom—which converts dollars to cents—begins with the reserved word FUNCTION, as shown in Figure 9.1*a*:

```
FUNCTION CentsFrom(Dollars: real):integer;
(* Converts dollars to cents *)
(* Use of trunc shows round off error *)
BEGIN
   CentsFrom:= trunc( Dollars * 100 )
END (* CentsFrom *);
```

This heading ends with a colon and then the type of function, here integer. Since the information to be passed back to the main program is stored in the location named by the function identifier, here CentsFrom, the function identifier must appear on the left-hand side of an assignment statement somewhere before the end of the function. In other words, a value must be assigned to the function identifier before control is transferred to the activating program, here the main program, so we write

```
CentsFrom:= trunc( Dollars * 100 )
```

The reason the transfer function trunc is used here is that you cannot assign a real, here Dollars * 100, to an integer (CentsFrom).

In the main program of Figure 9.1*a*, the function is activated when the statement containing the function identifier, CentsFrom, written with an argument, here Bucks, is activated.

The function can be placed anywhere that an expression can be placed (e.g., in an assignment statement, in a write or a writeln statement, or in the activation of a procedure or a function). In this program, it is activated by a writeln statement:

```
writeln('$', Bucks:5:2, ' = ', CentsFrom(Bucks):4, ' cents')
```

An example of using it in an assignment statement would be

```
EngPounds:= 1.8 * CentsFrom(Bucks);
```

and an example of using it in a procedure activation would be Print(Cent-From(Bucks)). Note that we have chosen the function name so that when the function is activated, the purpose of the function is self-explanatory. Thus the person who reads the program will interpret CentsFrom(Bucks) as meaning "cents from bucks."

INTRODUCTION TO FUNCTIONS

```
PROGRAM Intro(input, output);
(* Introduction to functions *)
VAR Bucks: real;

FUNCTION CentsFrom(Dollars: real):integer;
(* converts Dollars TO cents *)
(* Use of trunc shows roundoff error *)
BEGIN
   CentsFrom:= trunc( Dollars * 100 )
END (* CentsFrom *);

BEGIN (* MAIN *)
   writeln('Type in amount in Dollars');
   readln(Bucks);
   writeln('$', Bucks:5:2, ' = ', CentsFrom(Bucks):4, ' cents')
END.
```

FIGURE 9.1a.   The form of a function is similar to that of a procedure, except that the function name has a type and must be assigned a value in the body of the function.

Returning to our program, we note that when the program is run, all the statements in the main program are executed in the order in which they are written. When the last `writeln` is executed, the string $ and the value of `Bucks` are printed. The computer then encounters `CentsFrom(Bucks)` and executes the function. Just as in procedures, since `Bucks` is used in `CentsFrom(Bucks)` when the function is activated, `Bucks` is called the *actual parameter*. Similarly, since the corresponding parameter used in the function heading, `FUNCTION CentsFrom(Dollars: real):integer;`, is `Dollars`, it is called the *formal parameter*. Since VAR is not used in the function heading, `Dollars` and `Bucks` are corresponding value parameters. Consequently, as shown in the table for Figure 9.1*a*, they label two different memory locations. The value placed in `Bucks` in the main program is copied to the location named `Dollars` in the function; however, if the value in `Dollars` were changed in the function, the value in `Bucks` would not be changed.

When the function is executed, the value of the number of cents is stored in the location named by the function identifier, `CentsFrom`. This same location is named by `CentsFrom(Bucks)` in the main program. The computer then returns to the main program and continues from the point it left, printing the value of `CentsFrom(Bucks)` and then printing the string `cents`.

When the program is run as shown in Figure 9.1*b*, the result is off by one cent:

$$\$12.34 = 1233 \text{ cents}$$

The reason is that because of roundoff errors, the value of `Dollars * 100` is a number close to but less than the correct amount (1234.0)—for example, 1233.99999999—and `trunc( Dollars * 100 )` truncates this to 1233. When the `trunc` function is replaced with the `round` function, as shown in Figure 9.1*c*.

$$\text{CentsFrom} := \text{round}(\text{Dollars} * 100)$$

the correct result is obtained, as shown in Figure 9.1*d*. We will use the term *subprogram* to refer to procedures and functions.

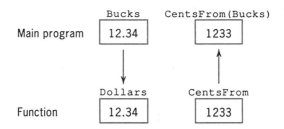

TABLE FOR FIGURE 9.1a. How the function name `CentsFrom` stores the result calculated in the function and returns it to the main program.

Type in amount in Dollars
12.34
$12.34 = 1233 cents

FIGURE 9.1b. Running the program of Figure 9.1a. Although we type in 12.34, it is stored as 12.3399999. Thus it is truncated in the function.

CORRECTING ROUNDOFF ERROR

```
PROGRAM Intro(input, output);
(* Introduction to functions *)
VAR Bucks: real;

FUNCTION CentsFrom(Dollars: real):integer;
(* converts Dollars TO cents *)
BEGIN
   CentsFrom:= round( Dollars * 100 )
END (* CentsFrom *);

BEGIN (* MAIN *)
   writeln('Type in amount in Dollars');
   readln(Bucks);
   writeln('$', Bucks:5:2, ' = ', CentsFrom(Bucks):4, ' cents')
END.
```

FIGURE 9.1c. We replace the `trunc` with the `round` function so that no roundoff error occurs.

Type in amount in Dollars
12.34
$12.34 = 1234 cents

FIGURE 9.1d. Running the program of Figure 9.1c. Now there is no roundoff error.

9.2

AVOIDING SIDE EFFECTS WHEN USING FUNCTIONS

When possible, you should use only value parameters* in functions, since only the function name should return information. If you use variable parameters, you run the risk of changing the value of the actual parameter in the activating program. Since you will be using value parameters, you can use expressions as the functions arguments. For instance, you can write CentsFrom(2.5 * Bucks).

9.3

A CHARACTER FUNCTION

Figure 9.2a shows a program that determines the Nth character after A in the character set your compiler is using. If your compiler uses the ASCII character set, the program will determine the Nth letter of the alphabet. The identifier Number refers to the position of a given letter in the alphabet. The function

```
FUNCTION GetLetter(Number: integer): char;
(* Gets the nth letter of the alphabet *)
VAR Letter: integer;
BEGIN
   Letter:= ord('A')+ Number - 1;
   GetLetter:= chr(Letter)
END(* GetLetter *);
```

determines what the letter is, and the main program in

```
writeln('Letter #', Number:3, ' is ', GetLetter(Number) )
```

prints the letter, as shown in Figure 9.2b. In this program, the same identifier, Number, is used as the actual and formal variable parameters. However, it is important to note that there are two separate locations. The location Number in the main program is not the same as the location Number used in the function, as shown in the table for Figure 9.2a.

Remember that a function may be used either in an expression or in a write or writeln statement, as it is here; it cannot be used alone. Thus the statement GetLetter(Number); will cause a syntax error.

*When we study arrays, we will see that it is more efficient to pass arrays as VAR parameters because the computer does not make copies of them.

A CHARACTER FUNCTION

```
PROGRAM ShowLetter(input, output);
VAR Number:integer;

FUNCTION GetLetter(Number: integer): char;
(* Gets the Nth letter of the alphabet *)
VAR Letter: integer;
BEGIN
  Letter:= ord ('A') + Number − 1;
  GetLetter:= chr(Letter)
END(* GetLetter *);

BEGIN(* MAIN *)
  writeln('Type the number corresponding to the required Letter');
  readln(number);
  writeln('Letter #', Number:3, ' is ', GetLetter(Number) )
END.
```

FIGURE 9.2a.   The function returns the Nth letter of the alphabet.

```
Type the number corresponding to the required letter
14
Letter # 14 is N
```

FIGURE 9.2b.   Running the program of Figure 9.2a.

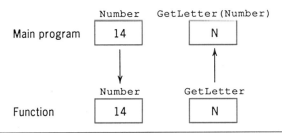

TABLE FOR FIGURE 9.2a.   Shows how the function name GetLetter stores the result calculated in the function and returns it to the main program.

9.4

BOOLEAN FUNCTIONS

Since the expression NOT odd(Number) determines whether or not an integer is even, it is assigned to the boolean identifier Even in

```
FUNCTION Even(number: integer): boolean;
BEGIN
   Even:= NOT odd(number)
END
```

Thus Even(4) will be evaluated as NOT odd(4), which is true.

In Figure 9.3a, a boolean function is used in a program that is a modification of procedure LabelColumns that labeled the columns (see Figure 7.2a). The function will determine whether or not the value of Column is a multiple of 10. In the function

```
FUNCTION Mod10(Column: integer): boolean;
BEGIN
   Mod10:= Column MOD 10 = 0
END (* Mod10 *);
```

the boolean expression Column MOD 10 = 0 is assigned to the function identifier Mod10. If the value of Column MOD 10 is not 0, then the value of Mod10 is false; otherwise, it is true. The function is activated in the main program in

```
FOR I:= 1 TO 35 DO
   IF Mod10(I) THEN
      write('-')
   ELSE
      write(I MOD 10:1);
```

The results, as shown in Figure 9.3b, are as follows:

123456789-123456789-123456789-12345

The Function Type
The function type may be either of the types learned so far: real or ordinal.

A BOOLEAN FUNCTION

```
PROGRAM LabelColumns(input, output);
(* Numbers the columns *)
VAR I, J:integer;

FUNCTION Mod10(Column: integer): boolean;
BEGIN
  Mod10:= Column MOD 10 = 0
END (* Mod10 *);

BEGIN (* LabelColumns *)
  (* Print units digit *)
  FOR I:= 1 TO 35 DO
    IF Mod10(I) THEN
      write('-')
    ELSE
      write(I MOD 10:1);
END.
```

FIGURE 9.3a. The function determines whether a number is a multiple of 10. We assign a boolean expression to the function identifier.

123456789–123456789–123456789–12345

FIGURE 9.3b. Running the program of Figure 9.3a. The program labels the columns such that every 10th column is labeled with a dash.

9.5

CALCULATING FACTORIALS

The next program, shown in Figure 9.4a, uses a function to calculate factorials for integers read as input. A factorial of an integer is the product of that integer with all the integers less than it but greater than 0. Thus 4 factorial, which is written as 4!, equals $4 \times 3 \times 2 \times 1$, and by definition, 0! equals 1.

BEFORE YOU BEGIN

Why learn how to calculate factorials? One reason is that they are important in theoretical computer science, since the amount of time a program requires for execution may depend on how many ways you can arrange the data. Let's look at a simple application of factorials.

The number of ways you can arrange N items, when none of them are identical, is $N!$. Thus the number of ways you can arrange the three letters A, B, and C is 3!, that is, six. The six arrangements are ABC, ACB, BAC, BCA, CAB, and CBA.

How did we know *a priori* that the number of ways we can arrange A, B, and C is 3!? The answer is that there are three choices for the first letter: A, B, or C (thus the first factor in the multiplication that forms the factorial is 3). For each of these, there are two choices for the second letter (thus the second factor is 2). For each of the second letters, there is one choice for the third letter—the remaining letter (thus the third factor is 1). For instance, if A is chosen as the first letter, you can choose B or C as the second. If you choose B for the second letter, the only choice you have for the third letter is C. The product of all the factors is $3 \times 2 \times 1$, or 3!

Factorials are very large numbers; for instance, 11! is greater than 39 million. Since the maximum integer (`maxint`) that your computer can accommodate is much less than the maximum real constant, we will use reals to store factorials.

If you realize that $4! = 4 \times 3!$ and $5! = 5 \times 4!$, the first version of our pseudocode in which factorials are stored in *Product* is

FOR J : = 1 TO *the integer read* DO BEGIN
    Multiply J by the previous Product and store
    the result in the present Product.
    Make the present Product the previous Product.
END (* FOR J *)

CALCULATING A FACTORIAL

```
PROGRAM Factorial(input, output);
(* Determines the factorial of a number *)
VAR N : integer;

FUNCTION FACTOR(L: integer): real;
VAR J: integer;
    Prod: real;
BEGIN (* Factor *)
IF L >= 0 THEN BEGIN
    Prod:= 1.0;
    FOR J:= 1 TO L DO
      Prod:=Prod * J;
    Factor:= Prod
  END(* IF *)
END (* Factor *);

BEGIN (* MAIN *)
    writeln('type N');
    readln (N);
    writeln(N:3, '! = ', Factor(N):6:0)
END.
```

FIGURE 9.4a.   The function calculates the factorial (!) of a number (3! = 3 × 2 × 1).
The function name cannot appear to the right of a ":=". Thus write Prod: =Prod * J;
in the loop and then Factor: = Prod.

This demands that the original value of *previous Product* be 1. Also, since each time the loop is executed the former *present Product* becomes the *previous Product*, we simply use *Product* to represent both, and therefore refine the pseudocode to

```
Product := 1;
FOR J := 1 TO the integer read DO
   Multiply J by the Product and again store the result in Product.
```

In the program, the function FACTOR calculates the factorial. Since the factorial of a negative number is infinite, we'll include a test for positive numbers in the function IF L >= 0 THEN BEGIN. Because this function calculates a product, it starts by setting the value of Prod equal to 1. Then in Prod := Prod * J in the J loop, the previous value of Prod is multiplied by the value of J and the result is again stored in Prod.

```
FUNCTION FACTOR(L: integer): real;
VAR J: integer;
    Prod: real;
BEGIN (* Factor *)
  IF L >= 0 THEN BEGIN
    Prod:=1.0;
    FOR J:= 1 TO L DO
      Prod:=Prod * J;
    Factor:= Prod
  END(* IF *)
END (* Factor *);
```

How the values are passed from the actual parameter N to the formal parameter L is shown in Table I for Figure 9.4a.

Since the value of J goes from 1 to the value of the number used as input, the function calculates the factorial of the inputted number. Table II for Figure 9.4a explains how the calculation proceeds for the first five times the loop is executed. If you examine any two consecutive lines, for instance,

Time executed	J	Prod
2nd	2	2.0
3rd	3	6.0

you see that the value of Prod for the third line equals the product of J for that line with the value of Prod for the previous line. This is the meaning of Prod := Prod * J.

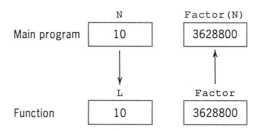

	N		Factor(N)
Main program	10		3628800
	L		Factor
Function	10		3628800

TABLE I FOR FIGURE 9.4a.   Shows how the function name Factor stores the result calculated in the function and returns it to the main program.

Time executed	J	Prod
1st	1	1.0
2nd	2	2.0
3rd	3	6.0
4th	4	24.0
5th	5	120.0

TABLE II FOR FIGURE 9.4a.   For a given line, the value of Prod is obtained from the product of J for that line and Prod from the preceding line.

In order to pass the final factorial to the main program, you must store the result in Factor, so we write Factor:= Prod. The reason we did not use Factor instead of Prod in the loop is that the function identifier cannot appear on the right-hand side of an assignment statement unless the function will activate itself (this is called *recursion*; see Chapter 16). Thus Factor:= Factor * J would produce a syntax error. The results of running the program are shown in Figure 9.4*b*.

TEST YOURSELF

QUESTION: What is wrong with using Factor(L):= Prod in the function Factor?

ANSWER: You can never use the function name with parameters on the left-hand side of an assignment statement.

QUESTION: What happens if we pass a negative number to function Factor?

ANSWER: Because of the IF, no value is stored in Factor. Thus the value printed in the main program will be unpredictable.

QUESTION: How would you rewrite the function to solve this problem?

ANSWER:

```
FUNCTION Factor(L: integer): real;
(* Calculates factorials *)
VAR J: integer;
       Prod: real;
BEGIN (* Factor *)
    IF L >= 0 THEN BEGIN
           Prod:= 1.0;
           FOR J:= 1 TO L DO
              Prod:=Prod * J;
           Factor:= Prod
        END (* THEN *)
    ELSE BEGIN (* Return -1 for negative numbers *)
        Factor:= -1;
        writeln('Negative input')
    END (* ELSE *)
END (* Factor *);
```

```
type N
10
10! = 3628800
```

FIGURE 9.4b. Running the program of Figure 9.4a.

TEST YOURSELF

QUESTION: How would you rewrite function GetLetter (Figure 9.2a) so that it will handle all values of Number?

ANSWER:

```
FUNCTION GetLetter(Number: integer): char;
(* Gets the Nth letter of the alphabet.
   If Number is out of range, a ''?'' is returned. *)
VAR Letter: integer;
BEGIN
    IF Number IN [1..26] THEN
       GetLetter: = chr( ord('A') + Number   1)
    ELSE
        GetLetter: = '?'
END {GetLetter};
```

9.6

WRITING A MOD AND A DIV FUNCTION

BEFORE YOU BEGIN

If you wanted to simulate the MOD and DIV operations on a computer that had only subtraction and addition available, you could do so by performing successive subtractions, as will now be shown.

The values of 7 DIV 3 and 7 MOD 3 can be obtained by determining the number of times you can subtract 3 from 7 while obtaining an answer greater than or equal to 0. In this division 7 is the numerator, 3 is the denominator, and the result, 2 is the quotient; in general, the quotient is the number of times you can subtract the denominator from the numerator. Thus $7 - 3 = 4$, and subtracting 3 from this yields $4 - 3 = 1$. If you subtract 3 again, you get $1 - 3 = -2$, a negative number. Since the number of times you can perform this subtraction and get a nonnegative result is two, we see that 3 goes into 7 two times. Thus 7 DIV 3 is 2, and since the remainder for the second subtraction is 1, the value of 7 MOD 3 is 1.

Figure 9.5a uses Dividend as the counter in Divide, the function that simulates the DIV. In 7 DIV 3, the original value of Numerator is 7 and the value of Denominator is 3. The test performed after each subtraction is whether Numerator − Denominator >= 0 is true. If you add Denominator to each side of this inequality, you get the equivalent expression Numerator >= Denominator. Since the result of the subtraction

```
Numerator: = Numerator − Denominator;
```

is assigned to Numerator, we write

```
WHILE Numerator >= Denominator DO BEGIN
   Numerator: = Numerator − Denominator;
   Dividend: = Dividend + 1
END (* WHILE *);
```

Since the number of times you can subtract 3 from 7 is stored in Dividend, assign it to the function name in Divide: = Dividend.

Modu, the function that simulates the MOD, is identical to the function Divide, except that it does not have a counter; the value of the MOD is the final value of Numerator. The results of running the program for a numerator of 7 and a denominator of 3 are shown in Figure 9.5b.

SIMULATING THE MOD AND THE DIV

```
PROGRAM Dividing(input, output);
(* Simulates the DIV and the MOD by using repeated subtraction *)
VAR Numerator, Denominator:integer;

FUNCTION Divide(Numerator, Denominator:integer):integer;
(* Calculates DIV *)
VAR Dividend:integer;
BEGIN
  Dividend:= 0;
  WHILE Numerator >= Denominator DO BEGIN
    Numerator:= Numerator - Denominator;
    Dividend:= Dividend + 1
  END (* WHILE *);
  Divide:= Dividend
END (* Divide *);

FUNCTION Modu(Numerator, Denominator:integer):integer;
(* Calculates MOD *)
BEGIN
  WHILE Numerator >= Denominator DO
    Numerator:= Numerator - Denominator;
  Modu:= Numerator
END (* Modu *);

BEGIN
  writeln('Type your numerator and denominator');
  readln(Numerator, Denominator);
  writeln(Numerator:2, ' DIV',Denominator:3, ' = ',
    Divide(Numerator, Denominator));
  writeln(Numerator:2, ' MOD',Denominator:3, ' = ',
    Modu(Numerator, Denominator))
END.
```

FIGURE 9.5a. The number of times you can subtract the denominator from the numerator is the value obtained from the DIV. The remainder after the last subtraction is the value obtained from the MOD.

```
Type your numerator and denominator
7  3
7 DIV 3 = 2
7 MOD 3 = 1
```

FIGURE 9.5b. Running the program of Figure 9.5a.

9.7

USING A FUNCTION IN AN EXPRESSION

Now let's use the most recent version of the function `Factor` to calculate the binomial coefficient

$$\binom{N}{M} = N! \; / \; [M! \; (N - M)!]$$

BEFORE YOU BEGIN

The symbol $\binom{N}{M}$ is also called a *combination symbol.* As an example, $\binom{52}{5}$ tells how many different ways you can choose 5 objects from a total of 52 objects, regardless of the order in which the 5 objects are chosen. Thus you can use this symbol to determine how many different three-card hands can be obtained from a deck of eight cards. Here M = 3 and N = 8, so

$$\binom{N}{M} = \binom{8}{3} = 8! \; / \; [5! \; * \; 3!]$$

or 56. There is a more efficient way of calculating combination symbols; however, we will not discuss it here.

The combination symbol is the basis of the field of mathematics called *combinatorics.* One of its applications is to predict how long certain types of programs will run.

The program in Figure 9.6a calculates *N! / [M! * (N − M)!]* in

```
Comb:=Factor(N) / (Factor(M) * Factor(N - M) );
```

This is the first time we use a function in a calculation and with different arguments. The values of N and M read are 8 and 5, respectively, as shown in Figure 9.6b, and the value of N − M is 8 − 5, or 3. The statement

```
Comb:=Factor(N) / (Factor(M) * Factor(N - M) );
```

is executed like any other statement that contains a mathematical expression. Thus since `Factor(M) * Factor(N - M)` is parenthesized, this part of the expression is executed first. The order of the steps is as follows:

A FUNCTION USED IN A CALCULATION

```
PROGRAM Combination(input, output);
(* Calculates combination symbol *)
VAR N, M : integer;
    Comb: real;

FUNCTION Factor(L: integer): real;
(* Calculates factorials *)
VAR J: integer;
    Prod: real;
BEGIN (* Factor *)
  IF L = 0 THEN BEGIN
    Prod:=1.0;
    FOR J:= 1 TO L DO
      Prod:= Prod * J;
    Factor:= Prod
    END (* THEN *)
  ELSE BEGIN (* Return -1 for negative numbers *)
    Factor := -1;
    writeln('Negative input')
  END (* ELSE *)
END (* Factor *);

BEGIN (* MAIN *)
    writeln('type N, M');
    readln(N, M);
    Comb:= Factor(N) / (Factor(M) * Factor(N - M) );
    writeln('# of ways of taking ', N:2, ' things ',
    M:2, ' at a time is', Comb:7:0)
END (* main *).
```

FIGURE 9.6a.   After a function is evaluated, the computer returns to the expression containing the function and evaluates the rest of the expression.

```
type N, M
8  5
# of ways of taking 8 things 5 at a time is 56
```

FIGURE 9.6b.   Running the program of Figure 9.6a. This shows, for instance, the number of five-card hands you can get from an eight-card deck.

1. $\text{Factor}(M)$, that is, $\text{Factor}(3)$, is evaluated and the function returns 3! Here M is the actual parameter and L is the formal parameter.

2. $\text{Factor}(N - M)$, that is, $\text{Factor}(5)$, is evaluated, and the function returns 5! The expression $N - M$ is the actual parameter and L is the formal parameter.

3. Then 3! is multiplied by 5!

4. $\text{Factor}(N)$, that is, $\text{Factor}(8)$, is evaluated, and the function returns 8! N is the actual parameter and L is the formal parameter.

5. Finally, 8! is divided by the product of 3! times 5! and the result is assigned to Comb.

9.8

WRITING A CALCULATOR

BEFORE YOU BEGIN

> One part of computer science is compiler design. In it, we study, among other things, how the compiler evaluates an expression like $3 * 4 - 8 / 4$. The following program shows how the computer does this for a restricted case. The more general case is covered in the computer science II course.

The next program represents a more sophisticated calculator than the one presented in Chapter 7. We will use the ">" and "<" as delimiters to denote the terms used. Define *<term>* as

$$<term> = <operand><operator><operand>$$

where *<operator>* can only be a "*" (the symbol for multiplication), a "/" (the symbol for division), or a "^" (the symbol for exponentiation). On the other hand, *<operand>* can only be a digit. Therefore $3 * 4$, $2 / 5$, and $3 \wedge 2$ (i.e., 3×3) are all examples of *<term>*s.

Our program will evaluate expressions of the type $\pm$ *<term>* $\pm$ *<term>* $\pm$ as many *<term>*s as we want.

In order for the expression to be evaluated the same way as a Pascal expression is, that is, according to the priorities assigned to the different operators, you must instruct the program to evaluate the *<term>*s first. Now we see why the operators used in their evaluation must have a higher priority than the "+" or "−", i.e., the operators used are the "*", "/", and "^". Because each term consists of three characters preceded by a plus or minus sign, the number of characters in the input must be a multiple of 4 (i.e., 4, 8, 12, etc.). Thus an example of valid input is the 12 characters $+3*4+5/6-3\wedge3$. The pseudocode for the calculator is shown in Figure 9.7a.

Since the resulting program will be somewhat complicated, we'll use the bottom-up approach by first writing and testing a program that evaluates *<term>*. The overall description of the test program is shown in Figure 9.7b. The pseudocode for the main program is shown in Figure 9.7c.

WRITING A CALCULATOR THAT SUMS TERMS—
STEP I. EVALUATING A TERM THE PSEUDOCODE

```
Sum:= 0;
WHILE NOT eoln DO BEGIN
  read(sign, operand1, operator, operand2);
  evaluate <term>;
  CASE sign OF
  "+": Sum:= Sum + <term>;
  "-": Sum:= Sum - <term>
  END (* CASE *)
END (* WHILE *);
writeln(Sum)
```

FIGURE 9.7a. Pseudocode for a calculator that sums terms containing "*"s, "/"s, and "^"s (exponentiations).

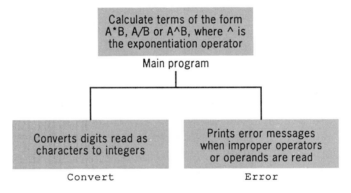

FIGURE 9.7b. The top-down diagram for a calculator that evaluates only one term.

```
Readln(operand1, operator, operand2);
Convert operands to digits;
IF the operands and operator are valid THEN BEGIN
    CASE operator OF
      '*': perform multiplication;
      '/': perform division;
      '^': perform exponentiation
    END (* CASE *);
    Write results
  END (* THEN *)
ELSE
    Write error message
```

FIGURE 9.7c. The pseudocode for a simple calculator that evaluates only one term.

Since exponentiation is simply repeated multiplication, evaluate Digit1 raised to the Digit2 by multiplying Digit1 by itself Digit2 times. Thus translate '∧': *perform exponentiation* to

```
'∧': BEGIN
         Term:=1;
         FOR J := 1 TO Digit2 DO
            Term:= Term * Digit1
       END (*∧BEGIN *)
```

as shown in Figure 9.7*d.* The conversion from operands to digits is done in procedure Convert.

The operands are read as characters, so that if an operand is not a digit, the program will produce an error message. Let's see how this is done. The program detects improper operands (e.g., a B) in procedure Convert in

```
ValidValue:= Operand IN ['0'..'9'];
```

If the first operand is not a digit, the program sets the actual parameter ValidOperand1 to False after it activates Convert the first time. If the second operand is not a digit, the program sets the actual parameter ValidOperand2 to False after it activates Convert the second time. These actual parameters correspond to the dummy parameter ValidValue in procedure Convert. Because information must be passed back to the main program, ValidValue must be a VAR parameter. Since it is best not to use VAR parameters in a function, we have written the subprogram Convert as a procedure.

In order to detect an improper operator (e.g., a #), let's first evaluate a boolean expression and then assign it to ValidOperator in the main program in

```
ValidOperator:= Operator IN ['*', '/', '∧'];
```

If the operator is not a valid one, the value of ValidOperator is false. The CASE statement that determines which operation to perform is placed in an IF statement beginning with

```
IF ValidOperator AND ValidOperand1 AND ValidOperand2 THEN BEGIN
```

and ending with

```
ELSE Error(ValidOperator, ValidOperand1, ValidOperand2)
```

WRITING A CALCULATOR THAT SUMS TERMS
STEP I. EVALUATING A TERM THE PROGRAM

```
PROGRAM Calculator(input, output);
(* Evaluates an expression that has one operator *)
   (* Checks for valid input *)
VAR Operandl, Operand2, Operator: char;
   Term: real;
   Digitl, Digit2, J: integer;
   ValidOperator, ValidOperandl, ValidOperand2: boolean;

PROCEDURE Convert( Operand: char; VAR ValidValue: Boolean; VAR
Digit: integer);
(* Converts character digit to integer *)
BEGIN
   ValidValue: = Operand IN ['0'..'9'];
   IF ValidValue THEN
      Digit: =ord(Operand) - ord('0')
END (* Convert *);

PROCEDURE Error(ValidOperator, ValidOperandl,
ValidOperand2: boolean);
(* Prints error messages *)
BEGIN
   IF NOT ValidOperator THEN
      writeln('Operator is not allowed.');
   IF (NOT ValidOperandl) OR (NOT ValidOperand2) THEN
      writeln('Operand is not a digit.')
END (* Error *);

BEGIN (* MAIN *)
   writeln('Type your 3 character expression');
   readln(Operandl, Operator, Operand2);
   Convert(Operandl, ValidOperandl, Digitl);
   Convert(Operand2, ValidOperand2, Digit2);
   ValidOperator: = Operator IN ['*', '/', '^'];
   IF ValidOperator AND ValidOperandl AND ValidOperand2 THEN BEGIN
       CASE Operator of
          '*': Term: =Digitl * Digit2;
          '/': Term: = Digitl / Digit2;
          '^': BEGIN
             Term: = 1;
             FOR J := 1 TO Digit2 DO
               Term: = Term * Digitl
          END (* ^BEGIN *)
       END (* CASE *);
       writeln( 'Value of ', Digitl, Operator, Digit2, ' is ',
Term :3:1);
       END (* THEN *)
     ELSE
       Error(ValidOperator, ValidOperandl, ValidOperand2)
END.
```

Before we calculate the sum, we write a program that evaluates terms
of the form A*B, A/B, or A^B, where ^ is our exponentiation operator.

where procedure Error writes error messages. The results of running the program with invalid and valid data are shown in Figure 9.7e. When a program can filter bad data (as this one eliminates illegal operators and operands), we say that the program is *robust*.

The next step is to rewrite the main program of Figure 9.7d as the function Term and use it to add all the terms in the sum. The overall description of the program which uses Term is

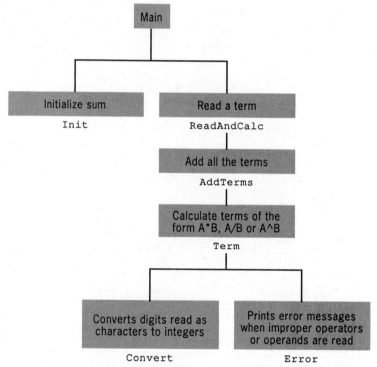

Activate the function Term in procedure AddTerms by writing

```
CASE sign OF
    '+':Sum:= Sum + Term(operand1, operator, operand2);
    '-':Sum:= Sum - Term(operand1, operator, operand2)
END (* CASE *);
```

as shown in Figure 9.8a(I).

Type your 3 character expression

3#4

Operator is not allowed.

Type your 3 character expression

A*5

Operand is not a digit.

Type your 3 character expression

5^6

Value of 5^6 is 15625.0

FIGURE 9.7e. Running the program of Figure 9.7d three times. The program detects improper operands and operators.

WRITING A CALCULATOR THAT SUMS TERMS
STEP II. EVALUATING THE SUM OF THE TERMS

```
PROCEDURE AddTerms(VAR Sum:real; Sign, Operandl, Operator, Operand2:
char);
(* Sums the terms in the expression *)
BEGIN
  IF Sign IN ['+', '-'] THEN
    CASE Sign OF
      '+':Sum:= Sum + Term(Operandl, Operator, Operand2);
      '-':Sum:= Sum - Term(Operandl, Operator, Operand2)
    END (* CASE *)
  ELSE
    writeln(Sign, ' is not a + or - Sign')
END (* AddTerms *);
```

FIGURE 9.8a(I). Sums the terms evaluated by the function Term and, depending on the value of Sign, either adds or subtracts the term. Since we have tested the main program of the previous program, we rewrite it as the function Term (see next page).

Since `Term` [see Figure 9.8a(II)] is now a function, the identifier `Term` cannot appear on the right-hand side of an assignment statement there, so we introduce a new variable, `Product`, to evaluate the exponentiation part of the function:

```
'^': BEGIN
        Product:=1;
        FOR J := 1 TO Digit2 DO
           Product:= Product * Digit1;
        Term:= Product
     END (*^BEGIN *)
```

The data are read and `AddTerms` is activated in procedure `ReadAndCalc`, as shown in Figure 9.8a(III), and the sum and the counter for the number of terms

```
FUNCTION Term( Operandl, Operator, Operand2: char): real;
(* Calculates <Term>, where <Term> = <Digit<Operator><Digit> *)
VAR product :real;
  Digitl, Digit2; J: integer;
BEGIN
  Convert(Operandl, ValidOperandl, Digitl);
  Convert(Operand2, ValidOperand2, Digit2);
  ValidOperator:= Operator IN ['*', '/', '^'];
  IF ValidOperator AND ValidOperandl AND ValidOperand2 THEN
    CASE operator OF
      '*': Term:= Digitl * Digit2;
      '/': Term:= Digitl / Digit2;
      '^': BEGIN
              Product:=1;
              FOR J := 1 TO Digit2 DO
                Product:= Product * Digitl;
              Term:= Product
            END (*^ BEGIN *)
      END (* CASE *)
  ELSE BEGIN
    Term:= 0;
    Error(ValidOperator, ValidOperandl, ValidOperand2)
  END (* ELSE *);
END (* Term *);
```

FIGURE 9.8a(II).   Calculates each term using the proper operator.

```
PROCEDURE ReadAndCalc(VAR Sum:real; Counter: integer);
(* Reads and calculates an expression *)
BEGIN
  WHILE NOT eoln DO
    BEGIN
      read(Sign, Operandl, Operator, Operand2);
      AddTerms(Sum, Sign, Operandl, Operator, Operand2);
      Counter:= Counter + 1;
      writeln('Sum of the first ', Counter:1, ' terms is ', Sum:7:2);
    END (* WHILE *)
END (* ReadAndCalc *);
```

FIGURE 9.8a(III).   Reads each set of data and activates the procedure that sums the evaluated term.

are initialized in Figure 9.8*a*(IV). The main program and the headings for all the subprograms used are shown in Figure 9.8*b*.

```
        PROCEDURE Init(VAR Sum: real; VAR Counter:integer);
        (* Initializes variables *)
        BEGIN
          Sum:= 0;
          Counter:= 0;
        END (* Init *);
```

FIGURE 9.8a(IV).   Initializes the counter and accumulator used in the program.

```
PROGRAM Calculator(input, output);
(* Evaluates an expression of the form (+/-)<Term>(+/-)<Term>, etc. *)
(* where <Term> = <Digit><Operator><Digit> *)
VAR Sign, Operand1, Operand2, Operator: char;
  Counter: integer;
  Sum: real;
  ValidOperator, ValidOperand1, ValidOperand2: boolean;

PROCEDURE Init(VAR Sum: real; VAR Counter:integer);          {On this page}
PROCEDURE Convert( Operand:char; VAR ValidValue:boolean; VAR
Digit:integer);                                              {See page 381}
PROCEDURE Error(ValidOperator, ValidOperand1, ValidOperand2:boolean);
                                                             {See page 381}
FUNCTION Term(Operand1, Operator, Operand2: char): real;     {See page 385}
PROCEDURE AddTerms(VAR Sum:real; Sign, Operand1, Operator,
Operand2:char);                                              {See page 383}
PROCEDURE ReadAndCalc(VAR Sum:real; Counter: integer);       {See page 385}

BEGIN (* MAIN *)
  writeln('Type your expression');
  Init(Sum, Counter);
  ReadAndCalc(Sum, Counter);
  writeln('The value of the expression is ', Sum :7:2)
END.
```

FIGURE 9.8b.   The main program and the headings for the procedures previously presented; however, the entire procedure must be used when actually running the program.

The results of running the program with valid input are shown in Figure 9.8c, and the results of running it with invalid data are shown in Figure 9.8d.

PITFALLS

1. A pitfall in using function subprograms is not listing all the actual parameters in the VAR declaration of the activating program or in the VAR declaration or heading of the activating subprogram. Thus if you used Count(one, two, three) in procedure Determine, you would have to declare each of the actual parameters, One, Two, and Three, in the VAR declaration of Determine or in its procedure heading.

2. Another pitfall is forgetting to assign a value to the function identifier if a boolean expression is false. For instance, in

```
FUNCTION FACTOR(L: integer): real;
VAR J: integer; Prod: real;
BEGIN (* Factor *)
IF L >= 0 THEN BEGIN
    Prod:=1.0;
    FOR J: = 1 TO L DO
        Prod:=Prod*J;
    Factor:= Prod
  END(* IF *)
END (* Factor *);
```

Factor is undefined if the value of L is negative.

3. Finally, initializing a factorial to 0 instead of 1 will yield a value of $N!$ equal to 0.

PROGRAMMING STYLE

At this point in the term, students usually ask themselves, "When should I write a subprogram as a function and when as a procedure?" If the result of a subprogram can be used in a calculation the way the factorial can be used in the evaluation of a combination symbol, then write the subprogram as a function.

The only identifier in the function that returns information to the activating program should be the function name. If you must also use variable parameters to return information, write the function as a procedure in which the role of the function identifier is taken by a variable parameter.

Any function can easily be written as a procedure. For instance, you can write a procedure Factor as

```
Type your expression
+3*4+5/6-3^3
Sum of the first 1 terms is 12.00
Sum of the first 2 terms is 12.83
Sum of the first 3 terms is -14.17
The value of the expression is -14.17
```

FIGURE 9.8c. Running the program of Figure 9.8b. We print the value of the running sum so that we can check the program.

```
Type your expression
+3+4-4*6*4+3
Operator is not allowed.
```

FIGURE 9.8d. Running the program of Figure 9.8b with invalid data.

```
        PROCEDURE Factor(L: integer; VAR Prod:real);
        (* calculates L! *)
        VAR J: integer;
        BEGIN (* Factor *)
          IF L >= 0 THEN BEGIN
                  Prod:=1.0;
                  FOR J:= 1 TO L DO
                      Prod:=Prod*J;
             END(* IF *)
           ELSE Prod:= -1
        END (* Factor *);
```

On the other hand, in general many procedures, and in particular those that produce output, cannot easily be written as functions. Thus VertLine and HorizLine from Chapter 6 are not candidates for being written as functions.

Summary of the Pascal Statements Used in This Chapter

FUNCTION Statement   The form of the function is FUNCTION followed by one or more blanks, followed by the function identifier, followed by a "(", followed by a list of variable identifiers, followed by ":" and the type describing the list. If there is more than one such list, these lists are separated from each other by semicolons. The type describing the last list is followed by a "):" and the function type. A ";" ends the statement. For example:

FUNCTION Price(Length, Width, Height:integer; Cost:real):real;

The function type can only be real, ordinal, subrange, or pointer. We will learn about subranges in Chapter 10 and about pointers in Chapter 17.

CHAPTER REVIEW

1. The function name must appear at least once on the left-hand side of an assignment statement in the function. It must appear without parentheses there. Thus Fact(N):= Product would be an error. Until you read Chapter 16, do not use the function name on the right-hand side of an assignment statement.

2. To avoid side effects, do not use variable parameters in functions.

3. The function should always return a value even if the information in the parameters sent to the function is not in the proper range.

NEW TERMS

argument

combination symbol

function

function name

robust

EXERCISES

1. What is wrong with the following function that cubes a number?

```
FUNCTION Cube(Number:real);
VAR Y:real;
BEGIN
  Y: = Number * Number * Number
END
```

2. What is wrong with the following function that squares a number?

```
FUNCTION Square(Number:real):real;
BEGIN
  Square: = Number * Number;
  writeln(Square)
END
```

3. Is the following function that raises a number to the fourth power correct?

```
FUNCTION Fourth(Number:real):real;
FUNCTION Square(Number:real):real;
BEGIN
  Square: = Number * Number
END (* Square *);
BEGIN (* Square *)
  Fourth: = Square(Number * Number)
END (* Fourth *);
```

4. What is wrong with the following function that raises a number to the fourth power?

```
FUNCTION Fourth(Number:real):real;
BEGIN
   Fourth:= Number * Number;
   Fourth:= Fourth * Fourth
END (* Fourth *);
```

5. What is wrong with the following programming segment that evaluates Digit1 raised to the Digit2 power?

```
Term:=Digit1;
FOR J := 1 TO Digit2 - 1 DO
   Term:= Term * Digit1
```

Programming Problems

6. Rewrite function GetLetter shown in Figure 9.2a so that the program checks whether Number is in the proper range.

7. Write a function that determines the maximum of two integer values.

8. Write a function that determines the minimum of two integer values.

9. Write a function that determines the maximum of three real values.

10. Write a function that determines the absolute value of an integer.

11. Write a function that rounds an integer to the nearest 10.

12. Write a function that rounds a real to the nearest 10th.

13. Write a function that finds the successor of a character.

14. Write a function that finds the predecessor of a character.

15. Write a function that evaluates the sin of an angle that is given in degrees instead of radians.

16. Write a function that converts cents to dollars.

17. Newton's method for determining the square root of a number is as follows: Let A represent your first approximation to the square root of X. Then the second approximation is given by $A = (A + X / A) / 2$. If you continue to execute this in a WHILE loop, the value of A will come closer and closer to the square root of X, or $X/(A * A)$ will approach 1.0. Because of roundoff error, it will never reach it. Since we don't know a priori whether $A * A$ is greater or less than X, we calculate abs(X/(A*A) - 1.0) and compare it with Epsilon, whose value is very small. Choose it as 10^{-6}. Using WHILE abs(X/(A*A) - 1.0) > Epsilon DO continuously approximates the square root of X until the boolean expression is false.

18. Write a function Comb(N, M) that uses the function Factor (see Figure 9.6a) to calculate the combination symbol.

19. When you expand $(a + b)^n$, the coefficient of $a^3 b^4$ is given, for instance, by `Comb(3, 4)` (see the previous exercise). Write a program that expands $(a + b)^n$, for instance,

$$(a + b)^2 = a^2 b^0 + ab + ab + a^0 b^2.$$

20. Write a function with the heading `Function Binary` that reads a binary number and returns its decimal equivalent.

21. The value of $\sin x$ is given by the series

$$\sin x = x - x^3/3! + x^5/5! - x^7/7! + x^9/9! \text{ f}$$

where x is measured in radians and the series has an infinite number of terms. For a finite number of terms, the series is more accurate the smaller x is. Write a function called `Sine` that sums the terms up to x raised to the 15th power term for 30 degrees. Hint: One way of getting the sign to change for each term is to place `Sign: = 1` before the loop and `Sign: = -Sign` at the end of the loop.

22. Because any given computer can accommodate only a certain number of digits in a number, it makes a roundoff error when it adds a very small number to a large one. For instance, if it can accommodate only five-digit numbers, when it adds 0.01 to 1234.5 the actual sum will be 1234.5 instead of 1234.51, the mathematical sum. The reason is that the computer aligns both numbers so that the decimal points correspond before it adds the two numbers; consequently, the 1 in .01 is lost. However, when the computer adds two small numbers, no roundoff error occurs. For example, when it adds .003 and .0005, the sum is .0035.

When a program performs a sum, such as the one in the series in the previous problem, if it adds the terms from left to right, at some point the term will be so small that when it is added to the sum, the sum will not change. However, if the sum is done from right to left, the small terms at the right will always contribute to the actual sum.

Do the previous problem with the terms summed from right to left. Is there any difference from the result obtained in problem 21?

23. Using the last exercise in Chapter 5, write a function that determines the area under the curve for the polynomial

$$z = x + x^2 + x^3 + x^4$$

24. The value of e, the base of the natural logarithm, is given by the following infinite series:

$$e = 1 + 1/1! + 1/2! + 1/3! + 1/4! + \ldots + 1/n!$$

Write a program that determines the sum of the first 9 terms of e.

25. Plywood, as the name implies, is constructed from various layers (or plies) of lumber. The two outside layers are called *faces* and, for interior plywood, are graded in three levels of quality: *A*, *B*, and *C*. An *A* face has no holes in it (these holes are caused by knots), where a *C* face does. A *B* face has holes that have been filled in; thus its quality is somewhere between that of *A* and *C*. A sheet that has an *A* face and a *C* face is designated as *A/C*. Write a function called `Price` that calculates the price of a piece of plywood. The function has as its parameters the length, width (both measured in feet), and quality of both sides of the plywood. An example of an activating statement is `Price(4, 8, A, C)`. The price for 1/2-inch-thick plywood given in dollars per square feet at the Montego Lumber Company for various qualities is *A/A* ($1.71), *A/B* ($1.28), *A/C* ($0.62), and *C/C* ($0.35).

An Example of the Bottom-Up Approach

Measurements cannot be taken with infinite accuracy. For instance, the length of a rod can be measured with a meter stick to an accuracy of 1/10th of a centimeter (1 millimeter), for instance, 12.3 cm. On the other hand, its weight can be measured by a balance to an accuracy of 1/1000th of a gram, for instance, 20.231 g. In order to calculate the density of the rod (weight per unit distance) in grams per centimeter, we divide the weight by the length—in this case, 20.231 / 12.3, or 1.6448 g/cm. This result, although mathematically correct, gives the impression that it is correct to five decimal places, although it is not. The proper way of doing the calculation is as follows:

a. Determine which of the two measurements is less accurate (here, the 12.3-cm length) and take as the precision of the calculation the number of decimal places to the right of the decimal point (here, 1).

b. Round the other measurement(s) to the same precision (here, round 20.231 to 20.2).

c. Then perform the calculation with these figures (here, 20.2 / 12.3, or 1.6423) and round the results to the precision of the calculation (here, 1.6).

Write a program in five steps that multiplies two numbers and obtains a result of the proper precision.

26. Step 1: Write a program that reads two real numbers and determines, for each the integer equivalent of the number with the decimal point removed, and the number of digits to the right of the decimal point. Thus if the program reads 12.345, the integer equivalent is 12345, and the number of digits to the right of the decimal point is three. Hint: See exercises 18 and 20 in Chapter 8.

27. Step 2: Incorporate the program you wrote for the previous exercise into one that determines which of the two numbers has more digits to the right of the decimal point.

28. Step 3: Incorporate the program you wrote for the previous exercise into one that truncates the number that has more digits to the right of the decimal point so that it has the same number of digits as the other one. Both numbers should be stored as their integer equivalents. Thus if the two numbers were 1.297 and 1.8, the program would truncate 1.297 and store the results as 12 and 18, respectively.

29. Step 4: Incorporate the program you wrote for the previous exercise into one that multiplies the two numbers after one has been truncated to the proper precision and then prints the results to the proper precision. Use 1.1 and 1.28 to test your program. The 1.1 would be stored as 11 and 1.28 as 12. The program would then multiply 11 by 12, obtaining 132, and divide this number by 10 ^ 2. Remember, if the product of the two numbers is greater than `maxint`, an error will result.

30. Step 5: Do the problem so that both the intermediate and final results are rounded to the proper precision.

10

ARRAYS; PROGRAMMING BY STAGES; THE TOOL BOX APPROACH

CHAPTER OVERVIEW

This chapter introduces a method of storing data in a group of locations in memory called an *array* so that one can access any of the locations by using an index and the array name. The type of array needed is defined in a TYPE statement or in a VAR declaration. The TYPE statement is also used to define subsets of the standard types.

Also discussed is a series of programs that determine the frequency of occurrence of the letters of the alphabet in a sentence. In writing these programs, we use the concept of building a tool box of subprograms that enables us to use the same subprogram in many programs.

10.1

AN INTRODUCTION TO ARRAYS; ARRAYS CONTAINING REAL VALUES

Let's explore a different method of representing variable identifiers. An example of the method involves the identifier Number, used in Figure 10.1a:

```
read( Number[1], Number[2], Number[3], Number[4], Number[5])
```

Number is called an *array variable* or, more simply, an *array*. It consists of five parts called the *elements* of the array. They are Number[1], Number[2], Number[3], Number[4], and Number[5] and are the names of five locations in the computer's memory, as shown in the table for Figure 10.1a. What distinguishes the elements of the array from each other are called *subscripts*; here, their values are 1, 2, 3, 4, and 5. The subscript must be enclosed in brackets and must be an expression of ordinal type.

In order for the computer to process a program that contains an array, it must allocate a memory location for each element of the array. One way of doing this is to use a TYPE definition, as, for example, in Figure 10.1a:

```
TYPE IntegerArray = ARRAY[1..5] OF integer;
```

This figure uses the TYPE definition to introduce a new type, here IntegerArray, which consists of an array. In the brackets that follow the reserved word ARRAY are specified the value of the lowest subscript (here, 1) followed by two periods, which, in turn, are followed by the value of the highest subscript (here, 5) that can be used in the array. This process is called *dimensioning an array*. These two values must be of the same ordinal type (here, integer) and dictate the type of expression that can be used as a subscript (again, here integer). Following the reserved word OF is the type of the values that will be stored in the array, here integer. If we had written TYPE TestArray = ARRAY['a'..'z'] OF integer, then a character expression must be used as a subscript. The dimension of an array is the number of elements in it. Thus the dimension of IntegerArray is 5.

IntegerArray is now a type that can be used in a VAR declaration or subprogram heading, just as the standard types integer, real, boolean, and char can. In Figure 10.1a VAR Number: IntegerArray; indicates that the identifier Number is of type IntegerArray. In other words, it is an array whose subscript ranges from 1 to 5 and that stores integer numbers. Thus an acceptable value for Number[2] would be 13.

When the program is run, as shown in Figure 10.1b, the integer numbers we type (12, 34, 56, 78 and 90) are assigned to the array, as shown in the table for Figure 10.1a. Note that only one type, the type indicated after the OF, can be assigned to an array. Thus you cannot assign, for instance, a character value to the first two elements and a real to the second three.

INTRODUCTION TO ARRAYS

```
PROGRAM IntroSubsc(input, output);
(* Reads five integers and prints them in reverse order *)
TYPE IntegerArray = ARRAY[1..5] OF integer;
VAR Number: IntegerArray;
BEGIN
  writeln('Type in 5 integers');
  read( Number[1], Number[2], Number[3], Number[4], Number[5]);
  write('The integers in reverse order are :');
  write(Number[5]:3, Number[4]:3, Number[3]:3, Number[2]:3, Number[1]:3)
END.
```

FIGURE 10.1a.   The array Number consists of five parts, Number[1], Number[2],...,and Number[5], called the *elements* of Number. What appears in the brackets is called a *subscript;* it distinguishes the elements from each other.

```
Type in 5 integers
12 34 56 78 90
The integers in reverse order are : 90 78 56 34 12
```

FIGURE 10.1b.   Running the program of Figure 10.1a. In the TYPE definition, we define IntegerType to be an array whose contents will be integer. The fact that [1..5] contains integers means that the subscripts must be integers and that 1 to 5 is their range.

Number[1]	Number[2]	Number[3]	Number[4]	Number[5]
12	34	56	78	90

TABLE FOR FIGURE 10.1a.   Shows how the values are stored in the elements of the array.

Using an array is one of the ways that allows us to declare variable identifiers that store more than one value. These types are called *structured types*. The structured type you've previously learned is the file type.

The program in Figure 10.1c, which reads five integers and then prints them in reverse order, shows one of the advantages of using an array: the ability to make the subscript a variable. This, in effect, allows us to change the identifier name during the program's execution. Let's see how this is done.

In order to read the five elements of Number[J], we place read(Number[J]) in a FOR–DO loop that has J as the control variable:

FOR J := 1 TO 5 DO
read(Number[J]);

The input of the program is shown in Figure 10.1d. When the value of J is 1, the computer interprets the read statement as read(Number[1]) and assigns the first number inputted, 12, to Number[1], as shown in the table for Figure 10.1c. Each time the read is executed, the computer assigns the next value read to the appropriate value of Number[J]. The left side of the table shows that when the value of J is 5, the value 90 is read and assigned to Number[5]:

J	Form of Number[J]	Value of Number[J]
5	Number[5]	90

The second FOR–DO loop

FOR K := 5 DOWNTO 1 DO
write(Number[K]:4)

prints the values in the reverse order in which they were read. The fact that the subscript is now K does not affect the running of the program. For instance, when the value of K is 5, the computer interprets the write as write(Number[5]:4). But Number[5] has been assigned the value 90 (in the preceding loop), so the computer has no difficulty printing the result. Thus it is the value of the subscript that is important; the identifier or expression used as the subscript is immaterial, provided that it is of the correct type.

BEFORE YOU PROCEED

Why do we learn about arrays? Because they are useful when we have a group of entities that are identical in form but are differentiated by the subscript. For instance, in the survey problem first discussed in Chapter 2 and done as a question in Chapter 7, the counters are called NorthCount, SouthCount, EastCount, and WestCount. They can, however, all be represented by one array, Count, with the following correspondence: Count[1] corresponds to NorthCount, Count[2] to SouthCount, and so on. To set the counters to 0, all we have to write is FOR K := 1 TO 4 DO Count[K] := 0.

PRINTS NUMBERS IN THE OPPOSITE ORDER IN WHICH THEY WERE READ

```
PROGRAM IntroArray(input, output);
(* Reads five integers and prints them in reverse order *)
(* Using a FOR-DO loop *)
TYPE IntegerArray = ARRAY[1..5] OF integer;
VAR Number: IntegerArray;
   J, K: integer;
BEGIN
   writeln('Type in 5 integers' );
   FOR J: = 1 TO 5 DO
      read( Number[J] );
   write('The integers in reverse order are :');
   FOR K: = 5 DOWNTO 1 DO
      write( Number[K]:4 )
END.
```

FIGURE 10.1c.   The program demonstrates the use of variables as subscripts. Each of the five times read(Number[J]) is executed, a different value is assigned to Number[J], as shown in the table.

```
Type in 5 integers
12 34 56 78 90
The integers in reverse order are : 90 78 56 34 12
```

FIGURE 10.1d.   Running the program of Figure 10.1c. The name of the subscript is not important; what is important is its value. Thus, when K and J have the same value, so do Number[K] and Number[J].

J	Form of Number[J]	Value of Number[J]	K	Value of Number[K]	Value of Number[K]
1	Number[1]	12	5	Number[5]	90
2	Number[2]	34	4	Number[4]	78
3	Number[3]	56	3	Number[3]	56
4	Number[4]	78	2	Number[2]	34
5	Number[5]	90	1	Number[1]	12

TABLE FOR FIGURE 10.1c.   Since the values of K are in reverse order in comparison to those of J, the results are printed in the reverse order in which they are read.

PITFALLS IN USING ARRAYS

1. Using a value of a subscript that is outside the range indicated in the TYPE statement will cause an execution error. Thus read(Number[6]) would cause an error in Figure 10.1c because the upper limit of the subscript is given in TYPE IntegerArray = ARRAY[1..5] OF integer;. What happens is that the number read is placed in the next allocatable location in memory, thus overwriting the previous contents.

2. Using a type as an array identifier will cause a syntax error. For example, read(IntegerArray[3]) is an error if IntArray has been defined in a TYPE definition. Write read(Number[3]) instead, where you have declared Number to be of type realArray.

3. Using the ":=" sign instead of the "=" sign in the TYPE statement will cause a syntax error. For example, TYPE IntegerArray := ARRAY[1..5] OF real; is incorrect.

4. Declaring an array with a dimension greater than that allowed for your computer will cause an error message. An example could be: Error 22: Structure too large.

5. Using parentheses—for example, Number(5)—instead of square brackets to indicate the subscript will cause a syntax error.

6. Using in the array definition a value for the lower limit of the subscript that is greater than the upper limit will cause a syntax error. For example, Value = ARRAY[True..False] OF integer is incorrect because the ordinal value of False is lower than that of True.

Placement of the TYPE Definition

The TYPE definition should be placed after the CONST definition and before the VAR declaration.

10.2

ARRAYS CONTAINING CHARACTER VALUES

The program in Figure 10.2a prints in reverse order the characters read into the program. Here

```
TYPE CharacterArray = ARRAY[1..8] OF char;
VAR Letter: CharacterArray;
```

indicates that Letter is an array whose subscripts vary from 1 to 8 and whose elements contain character values. For instance, Letter[3] := '*' is a valid assignment statement. Contrast this with an array we will use later in this chapter, defined as

AN ARRAY OF CHARACTERS

```
PROGRAM IntroCharArray(input, output);
(* Reads eight characters and prints them in reverse order *)
TYPE CharacterArray = ARRAY[1..8] OF char;
VAR Letter: CharacterArray;
  J: integer;
BEGIN
  writeln('Type in 8 characters' );
  FOR J: = 1 TO 8 DO
    read( Letter[J] );
  write('The characters in reverse order are :');
  FOR J: = 8 DOWNTO 1 DO
    write( Letter[J] )
END.
```

FIGURE 10.2a.   In the TYPE definition, we define CharacterArray to be an array whose contents will be characters. The fact that [1..8] contains integers means that the subscripts must be integers and that 1 to 8 is in their range.

```
TYPE CharacterArray = ARRAY['a'..'z'] OF integer;
VAR Freq:CharacterArray;
```

This indicates that Freq is an array whose subscripts vary from 'a' to 'z' and whose elements contain integer values. For instance, Freq['r']:=4 is a valid assignment statement.

The program being discussed reads as data eight contiguous characters (for example, THINKING) in

```
FOR J:= 1 TO 8 DO
   read( Letter[J] );
```

and print them in reverse order in

```
FOR J:= 8 DOWNTO 1 DO
   write( Letter[J] )
```

The table for Figure 10.2a shows how the assignments of the characters to the elements of the array are made. The results are shown in Figure 10.2b.

Other Examples of Defining Arrays

1. TYPE Temperature = ARRAY[−10..10] OF real; indicates that the subscript will have 21 values varying from −10 to 10, including 0.
2. TYPE Symbol = ARRAY['0'..'9'] OF integer; indicates that the subscript will have 10 values varying from '0' to '9'.
3. TYPE Symbol = ARRAY[10..20] OF char; indicates that the subscript will have 11 values varying from 10 to 20 and that the contents of each element is of char type.

TEST YOURSELF

QUESTION: Given

```
Value[1]:= True;
Value[2]:= False;
```

write (a) a valid TYPE definition and VAR declaration and (b) a statement that will print the two values of Value.

ANSWER: (a)

```
TYPE BooleanArray = ARRAY[1..2] OF boolean;
VAR Value: BooleanArray;
   I:integer;
```

(b)

```
FOR I:= 1 TO 2 DO writeln(Value[I]);
```

J	Form of Letter[J]	Value of Letter[J]	J	Value of Letter[J]	Value of Letter[J]
1	Letter[1]	T	8	Letter[8]	G
2	Letter[2]	H	7	Letter[7]	N
3	Letter[3]	I	6	Letter[6]	I
4	Letter[4]	N	5	Letter[5]	K
5	Letter[5]	K	4	Letter[4]	N
6	Letter[6]	I	3	Letter[3]	I
7	Letter[7]	N	2	Letter[2]	H
8	Letter[8]	G	1	Letter[1]	T

TABLE FOR FIGURE 10.2a.   Since the values of J in the loop containing the write are in reverse order in comparison to those of J in the read loop, the results are printed in the opposite order in which they were read.

```
Type in 8 characters
THINKING
The characters in reverse order are :GNIKNIHT
```

FIGURE 10.2b.   Running the program of Figure 10.2a.

10.3

SUBRANGES

You can define a type, called a *subrange type*, that is a subset of any ordinal type. For instance, TYPE Digit = 0 . 9; defines a subrange type that consists of the digits. Once you've defined a subrange type, you can declare a variable of that type, for example, VAR Number : Digit;. The compiler can now check whether the value of the variable falls within the subrange and thus can detect whether you made an error. Let's see how this is done.

For instance, if you accidentally assign a value to Number that is not within the subrange (e.g., Number : = 10), an execution error called a *range checking error* will occur. The compiler will also check whether you are using a subscript that is outside the range of a dimension. For instance, if you use 0 in Salary[0], where Salary is defined by

TYPE Income = ARRAY[1 . .10] OF integer;

VAR Salary: Income;

an execution error will occur.

As an example of a subrange of a character type, TYPE Alpha = 'a' . . 'z'; defines a subrange consisting of the characters from a to z in the collating sequence. For all subranges, the lower limit must be the same type as the upper limit and must have a value equal to or less than that of the upper limit. Thus 'z' . . 'a' would be illegal.

BEFORE YOU PROCEED

A subrange localizes the area of interest. For instance, the character type encompasses 256 different values, whereas Digits = '0' . . '9' narrows the range to the digits. This allows the program to check for the purity of the data before an out-of-range item creates havoc further down the line by causing an error that's difficult to detect. It also enables us to document the program. For example, the reader of the program knows that the value of Number declared in

VAR Number : Digits;

must be limited to a digit and cannot be simply an integer.

You can use a constant in a subrange definition. For instance, CONST MaxSubsc = 20; TYPE SubscRange = 0 . . MaxSubsc; defines a subrange for a subscript consisting of the integers from 0 to 20. As another example, Type

`PositiveIntegers = 0..maxint;` defines a subrange consisting of the positive integers.

A subrange type can be used to dimension an array, for instance,

> `TYPE SubscRange = 0..MaxSubsc;`
> `RealArray = ARRAY[SubscRange] OF real;`

which is equivalent to `TYPE RealArray = ARRAY[0..MaxSubsc] OF real;`, where `MaxSubsc` has been defined in a `CONST` definition. The subrange type must precede its use in the dimensioning of the array. Thus a syntax error would result from

> `TYPE RealArray = ARRAY[SubscRange] OF real;`
> `SubscRange = 0..MaxSubsc;`

Once you have defined an array or a subrange type in a `TYPE` statement, you can use that type in the heading of a procedure or a function, for example, `PROCEDURE Switch( Index:SubscRange; MarkArray:ScoreArray)`, where `SubscRange` and `ScoreArray` are types that have already been defined. On the other hand, it is illegal to define a subrange or a type in a subprogram heading. For example, `PROCEDURE Switch( Index:0..MaxSub; MarkArray:-4..4)` would cause a syntax error.

You may declare an array and a variable of a subrange type in a `VAR` declaration without having defined the array or the subrange type in a `TYPE` statement. Thus `VAR Index:0..MaxSubsc` and `VAR MarkArray:ARRAY [1..10] OF integer;` are both valid. However, as we have just seen, you cannot now pass `Index` or `MarkArray` to a subprogram. For instance, `PROCEDURE Add(MarkArray:ARRAY[1..10] OF integer)` will produce a syntax error.

Using the Standard Types to Dimension Arrays

Just as you can use a subrange type to dimension an array, you can use either of the ordinal types, `char` or `boolean`, to do this. Thus `TYPE CharacterArray = ARRAY[char] OF integer;` indicates that the dimension of `CharacterArray` is the same as the number of characters in the collating sequence. The lower bound for the subscripts is the first character in the collating sequence used by our compiler, and the upper bound is the last character in the sequence. Similarly, `TYPE BoolArray = ARRAY[boolean] OF integer;` is equivalent to `TYPE BoolArray = ARRAY[false..true] OF integer;`.

`TYPE IntegerArray = ARRAY[Integer] OF integer` is syntactically correct and is the equivalent of `TYPE IntegerArray = ARRAY[-maxint.. maxint] OF integer`. However, since the dimension is too large for the computer to accommodate, it produces a memory overflow message.

10.4

CALCULATING STANDARD DEVIATIONS

Although it would have been awkward, the previous two programs could have been written without arrays. Let's examine a program that cannot be written without an array. It reads an unknown number of marks, calculates their average, determines by how much each mark differs from the average, and finally, calculates a quantity called the *standard deviation,* which depends on these differences.

Once you calculate the average, you can determine the amount by which each element of the array varies from the average. This can't be done without an array. For instance, if you read and count marks in

```
Count:= 0;
WHILE NOT eoln DO BEGIN
    read(Mark);
    Count:= Count + 1
END (* WHILE *);
```

once the computer reads a new value of Mark, it erases the previous value. Thus you cannot subtract each value of Mark from the average.

Let's recall from high school mathematics the steps in calculating the standard deviation for a sample of five numbers consisting of 1, 4, 5, 6, and 9.

1. Calculate the average. Here, it is 5.
2. Calculate the difference between each number and the average: -4 (for the 1), -1 (for the 4), 0 (for the 5), 1 (for the 6), and 4 (for the 9).
3. Calculate the sum of these differences:

$$(-4)^2 + (-1)^2 + 0^2 + 1^2 + 4^2 = 34$$

4. Find the square root of the sum of these differences divided by the sample size* minus 1. Thus we have to find the square root of $34 / (5 - 1)$. The answer is 2.92; this is the standard deviation.

BEFORE YOU BEGIN

When you take an examination administered to many people, the results of all the examinations may be given in terms of the average grade and a number indicating how closely the grades are bunched together. This number is the standard deviation. For instance, if the average is 85 and the standard deviation is 10, a grade of 90 would not be considered as good as if the standard deviation were 2. The standard deviation is important in much of statistical studies. Let's see how to write a program that calculates it.

The top-down diagram is shown in the table for Figure 10.3*a.*

*The sample size is the number of pieces of data.

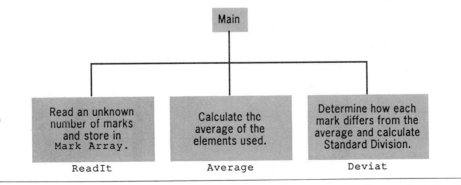

TABLE FOR FIGURE 10.3a.   The top-down diagram for a program that calculates the standard deviation.

We begin the program with

```
CONST MaxSubsc = 20;
TYPE Grade = 0..100;
     IntegerArray = ARRAY[1..MaxSubsc] OF Grade;
     SubscRange = 0..MaxSubsc;
```

where MaxSubsc is the maximum value of the subscript and SubscRange is the subrange for the variable, Count. This variable counts the marks and is the subscript for the array MarkArray.

Procedure ReadIt, shown in Figure 10.3a(I),

```
Count:= 0;
writeln('Type data on one line');
WHILE (NOT eoln) AND (count < MaxSubsc) DO BEGIN
   Count:= Count + 1;
   read( MarkArray[Count] )
END (* WHILE *);
BadCount:= (NOT eoln) OR (Count = 0)
```

reads the marks into the array MarkArray, which is of type IntegerArray. Each time it reads a mark, it increases the subscript Count by 1. Since the initial value of Count is 0 and its maximum value is MaxSubsc (here, 20), we declare that Count is of type SubscRange. If there are more than MaxSubsc marks to be read, the program will only read the first MaxSubsc marks and then Count < MaxSubsc will become false. Since the pointer will not be at the end of the buffer, NOT eoln will be true and so will BadCount—when control is returned to the main program, if BadCount is true, an error message is printed. Finally, since we want to return the value of Count, BadCount and all the elements of the array to the main program, we write the header as PROCEDURE ReadIt(VAR MarkArray:IntegerArray; VAR Count:SubscRange; VAR BadCount:boolean);.

When the computer sees that MarkArray is of type IntegerArray, it knows that the array has 20 elements, and since MarkArray is a variable parameter, the computer passes all 20 elements to the main program. The table for Figure 10.3a(I) shows how this is done. As it does with nonstructured variable parameters, the computer uses the same locations in the main program as in the procedure to store the array.

CALCULATING THE STANDARD DEVIATION

```
CONST MaxSubsc = 20;
TYPE Grade = 0..100;
     IntegerArray = ARRAY[1..MaxSubsc] OF Grade;
     SubscRange = 0..MaxSubsc;
PROCEDURE ReadIt(VAR MarkArray:IntegerArray; VAR Count:SubscRange;
                 VAR BadCount:boolean);
(* Reads MarkArray into array *)
(* If you call this procedure Read, it will try to call itself recursively *)
BEGIN
  Count:= 0;
  writeln('Type data on one line');
  WHILE (NOT eoln) AND (Count < MaxSubsc) DO BEGIN
    Count:= Count + 1;
    read( MarkArray[Count] )
  END (* WHILE *);
  BadCount:= (NOT eoln) OR (Count = 0);
  writeln
END (* ReadIt *);
```

FIGURE 10.3a(I).   The procedure reads a group of marks into an array. The definitions used in the main program are also given.

THE ALLOCATION OF A VAR PARAMETER ARRAY IN MEMORY

Main program ReadIt	MarkArray[1]	MarkArray[2]	MarkArray[3]	. . .	MarkArray[20]

TABLE FOR FIGURE 10.3a(I).   Because MarkArray is a VAR parameter, the corresponding elements in the main program and in ReadIt occupy the same locations.

Function Average shown in Figure 10.3*a*(II), averages the elements of the array with subscripts from 1 to the value of Count:

```
Sum: = 0.0;
FOR K: = 1 TO Count DO
  Sum: = Sum + MarkArray[K];
AvMark: = Sum / Count;
Average: = AvMark;
writeln('Sum= ', Sum:5:1, ' Count= ', Count:3, ' Average= ', AvMark:4:1)
```

The value of the sum must be printed in the function because Sum is not a parameter of the function:

```
FUNCTION Average(MarkArray:IntegerArray; Count:SubscRange): Real;
```

For convenience, we print the value of the average here too. This creates a problem. The inclusion of writeln(Average) in the function Average would create an error because it instructs the function to activate itself. In order to print the average's value, assign it to the local variable AvMark in AvMark: = Sum / Count and then print the value of AvMark.

Note that the value of Count can't be 0 in this function, since the function is activated in the main program only if the value of Count is not 0. Thus AvMark: = Sum / Count; will never create an error. Also note that MarkArray is a value parameter. In Standard Pascal, this means that there are MaxSubsc elements (here, 20) in the main program and that MaxSubsc separate elements are used in the function, as we see in the table for Figure 10.3*a*(II). For this reason, in order to pass arrays more efficiently in Standard Pascal, it is advisable to declare them as VAR parameters. Then only one-half the number of elements that would be allocated if a value parameter were used are allocated.

```
FUNCTION Average(MarkArray:IntegerArray; Count:SubscRange): Real;
(* Calculates the average of "Count" marks *)
VAR AvMark, Sum:real;
    K:integer;
BEGIN
    Sum:= 0.0;
    FOR K:= 1 TO Count DO
        Sum:= Sum + MarkArray[K];
    AvMark:= Sum / Count;
    Average:= AvMark;
    writeln('Sum= ', Sum:5:1, ' Count= ', Count:3, ' Average =', AvMark:4:1)
END (* Average *);
```

FIGURE 10.3a(II). MarkArray read in ReadIt is passed to Average, which calculates and prints the average. To save memory, we could have declared MarkArray as a VAR parameter. Then only 20 locations instead of 40 would be allocated.

THE ALLOCATION OF A VALUE PARAMETER ARRAY IN MEMORY

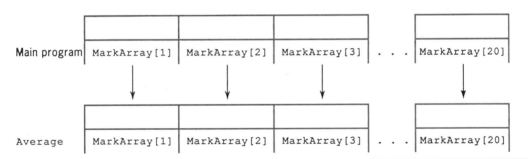

TABLE FOR FIGURE 10.3a(II). In Standard Pascal, because MarkArray is a value parameter, the corresponding elements in the main program and in ReadIt occupy two different locations. Thus the computer must allocate an additional 20 locations.

The function Deviat, shown in Figure 10.3a(III), which has the heading

```
FUNCTION Deviat(MarkArray:IntegerArray; Count:SubscRange;
   Average:real):real;
```

first calculates the difference between each mark and the average in Diff: = MarkArray[K] − Average, where the value of the subscript K is determined by FOR K: = 1 TO Count DO BEGIN. Since the value of the standard deviation is calculated from the sum of the squares of these differences, we write

```
Sum: = 0.0;
FOR K: = 1 TO Count DO BEGIN
   Diff: = MarkArray[K] − Average;
   Diff2: = sqr(Diff);
   Sum: = Sum + Diff2;
END (* FOR K *);
```

(where we have excluded the output statements), and since the actual value is the square root of this sum divided by the value of Count − 1, we write Deviat: = sqrt(Sum / (Count − 1)). If our data consisted of only one item, the value of Count would be 1 and the program would divide by 0. Since this would create an execution error, we write

```
IF Count = 1 THEN
   Deviat: = 0
ELSE
   Deviat: = sqrt(Sum / (Count − 1))
```

This will provide the correct answer for one or more pieces of data.

```pascal
FUNCTION Deviat(MarkArray:IntegerArray; Count:SubscRange; Average:real-
):real;
(* Finds the standard deviation *)
VAR Diff, Diff2, Sum:real;
  K:integer;
BEGIN
  Sum:= 0.0;
  writeln;
  writeln('K':3, 'Mark':10, 'Deviation':15, 'Deviat squared':20,'Sum':10);
  writeln('------------------------------------------------------------');
  FOR K:= 1 TO Count DO BEGIN
    Diff:= MarkArray[K] - Average;
    Diff2:= sqr(Diff);
    Sum:= Sum + Diff2;
    writeln(K:3, MarkArray[K]:10, Diff:12:1, Diff2:18:1, Sum:15:1)
  END (* FOR K *);
  writeln('------------------------------------------------------------');
  IF Count = 1 THEN
    Deviat:= 0
  ELSE
    Deviat:= sqrt(Sum / (Count - 1))
END (* Deviat *);
```

FIGURE 10.3a(III). MarkArray is passed to Deviat, and this function calculates the standard deviation.

Figure 10.3a(IV) shows the main program proceded by the headings of the functions and procedures used. The program tests for the possibility of there being no data or too much data. Note that all of the variable and array identifiers used in the main program must be declared there in the VAR statement; however, it would be a mistake to declare the functions (here, Deviat and Average) or procedure identifiers. For instance, VAR Deviat, Average: real

TEST YOURSELF

QUESTION: In procedure ReadIt (Figure 10.3a[I]), why didn't we test for Count being out of range by writing

BadCount:= (Count = 0) OR (Count > MaxSubsc)

ANSWER: Because of the presence of AND (Count < MaxSubsc) in the WHILE, the value of Count can never exceed MaxSubscr.

```
PROGRAM Standard(input, output);
(* Calculates the standard deviation *)
CONST MaxSubsc = 20;
TYPE Grade = 0..100;
   IntegerArray = ARRAY[1..MaxSubsc] OF Grade;
   SubscRange = 0..MaxSubsc;
VAR MarkArray:IntegerArray;
   Count:SubscRange;
   AverMark, Deviation:real;
   BadCount:boolean;

PROCEDURE ReadIt(VAR MarkArray:IntegerArray; VAR Count:SubscRange;
                 VAR BadCount:boolean);                    {See page 411}
FUNCTION Average(MarkArray:IntegerArray; Count:SubscRange): Real;
                                                           {See page 413}
FUNCTION Deviat(MarkArray:IntegerArray; Count:SubscRange; Average:
real):real;                                                {See page 415}

BEGIN (* Standard *)
   ReadIt( MarkArray, Count, BadCount);
   IF NOT BadCount THEN BEGIN
      AverMark:= Average(MarkArray, Count);
      Deviation:= Deviat(MarkArray, Count, AverMark);
      writeln('Standard Deviation =', Deviation:5:1);
      writeln('Average = ', AverMark:5:1, ' + or -', Deviation:5:1)
   END (* NOT BadCount *)
   ELSE
      writeln('subscript out of range')
END.
```

FIGURE 10.3a(IV).   The main program with all the headings of the subprograms. If you run the program you must also include the entire procedures.

would cause an error. The results of running the program are shown in Figure 10.3*b*.

In order for this program to be robust, it should check for situations in which there is one piece of data, no data or too much data. Figure 10.3*c* shows it testing for one piece of data, and Figure 10.3*d* shows it testing for no data.

To understand the theoretical significance of the standard deviation, let's consider the following. Certain distributions are shaped like a normal (bell-shaped) curve. An example is the plot of the heights of the male students in graduate school versus the number of students that fall within a certain height range:

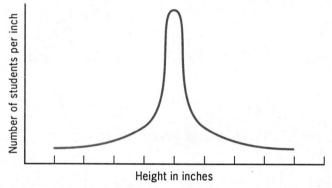

For a normal distribution, 68.3% of the data lie within one standard deviation of the average, 95.4 lie within two standard deviations, and 99.7% lie within three standard deviations. If exam marks are normally distributed, then the same percentages apply: 68.3% of the marks lie within one standard deviation of the average, and so on. If the average is 70 and the standard deviation is 5, then 68.3% of the marks will lie between 65 and 75.

Type data on one line
56 78 89 98 75 97 76 100 83 79
Sum = 831.0 Count = 10 Average = 83.1

K	Mark	Deviation	Deviat squared	Sum
1	56	−27.1	734.4	734.4
2	78	−5.1	26.0	760.4
3	89	5.9	34.8	795.2
4	98	14.9	222.0	1017.2
5	75	−8.1	65.6	1082.8
6	97	13.9	193.2	1276.1
7	76	−7.1	50.4	1326.5
8	100	16.9	285.9	1612.1
9	83	−0.1	0.0	1612.1
10	79	−4.1	16.8	1628.9

Standard Deviation = 13.5
Average = 83.1 + or − 13.5

FIGURE 10.3b.   Running the program of Figure 10.3a.

Type data on one line
89
Sum = 89.0 Count = 1 Average = 89.0

K	Mark	Deviation	Deviat squared	Sum
1	89	0.0	0.0	0.0

Standard Deviation = 0.0
Average = 89.0 + or − 0.0

FIGURE 10.3c.   Running the program of Figure 10.3a. Tests that the program can handle only one piece of data correctly.

Type data on one line

No marks read

FIGURE 10.3d.   Running the program of Figure 10.3a. Tests that the program can correctly handle no data. You should also check that the program correctly handles too much data (here more than 20 marks).

10.5

USING ARRAYS TO COUNT: PROGRAMMING BY STAGES; CREATING A TOOL BOX

BEFORE YOU BEGIN

The next program determines which letter occurs most frequently in a sentence and then produces a histogram of how many times each letter in the sentence occurs. This type of information is important in such applications as cryptography (code breaking), sophisticated spelling checkers, and programs that compare the style of two works in order to check the authenticity of authorship.

In order to make our task easier, we'll produce this program in three stages. Stage I is the bare-bones approach to the problem. Each successive stage adds another feature to the program.

1. Stage I counts how many times each lowercase letter occurs in the sentence.
2. Stage II determines which letter occurs most frequently.
3. Stage III includes a procedure that prints a histogram of the results.

TEST YOURSELF

QUESTION: The input for the following program is 67 89 97 87 98 85. What is the output?

```
Count:= 0;
WHILE NOT eoln DO BEGIN
  Count:= Count + 1;
  Read( MarkArray[Count] )
END (* WHILE *);
FOR K:= 1 TO Count DO write( MarkArray[Count] )
```

ANSWER: The output is 85 85 85 85 85 85.

QUESTION: Why does this code not produce the proper contents of Mark-Array?

ANSWER: The value of Count is 6, so the computer interprets the FOR–DO as FOR K:= 1 TO Count DO write(MarkArray[6]). The subscript of MarkArray in the FOR–DO should be the same as the control variable, K. The correct code is FOR K:= 1 TO Count DO write(MarkArray[K]).

Stage I

This stage uses the elements of the array Freq, defined by

```
TYPE CharacterArray = ARRAY['a'..'z'] OF integer;
VAR Freq:CharacterArray;
```

as counters. A primitive way of counting how many times a given letter occurs would be to write

```
WHILE NOT eoln DO BEGIN
  read(Letter);
  CASE Letter OF
    'a':Freq['a']:=Freq['a'] + 1;
    'b':Freq['b']:=Freq['b'] + 1;
    etc.
  END(* CASE *)
END(* WHILE *);
```

where all the elements of Freq would be set to 0 in previous statements. But this would require 26 statements in the CASE statement. A more elegant approach is to use Letter as the subscript and write

```
WHILE NOT eoln DO BEGIN
  read(Letter);
  Freq[Letter]:= Freq[Letter] + 1
END (* WHILE *);
```

Then, if the program reads a, it executes Freq['a']:= Freq['a'] + 1 and adds 1 to Freq['a'], the counter for the as; if it reads b, it executes Freq['b']:=Freq['b'] + 1 and adds 1 to Freq['b'], the counter for the bs; and so on. Before any counting is done, all the elements of the array must be set to 0; otherwise, Freq[Letter] on the right-hand side of the assignment statement will not have a value.

The pseudocode to determine how many times a letter occurs in a sentence is shown in Figure 10.4a.

Zero all counters;
WHILE NOT *end of sentence* DO BEGIN
   read character;
   IF *character is a letter* THEN *increment proper counter*
   ELSE *print the character*
END (* WHILE; *)
Print the contents of each counter.

FIGURE 10.4a. The pseudocode determines how many times a letter occurs in a sentence.

The top-down diagram is

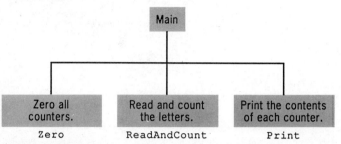

Figure 10.4*b*(I) presents Zero, the procedure that zeros the array, and Figure 10.4*b*(II) shows ReadAndCount, the procedure that reads and counts the letters. Since the program reads characters such as commas and periods that do not fall in the subrange 'a'..'z', we declare the variable used to read the characters, Letter, to be of char type and not to be in the subrange 'a'..'z'; otherwise, a nonletter like a blank or a comma will produce an execution error and terminate the program. The program checks whether Letter is in the subrange 'a'..'z' in

IF Letter IN ['a'..'z'] THEN
    Freq[Letter] := Freq[Letter] + 1
ELSE write(Letter:2)

COUNTS HOW MANY TIMES EACH LETTER OCCURS IN A SENTENCE

```
TYPE CharacterArray = ARRAY['a'..'z'] OF integer;
PROCEDURE Zero(VAR Freq:CharacterArray);
(* Zeros each element of 'Freq' *)
VAR Letter:char;
BEGIN
  FOR Letter:= 'a' TO 'z' DO
    Freq[Letter]:= 0
END (* Zero *);
```

FIGURE 10.4b(I).   The procedure zeros an array. The ARRAY['a'..'z'] in the TYPE definition indicates that the subscript will be of char type. The definitions used in the main program are also given.

```
PROCEDURE ReadAndCount(VAR Freq:CharacterArray);
(* Read letters in a line and determines the frequency of each letter *)
VAR Letter:char;
BEGIN (* ReadAndCount *)
  writeln( 'Type your sentence');
  WHILE NOT eoln DO BEGIN
    read(Letter);
    IF Letter in ['a'..'z'] THEN
      Freq[Letter]:= Freq[Letter] + 1
    ELSE write(Letter:2)
  END (* WHILE *);
  writeln(' are not letters.');
END (* ReadAndCount *);
```

FIGURE 10.4b(II).   In Freq[Letter]:= Freq[Letter] + 1, the procedure counts how many times each letter occurs. This statement is the equivalent of 24 counters.

Figure 10.4*b*(III) shows `Print`, the procedure that prints the results. In order to print only the counts for the letters that occur in the sentence (those letters with nonzero frequencies), we write

```
FOR Letter: = 'a' TO 'z' DO
   IF Freq[Letter] <> 0 THEN
      writeln( Letter ' occurs', Freq[Letter]:2, ' times')
```

Figure 10.4*b*(IV) shows the main program preceded by the headings of the

```
PROCEDURE Print(Freq:CharacterArray);
(* Prints frequencies *)
VAR Letter: char;
BEGIN
  FOR Letter:= 'a' TO 'z' DO
    IF Freq[Letter] <> 0 THEN
      writeln( Letter, ' occurs', Freq[Letter]:2, ' times')
END (* Print *);
```

FIGURE 10.4b(III).   The procedure prints each of the nonzero frequencies.

```
PROGRAM LetterCount(input, output);
(* Counts how many times each letter occurs in a sentence. *)
TYPE CharacterArray = ARRAY['a'..'z'] OF integer;
VAR Freq:CharacterArray;

PROCEDURE Zero(VAR Freq:CharacterArray);              {See page 425}
PROCEDURE ReadAndCount(VAR Freq:CharacterArray);  {See page 425}
PROCEDURE Print(VAR Freq:CharacterArray);             {On this page}

BEGIN (* LetterCount *)
  Zero(Freq);
  ReadAndCount(Freq);
  Print(Freq)
END.
```

FIGURE 10.4b(IV).   The main program with all the headings of the procedures. If you run the program, you must also include the procedures themselves.

procedures used, and Figure 10.4c displays the results of running the program.

QUESTION: Given VAR Count: ARRAY[1..4] OF INTEGER, write the loop to zero the array Count. What is the type of the subscript?

ANSWER: FOR J:= 1 TO 4 DO Count[J]:= 0;. The type of J is integer.

Stage II

The Stage II program determines which letter occurs most frequently; in other words, it determines the mode. This determination is done in a procedure whose pseudocode is

> *Set* Large *equal to the value of the first counter;*
>
> FOR *each subsequent counter* DO
>
> IF *the value of a counter is greater than* Large THEN
>
> > *Set* Large *equal to the value of that counter;*

where *counter* refers to an element of array of Freq.

At the end of the loop, the value of Large will equal the value of the counter with the largest value. Thus if that counter is Freq['e'] and has the value 8 (i.e., e occurred more times than any other letter—eight times), then the value of Large is 8. We now know how many times the most frequently occurring letter occurred; however, we still do not know which letter it is. Also, it is possible that more than one letter occurred with a frequency equal to the value of Large, so we add the following to the pseudocode:

> FOR *each letter* DO
>
> > IF *the counter for that letter equals* Large THEN
> >
> > > *print that letter and the value of its counter*

This pseudocode will become procedure Mode. The top-down diagram for the entire program is now

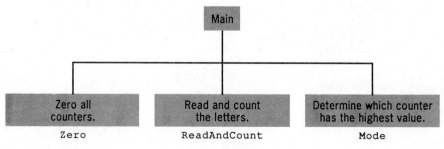

```
Type your sentence
we hold these truths to be self-evident.
            - . are not letters.
b occurs 1 times
d occurs 2 times
e occurs 7 times
f occurs 1 times
h occurs 3 times
i occurs 1 times
l occurs 2 times
n occurs 1 times
o occurs 2 times
r occurs 1 times
s occurs 3 times
t occurs 5 times
u occurs 1 times
v occurs 1 times
w occurs 1 times
```

FIGURE 10.4c.   Running the program of Figure 10.4b.

where Mode replaces Print in the top-down diagram for the previous program. Procedure Mode and the main program are shown in Figure 10.4*d* and the running of the program in Figure 10.4*e*.

DETERMINES THE MODE OF THE LETTER FREQUENCIES

```
PROGRAM ModeEval(input, output);
(* Determines which letter occurs most frequently in a sentence *)
TYPE CharacterArray = ARRAY['a'..'z'] OF integer;
VAR Freq:CharacterArray;

PROCEDURE Zero(VAR Freq:CharacterArray);                    {See page 425}
PROCEDURE ReadAndCount(VAR Freq:CharacterArray);           {See page 425}

PROCEDURE Mode(VAR Freq:CharacterArray);
(* Determines the mode *)
VAR Letter:'a'..'z';
  Large:integer;
BEGIN
  Large:= freq['a'];
  FOR Letter:= 'b' TO 'z' DO
      IF Freq[Letter] > Large THEN
        Large:= Freq[Letter];
  (* Now 'Large' is the greatest frequency *)
  (* Check for repetitions of Large *)
  writeln;
  FOR Letter:= 'a' TO 'z' DO
    IF Freq[Letter] = Large THEN
      writeln('"',Letter, '"', ' is the mode. It occurs ', Large, ' times')
END (* Mode *);
BEGIN (* ModeEval *)
  Zero(Freq);
  ReadAndCount(Freq);
  Mode(Freq)
END.
```

FIGURE 10.4d. Procedure MODE determines the letters or letters with the highest frequency. The main program and the headings of all the other procedures used are also included here.

```
we hold these truths to be self-evident, that all men are created equal.
        - ,              . are not letters.
  "e" is the mode. It occurs 12 times
```

FIGURE 10.4.e. Running the program of Figure 10.4d.

Stage III

The final stage includes a procedure that prints a histogram of the results. The top-down diagram for the resulting program is shown in Figure 10.5a.

The program will plot the histogram such that if, for instance, the letter a occurs five times in the sentence, the computer will print five as. If a letter does not occur in the sentence, the computer will not print anything for that letter. Thus if Freq['a'] is 5, Freq['b'] is 0, Freq['c'] is 1, and Freq['d'] is 3, the results will look like this:

Letter	Frequency
a	5 aaaaa
c	1 c
d	3 ddd

The pseudocode is

```
FOR each letter DO BEGIN
    IF letter occurs in sentence THEN
        print that letter the number of times it occurs in sentence;
    Start a new line
END
```

This translates to

```
FOR Letter:= 'a' TO 'z' DO BEGIN
   IF Freq[Letter] <> 0 THEN BEGIN
      write(Letter:6, Freq[Letter]:7, ' ':5);
      FOR J:= 1 TO Freq[Letter] DO
        write(Letter);
      writeln
   END (* IF *);
END (* FOR *)
```

The entire procedure, Histo, is shown in Figure 10.5b(I).

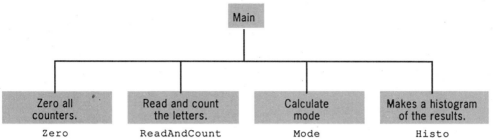

FIGURE 10.5a. The pseudocode determines how many times a letter occurs in a sentence.

```
PROCEDURE Histo(Freq:CharacterArray);
(* Produces a histogram *)
VAR Letter:'a'..'z';
    J:integer;
BEGIN
   writeln('Letter', 'Frequency':12);
   FOR Letter:= 'a' TO 'z' DO BEGIN
     IF Freq[Letter] <> 0 THEN BEGIN
       write(Letter:6, Freq[Letter]:7, ' ':5);
       FOR J:= 1 TO Freq[Letter] DO
         write(Letter);
       writeln
     END (* IF *);
   END (* FOR *)
END (* Histo *);
```

FIGURE 10.5b(I). The procedure prints a histogram of frequency versus letter. When Freq[Letter] is 0, the computer interprets FOR J:= 1 TO Freq[Letter] DO as FOR J:= 1 TO 0 DO and therefore prints nothing for that value of Letter.

When we write the main program, we add procedure Histo, just described, to procedures Zero, ReadAndCount, and Mode, used in Figure 10.4, and obtain

```
BEGIN ( * Histogram *)
   Zero(Freq);
   ReadAndCount(Freq);
   Mode(Freq);
   Histo(Freq)
END.
```

as shown in Figure 10.5b(II). The results of running the program are shown in Figure 10.5c.

When a collection of subprograms such as Zero, ReadAndCount, Mode, and Histo can be used in many programs, it's called a tool box. We used this approach in writing the word processing program in Chapter 7; however, at that time, we did not want to name the approach because we didn't want to burden you with another term to memorize.

TEST YOURSELF

QUESTION: Why will the following procedure not properly initialize Freq?

```
PROCEDURE Zero(Freq:CharacterArray);
VAR Letter:char;
BEGIN
  FOR Letter:= 'a' TO 'z' DO
    Freq[Letter]:= 0
END (* Zero *);
```

ANSWER: The array will be initialized in the procedure, but since Freq is not a variable parameter, its contents will not be returned to the main program.

```
PROGRAM Histogram(input, output);
(* Determines which letters occur most frequently *)
(* then makes a histogram of the letter frequencies. *)
TYPE CharacterArray = ARRAY['a'..'z'] OF integer;
VAR Freq:CharacterArray;
PROCEDURE Zero(VAR Freq:CharacterArray);          {See page 425}
PROCEDURE ReadAndCount(VAR Freq:CharacterArray);
                                                  {See page 425}

PROCEDUE Mode(Freq:CharacterArray);               {See page 431}
PROCEDURE Histo(Freq:CharacterArray);             {See page 433}
BEGIN (* Histogram *)
  Zero(Freq);
  ReadAndCount(Freq);
  Mode(Freq);
  Histo(Freq)
END.
```

FIGURE 10.5b(II). The main program with all the headings of the subprograms.

Type your sentence
we hold these truths to be self-evident, that all men are created equal.
"e" is the mode. It occurs 12 times

```
        Letter   Frequency

        a           5   aaaaa
        b           1   b
        c           1   c
        d           3   ddd
        e          12   eeeeeeeeeeee
        f           1   f
        h           4   hhhh
        i           1   i
        l           5   lllll
        m           1   m
        n           2   nn
        o           2   oo
        q           1   q
        r           3   rrr
        s           3   sss
        t           8   tttttttt
        u           2   uu
        v           1   v
        w           1   w
```

FIGURE 10.5c. Running the program of Figure 10.5b. We see that the letter e occurs the most frequently.

10.6

SORTING

BEFORE YOU BEGIN

In order to easily find a set of information, such as the checking account and savings account balances for a given depositor in a bank, amid all the other sets of information for depositors, it is first necessary to order these sets according to the depositors' IDs or names. The process is called *sorting*. In order to understand it, we introduce the process of sorting only numbers.

The next program sorts numbers in ascending order. Thus, if the list of numbers is 6, 3, 24, 15, 9, the sorted list will be 3, 6, 9, 15, 24. The crux of the program is to place the largest number at the right of the list. Start by comparing the first two numbers and, if necessary, switch them so that the larger one is at the right. In our list, 6 would be switched with 3. Then compare the second two numbers and, if necessary, switch them so that the larger one is at the right. Since 24 is greater than 6, do nothing. This process continues until the largest number is at the right of the list, as shown in Table 10.1. The number of comparisons (four) is one less than the number of items (five) in the list.

The pseudocode so far is

> FOR *each number in the list except the last* DO
> > IF *a number > the number to its right* THEN
> > > *Switch the two numbers in the list*

Repeat this process on the altered list shown in the last line of Table 10.1. You can save some steps by noting that in this altered list, the rightmost number (24) is in the position it should be in at the end of the sort. Consequently, when you repeat the process the second time, you do not have to switch this number. Thus the number of comparisons needed is now only three, as shown in Table 10.2.

Each time the switching process is performed, the number of comparisons will be one less than previously because one more number is in its proper position in the list. Let's incorporate this into the pseudocode by changing the FOR–DO so that the pseudocode becomes

> FOR *each number in the new list except the last* DO
> > IF *a number > the number to its right* THEN
> > > *Switch the two numbers in the list*

where *new list* does not include the last element of the previous version of the list.

6 3 24 15 9	6 is greater than 3, so switch them.
3 6 24 15 9	6 is less than 24, so do nothing.
3 6 24 15 9	24 is greater than 15, so switch them.
3 6 15 24 9	24 is greater than 9, so switch them.
3 6 15 9 24	

TABLE 10.1.   The first time the numbers are switched in the list. The ⌣ indicates the two numbers being compared.

3 6 15 9 24

3 6 15 9 24

3 6 15 9 24

3 6 9 15 24

TABLE 10.2.   The second time the numbers are switched in the list.

The last line of Table 10.2 shows that the elements in the list are in sorted order. Therefore if the FOR–DO is executed again, there will be no more switching. In general, when you sort a list of numbers, repeat the FOR–DO loop until there is no more switching. The list will then be sorted. Implement this by nesting the FOR–DO loop in a REPEAT loop, as shown in the pseudocode in Figure 10.6a. The type of sort we have just described is a *Bubble sort*.

Each time, before the items in the list are compared, we set an identifier, *Sorted*, to true in the hope that the list is sorted. If it is not, then the program will switch items in the list. Every time it does this, it sets the value of *Sorted* to false. The process continues until there is no more switching, that is, until *Sorted* remains true for a complete pass.

The top-down diagram for the resulting program is

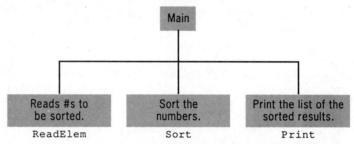

Procedure ReadElem is shown in Figure 10.6b(I). The procedure corre-

THE BUBBLE SORT

```
REPEAT
    Set Sorted to true;
    FOR each number in the new list except the last DO
        IF a number > the next number THEN BEGIN
            Switch the two numbers in the list;
            Set Sorted to false
        END (* IF *)
UNTIL Sorted is true
```

FIGURE 10.6a. The pseudocode for a sort.

```
CONST MaxSubsc=100;
TYPE IntegerArray = ARRAY[1..MaxSubsc] OF integer;
    SubRange = 0..MaxSubsc;
PROCEDURE ReadElem(VAR List:IntegerArray; VAR Count:SubRange;
                    VAR BadCount:boolean);
(* Reads integers into ARRAY *)
BEGIN(* ReadElem *)
    Count:=0;
    writeln('TYPE your numbers');
    WHILE (NOT eoln) AND (Count < MaxSubsc) DO BEGIN
        Count:=Count + 1;
        read( List[Count] );
        writeln('number', Count:2, ' is ', List[Count]:2 );
    END(* WHILE *);
    writeln( 'eoln encountered');
    BadCount:= (NOT eoln) OR (Count = 0);
    writeln
END(* ReadElem *);
```

FIGURE 10.6b(I). The procedure reads the numbers to be sorted. If the value of Count exceeds MaxSubsc, then Count will be out of the range defined by SubRange = 0..MaxSubsc and an error will ensue. The definitions used in the main program are also given.

sponding to the sorting is shown in Figure 10.6*b*(II). Since Sorted is boolean, we end the loop with the more appealing UNTIL Sorted instead of UNTIL Sorted = True. The identifier NumElem represents the number of items to be sorted, and List is the array in which the items are stored. The pseudocode for Sort translates to

```
REPEAT
    Sorted: = true;
    (* Don't sort elements already in place *)
    NumElem: = NumElem − 1;
    FOR J: = 1 to NumElem DO
        IF List[J] > List[J+1] THEN BEGIN
            Switch(List, J);
            Sorted: = False
        END(* THEN *)
UNTIL Sorted
```

where procedure Switch switches adjacent items in the list, that is, List[J] and List[J + 1]. We write the switching process as

```
Temp: =List[J];
List[J]: =List[J+1];
List[J+1]: =Temp;
```

The following shows how the switching is done.*

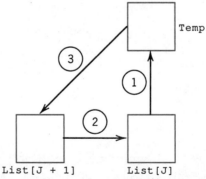

It would have been wrong to have written just

```
List[J]: = List[J + 1];
List[J + 1]: = List[J];
```

since the values of List[J] and List[J + 1] would be the same.

Procedure Print is shown in Figure 10.6*b*(III). The entire program is shown

*The circled numbers indicate the order of the steps in the switching process.

```
PROCEDURE Sort(VAR List:IntegerArray; NumElem: Subrange);
(* Performs a bubble sort on the array "List" *)
VAR J: Subrange;
  Sorted: boolean;

PROCEDURE Switch(VAR List: IntegerArray; J: Subrange);
VAR Temp: integer;
BEGIN
  Temp:=List[J];
  List[J]:=List[J+1];
  List[J+1]:=Temp;
END (* Switch *);

BEGIN(* Sort *)
  REPEAT
    Sorted:= true;
    (* Don't sort elements already in place *)
    NumElem:= NumElem - 1;
    FOR J:=1 to NumElem DO
      IF List[J] > List[J+1] THEN BEGIN
        Switch(List, J);
        Sorted:= False
      END(* THEN *)
  UNTIL Sorted
END; (* Sort *)
```

FIGURE 10.6b(II). The procedure switches adjacent elements in the list until the one with the greatest value is at the end of the list. This procedure is repeated until there is no more switching.

```
PROCEDURE Print( List:IntegerArray; Count:Subrange);
(* Prints a sorted list of integers *)
VAR K:Subrange;
BEGIN
  writeln('The sorted list is:');
  FOR K:= 1 TO Count DO
    write( List[K]:3 )
END (* Print *);
```

FIGURE 10.6b(III). The procedure prints the sorted list.

in Figure 10.6b(IV) and the results of running the program in Figure 10.6c.

AN INTERESTING FACT ABOUT ARRAYS

All the elements of arrays of the same type can be assigned to each other quite simply. For instance, if Name and Number are both of type IntegerArray, then the statement Name : = Number is equivalent to FOR K: = 1 TO 5 DO Name[J]:= Number[J].

Pitfalls

1. You cannot assign an array of one type to an array of another type even if the definitions are identical. For instance, in a program beginning with the definitions

```
TYPE One = ARRAY[1..5] OF integer;
     Two = ARRAY[1..5] OF integer;
     Sub = 0..9;
VAR Uno:One;
    Dos:Two;
    Digit:Sub;
    Number:integer;
```

even though the array definitions for Uno and Dos are identical, the assignment statement Dos: = Uno produces a type mismatch syntax error because Uno is of type One, whereas Dos is of type Two.

Note that we can assign a variable identifier of a subrange of an ordinal type to a variable identifier of that ordinal type. Thus Number : = Digit is legal, where Digit is of type Sub and Number is an integer. If, however, we do the reverse, that is, write Digit: = Number, a range checking error will occur if the value of Number does not fall within the range of Digit. For example, Digit: = 12 will cause such an error.

2. An actual parameter of one type cannot correspond to a formal parameter of another type even if the definitions of the types are identical. For instance, if we use the definitions from (1) and write the heading PROCEDURE Zero(Uno:One); and activate Zero with Zero(Dos); we obtain a syntax error like Error 26: Type mismatch because Uno is of type One, whereas Dos is of type Two.

Note that if the types of the corresponding formal and actual parameters are a type and a subrange of that type, no error will occur. Thus, if we write the heading PROCEDURE Assign(Number:integer); we can activate Assign with Assign(Digit);, where Number is an

```
PROGRAM Bubble(input,output);
(* Performs a bubble sort on integers *)
CONST MaxSubsc= 100;
TYPE IntegerArray = ARRAY[1..MaxSubsc] OF integer;
   SubRange = 0..MaxSubsc;
VAR Count, K: Subrange;
   List: IntegerArray;
   BadCount:boolean;
PROCEDURE ReadElem(VAR List:IntegerArray; VAR Count:SubRange;
                   VAR BadCount:boolean);          {See page 439}
PROCEDURE Sort(VAR List: IntegerArray; NumElem: Subrange);
                                                   {See page 441}
PROCEDURE Print( List:IntegerArray; Count:Subrange);
                                                   {See page 443}
BEGIN (* Bubble *)
   ReadElem(List, Count, BadCount);
   IF NOT BadCount THEN BEGIN
         Sort(List, Count);
         Print(List, Count)
         END (* IF *)
   ELSE writeln ('Count out of range')
END(* Bubble *).
```

FIGURE 10.6b(IV).   The main program with all the headings of the subprograms.

```
                     type your numbers
                     12 34 23 13 24 15 8 13 6
                     number 1 is 12
                     number 2 is 34
                     number 3 is 23
                     number 4 is 13
                     number 5 is 24
                     number 6 is 15
                     number 7 is 8
                     number 8 is 13
                     number 9 is 6
                     eoln encountered
                     The sorted list is:
                     6 8 12 13 13 15 23 24 34
```

FIGURE 10.6c.   Running the program of Figure 10.6b.

integer and Digit is of type Sub. If, however, we do the reverse, that is, write the heading as PROCEDURE Assign(Digit:Sub); and activate Assign with Assign(Number), a range checking error will occur if the value of Number does not fall within the range of Digit. For example, Number(12) will cause such an error.

3. You cannot declare a function to be an array type, only a real, ordinal, string, subrange, or pointer (see Chapter 15). Thus FUNCTION Zero—(Max:integer): IntegerArray;, where IntArray is defined in TYPE IntegerArray = ARRAY[1..5] OF integer;, will produce a syntax error.

4. You cannot define a subrange of a real. Thus Type Sub = 1.0..9.0 will produce a syntax error.

5. You cannot simply write X[J]:=0 to zero the array X. You must instead specify all the values of J, typically be inserting the assignment statement in a FOR or WHILE loop.

CHAPTER REVIEW

The TYPE Statement
In the TYPE statement you can define arrays and subranges. Just as you cannot use integer and real as variables, you cannot use the array type as a variable. The TYPE definition follows the CONST and precedes the VAR declaration.

Arrays
Arrays can be defined in a TYPE statement and then declared in the VAR declaration, or they can be declared in the VAR declaration, with the definition appearing instead of the type, as in VAR IntegerArray: ARRAY[1..5] OF integer.

Subscripts
The subscript range given in the array definition determines not only the limits but also the type of the subscript. Thus the 1..5 in TYPE One = ARRAY[1..5] OF integer indicates that the subscript must be an integer. You may use any ordinal type as a subscript.

Subrange
You can only define subranges of ordinal type. An example of a subrange type is

```
      CONST Low = -4;
             High = 4;
      TYPE ScoreRange = Low..High;
         ScoreArray = ARRAY[ScoreRange] OF ScoreRange;
```

This shows that the values to be stored in the array must be in the range -4 to 4, and the subscript must also be in this range.

Because the format of this book places a premium on the amount of space a program occupies, in future programs we will check whether a subscript is out of range simply by declaring a subscript to be of a subrange type. When you write such a program, however, we suggest that you use the techniques shown in Fig. 10.3a to check whether a subscript is out of range.

NEW TERMS

array

dimensioning an array

elements

range checking error

sorting

structured type

subrange type

subscript

tool box

EXERCISES

1. What is the output of the following program?

```
PROGRAM Probl(input, output);
VAR I:integer;
    X:ARRAY[1..5] OF integer;
BEGIN
    FOR I:= 1 TO 5 DO
        X[I]:= 2 * I;
    FOR I:= 1 TO 5 DO
        IF I < 3 THEN
            X[I]:= 2 * X[I] - X[I + 2]
        ELSE
            X[I]:= - X[I];
    FOR I:= 1 TO 5 DO
        writeln(X[I])
END.
```

2. What does the following program produce?

```
PROGRAM Prob2(input, output);
TYPE Vector = ARRAY[1..10] OF integer;
VAR Ray, L:Vector;
   j:integer;
PROCEDURE Box(M:Vector; VAR N:Vector);
VAR K:integer;
BEGIN
  FOR K:= 1 TO 10 DO
    N[K]:= M[K] + K * K
END (* BOX *);
BEGIN (* Main *)
  FOR J:= 1 TO 10 DO
    L[J]:= J * J;
  Box(L, Ray);
  FOR J:= 1 TO 10 DO
    writeln('J= ', J, ' Ray = ', Ray[J])
END.
```

3. Indicate whether each of the following is valid or not. If not, explain the reason.

a. VAR Ray:ARRAY[5..1] OF integer;

b. WHILE J[X] = J[X + 1] DO X:= succ(X);

c. Test:= Y[3] < Y[-8];

d. VAR Y: ARRAY[7.0...10.0] OF boolean;

e. TYPE Ray: ARRAY[1..100] OF boolean;

f. VAR Alphabet = ARRAY['A'..'Z'] OF boolean;

4. What is wrong with the following?

```
CONST X = 'X';
   0 = '0';
TYPE Symbol = ARRAY[X..0] OF integer;
```

Programming Problems

5. Write a program that reads up to 100 utility bills. The data consist of the amount to be paid, entered to the nearest dollar; thus the amount is an integer. The program should sort the bills according to the amount and print the number of customers who had the lowest bill and the number who had the highest bill.

6. Write a program that reads the ages of up to 100 people, and prints the number of people who are older than the average, and the number who are younger than the average.

7. Five candidates run for office. The voter presses a number that varies from 1 to 5 to indicate the candidate of his or her choice. The data consist of these numbers terminated by an end-of-line number. Write a program that determines how many votes each person received and who won. The program should indicate whether there is any type of tie (two-way, three-way, etc.)

8. Write a program that determines which of 12 channels is watched most frequently and the number of viewers who watch it; which channel is watched least frequently and the number of viewers who watch it; and the average number of viewers per channel. The input consists of integers ranging from 1 to 12, indicating the channel watched. Assume that there are no ties for first place or last place.

9. Write a program that reads the times in seconds of 10 runners in the 100-yard dash and determines the times of the 3 fastest runners.

10. Write a program that determines the average of the five highest grades for a student who has eight grades. Do this without sorting the grades.

11. Do problem 10 by sorting the data.

12. Write a program that determines the median income of a set of up to 100 incomes. The median is the item in a sorted list for which there is an equal number of items above it and below it.

13. Write a program that determines the largest element in an array X and the value of its subscript, given

```
VAR X: ARRAY[1..10] OF integer;
```

14. Given

```
TYPE Sorted = ARRAY[1..50] OF integer;
     Merged = ARRAY[1..100] OF integer;
```

and given two sorted arrays of type Sorted and the number of elements in each, write a procedure that merges the two arrays, storing the results in an array of type Merged. Thus the elements of Merged will be sorted. Note that when two sorted arrays are merged, the smallest value becomes the first element of the merged array, and the second smallest value becomes the second element and so on.

15. Write a program that determines whether two arrays of the same size have the same elements.

16. Write a program that takes an array and stores it in reverse order in another array.

17. Write a program that takes two arrays, One and Two, that have the same number of elements and interleaves them, storing the results in Three. Thus if One[1] is 4, One[2] is 3, Two[1] is 6, and Two[2] is 8, then the first four elements of Three would be 4, 3, 6, and 8.

18. Given the two arrays, Customer and Bad, that are of type ARRAY[1..25] OF integer;, where Customer contains the IDs of all the customers of a store and Bad contains the IDs of people who have passed back checks, write a program that prints the IDs in Customer that are not in Bad.

19. Write a program that prints the letters that were used in a sentence and then the letters that were not used.

20. Write a program that prints the letters used in one of two sentences and also in the other, that is, the union of the sets of letters used in both sentences.

21. Each pair of data in a set of input consists of a bank depositor's ID and the amount of the deposit. If there is more than one pair of data for a depositor, these pairs are consecutive. Write a program to print the total dollar amount of deposits for each depositor. There is no limit to the amount of deposits a depositor can make. Do not use arrays in writing this program. Use the following data set to test your program:

```
1002 456.34
1002 543.21
1000 345.39
1000 34.56
1000 456.67
1008 233.67
1009 341.23
1009 333.11
```

22. Alter the program for exercise 24 so that it reads a 10-character string variable instead of the ID. Use the following data set to test your program:

```
Corwin    567.89
Corwin    234.12
Bennet    322.33
Bennet    567.23
Bennet    256.45
Abrams    444.12
Lind      123.76
Lind      232.33
```

11

STRING PROCEDURES AND FUNCTIONS

CHAPTER OVERVIEW

Many compilers include predefined string functions and procedures, although they are not prescribed by the Pascal standard. These subprograms can assist you when you write string processing programs such as word processing programs; consequently, we'll write our own string subprograms and then use them in a word processing program. We'll write these subprograms so that, whenever possible, they have the same format and names as their Turbo Pascal equivalents. This will enable you to run them in the Turbo Pascal environment with as little change as possible. We'll conclude the chapter with a discussion of a type of array called a *packed array*, specified by the Pascal standard, that is helpful in comparing strings for alphabetical order.

11.1

AN INTRODUCTION TO STRING PROCEDURES AND FUNCTIONS

Let's begin by writing the following set of subprograms that will enable us to process strings stored in character arrays:

1. Procedure ReadString reads a string into a character array.*
2. Function Length determines how many characters are in a string.
3. Procedure Print prints a string.*

It's convenient to store the length of the string in the zeroth element of the array because it's natural to use the element whose subscript is 1 to store the first character in the string. Besides, this is the way it's done in Turbo Pascal, a popular compiler used with IBM-PCs. With this in mind, let's start our discussion with the procedure that reads a string.

Reading a String

The pseudocode for a procedure that reads a string is

> *Starting with element 1, place each character in successive elements of the array;*
> *Store the number of characters in element 0.*

Let's expand this to

> *Set Counter to one;*
> WHILE NOT eoln AND *dimension not exceeded* DO BEGIN
> *Read character into element designated by Counter;*
> *Add 1 to Counter*
> END (* WHILE *);
> *Store the value of Counter in the zeroth element.*

This translates to the procedure shown in Figure 11.1a(I), where we use TYPE Line = ARRAY[0..126] OF Char to define the array type and the identifier Stream to declare the array name.

BEFORE YOU PROCEED

> Why do we need to write a special procedure to read a string? Since Stream is an array, simply writing read(Stream) would produce an error.

*Turbo Pascal does this differently.

CHARACTER FUNCTIONS: PRINTING A STRING BACKWARD

```
CONST Max = 126;
TYPE Line = ARRAY[0..Max] OF Char;
PROCEDURE ReadString(VAR FileA:text; VAR Stream:Line);
(* Reads characters into a string array *)
VAR Count:Integer;
BEGIN
  Count:= 0;
  (*Place characters starting in second element *)
  WHILE NOT eoln(FileA) AND (Count < Max) DO BEGIN
    Count:= Count + 1;
    read(FileA, Stream[Count])
  END (* WHILE *);
  Stream[0]:= chr(Count)
END (* ReadString *);
```

FIGURE 11.1a(I).   Reads a string of characters either from the keyboard or from a file into an array of characters. It places in the zeroth element the character in the collating sequence corresponding to the number of characters in the string. The definitions used in the main program are also given. If we simply wrote read–(Stream), an error would result.

We're now going to use the fact that, as we learned in Chapter 8, the `input` file is a text file. Since the procedure should read strings either from the keyboard (the `input` file) or from another text file, we write the procedure heading as

```
PROCEDURE ReadString(VAR FileA:text; VAR Stream:Line);
```

Activating the procedure as `ReadString(input, Sentence)` will enable us to read the string from the keyboard. The reading and storing of the characters is done in

```
WHILE NOT eoln(FileA) AND (Count < Max) DO BEGIN
  Count:= Count + 1;
  read(FileA, Stream[Count])
END (* WHILE *);
Stream[0]:= chr(Count)
```

Each of the characters stored in `Stream` can be accessed by using a subscript. For example, if `think` is read into `Stream`,* then `Stream[1]` stores `t`, `Stream[2]` stores `h`, `Stream[3]` stores `i`, and so on.

Since the contents of `Stream` are of character type, you can't store the integer value of `Counter` in `Stream[0]`. Consequently, store `chr(Counter)` there. For instance, if there are 33 characters in the string, store the value of `chr(33)`, that is, a "!", in `Stream[0]`. Similarly, if there are eight characters in the string, store `chr(8)`, that is, the character representation of a backspace, in `Stream[0]`. Finally, if there are no characters in the string (i.e., you read the null string), store `chr(0)` in `Stream[0]`. Although the people who devised the ASCII table did not intend it as such, the fact that the character value of `chr(0)` in this table is given as "NULL" makes sense in view of our present discussion.

Finding the Length of a String

Since we've already stored `chr(Counter)` in `Stream[0]`, the length of the string is given as `ord(Stream[0])`, as shown in function Length in Figure 11.1a(II):

$$\text{Length:= ord(Stream[0])}$$

For instance, if the value of `Stream[0]` is "!", the length of the string is 33.

TEST YOURSELF

QUESTION: What is the length of chr(0)?

ANSWER: Although chr(0) is the character that corresponds to the length of the null string, because it consists of one character, its length is 1.

---

*Just as in Turbo Pascal, if you type more characters than the array can accommodate, these excess characters are not read.

```
FUNCTION Length(Stream:Line):integer;
(* Finds the length of a string *)
BEGIN
   Length:= ord(Stream[0])
END (* Length *);
```

FIGURE 11.1a(II).   Determines the number of characters in the string by obtaining the ordinal value of the character in the zeroth element.

Printing the Contents of a String

In order to print the contents of a string, write

```
FOR J:= 1 TO Length(Stream) DO
    write(Stream[J])
```

as shown in Figure 11.1a(III).

BEFORE YOU LEAVE

Why do we have to write a special procedure to print a string? Since Stream is an array, simply writing write(Stream) would produce an error.

Printing a String Backward

Now that we've written these subprograms, let's use them in a program. Remember the program in the previous chapter that used an array of char to read a string and then print it backward? The program of Figure 11.1b shows how to do it using a string. The loop

```
FOR Index:= Length(Sentence) DOWNTO 1 DO
    write(Sentence[Index])
```

```
PROCEDURE Print(Stream:Line);
(* Prints a string *)
VAR J:integer;
BEGIN
  FOR J:= 1 TO Length(Stream) DO
    write(Stream[J])
END (* Print *);
```

FIGURE 11.1a(III). **Prints the characters in the string.** If we simply wrote write (Stream), an error would result.

```
PROGRAM CharFunct(input, output);
(* Functions used with string arrays: Length, Print, ReadString *)
(* Prints a string backward *)

CONST Max = 126;

TYPE Line = ARRAY[0..Max] OF Char;

VAR Stream:Line;
  Count:integer;

FUNCTION Length(Stream:Line):integer;              {See page 453}

PROCEDURE Print(Stream:Line);                      {On this page}

PROCEDURE ReadString(VAR FileA:text; VAR Stream:Line);   {See page 451}

BEGIN (* CharFunct *)
  writeln('Type your sentence');
  ReadString(input, Sentence);
  writeln('The original sentence is ');
  Print(Sentence);
  writeln;
  writeln('The string backward is:');
  FOR Index:= Length(Sentence) DOWNTO 1 DO
    write(Sentence[Index])
END.
```

FIGURE 11.1b. The main program with all the headings of the subprograms. II prints a string backward. A string is similar to an array of characters. Thus Sentence [3] refers to the third character in the string. Since input is used as a parameter in ReadString, that procedure reads the string from the keyboard. If you run the program you must also include the procedures themselves.

prints the string backward, as shown in Figure 11.1c. The inputted string

```
A man, a plan, a canal, panama
```

is a palindrome, that is, it reads the same way backward as it does forward if you eliminate the blanks and punctuation marks and make all the uppercase letters lowercase.

In order to conform to the terminology used in Turbo Pascal and other compilers, we'll call the variables whose type is ARRAY OF char that are used with our string functions and procedures *string variables.* Thus Sentence is a string variable.

11.2

MORE STRING PROCEDURES AND FUNCTIONS: SEARCH AND REPLACE

A Word Processing Technique: Global Search and Replace

Before we proceed, let's define the term *substring.* A substring is any part of a string. Some examples of substrings for the string "Dear Sir" are "Dear", "De", "r S" and "Dear Sir".

An interesting program is one that will replace all occurrences of a substring in a string independent of whether or not the first letter of the substring is capitalized. If the first letter of the replaced substring is capitalized, then the first letter of the replacement substring will also be capitalized. For example, in

```
"My country tis of thee, Sweet land of liberty, Of thee I sing."
```

if you choose to replace the word "of" with "to", then "Of" would be replaced by "To" as well, resulting in

```
"My country tis to thee, Sweet land to liberty, To thee I sing".
```

where the underlined words are the ones that were changed. When this type of replacement is made for a word or substring in an entire text, the process is called *global search and replace.* It's helpful to solve the problem in the following stages:

1. Write the string on a disk file so that you can use the same string both to debug a given stage of the program and to test the different stages of the program.

2. Replace the first occurrence of the noncapitalized substring in the string. In our example, you would only replace the "of" in "My country tis of thee".

3. Write a program that capitalizes a word.

```
Type your sentence
A man, a plan, a canal, panama
The original sentence is
A man, a plan, a canal, panama
The string backward is:
amanap ,lanac a ,nalp a ,nam A
```

FIGURE 11.1c.   Running the program of Figure 11.1*b*.

4. Replace the first occurrence of the noncapitalized substring and the first occurrence of the capitalized substring in the string. Thus you would replace the "of" in "My country tis of thee" and the "Of" in "Of thee I sing".

5. Replace all the occurrences of the noncapitalized substring and the capitalized substring in the string.

Part I: Storing a Sentence on a Disk

The program of Figure 11.2a reads a string from the keyboard and writes it on a file. Since `Sentence` is a string variable, we can't use

```
writeln(SentenceFile, Sentence)
```

to write the string onto the file; consequently, we'll include procedure `Print-File` in our program to do this. Figure 11.2b shows the string used as input data.

Part II: Replacing a Word in a Sentence

The top-down diagram for the second stage is

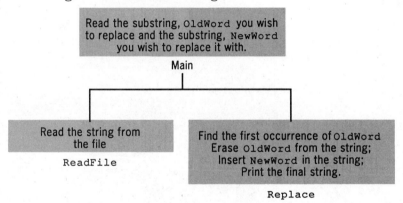

The program replaces the first occurrence of the noncapitalized substring in the string.

A WORD PROCESSING PROGRAM
PART I: STORING A SENTENCE ON A DISK

```
PROGRAM SetUp(input, output, SentenceFile);
(* Writes a sentence on a file *)
CONST Max = 126;
TYPE Line = ARRAY[0..Max] OF Char;
VAR SentenceFile :text;
  Sentence:Line;

PROCEDURE PrintFile(VAR SentenceFile:text; Sentence:Line);
(* Prints a string on a file *)
VAR J :integer;
BEGIN
  FOR J:= 1 TO Length(Sentence) DO
  write(SentenceFile, Sentence[J])
END (* PrintFile *);

FUNCTION Length(Stream:Line):integer;             {See page 453}
PROCEDURE ReadString(VAR Stream:Line);            {See page 451}

BEGIN (* SetUp *)
  rewrite(SentenceFile);
  writeln('Type your sentence');
  ReadString(input, Sentence);
  PrintFile(SentenceFile, Sentence);
END.
```

FIGURE 11.2a. Writes a sentence on a file. We must use PrintFile instead of a write to write a string on a file. The headings for ReadString and Length are also included. If you run the program, you must also include all of ReadString and Length.

```
                Type your sentence
                To be or not to be, To sce or not to see...
```

FIGURE 11.2b. Running the program of Figure 11.2a.

In order to translate this top-down diagram into Pascal, it is helpful to use the following three subprograms. To find the first occurrence of OldWord in the string, we use the pos function shown in Figure 11.3a. This function and the two procedures that follow are fairly complicated. Since they appear on the distribution disk for this book, we advise you to just learn how to use them and not worry about the details involved in writing them. The following is a description of the function.

The pos Function   This function finds the position in *string* of the first character in the first occurrence of the *substring*. Its form is Pos(*substring, string*). For example, if the string is

t	h	i	n	k	i	n	g
1	2	3	4	5	6	7	8

then the value of Pos('in', 'thinking') is 3. If the substring cannot be found, the value of pos is 0.

A WORD PROCESSING PROGRAM
PART II: REPLACING A WORD IN A SENTENCE

```
CONST Max = 126;
TYPE Line = ARRAY[0..Max] OF Char;
FUNCTION Pos(Substring, InString:Line):integer;
(* Finds position in string of substring; returns 0 if not found *)
VAR Index, SubIndex, Len1, Len2:integer;
  Match:Boolean;
BEGIN
  Index:= 1;
  Len1:= Length(InString);
  Len2:= Length(Substring);
  Match:= False;
  IF Len2 > 0 THEN BEGIN (* Substring not null *)
    WHILE (Index <= Len1) AND NOT Match DO BEGIN
      SubIndex:= 1;
      (* Find position of first character *)
      WHILE (Substring[SubIndex] <> InString[Index]) AND
        (Index <= Len1) DO (* Won't work without "=" here *)
          Index:= Index + 1;
      Pos:= Index; (* Save position if this begins match *)
      (* Match other characters *)
      Match:= True;
      WHILE (SubIndex <= Len2) AND Match DO BEGIN
      IF (Substring[SubIndex] = InString[Index]) AND (Index <= Len1)
        THEN BEGIN
            Index:= Index + 1;
            SubIndex:= SubIndex + 1
          END (* IF *)
        ELSE
          Match:= False
      END (* WHILE *)
    END (* WHILE *)
  END (* IF Len2 > 0 *);
  IF NOT Match THEN
      Pos:= 0
END (* Pos *);
```

FIGURE 11.3a.   Finds the first position in the string of a substring; returns 0 if not found. The definitions that must be used in the activating program are also included.

To erase `OldWord` from the string, we use procedure `delete`, shown in Figure 11.3*b*. The following is a description of the function.

The `delete` Procedure   This procedure deletes part of a string. Its form is `delete`(*string, starting position, length*), where *starting position* indicates where in the string the deletion should start and *length* indicates how many characters should be deleted. For instance, in `delete(Sentence, 3, 2)`, if the original value of `Sentence` is `thinking`, then the two-character string starting in the third position (the third and fourth characters, namely, `in`) would be deleted. The final value of `Sentence` would be `thking`:

Sentence	t	h	i	n	k	i	n	g		Sentence	t	h	k	i	n	g
	1	2	3	4	5	6	7	8			1	2	3	4	5	6

```
        original value                    final value
```

```
PROCEDURE Delete(VAR InString:Line; Index, Count:integer);
(* Deletes characters from a string *)
VAR I, J, Len:integer;
BEGIN
   Len:= Length(InString);
   IF Index <= Len THEN BEGIN
     J:= Index + Count; (* subscript of part to be shifted *)
     IF J > Len THEN (* Deleting to end of string *)
       InString[0] := chr(Index - 1)
     ELSE BEGIN (* Shift to deleted part *)
       FOR I:= Index TO Len - Count DO BEGIN
         InString[I]:= InString[J];
         J:= J + 1
       END (* FOR *);
       InString[0] := chr(Len - Count)
     END (* ELSE *)
   END (* IF *)
END (* Delete *);
```

FIGURE 11.3b. Deletes Count characters from a string starting in position Index.

To insert NewWord in the string, we use procedure insert, shown in Figure 11.3c. The following is a description of the function.

The insert Procedure   This procedure inserts a substring in a string. Its form is insert(*substring, string, starting position*), where *starting position* indicates where in the string the substring should be inserted. For instance, in insert('in', Sentence, 3), if the original value of Sentence is thking, then in would be inserted starting in the third position. The final value of Sentence would be thinking:

Sentence

t	h	k	i	n	g
1	2	3	4	5	6

original value

Sentence

t	h	i	n	k	i	n	g
1	2	3	4	5	6	7	8

final value

After the insertion, if the resulting string is longer than its dimension, it is truncated. For example, if the dimension of Sentence is 8, then insert('abcde', Sentence, 7) would change the value of Sentence to thinkiab.

TEST YOURSELF

QUESTION: If the value of Term is wonder, what is the result of the following if Term is declared as Term: ARRAY[0..7]OF char?

a.   Pos('won', Term)   **b.**   delete(Term, 4, 2)
c.   insert('ful', Term, 7)

ANSWER: **a.** 1   **b.** wonr   **c.** wonderf. Since the length of Term is 7, only the "f" in "ful" is appended to the string.

```
PROCEDURE Insert(SubString:Line; VAR InString:Line; Index:integer);
(* Inserts characters in a string *)
VAR I, J, Lenl, Len2:integer;
BEGIN
  Len2:= Length(SubString);
  Lenl:= Length(InString);
  (* If index > Length(InString) + 1 do nothing *)
  IF Index <= Lenl THEN BEGIN
    J:= Lenl + Len2;
    (* Shift array up by length(substring) *)
    FOR I:= Lenl DOWNTO Index DO BEGIN
      InString[J]:= InString[I];
      J:= J - 1
    END (* FOR *);
  END (* IF *);
  (* Allows you to also append a substring at end *)
  IF Index <= Lenl + 1 THEN BEGIN
    J:= 1;
    (* Insert substring *)
    FOR I:= Index TO Index + Len2 - 1 DO BEGIN
      InString[I]:= SubString[J];
      J:= J + 1
    END (* FOR *);
    InString[0] := chr(Lenl + Len2)
  END (* IF *)
END (* Delete *);
```

FIGURE 11.3c.   Inserts characters in SubString into InString starting in position Index.

Procedure ReadFile, shown in Figure 11.3*d*(I), reads a string from the file SentenceFile and then prints it. Therefore the first actual parameter in ReadString is now SentenceFile, as shown in ReadString(Sentence-File, Sentence).

Figure 11.3*d*(II) shows procedure Replace, which replaces the first occurrence of a word in the string with another word. The pseudocode for procedure Replace is

Find the first position of the old word in the sentence;

Delete the old word;

Insert the new word in the same position.

```
CONST Max = 126;
TYPE Line = ARRAY[0..Max] OF Char;
PROCEDURE ReadFile(VAR Sentence:Line);
(* Reads a sentence from a file *)
VAR SentenceFile:text;
BEGIN
  reset(SentenceFile);
  ReadString(SentenceFile, Sentence);
  writeln('The sentence read was:');
  Print(Sentence);
  writeln;
END (* ReadFile *);
```

FIGURE 11.3d(I).   The procedure reads a sentence from a file and prints it. Hence, the first parameter of ReadString is now SentenceFile instead of input.

```
PROCEDURE Replace(NewWord, OldWord:Line; VAR Sentence:Line);
(* Replaces a word in a string *)
BEGIN
  Position:= Pos(OldWord, Sentence);
  writeln('Position = ', Position);
  delete(Sentence, Position, Length(OldWord));
  insert(NewWord, Sentence, Position);
  Print(Sentence)
END; (* Replace *)
```

FIGURE 11.3d(II).   The procedure finds the first position of the old word in the sentence, then deletes the old word, and finally inserts the new word in the same position.

Figure 11.3*e* shows the main program and the headings for the procedures, and Figure 11.3*f* shows the running of the program.

```
PROGRAM Replacement(input, output, SentenceFile);
 (* Replaces substrings in a string *)
CONST Max = 126;
TYPE Line = ARRAY[0..Max] OF Char;

VAR NewWord, OldWord, Sentence:Line;
   Position:integer;
PROCEDURE ReadString(VAR Stream:Line);              {See page 451}
FUNCTION Length(Stream:Line):integer;              {See page 453}
PROCEDURE Insert(SubString:Line; VAR Instring:Line; Index:
   integer);                                        {See page 465}
PROCEDURE Delete(VAR InString:Line; Index,Count:integer);
                                                    {See page 463}
FUNCTION Pos(SubString, InString:Line):integer;    {See page 461}
PROCEDURE Replace(NewWord, OldWord:Line; VAR Sentence: Line);
                                                    {See page 467}

PROCEDURE ReadFile(VAR Sentence:Line);             {See page 467}
BEGIN (* Replacement *)
  ReadFile(Sentence);
  write('Type the word to be replaced: ');
  ReadString(input, OldWord);
  write('Type new word: ');
  ReadString(input, NewWord);
  writeln;

  write('The word replaced starts in ');
  Replace(NewWord, OldWord, Sentence);
END.
```

FIGURE 11.3e.   The main program and the headings for the procedures used. If you run the program, you must also include the procedures themselves.

```
The sentence read was:
To be or not to be, To see or not to see...

Type the word to be replaced: to
Type new word: three

The word replaced starts in Position = 14
To be or not three be, To see or not to see...
```

FIGURE 11.3f.   Running the program of Figure 11.3e. Replaces only the first occurrence of the old word.

Part III: Capitalizing a Word

The third stage, shown in Figure 11.4*a*, capitalizes a word. Function UpCase takes a lowercase letter, OldWord[1], and capitalizes it. We use OldWord[1], since the first letter of a word is stored in the first location of the string. The function assumes that your compiler uses the ASCII collating sequence. The capitalization is done in

$$Upcase := chr(ord(ch) - 32)$$

Note that if Ch is not a lowercase letter, the function returns the value of Ch. If your compiler doesn't use the ASCII sequence, you'll have to change the "−32" in ord(ch) − 32 as required. The running of the program is shown in Figure 11.4*b*.

TEST YOURSELF

QUESTION: If the difference in the ordinal values of each lowercase and uppercase letter was the same in a certain collating sequence, how would you write the statements that enable the program itself to determine this difference?

ANSWER:

$$Difference := ord('A') - ord('a');$$
$$Upcase := chr(ord(Ch) + Difference)$$

QUESTION: Would Upcase (see Figure 11.4*a*) work as required if your compiler used the EBCDIC table?

ANSWER: No. The non-letter characters falling between a and z would be treated incorrectly since Upcase would not return these non-letter characters.

A WORD PROCESSING PROGRAM
PART III: CAPITALIZING A WORD

```
PROGRAM Capitalize(input, output);
(* Capitalizes a word *)
CONST Quote = '"';

Max = 126;
TYPE Line = ARRAY[0..Max] OF Char;

VAR OldWord: Line;

PROCEDURE ReadString(VAR Stream:Line);            {See page 451}

FUNCTION Length(Stream:Line):integer;            {See page 453}

PROCEDURE Print(Stream:Line);                    {See page 455}


FUNCTION Upcase(Ch:char):char;
(* Converts lowercase to uppercase *)
BEGIN
   IF Ch IN ['a'..'z'] THEN
      Upcase:= chr(ord(ch) - 32)
   ELSE Upcase := Ch
END (* Upcase *);


BEGIN (* Capitalize *)
   writeln('Type a word ');
   ReadString(input, OldWord);
   OldWord[1]:= UpCase(OldWord[1]);
   write('The capitalized word is ', Quote);
   Print(OldWord);
   writeln(Quote)
END.
```

FIGURE 11.4a.   Capitalizes a word and makes the capitalized word the same length as the old word. The headings of the other subprograms used are also included. If you run the program, you must also include the procedures themselves.

```
Type a word
thinking
The capitalized word is "Thinking"
```

FIGURE 11.4b.   Running the program of Figure 11.4a.

Part IV: Replacing the First Occurrence of the Lowercase and Capitalized Word in a Sentence

The pseudocode to replace the first occurrence of the lowercase substring and the first occurrence of the uppercase substring in a sentence is

> *Read the substring,* OldWord, *you wish to replace;*
>
> *Read the substring,* NewWord, *you wish to replace it with;*
>
> *Replace* OldWord *with* NewWord;
>
> *Capitalize* OldWord;
>
> *Capitalize* NewWord;
>
> *Replace* OldWord *with* NewWord;

The program (see Figure 11.4c) uses procedures Replace and ReadFile.

A WORD PROCESSING PROGRAM
PART IV: REPLACING THE FIRST OCCURRENCE OF THE
LOWERCASE AND CAPITALIZED WORD IN A SENTENCE

```
PROGRAM ReplaceWord(input, output, SentenceFile);
(* Replaces a word in a string whether or not it is capitalized *)
CONST Max = 126;
TYPE Line = ARRAY[0..Max] OF Char;

VAR NewWord, OldWord, Sentence:Line;
    Position:integer;
    SentenceFile:text;

PROCEDURE ReadString(VAR Stream:Line);                              {See page 451}
FUNCTION Length(Stream:Line):integer;                              {See page 453}
PROCEDURE Insert(SubString:Line; VAR Instring:Line; Index:integer);
                                                                   {See page 465}
PROCEDURE Delete(VAR InString:Line; Index,Count:integer);         {See page 463}
FUNCTION Pos(SubString, InString:Line):integer;                   {See page 461}
FUNCTION Upcase(Ch:char):char;                                    {See page 471}
PROCEDURE Replace(NewWord, OldWord:Line; VAR Sentence:Line);      {See page 467}
PROCEDURE ReadFile(VAR Sentence:Line);                            {See page 467}

BEGIN (* ReplaceWord *)
  ReadFile(Sentence);
  writeln;
  write('Type the word to be replaced: ');
  ReadString(input, OldWord);
  readln;
  write('Type new word: ');
  ReadString(input, NewWord);
  writeln;
  write('The sentence with the lowercase word replaced starting in ');
  Replace(NewWord, OldWord, Sentence);
  writeln;
  OldWord[1]:= UpCase(OldWord[1]);
  NewWord[1]:= UpCase(NewWord[1]);
  write('The sentence with the capitalized word replaced starting in ');
  Replace(NewWord, OldWord, Sentence)
END.
```

FIGURE 11.4c.   Replaces the first occurrence of the lowercase word and then the first occurrence of the capitalized word. The headings of the subprograms used are also included. If you run the program you must also include the procedures themselves.

As we see when the program is run (Figure 11.4d)

> Three be or not three be, To see or not to see...

the first "To" and "to" have been replaced, respectively, with "Three" and "three".

Part V: Replacing All Occurrences of the Lowercase and Capitalized Word in a Sentence

In order to use the pos function to find all the occurrences of a substring in a string, you must replace an occurrence of the substring before you can find the next one (the reason is that pos finds only the first occurrence of a substring). Thus to find the positions of both "to's in the string Sentence

> To be or not to be, To see or not to see . . .

the program must replace the first "to" before it can locate the second one. Once all the "to"s have been replaced, the value of pos('to', Sentence) will be 0, so we write the following pseudocode for procedure Replace:

> *Find the position of the first occurrence of* OldWord;
> WHILE *the position is not zero* DO BEGIN
>   *Delete* OldWord *from the sentence;*
>   *Insert* NewWord *in that position;*
>   *Find position of next occurrence of* OldWord
> END (* WHILE *);

We translate this into procedure Replace, shown in Figure 11.5a.

Since we must replace both "to" and "To" in the sentence, we activate Replace twice; thus the pseudocode for the main program is

> *Read the substring,* OldWord, *you wish to replace;*
> *Read the substring,* NewWord, *you wish to replace it with;*
> *Replace all* OldWords *with* NewWord;
> *Capitalize* OldWord *and* NewWord;
> *Replace all* OldWords *with* NewWord;
> *Print the edited sentence.*

The sentence read was:

To be or not to be, To see or not to see...

Type the word to be replaced: to
Type new Word: three

The sentence with the lowercase word replaced starting in Position = 14
To be or not three be, To see or not to see...
The sentence with the capitalized word replaced starting in Position = 1
Three be or not three be, To see or not to see...

FIGURE 11.4d.   Running the program of Figure 11.4c.

A WORD PROCESSING PROGRAM
PART V: REPLACING ALL OCCURRENCES OF THE
LOWERCASE AND CAPITALIZED WORD IN A SENTENCE

```
PROCEDURE Replace(NewWord, OldWord:Line; VAR Sentence:Line);
(* Replaces a word in a string *)
VAR Position:integer;
BEGIN
  Position:= Pos(OldWord, Sentence);
  WHILE Position <> 0 DO BEGIN
    delete(Sentence, Position, Length(OldWord));
    insert(NewWord, Sentence, Position);
    Position:= Pos(OldWord, Sentence)
  END (* WHILE *);
END; (* Replace *)
```

FIGURE 11.5a.   The second version of Replace. As the procedure finds each occurrence of the desired word, it replaces it and then finds the next occurrence.

The program is shown in Figure 11.5b, and its running in Figure 11.5c.

```
PROGRAM ReplaceWord(input, output, SentenceFile);
(* Replaces all occurrences of a word in a string, whether or not it is
capitalized. If the replaced word is capitalized, so is the replacement *)
CONST Max = 126;
TYPE Line = ARRAY[0..Max] OF Char;
VAR NewWord, OldWord, Sentence:Line;
    SentenceFile:text;

PROCEDURE ReadString(VAR Stream:Line);                              {See page 451}
FUNCTION Length(Stream:Line):integer;                              {See page 453}
PROCEDURE Insert(SubString:Line; VAR Instring:Line; Index:integer);
                                                                  {See page 465}
PROCEDURE Delete(VAR InString:Line; Index,Count:integer);         {See page 463}
FUNCTION Pos(SubString, InString:Line):integer;                   {See page 461}
FUNCTION Upcase(Ch:char):char;                                    {See page 471}
PROCEDURE Replace(NewWord, OldWord:Line; VAR Sentence:Line);      {See page 475}
PROCEDURE ReadFile(VAR Sentence:Line);                            {See page 467}

BEGIN (* ReplaceWord *)
  ReadFile(Sentence);
  writeln;
  write('Type the word to be replaced: ');
  ReadString(input, OldWord);
  readln;
  write('Type new Word: ');
  ReadString(input, NewWord);
  writeln;
  writeln('The sentence with the lowercase word replaced: ');
  Replace(NewWord, OldWord, Sentence);
  Print(Sentence);
  writeln;
  writeln('The sentence with the capitalized word also replaced:');
  OldWord[1]:= Upcase(OldWord[1]);
  NewWord[1]:= Upcase(NewWord[1]);
  Replace(NewWord, OldWord, Sentence);
  Print(Sentence)
END.
```

FIGURE 11.5b.   Replaces all occurrences of a word in a string, whether or not it is capitalized. If the replaced word is capitalized, so is the replacement. The headings of the subprograms used are also included.

```
The sentence read was:
To be or not to be, To see or not to see...

Type the word to be replaced: to
Type new Word: three

The sentence with the lowercase word replaced:
To be or not three be, To see or not three see...

The sentence with the capitalized word also replaced:
Three be or not three be, Three see or not three see...
```

FIGURE 11.5c.   Running the program of Figure 11.5b.

The procedure, shown in Figure 11.6, is another string procedure we will use.

The copy Procedure This procedure copies a substring to a string variable. Its form is copy(*string, substring, starting position, length of substring*) where * *starting position* indicates where in the string the substring starts. For example, in copy('abcdef', Sub, 2, 3), the value of Sub is bcd. If *starting position* is greater than the string length, for example, copy('abcdef', Sub, 8, 3), the function returns the null string, that is, the string that has a length of 0. If *length of the substring* is greater than the length of the string, for example, copy('abcdef', Sub, 4, 20), only the part of the string up to the end is copied, here def.

11.3

PACKED ARRAYS

We've seen that an entire array can be referred to just by the array variable in two cases:

1. When you pass an array to a procedure or function, as in Switch–(List, J), where List is an array.
2. When you assign all the elements of an array to another array, as in Name := Number, where Name and Number are both arrays of the same type.

We'll now learn about the PACKED ARRAY, another case where we can use the array variable to refer to the entire array. A type is a PACKED ARRAY type if it is defined in terms of an array whose elements are of char type and if the words PACKED ARRAY replace ARRAY. For instance, in TYPE CharArray = PACKED ARRAY[1..5] OF char, CharArray is a packed array type. You can perform specific operations on variables—they fall within our definition of a string variable—whose type is a packed array simply by referring to the array variable. For our example, we'll declare the string variable Name in VAR Name : CharArray. These operations are as follows:

1. Assigning a string to the string variable, for example, Name := 'thing'; however, the string length must be the same as the dimension of the array, here 5. If the string is shorter than the length of the string

---

*The Turbo Pascal version of Copy is a function whose value is the substring.

```
PROCEDURE Copy(InString:Line; VAR Substring:Line; Index, Count:integer);
(* Copies a substring to a string *)
(* "Index" is starting point and "Count" is length *)
VAR IndexIn, IndexOut, Len:integer;
BEGIN
  Len:= Length(InString);
  IF Index <= Len THEN BEGIN (* Can't copy part beyond end *)
      IndexIn:= Index;
      FOR IndexOut:= 1 TO Count DO BEGIN
         Substring[IndexOut]:=InString[IndexIn];
         IndexIn:= IndexIn + 1
      END (* FOR *);
      IF Index + Count > Len THEN (* truncate at length *)
         Substring[0]:= Chr(Len - Index + 1)
      ELSE
         Substring[0]:= Chr(Count)
    END (* IF *)
    ELSE
      Substring[0]:= chr(0)
END (* Copy *);
```

FIGURE 11.6.   Copies a substring of InString to the string SubString. "Index" is the starting point and "Count" is the length of the substring in the original string.

variable, you must add trailing blanks to the string.* Thus we add two blanks to the in assigning it to Name in

$$\text{Name} := \text{'the\ \ '}.$$

2. Outputting the entire string variable without using a subscript; for example, `writeln(Name)` will write the string `thing`.

3. Comparing two string variables or a string variable and a string constant of the same length to determine the alphabetical order by using the relational operators. Thus if you've declared VAR Small, Letter : CharArray;, you can form the boolean expression Letter < Small and test whether the string stored in Letter alphabetically precedes the string stored in Small. Thus, if Letter stored 'cat' and Small stored 'dog', then Letter < Small would be true.

Beware of the following:

1. The lower subscript bound of a packed array must be 1. Thus TYPE CharArray = PACKED ARRAY[0..5] OF char would produce a syntax error.

2. You cannot** read a packed array simply by using the array identifier in a read or readln. Thus read(Name) would produce a syntax error.

Figure 11.6a shows a program that determines which six-character word typed as input has the lowest alphabetical value. First, we assign to Small the six-character word that has the highest value by writing Small := 'zzzzzz', since z is the last letter of the alphabet. Here we've used characteristic 1 of a packed array. Thus any other word read into the program has a lower alphabetical order than Small. Then we read subsequent six-character words in the WHILE loop in FOR K := 1 TO 6 DO read(Word[K]). Next, we use characteristic 3 of a packed array by writing IF Word < Small THEN Small := Word. Thus, if a word is lower alphabetically than Small, we assign it to Small (see the table for Figure 11.6a). Finally, we use characteristic 2 to print the value of Small in writeln('First word alphabetically is :', Small). The output is shown in Figure 11.6b.

Pitfalls

If the dimension of a string is not large enough, you may get the wrong answer in an insertion. Thus insert('abcdefgh', Term, 3), where the value of Term is bring and its length is 5, will produce brabc instead of brabcdefghing.

---

*VAX Pascal automatically pads the end of a string with blanks.

**You can do this in VAX Pascal.

PACKED ARRAYS

```
PROGRAM IntroToPack(input, output);
(* Uses packed array to find the first word in alphabetical order *)
TYPE CharArray = PACKED ARRAY[1..6] OF char;
VAR Small, Word:CharArray;
  K:1..6;
BEGIN
  Small:= 'zzzzzz';
  writeln('Type 6-character words on one line.');
  WHILE NOT eoln DO BEGIN (* Are subsequent words smaller? *)
    FOR K:= 1 TO 6 DO
      read(Word[K]);
    IF Word < Small THEN
      Small:= Word
  END (* WHILE *);
  writeln;
  writeln('First word alphabetically is :', Small)
END.
```

FIGURE 11.6a. Shows the use of packed arrays of string variables. We use them to (1) assign a string to the string variable, (2) output the entire string variable without using a subscript, and (3) compare two string variables or a string variable and a string.

Word	Small	Word < Small
thinkB	zzzzzz	True
likeBB	thinkB	True
mister	likeBB	False

TABLE FOR FIGURE 11.6a. The B represents a blank. The blank has a lower value in the collating sequence than any letter. The computer compares strings in the same way that you would compare two words when alphabetizing them for a dictionary. Thus thinkBB < thinker is true.

```
Type 6-character words on one line.
think like mister
First word alphabetically is :like
```

FIGURE 11.6b. Running the program of Figure 11.6a.

NEW TERMS

global search and replace   string variable
packed arrays   substring

EXERCISES

1. Given `StringA:= 'aaaabbbb'` and `SubString:= 'ab'`, what is the value of `Pos('ab', StringA)`?

2. What is the value of `Delete(StringA, 3, 3)` for the previous problem?

3. What is the value of `Insert(SubString, StringA, 3)` for the previous problem?

4. Write the `Copy` function that will produce substring bbb from the string `StringA`.

Programming Problems

5. Write a program that determines whether a string is a palindrome, assuming that the string has no blanks or punctuation marks and that all the letters in the string are of one case, either lowercase or uppercase.

6. Do the previous problem, assuming that the string contains punctuation marks and blanks. Hint: Remove the blanks and punctuation marks from the string and then use the solution to the previous problem as a procedure.

7. Do the previous problem, assuming that the string contains a mixture of uppercase and lowercase letters.

8. Write a program that removes all occurrences of a given word from a string.

9. Define an array of characters `StringArray` such that `StringArray = PACKED ARRAY[1..80] OF char`. Using this definition, write your version of function `Length`.

10. Using the definition in problem 9, write your version of function `pos`.

11. Using the definition in problem 9, write your version of function `copy`. Your version of `copy` will have to be a procedure, since the type of a function can't be an array.

12. Using the definition in problem 9, write your version of procedure `delete`.

13. Using the definition in problem 9, write your version of procedure `insert`.

14. Using these definitions, write your own version of a search and replace program.

Let's write a program that will find all the last names of married women in a paragraph stored on a file and on which line they were found. For instance, in

```
Hello Mrs. Smith, Mrs. Jones, and Mrs.
Abrams. Lend me your ears. How are
Mrs. Davis; and Mrs. Cook?
```

the last names of the married women appearing on the first line are "Smith" and "Jones". We'll write the program in four steps:

Step 1 finds the word (here, the last name) immediately following the first occurrence of "Mrs." in a sentence, assuming that the delimiter for this word is a blank. Thus given "Hello Mrs. Smith; and Mrs. Jones? Do you know Mrs. Abrams", the program would find "Smith;". In other words, the punctuation is included in the word.

Step 2 finds all the last names in a sentence (again, assuming that a blank is the delimiter). Thus in the sentence of Step 1, it would find "Smith;" and "Jones?", but not "Abrams" because "Abrams" is immediately followed by a carriage return. Again, the punctuation marks are included in the names found.

Step 3 finds all the last names in a sentence (assuming that any nonletter is a delimiter). Thus it would find "Smith", "Jones", and "Abrams".

Step 4 extends Step 3 to a paragraph. In addition, when a sentence ends with "Mrs.", the program will print the first word in the next sentence.

15. Write the program for Step 1.
The pseudocode is

> *Read* LeadWord;
> *Read sentence from the file;*
> *Find and print the word after* LeadWord

where in our case LeadWord is "Mrs.". This suggests the top-down diagram

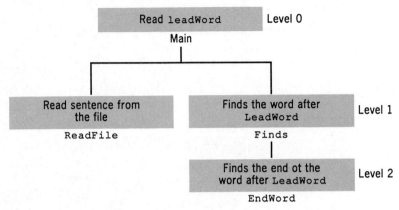

The pseudocode for procedure Finds is

> *Find the position of* LeadWord *in the sentence;*
> *Redefine the sentence so that the part from its beginning*
> *to the end of* LeadWord *is erased.*
> *Find the end of the first word in the redefined sentence;*
> *Copy that word to the printer.*

Implement *Find the end of the first word* by subtracting 1 from the position of the next blank, in function EndWord.

16. Write the program for Step II.

In order to find the words that follows each occurrence of LeadWord, let's rewrite procedure Finds. The pseudocode for the new version is

> *Find the position of* LeadWord *in the sentence;*
> WHILE *that position* <> 0 DO BEGIN
>   *Redefine the sentence so that the part from its beginning*
>   *to the end of* LeadWord *is erased.*
>   *Find the end of the first word in the redefined sentence;*
>   *Copy that word to the printer;*
>   *Find the position of* LeadWord *in the redefined sentence*
> END (* WHILE *) ;

In order to search for each occurrence of LeadWord, use

```
Copy(Sentence, Sentence, PosNextWord, ToEnd);
```

where the value of PosNextWord is the position of the beginning of the next word, and the value of ToEnd is 300 since only the part of the string up to its end is copied. Redefining Sentence this way erases the sentence up to the word following LeadWord and allows the program in

```
Copy(Sentence, TargetWord, 1, EndPosition);
```

to search for a new last name each time the loop is executed, where EndPosition indicates the end of the first word.

17. Write the program for Step III.

What's new here is that function EndWord is rewritten so that when it finds the end of the first word in the redefined Sentence, it looks for any nonletter as the delimiter. Its pseudocode is

> *Set* Index *to 1;*
> WHILE *the current character is a letter* DO
>   *Increment* Index *by 1;*
>   *Since the last value of* Index *is for a nonletter,*
>   *subtract 1 from* Index

Because the boolean expression in the translation of the WHILE should be (sentence[Index] IN ['a'..'z', 'A'..'Z']) AND (Index <= Length-(Sentence), so that the function finds the last word in the sentence even if it is immediately followed by a carriage return.

18. Write the program for Step IV.

This step extends Step III to a program that reads a paragraph. The top-down diagram for the program is

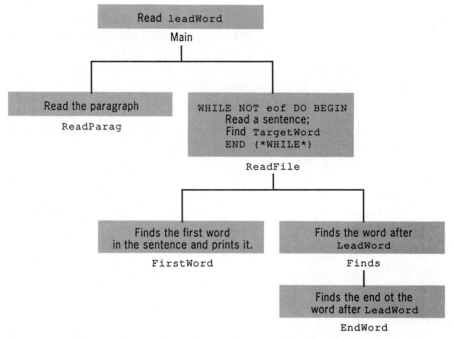

In order to find a last name (TargetWord) even if "Mrs." is the last word in the preceding sentence, do the following:

1. Alter procedure Finds so that it tests whether LeadWord is the last word in the sentence; this means that TargetWord will be the first word in the next sentence. If it is, set the boolean VAR parameter, NextSentence, to true in this procedure,

$$\text{IF PosNextWord} >= \text{length(Sentence) THEN}$$
$$\text{NextSentence}: = \text{True};$$

2. Add procedure FirstWord, which prints the first word in the sentence. This will be activated if the value of NextSentence is True.

3. Add procedure ReadParag so that you can see the paragraph before you make any alterations.

4. Add procedure ReadFile which reads each line of the paragraph. If the previous line ends with LeadWord, this procedure will direct the computer to print the first word in the next line.

The output should display the line number and the last names occurring on the line with that number. If you arrange this information in alphabetic order, you can construct an index.

12

USER-ENUMERATED TYPES

CHAPTER OVERVIEW

You have learned about the standard ordinal types:integer, boolean, and character. Did you know that you can define your own ordinal types to fit a given problem? This chapter shows you how to do so and applies this technique to a program that produces a calendar, to one that produces a series of Roman numerals, and finally, to the regional survey problem introduced in Chapter 2.

12.1

ENUMERATED TYPES

Pascal allows the programmer to define his own ordinal types, which are called *user-defined enumerated types*. In doing so, the programmer chooses the identifiers that define the type. For instance, in

    PartDescrip = (ScrewDriver, Pliers, Hammer, Wrench)

the programmer has defined a type, PartDescrip, that has four values, ranging from ScrewDriver to Wrench. This is a more meaningful description of the items than writing, for instance, the subrange definition Part = 1..4.

In the enumerated type definition, the ordinal value of the first identifier after the "(", here ScrewDriver, is 0, that of the second one, here Pliers, is 1 and so forth. This indicates for instance that the value of ord(Pliers) is 1 and that of Hammer > Pliers is true. Similarly, the value of succ(Pliers) is Hammer, which is also the value of pred(Wrench). As is the case with the ordinal types you have studied, you may use variable identifiers of enumerated types as the loop control variable in FOR–DO loops. For instance, given VAR Tool: PartDescrip, you can write FOR Tool:= Pliers TO Wrench DO. Another advantage of enumerated types is that since they are ordinal types, they can be used as subscripts.

Let's use both of these properties for the enumerated type PartDescrip to write a program that determines how many tools of each description a store has in inventory. To do this, we'll use an array of the type

    ToolArray = ARRAY[PartDescrip] OF integer

to count the number of tools of a given description. The array NumberOf will be of the type ToolArray. Thus NumberOf[ScrewDriver] will count the number of screwdrivers, NumberOf [Pliers] will count the number of pliers, and so on. The overall description of the three procedures in the program is shown in table for Figure 12.1.

Figure 12.1a(I) shows procedure Zero. Since PartDescrip is an ordinal type, you can zero the array NumberOf by writing

    FOR Part:= ScrewDriver TO Wrench DO
      NumberOf[Part]:=0;

where Part is of type PartDescrip and NumberOf is of type ToolArray.

AN INVENTORY PROGRAM THAT USES AN ENUMERATED TYPE

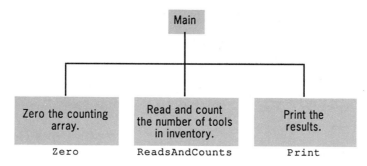

TABLE FOR FIGURE 12.1. The top-down diagram for an inventory program.

```
TYPE PartDescrip = (ScrewDriver, Pliers, Hammer, Wrench);
   ToolArray = ARRAY[PartDescrip] OF integer;

PROCEDURE Zero(VAR NumberOf:ToolArray);
(* Zeros the counting array *)
VAR Part: PartDescrip;
BEGIN
   FOR Part:= ScrewDriver TO Wrench DO (* zero all elements OF the ARRAY *)
      NumberOf[Part]:=0;
END (* Zero *);
```

FIGURE 12.1a(I). We define an enumerated type, PartDescrip, in the main program and specify the identifiers. ScrewDriver has an ordinal value of 0, and Wrench has an ordinal value of 3. This procedure zeros the four counters Number−Of[Part].

In Standard Pascal , you can use the user-defined identifiers everywhere in the program, except as input to the program or as output using a terminal or text file. For instance, the following would cause a syntax error

```
FOR Part:= ScrewDriver TO Wrench DO read(Part)
```

since `Part` is of type `PartDescrip`. Thus you have to read the input using the standard input types and then convert to the user-enumerated types subsequently in the program. The pseudocode for `ReadsAndCounts`, the procedure that does this, is

> WHILE NOT eoln DO BEGIN
>   *Read the part number;*
>   IF *the part number is a valid one* THEN
>   *Increment the proper counter*
> END

The code *Increment the proper counter* becomes

```
CASE PartNum OF
   1: NumberOf[ScrewDriver] := NumberOf[ScrewDriver] + 1;
   2: NumberOf[Pliers] := NumberOf[Pliers] + 1;
   3: NumberOf[Hammer] := NumberOf[Hammer] + 1;
   4: NumberOf[Wrench] := NumberOf[Wrench] + 1
END (* CASE *)
```

where the value of the part number, `PartNum`, is read as 1 for a screwdriver, 2 for pliers, 3 for a hammer, and 4 for a wrench. The procedure that reads and counts the tools is shown in Figure 12.1a(II).

Procedure `Print` converts from the user-defined enumerated types to strings in order to output the results. The pseudocode is

> FOR *each of the tools* DO
>   *Print the string corresponding to the identifier*
>   *representing the tool.*

This becomes the procedure shown in Figure 12.1a(III). The main program is

```
PROCEDURE ReadsAndCounts(VAR NumberOf:ToolArray);
VAR PartNum: integer;
    Part: PartDescrip;
BEGIN
  writeln('Type inventory number');
  WHILE NOT eoln DO BEGIN
        read(PartNum);
        IF PartNum IN [1..4] THEN
          CASE PartNum OF (* Place number in proper bin *)
            1: NumberOf[ScrewDriver] := NumberOf[ScrewDriver] + 1;
            2: NumberOf[Pliers] := NumberOf[Pliers] + 1;
            3: NumberOf[Hammer] := NumberOf[Hammer] + 1;
            4: NumberOf[Wrench] := NumberOf[Wrench] + 1
          END (* CASE *)
      ELSE
        writeln(PartNum, ' is not a valid part number')
END (* WHILE *);
writeln
END (* ReadsAndCounts *);
```

FIGURE 12.1a(II). This procedure counts the number of each item. You can't read (or print) an enumerated type, so this procedure reads an integer type and then increments the proper counter.

```
PROCEDURE Print(NumberOf:ToolArray);
(* Print results *)
VAR Part: PartDescrip;
BEGIN
  FOR Part:= ScrewDriver TO Wrench DO BEGIN
    write('number of ');
    CASE Part OF
      ScrewDriver: write('screw drivers');
      Pliers: write('pliers');
      Hammer: write('hammers');
      Wrench: write('wrenches')
    END (* CASE *);
    writeln( ' is ', NumberOf[Part])
  END(* FOR *)
END (* Prints *);
```

FIGURE 12.1a(III). This procedure translates the identifiers of the ordinal type into strings and prints the results of the program.

shown in Figure 12.1*b*, and the results of running the program are shown in Figure 12.1*c*.

Enumerated Subrange Types

You can define subranges of enumerated types. Thus given

```
TYPE DayOfWeek = (Sun, Mon, Tue, Wed, Thu, Fri, Sat);
```

the subrange TYPE First = Sun..Wed; will consist of Sun, Mon, Tue, and Wed. However, once you use an identifier in an enumerated type, you can't use the same identifier in another enumerated type in the same block. Thus once DayOfWeek is defined, you can't define WeekEnd as TYPE WeekEnd = (Sun, Sat); in the same block, because WeekEnd would contain two of the identifiers used in DayOfWeek. You can, however, define WeekEnd in a block in which DayOfWeek is not defined. For instance, if DayOfWeek were defined only in Figure 12.1*a* in procedure Zero, you could define WeekEnd in procedure Print.

Constant Identifiers of an Enumerated Type

You may define a constant of an enumerated type anywhere in the program after the enumerated type itself is defined. For instance, you can write

```
TYPE PartDescrip = (ScrewDriver, Pliers, Hammer, Wrench)
CONST FirstTool = ScrewDriver; LastTool = Wrench;
```

Illegal Enumerated Type Identifiers

Since the values of an enumerated type must be identifiers, they can't be digits or text constants (for example, 'Dog'. Thus the following enumerated types will cause a syntax error:

```
TYPE Vowel = ('a', 'e', 'i', 'o', 'u');
     Digits = (0, 1, 2, 3, 4, 5, 6, 7, 8, 9);
```

TEST YOURSELF

QUESTION: Why is 'a' an illegal enumerated value?

ANSWER: It contains a single quotation mark ('), which is an illegal character for an identifier.

```
PROGRAM ReadsAndCounts(input, output);
(* Histograms using the enumerated TYPE *)
TYPE PartDescrip = (ScrewDriver, Pliers, Hammer, Wrench);
  ToolArray = ARRAY[PartDescrip] OF integer;
VAR NumberOf:ToolArray;

PROCEDURE Zero(VAR NumberOf:ToolArray);                {See page 489}
PROCEDURE ReadsAndCounts(VAR NumberOf:ToolArray);      {See page 491}
PROCEDURE Print(NumberOf:ToolArray);                   {See page 491}

BEGIN
  Zero(NumberOf);
  ReadsAndCounts(NumberOf);
  Print(NumberOf)
END.
```

FIGURE 12.1b. The main program and the headings for the procedures used in the program. If you run the program, you must also include the procedures themselves.

```
          Type inventory number
          1 2 2 1 2 3 6 4 2 3 4 1 2 2 3 4 4 8 2 3
          6 is not a valid part number
          8 is not a valid part number
          number of screwdrivers is 3
          number of pliers is 7
          number of hammers is 4
          number of wrenches is 4
```

FIGURE 12.1c. Running the program of Figure 12.1b.

12.2

CALENDAR-RELATED PROGRAMS

BEFORE YOU BEGIN

One may ask, why do we use enumerated types if we cannot use them in input or output? One reason is that this is a way of implicitly documenting the program, thereby making it easier to understand. For instance, using

```
DayOfWeek = (Sun, Mon, Tue, Wed, Thu, Fri, Sat);
```

is more meaningful than using DayOfWeek = 0..6. In other cases, using an enumerated type makes the writing of a program easier. Let's see how it does.

Our next goal is to write a program that produces a calendar. Before we do that, let's write a simpler program that uses the same enumerated type. This program prints the day of the week corresponding to each day of a particular 30-day month. The pseudocode is

> *Assign a day of the week to the first day of the month;*
> FOR *day of the month varying from* 1 TO 30 DO BEGIN
>   *Print the string corresponding to the day of the week;*
>   *Advance the day of the week*
> END (* FOR *);

To translate *Advance the day of the week* to Pascal, you must first define the type:

```
TYPE DayOfWeek = (Sun, Mon, Tue, Wed, Thu, Fri, Sat);
```

as shown in Figure 12.2*a*. Then, if the day of the week is represented by the identifier Day of type DayOfWeek, *Advance the day of the week* can be translated into

```
IF Day = Sat THEN
   Day:= Sun
ELSE
   Day:= succ(Day)
```

The running of the program is shown in Figure 12.2*b*.

PRODUCING A CALENDAR—STEP I. CONVERTING THE DATE TO THE DAY OF THE WEEK

```
PROGRAM Day(input, output);
(* Produces day of week for each date in the month *)
TYPE
    DayOfWeek = (Sun, Mon, Tue, Wed, Thu, Fri, Sat);
VAR
    Day: DayOfWeek;
    DayOfMonth: integer;
BEGIN
    Day:=Tue;
    FOR DayOfMonth:= 1 TO 30 DO BEGIN
      write(' Day ', DayOfMonth:2, ' is ');
      CASE Day OF
          Sun: write('Sunday');
          Mon: write('Monday');
          Tue: write('Tuesday');
          Wed: write('Wednesday');
          Thu: write('Thursday');
          Fri: write('Friday');
          Sat: write('Saturday')
      END (* CASE *);
      write('.');
      IF DayOfMonth MOD 3 = 0 THEN (* Prints 3 days per line *)
        writeln;
      IF Day = Sat THEN
          Day:= Sun
      ELSE
          Day:= succ(Day)
    END (* FOR *)
END.
```

FIGURE 12.2a. The program uses the succ function to correlate the days of the month with the days of the week, the enumerated type identifiers.

```
Day 1 is Tuesday. Day 2 is Wednesday. Day 3 is Thursday.
Day 4 is Friday. Day 5 is Saturday. Day 6 is Sunday.
Day 7 is Monday. Day 8 is Tuesday. Day 9 is Wednesday.
Day 10 is Thursday. Day 11 is Friday. Day 12 is Saturday.
Day 13 is Sunday. Day 14 is Monday. Day 15 is Tuesday.
Day 16 is Wednesday. Day 17 is Thursday. Day 18 is Friday.
Day 19 is Saturday. Day 20 is Sunday. Day 21 is Monday.
Day 22 is Tuesday. Day 23 is Wednesday. Day 24 is Thursday.
Day 25 is Friday. Day 26 is Saturday. Day 27 is Sunday.
Day 28 is Monday. Day 29 is Tuesday. Day 30 is Wednesday.
```

FIGURE 12.2b. Running the program of Figure 12.2a.

The next program produces a calendar for a given month. The top-down diagram is

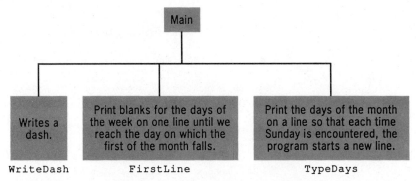

WriteDash   FirstLine   TypeDays

Refine the pseudocode in the top-down diagram for FirstLine to

FOR *weekday from Sun* TO *first weekday of the month* DO
    Print blanks

This becomes the Pascal code shown in Figure 12.3a(I). Refine the pseudocode for TypeDays to

Set weekday to first weekday of month;
FOR *each day of the month* DO BEGIN
  IF *weekday is* SAT THEN BEGIN
     write day number and start a new line;
     Print a line of dashes;
     Set weekday to Sun
   END (* THEN *)
  ELSE BEGIN (* *Any day but Sat* *)
     write day number;
     Set weekday to next weekday
  END (* ELSE *)
END (* FOR *)

This becomes the Pascal code shown in Figure 12.3a(II), where *Print a line*

PRODUCING A CALENDAR—STEP II. THE CALENDAR

```
TYPE
   DayOfWeek = (Sun, Mon, Tue, Wed, Thu, Fri, Sat);

PROCEDURE FirstLine(FirstDay: DayOfWeek);
(* Print blanks on the first line until the first of the month *)
VAR Day: DayOfWeek;
BEGIN
  FOR Day: = Sun TO pred(FirstDay) DO
    write( ' ':6);
END (* FirstLine *);
```

FIGURE 12.3a(I).   This procedure prints blanks on the first line of the calendar until the first day of the month. Here the enumerated type is defined in the main program.

```
PROCEDURE TypeDays(Day: DayOfWeek);
(* Types the days in the month on the calendar *)
VAR NumberOfDay: integer;

BEGIN
  (* Start typing the days in the month on the calendar *)
  FOR NumberOfDay := 1 TO 31 DO
    BEGIN (* FOR *)
      IF Day = Sat THEN (* Day is Sat, then finish line *)
        BEGIN
          writeln( NumberOfDay:4, ' ');
          WriteDash;
          Day: = Sun
        END (* THEN *)
      ELSE (* continue printing on the same line *)
        BEGIN
          write( NumberOfDay:4, ' ');
          Day: = succ(Day)
        END
    END (* FOR *);
  writeln;
END (* TypeDays *);
```

FIGURE 12.3a(II).   This procedure prints the days of the month in the proper column. The original value of Day is the first weekday of the month. When Day is Sat, the date is written and Day is advanced to Sun, a carriage return is executed, and the procedure that draws a line is activated.

of dashes becomes the procedure shown in Figure 12.3*a*(III). The main program is shown in Figure 12.3*b* and the results in Figure 12.3*c*.

TEST YOURSELF

QUESTION: Why doesn't the following version of procedure `FirstLine` produce the correct results?

```
PROCEDURE FirstLine(VAR Day: DayOfWeek);
VAR FirstDay: DayOfWeek;
BEGIN
  FirstDay:= Sat;
  FOR Day:= Sun TO pred(FirstDay) DO
    write(' ':6);
END (* FirstLine *)
```

ANSWER:

1. The `FOR` loop control variable must be a local variable.
2. The `FOR` loop control variable is undefined after the execution of the loop, so the value of `Day` cannot be returned to the program.

Using Enumerated Type Functions

You can write a function whose type is an enumerated type. For instance, the heading for a function that finds the day of the week for a given date would be

```
FUNCTION FindDay(FirstDay:DayOfWeek; Date:integer) :DayOfWeek;
```

TEST YOURSELF

QUESTION: Write a function that finds the day of the week for a given date. You must pass to the function the day on which the first day of the month falls.

ANSWER:

```
FUNCTION FindDay(FirstDay:DayOfWeek; Date:integer):DayOfWeek;
(* Finds the day of the week corresponding to the date *)
VAR Day: DayOfWeek;
  DateIndex: integer;
BEGIN
  Day:= FirstDay;
  FOR DateIndex:= 2 TO Date DO
    IF Day = Sat THEN
      Day:= Sun
    ELSE
      Day:= succ(Day);
  FindDay:= Day
END (* FindDay *);
```

```
    PROCEDURE WriteDash;
    BEGIN (* dash *)
       writeln('----------------------------------------------')
    END (* dash *);
```

FIGURE 12.3a(III).   This procedure writes a line of dashes in order to separate the lines of the calendar.

```
PROGRAM Calendar(input, output);
(* Produces a calendar *)
TYPE
   DayOfWeek = (Sun, Mon, Tue, Wed, Thu, Fri, Sat);
VAR FirstDay:DayOfWeek;
PROCEDURE WriteDash;                                      {On this page}
PROCEDURE FirstLine(FirstDay: DayOfWeek);                 {See page 497}
PROCEDURE TypeDays(Day: DayOfWeek);                       {See page 497}
BEGIN
   writeln( 'Sun':6, 'Mon':6, 'Tue':6, 'Wed':6, 'Thu':6, 'Fri':6,
   'Sat':6);
   WriteDash;
   FirstDay:= Tue;
   FirstLine(FirstDay);
   TypeDays(FirstDay);
   WriteDash
END.
```

FIGURE 12.3b.   The main program and the headings for the procedures used in the program. If you run the program, you must also include the procedures themselves.

Sun	Mon	Tue	Wed	Thu	Fri	Sat
						1
2	3	4	5	6	7	8
9	10	11	12	13	14	15
16	17	18	19	20	21	22
23	24	25	26	27	28	29
30	31					

FIGURE 12.3c.   Running the program of Figure 12.3b.

12.3

ROMAN NUMERALS

Next, we'll tackle a program that produces Roman numerals for the decimal numbers from 1 to 98. In order to plan the program, it is helpful to write the enumerated type first. The simplest way to do this is to convert the digits in the decimal number separately. For instance, for 23, convert the 2 to the Roman numeral for 20, namely, XX; and then convert the 3 to the Roman numeral for 3, namely, III. Thus it's natural to define the following two types:

```
FirstNumber = (none, X, XX, XXX, XL, L, LX, LXX, LXXX, XC);
SecondNumber = ( I, II, III, IV, V, VI, VII, VIII, IX, ten);
```

where None and Ten will be printed as a blank. The pseudocode is shown in Figure 12.4a.

The top-down diagram is

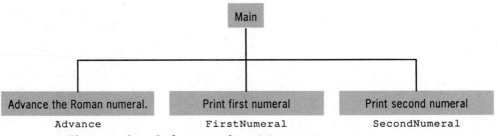

The pseudocode for procedure Advance is

> *Get the successor of Second numeral;*
> IF *Number is a multiple of 10* THEN
> *Get the successor of First numeral*

To understand this, consider the following example. When the value of *Second numeral* is V and the value of *First numeral* is X, the procedure advances *Second numeral* to VI and does nothing to *First numeral*. Thus the Roman numeral becomes XVI. However, if the value of *Second numeral* is ten and the value of *First numeral* is X, since the decimal number, *Number,* is a multiple of 10, the procedure not only advances *Second numeral* to I but also advances *First numeral* to XX. Procedure Advance is shown in Figure 12.4b(I). The statement part is

PRODUCING ROMAN NUMERALS

Set First numeral to None;
Set Second numeral to I;
FOR Number := 2 TO 98 DO BEGIN
   Advance the Roman numeral;
   Print First numeral;
   Print Second numeral
END (* FOR *);

FIGURE 12.4*a.* The pseudocode to print Roman numerals.

```
TYPE
   FirstNumber = (none, X, XX, XXX, XL, L, LX, LXX, LXXX, XC);
   SecondNumber = ( I, II, III, IV, V, VI, VII, VIII, IX, ten);

PROCEDURE Advance(VAR First: FirstNumber; VAR Second: SecondNumber;
Number:integer);
(* Gets the next Roman numeral *)
BEGIN
    IF Second = ten THEN
      Second := I
    ELSE
      Second := succ(Second);
    IF Number mod 10 = 0 THEN
      First := succ(First)
END (* Advance *);
```

FIGURE 12.4*b*(l). We define two enumerated types: FirstNumber describes the 10s digit and SecondNumber describes the units digits. This procedure advances the Roman numeral units digit (Second) for each increment in the decimal value and advances the Roman numeral 10 digit (First) when the decimal value is a multiple of 10.

```
                  IF Second = ten THEN
                     Second : = I
                  ELSE
                     Second : = succ(Second);
                  IF Number mod 10 = 0 THEN
                     First : = succ(First)
```

Procedures FirstNumeral and SecondNumeral both use a CASE statement to print the character equivalents (I, II, etc.) of the enumerated types. They are shown in Figure 12.4*b*(II) and Figure 12.4*b*(III), respectively. The main

```
PROCEDURE FirstNumeral(First: FirstNumber);
(* Prints the first numeral in a Roman numeral *)
BEGIN
  CASE First OF
    none: write(");
       X: write('X');
      XX: write('XX');
     XXX: write('XXX');
      XL: write('XL');
       L: write('L');
      LX: write('LX');
     LXX: write('LXX');
    LXXX: write('LXXX');
      XC: write('XC')
  END (* CASE *)
END (* FirstNumeral *);
```

FIGURE 12.4b(II). This procedure translates an enumerated 10s value to its string equivalent.

```
PROCEDURE SecondNumeral(Second: SecondNumber);
(* Prints the second numeral in a Roman numeral *)
BEGIN
  CASE Second OF
       I: write('I');
      II: write('II');
     III: write('III');
      IV: write('IV');
       V: write('V');
      VI: write('VI');
     VII: write('VII');
    VIII: write('VIII');
      IX: write('IX');
     ten: write(")
  END (* CASE *)
END (* SecondNumeral *);
```

FIGURE 12.4b(III). This procedure translates an enumerated units value into its string equivalent.

program is shown in Figure 12.4c, and the running of the program in Figure 12.4d.

```
PROGRAM Roman(input, output);
(* Converts decimals to numbers to Roman numerals *)
TYPE
  FirstNumber = (none, X, XX, XXX, XL, L, LX, LXX, LXXX, XC);
  SecondNumber = ( I, II, III, IV, V, VI, VII, VIII, IX, ten);
VAR
  First: FirstNumber;
  Second: SecondNumber;
  Number: integer;
PROCEDURE FirstNumeral(First: FirstNumber);                    {See page 503}
PROCEDURE SecondNumeral(Second: SecondNumber);                 {See page 503}
PROCEDURE Advance(VAR First: FirstNumber; VAR Second: SecondNumber;
                  Number:integer);                            {See page 501}

BEGIN
  First := none;
  Second:= I;
  FOR Number:= 2 TO 98 do
    BEGIN (* FOR *)
      Advance(First, Second, Number);
      FirstNumeral(First);
      SecondNumeral(Second);
      write ( ' is', Number:3, ' ');
      IF Number MOD 5 = 0 THEN (* carriage return after five numbers *)
        writeln
    END(* FOR *)
END.
```

FIGURE 12.4c.   The main program and the headings for the procedures used in the program. It directs the computer to print five Roman numerals per line.

```
II is 2   III is 3   IV is 4   V is 5
VI is 6   VII is 7   VIII is 8   IX is 9   X is 10
XI is 11   XII is 12   XIII is 13   XIV is 14   XV is 15
XVI is 16   XVII is 17   XVIII is 18   XIX is 19   XX is 20
XXI is 21   XXII is 22   XXIII is 23   XXIV is 24   XXV is 25
XXVI is 26   XXVII is 27   XXVIII is 28   XXIX is 29   XXX is 30
XXXI is 31   XXXII is 32   XXXIII is 33   XXXIV is 34   XXXV is 35
XXXVI is 36   XXXVII is 37   XXXVIII is 38   XXXIX is 39   XL is 40
XLI is 41   XLII is 42   XLIII is 43   XLIV is 44   XLV is 45
XLVI is 46   XLVII is 47   XLVIII is 48   XLIX is 49   L is 50
LI is 51   LII is 52   LIII is 53   LIV is 54   LV is 55
LVI is 56   LVII is 57   LVIII is 58   LIX is 59   LX is 60
LXI is 61   LXII is 62   LXIII is 63   LXIV is 64   LXV is 65
LXVI is 66   LXVII is 67   LXVIII is 68   LXIX is 69   LXX is 70
LXXI is 71   LXXII is 72   LXXIII is 73   LXXIV is 74   LXXV is 75
LXXVI is 76   LXXVII is 77   LXXVIII is 78   LXXIX is 79   LXXX is 80
LXXXI is 81   LXXXII is 82   LXXXIII is 83   LXXXIV is 84   LXXXV is 85
LXXXVI is 86   LXXXVII is 87   LXXXVIII is 88   LXXXIX is 89   XC is 90
XCI is 91   XCII is 92   XCIII is 93   XCIV is 94   XCV is 95
XCVI is 96   XCVII is 97   XCVIII is 98
```

FIGURE 12.4d.   Running the program of Figure 12.4c.

12.4

THE SURVEY PROBLEM REVISITED

At last, we can write the survey problem introduced in Chapter 2 using an enumerated type. The type is

```
Origin = (North, South, East, West);
```

and the array type is Population = ARRAY[Origin] OF integer.

The counter Box (which is of type Population) is zeroed in procedure ZeroBox:

```
FOR Region:= North TO West DO
    Box[Region]:= 0
```

as shown in Figure 12.5a(I).

The first thing done in procedure AskAndRecord is to read the data. A sample data set is NNSEWWSEN, where each of the four regions of the city is represented by the capital letter with which the name of the region begins. Thus, *N* represents north; *S*, south; *E*, east; and *W*, west. It then increments the proper counter. All of this is done in

```
WHILE NOT eoln DO BEGIN
    read(Direction);
    IF Direction IN ['N', 'S', 'E', 'W'] THEN
        CASE Direction OF
            'N': Box[North]:= Box[North] + 1;
            'S': Box[South]:= Box[South] + 1;
            'E': Box[East]:= Box[East] + 1;
            'W': Box[West]:= Box[West] + 1
        END (* CASE *)
    ELSE
        writeln(Direction, ' is an improper direction')
END (* WHILE *)
```

as shown in Figure 12.5a(II). The CASE statement translates the character type read, to the enumerated type used as the counter subscript.

THE SURVEY PROBLEM REVISITED

```
(* Records the results of a survey using the enumerated type *)
TYPE Origin = (North, South, East, West);
  Population= ARRAY[Origin] OF integer;

PROCEDURE ZeroBox(VAR Box:Population);
(* Zeros all the counters *)
VAR Region:Origin;
BEGIN
  FOR Region:= North TO West DO
    Box[Region]:= 0
END (* ZeroBox *);
```

FIGURE 12.5a(I). We use an enumerated type to define the four regions of the city. This procedure zeros the counters for each region.

```
PROCEDURE AskandRecord(VAR Box:Population);
(* Questions everyone and records their answers *)
VAR Direction: char;
BEGIN
  writeln('Type the origins for each person on line');
  WHILE NOT eoln DO BEGIN
    read(Direction);
    IF Direction IN ['N', 'S', 'E', 'W'] THEN
      CASE Direction OF
        'N': Box[North]:= Box[North] + 1;
        'S': Box[South]:= Box[South] + 1;
        'E': Box[East]:= Box[East] + 1;
        'W': Box[West]:= Box[West] + 1
      END (* CASE *)
    ELSE
      writeln(Direction, ' is an improper direction')
  END (* WHILE *)
END; (* AskAndRecord *)
```

FIGURE 12.5a(II). This procedure increments the proper counter for each character read.

QUESTION: Why can't IF Direction IN ['N', 'S', 'E', 'W'] THEN be written as

IF Direction IN [North..West] THEN

ANSWER: Because Direction is of type Char, whereas North is of type Origin.

Finally, the results are printed in procedure Print, as shown in Figure 12.5a(III). The main program is shown in Figure 12.5b, and the results of running the program are shown in Figure 12.5c.

CHAPTER REVIEW

Enumerated Types

An identifier for a user-defined enumerated type may be used the same way as that of an ordinal type. Thus we can use it as the control variable for a FOR–DO loop and as a subscript for an array.

The values for an enumerated type must be unique within the block in which the type is used. The values must be identifiers and therefore cannot be digits or text constants. Thus TYPE Pronoun = ('I', 'me', 'you'); would cause an error.

NEW TERM

user-defined enumerated types

EXERCISES

1. What is wrong with the following type?

Day = (S, M, T, W, T, F, S)

2. What is wrong with the following type?

TYPE Kansas = (Lawrence, Topeka, Emporia, Newton, Hutchinson, Dodge City, Garden City);

3. What is wrong with the following?

TYPE WeekEnd = ('Saturday', 'Sunday');

```
            PROCEDURE Print (Box:Population);
            (* Prints the results of the survey *)
            BEGIN
              writeln;
              writeln('Results of the survey:');
              writeln;
              writeln('Number from North ', Box[North]);
              writeln('Number from South ', Box[South]);
              writeln('Number from East ', Box[East]);
              writeln('Number from West ', Box[West]);
            END(* Print *);
```

FIGURE 12.5a(III).   This procedure prints the contents of each counter.

```
    PROGRAM Survey(input, output);
    (* Records the results of a survey using the enumerated type *)
    TYPE Origin = (North, South, East, West);
      Population= ARRAY[Origin] OF integer;

    VAR Box:Population;

    PROCEDURE ZeroBox(VAR Box:Population);            {See page 507}
    PROCEDURE AskandRecord(VAR Box:Population);       {See page 507}
    PROCEDURE Print (Box:Population);                 {On this page}
    BEGIN (* main program *)
      ZeroBox(Box);
      AskandRecord(Box);
      Print (Box);
    END.
```

FIGURE 12.5b.   The main program and the headings for the procedures used in the program.

```
            Type the origins for each person on line
            NSEEWeesWN
            e is an improper direction
            e is an improper direction
            s is an improper direction

            Results of the survey:

            Number from North 2
            Number from South 1
            Number from East 2
            Number from West 2
```

FIGURE 12.5c.   Running the program of Figure 12.5b.

4. What does the following program produce for the input 1 2 3 4 5 6?

```
PROGRAM Prob1;
TYPE StateName = (Mass, Conn, RI, NH, Maine, Vermont);
   Population = ARRAY[StateName] OF integer;
VAR D, E, G, H:integer;
   State: StateName;
   Pop: Population;
PROCEDURE Scope(D:integer; VAR E:integer);
VAR G:integer;
BEGIN
   G:= 8;
   WHILE (D > 0) AND (E > 0) DO BEGIN
      D:= D - 4;
      E:= E + 1;
      G:= G DIV E;
      H:= H + 3;
      writeln(' Line D ', D:2, E:2, G:2, H:2)
   END (* WHILE *)
END (* Scope *);
BEGIN (* Main *)
   FOR State:= Mass TO Vermont DO
      read(Pop[State]);
   write(' Line 1');
   FOR State := Maine DOWNTO Conn DO
      write(ord(State):2, Pop[State]:2);
   writeln;
   D:= 7;
   E:= 5;
   G:= 3;
   H:= D DIV E;
   writeln(' Line 2 :', H:2, (D MOD E):2);
   Scope(E, D);
   writeln(' Line 3 :', D:2, E:2, G:2, H:2)
END.
```

Programming Problems

5. Rewrite the program of Figure 12.3 so that it counts the number of Sundays, Mondays, and so on in the month.

6. Write a program that, given a month, will print the names of the next 11 months.

7. Rewrite the program of Figure 12.5a so that it takes both lowercase and uppercase input.

8. Write a program that uses an enumerated type to generate the octal numbers from 1 to 63.

9. Write a program that uses an enumerated type to generate the hexadecimal numbers from 1 to 99.

10. Write a program that generates the decimal numbers from 1 to 99.

11. Write a program that uses an enumerated type to calculate a person's wage in a given week, where the worker gets straight time for working on a weekday, time and one-half for working on Saturday, and double time for working on Sunday. The input to the program is the worker's ID, his hourly wage, and the first and last days of the week on which he worked. Use the following abbreviations for the days of the week: Sun, Mon, Tue, Wed, Thu, Fri, Sat. Sample input is

```
1002 7.50 Mon Fri
1005 6.45 Mon Sat
1006 7.25 Sun Wed
1008 8.00 Sat Sat
1009 7.50 Sun Sun
1010 9.00 Sun Sat
```

Note that some systems require the two days for each ID to be typed on separate lines, for example,

```
1002 5.50
Mon
Fri
```

Bottom-Up Design

12. Using the following definitions

```
Food = (Apple, Pear, Orange, Grape, Lemon, Peach,
    Lettuce, Spinach, Tomato, Potato, Pea, Unknown);
```

write a program that reads seven characters representing an edible and determines whether it is a fruit, a vegetable, or an unknown.

13. Write a program that determines how many of each edible are read into the program.

14. Write a program that makes a histogram of each edible read. If only three pears, four peas, and six peaches are read, the histogram would look like this:

```
3 pear   pear   pear
4 pea   pea   pea   pea
6 peach   peach   peach   peach   peach   peach
```

15. The Amtrak train called the *Southwest Chief* makes the following stops at the following times (A.M.) in Kansas: Lawrence, 12:45, Topeka, 2:10; Emporia, 3:15; Newton, 4:30; Hutchinson, 5:12; Dodge City, 6:55; and Garden City, 7:37. Define an enumerated type called Kansas that has these cities as the constants. Write a program that reads two 1-digit codes for two of these cities and finds the times required to travel between them. Assign 0 to Lawrence, 1 to Topeka, and so on. The times should be assigned in the program as the elements of an array that has subscripts of type Kansas.

13

MULTIDIMENSIONAL ARRAYS

CHAPTER OVERVIEW

Now that you've learned about arrays that have one subscript, you are ready to learn about arrays that have more than one subscript and arrays whose elements are themselves arrays. We'll use the latter type in two programs that sort words.

13.1

TWO-DIMENSIONAL ARRAYS

Some situations require an array when a one-dimensional array—an array that has only one subscript—is not suited to solving the problem. For instance, it's easier to visualize board games such as chess and checkers with a two-dimensional grid that shows where the pieces (men) are located. As another example, in storing the likeness of a tic-tac-toe board in memory it is helpful to use two subscripts: one representing a row (to designate the horizontal line) and one representing a column (to designate the vertical line), as shown in Table 13.1. The mathematical term for an array is a *matrix*. If the number of dimensions is not specified when the word *matrix* is used, it is assumed that the matrix has two dimensions.

To describe this pattern, define a two-dimensional array type

```
TYPE Grid = ARRAY[1..3, 1..3] OF Char;
```

where the first `1..3` designates that the first subscript will range from 1 to 3 and the second `1..3` designates that the second subscript will also range, in this case, from 1 to 3. We'll follow the convention that the first subscript represents the rows and the second one represents the columns. Thus if we declare `Display` to be of type `Grid`, then `Display[1, 3]` represents the location designated by the intersection of the first row and the third column and `Display[1, 3]:= 'X'` places an *X* there, as shown in Table 13.1. Similarly, `Display[3, 1]:= '0'` places a 0 in the third row, first column. An array that has the same number of rows as columns, as this one does, is called a *square* array. Let's begin by planning a program that displays two tic-tac-toe boards.

First Board

The pseudocode for the first board is

> *Set the first column to Xs;*
>
> *Set the second and third columns to 0s.*

The first refinement is

> *(* Set the first column to Xs *)*
> FOR Row := 1 TO 3 DO BEGIN
>   *Fix the column number to 1;*
>   *Place an X in display;*
> END;
> *(* Set the second and third columns to 0s *)*
> FOR Row := 1 TO 3 DO
>   *For columns 2 and 3: Place a 0 in display*
> END

	Col 1	Col 2	Col 3
Row 1			X
Row 2			
Row 3	0		

TABLE 13.1.   The tic-tac-toe pattern labeled according to rows and columns.

We fix the column number to 1 and let the row vary by writing `Display[Row, 1]`, and thus place an *X* in column 1 for all three rows by writing

```
FOR Row: = 1 TO 3 DO
    Display[Row, 1]: = 'X';
```

as shown in the main program of Figure 13.1*a*. To set the second and third columns to 0s, write the nested FOR loop

```
FOR Row: = 1 TO 3 DO
    FOR Col: = 2 TO 3 DO
        Display[Row, Col]: = '0';
```

Since the outer loop (rows) is incremented more slowly than the inner loop (columns), the order in which the elements are set to 0 is `Display[1,2]`, `Display[1,3]`, `Display[2,2]`, `Display[2,3]`, `Display[3,2]`, and `Display[3,3]`. Since the order is not important when a value is assigned to the elements of an array, you can obtain the same results by reversing the order of the two FORs by writing

```
FOR Col: = 2 TO 3 DO
    FOR Row: = 1 TO 3 DO
        Display[Row, Col]: = '0';
```

When you print the tic-tac-toe board, however, the order is important. The pseudocode for the printing is

```
FOR each Row DO BEGIN
    FOR Col: = 1 TO 3 DO
        write( Display[Row, Col]:3 );
    Start a new line
END
```

This translates into the code for procedure `Print`.

Second Board

The pseudocode for the second board is

> *Set all the elements to 0;*
> *Place Xs on the diagonal.*

where the diagonal is the line going from the upper left to the lower right of a square array, here the representation of the board. Set all the elements to 0 by writing

SETTING UP AND PRINTING A TWO-DIMENSIONAL ARRAY

```
PROGRAM TicTac(input, output);
(* Stores and prints the tic-tac-toe grid *)
TYPE Grid = ARRAY[1..3, 1..3] OF Char;
VAR Row, Col:1..3;
   Display:Grid;
PROCEDURE Print(Display: Grid);
(* Prints tic-tac-toe grid *)
VAR Row, Col:1..3;
BEGIN
  FOR Row:= 1 TO 3 DO BEGIN
    FOR Col:= 1 TO 3 DO
      write( Display[Row, Col]:3 );
    writeln
  END (* FOR Row *)
END (* Print *);
BEGIN (* TicTac *)
  (* Set up first board *)
  FOR Row:= 1 TO 3 DO
    Display[Row, 1]:= 'X';
  FOR Row:= 1 TO 3 DO
    FOR Col:= 2 TO 3 DO
      Display[Row, Col]:= 'O';
  Print(Display);
  writeln;
  (* Set up second board *)
  FOR Row:= 1 TO 3 DO
    FOR Col:= 1 TO 3 DO
      Display[Row, Col]:= 'O';
  FOR Row:= 1 TO 3 DO
    Display[Row, Row]:= 'X';
  Print(Display);
END.
```

FIGURE 13.1a. In procedure `Print,` the fact that the `Col` loop is nested in the `Row` loop means that the columns are printed for each row. The `writeln` there starts a new row. You can't interchange the two `FOR` statements here. When you assign the values to the elements of the array, however, you can interchange the two `FOR`s if you wish.

```
FOR Row:= 1 TO 3 DO
   FOR Col:= 1 TO 3 DO
      Display[Row, Col]:= '0';
```

The elements on the diagonal of a square array have the same row as column number, for example, `Display[1,1]`, `Display[2,2]`, and in general `Display[Row, Row]`. Thus in order to place Xs on the diagonal, write

```
FOR Row:= 1 TO 3 DO
   Display[Row, Row]:= 'X';
```

The results of running the program are shown in Figure 13.1b.

TEST YOURSELF

QUESTION: If the array `Display` is configured so that procedure `Print` produces the following output

```
          X 0 0
          X 0 0
          X 0 0
```

what output would the following produce?

```
FOR Row:= 1 TO 3 DO BEGIN
   FOR Col:= 1 TO 3 DO
      write( Display[Col, Row]:3 );
   writeln
END (* FOR Row *)
```

(We have interchanged the subscripts Row and Col of `Display` compared to their order in Figure 13.1a.)

ANSWER:

```
          X X X
          0 0 0
          0 0 0
```

Interchanging the rows and columns produces what is called the *transpose* of the array.

```
X 0 0
X 0 0
X 0 0

X 0 0
0 X 0
0 0 X
```

FIGURE 13.1*b*.   Running the program of Figure 13.1*a*.

ANALOGY

Two-dimensional arrays allow us to categorize something by two classifications, for instance, streets and avenues or the X and Y coordinates. A three-dimensional array is like the X-Y-Z coordinate system.

13.2

WRITING A TABLE LOOK-UP PROGRAM: PROGRAMMING BY STAGES

BEFORE YOU BEGIN

Many applications require you to look up values in a table stored in memory. Two examples of such tables are insurance tables and tax tables. Let's examine the technique used to do this.

Next, let's plan a program that will use a table, such as the ones found on maps, to determine the distance between two cities (Table 13.2). This type of program is called a *table look-up program.*

The reason there are no entries above the diagonal is that the distance between, for instance, Cleveland and Boston is the same as the distance between Boston and Cleveland. Because the distance between Cleveland and Boston (look across the row marked *Clevel* until you find the column marked *Boston* and obtain 654 miles) is given, the distance between Boston and Cleveland is left blank (look across the row marked *Boston* until you find the column marked *Clevel*). The reason the diagonal entries are all zeros is that the distance between a given city and itself must be 0.

PROGRAM PLANNING

As we have seen in previous chapters, one way of solving a difficult problem is to write the program in several steps such that each step produces output that is closer to the desired output. We'll apply this technique to the distance table problem. The steps are:

STEP I   Produces a table that has no entries above the diagonal.

STEP II   Generates a simplified version of the table such that numbers instead of city names label the table. The program also determines the distance between two cities by referring to the table.

STEP III   The same as Step II, except that city names label the table. However, the program does not determine the distance between two cities.

STEP IV   The same as Step III, except that now the program determines the distance between two cities.

	Albuqu	Atlant	Boston	Chicag	Clevel
Albuqu	0				
Atlant	1424	0			
Boston	2248	1115	0		
Chicag	1351	722	1009	0	
Clevel	1616	734	654	355	0

TABLE 13.2. The distances between cities given in table form. There are no entries above the diagonal because the distance between cities A and B is the same as that between cities B and A.

Step I

The first program in the series will be an exercise in producing part of a square display that satisfies the following condition:

If the array is considered a square array, the first element in the first row contains the number 1; the elements in a row contain sequential integers; and the next row continues the sequence.

An array that had four rows and four columns, satisfying this condition, is

```
 1  2  3  4
 5  6  7  8
 9 10 11 12
13 14 15 16
```

If `NumCol` represents the number of columns, then

$$\text{Matrix[Row, Col]} := \text{NumCol} * (\text{Row} - 1) + \text{Col};$$

gives the numbers in the square for a value of `NumCol` of 4. For instance, for row 1, since $(\text{Row} - 1)$ is 0, the elements are just the column numbers. For row 2, the elements are the column numbers added to 4, the value of `NumCol`. For row 3, the elements are the column numbers added to 8, and so on.

If you add the criterion that the array must have 0s on the diagonal, and no elements above the diagonal (in conformance with the distance table), you obtain

```
 0
 5  0
 9 10  0
13 14 15 0
```

Since this matrix looks like a triangle, it is called a *triangular matrix* or *triangular array.*

The pseudocode for obtaining this triangular array is

```
FOR each row DO BEGIN
  FOR Column:= 1 TO that row DO
     Matrix[row, Column]:= NumCol * (row - 1) + Column;
  IF on the diagonal THEN
     Matrix[row, Col] := 0
END
```

Note that the upper limit for `Column` in `FOR Column:= 1 TO` *that row* DO is the row number. Thus in row 1, `Column` ranges from 1 to 1; in row 2, from 1 to 2; in row 3, from 1 to 3, and so on. The IF translates to IF Row = Col THEN `Matrix[Row, Col] := 0`. The program is shown in Figure 13.2a and the results in Figure 13.2b.

FINDING THE DISTANCE BETWEEN TWO CITIES—STEP I. PRODUCING A TRIANGULAR MATRIX

```
PROGRAM Rectangle2(input, output);
(* Produces a rectangle with each cell containing the next integer.
Only elements above the diagonal are printed. Elements on the
diagonal are set to 0 *)
CONST NumRow = 10;
  NumCol = 10;
TYPE RowType = 1..NumRow;
  ColType = 1..NumCol;
  Grid = ARRAY[RowType, ColType] OF integer;
VAR Matrix:Grid;
  Row:RowType;
  Col:ColType;
PROCEDURE Print(Matrix:Grid);
VAR Row:RowType;
  Col:ColType;
BEGIN
  (* Write matrix *)
  FOR Row:= 1 TO NumRow DO BEGIN
    FOR Col:= 1 TO Row DO
      write(Matrix[Row, Col]:3);
    writeln
  END (* FOR Row *)
END (* Print *);
BEGIN
  (* Generate matrix *)
  FOR Row := 1 TO NumRow DO
    FOR Col := 1 TO Row DO BEGIN
      Matrix[Row, Col]:= NumCol * (Row - 1) + Col;
      IF Row = Col THEN (* Zero elements on diagonal *)
        Matrix[Row, Col] := 0
    END (* FOR Col *);
  Print(Matrix)
END.
```

FIGURE 13.2a. For the first row, the value of `Matrix[Row, Col]` is the column number `Col`. For the second row, it is the number of columns, `NumCol` (here, 10) plus `Col`. In the third row, it is 2 * `NumCol` (here, 20) plus `Col`.

```
 0
11  0
21 22  0
31 32 33  0
41 42 43 44  0
51 52 53 54 55  0
61 62 63 64 65 66  0
71 72 73 74 75 76 77  0
81 82 83 84 85 86 87 88  0
91 92 93 94 95 96 97 98 99  0
```

FIGURE 13.2b. Running the program of Figure 13.2a. Since `Col` goes from 1 to Row, we get a triangular array. The 0s lie on the diagonal, which is defined by Row = Col.

Step II

The next program reads a table of distances between two cities in procedure ReadMatrix, prints the table in procedure WriteMatrix, and determines the distance between two given cities in procedure FindDist. A typical table of distances produced by WriteMatrix is

		#1	#2	#3	#4	#5
#1	:	0				
#2	:	1424	0			
#3	:	2248	1115	0		
#4	:	1351	722	1009	0	
#5	:	1616	734	654	355	0

where, for instance, 1424 is the distance between city #2 and city #1, and 2248 is the distance between city #3 and city #1.

The pseudocode for ReadMatrix is

Read each of the distances between two cities.

Because you do not need the distances on and above the diagonal, refine this to

FOR Row: = 2 TO *number of rows* DO
   FOR Col: = 1 TO *one less than the column # for the diagonal* DO
    read the distances.

which becomes the procedure in Figure 13.3*a*(I).

The pseudocode for WriteMatrix is

FOR Row: = 1 TO *number of rows* DO BEGIN
   FOR Col: = 1 TO *the column # of the diagonal* DO
    print the distances;
   Start a new line
END

which becomes the procedure in Figure 13.3*a*(II).

FINDING THE DISTANCE BETWEEN TWO CITIES—STEP II. USING A NUMERICAL CODE TO REPRESENT THE CITIES

```
CONST NumRow = 5;
   NumCol = 5;
TYPE RowType = 1..NumRow;
   ColType = 1..NumCol;
   Grid = ARRAY[RowType, ColType] OF integer;

PROCEDURE ReadMatrix(VAR Matrix:Grid);
(* Only elements below the diagonal are read.
Elements on the diagonal are set to 0 *)
VAR Row:RowType;
   Col, Limit:ColType;
BEGIN
  (* First row contains no entries *)
  FOR Row := 2 TO NumRow DO BEGIN
    write('Type ', Row - 1:2, ' distances for row ', Row:1, ' : ');
    FOR Col := 1 TO Row - 1 DO
      Read( Matrix[Row, Col] );
    readln; (* Read next line *)
  END (* FOR Row *);
  FOR Row := 1 TO NumRow DO (* Set diagonal to 0 *)
    Matrix[Row, Row]:= 0;
  writeln
END (* ReadMatrix *);
```

FIGURE 13.3a(I).   In this procedure, FOR Col := 1 TO Row − 1 DO instructs the computer to read the distances between cities only for elements below the diagonal. The definitions given in the main program are also shown.

```
PROCEDURE WriteMatrix(VAR Matrix:Grid);
VAR Row:RowType;
   Col:ColType;
BEGIN
  write('    '); (* Label table top *)
  FOR Col := 1 TO NumCol - 1 DO
    write(' #',Col:1);
  writeln;
  writeln('-------------------------------');
  (* Write matrix *)
  FOR Row := 1 TO NumRow DO BEGIN
    write('#', Row:1, ' :');
    FOR Col := 1 TO Row DO
      write(Matrix[Row, Col]:5);
    writeln
  END (* FOR Row *);
  writeln(-----------------------------');
  writeln
END (* WriteMatrix *);
```

FIGURE 13.3a(II).   We label the top and side of the table with numbers. FOR Col := 1 TO Row DO produces output that falls on and below the diagonal.

Since the column number must be less than or equal to the row number, the pseudocode for FindDist (where *Code2* represents the column number and *Code1* represents the row number for the distance required) is

> *Read Code1, Code2*
> If Code2 > Code1 THEN
>   *Switch Code2 with Code1;*
> *Print distance corresponding to Code1 and Code2.*

Thus an input of 2 (as the row number) and 5 (as the column number), since the latter is larger than the former, will cause the program to switch these two numbers and find the distance in the fifth row and the second column. This pseudocode translates into the procedure in Figure 13.3*a*(III).

```
PROCEDURE FindDist( Matrix:Grid);
(* Finds the distance between two cities *)
VAR Code1, Code2: Row Type;
    Dist: integer;

PROCEDURE Switch( VAR Code1, Code2:RowType);
(* Switch the two codes if Code2 > Code1 so that table can be used *)
VAR Temp:RowType;
BEGIN
    Temp:= Code1;
    Code1:= Code2;
    Code2:= Temp
END (* Switch *);

BEGIN
  write('Type the codes for the two cities; Ctrl—Break to end:');
  WHILE NOT eof DO BEGIN
    read(Code1, Code2);
    IF Code2 > Code1 THEN
      Switch(Code1, Code2);
    Dist:= Matrix[Code1, Code2];
    writeln('The distance between the cities is ', Dist:5, ' miles');
    write('Type the codes for the two cities; Ctrl—Break to end:');
  END (* WHILE *);
END (* FindDist *);
```

FIGURE 13.3a(III).   Since the array is triangular, we must switch the codes if Code > Code1.

Finally, the main program is shown in Figure 13.3*b*, and the results of running the program are shown in Figure 13.3*c*.

TEST YOURSELF

QUESTION: In procedure FindDist, why must the write statement that produces the prompt precede the WHILE loop?

ANSWER: If the write is in the WHILE loop

```
WHILE NOT eof DO BEGIN
   write('Type the codes for the two cities; RETURN to end:');
   read(Code1, Code2);
   IF Code2 > Code1 THEN
     Switch(Code1, Code2);
   Dist:= Matrix[Code1, Code2];
   writeln('The distance between the cities is ', Dist:5, '
   miles');
END (* WHILE *);
```

since nothing is in the buffer, the computer pauses until something is placed there. Only after data are typed will the computer execute the write.

```
PROGRAM Distance(input, output);
(* Finds the distance between two cities *)
CONST NumRow = 5;
  NumCol = 5;
TYPE RowType = 1..NumRow;
  ColType = 1..NumCol;
  Grid = ARRAY[RowType, ColType] OF integer;
VAR Matrix:Grid;
PROCEDURE ReadMatrix(VAR Matrix:Grid);        {See page 525}
PROCEDURE WriteMatrix(VAR Matrix:Grid);       {See page 525}
PROCEDURE FindDist( Matrix:Grid);             {See page 527}
BEGIN (* Distance *)
  ReadMatrix(Matrix);
  WriteMatrix(Matrix);
  FindDist( Matrix);
END.
```

FIGURE 13.3*b*.   The main program and the headings for the procedures used. If you run the program, you must also include the procedures themselves.

```
Type 1 distances for row 2 : 1424
Type 2 distances for row 3 : 2248 1115
Type 3 distances for row 4 : 1351 722 1009
Type 4 distances for row 5 : 1616 734 654 355
        #1  #2  #3  #4
     -------------------------------

#1 :    0
#2 : 1424    0
#3 : 2248 1115    0
#4 : 1351  722 1009   0
#5 : 1616  734  654 355   0
     -------------------------------

Type the codes for the two cities; Ctrl-Break to end:2 5
The distance between the cities is 734 miles
Type the codes for the two cities; Ctrl-Break to end:5 2
The distance between the cities is 734 miles
Type the codes for the two cities; Ctrl-Break to end:2 2
The distance between the cities is 0 miles
Type the codes for the two cities; Ctrl-Break to end:
```

FIGURE 13.3*c*.   Running the program of Figure 13.3*b*. We check that the input 2 5 gives the same results as 5 2 and that 2 2 produce a distance of 0.

Step III

The next program labels the rows and columns of the table with the first six letters of city names instead of digits (however, this version of the program will not look up distances). To do this, the program reads the first six letters in the city name into successive elements of the array Abbrev in

```
FOR J: = 1 TO AbbrevLen DO
   read( Letter[J] );
readln;
Abbrev[CityCount]: = Letter:
```

as shown in Figure 13.4a(I). The type of Abbrev is City, defined by City = ARRAY[1..5] OF List, where List is defined in List = PACKED ARRAY[AbbrevLen] OF char. The value of AbbrevLen is 6, and the value of the subscript CityCount ranges from 1 to 5. For instance, if *Albuquerque* is the first name, the first six letters, that is, *Albuqu*, will be stored in Abbrev[1]:

Abbrev[1]

A	l	b	u	q	u
1	2	3	4	5	6

When we run the program, the contents of the elements of Abbrev are

$$Abbrev[1] \longleftarrow Albuqu$$
$$Abbrev[2] \longleftarrow Atlant$$
$$Abbrev[3] \longleftarrow Boston$$
$$Abbrev[4] \longleftarrow Chicag$$
$$Abbrev[5] \longleftarrow Clevel$$

This will enable us to label the top of the table with

```
FOR Col : = 1 TO NumCol DO
   write(Abbrev[Col]:AbbrevLen + 1);
```

where the value of NumCol is 5, as shown in procedure WritMatrix (Figure 13.4a(II)).

FINDING THE DISTANCE BETWEEN TWO CITIES—STEP III. LABELING THE CITIES WITH STRINGS

```
CONST NumRow = 5;
  NumCol = 5;
  AbbrevLen = 6;
TYPE RowType = 1..NumRow;
  ColType = 1..NumCol;
  Grid = ARRAY[RowType, ColType] OF integer;
  List = PACKED ARRAY[1..AbbrevLen] OF char;
  City = ARRAY[1..NumCol] OF List;
  NumCity = 0..NumCol;
  NumLetter = 0..AbbrevLen;
PROCEDURE FormWord( VAR Abbrev: City);
(* Places city abbreviation in an array *)
VAR J: NumLetter;
  Letter: List;
  CityCount: ColType;
BEGIN
  FOR CityCount := 1 to NumCol DO BEGIN
    write('Type city', CityCount:2, ' in', AbbrevLen:2, ' letters:');
    FOR J := 1 TO AbbrevLen DO
      read( Letter[J] );
    readln;
    Abbrev[CityCount] := Letter;
  END (* FOR *)
  writeln;
END (* FormWord *);
```

FIGURE 13.4a(I).   We read the first six letters in the city name into successive elements of the array `Abbrev`, whose elements are packed arrays of char. The definitions given in the main program are also shown.

```
PROCEDURE WriteMatrix(Matrix:Grid; Abbrev:City);
CONST Blank = ' ';
VAR Row:RowType;
  Col:ColType;
BEGIN
  write(Blank:AbbrevLen + 1 ); (* Label table top *)
  FOR Col := 1 TO NumCol DO
    write(Abbrev[Col]:AbbrevLen + 1);
  writeln;
  writeln('--------------------------------------------');
  (* Write matrix *)
  FOR Row := 1 TO NumRow DO BEGIN
    write(Abbrev[Row]:AbbrevLen + 1);
    FOR Col := 1 TO Row DO
      write(Matrix[Row, Col]:AbbrevLen + 1);
    writeln
  END (* FOR Row *);
  writeln('--------------------------------------------')
END (* WriteMat *);
```

FIGURE 13.4a(II).   Because `List` is a packed array, when the computer prints `Abbrev[Row]`, it prints the six characters assigned to `Abbrev[Row]`.

The main program is shown in Figure 13.4*b*, and the results of running the program are shown in Figure 13.4*c*.

```
PROGRAM Labeled(input, output);
(* Uses arrays of strings *)
CONST NumRow = 5;
    NumCol = 5;
    AbbrevLen = 6;
TYPE RowType = 1..NumRow;
    ColType = 1..NumCol;
    Grid = ARRAY[RowType, ColType] OF integer;
    List = PACKED ARRAY[1..AbbrevLen] OF char;
    City = ARRAY[1..NumCol] OF List;
    NumCity = 0..NumCol;
    NumLetter = 0..AbbrevLen;
VAR Matrix:Grid;
    Abbrev: City;
PROCEDURE ReadMatrix(VAR Matrix:Grid);                {See page 525}
PROCEDURE FormWord( VAR Abbrev: City);                {See page 531}
PROCEDURE WriteMatrix(Matrix:Grid; Abbrev:City);      {See page 531}
BEGIN (* Distance *)
    FormWord(Abbrev);
    ReadMatrix(Matrix);
    WriteMatrix(Matrix, Abbrev);
END.
```

FIGURE 13.4b.   The main program and the headings for the procedures used. If you run the program, you must also include the procedures themselves.

```
Type city 1:Albuquerque
Type city 2:Atlanta
Type city 3:Boston
Type city 4:Chicago
Type city 5:Cleveland

Type 1 distances for row 2 :1424
Type 2 distances for row 3 :2248 1115
Type 3 distances for row 4 :1351 722 1009
Type 4 distances for row 5 :1616 734 654 355
      Albuqu Atlant Boston Chicago Clevel
------------------------------------------------
Albuque     0
Atlant   1424     0
Boston   2248  1115     0
Chicag   1351   722  1009     0
Clevel   1616   734   654   355     0
------------------------------------------------
```

FIGURE 13.4c.   Running the program of Figure 13.4b.

Step IV

Now let's include procedure `FindDist` in the preceding program. However, we alter the procedure so that the array containing the city names, `Abbrev`, is sent to the procedure, as shown in Figure 13.5*a*:

```
PROCEDURE FindDist( Matrix:Grid; Abbrev: City);
```

This will allow the procedure to print the names of the cities when it prints the distance between them; for instance:

```
Type the codes for the two cities; Ctrl-Break to end:2 3
The distance between Boston and Atlant is 1115 miles
```

FINDING THE DISTANCE BETWEEN TWO CITIES—STEP IV. LABELS THE CITIES WITH STRINGS & FINDS THE DISTANCE BETWEEN THEM

```
CONST NumRow = 5;
   NumCol = 5;
   AbbrevLen = 6;
TYPE RowType = 1..NumRow;
   ColType = 1..NumCol;
   Grid = ARRAY[RowType, ColType] OF integer;
   List = PACKED ARRAY[1..AbbrevLen] OF char;
   City = ARRAY[1..NumCol] OF List;
   NumCity = 0..NumCol;
PROCEDURE Find Dist( Matrix:Grid; Abbrev: City);
(* Finds the distance between two cities *)
VAR Code1, Code2: RowType;
   Dist: integer;
PROCEDURE Switch( VAR Code1, Code2:RowType);                    {See page 527}
BEGIN
   write('Type the codes for the two cities; Ctrl-Break twice to end:');
   WHILE NOT eof DO BEGIN
      read(Code1, Code2);
      IF Code2 > Code1 THEN
         Switch(Code1, Code2);
      Dist:= Matrix[Code1, Code2];
      writeln('The distance between ', Abbrev[Code1],' and ',
      Abbrev[Code2],
      ' is', Dist:5, ' miles');
      write('Type the codes for the two cities; Ctrl-Break to end:');
   END (* WHILE *);
END (* FindDist *);
```

FIGURE 13.5a.   Now when the procedure calculates the distance between the two cities, it prints their names as well. Procedure Switch is given in Figure 13.3a(III). The definitions given in the main program are also shown.

The main program, with all the procedure headings, is shown in Figure 13.5*b*, and the results of running the program are shown in Figure 13.5*c*.

13.3

SORTING WORDS

BEFORE YOU BEGIN

If you wanted to place in alphabetical order the last names of all the depositors in a branch bank, you would have to sort them. The following section explains how to perform an alphabetical sort.

The next program sorts words in alphabetical order. It uses the following definitions

```
CONST MaxLen=20;
      MaxElem= 100;
TYPE List= PACKED ARRAY[1..MaxLen] OF char;
     Grid = ARRAY[1..MaxElem] of List;
     Range = 0..MaxElem;
     NumLetter = 0..MaxLen;
```

Because we form words using

```
VAR Word:grid;
    Letter: List;
```

each letter is stored in an element of Letter, and each word is stored in an element of Word. Thus Word is an array that has as its elements another array. Let's see what this means. The first word will be read in array Letter. Then this entire array will be placed in the first element of Word:

Words[1] ⟵
t	h	i	n	k
1	2	3	4	5

The second word will then be read into Letter, and this entire array will be placed into the second element of Word:

Words[2] ⟵
r	i	n	k
1	2	3	4

This process continues until all the words are read.

```
PROGRAM Labeled(input, output);
(* Uses arrays of a packed array *)
(* Also finds distance between cities *)
CONST NumRow = 5;
   NumCol = 5;
   AbbrevLen = 6;
TYPE RowType = 1..NumRow;
   ColType = 1..NumCol;
   Grid = ARRAY[RowType, ColType] OF integer;
   List = PACKED ARRAY[1..AbbrevLen] OF char;
   City = ARRAY[1..NumCol] OF List;
   NumCity = 0..NumCol;
VAR Matrix:Grid;
   Abbrev: City;

PROCEDURE ReadMatrix(VAR Matrix:Grid);              {See page 525}
PROCEDURE FormWord( VAR Abbrev: City);              {See page 531}
PROCEDURE WriteMatrix(Matrix:Grid; Abbrev:City);    {See page 531}
PROCEDURE FindDist( Matrix:Grid; Abbrev: City);     {See page 535}

BEGIN (* Distance *)
   FormWord(Abbrev);
   ReadMatrix(Matrix);
   WriteMatrix(Matrix, Abbrev);
   FindDist(Matrix, Abbrev)
END.
```

FIGURE 13.5b.   The main program and the headings for the procedures used. If you run the program, you must also include the procedures themselves.

```
Type city 1 in 6 letters:Albuqu
Type city 2 in 6 letters:Atlant
Type city 3 in 6 letters:Boston
Type city 4 in 6 letters:Chicag
Type city 5 in 6 letters:Clevel

Type 1 distances for row 2 :1424
Type 2 distances for row 3 :2248 1115
Type 3 distances for row 4 :1351 722 1009
Type 4 distances for row 5 :1616 734 654 355
            Albuqu Atlant Boston  Chicago Clevel
         ---------------------------------------------
Albuqu      0
Atlant    1424     0
Boston    2248   1115      0
Chicago   1351    722   1009      0
Clevel    1616    734    654    355      0
         ---------------------------------------------
Type the codes for the two cities; Ctrl-Break to end:2 3
The distance between Boston and Atlant is 1115 miles
```

FIGURE 13.5c.   Running the program of Figure 13.5b.

Upon examining the reading process more closely, we see that since the elements of Word are packed arrays, each word must contain the same number of characters, here 20. In order to understand the complications that can arise from this situation, consider the first two words read. The five letters in the first word think are stored in the first five locations of array Letter. The contents of the 6th to the 20th locations are undefined; they could contain any characters (here depicted by "&," "%," and "$").

Letter	t	h	i	n	k	&	%	. . .	$
	1	2	3	4	5	6	7	. . .	20

If we did nothing else at this time and assigned Letter to the first element of array Word, all of these elements, including the undefined ones, would be assigned to the first element of array Word. This would create difficulties when we print the word and would make it impossible to sort the words.

The second word read is rink. Its four letters replace the characters in the first four locations of array Letter; however, the 5th to 20th locations contain the same characters they did when think was read, namely, "k" and "& %...$":

Letter	r	i	n	k	k	&	%	. . .	$
	1	2	3	4	5	6	7	. . .	20

This would create difficulties when the words are sorted. In order to make sure that there are no spurious characters in the elements of Letter that will cause difficulties in the sorting and printing of the words, after we read a word we add blanks to its end. The second word read, for instance, would now be stored as

Letter	r	i	n	k				. . .	
	1	2	3	4	5	6	7	. . .	20

Note that placing blanks at the end of the word will not affect the sorting because a blank has a lower ordinal position in the collating sequence than the letters do.

Since the words will be typed one per line, our pseudocode for reading and storing the words is

WHILE NOT eof DO BEGIN
    Read the letters in a word;
    Add blanks to the word end;
    Store the word in the next element of array to be sorted;
    Carriage return in order to read next word.
END

We refine this to:

> *Set word counter to 0;*
> WHILE NOT eof DO BEGIN
>   *Increment word counter;*
>   *Set letter counter to 0;*
>   WHILE NOT eoln DO BEGIN
>   *Increment letter counter;*
>   *Read the next letter and store in the next location*
>   *of the array* Letter
>   END;
>   *Store blanks in the next through the last location of*
>   Letter;
>   *Store the contents of array* Letter *in the*
>   *next element of array to be sorted;*
>   *Hit carriage return in order to read next word*
> END

We expand this into procedure FormWord, shown in Figure 13.6a(I). We translate *Store blanks in the next through the last location of* Letter into procedure Full, shown in Figure 13.6a(II).

The pseudocode for the sorting procedure is

> REPEAT
>   *Set Sorted to true;*
>   FOR *each word in the new list except the last word* DO
>   IF *a word* > *the next word* THEN BEGIN
>   *Switch the two words in the list;*
>   *Set Sorted to false*
>   END
> UNTIL *Sorted is true*

```
CONST MaxLen=20;
  MaxElem= 100;
TYPE List= PACKED ARRAY[1..MaxLen] of char;
  grid = ARRAY[1..MaxElem] of List;
  Range = 0..MaxElem;
  NumLetter = 0..MaxLen;


PROCEDURE FormWord( VAR Words: Grid; VAR WordNumber:Range);
(* Makes string an element of array word *)
VAR J: NumLetter;
  Letter: List;
BEGIN
  WordNumber:= 0;
  writeln('Type your words, 1 per line ');
  WHILE NOT eof(input) DO BEGIN
      WordNumber:= WordNumber + 1;
      J:= 0;
      WHILE NOT eoln DO BEGIN
        J := J + 1;
        read( Letter[J] );
      END (* eoln *);
    readln;
    Full( Letter, J + 1, MaxLen );
    writeln( 'unsorted word #', WordNumber , ' is ', Letter);
    Word[WordNumber] := Letter;
  END (* WHILE *)
END (* FormWord *);
```

FIGURE 13.6a(I).   The procedure reads words into successive elements of `Words`, which is an array whose elements are a packed array. The definitions given in the main program are also shown here.

```
PROCEDURE Full( VAR Letter:List; Beg, Lmax: NumLetter);
(* Fills the unused part of the array with blanks because
the compiler can only compare packed arrays of same length*)
VAR J: NumLetter;
BEGIN(* Full *)
  FOR J:= Beg TO Lmax DO
    Letter[J] := ' ';
END; (* Full *)
```

FIGURE 13.6a(II).   The procedure pads the array with blanks so that all words have the same length.

where *new list* is a list that does not include the last element of the previous version of the list, and *word > the next word* is true if *word* follows *next word* in a dictionary that alphabetizes words such that all the uppercase letters precede the lowercase ones. Thus the following would all be true: (*dog > DOG*), (*dog > cat*), and (*dog > doG*). The pseudocode translates to the procedure shown in Figure 13.6*a*(III).

Since the elements of `Word` are of type `List`, when adjacent elements of `Word` are switched in procedure `Switch`, starting with `Temp:=Word [J]`, the temporary location `Temp` must be defined as type `List`. Procedure `Print`, shown in Figure 13.6*a*(IV) prints the results.

```
PROCEDURE Sort(VAR Word: grid; MaxEl: Range);
(* Sorts words alphabetically *)
VAR J: Range;
    Unsorted: boolean;
PROCEDURE Switch(VAR Word: Grid; J: Numword);
VAR Temp: List;
BEGIN
    Temp:=Word[J];
    Word[J]:=Word[J+1];
    Word[J+1]:=Temp
END (* Switch *);
BEGIN(* Sort *)
  Unsorted:=true;
  WHILE Unsorted DO BEGIN
    Unsorted:=false;
    FOR J:= 1 TO MaxEl - 1 DO
      IF Word[J] > Word[J+1] THEN BEGIN
          Switch(Words, J);
          Unsorted:=true
        END(* THEN *)
    END;(* WHILE *)
END;(* Sort *)
```

FIGURE 13.6a(III).   Uses the bubble sort to sort the elements of the array Words so that they are in alphabetical order.

```
PROCEDURE Print(Word: Grid; WordNumber:Range);
VAR L: Range;
BEGIN
  FOR L:= 1 TO WordNumber DO
    writeln( Word[L], ' is sorted word #', L);
END (* Print *);
```

FIGURE 13.6a(IV).   Prints the sorted words.

The entire program is shown in Figure 13.6*b*, and its running in Figure 13.6*c*.

13.4

USING TEXT FILES: SORTING WORDS IN A PARAGRAPH

BEFORE YOU BEGIN

In the real world, most sets of data are stored on files; consequently, let's modify the last program so that it sorts words in a paragraph stored on a file.

The next program is similar to the previous one, except that now procedure FormWord reads words from a paragraph stored on a text file and, as before, stores them as words in an array. The program assumes that a word is terminated by either a blank, punctuation, or a carriage return and that only one blank separates words. If one or more blanks separate words (see, e.g., Figure 7.7*a*), the program is only slightly more difficult to write. The pseudocode for procedure FormWord is

Rewind file;
Set word count to 0;
Set letter count to 0;
WHILE NOT eof(file) DO BEGIN
   Set counter for characters in the line to 0;
   WHILE NOT eoln(file) DO
   Read a character from the file and store in array Sentence
   END
   FOR *each character in* Sentence DO BEGIN
      IF NOT *end of word* THEN BEGIN
         Increment letter count by 1;
         Store the character in the next location in letter array
      END (* THEN *)
      ELSE
      Perform end-of-word procedure
   END (* FOR *);
   Since an eoln has been encountered, perform end-of-word procedure;
   Proceed to the beginning of the next line on the file.
END (* WHILE NOT eof *);

```
PROGRAM Bubble(input, output);
(* Performs bubble sort on strings *)
CONST MaxLen= 20;
  MaxElem= 100;

TYPE List= STRING[MaxLen];
  grid = ARRAY[1..MaxElem] of List;
  Range = 0..MaxElem;
  NumLetter = 0..MaxLen;

VAR Word: grid;
  Letter: List;
  WordNumber:Range;

PROCEDURE Full( VAR Letter:List, Beg, Lmax: integer);
                                              {See page 541}
PROCEDURE Sort(VAR Word: grid; MaxEl: Range);    {See page 543}
PROCEDURE FormWord( VAR Word: Grid; VAR WordNumber:Range);
                                              {See page 541}
PROCEDURE Print(Word: Grid; WordNumber:Range);   {See page 543}

BEGIN(* Bubble *)
  FormWord(Words, WordNumber);
  Sort( Words, WordNumber);
  Print(Words, WordNumber)
END.
```

FIGURE 13.6*b*.   The main program and the headings for the procedures used.

```
Type your words, 1 per line.
think
unsorted word #1 is think
rink
unsorted word #2 is rink
car
unsorted word #3 is car
shirt
unsorted word #4 is shirt
car       is sorted word #1
rink      is sorted word #2
shirt     is sorted word #3
think     is sorted word #4
```

FIGURE 13.6*c*.   Running the program of Figure 13.6*b*.

The pseudocode becomes procedure `FormWord`, shown in Figure 13.7a(I). We translate IF NOT *end of word* THEN to IF `Sentence[J]`IN `['a'..'z',` `'A'..'Z', "", '-']` THEN so that a word can contain a hyphen or an apostrophe as well as letters. The reason we also perform the end-of-word procedure at the end of a line is that if no punctuation but only a carriage return follows the last letter of the last word in a line, then `Sentence[J]`IN `['a'..'z', 'A'..'Z',` `"", '-']` can't be used to test for the end of the last word.

The entire IF–THEN–ELSE translates to

```
IF Sentence[J] IN ['a'..'z', 'A'..'Z', "", '-'] THEN
   Letter:= Letter + Sentence[J]
ELSE (* end of word *)
   EndOfWord(Words, WordCount, Letter)
```

This could create difficulties, since when the Jth character is a blank preceded by punctuation, the program activates procedure `EndOfWord` and stores a string consisting of blanks as the next element in array `Word`. The reason is that `EndWord` is activated when the punctuation is encountered and then again when the blank is encountered. If there are many midline punctuation marks in the paragraph, there will be an equal number of entries consisting of blanks in this array. Similarly, unnecessary blank entries would be produced when a punctuation terminates a line. To avoid this situation, test that the letter counter has not already been set to zero. This is accomplished by writing the pseudocode for the end-of-word procedure, `EndOfWord`, as

```
IF the letter count <> 0 THEN BEGIN
   Store blanks in the next through the last location of letter array;
   Increment word counter;
   Store the word in the next element of word array;
   Set letter counter to 0;
END
```

```
CONST MaxLen=80;
   MaxElem= 100;
TYPE List = PACKED ARRAY[1..MaxLEN] OF char;
   grid = ARRAY[1..MaxElem] of List;
   Range = 0..MaxElem;
   NumOfLetter = 0..MaxLen;

PROCEDURE FormWord(VAR Word: grid; VAR WordCount:Range; VAR Parag:text);
(* Places words in paragraph into array Word *)
CONST Blank = ' ';

VAR J, Count, LetterCount: NumOfLetter;
   Sentence, Letter: List;
   Ch: char;

PROCEDURE EndOfWord(VAR Word: grid; VAR WordCount:Range);
(* Used when the end of the word is encountered *)
BEGIN
   IF LetterCount <> 0 THEN BEGIN
      WordCount := WordCount + 1;
      Full( Letter, LetterCount + 1, MaxLen );
      LetterCount:=0;
      Word[WordCount] := Letter;
   END (* IF *)
END (* EndOfWord *);

BEGIN (* FormWord *)
   WordCount:= 0;
   LetterCount:= 0;
   reset(Parag); (* rewind file so that we can read it again *)
   WHILE NOT eof(Parag) DO BEGIN
      Count:= 0;
      WHILE NOT eoln(Parag) DO BEGIN
      (* Read characters in a line into array Sentence *)
         read(Parag, Ch);
         Count:= Count + 1;
         Sentence[Count]:= Ch
      END (* WHILE *);
      readln(Parag);
      FOR J:= 1 TO Count DO BEGIN
         IF Sentence[J] IN ['a'..'z', 'A'..'Z', "", '-'] THEN BEGIN
            LetterCount:= LetterCount + 1;
            Letter[LetterCount]:= Sentence[J]
         END (* IF *)
      ELSE (* end of word, but previous character not punctuation *)
            EndOfWord(Word, WordCount)
      END (* FOR *);
      (* End of word at end of line *)
      EndOfWord(Word, WordCount);
   END (* WHILE NOT eof *)
END (* FormWord *);
```

FIGURE 13.7a(I).   Reads a string from a text file and forms a word each time a nonletter is encountered. The nested procedure EndOfWord places the next word in the next element of the array. The definitions given in the main program, are also shown here.

Since procedure EndOfWord is nested in FormWord, we translate all of this into procedure FormWord, shown in Figure 13.7a(I). Procedure Full is as shown in the previous program. The table for Figure 13.7a(I) shows how the first word read is stored.

TEST YOURSELF

QUESTION:　What happens if the end-of-word procedure is not performed at the end of the line?

ANSWER:　If the last word in a line does not end with punctuation, as in the *thee* in the first line in

my country tis of thee

sweet land of liberty,

the program merges that word with the first word in the next; here *thee* and *sweet* would be merged into *theesweet*.

QUESTION:　What happens if the words are separated by more than one blank? How do you correct for this?

ANSWER:　The program activates EndOfWord too many times, thereby generating null strings in the output. To avoid this, change the ELSE IF to

```
ELSE IF NOT (Sentence[J - 1] IN [',', '.', ';', ':', Blank]) THEN
   EndOfWord(Words, WordCount, Letter)
```

The paragraph is printed in procedure ReadParag, shown in Figure 13.7a(II). The procedure that prints the results is shown in Figure 13.7a(III),

Sentence[J]	Letter
m	m
y	my

TABLE FOR FIGURE 13.7a(I).   Shows how LetterCount:= LetterCount + 1; Letter[LetterCount]:= Sentence[J] works for the first word read.

```
PROCEDURE ReadParag(VAR Parag:text);
(* Reads and prints a paragraph from a file *)
VAR Ch:char;
BEGIN
  WHILE NOT eof(Parag) DO BEGIN
    WHILE NOT eoln(Parag) DO BEGIN
      read(Parag,ch);
      write( ch)
    END (* WHILE NOT eoln *);
    readln(Parag);
    writeln
  END (* WHILE NOT eof *)
END (* ReadParag *);
```

FIGURE 13.7a(II).   Reads the paragraph from the text file and prints it so that we can see the words that will be sorted.

```
PROCEDURE Print(Word: Grid; WordNumber:Range);
VAR L: Range;
BEGIN
  writeln;
  writeln('THE SORTED WORDS ARE:');
  FOR L:= 1 TO WordNumber DO
    write( Word[L]);
  writeln('The number of words is ', WordNumber)
END (* Print *);
```

FIGURE 13.7a(III).   Prints the sorted words.

and the main program in Figure 13.7*b*; procedure Sort is as shown in the previous program. For the results of running the program, see Figure 13.7*c*. Since the uppercase letters appear before the lowercase ones in the ASCII table, and consequently after a sort all the capitalized words would appear before the noncapitalized ones, we wrote the paragraph using only lowercase letters.

```
PROGRAM ArrayPractice(input, output, Parag);
(* Reads the words in a paragraph from a text file *)
(* Then sorts the words *)
CONST MaxLen=80;
   MaxElem= 100;
TYPE List = PACKED ARRAY[1..MaxLEN] OF char;
   grid = ARRAY[1..MaxElem] of List;
   Range = 0..MaxElem;
   NumOfLetter = 0..MaxLen;
VAR
   Word:grid;
   Letter: List;
   WordNumber:Range;
   Parag:text;

PROCEDURE ReadParag(VAR Parag:text);                                    {See page 549}
PROCEDURE Full( VAR Letter:List; Beg, Lmax: integer);                   {See page 541}
PROCEDURE FormWord(VAR Word: grid; VAR WordCount:Range; VAR Parag:text);
                                                                        {See page 547}
PROCEDURE Sort(VAR Word: grid; MaxEl: Range);                          {See page 543}
PROCEDURE Print(Word: Grid; WordNumber:Range);                         {See page 549}

BEGIN
   reset(Parag);
   writeln('THE PARAGRAPH READ WAS:');
   ReadParag(Parag);
   FormWord(Words, WordNumber, Parag);
   Sort(Words, WordNumber);
   Print(Words, WordNumber);
END.
```

FIGURE 13.7b. The main program and the headings for the procedures used. For procedure Sort, see Figure 13.6a(III); for procedure Full, see Figure 13.6a(II). If you run the program, you must also include the procedures themselves.

```
THE PARAGRAPH READ WAS:
my country tis of thee,
sweet; land of liberty,
of thee i sing.
THE SORTED WORDS ARE:
country i land liberty my of of of sing sweet thee thee tis
```

FIGURE 13.7c. Running the program of Figure 13.7b.

13.5

USING ONE OR TWO SUBSCRIPTS TO DESCRIBE AN ARRAY

BEFORE YOU BEGIN

In order for a word processing program, for instance, to move a phrase from one part of a text to another, it must use a two-dimensional array. The following program reads a text file into a two-dimensional array and then prints the array. This prepares the reader for a word processing program that follows in a later chapter.

The two-dimensional array Screen of type Page is defined using

```
TYPE Line = ARRAY[1..NumChar] OF char;
     Page = ARRAY[1..NumLine] OF Line;
```

Procedure ReadSong, shown in Figure 13.8a(I), does the reading. In

```
CharCounter:= 0 (* Initialize character counter *);
WHILE NOT eoln(Song) DO BEGIN
   CharCounter:= CharCounter + 1;
   read(Song, Phrase[CharCounter]);
END (* WHILE NOT eoln *);
readln(Song);
LineCount:= LineCount + 1;
NumLetter[LineCount]:= CharCounter;
Screen[LineCount]:= Phrase;
```

the line of text just read is assigned to the element of Screen for the current value of LineCount.

If Line were defined as a packed array, then in procedure Print, shown in Figure 13.8a(II), we could treat Screen as a one-dimensional array of elements of type Line. We could then print the paragraph by writing

```
FOR Row:= 1 TO LineCount DO
   writeln( Screen[Row])
```

This would print the paragraph line by line; however, it would print the extraneous characters stored at the end of each line. The following is a better

STORING A PARAGRAPH READ FROM A FILE IN AN ARRAY

```
CONST NumChar = 80;
   NumLine = 25;
TYPE Line = ARRAY[1..NumChar];
   Page = ARRAY[1..NumLine] OF Line;
   EndOfLine = ARRAY[1..NumLine] OF integer;
   CharRange = 1..NumChar;
   LineRange = 0..NumLine;

PROCEDURE ReadSong(VAR Song:text; VAR Screen:Page; VAR LineCount:
LineRange VAR NumLetter:EndOfLine);
(* Reads a paragraph from a file *)
VAR CharCounter: CharRange;
   Phrase: Line;
BEGIN
   LineCount:=0 (* Set Line counter = 0 *);
   WHILE NOT eof(Song) DO BEGIN (* read Text into ARRAY *)
     CharCounter:= 0 (* Initialize character counter *);
     WHILE NOT eoln(Song) DO BEGIN
        CharCounter:= CharCounter + 1;
        read(Song, Phrase[CharCounter] );
     END (* WHILE NOT eoln *);
     readln(Song);
     LineCount:= LineCount + 1;
     NumLetter[LineCount]:= CharCounter;
     Screen[LineCount]:= Phrase;
   END (* WHILE NOT eof *);
END (* ReadSong *);
```

FIGURE 13.8a(I).   Each time a line of input is read from the file, it is stored in the next element of Screen. The definitions given in the main program are also given.

```
PROCEDURE Print(LineCount:LineRange; Screen:Page; NumLetter:EndOfLine);
(* Prints a paragraph on the screen *)
VAR Column: CharRange;
   Row: LineRange;
BEGIN
   FOR Row:= 1 TO LineCount DO BEGIN (* Print results *)
     FOR Column:= 1 TO NumLetter[Row] DO
        write( Screen[Row, Column ]);
     writeln;
   END (* FOR Row *);
END (* Print *);
```

FIGURE 13.8a(II).   Since Screen is an array of a string variable, we can refer to a character in a given line by using two subscripts for Screen. The write prints one character at a time.

way. Since Screen is implicitly a two-dimensional array whose first element is the row number and whose second element is the column number (or character number in the string), we can print the paragraph as shown:

```
FOR Row:= 1 TO LineCount DO BEGIN (* Print results *)
   FOR Column:= 1 TO NumLetter[Row] DO
      write( Screen[Row, Column ]);
   writeln
END (* FOR Row *)
```

We use a write instead of a writeln in write(Screen[Row, Colunn]) here to contiguously print the characters on a line. The main program and the headings for the procedures used are shown in Figure 13.8*b*. The results of running the program are shown in Figure 13.8*c*.

13.6

ARRAYS THAT HAVE MORE THAN TWO SUBSCRIPTS

You can use more than two subscripts in an array definition. For instance, in

```
TYPE Volume = ARRAY[1..10, 1..10, 1..10] OF integer;
```

all the subscripts must be integers, whereas in

```
TYPE WeekDay = (Mon, Tue, Wed, Thu, Fri);
   Cube = ARRAY[1..10, 'A'..'Z', Mon..Fri] OF integer;
```

the type of the first subscript is integer, the type of the second one is a character ranging between 'A' and 'Z', and the type of the third one is WeekDay. The definition of Cube can be written alternatively as Cube = ARRAY[1..10, 'A'..'Z', WeekDay] OF integer.

```
PROGRAM ArrayPractice(input, output, Song);
(* Reads a text file into a two-dimensional array *)
(* Then prints the words in the paragraph *)
CONST NumChar = 80;
   NumLine = 25;

TYPE Line = ARRAY[1..NumChar] OF char;
   Page = ARRAY[1..NumLine] OF Line;
   EndOfLine = ARRAY[1..NumLine] OF integer;
   CharRange = 0..NumChar;
   LineRange = 0..NumLine;
VAR Screen: Page;
   LineCount:LineRange;
   NumLetter: EndOfLine;
   Song:text;

PROCEDURE ReadSong(VAR Song:text; VAR Screen:Page; VAR LineCount:
LineRange; VAR NumLetter:EndOfLine);                    {See page 553}
PROCEDURE Print(LineCount:LineRange; Screen:Page; NumLetter:EndOfLine);
                                                       {See page 553}


BEGIN
   reset(Song);
   ReadSong(Song, Screen, LineCount);
   writeln('THE PARAGRAPH READ WAS:');
   writeln;
   Print(LineCount, Screen);
END.
```

FIGURE 13.8b. The main program and the headings for the procedures used. If you run the program, you must also include the procedures themselves.

THE PARAGRAPH READ WAS:

My country tis of thee,
Sweet land of liberty,
Of thee I sing.
Land where my fathers died,
Land of the pilgrims pride,
From every mountain side,
Let freedom ring.

FIGURE 13.8c. Running the program of Figure 13.8b.

13.7

USING ENUMERATED TYPES TO OVERCOME THE LIMITATIONS OF MULTIPLE-DIMENSIONED ARRAYS

In the exercises, you are asked to write a program that stores a railroad timetable and then prints the arrival time when you input the string consisting of a given town on the route. To store a town's name, you can define the type TownName in TownName = PACKED ARRAY[1..15] OF char. However, you can't use it as the subscript of an array, since TownName is not an ordinal type. For instance, you cannot define the array for the timetable as TimeTable = ARRAY[TownName] OF integer. The most convenient way to do this is to first define an enumerated type, for instance, Colorado = (Akron, FortMorgan, Denver, WinterPark, Granby). Then you may define the timetable array in TimeTable = ARRAY[Colorado] OF integer;.

Somewhere in the program, you have to convert the inputted string, consisting of a town's name, into the corresponding enumerated type identifier. For instance, you can write the procedure shown in Figure 13.9.

Pitfalls

1. Interchanging the position of the FOR statement that increments the rows with the one that increments the columns when printing a square array will produce incorrect results. For instance, if the array Map contains

1 2 3

4 5 6

7 8 9

and if, in error, you place the FOR Col := 1 TO 3 DO statement before the FOR Row := 1 TO 3 DO statement, thus writing

```
FOR Col := 1 TO 3 DO BEGIN
   FOR Row := 1 TO 3 DO
      write( Map[Row, Col]:3 );
   writeln
END (* FOR Col *)
```

you will obtain the incorrect array as output:

1 4 7

2 5 8

3 6 9

Remember that this array is called the *transpose* of the original array; the rows and columns are interchanged.

USING ENUMERATED TYPES TO OVERCOME THE LIMITATIONS OF MULTIPLE-DIMENSIONED ARRAYS

```
TYPE TownName = PACKED ARRAY[1..15]OF char;
  Colorado = (Akron, FortMorgan, Denver, WinterPark, Granby).
  TimeTable = ARRAY[Colorado] OF integer;
PROCEDURE TownName(Code:TownName; VAR Town:Colorado);
(* Converts a string into the corresponding enumerated type *)
BEGIN
  IF Code = 'Akron       ' THEN Town:= Akron;
  IF Code = 'Fort Morgan  ' THEN Town:= FortMorgan;
  IF Code = 'Denver      ' THEN Town:= Denver;
  IF Code = 'Winter Park  ' THEN Town:= Winterpark;
  IF Code = 'Granby      ' THEN Town:= Granby;
END
```

FIGURE 13.9. You can't use a nonordinal type like TownName (which stores strings consisting of a town's name) as the subscript of an array, for instance, TimeTable = ARRAY[TownName] OF integer. To do this, define the towns' names in Colorado = (Akron, FortMorgan, Denver, WinterPark, Granby). Then you may define TimeTable = ARRAY[Colorado] OF integer. This procedure converts the inputted string, consisting of a town's name, into the corresponding enumerated type identifier.

2. Interchanging the subscripts when printing a nonsquare rectangular array will produce an execution error. For example, if the array Rectangle is of type TYPE Grid = ARRAY[1..2, 1..4] OF integer; and should look like

1 2 3 4

5 6 7 8

when printed, then

```
FOR Row:= 1 TO 2 DO BEGIN
  FOR Col:= 1 TO 4 DO
    write( Rectangle[Col, Row]:3 );
  writeln
END (* FOR Row *)
```

will produce an error. Since the first subscript ranges only from 1 to 2, when the value of Col is 3, the computer will produce a subscript out-of-range message.

CHAPTER REVIEW

Arrays Definable as Multiple-Dimensioned Arrays or as Arrays of Arrays

Some arrays can be explicitly defined as multiple-dimensioned arrays; that is, all the subscripts can be placed in the brackets after the word ARRAY. An example is the type Grid, defined in TYPE Grid: ARRAY[1..3, 1..4] OF Char;, an array that has three rows and four columns. You can, however, define Grid in two steps

```
TYPE Row: ARRAY[1..4] OF Char;
     Grid: ARRAY[1..3] OF Row;
```

(where the elements of Row are characters positioned in successive columns). If you do this, you can refer to any of the rows of the array in compact notation. For instance, if you declare the array Matrix to be of type Grid, then Matrix[2] refers to the second row. Thus if you declare Line to be of type Row, you can write Line:= Matrix[2], thereby assigning the second row to the identifier Line. You can still, however, refer to individual elements of the array. Thus Matrix[2, 3] refers to the element in the second row, third column. Therefore defining an array as an array of an array has an advantage.

Note that you can define the array Matrix in the VAR declaration: VAR Matrix:ARRAY[1..3] OF ARRAY[1..4] OF integer;.

Arrays Definable Only as Arrays of Arrays

Some arrays, whose elements are themselves arrays, can't effectively be defined explicitly as multiple-dimensioned arrays. For instance, in

```
TYPE List = ARRAY[1..AbbrevLen] OF char;
     City = ARRAY[1..NumCol] OF List;
```

the elements of City are names of cities, whereas the elements of List are letters. If you define City as City = ARRAY[1..NumCol, 1..AbbrevLen] OF char;, you can't refer easily to a city in the program.

Assigning Values to Elements of Multiple-Dimensioned Arrays

Given

```
TYPE Row: ARRAY[1..4] OF Char;
     Grid: ARRAY[1..3] OF Row;
```

where we declare the array Matrix to be of type Grid, if you want to assign the second row of Matrix to the identifier Line, what is the type of Line? Since the elements of Matrix are of type Row, you must declare Line to also be of type Row.

NEW TERMS

matrix	transpose
square array	triangular matrix (array)
table look-up program	

EXERCISES

1. Given

```
CONST CityLength = 20;
      AbbrevLen = 3;
TYPE List = ARRAY[1..CityLength] OF char;
     NumLetter = 0..CityLength;
PROCEDURE FormWord;
(* Places a city abbreviation in an array *)
VAR J: NumLetter;
```

```
    BEGIN
      writeln('Type city abbreviation in ', AbbrevLen, '
      letters');
      FOR J: = 1 TO AbbrevLen DO
        read( Letter[J] );
      readln;
      writeln;
    END (* FormWord *);
```

if FormWord(Letter) is executed from the main program and Den is typed as data for the procedure, what are the contents of Letter when it is passed back to the main program?

2. Given

```
        TYPE List = ARRAY[1..10] OF char;
          City = ARRAY[1..4] OF List;
        VAR CityName:City;
```

and the statement CityName[2]: = 'ABCDEFGHIK', write the program segment that prints the letters A to G. Hint: Place CityName[2, J] in a loop that has J as the control variable.

3. Given

```
        TYPE City = ARRAY[1..4] OF List;
        VAR CityName:City;
```

and the statement CityName[2]: = Temp, what should be the type of CityName?

4. Given

```
        TYPE List = ARRAY[1..2] OF char;
          StateAbbrev = (NY, NJ, CO, IA);
        VAR State:List;
          Region:StateAbbrev;
```

what is wrong with the following?

```
        CASE State OF
            'NY': Region: = NY;
            'NJ': Region: = NJ;
            'CO': Region: = CO;
            'IA': Region: = IA;
    END (* CASE *);
```

5. What is wrong with the following?

```
TYPE List = ARRAY[1..5] OF char;
     Table = ARRAY[List] OF integer
```

Programming Problems

6. Given

```
TYPE SAT = 200..800;
Sex = (Male, Female);
ScoreType = ARRAY[SAT, Sex] OF integer;
```

the input to the program is the sex ('M' of 'F') and the SAT score of students in a sample. Write a program that reads all the data for the sample (use the eof function). Count the number of students who got each possible SAT score by sex. At the end of the program, print the total number of students (regardless of sex) who got each SAT score and the sex and SAT score for the lowest count.

7. Write a program that determines the number of words in a paragraph.

8. Given VAR Grid : ARRAY[1..10, 'A'..'Z'] OF integer, write a program that determines the largest element of the array and its location.

9. Given

```
TYPE Day = (S, M, T, W, TH, F, SA);
VAR Matrix: ARRAY[1..10, 'A'..'Z', S..SA] OF integer;
    WeekDay:Day;
```

write a program that determines the largest element of the array and its location.

10. Write a program that uses a counter to store the following in an array:

```
1 2 3 4
5 6 7 8
9 10 11 12
13 14 15 16
```

11. Write a program that produces the following display:

```
1
2 3
4 5 6
7 8 9 10
```

12. Write a program that produces the following display:

```
1 2 3 4
  5 6 7
    8 9
     10
```

13. Will the following programming segment check whether all the diagonal elements have the same value as that stored in Symbol?

```
Win:=False;
FOR Row:= 1 TO 3 DO
    IF Score[Row, Row] = Symbol THEN
Win:= True;
```

Rewrite the segment using a FOR–DO loop so that it tests the diagonal elements correctly.

14. Rewrite the previous programming segment using a WHILE loop so that it tests the diagonal elements correctly. As soon as the program encounters an improper diagonal value, it should quit the loop.

15. Write a program that reads a paragraph written on a file into a two-dimensional array. Copy the words from the two-dimensional array into a one-dimensional array and then sort this one-dimensional array.

16. Write a program that makes a histogram of the length of words in a paragraph.

17. Write a program that reads a sentence and prints the number of times a letter has occurred. For instance, the first time the program encounters an *a*, it prints "first *a*"; the second time, it prints "second *a*"; and so on. Hint: Use an array that has elements of the packed array type.

18. Write a program that uses an array that has elements of the packed array type to produce the numbers in English from 1 to 99. Each number less than 20 is stored in an element of the array. Your program should, for instance, separate 20 into a 2 and a 0. The 2 should cause the program to print "twenty"; the 0 should cause it to print a blank.

19. Write a program that determines the average length of words in a paragraph.

Bottom-Up Approach

20. Write a program that reads the first three letters of the following towns in Colorado on the route of the AMTRAK train *Desert Wind* and prints the entire name as output: Fort Morgan, Denver, Winter Park, Granby, Glenwood Springs, and Grand Junction. To make your task easier, type the first letter in uppercase and the next two in lowercase.

21. Rewrite the previous program so that you can type the first three letters in any combination of uppercase and lowercase you want; for example, in order to have the program type Denver, you may type DEN, deN, and so on.

22. Rewrite the previous program so that if you type all, the program prints the names of all the towns at which the *Desert Wind* stops. However, if you type the first three letters of the town's name, the program will print the entire name.

23. Rewrite the previous program so that it reads as many letters as you type for a town's name and then prints the entire name as output. For example, if you type F, Fo, For, and so on, the program will print "Fort Morgan."

24. Rewrite the previous program so that it prints the arrival time for each of the cities. These times are: Akron, 5:30 A.M.; Fort Morgan, 6:00 A.M.; Denver, 8:05 A.M.; Winter Park, 10:40 A.M.; Granby, 11:05 A.M.; Glenwood Springs, 2:10 P.M.; and Grand Junction, 4:15 P.M.

25. Rewrite the previous program so that it prints the time required to travel between the two inputted towns.

26. Rewrite the previous program so that if the city names are entered in the wrong order, the program switches them.

27. Rewrite the previous program so that if more than one city name corresponds to the first few letters you type, the program asks for clarification and then calculates the proper time.

14
RECORDS

CHAPTER OVERVIEW

This chapter introduces the record, a structured type that allows us to store data of different types in one structure. It concludes with a program that forms an index of the words in a text file.

14.1

RECORDS

BEFORE YOU BEGIN

You may be familiar with the term *data base*. It refers to a group of data arranged so that they can be conveniently analyzed. An example of a data base used by a bank is the collection of deposit information for each of the many depositors in the bank. This collection might include the name of the depositor (a packed array of characters), the bank branch (defined by a subrange type, for instance, 1..50), the type of account (defined by an enumerated type, for instance, MoneyMarket, Checking, or Savings), and the balance (a real). The *record* data type allows us to lump these different types under one identifier and therefore process them easily.

In an array, all the elements have to be of the same type. For instance, in TYPE Line = ARRAY[1..10] OF Char, all the elements of the type Line must be of type char. The record data type allows us to refer to an entity that can have at the same time real, integer, character, boolean, and any other type we define as a component. The components of a record are called *fields*. For instance, in Figure 14.1*a* the record DepositRecord

```
TYPE DepositRecord = RECORD
     ID, Branch, TypAcct: integer;
     Dep: real
END; (* DepositRecord *)
```

has four fields; three (ID, Branch, and TypAcct) are integers, and one (Dep) is a real. Each record describes the information for a depositor. ID represents the depositor's account number; Branch, the bank's branch number; TypeAcct, the type of account; and Dep, the amount deposited. Note that the field declarations (here, ID, Branch, TypAcct: integer, and Dep: real) are sandwiched between the beginning of the definition (DepositRecord = RECORD) and the delimiter, END. It is an error to place a BEGIN in the record definition. For instance,

```
TYPE DepositRecord = RECORD
     BEGIN
     ID, Branch, TypAcct: integer;
     Dep: real
END; (*DepositRecord*)
```

will cause a compilation error. Before you refer to a record, you must declare an identifier of the record type. For instance, VAR Large, Present : DepositRecord declares two variable identifiers to be of type DepositRecord.

AN INTRODUCTION TO RECORDS

```
PROGRAM IntroToRecords;
(* Determines the account number with the greatest deposit *)
TYPE DepositRecord = RECORD
            ID, Branch, TypAcct: integer;
            Dep: real;
        END; (* DepositRecord *)
VAR Large, Present : DepositRecord;
BEGIN
  Large.Dep:= 0.0;
  writeln('Type ID, Deposit, Branch, Type of account');
  WHILE NOT eof DO BEGIN
    read( Present.ID, Present.Dep, Present.Branch, Present.TypAcct);
    IF Present.Dep > Large.Dep THEN
      Large:= Present;
  END; (* WHILE *)
  writeln;
  writeln('Largest depositor is:');
  writeln( 'ID#=', Large.ID, 'Deposit = $', Large.Dep:7 :2)
END.
```

FIGURE 14.1a.   A record consists of components of different types called *fields*. Once you declare a variable (e.g., Large) of the record type, you refer to a field by writing the record identifier, a period, and then the field, for example, Large.Dep. This is called *dot notation*.

In order to refer to a given field of, for instance, the record Present in the program, you must follow the record identifier by a period and then by the field identifier. For example, Present.ID represents the ID field of the variable Present. This technique is called *dot notation*. How do you read information into the locations represented by the record's four fields? Simply by writing

```
readln( Present.ID, Present.Dep, Present.Branch, Present.TypAcct);
```

Let's write a program to identify the person who deposited the most money in a given set of data. The pseudocode is

> *Set the deposit for the record Large to zero;*
> WHILE NOT eof DO BEGIN
>   *Read the fields for the record Present;*
>   IF *deposit for Present* > *deposit for Large* THEN
>   *Assign all the fields of Present to Large*
> END (* WHILE *);
> *Print all the fields of Large.*

The advantage of using records in this program is evident when you translate *assign all the fields of Present to* Large to Pascal. As shown in Figure 14.1*a*, this becomes

```
Large:= Present;
```

This is the same thing you do when you assign all the elements of one array (for instance, Phrase) to the corresponding elements of another array (for instance, Stream) of the same type by writing Stream:= Phrase. The results of running the program are shown in Figure 14.1*b*. The storage of the data in the different fields of the record is shown in the table for Figure 14.1*a*. Note that if more than one depositor made the same largest deposit, the program would detect only the first such depositor in the data set.

```
TypeID, Deposit, Branch, Type of account
1002 345.66 2 4 1007 123.45 3 5 1003 345.66 4 7 1006 322.11 3 3
1009 213.22 4 5 1008 134.33 4 5
Largest depositor is:
ID#= 1002 Deposit = $ 345.66
```

FIGURE 14.1b. Running the program of Figure 14.1a. When the program encounters a record (Present) with a deposit larger than the value of Large.Dep, it copies all the field values from that record to Large when Large: = Present is executed.

Present	1002	345.66	2	4
	ID	Dep	Branch	TypAcct

TABLE FOR FIGURE 14.1a. The contents of the locations for the fields of record Present for the first set of data read.

14.2

USING THE WITH

> Throughout much of this chapter, we will be using various versions of the bank account problem to study the different facets of record manipulation. Thus the student will not have to become acquainted with a new problem each time a new programming principle is introduced.

Can the program of Figure 14.1*a* be rewritten without using the dot notation to refer to the fields in the record? Figure 14.2*a* shows how this is done. Anytime you refer to a field of the record Present in the statement or compound statement that follows WITH Present DO, you write only the field identifier. Thus

                    WITH Present DO
                        read(ID, Dep, Branch, TypAcct);

is equivalent to

    read(Present.ID, Present.Dep, Present.Branch, Present.TypAcct);

and is much easier for the programmer to both write and subsequently read. Since

                    IF Dep > Large.Dep then

lies within the first compound statement following WITH Present, the computer interprets it as IF Present.Dep > Large.Dep THEN. The results of running the program are shown in Figure 14.2*b*.

> The WITH simplifies notation, saves typing, eliminates the need to type statements that because of the dot notation require more than one line, and is more efficient for the computer.

```
PROGRAM UsingTheWith;
(* Determines the account number with the greatest deposit *)
(* Uses the WITH to avoid dotting everything *)
TYPE DepositRecord = RECORD
            ID, Branch, TypAcct: integer;
            Dep: real
         END; (* DepositRecord *)
VAR Large, Present : DepositRecord;
BEGIN
Large.Dep:= 0.0;
writeln('Type ID, Deposit, Branch, Type of account');
  WHILE NOT eof DO
    WITH Present DO BEGIN
    read( ID, Dep, Branch, TypAcct);
    IF Dep > Large.Dep then
      Large:= Present;
    END (* WITH *)
  writeln;
  writeln( 'Largest depositor is:');
  WITH Large DO
    writeln( 'ID#=', ID, 'Deposit = $', Dep:8:2)
END.
```

FIGURE 14.2a.   By preceding the statement that uses the record fields with WITH Present DO, we can refer to the fields without using dot notation.

```
TypeID, Deposit, Branch, Type of account.
1002 345.66 2 4   1007 123.45 3 5   1003 345.66 4 7   1006 322.11 3 3
1009 213.22 4 5   1008 134.33 4 5
Largest depositor is:
ID#=1002 Deposit = $ 345.66
```

FIGURE 14.2b.   Running the program of Figure 14.2a.

14.3

PASSING RECORDS TO SUBPROGRAMS

Next, we'll write a program that identifies the student with the highest grade average for three grades. Let's start by defining the record GradeRecord, as shown in Figure 14.2c:

```
CONST MaxNum = 10;
   MaxChar = 20;
   GradeNumber = 3;
TYPE GradeRange = 0..100;
   NameRange = 1..MaxChar;
   List = PACKED ARRAY[NameRange] OF char;
   GradeRecord = RECORD
     Name: List;
     Grade: ARRAY[1..GradeNumber] OF GradeRange;
     Average: GradeRange;
     END; (* GradeRecord *)
   RecArray = ARRAY[1..MaxNum] OF GradeRecord;
   RecRange = 0..MaxNum;
```

The field Grade is an array that has three elements. Procedure ReadRecord reads these three elements and the string for Name. It also calculates the value of Average. The top-down diagram for the program is

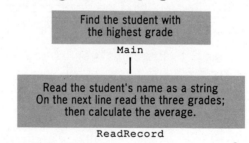

Because of the WITH, the read in

```
WITH Present DO BEGIN {read record}
   K:= 0;
   WHILE NOT eoln DO BEGIN
     K:= K + 1;
     read(Name[K])
   END (* WHILE *);
```

PASSING RECORDS TO SUBPROGRAMS

```pascal
PROGRAM ProceduresWithRecords;
(* Passes records to subroutines *)
(* Determines the student with the highest average *)
CONST MaxChar = 20;
  GradeNumber = 3;
TYPE GradeRange = 0..100;
  NameRange = 1..MaxChar;
  List = PACKED ARRAY[NameRange] OF char;
  GradeRecord = RECORD
      Name: List;
      Grade:ARRAY[1..GradeNumber] OF GradeRange;
      Average:GradeRange;
    END; (* GradeRecord *)
VAR Large, Present : GradeRecord;
PROCEDURE Full( VAR Letter:List; Beg, Lmax: NameRange);
(* Fills the unused part of the array with blanks *)
VAR J: NameRange;
BEGIN
  FOR J:= Beg TO Lmax DO
    Letter[J]:= ' ';
END; (* Full *)
PROCEDURE ReadRecord(VAR Present:GradeRecord);
(* Reads a record and gets the average *)
VAR Mark, Sum:integer;
  K:0..MaxChar;
BEGIN
  WITH Present DO BEGIN (* read record *)
    K:= 0;
    WHILE NOT eoln DO BEGIN
      K:= K + 1;
      read(Name[K])
    END (* WHILE *);
    Full(Name, K + 1, MaxChar);
    FOR Mark:= 1 TO GradeNumber DO
      read(Grade[Mark]);
    readln;
    Sum:= 0;
    (* Calculate the average *)
    FOR Mark:= 1 TO GradeNumber DO
      Sum:= Sum + Grade[Mark];
    Average:= round(Sum / GradeNumber)
  END (* WITH *)
END (* ReadRecord *);
BEGIN (* Main *)
  writeln('Type Name hit ENTER, then', GradeNumber, 'grades');
  WITH Large DO BEGIN
    Average:= 0;
    WHILE NOT eof DO BEGIN
      ReadRecord(Present);
      IF Present.Average > Average then
        Large:= Present;
    END (* NOT eof *);
    writeln;
    writeln(Name, 'received the highest average:', Average:4)
  END (* WITH *)
END.
```

FIGURE 14.2c.   When we pass a record to a subprogram, we pass the values of all the fields. If the average for the student's record just read is greater than the average for Large, then Large is assigned the record for that student. Procedure Full pads the packed array with blanks so that the names will be printed without undesirable characters.

is equivalent to read(Present.Name[K]). Similarly, since read(Grade-[Mark]) is in the FOR loop and is also effected by the WITH, it is equivalent to read(Present.Grade[1]), read(Present.Grade[2]), and read(Present.Grade[3]). Because Average is assigned a value within the WITH, this value becomes part of the record as well. Since Present is a VAR parameter, after the procedure is finished, the computer passes the fields of the record to the main program, the major part of which is

```
WITH Large DO BEGIN
   Average:= 0;
   WHILE NOT eof DO BEGIN
     ReadRecord(Present);
     IF Present.Average > Average THEN
       Large:= Present;
   END (* NOT eof *);
   writeln;
   writeln(Name,' received the highest average:', Average:4)
END (* WITH *)
```

If the average for the student's record just read is greater than the average for Large, then Large is assigned the record for that student. The results of running the program are shown in Figure 14.2d. The reason we type the name on one line and the grades on another is that we do not want the grades to be part of the string used for the name. Procedure Full pads the packed array with blanks so that the names will be printed without undesirable characters.

TEST YOURSELF

QUESTION: Rewrite the part of the program within the WITH so that it doesn't need a WITH.

ANSWER:

```
Large.Average:= 0;
WHILE NOT eof DO BEGIN
   ReadRecord(Present);
   IF Present.Average > Large.Average THEN
     Large:= Present;
END (* NOT eof *);
writeln;
writeln(Large.Name, 'received the highest average:',
        Large.Average:4)
```

A hand calculation shows that both Nathan Hull and David McQueen got an average of 93; however, the program detects only the first student to get the highest average. The next section shows how to correct this problem.

```
Type Name hit ENTER, then 3 grades
Abrams, S. L.
80 90 100
Hull, Nathan
95 90 95
McQueen, David
90 95 95
Jones, L.
85 88 100
Hull, Nathan        received the highest average : 93
```

FIGURE 14.2d. Running the program of Figure 14.2c. We type the name on a separate line so that the program can read the numerical data into the proper variables; otherwise, the numerical data could become part of the string.

14.4

ARRAYS OF RECORDS

Compared to the previous program, the current one determines all the students who got the highest average. It does this by storing all records read in consecutive elements of an array defined in RecordArray = ARRAY [1..MaxNum] OF GradeRecord. This definition must follow the definition of GradeRecord. The top-down diagram for the program is

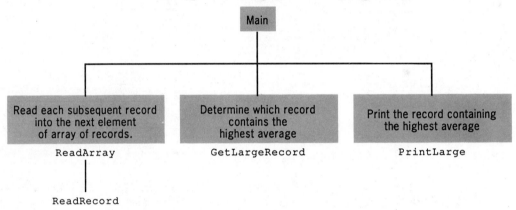

Refining the pseudocode for ReadArray produces

> *Set Number of records to zero;*
> WHILE NOT eof DO BEGIN
>   *Increment Number of records by 1;*
>   *Read the data for the array element for that record*
> END (* WHILE *)

The pseudocode *Read the data for the array element for that record* becomes

ReadRecord(PresentElem[RecNumber])

as shown in Figure 14.3a(I), where PresentElem is of type RecordArray. We've already written procedure ReadRecord in the previous program. Thus ReadArray takes the records read by ReadRecord and assigns them to the elements of PresentElem. For instance, the contents of the record stored in PresentElem[1] and PresentElem[2] are shown in the table for Figure 14.3a:

USING AN ARRAY OF RECORDS

```
CONST MaxNum = 10;
   Max Char = 20;
   GradeNumber = 3;
TYPE GradeRange = 0..100;
   NameRange = 1..MaxChar;
   List = PACKED ARRAY[NameRange] OF char;
   GradeRecord = RECORD
       Name: List;
       Grade: ARRAY[1..GradeNumber] OF GradeRange;
       Average: GradeRange;
     END; (* GradeRecord *)
   RecArray = ARRAY[1..MaxNum] OF GradeRecord;
   RecRange = 0..MaxNum;

PROCEDURE ReadArray(VAR PresentElem: RecordArray;
                    VAR RecNumber:RecRange);
(* Assigns student records to an element of an array *)
BEGIN
   RecNumber:= 0;
   writeln('Type Name hit ENTER, then', GradeNumber, 'grades');
   WHILE (NOT eof(input) ) AND (RecNumber < MaxNum) DO BEGIN
     RecNumber:= RecNumber + 1;
     ReadRecord(PresentElem[RecNumber])
   END (* WHILE *)
END (* Readecord *);
```

FIGURE 14.3a(I).   Uses procedure ReadRecord (Figure 14.2c) to read a record and assigns it the current element of PresentElem. Since the array PresentElem is a variable parameter, all the records in the array are passed back to the main program. The definitions given in the main program are also shown.

Record PresentElem[1]	Abrams, S.L.	80	90	100
	Name	Grade[1]	Grade[2]	Grade[3]

Record PresentElem[2]	Hull, Nathan	95	90	95
	Name	Grade[1]	Grade[2]	Grade[3]

TABLE FOR FIGURE 14.3a.   The contents of the first two records in the array.

TEST YOURSELF

QUESTION: Why is the following procedure that reads the elements of the array incorrect?

```
PROCEDURE ReadArray(VAR PresentElem: RecordArray;
                         VAR RecNumber:RecRange);
(* Assigns student records to an element of an array *)
VAR Mark:integer;
BEGIN
  RecNumber:= 1;
  WHILE (NOT eof(input) ) AND (RecNumber < MaxNum) DO
    WITH Present[RecNumber] DO BEGIN
      RecNumber:= RecNumber + 1;
      FOR Mark:= 1 TO GradeNumber DO
        read(Grade[Mark]);
      readln;
  END (* WITH *)
END (* ReadRecord *);
```

ANSWER: The record specified in the WITH (here, Present[RecNumber]) cannot be changed by a statement in the compound statement following the WITH (here, RecNumber: = RecNumber + 1). If it is, the results are unpredictable.

The pseudocode for GetLargeRecord is

> *Assign the first record to Large;*
> FOR *the rest of the records* DO
>   IF *the average for a record* > *the average for Large* THEN
>   *Assign that record to Large.*

The last line becomes Large: = PresentElem[K], where K is the loop index. This assignment makes sense because PresentElem is an array whose elements are of type GradeRecord, and the type of Large is GradeRecord. The procedure is shown in Figure 14.3a(II).

The pseudocode for PrintLarge is

> FOR *all records* DO
>   *Write the information for records with average equal to the*
>   *average for Large.*

The resulting procedure is shown in Figure 14.3a(III). Here

> WITH PresentElem[K] DO
>   IF Average = Large.Average THEN

```
PROCEDURE GetLargeRecord(PresentElem: RecordArray; RecNumber:RecRange;
                         VAR Large:GradeRecord);
(* Finds the record with the largest average *)
VAR K:RecRange;
BEGIN
  Large:= PresentElem[1];
  FOR K:= 2 TO RecNumber DO
    IF PresentElem[K].Average > Large.Average THEN
      Large:= PresentElem[K];
END (* GetLargeRecord *);
```

FIGURE 14.3a(II).   Since PresentElem is an array of GradeRecord, the type of Large must be GradeRecord in order for Large:= PresentElem[k] to be correct.

```
PROCEDURE PrintLarge(PresentElem: RecordArray; RecNumber:RecRange;
                     Large:GradeRecord);
(* Prints all records with an average equal to the maximum average *)
VAR K:RecRange;
BEGIN
    writeln('The largest average is for:');
    FOR K:= 1 TO RecNumber DO (* check FOR duplicates OF Large *)
      WITH PresentElem[K] DO
        IF Average = Large.Average THEN
          writeln( Name,'; Average is', Average:6)
END (* PrintLarge *);
```

FIGURE 14.3a(III).   The meaning of WITH PresentElem[K] DO is "with the Kth element of the array of records DO".

is equivalent to IF PresentElem [K].Average = Large.Average THEN. The main program is shown in Figure 14.3*b* and the running of the program in Figure 14.3*c*.

```
PROGRAM RecordPractice;
(* Using an array of records to find all students with a high mark *)
CONST MaxNum = 10;
   MaxChar = 20;
   GradeNumber = 3;
TYPE GradeRange = 0..100;
   NameRange = 1..MaxChar;
   List = ARRAY[NameRange] OF char;
   GradeRecord = RECORD
      Name: List;
      Grade:ARRAY[1..GradeNumber] OF GradeRange;
      Average:GradeRange;
   END; (* GradeRecord *)
   RecArray = ARRAY[1..MaxNum] OF GradeRecord;
   RecRange = 0..MaxNum;

PROCEDURE Full( VAR Letter:List; Beg, Lmax: NameRange);        {See page 573}

PROCEDURE ReadRecord(VAR Present:GradeRecord);                 {See page 573}

PROCEDURE ReadArray(VAR PresentElem: RecArray;
                    VAR RecNumber:RecRange);                   {See page 577}

PROCEDURE GetLargeRecord(PresentElem: RecArray; RecNumber:RecRange;
         VAR Large:GradeRecord);                               {See page 579}

PROCEDURE PrintLarge(PresentElem: RecArray; RecNumber:RecRange;
         Large:GradeRecord);                                   {See page 579}

BEGIN
   ReadArray(PresentElem, RecNumber);
   GetLargeRecord(PresentElem, RecNumber, Large);
   PrintLarge(PresentElem, RecNumber, Large)
END.
```

FIGURE 14.3b. The main program and the headings of the procedures used. If you run the program, you must also include the procedures themselves.

```
Type Name hit ENTER, then 3 grades
Abrams, S. L.
80 90 100
Hull, Nathan
95 90 95
McQueen, David
90 95 95
Amico, R.
92 90 90
Jones, L.
85 88 100
The largest average is for:
Hull, Nathan     ; Average is   93
McQueen, David   ; Average is   93
```

FIGURE 14.3c.   Running the program of Figure 14.3b.

14.5

THE SELECTION SORT (PROGRAM DESIGN BY INDUCTION)

BEFORE YOU BEGIN

An array of records can be sorted according to the value of one of the fields. For instance, you can sort the array used in the previous section such that the IDs are in ascending order: 1002 345 2 4, 1003 345 4 7, 1006 322 3 3, 1007 123 3 5, 1008 134 4 5, 1009 213 4 5.

The bubble sort is an efficient way to do this if the inputted array is almost sorted. If it is completely unsorted, however, the sort will interchange many records, thereby requiring a long time to execute. Let's study a sort that minimizes record interchanges, namely, the *selection sort*.

Stage I

The program for the selection sort appears in three stages. The first stage searches a list of numbers for the smallest one and interchanges it with the first number in the list. For example, given 8, 6, 3, 1, 2, since 1 is the smallest number, we interchange it with 8 and obtain 1, 6, 3, 8, 2. The pseudocode for this is

> *Assign 1 to the SubscriptOfSmall;*
> FOR *the second to the last element* DO
>   IF *the element is smaller than* Small THEN
>   *Assign its subscript to SubscriptOfSmall;*
> *Interchange the first and the smallest element.*

where *Small* is the element whose subscript is SubscriptOfSmall. This becomes procedure Select1, shown in Figure 14.4a(I). Note that only one interchange was done.

Procedure ReadArray [Figure 14.4a(II)] reads the elements into the array,

THE SELECTION SORT
STEP I. PLACING THE SMALLEST VALUE IN THE FIRST ELEMENT

```
CONST MaxElem = 30;
TYPE Range = 0..MaxElem;
   IntegerArray = ARRAY[1..MaxElem] OF Integer;

PROCEDURE Select1(VAR X:IntegerArray; NumElements:Range);
(* Places the smallest element in X[1] )
VAR SubscriptOfSmall, Index:Range;
  Small:Integer;
BEGIN (* Select *)
  SubscriptOfSmall:= 1;
  FOR Index:= 2 to NumElements DO
    IF X[Index] < X[SubscriptOfSmall] THEN
       SubscriptOfSmall:=Index;
  (* Switch first and smallest elements *)
  Small:= X[1];
  X[1]:= X[SubscriptOfSmall];
  X[SubscriptOfSmall]:= Small
END (* Select *);
```

FIGURE 14.4a(I). We originally call SubscriptOfSmall the subscript of the first element. When we find an element smaller than this, we call it SubscriptOfSmall. At the end, we swap the smallest element with the first one. The definitions given in the main program are also shown.

```
PROCEDURE ReadArray(VAR X:IntegerArray; VAR NumElements:Range);
(* Reads an array *)
BEGIN
  writeln('Type Integer values');
  NumElements:= 0;
  WHILE NOT eoln DO BEGIN
    NumElements:= NumElements + 1;
    read(X[NumElements])
  END (* WHILE *)
END (* ReadArray *);
```

FIGURE 14.4a(II). This procedure reads the elements into the array.

and procedure Print [Figure 14.4a(III)] prints the results. Figure 14.4a(IV) shows the main program and the headings of the procedures used. Finally, the results of running the program are shown in Figure 14.4b.

```
PROCEDURE Print(X:IntegerArray; NumElements:Range);
(* Prints an array *)
VAR Index:Range;
BEGIN
  FOR Index:= 1 TO NumElements DO
    write(X[Index]:3)
END; (* Print *)
```

FIGURE 14.4a(III). This procedure prints the elements of the array.

```
PROGRAM Selection1;
(* Places the smallest value in the first element *)
CONST MaxElem = 30;
TYPE Range = 0..MaxElem;
  IntegerArray = ARRAY[1..MaxElem] OF Integer;
VAR X:IntegerArray;
  NumElements:Range;
PROCEDURE ReadArray(VAR X:IntegerArray; VAR NumElements:Range);
                                                    {See page 583}
PROCEDURE Print(X:IntegerArray; NumElements:Range);   {On this page}
PROCEDURE Select1(VAR X:IntegerArray; NumElements:Range);
                                                    {See page 583}
BEGIN (* Main *)
    ReadArray(X, NumElements);
    Select1(X, NumElements);
    writeln('The Final array is');
    Print(X, NumElements)
END.
```

FIGURE 14.4a(IV). The main program and the headings of the procedures used. If you run the program, you must also include the procedures themselves.

```
                Type Integer values
                8 6 3 1 2
                The Final array is
                1 6 3 8 2
```

FIGURE 14.4b. Running the program of Figure 14.4a(IV).

Stage II

Since the smallest number (here, 1) is now in its correct place in the list (1, 6, 3, 8, 2), you can ignore it. Search the rest of the list (here, 6, 3, 8, 2) for the smallest number (here, 2) and interchange it with the second number in the original list (here, 6.) Our list thus becomes 1, 2, 3, 8, 6. In Figure 14.4c, we see that procedure Select2 does this. Using the reading and the printing procedures from Figure 14.4a, and inputting the partially sorted results shown in Figure 14.4b, we get the results shown in Figure 14.4d. Now the first two elements are in their proper position in the list.

THE SELECTION SORT
STEP II. PLACING THE SECOND SMALLEST VALUE IN THE SECOND ELEMENT

```
PROGRAM Selection2;
(* Places the smallest value in the second element *)
CONST MaxElem = 30;
TYPE Range = 0..MaxElem;
   IntegerArray = ARRAY[1..MaxElem] OF Integer;
VAR X:IntegerArray;
  NumElements:Range;
PROCEDURE ReadArray(VAR X:IntegerArray; VAR NumElements:Range);
                                                      {See page 583}
PROCEDURE Print(X:IntegerArray; NumElements:Range);     {See page 585}
PROCEDURE Select2(VAR X:IntegerArray; NumElements:Range);
(* Places the smallest element in X[2] *)
VAR SubscriptOfSmall, Index:Range;
  Small:Integer;
BEGIN (* Select *)
   SubscriptOfSmall:=2;
   FOR Index:= 3 to NumElements DO
     IF X[Index] < X[SubscriptOfSmall] THEN
       SubscriptOfSmall:=Index;
   (* Switch the second and smallest elements *)
   Small:= X[2];
   X[2]:= X[SubscriptOfSmall];
   X[SubscriptOfSmall]:= Small
END (* Select *);
BEGIN (* Main *)
   ReadArray(X, NumElements);
   Select2(X, NumElements);
   writeln('The Final array is');
   Print(X, NumElements)
END.
```

FIGURE 14.4c. We now call `SubscriptOfSmall` the subscript of the second element. When we find an element smaller than this, we call Its subscript `SubscriptOfSmall`. At the end, we swap the smallest element with the second one. Note that the two procedures are given in the previous figure.

```
Type Integer values
1 6 3 8 2
The Final array is
1 2 3 8 6
```

FIGURE 14.4d.   Running the program of Figure 14.4c. We input to this program the partially sorted list that is the output of the previous program. The next smallest value and the value in the second element are swapped. Now the first two elements are in their proper place.

Stage III

If you examine the selection procedures used to place the lowest and next to lowest elements in the first two positions in the list, you see the following: The statements required to place the Nth element in its proper position in the list (assuming that the previous $N - 1$ elements have been placed in their proper position) are

```
SubscriptOfSmall := N;
FOR Index := N + 1 to NumElements DO
   IF X[Index] < X[SubscriptOfSmall] THEN
      SubscriptOfSmall := Index;
(* Switch the leading and smallest elements *)
Small := X[N];
X[N] := X[SubscriptOfSmall];
X[SubscriptOfSmall] := Small
```

If you do this for all but the last element in the list, all the elements will be in their proper position. Consequently, in order to sort a list of numbers, place these statements in a loop starting with FOR N := 1 TO NumElements −1 DO BEGIN, as shown in Figure 14.4e. The results of running the program are shown in Figure 14.4f.

TEST YOURSELF

QUESTION: Why is the FOR in the outer loop

FOR N := 1 TO NumElements −1 DO BEGIN

instead of FOR N := 1 TO NumElements DO BEGIN?

ANSWER: After the loop is executed for N equal to NumElements − 1, all the elements are sorted.

Induction   By writing the process for the first few steps of an involved operation, we can induce the form for the Nth step. In mathematics, this process is called *induction*.

Appendix B shows that the number of steps needed to sort an array of N elements is approximately N^2 for both the bubble sort and the selection sort.

THE SELECTION SORT
STEP III: GENERALIZING THE FIRST TWO STEPS

```
PROGRAM Selection3;
(* Performs the selection sort *)
CONST MaxElem = 30;
TYPE Range = 0..MaxElem;
   IntegerArray = ARRAY[1..MaxElem] OF Integer;
VAR X:IntegerArray;
   NumElements:Range;
PROCEDURE ReadArray(VAR X:IntegerArray; VAR NumElements:Range);
                                                   {See page 583}
PROCEDURE Print(X:IntegerArray; NumElements:Range);     {See page 585}
PROCEDURE Sort(VAR X:IntegerArray; NumElements:Range);
(* Selection sort *)
VAR SubscriptOfSmall, Index, N:Range;
   Small:Integer;
BEGIN
  FOR N:= 1 TO NumElements - 1 DO BEGIN
    SubscriptOfSmall:= N;
    FOR Index:= N + 1 to NumElements DO
      IF X[Index] < X[SubscriptOfSmall] THEN
        SubscriptOfSmall:=Index;
    (* Switch the leading and smallest elements *)
    Small:= X[N];
    X[N]:= X[SubscriptOfSmall];
    X[SubscriptOfSmall]:= Small
  END (* FOR N *)
END (* Sort *);
BEGIN (* Selection2 *)
  ReadArray(X, NumElements);
  Sort(X, NumElements);
  writeln('The Final array is');
  Print(X, NumElements)
END.
```

FIGURE 14.4e.   We write the code for the *N*th step and place it in a loop. If the *N*th step were a program, its input would be the output of the *N*th − 1 step. Thus the final result is a sorted list.

```
Type Integer values
8 6 3 1 2
The Final array is
1 2 3 6 8
```

FIGURE 14.4f.   Running the program of Figure 14.4e. The final array is sorted.

14.6

SORTING RECORDS

Let's use the selection sort to sort bank records according to ID number. In order to make the sorting procedure as general as possible, we'll use the generic identifier Key to represent the ID. This will allow us later to sort on other fields as well. How do we alter the selection sort? We change it so that it will sort the elements of an array Account of type Grid defined by

```
CONST MaxElem = 100;
TYPE RecordType = record
              Branch, TypeAcct, Key: integer;
              Deposit: real
      END (* record *)
Range = 0..MaxElem;
Grid= ARRAY[1..MaxElem] OF RecordType;
```

whose elements are records. Since the program will compare the Key field of one element of the array with the Key field of the next element, we write the switching loop as

```
FOR N:= 1 TO NumElements − 1 DO BEGIN
   SubscriptOfSmall:= N;
   FOR Index:= N + 1 to NumElements DO
     IF Account[Index].Key < Account[SubscriptOfSmall].Key THEN
       SubscriptOfSmall:=Index;
   (* Switch leading and smallest elements *)
   Small:= Account[N];
   Account[N]:= Account[SubscriptOfSmall];
   Account[SubscriptOfSmall]:= Small
END (* FOR N *)
```

as shown in Figure 14.5a. Since elements of Account are stored in Small, the

SORTING RECORDS

```
CONST MaxElem = 100;
TYPE RecordType = record
          Branch, TypeAcct, Key: integer;
          Deposit: real
     END (* record *);
     Range = 0..MaxElem;
     Grid= ARRAY[1..MaxElem] OF RecordType;

PROCEDURES Sort(VAR Account:RecordArray; NumElements:Range);
(* Selection sort *)
VAR SubscriptOfSmall, Index, N:Range;
  Small:RecAcct;
BEGIN
  FOR N:= 1 TO NumElements - 1 DO BEGIN
    SubscriptOfSmall:= N;
    FOR Index:= N + 1 to NumElements DO
      IF Account[Index].Key < Account[SubscriptOfSmall].Key THEN
        SubscriptOfSmall:=Index;
    (* Switch the leading and smallest elements *)
    Small:= Account[N];
    Account[N]:= Account[SubscriptOfSmall];
    Account[SubscriptOfSmall]:= Small
  END (* FOR N *)
END (* Sort *);
```

FIGURE 14.5a.   Since we are sorting elements of an array on the Key field, we alter the previous program by writing IF Account[Index].Key < Account[SubscriptOfSmall].Key THEN. The definitions given in the main program are also shown.

type of Small must be the same as the type of the array's elements, namely, RecordType. The main program and the printing procedure are shown in Figure 14.5b. The running of the program is shown in Figure 14.5c.

```
PROGRAM Sorter;
(* Performs a selection sort on records *)
CONST MaxElem = 100;
TYPE RecordType = record
        Branch, TypeAcct, Key: integer;
        Deposit: real
     END (* record *);
     Range = 0..MaxElem;
     Grid= ARRAY[1..MaxElem] OF RecordType;
VAR Account: Grid;
    NumElem: Range;
PROCEDURE ReadIt( VAR Account:RecordArray; VAR RecNumber: Range);
(* Reads records into an array *)
BEGIN
    RecNumber: = 0;
    writeln('type ID, DEPOSIT, BRANCH, TYPE OF ACCOUNT');
    WHILE NOT eof DO BEGIN
        RecNumber: = RecNumber + 1;
        WITH Account[RecNumber] DO
            read(Key, Deposit, TypeAcct, Branch)
    END; (* WHILE *)
    writeln;
END;(* ReadIt *)
PROCEDURE Print(Account:RecordArray; NumElem: Range);
(* Prints an array of records *)
VAR j: Range;
BEGIN
    writeln;
    FOR j: = 1 to NumElem DO BEGIN
        WITH Account[j] DO
            write( 'ID = ', Key:3, Deposit:7:2, TypeAcct:3, Branch:3);
        writeln
    END(* FOR *)
END; (* Print *)
PROCEDURE Sort(VAR Account:RecordArray; NumElements:Range);
BEGIN (* Sorted *)
    ReadIt(Account, NumElem);
    writeln('Unsorted ARRAY');
    Print(Account, NumElem);
    Sort(Account, NumElem);
    writeln('Sorted ARRAY');
    Print( Account, NumElem)
END.
```

FIGURE 14.5b. The main program, procedures ReadIt and Print, and the heading for procedure Sort. If you run the program, you must include procedure Sort in its entirety.

```
Type:ID, Deposit, Branch, TypeAcct
1002 345.66 2 4    1007 123.45 3 5    1002 478.20 4 7    1006 322.11 3 3
1009 213.22 4 5    1008 134.33 4 5
Unsorted ARRAY

ID = 1002 345.66 2 4
ID = 1007 123.45 3 5
ID = 1002 478.20 4 7
ID = 1006 322.11 3 3
ID = 1009 213.22 4 5
ID = 1008 134.33 4 5
Sorted ARRAY

ID = 1002 345.66 2 4
ID = 1002 478.20 4 7
ID = 1006 322.11 3 3
ID = 1007 123.45 3 5
ID = 1008 134.33 4 5
ID = 1009 213.22 4 5
```

FIGURE 14.5c.   Running the program of Figure 14.5b.

14.7

SORTING RECORDS ON A KEY

BEFORE YOU BEGIN

The field on which a group of records is sorted is called a *key*. In the previous program, we sorted the bank records using the ID field as the key. In a banking environment it is necessary to be able to sort a group of records on more than one key. Let's alter our bank deposit sorting program so that we can sort on either the ID, the branch number, or the type of account.

The crux of the previous sorting problem was the IF statement in procedure Sort:

IF Account[Index].Key < Account[SubscriptOfSmall].Key THEN

To sort on a given key, we must replace Key in the previous sorting program with something that can represent any one of the desired integer fields. The solution is to make each of the fields an element of an array (here, the type of this array is Bank Array). We thus write

```
TYPE KeyRange = 1..KeyNum;
      BankArray = ARRAY[KeyRange] of integer;
      DepositRecord = RECORD
        Field: BankArray;
        Deposit: real
      END (* DepositRecord *);
```

where Field[1] represents the branch, Field[2] the type of account, and Field[3] the ID. Since BankArray is a field type in the record, it must be defined before the record. To do the previous problem, the first thing you must do is to set the value of KeyNum to 3.

Once we have written our data structure definition, the formulation of the program is straightforward. Since the program now reads a variable number of fields (this number varies from 1 to the value of KeyNum), we must change our record reading procedure accordingly, as shown in Figure 14.6a(I). Each record is now read by

SORTING RECORDS ON A KEY

```
CONST KeyMax = 3;
TYPE KeyRange = 1..KeyMax;
     BankArray = ARRAY[KeyRange] of integer;
     DepositRecord = RECORD
       Field: BankArray;
       Deposit: real
     END (* DepositRecord *);
     Range = 0..100;
     RecordArray = ARRAY[Range] OF DepositRecord;
PROCEDURE ReadIt( VAR Account:RecordArray; VAR RecNumber: Range; VAR
SortKey:KeyRange);
(* Reads records into an array *)
VAR FieldNumber:KeyRange;
BEGIN
    RecNumber:= 0;
    writeln( 'To sort on ID, type 1; on Branch, type 2; on Typacct, type 3');
    readln( SortKey);
    CASE SortKey OF
     1: writeln('You have chosen to sort on ID');
     2: writeln('You have chosen to sort on Branch');
     3: writeln('You have chosen to sort on TypAcct')
    END (* CASE *);
    writeln('type ID, BRANCH, TYPE OF ACCOUNT, DEPOSIT');
    WHILE NOT eof DO BEGIN
      RecNumber:= RecNumber + 1;
      WITH Account[RecNumber] DO BEGIN
        FOR FieldNumber:= 1 TO KeyMax DO
          read( Field[ FieldNumber ]);
        read( Deposit );
      END (* WITH *)
    END (* WHILE *);
    writeln
END; (* ReadIt *)
```

FIGURE 14.6a(I). The definition of *key* is a field on which we sort. Since we are sorting on a key, we have to read the three fields on which we may sort as the elements of an array. The definitions given in the main program are also shown.

```
WITH Account[RecNumber] DO BEGIN
   FOR FieldNumber:= 1 TO KeyNum DO
      read( Field[ FieldNumber ]);
   read( Deposit );
END {WITH}
```

The switching loop in procedure Sort must be altered accordingly to

```
FOR Index:= N + 1 to NumElements DO
   IF Account[Index].Field[key] < Account[SubscriptOfSmall].Field[key]
      THEN SubscriptOfSmall:=Index;
```

as shown in Figure 14.6a(II). The computer interprets this when the value of Key is 1 as follows: Compare the value of the first field of one record in the array with the value of the first field of the next record. If these values are not in order, switch the records.

The procedure to print the sorted arrays is similar to the reading procedure and is shown in Figure 14.6a(III). The main program and the headings of the

```
PROCEDURE Sort(VAR Account:RecordArray; NumElements:Range;key:KeyRange);
(* Selection sort *)
VAR SubscriptOfSmall, Index, N:Range;
    Small:DepositRecord;
BEGIN
  FOR N:= 1 TO NumElements −1 DO BEGIN
      SubscriptOfSmall:= N;
      FOR Index:= N + 1 to NumElements DO
       IF Account[Index].Field[key]<Account[SubscriptOfSmall].Field[key]
          THEN SubscriptOfSmall:=Index;
      (* Switch leading and smallest elements *)
      Small:= Account[N];
      Account[N]:= Account[SubscriptOfSmall];
      Account[SubscriptOfSmall]:= Small
    END (* FOR N *)
END (* Sort *);
```

FIGURE 14.6a(II). Because of the IF statement, the program can sort the records on one of three keys.

```
PROCEDURE Print(Account:RecordArray; NumElem: Range);
(* Prints an array of records *)
VAR j: Range;
    FieldNumber:KeyRange;
BEGIN
  writeln;
  FOR j:= 1 to NumElem DO
    WITH Account[j] DO BEGIN
      FOR FieldNumber:= 1 TO KeyMax DO
        write(field[ FieldNumber ]:3);
      writeln(Deposit:8:2);
    END (* WITH *)
END; (* Print *)
```

FIGURE 14.6a(III). The procedure prints the sorted array.

procedure are shown in Figure 14.6*b*. Finally, the running of the program is shown in Figure 14.6*c*.

14.8

DETERMINING THE FREQUENCY OF LETTERS IN A SENTENCE

BEFORE YOU BEGIN

In Chapter 10 we made a histogram of the frequencies of the occurrence of each letter in a sentence. However, we can't sort the frequencies so that the letter most often used is the subscript of the first element and the one least often used is the subscript of the last element. The reason is that if we don't use an array of records, once two elements have been switched, we lose track of the original letter associated with each element. For instance, if the content before the switch of Bin['a'] is 10 and that of Bin['b'] is 3, after the switch the content of Bin['a'] will be 3 and that of Bin['b'] will be 10. Thus the value originally associated with 'a' (or any letter) is lost. However, if we use an array of records, we can keep track of the letters associated with each element. Here's how it's done.

We'll use a record containing two fields. The first will store the frequency of occurrence of a given letter, and the second will store the letter itself. These records will be the elements of an array defined by

```
TYPE Alphabet = 'a'..'z';
     FreqRecord = RECORD
        Frequency:integer;
        Let:Alphabet
     END (* FreqRecord *);
     RecoArray = ARRAY[Alphabet] of FreqRecord;
```

and the array will be declared in VAR RecInfo:RecoArray. An example of two adjacent elements of the array is

4	'a'	RecInfo['a']		6	'b'	RecInfo['b']
Frequency	Let			Frequency	Let	

We'll sort the records of this array according to frequency and then make a histogram of the sorted frequencies. Our top-down diagram is

```
PROGRAM Sorter;
(* Performs a selection sort on records, sorting on a key *)
CONST KeyMax = 3;
TYPE KeyRange = 1..KeyMax;
  BankArray = ARRAY[KeyRange] of integer;
  DepositRecord = RECORD
    Field: BankArray;
    Deposit: real
  END (* DepositRecord *);
  Range = 0..100;
  RecordArray= ARRAY[Range] OF DepositRecord;
VAR Account: RecordArray;
  NumElem: Range;
  Key:KeyRange;
PROCEDURE ReadIt( VAR Account:RecordArray;
                  VAR RecNumber: Range; VAR SortKey:KeyRange);
                                              {See page 595}
PROCEDURE Print(Account:RecordArray; NumElem: Range);
                                              {See page 597}
PROCEDURE Sort(VAR Account:RecordArray; NumElements:Range;
              key:KeyRange);                  {See page 597}
BEGIN (* Sorter *)
  ReadIt(Account, NumElem, Key);
  writeln('Unsorted ARRAY');
  Print(Account, NumElem);
  Sort(Account, NumElem, Key);
  writeln('Sorted ARRAY');
  Print( Account, NumElem)
END.
```

FIGURE 14.6b.   The main program and the headings of the procedures used. If you run the program, you must also include the procedures themselves.

```
To sort on ID, type 1; on Branch, type 2; on Typacct, type 3
1
You have chosen to sort on ID
type ID, BRANCH, TYPE OF ACCOUNT, DEPOSIT
1002 2 4 345.66   1007 3 5 123.45   1003 4 7 432.11   1006 3 3 322.89
1009 4 5 674.33   1008 4 5 134.00
Unsorted ARRAY

1002 2 4 345.66
1007 3 5 123.45
1003 4 7 432.11
1006 3 3 322.89
1009 4 5 674.33
1008 4 5 134.00
Sorted ARRAY

1002 2 4 345.66
1003 4 7 432.11
1006 3 3 322.89
1007 3 5 123.45
1008 4 5 134.00
1009 4 5 674.33
```

FIGURE 14.6c.   Running the program of Figure 14.6b.

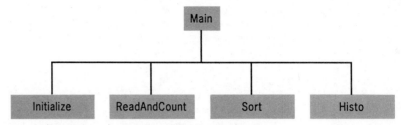

The pseudocode for procedure Initialize is

> FOR *the record for each letter of the alphabet* DO
> *Set frequency field to zero;*
> *Assign letter to letter field.*

This becomes the procedure shown in Figure 14.7a(I). The pseudocode for ReadAndCount is

> FOR *each character in the sentence* DO
> IF *the character is in the alphabet* THEN
> *Add 1 to the frequency field of the record for that letter.*

and it becomes

```
WHILE NOT eoln DO BEGIN
   read(Character);
   IF Character in ['a'..'z'] THEN
      WITH RecInfo[Character] DO
         Frequency:= Frequency + 1
END (* WHILE *)
```

as shown in Figure 14.7a(II).

SORTING LETTERS IN A SENTENCE ACCORDING TO FREQUENCY

```
TYPE Alphabet = 'a'..'z';
   FreqRecord = RECORD
      Frequency:integer;
      Let:Alphabet
   END (* FreqRecord *);
   RecoArray = ARRAY[Alphabet] of FreqRecord;

PROCEDURE Initialize(VAR RecInfo:RecoArray);
(* Zeros frequencies and initializes letters in elements of 'RecInfo' *)
VAR Letter:Alphabet;
BEGIN
   FOR Letter:= 'a' TO 'z' DO
      WITH RecInfo[Letter] DO BEGIN
         Frequency:= 0;
         Let:= Letter
      END (* WITH *);
END (* Initialize *);
```

FIGURE 14.7a(I).   We wish to sort the records in an array according to the frequency of occurrence of each letter in a sentence. In order to mark each element, we place a letter in each record. We also zero the frequency field. The definitions given in the main program are also shown.

```
PROCEDURE ReadAndCount(VAR RecInfo:RecoArray);
(* Reads the letters in a line and determines the frequency of each letter *)
VAR Character:char;
BEGIN (* ReadAndCount *)
   writeln('Type your sentence');
   WHILE NOT eoln DO BEGIN
      read(Character);
      IF Character in ['a'..'z'] THEN
         WITH RecInfo[Character] DO
            Frequency:= Frequency + 1
   END (* WHILE *);
END (* ReadAndCount *);
```

FIGURE 14.7a(II).   We add 1 to Frequency for the letter just read.

Let's use the bubble sort to sort the records. To refresh your memory, we'll repeat the form of the sorting procedure used in Chapter 10:

```
REPEAT
    Sorted: = true;
    (* Don't sort elements already in place *)
    NumElem: = NumElem − 1;
    FOR J: =1 to NumElem DO
        IF List[J] > List[J + 1] THEN BEGIN
            Switch(List, J);
            Sorted: = False
        END (* THEN *)
UNTIL Sorted
```

The analog of NumElem: = NumElem − 1, here, is

```
LastLetter: =pred(LastLetter);
```

as shown in Figure 14.7a(III), where the original value of LastLetter is 'z'. We must compare the frequency field of the record for a given letter with the frequency field of the record for the next letter of the alphabet, that is, succ(Letter). Moreover, since we want a record with a higher frequency to precede one with a lower frequency, we use "<" instead of ">" and write

```
IF RecInfo[Letter].Frequency < RecInfo[succ(Letter)].Frequency THEN
    BEGIN(* THEN *)
        Switch( RecInfo, Letter);
        Sorted: = False
    END(* THEN *)
```

```
PROCEDURE Sort(VAR RecInfo: RecoArray);
(* Performs a bubble sort on the array *)
VAR LastLetter, Letter:Alphabet;
  Sorted: boolean;

PROCEDURE Switch(VAR RecInfo: RecoArray; Letter: Char);
(* Switches records *)
VAR temp: FreqRecord;
BEGIN
  temp:= RecInfo[Letter];
  RecInfo[Letter]:= RecInfo[succ(Letter)];
  RecInfo[succ(Letter)]:= temp;
END (* Switch *);

BEGIN(* sort *)
  LastLetter:= 'z';
  REPEAT
    Sorted:= true;
    (* Don't sort elements already in place *)
    LastLetter:= pred(LastLetter);
    FOR Letter:= 'a' to LastLetter DO
      IF RecInfo[Letter].Frequency < RecInfo[succ(Letter)].Frequency
        THEN BEGIN
          Switch( RecInfo, Letter);
          Sorted:= False
        END(* THEN *)
  UNTIL Sorted
END; (* sort *)
```

FIGURE 14.7a(III).   We sort the records according to frequency. The original subscript is the letter associated with that frequency. After the sort, the final subscript will be different. However, the value of the Letter field is the value of the original subscript.

After the program executes procedure Switch, the elements shown in the previous array diagram become

6	'b'

RecInfo['a']

4	'a'

RecInfo['b']

Frequency   Let   Frequency   Let

and thus each record retains the original value of the Let field.

The pseudocode for procedure Histo is

> FOR *each letter of the alphabet* DO
>   IF *the frequency is not zero* THEN
>   FOR *number of times equal to frequency* DO
>   *Write that letter;*
>   writeln

This becomes the procedure shown in Figure 14.7a(IV). The main program is

```
PROCEDURE Histo(RecInfo:RecoArray);
(* Produces a histogram *)
VAR Letter:Alphabet;
    J:integer;
BEGIN
   writeln;
   writeln('Letter', 'Frequency':12);
   FOR Letter:= 'a' TO 'z' DO
     WITH RecInfo[Letter] DO
     IF Frequency <> 0 THEN BEGIN
        write(let:6, Frequency:7, ' ':5);
        FOR J:= 1 TO Frequency DO
           write(let);
        writeln
     END (* IF *);
END (* Histo *);
```

FIGURE 14.7a(IV).   Prints a histogram of the frequency of occurrence of each letter, sorted on the frequency. If the frequency is 0, the letter is not printed.

shown in Figure 14.7b, and the running of the program is shown in Figure 14.7c. The reason we wrote the letters in lowercase is that we want to make a histogram only for the lowercase letters.

14.9

GENERATING AN INDEX; STABLE SORTS

Have you ever wondered how to make an index of the terms used in a book? We'll now show you how to write a program to do a similar task, namely, to generate an index for the words read from a text file. An entry in the index consists of a word and the line it occurs on. Thus given the text

```
my country tis of thee
sweet; land of liberty,
of thee i sing.
```

the entry for "country" would be "country 1", and the one for "of" would be "of 1, 2, 3". To do this, we'll sort records consisting of two fields (one for the word and one for the line number), such that the words will be in alphabetical order.

As you remember, the program of Figure 13.7a read a text file and placed each word in an element of an array called Grid. We will use procedures FormWord, EndOfWord, and ReadParag from that program; however, we'll alter EndOfWord so that it now forms a record consisting of both the word and the line number and places it in an element of Grid. Thus we've altered the definition of Grid which was

```
TYPE List = PACKED ARRAY[1..MaxLen] OF char;
     Grid = ARRAY[1..MaxElem] OF list;
```

so that it is now

```
CONST MaxLen= 10;
   MaxElem= 100;

TYPE List = PACKED ARRAY[1..MaxLen] OF char;
   Line= PACKED ARRAY[1..80] OF char;
   NumOfLetter = 0..MaxLen;
   RecordType = RECORD
     Key:List;
     LineNumber:integer
   END (* RecordType *);
   Grid = ARRAY[1..MaxElem] of RecordType;
   Range = 0..MaxElem;
```

where the definitions from RecordType = RECORD down are the same as those that were used in the record-sorting program (Figure 14.5a), except that the

```
PROGRAM Histogram;
(* Reads a sentence and then sorts the letters according to frequency;
   finally, makes a histogram of the letter frequencies *)
TYPE Alphabet = 'a'..'z';
  FreqRecord = RECORD
     Frequency:integer;
     Let:Alphabet
  END (* FreqRecord *);
  RecoArray = ARRAY[Alphabet] of FreqRecord;

VAR RecInfo:RecoArray;
PROCEDURE Initialize(VAR RecInfo:RecoArray);            {See page 601}
PROCEDURE ReadAndCount(VAR RecInfo:RecoArray);          {See page 601}
PROCEDURE Sort(VAR RecInfo: RecoArray);                 {See page 603}
PROCEDURE Histo(RecInfo:RecoArray);                     {See page 605}
BEGIN(* Histogram *)
  Initialize(RecInfo);
  ReadAndCount(RecInfo);
  Sort(RecInfo);
  Histo(RecInfo)
END.
```

FIGURE 14.7b. The main program and the headings of the procedures used. If you run the program, you must also include the procedures themselves.

```
Type your sentence
we hold these truths to be self-evident, that all men are created
equal.
Letter  Frequency
   e      12   eeeeeeeeeeee
   t       8   tttttttt
   a       5   aaaaa
   l       5   lllll
   h       4   hhhh
   d       3   ddd
   r       3   rrr
   s       3   sss
   n       2   nn
   o       2   oo
   u       2   uu
   b       1   b
   c       1   c
   f       1   f
   i       1   i
   m       1   m
   q       1   q
   v       1   v
   w       1   w
```

FIGURE 14.7c. Running the program of Figure 14.7b. The letters are sorted according to frequency.

fields in the record (except for Key) are different and Key is now of type List.

However, since the record identifier RecordType, the subrange Range, and the field identifier Key are the same ones used in both the sorting program and this one, we can use procedure Sort of Figure 14.5a as is to sort the records so that the words will be in alphabetical order. Remember, its heading is

PROCEDURE Sort(VAR Account:Grid; NumElements:Range);

Note that we wrote procedures FormWord, ReadParag, and Sort so that they can be used with the new TYPE definitions.

The top-down diagram for our program is

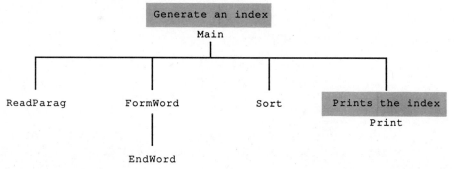

Since most of the procedures have already been tested, this is an example of the bottom-up approach. The procedures used are shown in Figures 14.8a(I), 14.8a(II), and 14.8a(III). The main program is shown in Figure 14.8b and the

GENERATING AN INDEX

```
CONST MaxLen=10;
      NumOfLetter = 0..MaxLen;
      TYPE List = PACKED ARRAY[1..MaxLen] OF char;
PROCEDURE ReadParag(VAR Parag:text);
(* Reads and prints a paragraph from a file *)
VAR Ch:char;
BEGIN
   WHILE NOT eof(Parag) DO BEGIN
     WHILE NOT eoln(Parag) DO BEGIN
       read(Parag,ch);
       write( ch)
     END (* WHILE NOT eoln *);
     readln(Parag);
     writeln
   END (* WHILE NOT eof *)
END (* ReadParag *);
PROCEDURE Full( VAR Letter:List; Beg, Lmax: NumOfLetter);
(* Fills the unused part of the array with blanks because
   the compiler can only compare packed arrays of same length *)
VAR J: NumOfLetter;
BEGIN{ Full}
   FOR J:= Beg TO Lmax DO
     Letter[J] := ' ';
END; (* Full *)
```

FIGURE 14.8a(l). Procedure ReadParag, used in the last chapter, and procedure Full, used in this chapter and the last one. The definitions given in the main program that are used in these procedures are also shown.

```
CONST MaxLen=10;
  MaxElem= 100;
TYPE List = PACKED ARRAY[1..MaxLen] OF char;
  Line= PACKED ARRAY[1..80] OF char;
  RecordType = RECORD
    Key:List;
    LineNumber:integer
  END (* RecordType *);
  Grid = ARRAY[1..MaxElem] of RecordType;
  Range = 0..MaxElem;
  NumOfLetter = 0..MaxLen;

PROCEDURE Form Word(VAR Word: grid; VAR WordCount:Range; VAR Parag;text);
(* Places words in a paragraph in the array "Word" *)
CONST Blank = ' ';

VAR J, Count, LetterCount: NumOfLetter;
  Sentence: Line;
  Letter: List;
  Ch: char;
  LineCount:integer;
PROCEDURE EndOfWord(VAR Word: grid; VAR WordCount:Range);
(* Used when the end of the word is encountered *)
BEGIN
  If LetterCount <> 0 THEN BEGIN
    WordCount := WordCount + 1;
    Full( Letter, LetterCount + 1, MaxLen );
    With Word[WordCount] DO BEGIN
        Key:= Letter;
        LineNumber:= LineCount
    END (* WITH *);
    LetterCount:=0;
  END (* IF *)
END (* EndOfWord *);
BEGIN (* FormWord *)
  WordCount:= 0;
  LetterCount:=0;
  LineCount:= 0;
  reset(Parag); (* rewind file so that we can read it again *)
  WHILE NOT eof(Parag) DO BEGIN
    LineCount:= LineCount + 1;
    Count:= 0;
    WHILE NOT eoln(Parag) DO BEGIN
    (* read characters in a line into the array "Sentence" *)
      read(Parag, Ch);
      Count:= Count + 1;
      Sentence[Count]:= Ch
    END (* WHILE *);
    readln(Parag);
    FOR J:= 1 TO Count DO BEGIN
      IF Sentence[J] IN ['a'..'z', 'A'..'Z',"",'-'] THEN BEGIN
        LetterCount := LetterCount + 1;
        Letter[LetterCount]:= Sentence[J]
      END (* IF *)
      ELSE (* end of word, but previous character not punctuation *)
          EndOfWord(Word, WordCount)
    END (* FOR *);
    (* end of word at end of line *)
    EndOfWord(Word, WordCount)
  END (* WHILE NOT eof *)
END (* FormWord *);
```

FIGURE 14.8a(II).   Procedure FormWord is the same as in the last chapter, except that now we include a line counter, LineCount, so that we can include the line number in the index. We've changed the fields in RecordType so that Key is now a packed array, and a new field, LineNumber, represents the line number. EndOf–Word has been altered to reflect these changes.

```
PROCEDURE Sort(VAR Account:Grid; NumElements:Range);
(* Selection sort *)
VAR SubscriptOfSmall, Index, N:Range;
  Small:RecordType;
BEGIN
  FOR N:= 1 TO NumElements -1 DO BEGIN
    SubscriptOfSmall:=N;
    FOR Index:= N + 1 to NumElements DO
      IF Account[Index].Key < Account[SubscriptOfSmall].Key THEN
        SubscriptOfSmall:=Index;
    (* Switch leading and smallest elements *)
    Small:= Account[N];
    Account[N]:= Account[SubscriptOfSmall];
    Account[SubscriptOfSmall]:= Small
  END (* FOR N *)
END (* Sort *);
```

FIGURE 14.8a(III). Since Account is of type Grid, identifier NumElements is of type Range and procedure Sort sorts on the field Key, we can use Sort (repeated here) from Figure 14.5a in the present program.

```
PROCEDURE Print(Word: Grid; WordNumber:Range);
(* Prints the index *)
VAR L: Range;
BEGIN
  writeln;
  writeln('THE SORTED WORDS ARE:');
  FOR L:= 1 TO WordNumber DO
    WITH Word[L] DO
    write(Key, LineNumber, Colon)
END (* Print *);
```

Figure 14.8a(IV)   Procedure Print prints the index.

running of the program in Figure 14.8c. When a word occurs on more than one line, the line numbers are unfortunately out of order; for instance, the entry for of is

of 2: of 1: of 3:

Originally, the records in the array were automatically sorted according to line number because the words on the first line are read first, then the words on the second line, and so forth. How, then, was the order changed?

In the following discussion, we'll use the notation ('Key' , LineNumber) to represent a record. If we trace the execution of procedure Sort, we see that when the first three records of Account, that is, ('country',1), ('i',3), and ('land',2), are in their sorted positions, the next record, ('of',1), will be the next one to be interchanged:

```
Account: ('country',1),('i',3),('land',2),('of',1),('thee',1),
('sweet',2),('tis',1),('of',2),('liberty',2),('of',3),('thee',3),
('my',1),
```

where the contents of each record are placed in parentheses, for example, ('sweet',2).

The record that will be swapped with ('of',1) is ('liberty',2). This means that the order of the three records for *of* after the swap will be ('of',2), ('of',1), ('of',3); thus they will not be sorted according to line number. This is a result of the nature of the selection sort. Because of this, the selection sort is called *unstable*. The bubble sort, on the other hand, maintains the line number order for records that contain the same word. Thus it is called a *stable* sort. So, in order to generate an index, we must include a bubble sort instead of a selection sort in procedure Sort.

```
PROGRAM ArrayPractice;
(* Reads the words in a paragraph from a text file
Then makes an index of words according to line number, using selection sort.
The identifier "Key" represents the word *)
CONST MaxLen=10;
  MaxElem= 100;
  Colon: ':';
TYPE List = PACKED ARRAY[1..MaxLen] OF char;
  Line= PACKED ARRAY[1..80] OF char;
  RecordType = RECORD
    Key:List;
    LineNumber:integer
  END (* RecordType *);
  Grid = ARRAY[1..MaxElem] of RecordType;
  Range = 0..MaxElem;
  NumOfLetter = 0..MaxLen;
VAR Word:Grid;
  WordNumber:Range;
  Parag:text;
PROCEDURE ReadParag(VAR Parag:text);                         {See page 609}
PROCEDURE Full( VAR Letter:List; Beg, Lmax: integer);        {See page 609}
PROCEDURE FormWord(VAR Word: grid; VAR WordCount:Range; VAR Parag:text);
                                                             {See page 610}
PROCEDURE Sort(VAR Account:Grid; NumElements:Range);         {See page 611}
PROCEDURE Print(Word: Grid; WordNumber:Range);               {See page 611}
BEGIN
  reset(Parag);
  writeln ('THE PARAGRAPH READ WAS:');
  ReadParag(Parag);
  FormWord(Word, WordNumber, Parag);
  Sort(Word, WordNumber);
  Print(Word, WordNumber);
END.
```

FIGURE 14.8b. The main program with the procedure headings. If you run the program, you must also include the procedures themselves.

```
THE PARAGRAPH READ WAS:
my country tis of thee
sweet; land of liberty,
of thee i sing.
THE SORTED WORDS ARE:
country 1: i 3: land 2: liberty 2: my 1: of 2: of 1: of 3: sing 3:
sweet 2: thee 3: thee 1: tis 1:
```

FIGURE 14.8c. Running the program of Figure 14.8b. We see that the line numbers for of and thee are out of order. This is because we used a selection sort instead of a bubble sort.

Figure 14.9*a* shows the bubble sorting procedure we will use in procedure Sort. Figure 14.9*b* shows the results of running the program of Figure 14.8*b* using the revised procedure Sort.

Printing the Index in the Standard Index Form

The standard form of an index has the word followed by the line numbers on which it appears. If the word appears more than once in the text, the word appears only once in the index, so let's use the following pseudocode:

> *Set First to first word*
>
> WHILE *the record number* < = *total number of records* DO BEGIN
>
> > *Print First and line number;*
> >
> > WHILE *subsequent records have the same word* DO BEGIN
> >
> > > *Print the line number;*
> > >
> > > *Set First to next word*
> >
> > END (* WHILE *)
>
> END (* WHILE *);

If three consecutive records were ('of', 1), ('of', 1), ('of', 3), a program based on this pseudocode would produce the index entry: "of 1, 1, 3"; that is, "1" would be unnecessarily repeated. To avoid this, refine the pseudocode to

> *Set First to first word*
>
> WHILE *the record number* < = *total number of records* DO BEGIN
>
> > *Print First and line number;*
> >
> > *Set FirstLine to the first line number;*
> >
> > WHILE *subsequent records have the same word* DO BEGIN
> >
> > > IF *line number* <> *FirstLine* THEN
> > >
> > > > *Print the line number;*
> > >
> > > *Set FirstLine to the present line number;*
> > >
> > > *Set First to next word*
> >
> > END (* WHILE *);
>
> END (* WHILE *);

A STABLE SORT:
USING A BUBBLE SORT IN THE Sorter UNIT TO SORT THE ENTRIES ON
LINE NUMBER

```
PROCEDURE Sort(VAR Words: grid; MaxEl: Range);
(* Sorts words alphabetically *)
VAR J: Range;
  Unsorted: boolean;
PROCEDURE Switch(VAR Words: Grid; J: Range);
VAR Temp: RecordType;
BEGIN
  Temp:= Words[J];
  Words[J]:= Words[J + 1];
  Words[J + 1]:= Temp
END (* Switch *);
BEGIN(* Sort *)
  Unsorted:= true;
  WHILE Unsorted DO BEGIN
    Unsorted:= false;
    FOR J:= 1 TO MaxEl - 1 DO
      IF Words[J].Key > Words[J + 1].Key THEN BEGIN
          Switch(Words, J);
          Unsorted:= true
        END (* THEN *)
      END; (* WHILE *)
END; (* Sort *)
```

FIGURE 14.9a.   A bubble sort that sorts on the field Key. Since Words is of type Grid and MaxEl is of type Range, we can use the procedure in our program.

```
THE PARAGRAPH READ WAS:
my country tis of thee
sweet; land of liberty,
of thee i sing.
THE SORTED WORDS ARE:
count 1: i 3: land 2: liberty 2: my 1: of 1: of 2: of 3: sing 3:
sweet 2: thee 1: thee 3: tis 1:
```

FIGURE 14.9b.   Running the program of Figure 14.8b with the procedure of Figure 14.9a. The words are now also sorted on line numbers.

This becomes procedure Print, shown in Figure 14.9c. When we run the program, we test it with a larger text file and get the results shown in Figure 14.9d.

```
PROCEDURE Print(Words: Grid; WordNumber:Range);
(* Prints an index in standard form *)
VAR L: Range;
  First: RecordType;
  FirstLine:integer;
BEGIN
  writeln;
  writeln('INDEX OF WORDS OCCURRING IN THE PARAGRAPH:');
  L:=1;
  WHILE L <= WordNumber DO BEGIN
    First:= Words[L];
    WITH Words[L] DO {print word}
      write(Key, Blank, LineNumber);
    FirstLine:= First.LineNumber;
    L:=L + 1;
    (* Print line numbers *)
    WHILE Words[L].Key = First.Key DO BEGIN
      IF Words[L].LineNumber <> FirstLine THEN
        write(Comma, Words[L].LineNumber);
      FirstLine:= Words[L].LineNumber;
      L:=L + 1
    END (* WHILE *);
    writeln
  END (* WHILE *)
END (* Print *);
```

FIGURE 14.9c. This version of procedure Print prints the index in the customary form.

```
THE PARAGRAPH READ WAS:
my country tis of thee, sweet land of liberty, of thee i sing.
land of the pilgrim's pride, land where my fathers died,
from every mountain side, let freedom ring.
INDEX OF WORDS OCCURRING IN THE PARAGRAPH:
country 1
died 2
every 3
fathers 2
freedom 3
from 3
i 1
land 1,2
let 3
liberty 1
mountain 3
my 1,2
of 1,2
pilgrim's 2
pride 2
ring 3
side 3
sing 1
sweet 1
the 2
thee 1
tis 1
where 2
```

FIGURE 14.9d.   Running the program of Figure 14.8b with the new Sort and Print procedures.

14.10

VARIANT RECORDS

BEFORE YOU BEGIN

The purpose of a data structure is to allow you to refer to a group of data by using only one identifier. If the group of data consists of different types, we use a record as the data structure. We have not yet learned the technique that would enable us, for instance, to store in the same record either the set of data to calculate the area of a rectangle (length and width) or the area of a circle (the radius), but not both sets of information at the same time. If we use an ordinary record to store one of several sets of data, the computer must allocate memory for the fields for all the sets of data. For instance, in

```
CarpetData = RECORD
   Length, Width: real;
   Radius: real;
   Yardage: integer
END (* CarpetData *);
```

memory is allocated for the set consisting of Length and Width, the one consisting of Radius, and the one consisting of Yardage. We now introduce a data structure, consisting of several sets of data, that allocates memory only for the one requiring the most memory—here, the one consisting of Length and Width—but still allows us to refer to any of the sets of data. This data structure is called a *variant record*. A less popular term for this is *record variant*.

Although the amount of memory saved here by using a variant record is negligible, it becomes significant when you use a data base. A data base record can consist of hundreds of fields. If you don't use a variant record to represent the data, the data base may not fit into the memory.

Let's define the following types

```
TYPE Shape = (Rectangle, Circle, Irregular);
   CarpetData = RECORD
      Cost: real;
      CASE Figure:Shape OF
         Rectangle:( Length, Width: real);
         Circle: (Radius:real);
         Irregular:(Yardage:integer);
   END (* CarpetData *);
```

as shown in Figure 14.10*a*(I). The first part of the record, Cost: real, is called the *fixed part*, and the rest—the part starting with CASE—is called the *variant part*. In our example, Figure is called the *tag field*, and Rectangle, Circle, and Irregular (the possible values of the tag field) are called the *selectors*.

VARIANT RECORD

```
TYPE Shape = (Rectangle, Circle, Irregular);
   CarpetData = RECORD
       Cost: real;
       CASE Figure:Shape OF
          Rectangle:( Length, Width: real);
          Circle: (Radius:real);
          Irregular:(Yardage:integer);
   END (* CarpetData *);
```

FIGURE 14.10*a*(I). Depending on the value of Figure—it's called the *tag*—only the fields for Rectangle, Circle, or Irregular will be used. These fields are called the *variant fields*; Cost is called the *fixed part*.

What follows the tag field indicates the tag field's type (here, Shape). If during execution the value of Figure is set to Rectangle, the fields used in the variant part of the record are Length and Width. If the value of Figure is set to Circle, the field used in the variant part of the record is Radius. Finally, if the value of Figure is set to Irregular, the field used in the variant part of the record is Yardage.

The CASE used here is different from the CASE statement in the following ways:

1. The tag is defined by a type (here, Shape).

2. Instead of executable statements, to the right of each selector are fields described by types.

3. The END following the selectors concludes the record definition and not the CASE.

The memory that the computer allocates for the variant part of the record is that needed to store the fields for the selector requiring the most memory— here, the fields for the selector Rectangle, as shown in the table for Figure 14.10. The computer doesn't have to allocate memory for the fields for all the selectors. The fields appearing between the parentheses are called the *variant fields*. Thus Length, Width, Radius, and Yardage are variant fields.

It is important to note that the variant part of a record must follow the fixed part. Thus cost:real precedes the variant part. Remember that the CASE in the variant part does not terminate with the delimiter END. However, as always, the record terminates with an END.

Procedure ReadIt reads the cost per square yard, the shape of the carpet, and the information (length and width or radius) enabling the program to calculate the area of the rug. We pass all the information for only the selected shape back to the main program by using the parameter Data. We write

```
PROCEDURE Readit( VAR Data: CarpetData);
```

MEMORY ALLOCATION FOR VARIANT RECORDS

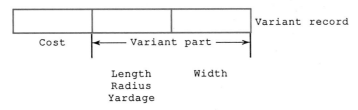

TABLE FOR FIGURE 14.10   The memory that the computer allocates for the variant part of the record is that needed to store the fields for the selector requiring the most memory—here, the fields for selector Rectangle. If we use a regular record, the computer must allocate memory for all the fields, even though it will use only one set of fields.

In the procedure, we must identify which variant field we wish to use, in other words, which shape we will use for the calculation. The user types a number indicating the shape, and this number is assigned to Code. If this number is 1, the program assigns Rectangle to the tag field Figure and reads the real values for Data.Length and Data.Width; if it is 2, the program assigns Circle to Figure and reads the real value for Data.Radius; and if it is 3, the program assigns Irregular to Figure and reads the integer value for Data.Yardage, as we see in Figure 14.10a(II):

```
WITH Data DO BEGIN
  CASE Code OF
    1: BEGIN
        Figure:= Rectangle;
        writeln('Type in Length, Width');
        read(Length, Width)
      END;
    2: BEGIN
        Figure:= Circle;
        writeln('Type in Radius');
        read(Radius)
      END;
    3: BEGIN
        Figure:= Irregular;
        writeln('Type in area');
        read(Yardage)
      END
  END (* CASE *);
```

In function Price, the computer calculates the area using the variant fields and the price, using the fixed field Cost:

```
WITH Data DO BEGIN
  CASE Figure OF
    Rectangle: Area:= Length * Width;
    Circle: Area:= 3.14159 * sqr(Radius);
    Irregular: Area:= Yardage
  END(* CASE *);
  Price:= Cost * Area
END (* WITH *)
```

```
PROCEDURE Readit( VAR Data: CarpetData);
(* Reads the data for different shapes *)
VAR Code : integer
BEGIN
  writeln('Type in code');
  writeln( '1: Figure:= Rectangle, ',
      '2: Figure:= Circle, ',
      '3: Figure:= Irregular shape');
  read(Code);
  WITH Data DO BEGIN
  CASE Code OF
    1: BEGIN
        Figure:= Rectangle;
        writeln('Type in Length, Width');
        read(Length, Width)
      END;
    2: BEGIN
        Figure:= Circle;
        writeln('Type in Radius');
        read(Radius)
      END;
    3: BEGIN
        Figure:= Irregular;
        writeln('Type in area');
        read(Yardage)
      END
    END (* CASE *);
    writeln('Type cost per square yard');
    readln(Cost)
  END (* WITH *)
END; (* Readit *)
```

FIGURE 14.10a(II).   The code you type in determines the value of the tag, `Figure`, and thus which of the variant fields the program will read.

as shown in Figure 14.10*a*(III). Note that since the value of the tag field Figure has been passed to the function Price, it calculates the proper area. The main program is shown in Figure 14.10*b* and its running in Figure 14.10*c*.

14.11

RECORDS OF RECORDS; DATA ABSTRACTION

BEFORE YOU BEGIN

> As we've seen, it's convenient to have the information for a depositor stored in a record. An elegant way of doing this is to have the record store the name of the depositor, his or her social security number, and a record consisting of all the depositor's account information. This, however, would require using records of records. Let's see how to use them.

You can define a record that has a field identifier that is itself a record; for example, in

```
TYPE DepositRecord = RECORD
          ID, Branch, TypAcct: integer;
          Dep: real;
     END; (* DepositRecord *)
     AccountRecord = RECORD
        Name: PACKED ARRAY[1..20] OF char;
        DepositInfo:DepositRecord
     END (* AccountRecord *);
```

the identifier DepositInfo is of type DepositRecord. Note that the definition of DepositRecord must precede its use (as it does here) in the definition of another record. When a record is nested in another record (as DepositRecord is nested in AccountRecord here), the structure is called a *hierarchical record*.

In the first stages of designing the program, we would define Account-Record as shown here:

```
     AccountRecord = RECORD
        Name: PACKED ARRAY[1..20] OF char;
        DepositInfo:DepositRecord
     END (* AccountRecord *);
```

Only when we come to the actual coding would we define DepositRecord. The process of leaving the coding of a data structure until the last stage of the design is called *data abstraction*.

```
FUNCTION Price( Data: CarpetData): real;
(* Calculates the cost for carpets of different shapes *)
VAR Area: real;
BEGIN
  WITH Data DO BEGIN
    CASE Figure OF
      Rectangle: Area:= Length * Width;
      Circle: Area:= 3.14159 * sqr(Radius);
      Irregular: Area:= Yardage
    END(* CASE *);
    Price:= Cost * Area
  END (* WITH Data *)
END (* Price *);
```

FIGURE 14.10a(III). The value of the tag, `Figure`, determines which of the areas will be calculated.

```
PROGRAM Variant;
(* Calculates the cost for carpets of different shapes
   using variant records *)
TYPE Shape = (Rectangle, Circle, Irregular);
  CarpetData = RECORD
    Cost: real;
    CASE Figure:Shape OF
      Rectangle:( Length, Width: real);
      Circle: (Radius:real);
      Irregular:(Yardage:integer);
  END (* CarpetData *);
VAR Data: CarpetData;
FUNCTION Price( Data: CarpetData): real;        {On this page}
PROCEDURE Readit( VAR Data: CarpetData);        {See page 623}
BEGIN
  Readit(Data);
  writeln('The price is', Price(Data):6:2 )
END.
```

FIGURE 14.10b. The main program and the headings of the procedures used. If you run the program, you must also include the procedures themselves.

```
Type in code
1: Figure:= Rectangle, 2: Figure:= Circle, 3: Figure:=
Irregular shape
1
Type in Length, Width
12 10
Type cost per square yard
3.50
The price is 420.00
```

FIGURE 14.10c. Running the program of Figure 14.10a.

When we write the code, if we declare VAR Account: AccountRecord;, then we can assign 345.67 to the Dep field by writing Account.DepositInfo.Dep:=345.67, or we can write the more elegant

```
        WITH Account DO
          WITH DepositInfo DO
            Dep:=345.67
```

or, better yet, we can write this using one WITH

```
        WITH Account, DepositInfo DO
          Dep:=345.67
```

where the second record identifier (here, DepositInfo) is the one used in the second WITH in the previous formulation. Note that we cannot switch these two WITHs. Thus

```
        WITH DepositInfo DO
          WITH Account DO
            Dep:=345.67
```

would cause a syntax error, since DepositInfo is a field of AccountRecord. Similarly, if we reverse the order of the two records in the one WITH formulation and thus write

```
        WITH DepositInfo, Account DO
          Dep:=345.67
```

we obtain a syntax error.

TEST YOURSELF

QUESTION: If we define the variant record in the preceding program using data abstraction, and therefore nest the record FormRec in the record CarpetData, that is,

```
        TYPE Shape = (Rectangle, Circle, Irregular);
          FormRec = RECORD
            CASE Figure:Shape OF
                Rectangle:( Length, Width: real);
                Circle: (Radius:real);
                Irregular:(Yardage:real)
          END (* FormRec *)
```

```
        CarpetData = RECORD
              Cost: real;
              Form: FormRec
          END (* CarpetData *)
        VAR Data: CarpetData;
```

how do we write function `Price`?

```
        FUNCTION Price( Data: CarpetData): real;
        VAR Area: real;
        BEGIN
          WITH Data DO BEGIN
            WITH Form DO
              CASE Figure OF
                Rectangle: Area:= Length * Width;
                Circle: Area:= 3.14159 * sqr(Radius);
                Irregular: Area:= Yardage
              END(* CASE *)
            Price:= Cost * Area
          END (* WITH Data *)
        END (* Price *);
```

14.12

ADVANCED USE OF RECORDS

You can define a record in a VAR declaration. For instance, in

```
        VAR X: RECORD
                L, M:integer
              END (* RECORD *);
            Y: RECORD
                M, N:integer
              END (* RECORD *)
```

X and Y are record identifiers (not types). Given these definitions, consider the following code fragment:

```
WITH X, Y DO BEGIN
   L: = 3;
   M: = 4
END (* WITH *);
```

Since M is used as a field identifier in both records, in which record will the value of M be stored? The rule that is followed is that when more than one record identifier is used in the list of a WITH statement, the last record listed takes precedence over the next to last one. Furthermore, that record identifier takes precedence over the one that precedes it, and so on. Thus, since M is a field identifier in both records, the value 4 is stored in record Y, since Y is the last record in the list in WITH X, Y DO. The value 3 is stored in X, since there is no duplicate field identifier in Y. The same assignments would occur if we wrote

```
WITH X DO
   WITH Y DO BEGIN
      L: = 3;
      M: = 4
   END (* WITH *);
```

On the other hand, if we wrote

```
WITH Y, X DO BEGIN
   L: = 3;
   M: = 4
END (* WITH *);
```

or

```
WITH Y DO
   WITH X DO BEGIN
   L: = 3;
   M: = 4
END (* WITH *);
```

the values of 3 and 4 would both be stored in record X.

PITFALLS

1. Although you can use the same field identifier for two different records, such as ID and Dep, in

```
TYPE DepositRecord = RECORD
        ID, Branch, TypAcct: integer;
        Dep: real;
    END; (* DepositRecord *)
    BankRecord = RECORD
        Name: PACKED ARRAY[1..20] OF char;
        ID :integer;
        Dep: real
    END; (* BankRecord *)
```

it is not advisable because it can lead to confusion. Once you use an identifier in a record, you can also use it in a VAR declaration. Thus, given the preceding definition of the type DepositRecord, the declaration of the identifier ID in

```
VAR ID: integer;
    TransRec:BankRecord;
```

is legal but may confuse someone reading the program.

2. Every record definition must end with an END, even if there is only one field type. Thus

```
TYPE DepositRecord = RECORD
            ID, Branch, TypAcct: integer;
VAR BankRec:DepositRecord
```

would produce a syntax error.

3. It is an error to place a BEGIN in the record definition. For instance,

```
TYPE DepositRecord = RECORD
        BEGIN
            ID, Branch, TypAcct: integer;
            Dep: real
        END; (* DepositRecord *)
```

will cause a compilation error.

SUMMARY OF PASCAL STATEMENTS STUDIED

Record   The form of the record is the record identifier, followed by "=", followed by one or more blanks, followed by the reserved word RECORD. This is followed by one or more declarations. Each declaration consists of a list of field identifiers, followed by a ":", followed by a type. The declarations are separated by a semicolon. The record concludes with an END followed by a semicolon. Examples:

```
BankRecord = RECORD
    ID, Branch, TypAcct: integer;
    Deposit: real
  END; (* BankRecord *)

DepositRecord = RECORD
    Name: PACKED ARRAY[1..40] OF char;
    Branch: 1..5;
    TypAcct: (MoneyMarket, Checking, Savings);
    Deposit: real
  END; (* DepositRecord *)
```

Variant Record   The form of the variant part of the record is CASE, followed by one or more blanks, followed by the tag identifier and a colon, followed by the tag identifier's type, followed by one or more blanks and OF. This is followed by a group of lines, each of which begins with a tag selector, a colon, and parenthesized items. These items consist of a list of variant field identifiers, followed by a colon and then a type. There can be several types for a given selector. Each line but the last must conclude with a semicolon. You may define the tag field identifier in the CASE statement. Example:

```
CASE Item: (Ch, Re, Bool) OF
  Ch: (ChItem, Figure:char);
  Re: (ReItem:real; ReArray: ARRAY[1..10] OF integer);
  Bool: ()
```

If nothing is to be done for a certain value of the tag field identifier, then nothing appears in the parentheses; however, the parentheses must still be inserted. See, for example, the line beginning with Bool. A record can have only one variant part.

CHAPTER REVIEW

Record Definition

Any type may be used for the field type. If the type is user defined, it must be defined before the definition of the record. For example, in

```
List = PACKED ARRAY[1..40] OF char;
DepositRecord = RECORD
    Name: List;
    Branch, TypAcct: integer;
    Dep: real
END; (* DepositRecord *)
```

List is defined in the line that precedes the record definition.

Accessing Fields

You refer to a field in a record by following the record identifier with a period and then by the field identifier. For example, in

```
List = PACKED ARRAY[1..40] OF char;
DepositRecord = RECORD
    Name: List;
    Branch, TypAcct: integer;
    Dep: real
END; (* DepositRecord *)
```

if we declare Present to be of type DepositRecord, then Present.Dep refers to the Dep field for record Present. This dot notation can be cumbersome. We can simplify it by using the WITH.

The WITH Statement

You can eliminate the record identifier in the dot notation by preceding all references to any field in the record with a WITH. For example,

```
WITH Present DO
    writeln(Name, Branch, TypAcct, Dep)
```

prints all the fields of the record Present. If we have another type record to which we wish to refer, for instance,

```
WithDrawRec = RECORD
    Name: List;
    Branch, TypWithDraw: integer;
    WithDraw: real
END; (* WithDrawRecord *)
```

we can refer to the fields of records of both types by doing the following: If we declare Draw to be of type WithDrawRec, we can write

```
WITH Present, Draw DO
    writeln(Name, Branch, TypAcct, TypeWithDraw, Dep, WithDraw)
```

Since Name and Branch are used in both records, if they do not have the same values for both records, the values printed will be those for record Draw.

Using Enumerated Types in Records

We may use the definition of an enumerated type as the field type in a record; for instance, in

```
TYPE DepositRecord= RECORD
    ID, Branch: integer;
    TypAcct: (Savings, Checking, MoneyMarket);
    Dep: real
END; (* DepositRecord *)
```

we use TypAcct: (Savings, Checking, MoneyMarket). If we declare VAR BankRecord:DepositRecord, then we can write, for instance,

```
CASE BankRecord.TypAcct OF
    Savings: Interest:= 0.06;
    Checking: Interest:= 0.02;
    MoneyMarket: Interest:= DiscountRate
END (* CASE *);
```

Variant Record

Normally, we use variants record when we use only one set of a number of sets of fields at a time. These fields are called the *variant fields*. The value of the tag identifier determines which set of variant fields will be used.

NEW TERMS

data abstraction	field
dot notation	hierarchical record

key	tag field
record	variant field
selection sort	variant record
selectors	

EXERCISES

1. What is wrong with the following?

   ```
   TYPE Employee = RECORD
                  Age:integer;
                  Name:NameType
          END (* RECORD *);
      NameType: PACKED ARRAY[1..20] OF char;
   ```

2. Correct the following:

   ```
   TYPE NumberOfExams = 5;
      Student = RECORD
        Name:PACKED ARRAY[20] OF char;
        Exams:ARRAY[1..NumberOfExams] of integer
      END (* RECORD *);
   ```

3. Given

   ```
   TYPE NameRecord = RECORD
        First, Last: PACKED ARRAY[1..20] OF char;
        MiddleInitial:char
      END (* NameRecord *);
      Employee = RECORD
        Age:integer;
        Name:NameRecord
      END (* RECORD *);
   VAR EmployeeName: Employee
   ```

   write the statement that assigns the middle initial to an employee.

4. Do the previous problem using the WITH statement.

5. In the previous problem, could we use WITH EmployeeName, Name-Record DO or WITH Name, EmployeeName DO?

6. Given

```
TYPE StudentRec = RECORD
        Name: PACKED ARRAY[1..20] OF char;
        Exams: ARRAY[1..4] OF real
     END (* RECORD *);

     ExamRec = RECORD
        Name: PACKED ARRAY[1..20] OF char;
        Exams: ARRAY[1..4] OF real
     END (* RECORD *);

VAR Info1:StudentRec;
    Info2:ExamRec;
```

can you write Info1:= Info2?

7. What is wrong with the following?

```
StudentData = RECORD
  Name:PACKED ARRAY[1..20] OF char;
  CASE Life OF
    Academic:(Exam1, Exam2, Exam3:0..100);
    Work:(Hours, Rate:real);
    Social:(Phone1, Phone2, Phone3:ARRAY[1..7] OF char)
  END (* Case *);
END (* StudentData *);
```

8. Rewrite the following so that the values read are correct

```
NumOfRecords:= 1;
WHILE (NOT eof) AND (NumOfRecords <= MaxNum) DO
   WITH Present[NumOfRecords] DO BEGIN
     NumOfRecords:= NumOfRecords + 1;
     readln(ID, Dep, Branch, TypeAcct);
   END (* WITH *);
```

where ID, Dep, Branch, and TypeAcct are fields of Present[NumOf-Records].

Programming Problems

9. Given the following definitions

```
TYPE NameType = PACKED ARRAY[1..20] OF char;
   Employee = RECORD
     LastName:NameType;
     SocSec:integer;
     Married:boolean;
     Dependents:integer;
     Salary:real
   END (* RECORD *);
   Staff = ARRAY[1..200] OF Employee;
VAR Personnel:Staff;
```

write a function that accepts as parameters the array and SocSec and returns the subscript of the array with the same value of SocSec or 0 if that value cannot be found.

10. Write a program to determine the ID of the depositor with the largest account in a bank that has 40 depositors, each with three accounts.

11. Write a program to determine which depositor has the largest account in a bank having 40 depositors, each with up to three accounts. Use

```
TYPE BankRec = RECORD
       Name: PACKED ARRAY[1..20] OF char;
       NumberOfAccts:1..3;
       Balance: ARRAY[1..3] OF real
     END (* RECORD *);
```

12. Write a program that sorts deposit records on the last name, followed by the first name. Use

```
TYPE BankRec = RECORD
       LastName, First: PACKED ARRAY[1..20] OF char;
       Balance: real
     END (* RECORD *);
```

13. Given

```
TYPE Card = RECORD
       NameX, NameO: PACKED ARRAY[1..20] OF char;
       Score: ARRAY[1..3, 1..3] OF char
     END (* RECORD *);
VAR TicTacToe:Card;
```

write the statement that stores the final appearance of the tic-tac-toe grid in the record `TicTacToe`. Note that `NameX` is the name of the person who used X and `Name0` is the name of the one who used O.

14. Write a program that determines whether or not a person won, where the winning configuration consists of three Xs (or three Os) on the diagonal.

15. Rewrite the previous program so that the array `Name` replaces `NameX` and `Name0`. Can we write `ARRAY[X..0] OF char`, where we are given `CONST X = 'X'; 0 = '0'`? How many elements does `ARRAY[0..X] OF char` have?

16. Write a program that searches an array of the records defined in problem 13 and prints the names of the people who won because their mark (X or O) was on each square of the diagonal. Use a file to store the names of the players and the corresponding boards.

17. Rewrite the previous program so that it searches for any winning combination. Hint: Use the symmetry of the board to simplify your program.

18. Given

```
TYPE Employee = RECORD
     Age:integer;
     Name:PACKED ARRAY[1..20] OF char
  END (* RECORD *);
```

write a procedure that prints the age of the oldest employee and the names of all the employees of that age in alphabetical order.

19. Write a program to determine which student has the largest cumulative exam scores in a class of up to 60 students. Each student takes four exams. Use

```
TYPE StudentRec = RECORD
      Name: PACKED ARRAY[1..20] OF char;
      Exams: ARRAY[1..4] OF real
  END (* RECORD *);
```

20. Given the following selectors and their associated variant fields for a variant record

```
Academic:(Exam1, Exam2, Exam3:0..100);
Work:(Hours, Rate:real)
```

write a program that calculates the person's exam average when the value of the tag field is `Academic` and the person's salary when the value of the tag field is `Work`.

Bottom-Up Design

21. Write a program that sorts the words in a paragraph and prints the words such that if a word occurs more than once, it is printed only once. See Figure 13.7*a*.

22. Using the previous program, write a program that determines how many unique words are used in a paragraph.

23. Using the previous program, write a program that determines how many times each words occurs in a paragraph. Use the following data structures:

```
List = PACKED ARRAY[1..MaxLen] OF char; (* Stores word *)
WordRecord = RECORD (* Stores unique word and
frequency *)
   HistoWord:List;
   Frequency:integer
END (* WordRecord *);
WordCount = ARRAY[1..MaxElem] OF WordRecord
```

Hint: Each time a new word is executed, Frequency is increased by 1 and the word is stored in HistoWord. When a word is repeated, only Frequency is incremented.

24. Write the previous program so that it makes a histogram of the words in a paragraph. For example, an input of "to be or not to be that is the question" produces:

```
be          2 be be
is          1 is
not         1 not
or          2 or or
question    1 question
that        1 that
the         1 the
to          2 to to
```

15

FILES AND SETS

CHAPTER OVERVIEW

In Chapter 8 we were introduced to text files. There is another type of file, one containing information written in binary; these files are appropriately called *binary files*. We'll use a binary file to write a program that simulates dealing a rummy hand from a shuffled deck. Finally, we'll introduce sets and the operations that can be performed on them. First, let's review text files.

15.1

TEXT FILES

Let's begin with a review of the procedures and functions that can be used with text files (Table 15.1).

reset(FileA)	Opens the file and resets the pointer to the beginning of the file. If FileA is empty, then eof(FileA) is true after reset is performed. If the file is a text file, it is now a read-only file.
rewrite(FileA)	Opens the file, erases it, and resets the pointer to the beginning of the file. If the file is a text file, it is now a write-only file.
writeln(FileA)	Writes the end-of-line mark, thereby positioning the file pointer at what is in effect the beginning of the next line in the file.
writeln(FileA, C)	Appends the value of C to the end of the file and then writes the end-of-line mark, thus positioning the file pointer at what is in effect the beginning of the next line in the file.
readln(FileA)	Instructs the computer to skip the end-of-line mark and advance the pointer to what is in effect the beginning of the next line.
readln(FileA, C)	Copies the next element to be read into C and advances the pointer to what is in effect the beginning of the next line on the file.
write(FileA, C)	Appends the value of C to the end-of-file FileA and moves the pointer to the new end of the file.
read(FileA, C)	Copies the next element to be read into C and advances the pointer.
eoln(FileA)	If the pointer is at the end-of-line mark, then the function is true.
eof(FileA)	If the pointer is at the end of the file, then the function is true.

TABLE 15.1.   A review of predefined subprograms used with text files.

Let's recall what we've learned about text files:

1. A file can be passed to a subprogram only as a variable parameter.
2. You cannot assign one file to another. Thus if Parag and Temp are two text files, Parag: = Temp is illegal.

Also, once you have opened a file for reading, you must execute a rewrite in order to write on it. This, of course, will erase the file. Once you have opened a file for writing, you must execute a reset in order to read from it. This will not erase the file.

15.2

BINARY FILES (STRUCTURED FILES)

A text file can be an image of a paragraph of text that appears on a screen or it can consist of numbers. Thus it always consists of characters. A binary file, on the other hand, consists of the binary representation of numbers and/or characters. We normally create and print text files using a Pascal program. However, they can be created and printed using a program such as a word processing program. A binary file, on the other hand, can be written and printed only by using a Pascal program.

A binary file is a file of any type other than char or text.

The following are all examples of binary files of simple types:

```
VAR IntFile:FILE OF integer;
    RealFile:FILE OF real;
    BoolFile:FILE OF boolean;
    StringFile:FILE OF PACKED ARRAY[1..80] OF char;
```

If you want to pass these files to subprograms, you must first define a type in a TYPE definition, for example, TYPE NumbersFile = FILE OF integer. The heading for a procedure to which you want to pass a file of type NumbersFile could be, for instance, PROCEDURE PrintFile(VAR IntFile: NumbersFile). You cannot write PROCEDURE PrintFile(VAR IntFile: FILE OF integer) instead.

Given the types

```
TYPE WeekDays = (Mon, Tue, Wed, Thu, Fri);
     Words = PACKED ARRAY[1..10] OF char;
     DepRecord = RECORD
       ID, Branch, TypAcct: integer;
       Dep: real
     END; (* DepRecord *)
```

the following are examples of binary files of these user-defined types:

```
VAR DayFile: FILE OF WeekDays;
    WordFile: FILE OF Words;
    BankFile: FILE OF DepRecord;
```

Since, as we see here, binary files can also be files of structured types, they are also called *structured files*. Unlike a text file, a binary file does not have a line structure, so you cannot use the readln or writeln procedures or the eoln functions with it. If

```
VAR Days:Weekdays; Nouns:Words; DepositInfo: DepRecord;
```

is used, then the following are valid examples of writing on a file:

```
write(DayFile, Days),
write(WordFile, Nouns)
write(BankFile, DepositInfo).
```

The component of a file is the identifier following OF in FILE OF. Thus the component of WordFile described in WordFile: FILE OF Words is Words, that is, a PACKED ARRAY[1..10] OF char. Thus a binary file consists of components of equal length (in bytes).

If the computer can't read information of enumerated type from the keyboard and write it to an output device, why can the computer read and write a file of a user-defined enumerated type such as DayFile? The reason is that the computer is reading and writing binary information here, not characters. The only restriction on a file type is that you can't declare or define a file of a file. Thus given TYPE NumbersFile = FILE OF integer, declaring IntFile: FILE OF NumbersFile is not allowed.

As with text files, you may write more than one element (here, a component) at a time on a binary file, for instance, write(BankFile, Record1, Record2). The following standard subprograms we have used can also be used with binary files: reset(FileA), rewrite(FileA), write(FileA, C), read(FileA, C), and eof(FileA). They have the same functions as they do when they are used with a text file (see Table 15.1).

15.3

AN ELEMENTARY PROGRAM USING BINARY FILES

Figure 15.1a shows a program that writes the bank information given in Figure 15.1b onto a file of records called BankFil. Before writing on the file, we prepare it for writing by typing rewrite(BankFil). Then we write the file in the WHILE loop:

```
WITH CustomerRec DO
    WHILE NOT eof DO BEGIN
        readln(ID, Dep, Branch, TypAcct);
        write(BankFil, CustomerRec)
    END (* WHILE *);
```

COPYING RECORDS TYPED AT A CONSOLE TO A BINARY FILE

```
PROGRAM WriteRec(input, BankFil);
(* Writes record information to a file *)
TYPE DepRecord = RECORD
        ID, Branch, TypAcct: integer;
        Dep: real
      END; (* DepRecord *)
VAR CustomerRec : DepRecord;
    BankFil: FILE OF DepRecord;
BEGIN (* use the WITH to avoid dotting everything *)
  rewrite( BankFil);
  writeln('Type ID, Deposit, Branch, Type of Acct');
  WITH CustomerRec DO
    WHILE NOT eof DO BEGIN
      readln(ID, Dep, Branch, TypAcct);
      write(BankFil, CustomerRec)
    END (* WHILE *);
END.
```

FIGURE 15.1*a*.   Reads the records from the console and writes them to the binary file.

```
Type ID, Deposit, Branch, Type of Acct
101 23.45 6 4
104 234.56 3 4
105 231.33 4 4
106 234.56 3 5
107 345.00 6 7
108 222.32 3 4
109 876.67 3 3
110 765.44 2 3
111 345.32 4 4
112 345.66 7 8
125 654.39 4 4
```

FIGURE 15.1*b*.   Running the program of Figure 15.1*a*.

Unlike the method used when you write records to the output file or any other text file, you don't have to specify the fields (here ID, Dep, Branch, and TypAcct) of the record when you write it on a binary file. Thus write(Bank-Fil, CustomerRec) does the job.

Figure 15.2*a* displays a program that reads the file BankFil and writes the records onto the screen. We prepare the file for reading by typing reset(BankFil) and then read the file in the WHILE loop:

```
WHILE NOT eof(BankFil) DO
  WITH CustomerRec DO BEGIN
    read(BankFil, CustomerRec);
    writeln(ID:4, Dep:7:2, Branch:2, TypeAcct:2 )
  END (* WITH *);
```

Again, unlike the method used when you read records from the input file or any other text file, you don't have to specify the fields of the record when you read it from a binary file; you simply specify the record identifier in the read statement.

The results of running the program are shown in Figure 15.2b.

READING FROM A BINARY FILE

```
PROGRAM ReadRec(BankFil, output);
(* Reads all records on a file *)
TYPE DepRecord = RECORD
        ID, Branch, TypAcct: integer;
        Dep: real
     END; (* DepRecord *)

VAR CustomerRec : DepRecord;
    BankFil: FILE OF DepRecord;

BEGIN (* use the WITH to avoid dotting everything *)
   reset( BankFil);
   WHILE NOT eof(BankFil) DO
     WITH CustomerRec DO BEGIN
       read(BankFil, CustomerRec);
       writeln(ID:4, Dep:7:2, Branch:2, TypAcct:2 )
     END (* WITH *);
  END.
```

FIGURE 15.2a.   Since we are reading from a binary file, we don't have to specify the fields, just the record identifier.

```
101 23.45 6 4
104 234.56 3 4
105 231.33 4 4
106 234.56 3 5
107 345.00 6 7
108 222.32 3 4
109 876.67 3 3
110 765.44 2 3
111 345.32 4 4
112 345.66 7 8
125 654.39 4 4
```

FIGURE 15.2b.   Running the program of Figure 15.2a. The first component is in the zeroth position, and so on.

15.4

GENERATING SEVEN-CARD RUMMY HANDS

Have you ever wondered how a program that plays a card-playing game with a computer user is written? If so, you should be interested in the next program. It generates seven-card hands from a shuffled deck and determines whether the hands contain any lays in the card game of rummy. A *lay* is defined as follows:

1. Three or four cards that have the same rank. For example, the five of clubs, the five of spades, and the five of hearts all have the rank of five.

2. Three or more cards of the same suit that have consecutive ranks. An example is the five of clubs, the six of clubs, and the seven of clubs.

We will write the program in six steps:

Step I generates 52 distinct random integers between 1 and 52. In future steps, these integers will correspond to the shuffled deck.

Step II deals three 7-card hands from a shuffled deck and prints each hand as a 4 × 13 array. The 4 here corresponds to the four suits and the 13 to the thirteen ranks (two, three, . . . , ace) for a given suit.

Step III displays the card arrays so that the elements are printed with their ranks and suit values.

Step IV prints sample hands onto a file so that we can test the next step.

Step V detects the lays in the sample hands.

Step VI detects the lays in the hands dealt from a shuffled deck.

Step I. Generating a Shuffled Deck

The top-down diagram in Figure 15.3a(I) describes how to generate 52 distinct random integers between 1 and 52. In future steps we will associate a different card with each of these integers. The two of clubs will correspond to 1, the two of spades to 2, the two of hearts to 3, and so forth. Since the 52 integers are in random order, our simulated deck is shuffled.

When you generate 52 random integers, there will be repetitions. For instance, if the first integer is a 12, the twentieth one may also be a 12. To avoid this, we define a type WasDealt = ARRAY[1..52] OF boolean and originally set all of the elements of array Dealt (whose type is WasDealt) to false. This is done in procedure Zero [see Figure 15.3a(II)]. The array is used in procedure Shuffle, whose pseudocode is

FOR *each card in the deck* DO

    Generate a random integer that has not been used;

    Associate that number with the card

END (* FOR *)

as shown in Figure 15.3a(III). The pseudocode *Generate a random integer that has not been used* becomes

REPEAT

    Card: = random(52) + 1

UNTIL Dealt[Card] = False;

and *Associate that number with the card* becomes Deck[Number]:= Card, where Number is the position of the card in the deck, Card is one of the 52 random integers, and Deck is the array representing the shuffled deck. For instance, when the value of Number is 1, Deck[Number] is the first card in the deck. Its value is the value of Card, for instance, 12. Once a card has been generated, the program sets Dealt[Card] to True to ensure that the card will not be generated again.

Procedure Print, shown in Figure 15.3a(IV), prints the 52 random numbers. The main program and the headings of the procedures used are shown in Figure 15.3a(V), and the results are shown in Figure 15.3b.

GENERATING SEVEN-CARD RUMMY HANDS
STEP I. GENERATING A SHUFFLED DECK

FIGURE 15.3a(I).   The top-down diagram for generating a shuffled deck.

```
TYPE Range = 1..52;
    WasDealt = ARRAY[Range] OF boolean;
    FullDeck = ARRAY[Range] OF Range;

PROCEDURE Zero(VAR Dealt: WasDealt);
(* Initializes a dealt array *)
BEGIN
    FOR Index:= 1 TO 52 DO
        Dealt[Index]:= False
END (* ZERO *);
```

FIGURE 15.3a(II).   Sets all elements of Dealt to false so that the same card won't be dealt twice.

```
PROCEDURE Shuffle(Dealt: WasDealt; VAR Deck: FullDeck);
(* Shuffles a deck *)
VAR Card, Number:Range;
BEGIN
    FOR Number:= 1 TO 52 DO BEGIN
        REPEAT
            Card:= random(52) + 1
        UNTIL Dealt[Card] = False;
        Deck[Number]:= Card;
        Dealt[Card]:= True
    END (* FOR *);
END (* Shuffle *);
```

FIGURE 15.3a(III).   Generates random numbers between 1 and 52 until one that hasn't been used is generated.

```
                    PROCEDURE Print(Deck: FullDeck);
                    (* Prints the deck *)
                    VAR Index:Range;
                    BEGIN
                      writeln;
                      writeln('The results are:');
                      FOR Index:= 1 TO 52 DO
                        write(Deck[Index]:4)
                    END (* PRINT *);
```

FIGURE 15.3a(IV). Prints the result of the shuffle.

```
          PROGRAM Dealer(input, output);
          (* Generates a shuffled deck *)
          TYPE Range = 1..52;
            WasDealt = ARRAY[Range] OF boolean;
            FullDeck = ARRAY[Range] OF Range;
          VAR Dealt: WasDealt;
            Deck: FullDeck;
            Card, Index, Number:Range;
          PROCEDURE Zero(VAR Dealt: WasDealt);          {See page 646}
          PROCEDURE Shuffle(Dealt: WasDealt; VAR Deck: FullDeck);
                                                        {See page 646}
          PROCEDURE Print(Deck: FullDeck);              {On this page}
          BEGIN
            randomize;
            Zero(Dealt);
            Shuffle(Dealt, Deck);
            Print(Deck)
          END.
```

FIGURE 15.3a(V). The main program and the headings of the procedures used.

```
          The results are:
          4 20 34 31 23 7 16 13 17 3 46 44 22 36 39 8 9 26 32 33
          30 35 41 5 28 51 2 49 48 6 52 24 47 42 29 11 50 38 19 1
          15 10 21 25 27 18 43 37 40 12 14 45
```

FIGURE 15.3b. Running the program of Figure 15.3a. The results consist of the integers from 1 to 52 in random order.

Step II. Dealing Hands from a Shuffled Deck

As outlined in Figure 15.3c(I), the program for this step deals the hands. To do this, we first define the type used to designate the cards in

```
RankType = (Two, Three, Four, Five, Six, Seven, Eight, Nine,
           Ten, Jack, Queen, King, Ace, Temp);
SuitType = (Clubs, Spades, Hearts, Diamonds);
```

(where the value Temp follows Ace in the RankType definition to facilitate finding lays in Step V). This allows us to define

```
Hands = ARRAY[1..NumOfHands, Clubs..Diamonds, Two..Ace] OF integer;
```

as the three-dimensional array that will hold from one to NumOfHands hands, where the part of the array that stores each hand is the

,Clubs..Diamonds, Two..Ace] OF integer

part. Before the program deals the hands, we set all the elements of this array to zero in procedure ZeroHands [see Figure 15.3c(II)]. We do this so that when the program deals a hand (in procedure DealCards) and sets the elements of the array representing the cards dealt to 1, we will be able to see which cards have been dealt. We must first, however, convert the random integers representing the shuffled cards to their card values. Here's how it's done: We associate the numbers from 1 to 4 with the 4 twos in the deck, 5 to 8 with the 4 threes, 9 to 12 with the 4 fours . . . , and 49 to 52 with the four aces, as indicated in Table I for Figure 15.3c.

Two of Clubs	Two of Spades	Two of Hearts	Two of Diamonds	Three of Clubs	Three of Spades	Three of Hearts	Three of Diamonds
1	2	3	4	5	6	7	8

TABLE I FOR FIGURE 15.3c.   How we associate the random integers with the cards.

Deck[Number]	SuitIndex:= (Deck[Number] − 1) MOD 4	RankIndex:= (Deck[Number] − 1) DIV 4
1	0	0
2	1	0
3	2	0
4	3	0
5	0	1
6	1	1
7	2	1
8	3	1
9	0	2
10	1	2

TABLE II FOR FIGURE 15.3c.   How SuitIndex:= (Deck[Number] − 1) MOD 4 associates a suit and RankIndex:= (Deck[Number] − 1) DIV 4 associates a rank with a random number (Deck[Number]).

Since the ordinal values of Clubs, Spades, Hearts, and Diamonds are 0, 1, 2, and 3, respectively, if we calculate Deck[Number] − 1) MOD 4 (where Deck[Number] is the integer representing the card), we obtain the proper ordinal value of the suit (see Table II for Figure 15.3c). Similarly, since the ordinal values of Two, Three, Four, . . . , Ace are 0, 1, 2, . . . , 12, respectively, if we calculate (Deck[Number] − 1) DIV 4, we obtain the proper ordinal value of the rank.

Then by using CASE statements, for instance,

```
CASE SuitIndex OF
    0: Suit:= Clubs;
    1: Suit:= Spades;
    2: Suit:= Hearts;
    3: Suit:= Diamonds
END (* CASE *);
```

we can convert these ordinal values back to the enumerated types. For instance, if the random integer generated is 7, the value of SuitIndex is 2 and the value of RankIndex is 1. This means that the value of Suit is Hearts and that of Rank is Three.

Procedure DealHands, shown in Figure 15.3c(III), takes the first seven random numbers generated (the first seven cards in the deck) and sets the elements of array Result for I equal to 1 (the first hand) and those of the seven pairs of Suit and Rank equal to 1. It does this also for the second and third hands. The results are printed by PrintCards [see Figure 15.3c(IV)]. Figure 15.3c(V) shows the main program and the headings for the procedures used.

The results are displayed in Figure 15.3d. We see after inspecting the first hand

```
Hand # 1
0000010011000
0000000000000
0000010010000
0000100000100
```

that it contains three clubs (the seven, ten, and jack, corresponding, respectively, to the 1s in the 6th, 9th, and 10th columns of the first row), no spades (all 0s in the second row), two hearts (the seven and ten), and two diamonds (the six and queen). To make it easier to read the hands, in the next program we'll print the hands using the card name. For instance, 3–C will represent the three of clubs.

STEP II. DEALING HANDS FROM A SHUFFLED DECK

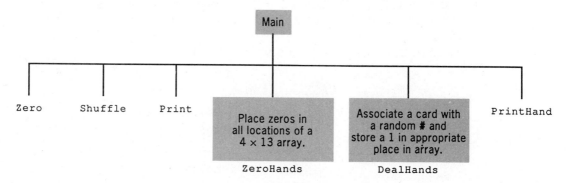

FIGURE 15.3c(I). The top-down diagram for dealing a hand from the deck.

```
CONST NumPerHand = 7;
NumOfHands = 3;
TYPE Range = 1..52;
  WasDealt = ARRAY[Range] OF boolean;
  FullDeck = ARRAY[Range] OF Range;
  RankType = (Two, Three, Four, Five, Six, Seven, Eight, Nine,
              Ten, Jack, Queen, King, Ace, Temp);
  SuitType = (Clubs, Spades, Hearts, Diamonds);
  Hands = ARRAY[1..NumOfHands, Clubs..Diamonds, Two..Ace] OF integer;
  Hand = 1..NumOfHands;
PROCEDURE ZeroHands(VAR Results:Hands);
(* Places zeros in the suit X rank matrix for each hand *)
VAR I:Hand;
  Suit: SuitType;
  Rank: RankType;
BEGIN
  FOR I:= 1 TO NumOfHands DO
    FOR Suit:= Clubs TO Diamonds DO
      FOR Rank:= Two TO Ace DO
        Results[I, Suit, Rank]:= 0
END (* ZeroHands *);
```

FIGURE 15.3c(II). Places zeros in the three-dimensional array that represents the cards dealt for each hand. For each hand there is a 4 × 13 submatrix (suit X rank) that represents the cards dealt.

```
PROCEDURE DealHands(VAR Results:Hands; Deck: Full_Deck);
(* Deals three hands *)
VAR Suit: SuitType;
  Face: FaceType;
  I:Hand;
  SuitIndex:0..NumOfHands;
  FaceIndex:0..12;
  Initial, Number:Range;
BEGIN
  FOR I:= 1 TO NumOfHands DO BEGIN
    Initial:= NumPerHand * I - (NumPerHand - 1);
    FOR Number:= Initial TO NumPerHand * I DO BEGIN
      SuitIndex:= (Deck[Number] - 1) MOD 4;
      FaceIndex:= (Deck[Number] - 1) DIV 4;
      (* Convert to a suit *)
      CASE SuitIndex OF
        0: Suit:= Clubs;
        1: Suit:= Spades;
        2: Suit:= Hearts;
        3: Suit:= Diamonds
      END (* CASE *);
      (* Convert to a rank *)
      CASE FaceIndex OF
        0: Face:= Two;
        1: Face:= Three;
        2: Face:= Four;
        3: Face:= Five;
        4: Face:= Six;
        5: Face:= Seven;
        6: Face:= Eight;
        7: Face:= Nine;
        8: Face:= Ten;
        9: Face:= Jack;
        10: Face:= Queen;
        11: Face:= King;
        12: Face:= Ace
      END (* CASE *);
      Results[I, Suit, Face]:= 1
    END (* FOR Number *)
  END (* FOR I *)
END (* Deal hands *);
```

FIGURE 15.3c(III).   Converts the random number representing a card to a specific rank and suit. Then places 1s for the seven cards dealt into the 4 × 13 submatrix for each hand.

```
PROCEDURE PrintHands(Results:Hands);
(* Prints the matrix for the hands dealt *)
VAR I: integer;
   Suit: SuitType;
   Rank: RankType;
BEGIN
  FOR I:= 1 TO NumOfHands DO BEGIN
    writeln('Hand # ', I);
    FOR Suit:= Clubs TO Diamonds DO BEGIN
      FOR Rank:= Two TO Ace DO
        write(Results[I, Suit, Rank]);
      writeln
    END (* FOR-Suit *);
    writeln
  END (* FOR I *);
  writeln
END (* PrintHands *);
```

FIGURE 15.3c(IV).   Prints the 4 × 13 submatrix for each hand.

```
PROGRAM Dealer(input, output);
(* Generates and prints the shuffled hands *)
CONST NumPerHand = 7;
  NumOfHands = 3;
TYPE Range = 1..52;
  WasDealt = ARRAY[Range] OF boolean;
  FullDeck = ARRAY[Range] OF Range;
  RankType = (Two, Three, Four, Five, Six, Seven, Eight, Nine,
        Ten, Jack, Queen, King, Ace);
  SuitType = (Clubs, Spades, Hearts, Diamonds);
  Hands = ARRAY[1..NumOfHands, Clubs..Diamonds, Two..Ace] OF integer;
  Hand = 1..NumOfHands;
VAR Dealt: WasDealt;
  Deck: FullDeck;
  Results:Hands;
```

`PROCEDURE Zero(VAR Dealt: WasDealt);`	{See page 646}
`PROCEDURE Shuffle(Dealt: WasDealt; VAR Deck: FullDeck);`	{See page 646}
`PROCEDURE Print(Deck: FullDeck);`	{See page 647}
`PROCEDURE ZeroHands(VAR Results:Hands);`	{See page 650}
`PROCEDURE DealHands(VAR Results:Hands; Deck: FullDeck);`	{See page 651}
`PROCEDURE PrintHands(Results:Hands);`	{On this page}

```
BEGIN
  randomize;
  Zero(Dealt);
  Shuffle(Dealt, Deck);
  Print(Deck);
  ZeroHands(Results);
  DealHands(Results, Deck);
  PrintHands(Results)
END.
```

FIGURE 15.3c(V).   The main program and the headings for the procedures used.

```
The results are:
33 44 37 20 35 21 23 22 25 42 45 47 9 2 31 19 10 11 40 29
3 7 43 28 27 46 17 24 8 41 38 50 52 14 16 6 34 13 32 4
12 15 5 30 39 49 18 48 26 1 36 51
Hand # 1
0000010011000
0000000000000
0000010010000
0000100000100

Hand # 2
0010001000010
1000010000100
0000000000010
0000000000000

Hand # 3
0000000100000
0010000000000
1010100100000
0000000001000
```

FIGURE 15.3d.   Running the program of Figure 15.3c.

Step III. Printing the Hands Using the Card Names

To print the results using the card names, we assign the appropriate strings to
SuitName and RankName in procedure PrintName, shown in Figure 15.3e(I).

STEP III. PRINTING THE HANDS USING THE CARD NAMES

```
PROCEDURE PrintName(Suit:SuitType; Rank:RankType);
CONST Space = ' ';
(* Prints card names *)
VAR SuitName :ARRAY[Clubs..Diamonds] OF String[10];
    RankName :ARRAY[Two..Ace] OF String[10];
BEGIN
    RankName[Two]:= '2'; RankName[Three]:= '3';
    RankName[Four]:= '4'; RankName[Five]:= '5';
    RankName[Six]:= '6'; RankName[Seven]:= '7';
    RankName[Eight]:= '8'; RankName[Nine]:= '9';
    RankName[Ten]:= '10'; RankName[Jack]:= 'J';
    RankName[Queen]:= 'Q'; RankName[King]:= 'K';
    RankName[Ace]:= 'A';
    SuitName[Clubs]:= 'C'; SuitName[Spades]:= 'S';
    SuitName[Hearts]:= 'H'; SuitName[Diamonds]:= 'D';
    write(RankName[Rank], '-', SuitName[Suit], Space)
END (* PrintName *);
```

FIGURE 15.3e(I).   Converts enumerated type values to string values.

When procedure PrintCards detects that the value of an element of Result is 1, it prints the appropriate card name; otherwise, it prints blanks. The pseudocode is

> FOR *each hand* DO BEGIN
>   FOR *each suit* DO
>   FOR *each face* DO
>   IF *element of array is 1* THEN
>   *Print the card name*
>   ELSE *Print blanks;*
>   writeln;
>   END *(* FOR each suit *);*
>   writeln;
> END FOR *each hand *)*

This becomes the program in Figure 15.3*e*(II). If we place PrintCards(Results) at the end of the main program in Figure 15.3*c*(V), and include PrintName and PrintCards as procedures, we get the results shown in Figure 15.3*f*. The value of NumOfHands is 2, so only two hands are printed.

```
PROCEDURE PrintCards(Results:Hands);
(* Prints the suit and rank matrix for three hands *)
CONST Blank = ' ';
VAR I: integer;
  Suit: SuitType;
  Rank: RankType;
BEGIN
  FOR I:= 1 TO NumOfHands DO BEGIN
    writeln('Hand # ', I);
    writeln('---------------------------');
    FOR Suit:= Clubs TO Diamonds DO BEGIN
      FOR Rank:= Two TO Ace DO
        IF (Results[I, Suit, Rank]) = 1 THEN
          PrintName(Suit, Rank)
        ELSE
          write(Blank);
      writeln
    END (* FOR - Suit *);
    writeln
  END (* FOR I *);
  writeln
END (* PrintCards *);
```

FIGURE 15.3e(II).   Prints the suit X rank matrix using abbreviations for the card names.

```
The results are:
15 13 37 20 6 51 28 16 45 10 21 52 23 34 41 49 47 43 29 19
1 18 8 30 12 38 17 42 4 14 36 48 24 25 26 11 40 44 50 31
27 32 5 3 35 33 46 2 9 39 22 7
Hand #1
```
```
                5-C                           J-C
        3-S
                5-H                                   A-H
                        6-D       8-D
        Hand # 2
```
```
                        7-C                   K-C
            4-S                       10-S
                        7-H
                5-D                                   A-D
```

FIGURE 15.3*f*.   Running the program of Figure 15.3c(V) with the procedures Print-Name and PrintCards.

Step IV. Writing Test Hands to a File

The next step is to expand the program so that it detects lays. If we have to rely on the random integers to generate hands that have, for instance, seven cards that form a lay of consecutive cards, we might have to wait for several days for the desired results. To simplify the testing, we will write various combinations of cards to a file, as shown in Figure 15.3*g*. Each component of the file will be defincd by

```
CardRecord = RECORD
    HandNumber:Hand;
    Rank:RankType;
    Suit:SuitType
END (* RECORD *);
```

STEP IV. WRITING TEST HANDS TO A FILE

```pascal
PROGRAM Dealer(input, output, CardFile);
(* Writes three hands to a binary file *)
CONST NumOfHands = 3;
TYPE RankType = (Two, Three, Four, Five, Six, Seven, Eight, Nine,
          Ten, Jack, Queen, King, Ace, Temp);
   SuitType = (Clubs, Spades, Hearts, Diamonds);
   Hand = 1..NumOfHands;
   CardRecord = RECORD
     HandNumber:Hand;
     Rank:RankType;
     Suit:SuitType
   END (* RECORD *);
   CardFile = FILE OF CardRecord;
VAR Cards:CardFile;
PROCEDURE WriteFile( VAR Cards:CardFile);
(* Deals three hands *)
VAR Card:CardRecord;
BEGIN
  WITH Card DO BEGIN
    HandNumber:= 1; (* First hand *)
    Rank:= Three;
    FOR Suit:= Clubs TO Diamonds DO
       write(Cards, Card);
    Rank:= Ace;
    FOR Suit:= Spades TO Diamonds DO
       write(Cards, Card);
    HandNumber:= 2; (* Second hand *)
    Suit:= Hearts;
    FOR Rank:= Eight TO Ace DO
       write(Cards, Card);
    HandNumber:= 3; (* Third hand *)
    Suit:= Clubs;
    FOR Rank:= Two TO Five DO
       write(Cards, Card);
    Rank:= Two;
    FOR Suit:= Spades TO Diamonds DO
       write(Cards, Card);
  END (* WITH *)
END (* WriteFile *);
BEGIN
  rewrite(cards);
  WriteFile(Cards);
END.
```

FIGURE 15.3g.   Writes three sample hands to a binary file.

Step V. Reading Test Hands and Detecting Lays

We alter procedure Dealhands, as shown in Figure 15.4a(I), so that it reads the test data from the file, and alter PrintCards [Figure 15.4a(II)] so that it checks for lays. A lay of cards of the same suit that have consecutive ranks is detected in procedure WinRank. Its pseudocode is

```
FOR each suit DO BEGIN
    Starting with "Two", search the hand array for the first card;
    Set Sum to zero;
    WHILE there are consecutive ranks DO
        Add 1 to Sum;
    IF Sum is greater than 2 THEN
        Print the lay
END (* FOR each suit *)
```

This becomes the code shown in Figure 15.4a(III). If the highest value in a lay is Ace, the value of Rank in the WHILE loop that increments Sum will be Temp; if Ace were the highest value in the RankType definition, an error would occur in the WHILE loop in this case.

A lay of cards that have the same ranks is detected in procedure WinSuit. Its pseudocode is

```
FOR each face DO BEGIN
    Set Sum to zero;
    FOR each suit DO
        IF element of the hand array is 1 THEN
            Add 1 to Sum;
    IF Sum is greater than 2 THEN
        Print the lay
END (* FOR each face *)
```

This becomes the code shown in Figure 15.4a(IV). The main program and the headings of the procedure used are shown in Figure 15.4a(V). The results of running the program are shown in Figure 15.4b.

STEP V. READING TEST HANDS AND DETECTING LAYS

```
PROCEDURE DealHands(VAR Results:Hands; VAR Cards:CardFile);
(* Reads three sample hands from the file *)
VAR
  I:1..NumOfHands;
  SuitIndex:0..NumOfHands;
  RankIndex:0..12;
  Initial, Number:Range;
  Card:CardRecord;
BEGIN
  FOR I:= 1 TO NumOfHands DO BEGIN
    Initial:= NumPerHand * I - (NumPerHand - 1);
    FOR Number:= Initial TO NumPerHand * I DO BEGIN
      read(Cards, Card);
      WITH Card DO
        Results[HandNumber, Suit, Rank]:= 1
    END (* FOR Number *)
  END (* FOR I *)
END (* DealHands *);
```

FIGURE 15.4a(I).   Reads the sample hands from the file and places each of them in a suit X rank submatrix.

```
PROCEDURE PrintCards(Results:Hands);
(* Prints three hands *)
CONST Blank = ' ';
VAR I: Hand;
  Suit: SuitType;
  Rank: RankType;
BEGIN
  FOR I:= 1 TO NumOfHands DO BEGIN
    writeln('Hand # ', I);
    writeln('-----------------------------');
    FOR Suit:= Clubs TO Diamonds DO BEGIN
      FOR Rank:= Two TO Ace DO
        IF (Results[I, Suit, Rank]) = 1 THEN
          PrintName(Suit, Rank)
        ELSE
          write(Blank);
      writeln
    END (* FOR-Suit *);
    WinRank(Results, I);
    WinSuit(Results, I);
    writeln
  END (* FOR I *);
  writeln
END (* PrintCards *);
```

FIGURE 15.4a(II).   Prints three hands and determines whether there are any lays.

```
PROCEDURE WinRank(Results:Hands; I:Hand);
(* Determines whether there is a lay of three consecutive cards *)
VAR Suit: SuitType;
  RankIndex, Rank, First: RankType;
  Sum:0..NumPerHand;
BEGIN
  FOR Suit:= Clubs TO Diamonds DO BEGIN
    Rank:= Two;
    WHILE Rank <= Queen DO BEGIN
      (* Look for the first card *)
      WHILE (Results[I, Suit, Rank] = 0) AND (Rank <= Queen) DO
        Rank:= succ(Rank);
      Sum:= 0;
      First:= Rank;
      (* Look for consecutive cards *)
      WHILE (Results[I, Suit, Rank] = 1) AND (Rank <= Ace) DO BEGIN
        Sum:= Sum + 1;
        Rank:= succ(Rank)
      END (* WHILE *)
      IF Sum >= 3 THEN BEGIN (* Print the lay *)
        write('lay for same suit: ');
        FOR RankIndex:= First TO pred(rank) DO
          PrintName(Suit, RankIndex);
        writeln
      END (* THEN *)
    END (* WHILE *)
  END (* FOR - Suit *)
END (* WinRank *);
```

FIGURE 15.4a(III). Determines whether there is a lay of three or more consecutive cards.

```
PROCEDURE WinSuit(Results:Hands; I:Hand);
(* Determines whether there is a lay for a given rank *)
VAR Suit: SuitType;
  Rank: RankType;
  Sum:0..4;
BEGIN
  FOR Rank:= Two TO Ace DO BEGIN
    Sum:= 0;
    FOR Suit:= Clubs TO Diamonds DO
      Sum:= Sum + Results[I, Suit, Rank];
    IF Sum >= 3 THEN BEGIN
      write('lay for same face:');
      FOR Suit:= Clubs TO Diamonds DO
        IF Results[I, Suit, Rank] <> 0 THEN
          PrintName(Suit, Rank),
      writeln
    END (* IF *)
  END (* FOR Rank *)
END (* WinSuit *);
```

FIGURE 15.4a(IV). Determines whether there is a lay for a given rank.

```
PROGRAM Dealer(input, output, CardFile);
(* Reads sample hands from a file and prints the hands in a card
notation in matrix form. Determines the type of lays. Can have
three or more consecutive cards for a lay. *)
CONST NumPerHand = 7;
  NumOfHands = 3;
TYPE Range = 1..52;
  WasDealt = ARRAY[Range] OF boolean;
  FullDeck = ARRAY[Range] OF Range;
  RankType = (Two, Three, Four, Five, Six, Seven, Eight, Nine,
        Ten, Jack, Queen, King, Ace, Temp);
  SuitType = (Clubs, Spades, Hearts, Diamonds);
  Binary = 0..1;
  Hands = ARRAY[1..NumOfHands, Clubs..Diamonds, Two..Ace] OF integer;
  Hand = 1..NumOfHands;
  CardRecord = RECORD
    HandNumber:Hand;
    Rank:RankType;
    Suit:SuitType
  END (* RECORD *);
  CardFile = FILE OF CardRecord;
VAR Dealt: WasDealt;
  Deck: FullDeck;
  Results:Hands;
  Cards:CardFile;
```

`PROCEDURE ZeroHands(VAR Results:Hands);`	{See page 650}
`PROCEDURE PrintName(Suit:SuitType; Rank:RankType);`	{See page 653}
`PROCEDURE DealHands(VAR Results:Hands; VAR Cards:CardFile);`	{See page 658}
`PROCEDURE WinRank(Results:Hands; I:Hand);`	{See page 659}
`PROCEDURE WinSuit(Results:Hands; I:Hand);`	{See page 659}
`PROCEDURE PrintCards(Results:Hands);`	{See page 658}

```
BEGIN
  randomize;
  reset(cards);
  ZeroHands(Results);
  DealHands(Results, Cards);
  PrintCards(Results);
END.
```

FIGURE 15.4a(V).   The main program and the headings for the procedures used.

```
Hand # 1
_____
        3–C
        3–S                                                  A–S
        3–H                                                  A–H
        3–D                                                  A–D
lay for same face: 3–C 3–S 3–H 3–D
lay for same face: A–S A–H A–D

Hand # 2
_____
                                    8–H 9–H 10–H J–H Q–H K–H A–H
lay for same suit: 8–H 9–H 10–H J–H Q–H K–H A–H

Hand # 3
_____
2–C 3–C 4–C 5–C
2–S
2–H
2–D
lay for same suit: 2–C 3–C 4–C 5–C
lay for same face: 2–C 2–S 2–H 2–D
```

FIGURE 15.4b. Running the program of Figure 15.4a(V).

Step VI. Detecting Lays from the Shuffled Deck

If we use the original version of DealCards in Figure 15.3c so that the hands are dealt from the shuffled deck, and the other procedure headings shown in Figure 15.5a, we have a program that detects lays in a shuffled deck. The results of running the program are shown in Figure 15.5b.

STEP VI. DETECTING LAYS FROM THE SHUFFLED DECK

```
PROGRAM Dealer(input, output);
(* Deals a shuffled hand and prints the hands in the card notation
in matrix form. Determines the type of lays. Can have three or more
consecutive cards for a lay. *)
CONST NumPerHand = 7;
   NumOfHands = 2;
TYPE Range = 1..52;
   WasDealt = ARRAY[Range] OF boolean;
   FullDeck = ARRAY[Range] OF Range;
   RankType = (Two, Three, Four, Five, Six, Seven, Eight, Nine,
         Ten, Jack, Queen, King, Ace, Temp);
   SuitType = (Clubs, Spades, Hearts, Diamonds);
   Binary = 0..1;
   Hands = ARRAY[1..NumOfHands, Clubs..Diamonds, Two..Ace] OF integer;
   Hand = 1..NumOfHands;
VAR Dealt: WasDealt;
   Deck: FullDeck;
   Results:Hands;
```

```
PROCEDURE Zero(VAR Dealt: WasDealt);                          {See page 646}
PROCEDURE Shuffle(Dealt: WasDealt; VAR Deck: FullDeck);       {See page 646}
PROCEDURE Print(Deck: FullDeck);                              {See page 647}
PROCEDURE ZeroHands(VAR Results:Hands);                       {See page 650}
PROCEDURE DealHands(VAR Results:Hands; Deck: FullDeck);       {See page 658}
PROCEDURE PrintName(Suit:SuitType; Rank:RankType);           {See page 653}
PROCEDURE PrintCards(Results:Hands);                          {See page 658}
```

```
BEGIN
   randomize;
   Zero(Dealt);
   Shuffle(Dealt,Deck);
   Print(Deck);
   ZeroHands(Results);
   DealHands(Results, Deck);
   PrintCards(Results)
END.
```

FIGURE 15.5a. The main program and the headings for the procedures used. Detects lays from the shuffled deck.

```
The results are:
16 12  8  1 23 52 48 31 21 20 17  2 14 6 49 43 45 28 33 42
35 19 51 36  4 29  3 26 44 50 37 47 10 9 38 25 41 39 27 13
34 22 30 18 46  5  7 32 11 24 15 40
Hand # 1
------------------------------------------------------------
2-C
                        7-H
      3-D 4-D 5-D                           K-D A-D
lay for same suit: 3-D 4-D 5-D
Hand # 2
------------------------------------------------------------
                     6-C 7-C
2-S 3-S        5-S
                              9-H
               6-D
```

FIGURE 15.5b. Running the program of Figure 15.5a.

15.5

THE BINARY SEARCH

In computer science, the process of looking through a group of items (for instance, a file or an array) for a given item is called a *search*. The search is made easier if the items are sorted on a key. For instance, Table I for Figure 15.6*a* shows an array of records in which each record is defined by

```
DepRecord = RECORD
      ID, Branch, TypAcct: integer;
      Dep: real
   END; (* DepRecord *)
```

and the array is sorted on the first field, the ID.

Suppose that we want to know the contents of the record with ID equal to 110. One way of getting this information would be to examine every record sequentially until we found the one with an ID of 110. This is called a *linear* or *sequential* search. The more elements there are in the array, the less feasible this becomes. What follows is a description of a more efficient method.

In the *binary search*, the program continually narrows the range of elements it examines until either it has found the requested item or it is sure that it is not in the array. We'll use three subscripts in the search: First, the

Element Number	Record
1	101 23.45 6 4
2	104 234.56 3 4
3	105 231.33 4 4
4	108 222.32 3 4
5	109 876.67 3 3
6	110 765.44 2 3
7	111 345.32 4 4
8	112 345.66 7 8
9	125 654.39 4 4
	BankArray

TABLE I FOR FIGURE 15.6*a*. Shows the elements of BankArray. Look for ReqID 110. Middle is 5 and ReqID > 109, so First becomes 6 and Last remains 9. Thus the range of elements we search is narrowed.

Element Number	Record
6	110 765.44 2 3
7	111 345.32 4 4
8	112 345.66 7 8
9	125 654.39 4 4
	BankArray

TABLE II FOR FIGURE 15.6a. `Middle` is 7 and `ReqID` < 111, so `Last` becomes 6 and `First` remains 6. Thus the range is narrowed again.

subscript of the first element in the range of examined elements; `Last`, the subscript of the last one; and `Middle`, that of the middle one. We originally set `First` to 1 and `Last` to N, the subscript of the last element in the array—in our case, 9. The subscript of the middle element is then given by `Middle = (First + Last) DIV 2`, which in our case is 5 (See Table I for Figure 15.6a).

If the value of the ID we are looking for—we will call it *ReqID*—is greater than the ID of the middle record, we redefine `First` so that the program searches the records with subscripts higher than that of the middle record. This means that in our case the program focuses on the sixth to the ninth elements (see Table II for Figure 15.6a). On the other hand, if the value of *ReqID* is less than that of the ID of the middle record, we redefine `Last` so that the program searches the records with subscripts lower than that of the middle record. This means that in our case the program focuses on the first to the fourth elements. The process is repeated and the value of `Middle` is redefined, enabling the search to continue. The search ends when either the program has found the desired record (see Table III for Figure 15.6a) or it ascertains that the record is not in the array. This suggests the following pseudocode:

Element Number	Record
6	110 765.44 2 3
	BankArray

TABLE III FOR FIGURE 15.6a. `Middle` is 6 and `ReqID` is 110, so the search stops.

Set First *to 1 and* Last *to the number of elements;*
WHILE *we are sure that the requested ID is still in array* DO BEGIN
   Middle:= (First + Last) DIV 2;
  IF *the ID for element* Middle *equals the requested ID* THEN
     Quit the loop
  ELSE IF *the requested ID is greater than the ID for element* Middle
     THEN *redefine* First *to examine elements above* Middle
  ELSE
     Redefine Last *to examine elements below* Middle
  END

Let's refine the code. In order to examine only the records above Middle, we set First to the subscript of the first element above Middle, that is, Middle + 1. Conversely, in order to examine only the records below Middle, we set Last to Middle − 1. Note that each time either First or Last is redefined, the number of records the program considers is halved. Also, if a record with the requested ID is not in the array, the value of First will eventually exceed the value of Last. Thus the second step in the refinement of the pseudocode is

Set First *to 1 and* Last *to the number of elements.*
Set Found to false
WHILE (First < = Last) AND NOT Found DO BEGIN
  Middle:= (First + Last) DIV 2;
  IF *the ID for element* Middle *equals the requested ID* THEN
    Set Found to true
  ELSE IF *the requested ID is greater than the ID for element* Middle
    THEN *Set* First *to* Middle + 1
  ELSE
    Set Last *to* Middle − 1
  END (* WHILE *)

This becomes procedure Binary, shown in Figure 15.6a(I), where the boolean identifier Found is global.

The reason we discuss this technique in this chapter is that the program reads the records into the array from a file. This is done in procedure ReadFile, which also computes the number of records in the file, as shown in Figure 15.6a(II). This number will become the initial value of Last. The main program is shown in Figure 15.6b, and the running of the program is shown in Figure 15.6c.

The part of the program requiring the most time is procedure ReadFile. Once a file has been read into an array, however, you can quickly search for as many requested IDs as you want.

THE BINARY SEARCH

```
CONST MaxElem = 100;

TYPE DepRecord = RECORD
            ID BRANCH TypAcct: integer;
            Dep: real
          END; (* DepRecord *)
     FileType = FILE OF DepRecord;
     RecordArray = ARRAY[1..MaxElem] OF DepRecord;

PROCEDURE Binary(BankArray:RecordArray; NumRec, ReqID: integer;
        VAR CustomerRec:DepRecord);
(* Performs a binary search *)
VAR Middle, First, Last: integer;
BEGIN
  First:= 1;
  Last:= NumRec;
  Found:= False;
  WHILE (First <= Last) AND (NOT Found) DO BEGIN
    Middle:= (First + Last) DIV 2;
    CustomerRec:= BankArray[Middle];
    WITH CustomerRec DO
      IF ID = ReqID THEN
        Found:= true
      ELSE IF ReqID > ID THEN
        First:= Middle + 1
      ELSE
        Last:= Middle - 1
  END (* WHILE *)
END (* Binary *);
```

FIGURE 15.6a(I).   If ReqID is greater than the ID read from the element with subscript Middle, then the value of First is set to Middle + 1. If it is less, then Last is set to Middle − 1. This narrows the range of elements in which the program searches for ReqID.

```
PROCEDURE ReadFile(VAR BankFil: FileType; VAR BankArray:RecordArray;
        VAR NumberOfRecords:integer);
(* Reads records from a file and stores them in an array *)
VAR CustomerRec : DepRecord;
BEGIN
  reset( BankFil);
  NumberOfRecords:= 0;
  writeln;
  writeln('The records read are');
  WHILE NOT eof(BankFil) DO BEGIN
    NumberOfRecords:= NumberOfRecords + 1;
    read(BankFil, CustomerRec);
    BankArray[NumberOfRecords]:= CustomerRec;
    WITH CustomerRec DO
      writeln(ID, Dep:7:2, Branch:2, TypAcct:2 )
  END (* WHILE *);
  writeln('Number of records read is ', NumberOfRecords:3)
END (* ReadFile *);
```

FIGURE 15.6a(II).   Reads records from file and copies them into array BankArray.

```
PROGRAM BinSearch(input, output, BankFil);
(* Performs a binary search on an array read from a file *)
CONST MaxElem = 100;

TYPE DepRecord = RECORD
          ID, Branch, TypAcct: integer;
          Dep: real
        END; (* DepRecord *)
  FileType = FILE OF DepRecord;
  RecordArray = ARRAY[1..MaxElem] OF DepRecord;

VAR CustomerRec : DepRecord;
  BankFil: FileType;
  NumberOfRecords, ReqID: integer;
  Found: boolean;
  BankArray:RecordArray;

PROCEDURE ReadFile(VAR BankFil: FileType; VAR BankArray:RecordArray;
      VAR NumberOfRecords:integer);                    {See page 666}
PROCEDURE Binary(BankArray:RecordArray; NumRec, ReqID: integer;
      VAR CustomerRec:DepRecord);                      {See page 666}
BEGIN (* Main *)
  writeln('Type required ID');
  readln(ReqID);
  ReadFile(BankFil, BankArray, NumberOfRecords);
  Binary(BankArray, NumberOfRecords, ReqID, CustomerRec);
  IF Found THEN BEGIN
    writeln;
    writeln('The desired record is');
    WITH CustomerRec DO
      writeln(ID, Dep:7:2, Branch:2, TypAcct:2 )
    END (* IF-THEN *)
  ELSE
    writeln(ReqID, ' not found');
  close(BankFil)
END.
```

FIGURE 15.6b.   The main program and the headings for the procedures used.

```
Type required ID
108
The records read are
101 23.45 6 4
104 234.56 3 4
105 231.33 4 4
108 222.32 3 4
109 876.67 3 3
110 765.44 2 3
111 345.32 4 4
112 345.66 7 8
125 654.39 4 4
Number of records read is 9
The desired record is
108 222.32 3 4
```

FIGURE 15.6c.   Running the program of Figure 15.6b.

15.6

SETS AND SET OPERATIONS (UNION AND DIFFERENCE)

In Section 6.6 we defined a set in Pascal as a collection of items of a given ordinal type. These items are called the *elements* of the set, and their type is called the *base type*. You can define a set type in one of two ways. For instance, you can define a set type, LetterSet, consisting of lowercase letters of the alphabet by writing TYPE LetterSet = ['a'..'z'] or by defining first the base type Alphabet = 'a'..'z' and then LetterSet = SET OF Alphabet. The set is another example of a structured type we can use. Table 15.3 shows examples of sets.

Examples of Sets

Set definition	Base type
TYPE DigSet= SET OF 0..9;	The integers from 0 to 9
TYPE LowerCase = ['a'..'z];	The lowercase letters
TYPE Letters = ['a'..'z', 'A'..'Z'];	All the letters
TYPE BoolSet = [False, True];	The boolean constants
TYPE Part = (Pliers, Hammer, Wrench);	
PartSet = SET OF Part;	Part

TABLE 15.3.   The type of the elements of the set is called the *base type*.

Pascal does not allow a set of reals or a set that consists of two base types. Thus, although TYPE Letters = ['a'..'z', '0'..'9'] is allowed, TYPE Letters = ['a'..'z', 0..9] is not because the base types of 'a'..'z' and 0..9 are different. Pascal also does not allow a set of a structured type. Thus TYPE Word = SET OF PACKED ARRAY[1..10] OF char is not allowed.

A set that contains no elements is called an *empty set* and is represented by [] in Pascal. Note that elements are not repeated in a set; it would make no sense to list the set of vowels as ['a', 'e', 'e', 'a', 'i', 'o', 'u']. Also, the order in which the elements appear in a set is immaterial. Thus [2, 3, 4] and [4, 3, 2] represent the same set. The maximum number of elements in a set in Turbo Pascal is 256. Therefore the base type integer, is not allowed since there are *2 * maxint + 1* integers.

In order to reinforce our understanding of sets, let's determine which first names had been given to students in a college class. If the names of the 10 students in a section of Computer Science I were Mary, Scott, Bill, Beth, Jennifer, Scott, Jennifer, David, Bill, and Mike, then the set of names would consist of seven elements, that is, [Mary, Scott, Bill, Beth, Jennifer, David, Mike].

Next, let's write a program that lists the letters used and the ones not used in a sentence. Since we are not interested in repetitions, we choose the set as our data structure and define the following types

```
TYPE Alphabet = 'a'..'z';
     LetterSet = SET OF Alphabet;
```

and declare the identifiers in VAR Used, Letters: LetterSet. We will use the set operations "+" and "−". The "+" operation is called the *union* and is used as follows: If A and B are sets—for instance, A is [1, 3, 4] and B is [3, 4, 7, 8]—then A + B is the set consisting of all of the elements in A and B—here, [1, 3, 4, 7, 8]. Note again that a given element is not repeated because the structure we are using is a set. Note that in mathematics A + B is written as $A \cup B$.

The minus sign (−) is used to obtain the difference of two sets. A − B is the set consisting of all those elements that A and B have in common subtracted from A, in other words, those elements in A that are not in B. In our case, A − B is [1]. A set operation can be performed only on sets of the same base type. Thus it would be an error to write [1..9] + ['a'..'f'].

The top-down diagram is

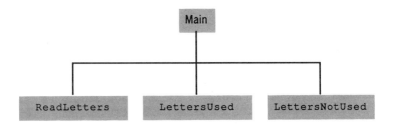

where

1. procedure ReadLetters reads the characters in the inputted sentence and places the letters in a set.
2. procedure LettersUsed prints the set of letters used in the sentence.
3. procedure LettersNotUsed prints the set of letters not used in the sentence.

The pseudocode for ReadLetters is

> *Set* Used *to the empty set;*
> WHILE NOT eoln DO BEGIN
>   *read a character;*
>   IF *the character is a letter* THEN
>   *Add the character to the set* Used
>   ELSE IF *the character is not a blank* THEN
>   *Print the character*
> END (* WHILE *)

This becomes the procedure shown in Figure 15.7a(I). We initialize the set Used in Used: = [ ] and code *Add the character to the set* Used as Used: = Used + [Character]. The type of all of the terms used in this set assignment statement must be the same, namely, LetterSet. Thus the type of Used is LetterSet (which is set of Alphabet), and since the type of Character is Alphabet, then the type of [Character] is also LetterSet. We declare Used as a variable parameter, since it must be passed back to the main program in order for its elements to be printed in LettersUsed and used to determine the letters not used in procedure LettersNotUsed.

The pseudocode for LettersUsed is

> FOR *each letter of the alphabet* DO
> IF *letter in the set* Used THEN
> *Print the letter*

This becomes the procedure shown in Figure 15.7a(II). The only reason that the elements of Used are printed in alphabetical order is that the control variable in the FOR–DO goes from 'a' to 'z'.

The pseudocode for LettersNotUsed is

> *Subtract the letters in* Used *from set of letters of the alphabet*
> *and assign it to* NotUsed;
> FOR *each letter of the alphabet* DO
> IF *letter in the set* NotUsed THEN
> *Print the letter*

This becomes the procedure shown in Figure 15.7a(III). The main program is shown in Figure 15.7b and the running of the program in Figure 15.7c. In order to simplify the program, we have used only lowercase letters.

TEST YOURSELF

QUESTION: How would you write procedure LettersNotUsed without using the difference of two sets?

ANSWER:

```
PROCEDURE LettersNotUsed(Used:LetterSet);
VAR Let: Alphabet;
BEGIN
  writeln('The following were not used ');
  FOR Let:= 'a' TO 'z' DO
    IF NOT (Let IN Used) THEN
      write(Let)
END (* LettersNotUsed *);
```

QUESTION: Is IF Let NOT IN Used THEN correct?

ANSWER: It is wrong because IN Used is only part of a boolean expression; it is not a boolean expression. Hence NOT can't immediately precede it.

USING SETS TO DETERMINE THE LETTERS USED IN A SENTENCE

```
TYPE Alphabet = 'a'..'z';
  LetterSet = SET OF Alphabet;
PROCEDURE ReadLetters(VAR Used: LetterSet);
(* Reads a sentence *)
CONST Blank = ' ';
VAR Character: Alphabet;
  Letters:LetterSet;
BEGIN
  Used:=[ ]; (* letters used so far *)
  Letters:= ['a'..'z'];
  writeln('Type your sentence');
  WHILE NOT eoln(input) DO BEGIN
    read(Character);
    IF Character IN Letters THEN
      Used:= Used + [Character]
    ELSE IF Character <> Blank THEN
      writeln(Character, ' is not a letter');
  END (* WHILE *);
  readln
END (* ReadLetters *);
```

FIGURE 15.7a(I). Each time a letter is read, it is added to the set Used. If a given letter is already in the set, it is not added because of the property of a set.

```
PROCEDURE LettersUsed(Used: LetterSet);
(* Prints the letters used in the sentence *)
VAR Let: Alphabet;
BEGIN
  writeln('The following letters were used');
  FOR Let:= 'a' TO 'z' DO
    (* List the letters used *)
    IF Let IN Used THEN
      write(Let);
  writeln
END (* LettersUsed *);
```

FIGURE 15.7a(II). Prints only the letters that are in the set.

```
PROCEDURE LettersNotUsed(Used:LetterSet);
(* Prints the letters not used *)
VAR Let: Alphabet;
  NotUsed:LetterSet;
BEGIN
  NotUsed:= ['a'..'z'] − Used;  (* Set of letters not used *)
  writeln('The following were not used ');
  FOR Let:= 'a' TO 'z' DO
    IF Let IN NotUsed THEN
       write(Let)
END (* LettersNotUsed *);
```

FIGURE 15.7a(III).   We subtract the letters used from the set of all letters to get the set of letters not used.

```
PROGRAM SetOperations(input, output);
(* Lists the letters used in a sentence *)
(* and the letters not used *)
TYPE Alphabet = 'a'..'z';
  LetterSet = SET OF Alphabet;
VAR Used, Letters: LetterSet;
PROCEDURE ReadLetters(VAR Used: LetterSet);  {See page 671}
PROCEDURE LettersUsed(Used: LetterSet);      {See page 671}
PROCEDURE LettersNotUsed(Used:LetterSet);    {On this page}
BEGIN
  ReadLetters(Used);
  LettersUsed(Used);
  LettersNotUsed(Used)
END.
```

FIGURE 15.7b.   The main program and the headings for the procedures used.

```
Type your sentence
we hold these truths to be self−evident, that all men are created
equal.
− is not a letter
, is not a letter
The following letters were used
abcdefhilmnoqrstuvw
The following were not used
gjkpxyz
```

FIGURE 15.7c.   Running the program of Figure 15.7b.

15.7

ANOTHER SET OPERATION: THE INTERSECTION

The *intersection* of two sets is the set consisting of the common elements of both sets. The symbol for the intersection is "*". If A is [1, 3, 4] and B is [3, 4, 7, 8], then A * B is the set [3, 4]. Note that A * B is written in mathematics as A ∩ B.

The next program determines which letters two sentences have in common, that is, it finds the intersection of the set of the letters in the first sentence with the set of the letters in the second sentence. We use the following declaration with the data type definitions used in the previous program:

```
VAR Sentence1, Sentence2, Intersection: LetterSet;
```

The main program uses some of the procedures of the last program, as shown in Figure 15.8a:

```
ReadLetters(Sentence1);
ReadLetters(Sentence2);
Intersection: = Sentence1 * Sentence2;
LettersUsed(Intersection)
```

The running of the program is shown in Figure 15.8b.

```
PROGRAM SetOperations(input, output);
(* Lists the letters used in the intersection of two sentences *)
TYPE Alphabet = 'a'..'z';
  LetterSet = SET OF Alphabet;
VAR Sentence1, Sentence2, Intersection: LetterSet;
PROCEDURE ReadLetters(VAR Used: LetterSet);        {See page 671}
PROCEDURE LettersUsed(Used: LetterSet);            {See page 671}
BEGIN
  ReadLetters(Sentence1);
  ReadLetters(Sentence2);
  Intersection: = Sentence1 * Sentence2;
  LettersUsed(Intersection)
END.
```

FIGURE 15.8a. We form `Sentence1` and `Sentence2`, two sets of letters read from each of two sentences. We then perform the intersection operation, obtain the letters used in both, and print the result.

```
Type your sentence
we hold these truths to be self-evident
- is not a letter
Type your sentence
that all men are created equal
The following letters were used in the Intersection.
dehlnrtu
```

FIGURE 15.8*b*.   Running the program of Figure 15.8*a*.

15.8

OTHER SET OPERATIONS

When sets appear in a boolean expression, the relational operators "=", "<=", ">=," and "<>" can be used to compare them, as shown in Table 15.4.

Operation	Mathematical Equivalent	Name	Example
=	=	Equality	[1, 2, 3] = [3, 2, 1] is true, since the two sets are equal
<>	≠	Nonequality	[1, 2, 3] <> [1, 2] is true, since the two sets are not equal
<=	⊂	Contained in	[1, 2] <= [1, 2, 3] is true, since the first set is contained in the second one
>=	⊃	Contains	['a', 'b', 'c'] >= ['a', 'b'] is true, since the first set contains the second one
IN	∈	Set membership	'1' IN ['1', '2', '3'] is true, since '1' is an element of the set

TABLE 15.4.   The set relational operations that can be used in boolean expressions.

If A <= B is true, we say that set A is contained in set B. That means that all the elements of set A are also elements of set B. On the other hand, if A >= B is true, we say that set A contains set B. That means that all the elements of set B are also elements of set A.

PROGRAMMING PITFALLS

Files
The following mistakes will cause errors:

1. Using readln and writeln with a binary file.
2. Not using reset before the first read or readln is executed for a file.

3. Not using `rewrite` before the first `write` or `writeln` is executed for a file.

4. Executing a `rewrite` by mistake for a file you do not want to erase.

5. Declaring a file to be a FILE OF text instead of just text.

6. Although a text file is a file of characters, it is not equivalent to FILE OF char on many compilers. Thus given the following declaration

```
VAR FileA:FILE OF char;
    Number:integer;
```

the statement `write(FileA, Number)` will cause a compiler error indicating a type mismatch because Number is an integer. Had we declared FileA-:text, we could have written an integer on the file.

Sets

The following mistakes will cause errors:

1. Not initializing a set.

2. Performing a set operation on sets of different base types.

CHAPTER REVIEW

The following applies to both text and binary files:

1. A file can be passed to a subprogram only as a variable parameter.

2. You cannot assign one file to another. Thus if Parag and Temp are two files, Parag:= Temp is illegal.

Text Files

A text file is a file consisting of characters. The following standard subprograms can be used with text files: `reset(FileA)`, `rewrite(FileA)`, `writeln-(FileA)`, `writeln(FileA, C)`, `readln(FileA)`, `readln(FileA, C)`, `write-(FileA, C)`, `read(FileA, C)`, `eoln(FileA)`, and `eof(FileA))`.

Binary Files

A binary file is a file of any type but char. The following standard subprograms can be used with binary files: `reset(FileA)`, `rewrite(FileA)`, `write-(FileA, C)`, `read(FileA, C)`, and `eof(FileA)`.

You can't declare or define a file of a file. Thus given TYPE NumbersFile= FILE OF integer, declaring IntFile: FILE OF NumbersFile is not allowed.

Unlike a text file, a binary file does not have a line structure, so you may not use the `readln` and `writeln` procedures or the `eoln` function.

Sets

The base types used for a set must all be of the same type. The number of elements in a set is limited and depends on the computer being used. The Pascal operations that can be used on sets are as follows:

Operation	Symbol
Union	+
Intersection	*
Difference	−
Membership test	IN
Inclusion	<= and >=
Equality	=

To add an element to a set, you must place the element or the identifier representing it in brackets ([]).

NEW TERMS

base type   linear search
binary files   search
binary search   sequential search
elements   structured files
empty set   union
intersection

EXERCISES

1. Given

   ```
   TYPE LibraryFile = FILE OF LibraryRecord;
   VAR Info:LibraryRecord;
   ```

   what is wrong with write(LibraryFile, Info)?

2. Given

   ```
   VAR LibraryFile:FILE OF LibraryRecord;
       Info:LibraryRecord;
   ```

   what is wrong with writeln(LibraryFile, Info)?

3. Given

```
TYPE LibraryRecord = RECORD
    LastName, FirstName: ARRAY[1..20] OF char;
    BooksOut:integer
END (* RECORD *);

VAR LibraryFile:FILE OF LibraryRecord;
    Info:LibraryRecord;
```

what is wrong with the following?

```
WITH Info DO BEGIN
    write(LibraryFile, FirstName, LastName, BooksOut);
```

4. Given the following data for a program that performs a binary search using the last name as the key and the definitions and declarations of the previous problem

Abrams	David	4
Abrams	Herman	9
Abrams	Samuel	7
Cowen	Claudia	0
Marateck	Samuel	3
Simon	Javier	6
Simon	Noel	6

what record will the program print if Abrams is entered as data?

5. What is wrong with the following expression:

$$NotUsed < Used$$

where VAR Used, NotUsed: ['a'..'z'];?

6. Given A:= [1, 3, 2, 7] and B:= [3, 9, 6], evaluate the following:
   a. A + B **b.** A − B **c.** A * B

7. Given A:= [1, 3, 2] and B:= [1, 3, 9, 2, 6], evaluate the following:
   a. A <= B **b.** A >= B **c.** B IN A

8. Given VAR SetA: [0..9], what is the original value of SetA?

9. Rewrite (Letter IN ['a'..'z']) AND (Letter IN ['A'..'Z']) without using the AND.

10. What is the value of ['a'..'z'] + ['A'..'Z'] = ['A'..'z']?

Programming Problems

11. Write a program that takes a paragraph written on a text file and reformats it so that the paragraph is written between two specified

columns read by the program. For example, if the beginning of the paragraph is

```
My country tis of thee,
Sweet land of liberty,
```

and we specify that the paragraph should appear between columns 12 and 42, then the beginning of the reformatted paragraph appears as follows:

```
12345678901234567890123456789012345678901234567890123456789
           My country tis of thee, Sweet
           land of liberty, Of thee I
           sing.
```

12. If your compiler uses an ASCII table, rewrite the previous program so that only the first word in each line of the reformatted paragraph is capitalized.

13. Rewrite the program of Figure 15.6*a* so that if the records on `File1` are sorted according to ID, you will not have to enter the ID after which you want a record inserted.

14. Given the following record, which stores the titles of an author's books

```
TYPE Book: ARRAY[1..20] OF char;
   LibrayRecord = RECORD
      FirstName, LastName:ARRAY[1..20] OF char;
      Title:ARRAY[1..4] OF Book
   END (* RECORD *);
```

write a program that searches an array for the author's last name and then prints the titles of all his books. A sample record for your test file would have the following information:

```
Abrams         Samuel        Chemistry
   Basic Chemistry      Algebra      Remedial Reading
```

where each title requires 20 characters.

15. Do the previous program so that it searches the array for the author's entire name.

16. Assuming that the `Title` field becomes `ARRAY[1..40] OF Book`, do the previous program so that it searches a given author's books for a specific title.

The following questions ask you to write procedures that will lead up to a program that replaces all occurrences of a given word in the paragraph with a word of your choosing. This is called *global search and replace.* The final program will also then reformat the altered paragraph.

The headings included in the following questions use the definitions in the TYPE statement

```
TYPE Line = array[1..80] of char;
     Page = array[1..20] of Line;
     EndOfLine = array[1..20] of integer;
     CharRange = 1..80;
     LineRange = 1..20;
```

17. Write a procedure that shifts elements of Phrase to the right, from the end of the replaced word to the last element of Phrase used, in order to make room for the new larger word. Use

```
PROCEDURE ShiftRight(VAR Phrase: Line; Start, LenWord,
LenSubst: CharRange);
```

where LenWord is the length of the word in text, Start is the column in which that word starts, and LenSubst is the length of the substitute word. Test your procedure with a sentence stored in a text file.

18. Using

```
PROCEDURE ShiftLeft(VAR Phrase: Line; Start, LenWord,
LenSubst: CharRange);
```

write a procedure that shifts elements of Phrase to the left in order to take up the slack for a new smaller word. Test your procedure with a sentence stored in a text file.

19. Using

```
PROCEDURE Shift(VAR Phrase: Line; Start, LenWord,
LenSubst: CharRange);
```

write a procedure that determines how to shift the line and then uses ShiftLeft or ShiftRight to do it.

20. Using

```
PROCEDURE Replace(VAR Phrase, Subst: Line; Start,
LenSubst: CharRange);
```

write a procedure that inserts a new word in the line, where Subst contains the new word. Test this procedure by writing

```
Shift ( Phrase, Start, LenWord, LenSubst) ;
NumLetter[I]:= NumLetter[I] + LenSubst - LenWord;
Replace(Phrase, Subst, Start, LenSubst );
```

where NumLetter is of type EndOfLine and is used to reset the length of the line.

21. Write a procedure that seeks a match between the inputted word and a word in the text and, if successful, makes the substitution.

22. Using the previous procedures, write a program that performs a global search and replace for a paragraph stored on a text file and then reformats the paragraph between the columns you designate.

When two files that are sorted on a key are merged, the resulting file will have the records of the two constituent files interleaved so that this file is also sorted on the key. For instance, if the IDs of the records of the first file are in the order 101, 104, 107, 110 and those of the second file are in the order 102, 103, 104, 105, 109, then the order on the merged file is 101, 102, 103, 104, 105, 107, 109, 110.

Write a program that merges two binary files, where each file consists of records of the following type:

```
TYPE DepositRecord = RECORD
        ID, Branch, TypeAccount:integer;
        Deposit:real
    END (* RECORD *);
```

Each file is sorted on the ID, and there is only one record for an ID. Assume that if two records appearing on each file have the same ID, then they are identical. Perform the merge so that the merged file has no duplicate records, that is, only one record appears for an ID.

23. Write a program that processes a file sorted on the ID (where the type of the records is given in the previous problem) such that if there is more than one record with the same ID, the program removes all but the first record from the file.

24. Write a program that first forms a set of the IDs of people who passed bad checks (this information is read from a file). It then reads another file of IDs of people who want to pay for items by check in a certain store and determines which of these people are in the original set.

25. Write a program that reads a check amount, for instance $123,45.67, and replaces each digit with an asterisk. The result here is

$$\$***,**.**.*.$$

26. Given TYPE CharSet = SET OF char;, use the following heading to write a procedure that counts the number of elements in a set:

```
FUNCTION Count(InputSet:CharSet):integer;
```

16

RECURSION

CHAPTER OVERVIEW

When you learned about writing functions in Chapter 9, you were told not to use the function name in a function subprogram on the right-hand side of an assignment statement. If you do this, the function will try to activate itself. If you do this accidentally, it leads to errors; however, when done purposely, it is an important technique that simplifies programming. This chapter explores *recursion*—the process by which either a function or a procedure activates itself—and explains how a given local variable is stored in a separate location for each recursive activation of the subprogram.

Normally, a subprogram can only activate a subprogram that precedes it. This chapter shows you how to use the FORWARD declaration to allow a subprogram to activate a subprogram that follows it. It concludes with a discussion of a calculator written using a recursive function.

16.1

RECURSIVE PROCEDURES

A subprogram that activates itself is called a *recursive* subprogram. For instance, procedure Print in Figure 16.1*a*

```
PROCEDURE Print;
VAR Ch:char;
BEGIN
    IF NOT eoln THEN BEGIN
        read(Ch);
        Print;
        write(Ch)
    END (* IF *)
END (* Print *);
```

activates itself when the statement Print in the procedure is executed. In order to explain how this works, let's explore how the program handles the input think.

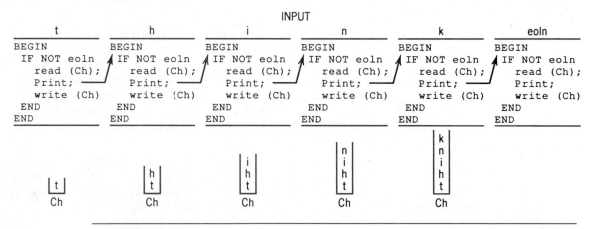

INPUT

TABLE I FOR FIGURE 16.1*a*.   Each time the procedure is activated, the character just read is placed on a data structure called a *stack* (each new character is placed on top of the previously stored character). The procedure activates itself, as indicated by the arrows.

It is helpful to think of each of the activations of the procedure as a link in a chain, as shown in Table I for Figure 16.1*a*. Since the program reads five letters and then detects the end-of-line mark, we draw six links, each of which contains the statements in the procedure. The first link represents the first time the procedure is activated; it reads the letter *t* and stores it in the location Ch for that procedure. The procedure then activates itself, so we draw an arrow from Print in the first link to the second link in the chain. Each time the procedure recursively activates itself, it allocates a new location for each of the local identifiers, here Ch.

In the second activation of the procedure, the program reads the second letter, *h*, and stores it in the location Ch for that activation of the procedure. The procedure activates itself again, so we draw an arrow from Print to the third link in the chain, where the procedure reads the third letter, *i*, and stores it in the location Ch for that activation of the procedure.

This process continues until the procedure reads the fifth letter, *k*. The procedure activates itself again, so we draw an arrow from Print to the sixth link. The program then detects the end-of-line mark. Since the NOT eoln is false, the computer skips the IF statement and reaches the end of the procedure. Now, for the first time, the computer has finished executing the complete procedure. Therefore the Print activated in the fifth link in the chain has been completely executed. The computer then executes the statement following the Print in the fifth link, namely, Write(Ch), and prints the contents of Ch, that is, k, for that activation of the procedure.

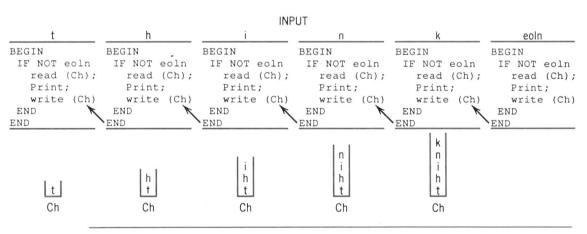

TABLE II FOR FIGURE 16.1a.   When the end of the line is encountered, control is returned to the statement following the Print, and the character on top of the stack is printed.

The Print activated in the fourth link in the chain has been completely executed. The computer then executes the statement following the Print in the fourth link, namely, Write(Ch), and prints the contents of Ch, that is, n, for that activation of the procedure. This process continues until the first activation of Print is completely executed and the computer prints the t. Consequently, the word *think* has now been spelled backward, as shown in Figure 16.1b. The program then returns to the main program and terminates.

INTRODUCTION TO RECURSION

```
PROGRAM Recursion1(input, output);
(* Prints a string in reverse order using recursion *)
PROCEDURE Print;
(* Recursive print *)
VAR Ch:char;
BEGIN
   IF NOT eoln THEN BEGIN
      read(Ch);
      Print;
      write(Ch)
   END (* IF *)
END (* Print *);
BEGIN
   writeln('Type a string, then hit return.');
   Print;
   writeln(' is the string spelled backward')
END.
```

FIGURE 16.1a.   Each time the procedure is activated, it reads another character and then activates itself. When it encounters the end of the line, it returns to the previous activation and prints the character read for that activation. A recursive subprogram must have a statement that terminates the recursive activations.

```
Type a string, then hit return.
think
kniht is the string spelled backward
```

FIGURE 16.1b.   Running the program of Figure 16.1a. Because the `writeln` follows the recursive activation, the input is printed backward.

The computer allocates a different variable for each recursive activation of a procedure by placing each new value of a given local variable (here, Ch) in the next position of a data structure called a *stack.* This is not done for the global variables.

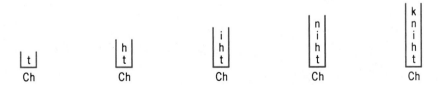

Each new value is placed on top of the stack, as shown in Table I when we read it from left to right. When a value is removed, it is removed from the top, as we see in Table II when we read it from right to left as we return from the end of the chain to its beginning. Thus if *i* was placed on the stack when Ch was read in the second recursive activation, and *n* was placed on the stack when Ch was read in the third recursive activation, then *n* will be removed from the stack when the program returns to the second recursive activation. Thus the value of Ch for the second activation will be the letter on top of the stack, *i*. This is the value printed there.

Although writing this procedure recursively is more difficult than writing it using an array, as done in Figure 10.2*a*, the recursive approach has an advantage: You don't have to dimension an array to a specific length; the computer automatically allocates locations to the stack as they are required up to a maximum value dictated by the size of a storage area in the memory called the *runtime stack*. Thus the recursive approach will accommodate an input of 30 characters or 3 characters equally well, whereas the array approach will only accommodate a number of characters up to the dimension of the array.

Two things are crucial to writing a recursive procedure or function:

1. The subprogram must activate itself, as in the execution of Print in procedure Print.

2. The subprogram must include a statement that ends the recursive linked chain when a certain boolean expression is false, as in IF NOT eoln THEN BEGIN. Here, when the program detects the end of a line, it finishes executing the procedure and returns to the previous execution of the procedure.

QUESTION: What will the following recursive procedure produce if it is substituted for procedure Print in Figure 16.1*a*?

```
PROCEDURE Print;
(* Recursive print *)
VAR Ch:char;
BEGIN
   IF NOT eoln DO BEGIN
      read(ch);
      Print;
   END(* IF *);
   write(Ch)
END (* Print *);
```

ANSWER: The end-of-line mark is encountered in the last activation of the procedure. Since read(ch) is not executed for this activation, no character is assigned to Ch. Thus the first value printed is unpredictable. However, in previous activations of the procedure, the value of Ch is the one read for that activation. Thus if the input is abcd, the output is #dcba, where "#" represents the unpredictable symbol.

QUESTION: What happens if we omit the test for the end of the line here or in Figure 16.1a?

ANSWER: The program continually activates itself until the runtime stack is full. The computer then prints an error message. If the runtime stack has an infinite capacity, the recursion will continue forever. For that reason, a recursive algorithm that lacks a statement that stops the recursion produces what is called *infinite recursion.*

Using the same analysis as we did for Figure 16.1a, we see why the IF in Figure 16.2a prints the input in the same order in which it was written:

```
IF NOT eoln THEN BEGIN
   read(Ch);
   write(Ch);
   Print
END (* IF *)
```

In each recursive activation of the procedure, since read(Ch) is immediately followed by write(Ch), whatever character is read is immediately printed. Then and only then does the procedure activate itself in Print. When the computer returns from the end of the linked chain to its beginning, it does not execute any statements, since no statements follow Print in the procedure. When this occurs, the type of recursion is called *tail recursion.* The results of running the program are shown in Figure 16.2b.

TEST YOURSELF

QUESTION: What is wrong with the following recursive procedure, which was written to print the input in the same order in which it is read?

```
PROCEDURE Print;
(* Recursive print *)
VAR Ch:char;
BEGIN
   IF NOT eoln THEN BEGIN
      Print
      read(Ch);
```

```
                 write(Ch);
             END (* IF *)
         END (* Print *);
```

ANSWER: Because the activation of Print immediately follows IF NOT eoln
THEN BEGIN, no characters are read by the program (nothing is transferred
from the buffer to location Ch) and an infinite loop occurs. The program will
terminate only if the first character read is an end-of-line character.

QUESTION: What will the procedure in the program of Figure 16.1*a* produce
if Ch is made a global instead of a local variable, in other words, if Ch is
declared in the main program instead of the procedure?

ANSWER: Since no stack is established for global variables, each new value of
Ch read will replace the previous one. Since K is the last value of Ch read, that
is the value that remains stored in Ch. Thus the program will print K the same
number of times that letters are inputted.

PRINTING A STRING IN THE ORDER IN WHICH IT IS WRITTEN

```
PROGRAM Recursion2(input, output);
(* Prints a string in order using recursion *)
PROCEDURE Print;
(* Recursive print *)
VAR Ch:char;
BEGIN
  IF NOT eoln THEN BEGIN
    read(Ch);
    write(Ch);
    Print
  END (* IF *)
END (* Print *);

BEGIN
  writeln('Type a string, then hit return.');
  Print;
  writeln(' is the string in the same order')
END.
```

FIGURE 16.2*a*.   Because the write precedes Print, the character is printed
before Print recursively activates itself.

```
Type a string, then hit return.
thinking
thinking is the string in the same order
```

FIGURE 16.2*b*.   Running the program of Figure 16.2*a*. When the end of the line is
encountered, the computer returns to the previous activation. Since there are no
statements left to be executed there, it continues back to the main program.

The next program uses a recursive procedure that contains a parameter. The program prints the letters of the alphabet from *a* to *e* and then from *e* back to *a*. The pseudocode is

Print successive letters of the alphabet using the linked chain
   going from left to right, until you reach "f".
Print the letters encountered when returning, using the linked chain going
   from right to left.

In order to print the letters up to *f*, the procedure must terminate itself when the letter passed to it—the contents of Ch—is *f*. So we start the body of the procedure—called Alpha—with IF Ch <> 'f' THEN BEGIN. The program then writes the letter, using write(Ch). In order to get the next activation of the procedure to write the succeeding letter, we write Alpha(Succ(Ch)), as shown in Figure 16.3*a*:

```
PROCEDURE Alpha(Ch:Char);
BEGIN
   IF Ch <> 'f' THEN BEGIN
     write(Ch);
     Alpha(Succ(Ch));
     write(Ch)
   END (* IF *)
END (* Alpha *);
```

The first time the program returns from the procedure to the previous activation is when the value of Ch is *f*. In order to print the letter that was at the top of the stack for that activation, we insert write(Ch) after Alpha(Succ-(Ch)). Each time the program returns to that write, it prints the letter at the top of the stack for that activation, and so prints the letters from *e* down to *a*, as shown in Figure 16.3*b*:

abcdeedcba

PRINTING THE LETTERS OF THE ALPHABET BACKWARD

```
PROGRAM RecurAlpha(input, output);
(*Prints the letters to e and back *)
VAR Ch:char;

PROCEDURE Alpha(Ch:Char);
BEGIN
  IF Ch <> 'f' THEN BEGIN
    write(Ch);
    Alpha(Succ(Ch));
    write(Ch)
  END (* IF *)
END (* Alpha *);

BEGIN
  Alpha('a')
END.
```

FIGURE 16.3a. The procedure first prints the letter passed to it and then activates itself, using the next letter of the alphabet. When it encounters the end of the line, it returns to the previous activation and prints the letter that was originally printed there.

```
abcdeedcba
```

FIGURE 16.3b. Running the program of Figure 16.3a. Because the procedure contains only write statements, the letters printed by the first and second writes are printed on the same line.

16.2

RECURSIVE FUNCTIONS

We've seen that all you have to do to make a procedure recursive is to place the procedure identifier and its parameters in the procedure itself. For instance, `Alpha(Succ(Ch))` recursively activated the procedure in the previous program. To make a function recursive, you must place the function identifier in an expression in the function's subprogram. Let's start by using recursion in rewriting the factorial problem we studied in Chapter 9.

The program, shown in Figure 16.4a, will calculate $N!$. Since, for instance, 5! is 5*4*3*2*1, then 5! = 5 * 4!. This is the recursive definition of a factorial, since it defines the factorial function (5!) in terms of itself (5 * 4!). We generalize the definition to $N! = N * (N-1)!$. Thus if the function heading is FUNCTION `Factor(N: integer):integer`, the statement that represents the recursive definition of the factorial is

$$\text{Factor} := N * \text{Factor}(N - 1)$$

Note two things here:

1. As always, when the function identifier appears on the left-hand side of an assignment statement, it is written without its argument.

2. When the function identifier appears on the right-hand side of an assignment statement, it must be written with its argument, here, `Factor(N - 1)`.

Like a recursive procedure, a recursive function must contain a statement that stops the traversal of the recursive linked chain. In order to write this statement, we must know that by definition 0! is 1. So we write

```
IF N = 0 THEN
   Factor := 1
ELSE
   Factor := N * Factor(N - 1)
```

The recursive linked chain is shown in the table for Figure 16.4a for the evaluation of 3!, where F represents `Factor`. When the program calculates 3!, the recursive statement activates `Factor(2)`. This, in turn, activates `Factor(1)`, which, in turn, activates `Factor(0)`. Here the recursive linked chain stops, and the value of `Factor` for N equals 0 is set equal to 1. The program then returns to the previous activation of `Factor` and evaluates `Factor := 1 * Factor(0)` as 1. Note that in contrast to a recursive procedure, when the program returns to the previous activation of a recursive function, it returns to the activating statement, here, Factor:= N * Factor(N − 1), not the statement following it. It does this so that it can evaluate the entire expression on the right side of the ":=".

As the program traverses the linked chain from right to left, it evaluates 2! and finally 3!. It then returns to the main program.

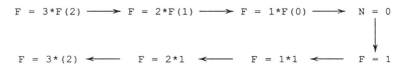

```
F = 3*F(2) ———→ F = 2*F(1) ———→ F = 1*F(0) ———→ N = 0

                                                    │
                                                    ↓
F = 3*(2)  ←——  F = 2*1  ←——  F = 1*1  ←——  F = 1
```

TABLE FOR FIGURE 16.4a.   The recursive linked chain for the evaluation of 3!.

The results of running the program are shown in Figure 16.4b.

When you use the function identifier in a writeln or write, it must also be written with its argument. Thus you could not write

$$writeln(N − 1, '!=', Factor)$$

because Factor is not written with its argument. However, if you wrote writeln(N − 1, '!=', Factor(N − 1)) in the function, you would be recursively activating the function in the writeln as well—which you do not want to do.

In Figure 16.4c, we show how to get the function itself to print the value of the factorial. We assign the value of Factor(N − 1) to Term in Term:= Factor(N − 1) and then calculate the factorial in Factor:= N * Term. The results of running the program are shown in Figure 16.4d.

TEST YOURSELF

QUESTION: What does the following procedure produce for a value of N equal to 3?

```
FUNCTION Factor(N: integer):integer;
(* Sums the numbers from 1 to N *)
BEGIN
   IF N = 0 THEN
      Factor:= 1
   ELSE BEGIN
      Factor:= N * Factor(N − 1);
      writeln(N − 1, '! = ', Factor(N − 1))
   END (* ELSE *)
END (* Factor *);
```

ANSWER:

$$0! = 1$$
$$1! = 0! = 1$$
$$1$$
$$2! = 0! = 1$$
$$1! = 0! = 1$$
$$1$$
$$2$$

THE RECURSIVE FACTORIAL FUNCTION

```
PROGRAM FacOtorial(input, output);
(* Calculates a factorial recursively *)
VAR N: integer;

FUNCTION Factor(N: integer):integer;
(* Sums the numbers from 1 to N *)
BEGIN
  IF N = 0 THEN
    Factor:= 1
  ELSE
    Factor:= N * Factor(N - 1)
END (* Factor *);

BEGIN
  writeln('Type the integer for Factorial');
  readln(N);
  writeln(N:2, '! = ', Factor(N):3);
END.
```

FIGURE 16.4a.   In order for a function to activate itself in an assignment statement, it must do so on the right-hand side.

```
Type the integer for Factorial
5
5! = 120
```

FIGURE 16.4b.   Running the program of Figure 16.4a. The recursion stops at the value of N equal to 0. There the value of Factor is set to 1.

PRINTING THE VALUE OF THE FUNCTION IN THE FUNCTION ITSELF

```
PROGRAM Factorial(input, output);
(* Calculates a factorial recursively *)
VAR N: integer;

FUNCTION Factor(N: integer):integer;
(* Sums the numbers from 1 to N *)
VAR Term:integer;
BEGIN
  IF N = 0 THEN
    Factor:= 1
  ELSE BEGIN
    Term:= Factor(N - 1);
    writeln(Term :3, ' = ', N - 1, '!');
    Factor:= N * Term
  END (* ELSE *)
END (* Factor *);

BEGIN
  write('Type the integer for Factorial ');
  readln(N);
  writeln(Factor(N):3, ' = ',N:2, '!');
END.
```

FIGURE 16.4c. You can't place the function name without an argument in a `writeln` or `write` statement; if you do, a syntax error will occur.

```
Type the integer for Factorial 5
  1 = 0!
  1 = 1!
  2 = 2!
  6 = 3!
 24 = 4!
120 = 5!
```

FIGURE 16.4d. Running the program of Figure 16.4c.

16.3

THE FIBONACCI SEQUENCE

A sequence of numbers is a set of numbers that are placed in a given order. Thus 2, 6, 9 is a sequence and 6, 9, 2 is a different sequence. The next program, shown in Figure 16.5a, generates a sequence of numbers such that the first two numbers are 0 and 1, respectively. Any higher number in the sequence is the sum of the two numbers preceding it. This sequence is called the *Fibonacci sequence.* It is 0, 1, 1, 2, 3, 5, 8, 13, 21, and so on.

The pseudocode is

> *The first number is 0;*
> *The second number is 1;*
> *Any other number is the sum of the preceding two.*

Using N to represent the order of the numbers, that is, the zeroth, first, second, and so on, we refine *Any other number is the sum of the preceding two* to

> *The Nth number is the sum of the N − 1st number plus*
> *the N − 2nd number.*

This, in turn, translates into the Pascal statement `Fibon: = Fibon(N − 1) + Fibon(N − 2)`, where `Fibon` represents the function. Since `Fibon` calls itself, it is a recursive function. The statement part of the function is

```
IF N = 0 THEN
   Fibon: = 0
ELSE IF N = 1 THEN
   Fibon: = 1
ELSE
   Fibon: = Fibon(N − 1) + Fibon(N − 2)
```

The results are shown in Figure 16.5*b*.

WHILE YOU ARE READING

The Fibonacci sequence is of interest to mathematicians working in number theory. It also has applications in computer science. In later courses you will study a search that uses Fibonacci numbers.

Calculating the Fibonacci sequence using recursion is very inefficient, as Table I for Figure 16.5*a* shows

THE FIBONACCI SEQUENCE

```
PROGRAM Fibonacci(input, output);
(* Calculates a Fibonacci series recursively *)
VAR J, N: integer;

FUNCTION Fibon(N: integer):integer;
(* Sums the Fibonacci numbers for N - 1 and N - 2 *)
BEGIN
  IF N = 0 THEN
    Fibon: = 0
  ELSE IF N = 1 THEN
    Fibon: = 1
  ELSE
    Fibon: = Fibon(N - 1) + Fibon(N - 2)
END (* Fibon *);

BEGIN
  writeln('Type the number of terms desired in the Fibonacci series');
  readln(N);
  FOR J: = 0 TO N DO
    write(Fibon(J):5)
END.
```

FIGURE 16.5a.   The definition of the Fibonacci sequence is that a given number is the sum of the preceding two, and the first and second numbers are 0 and 1, respectively.

```
Type the number of terms desired in the Fibonacci series
10
    0   1   1   2   3   5   8  13  21  34  55
```

FIGURE 16.5b.   Running the program of Figure 16.5a.

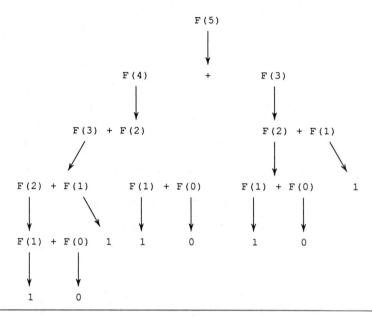

TABLE I FOR FIGURE 16.5a.   Shows how the function activates itself until the value of N is 0 or 1.

since F(3) is calculated twice; F(2) and F(0) three times; and F(1) four times. An efficient algorithm would evaluate each of these values only once. The saving feature of the recursive approach is that it is easy to write.

If you read Table II for Figure 16.5a from the bottom up, you see that next to each vertical line is a number in brackets representing the value of the expression immediately below it. From this it is evident that the value of F(5) is 5.

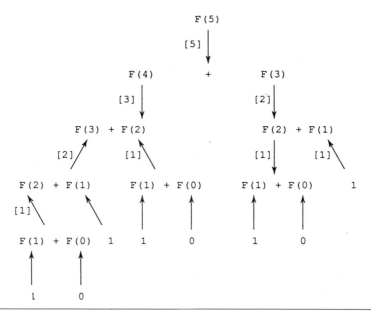

TABLE II FOR FIGURE 16.5a. Shows how values are assigned to the function on its way back to the main program. If you read the table from the bottom up, next to each vertical line is a number in brackets representing the value of the expression immediately below it.

BEFORE YOU LEAVE

Why do we learn recursion? It provides an elegant solution to a problem that may be done later by iteration.

16.4

THE FORWARD DECLARATION

Ordinarily, a procedure or a function can only activate a subprogram that appears before it. However, sometimes it is necessary to activate a subprogram that follows a given procedure. For instance, if procedure One activates Two, Two activates Three, and Three activates One

```
PROCEDURE One;
BEGIN
    Two;

        .

        .
END;
PROCEDURE Two;
BEGIN
    Three;

        .

        .
END;
PROCEDURE Three;
BEGIN
    One;

        .

        .
END .
```

then only procedure Three will be activating a procedure that precedes it. This process, whereby subprograms activate each other such that the last one activates the first, as is the case with One, Two, and Three here, is called a *recursive chain* or *mutual recursion*.

In order to allow one subprogram to activate a second subprogram that follows it, we must place the subprogram heading for the second one (slightly modified by appending Forward to it) before the first subprogram. The subprogram itself, however, remains in its original position. Thus if procedure ToRight activates ToLeft and precedes ToLeft, we place the heading PROCE-DURE ToLeft(Left, Right:integer);Forward; before procedure ToRight. When we write procedure ToLeft, we eliminate the arguments from the heading and simply write PROCEDURE ToLeft; instead. All of this is shown in Figure 16.6a.

This program prints a zigzag pattern consisting of diagonals of decreasing length. Its pseudocode is

```
PROCEDURE ToRight;
    Print a diagonal to the right;
    Activate ToLeft to print a smaller diagonal to the left
END;
PROCEDURE ToLeft;
    Print a diagonal to the left;
    Activate ToRight to print a smaller diagonal to the right
END;
```

We refine this to

```
PROCEDURE ToRight;
  FOR J: = Left TO Right DO
    Print a diagonal to the right;
    Activate ToLeft to print diagonal from (Right − 1) down to Left
END;
PROCEDURE ToLeft;
  FOR J: = Right DOWNTO Left DO
    Print a diagonal to the left;
    Activate ToRight to prints a diagonal from (Left + 1) to Right
END;
```

where the values of *Left* and *Right* are the leftmost and rightmost column numbers for a given diagonal.

As with a recursive subprogram, you must include in a recursive chain of procedures a statement that will stop the chain of activations. The procedures in the last version of the pseudocode will continue to activate each other forever. So we nest the statements in the Pascal versions of each of the procedures in the IF beginning with

IF Left <= Right THEN BEGIN.

As the computer draws the zigzag line, the value of Left increases while that of Right decreases. When the column number corresponding to Left is greater than the one corresponding to Right, the program will traverse the recursive linked chain back to the main program. In order to show this path, we include a write statement at the end of the compound statement in the procedures in order to print the name of the procedure. For instance, in ToLeft, we write write('ToLeft'):

```
         IF Left <= Right THEN BEGIN
           FOR J := Right DOWNTO Left DO
             writeln('X': J);
           ToRight(Left + 1, Right);
           write('ToLeft ')
         END (* IF *);
```

The results of running the program are shown in Figure 16.6b. The order of the procedure names printed as the program traverses its way back to the main program is ToLeft ToRight ToLeft ToRight ToLeft ToRight. If you read this list from right to left, you see the activations of the procedures in the order that produced the pattern.

You do not have to use a recursive chain of activations in order to use the Forward declaration. If for some reason you want to place subprogram One after subprogram Two, although Two activates One, you must forward declare One.

THE FORWARD DECLARATION

```
PROGRAM Pattern(input, output);
(* Demonstrates the forward declaration *)
VAR left, Right:integer;
PROCEDURE ToLeft(Left, Right:integer);Forward;
PROCEDURE ToRight(Left, Right:integer);
VAR k:integer;
BEGIN
  IF Left <= Right THEN BEGIN
    FOR k := Left TO Right DO
      writeln('X': k);
    ToLeft(Left, Right - 1);
    write('ToRight ')
  END (* IF *);
END (* ToRight *);
PROCEDURE Toleft;
VAR J:integer;
BEGIN
  IF Left <= Right THEN BEGIN
    FOR J := Right DOWNTO Left DO
      writeln('X': J);
    ToRight(Left + 1, Right);
    write('ToLeft ')
  END (* IF *);
END (* ToLeft *);
BEGIN
  writeln('Type left-hand and right-hand limits');
  readln(Left, Right);
  ToRight(Left, Right)
END.
```

FIGURE 16.6a. In order for a subprogram to activate another subprogram that follows it, you must precede the first subprogram with a FORWARD declaration containing the second one's name and its parameters. When you write the referenced subprogram, you omit its parameters from the heading.

```
Type left-hand  and right-hand limits
  2   7
    x
     x
      x
       x
        x
         x
          x
          x
          x
          x
         x
        x
       x
        x
         x
          x
          x
          x
          x
         x
        x
       x
        x
         x
          x
          x
ToLeft  ToRight  ToLeft  ToRight  ToLeft  ToRight
```

FIGURE 16.6b.   Running the program of Figure 16.6a. The last line indicates the opposite order in which the procedures were activated.

16.5

THE BUCKETS AND WELL PROBLEM

What follows is a problem* that requires you to write a nontrivial recursive procedure as its solution. You are given two empty buckets with capacities Cap1 and Cap2 gallons, respectively, and a well that has an infinite supply of water. The task is to write a recursive procedure to pour water into the buckets so that the total in the buckets is Amount gallons. The procedure may

1. fill either bucket to capacity from the well.
2. empty either bucket.
3. pour the water from one bucket into the other one until either the first one is empty or the second one is full. For instance, if the capacities of the buckets are 4 and 1 gallons, respectively, and the 4-gallon bucket is

*See also J.T. Schwartz, R.B.K. Dewar, E. Dubinsky, and E. Schonberg, *Programming with Sets: An Introduction to SETL*, Springer-Verlag, New York (1986), p. 177.

full and the 1-gallon one is empty, the situation before and after the pouring will be as shown in the table for Figure 16.7:

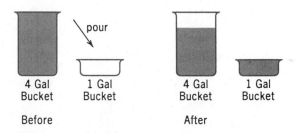

4 Gal   1 Gal   4 Gal   1 Gal
Bucket   Bucket   Bucket   Bucket

Before   After

TABLE FOR FIGURE 16.7.   The states of the bucket before and after one gallon is poured into the smaller bucket.

If our goal is to have the buckets contain a total of 3 gallons, one solution is the following sequence of states: (0,0), (4,0), (4,1), (0,1), (1,0), (1,1), (2,0), (2,1), where the first number in parentheses [for instance, the 4 in (4,1)] is the amount in the first bucket and the second number [here, the 1 in (4,1)] is the amount in the second bucket, and the term *state* refers to the description of the amount of water in the buckets.

This problem is similar to a maze problem. We don't know the sequence of steps required to get out of the maze, so at every point in the maze, we try all the possibilities. Similarly in the buckets problem, we try (**1**), (**2**), and (**3**) for both buckets. To avoid an infinite loop due to repeatedly visiting a sequence of states, we use a global boolean array, Visited[Bucket1, Bucket2], to determine whether we have already visited a state. If we have, we quit the procedure and try the next possibility.

Let's use PROCEDURE Pour(Bucket1, Bucket2, Goal) as the heading of our procedure, where Bucket1 and Bucket2 are the current contents of the respective buckets. Goal is a boolean variable that is true when our goal has been reached; otherwise, it is false. Translating (**1**) for bucket 1 into pseudocode produces

IF *bucket 1 is not full* THEN *fill it;*

which in Pascal becomes IF Bucket <> Cap1 THEN Pour(Cap1, Bucket2, Goal), as shown in Figure 16.7a. Translating (**2**) for bucket 1 into pseudocode produces

IF *bucket 1 is not empty* THEN *empty it;*

which in Pascal becomes IF B1 <> 0 THEN Pour(0, B2, Goal). Translating (**3**) for bucket 1 into pseudocode produces the following for the process of pouring from bucket 1 into bucket 2:

IF *the sum of the contents of bucket 1 and bucket 2* > Cap2 THEN
   Pour from bucket 1 into bucket 2 until bucket 2 is full
ELSE *Pour all of bucket 1 into bucket 2.*

which in Pascal becomes

```
IF B1 <> 0 THEN
   IF B1 + B2 > Cap2 THEN Pour(B1 - (Cap2 - B2), Cap2, Goal)
      ELSE Pour(0, B1 + B2, Goal);
```

where IF B1 <> 0 THEN avoids an unnecessary activation of Pour to empty the already emptied bucket 1. We must list these statements for both buckets in the procedure. Since Cap1 and Cap2 are like constants, we use them as global variables.

Since we don't want to repeat visited states and want to stop when we reach our goal, we start the procedure with IF NOT Visited[B1, B2] AND NOT Goal THEN BEGIN. If we input data for which no solution is possible, the final value of Goal will be false. We therefore include

```
IF NOT Goal THEN
   writeln(Amount, ' not attainable')
```

at the end of the main program to detect such data. The results of running the program are shown in Figure 16.7b.

THE BUCKETS AND WELL PROBLEM

```
PROGRAM Buckets(input, output);
VAR Row, Column, Cap1, Cap2, Amount:integer;
  Visited:ARRAY[0..10, 0..10] OF boolean;
  Goal:boolean;
PROCEDURE Pour(B1, B2:integer; VAR Goal:boolean);
(* Solves Buckets and Well problem recursively *)
BEGIN
  IF NOT Visited[B1, B2] AND NOT Goal THEN BEGIN
    writeln('Bucket1 = ', B1, 'Bucket2 = ', B2);
    Goal:= B1 + B2 = Amount;
    IF NOT Goal THEN BEGIN
      Visited[B1, B2]:= True;
      IF B1 <> Cap1 THEN Pour(Cap1, B2, Goal);
      IF B2 <> Cap2 THEN Pour(B1, Cap2, Goal);
      IF B1 <> 0 THEN Pour(0, B2, Goal);
      IF B2 <> 0 THEN Pour(B1, 0, Goal);
      IF B1 <> 0 THEN
        IF B1 + B2 > Cap2 THEN Pour(B1 - (Cap2 - B2), Cap2, Goal)
          ELSE Pour(0, B1 + B2, Goal);
      IF B2 <> 0 THEN
        IF B1 + B2 > Cap1 THEN Pour(Cap1, B2 - (Cap1 - B1), Goal)
          ELSE Pour(B1 + B2, 0, Goal)
    END (* IF NOT Goal THEN *)
  END (* IF NOT Visited *)
END (* Pour *);
BEGIN (* Main *)
  Goal:= False;
  writeln('Type the capacities of the two buckets and the goal');
  readln(Cap1, Cap2, Amount);
  FOR Row:= 0 TO Cap1 DO
    FOR Column:= 0 TO Cap2 DO
        Visited[Row, Column]:= False;
  Pour(0, 0, Goal);
  IF NOT Goal THEN
    writeln(Amount, ' not attainable')
END.
```

FIGURE 16.7a.   Since `Cap1` and `Cap2` are like constants, we use them as global variables.

```
Type the capacities of the two buckets and the goal
4 1 3
Bucket1 = 0 Bucket2 = 0
Bucket1 = 4 Bucket2 = 0
Bucket1 = 4 Bucket2 = 1
Bucket1 = 0 Bucket2 = 1
Bucket1 = 1 Bucket2 = 0
Bucket1 = 1 Bucket2 = 1
Bucket1 = 2 Bucket2 = 0
Bucket1 = 2 Bucket2 = 1
```

FIGURE 16.7b.   Running the program of Figure 16.7a.

16.6

AN APPLICATION

Remember that in Chapters 8 and 9 we wrote two calculators? Now let's write a calculator that uses recursion. It will evaluate expressions of the following form: An expression must be preceded by a "=" sign and must contain single digits representing operands, as well as "*" or "/" representing operators. Examples of such expressions would be "=3" and "=3*5/4*5". Each of these expressions is evaluated from left to right as a real.

The representation we will use to plan the program is as follows: A term in angle brackets will represent the definition of the term. Thus *<expression>* means the definition of an expression. The following is a recursive definition of an expression:

$$<expression> := <operand>$$

or

$$<expression> := <operand> <operator> <expression>$$

If "|" represents *or,* our definition* becomes

<expression> := *<operand>*|*<operand>* *<operator>* *<expression>*
<operator> := * | /
<operand> := 0 | 1 | 2 | 3 | 4 | 5 | 6 | 7 | 8 | 9

Some expressions you can obtain using this definition are the following:

1. 4, from *<expression>* := *<operand>*.
2. 4 * 5, from *<expression>* := *<operand>* *<operator>* *<expression>*, that is, *<expression>* := 4*<expression>*, where we then use *<expression>* := *<operand>* to evaluate the *<expression>* that appears on the right-hand side of the ":=".
3. 3 * 4 * 5, from *<expression>* := *<operand>* *<operator>* *<expression>*, that is, *<expression>* := 3*<expression>*, where we use *<expression>* := *<operand>* *<operator>* *<expression>* to evaluate the *<expression>* that appears on the right-hand side of the ":=", and obtain 3 * 4 * *<expression>*. We then use *<expression>* := *<operand>*.

*This representation is called *Backus Nauer form.*

The function that evaluates these expressions accepts two parameters—an operand and a string representing the part of the string that has not yet been evaluated. Let's use the string "=2*3*4" to explain our algorithm. The value of the operand (here, 0 or any digit) and the string "=2*3*4" are originally passed as parameters to the function. The first version of the pseudocode for the recursive function is

Set Operator *to 1st element of string;*
Set 2nd operand to 2nd element of string;
Set Rest *to rest of string;*
CASE *Operator* OF
    "=": *Set* Value *to 2nd operand;*
    "*", "/": *Set* Value *to result of calculation using the operand passed as a parameter,* Operator, *and 2nd operand*
END (* CASE *) ;
Recursively activate with the function, with Value *and* Rest *as parameters.*

Since the string is "=2*3*4", the function sets *Operator* to "=," *2nd operand* to 2, and the string *Rest* to "*3*4". It then sets Value to 2. When the function activates itself recursively, the value of the operand passed as a parameter is 2. The value of operator is "*", that of the second operand is 3, and that of Rest is "4". Value is calculated as 6 and, with Rest, is passed to the next activation of the function. The value of the first operand is now 6, that of the operator is "*", that of the second operand is 4, and Rest is the empty string. Value is calculated as 24 and, with Rest, is passed to the next activation of the function. In this final activation of the function, 24 is returned as the value of the function. Thus the second version of our function—we will call it Express—becomes

IF *string is not empty* THEN BEGIN
    Set Operator *to 1st element of string;*
    Set 2nd operand to 2nd element of string;
    Set Rest *to rest of string;*
    CASE Operator OF
        "=": *Set* Value *to 2nd operand;*
        "*", "/": *Set* Value *to result of calculation, using the operand passed as a parameter,* Operator, *and 2nd operand*
    END (* CASE *) ;
    Recursively activate with Rest *and* Value
    END THEN
ELSE Set Express *to the value of the 1st operand.*

To facilitate our programming effort, let's use the string subprograms Copy, Length, and ReadString written in Chapter 11. If the identifier Stream represents the string, the pseudocode IF *string is not empty* THEN becomes IF Length(Stream) > 0 THEN BEGIN.

In order to translate *Set* Rest *to rest of string* to Pascal, you must realize that the rest of the string consists of the substring from the third to the last characters (since the first two characters are used for *Operator* and *2nd operand*, respectively). Thus the Pascal code becomes Copy(Stream, Rest, 3, EndPoint), where the value of EndPoint is 80. We chose this value for EndPoint because it's the maximum number of characters that can fit on a line. Remember that if the value of EndPoint is greater than the number of characters left in the string (as it is here), only the part of the string from the third character to the end of the string will be copied to Rest.

Since the next to the last time the function is activated the length of Rest is 2 (it's value is "*4"), the computer evaluates that activation of the Copy procedure as Copy(Stream, Rest, 3, 80). The position where the substring should begin is 3, but its length is only 2; therefore, the program sets the value of Rest to the null string. This means that the value of the length of Rest is 0. The next time the function is activated, the value of the function will be the value of the expression, and the recursion will stop.

The program is shown in Figure 16.8*a* and the results of running it in Figure 16.8*b*. The table for Figure 16.8*a* shows how the expression is evaluated.

TEST YOURSELF

QUESTION: Why does an input of =1/2/3/4/5/6 produce the result 0.0?

ANSWER: The field specification for the result is 5:1, so the result of 0.0014 is printed as 0.0.

QUESTION: What happens if the input is the null string?

ANSWER: The function Expression returns the value of First, which is 0 the first time the function is activated.

QUESTION: Write an iterative solution to the calculator problem. To simplify matters, assume that the expression starts with an operand. For instance, a valid expression would be "3/4*5*6".

ANSWER:

```
PROGRAM Iterate;
(* Iterative approach to calculator *)
VAR Factor, Fact:real;
    Operator, Operand:char;
```

```
                    FUNCTION Convert(Ch:Char):integer;
                    BEGIN
                      Convert:= ord(Ch) − ord('0')
                    END (* Convert *);

                    BEGIN
                      writeln('type your string');
                      read(Operand);
                      Fact:= Convert(Operand);
                      WHILE NOT eoln DO BEGIN
                        read(Operator, Operand);
                        Factor:= Convert(Operand);
                        CASE Operator OF
                          '*': Fact:= Fact * Factor;
                          '/': Fact:= Fact / Factor
                        END (* CASE *);
                      END (* WHILE *);
                      writeln('expression value =', Fact:4:1)
                    END.
```

A RECURSIVE CALCULATOR

```
PROGRAM Calculator(input, output);
(* Program evaluates any expression with only * and / signs *)
(* The expression must begin with " = ")
(* Uses the Copy, Length, and Read String subprograms written
in Chapter 11 *)
CONST EndPoint = 80;
TYPE CharacterArray = ARRAY[0..EndPoint] OF char;
VAR Expression: CharacterArray;

FUNCTION Convert(Ch:Char):integer;
BEGIN
  Convert:= ord(Ch) − ord('0')
END (* Convert *);
```

```
FUNCTION Express(First: real; Stream:CharacterArray):real;
VAR Len:integer;
  Second, Value:real;
  Operator:Char;
  Rest:CharacterArray;
BEGIN
  IF Length(Stream) > 0 THEN BEGIN
     (* Ends recursion if operand is encountered *)
     Operator:= Stream[1];
     Second:= Convert(Stream[2]);
     Copy(Stream, Rest, 3, EndPoint);
     CASE Operator OF
       '=': Value:= Second;
       '-': Value:= First - Second;
       '*': Value:= First * Second;
       '/': Value:= First / Second
     END (* CASE *);
     Express:= Express(Value, Rest)
   END (* IF Len.. *)
  ELSE Express:= First;
END (* Express *);
BEGIN
  writeln('Type your expression');
  ReadString(input, Expression);
  writeln('The result is ', Express(0, Expression):5:1)
END.
```

FIGURE 16.8a. The recursive function evaluates expressions beginning with an "="
and containing only "*" and "/" and digits.

```
Type your expression
=2*3/4
The result is 1.5
```

FIGURE 16.8b. Running the program of Figure 16.8a.

Stream	First	Operator	Second	Rest
=2*3/4	0	=	2	*3/4
3/4	2	*	3	/4
/4	6	/	4	Null string
Null	1.5			

TABLE FOR FIGURE 16.8a. How the string is evaluated.

CHAPTER REVIEW

Recursive Subprograms

Two things are crucial to writing a recursive procedure or function:

1. The subprogram must activate itself.
2. The subprogram must include a statement that ends the recursion when a certain boolean expression is false.

Forward Declaration

In order to allow one subprogram to activate a second subprogram that follows it, we must place the subprogram heading for the second one (slightly modified by appending Forward to it) before the first subprogram. When we write the second procedure, we eliminate the arguments from the heading.

NEW TERMS

Fibonacci sequence	recursive chain
infinite recursion	runtime stack
mutual recursion	stack
recursion	tail recursion

EXERCISES

1. What is the consequence of using a local or global variable in a recursive subprogram?
2. What does the following program produce for an input of 2 4?

```
PROGRAM Prob1(input, output);

FUNCTION Test(N:integer):integer;
BEGIN
  IF N > 0 THEN
    Test:= N + test(N − 3)
  ELSE IF N = 0 THEN
    Test:= 0
  ELSE
    Test:= Test(N + 2) − N
END (* Test *);
```

```
BEGIN (* Main *)
  writeln(6:2, Test(6):6 );
  writeln(-2:2, Test(-2):6 );
  writeln(5:2, Test(5):6 );
END.
```

Programming Problems

3. Write a program that recursively calculates the sum of the integers from 1 to N.

4. The combination symbol is defined by

```
C(N, 0) = 1 for all N.
C(N, N) = 1 for all N.
C(N, K) = C(N - 1, K) + C(N - 1, K - 1) for 0 < K < N
```

Write a recursive function that computes the combination symbol.

5. Write a recursive function to compute X^n, where n is an integer and using the fact that $x^n = x^{n/2} * x^{n/2}$ for n even and $x^{n/2} * x^{n/2} * x$ for n odd.

6. Given the function header

```
FUNCTION SUM(VAR X:Matrix; M, N:integer);real;
```

with the definition `Matrix = ARRAY[1..10] OF real` and $N > M$, write a recursive function that sums the Mth to the Nth elements.

7. Write a program that produces the six permutations of ABC, that is, ABC, ACB, BAC, BCA, and so on.

The following three classic recursion problems are known by their names.

The Towers of Hanoi Problem

8. The Towers of Hanoi game is played with three pegs and a stack of N rings initially on peg A.

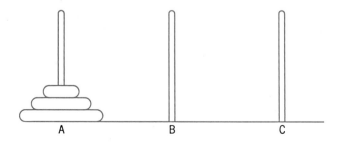

The *N* rings are of increasing sizes. The goal of the game is to transfer the rings one at a time until they are all on peg C. The following must be true when the rings are on any peg: The largest ring must always be on the bottom of the stack. The next largest ring must rest on the largest ring, and so forth, so that the smallest ring is on top of the stack.

For two rings, the sequence of actions would be: A to B, A to C, B to C. An action applies to the ring that is on top of the stack on the peg that precedes the *to*. For three rings, the initial sequence of actions would be A to C, A to B, C to B. What we've done is to transfer two rings from A to B using C. This brings us to the following state:

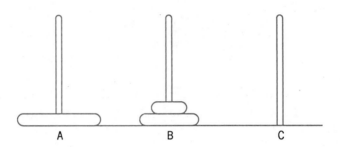

We then transfer the last ring from A to C and, finally, transfer the two rings from B to C using A. For *N* rings the algorithm is:

> *Transfer N − 1 rings from A to B using C.*
> *Transfer the last ring from A to C*
> *Transfer N − 1 rings from B to C using A*

Using PROCEDURE Transfer(N:integer; Initial, Final, Using:char), write a recursive procedure that transfers *N* rings from A to C. Note that when *N* is 1, the procedure should execute writeln ('Transfer a ring from', Initial, ' to ', Final). Otherwise, it should recursively activate the algorithm twice (corresponding to the two *Transfer N − 1 rings* statements in the algorithm). The A, B, and C should be replaced by the corresponding formal parameters. The main program should execute Transfer(N, 'A', 'C', 'B').

The Maze Problem

9. The problem of finding a path out of a maze is similar to the buckets and well problem in that you recursively try several actions until you have exited the maze. If the maze pattern has *M* rows and *N* columns, you have exited when you are in the first or *M*th rows or in the first or *N*th columns. At that point, you print the maze. A sample of a maze pattern that you could read into the program is

```
######## ####
######## ####
######   ####
####     ######
####          ##
#### ##### ##
#### ##### ##
####*##### ##
############
```

The starting point in the maze indicated by the "*" is also read into the program. The possible actions are "go up," "go down," "go left," and "go right." Use the heading PROCEDURE Find(Row, Column:integer; Maze:MazeArray), so that "go up" becomes:

IF Maze[Row + 1, Column] = ' ' THEN Find(Row + 1, Column, Maze)

The first statement in the procedure should store an "*" at your current position in the maze.

10. In the previous program, what would happen if the array Maze were a variable parameter?

The Eight Queens Problem

11. In the game of chess, a queen can move on the column and row at the intersection of which it's positioned. It can also move diagonally. Write a program that positions eight queens on a chessboard so that none of the queens can capture any of the other queens. Start by positioning the first queen in the first row and first column. Then position the second queen in the second column so that it won't be captured by the first queen. Position the third queen in the third column. If it can be captured by the second queen, backtrack as you do in the maze problem, reposition the second queen, and then position the third queen. Continue in this manner until all the queens are positioned.

12. Write a program that performs a recursive binary search.

13. Rewrite Figure 16.7a so that it checks for invalid input.

14. Write a program that performs the quick sort, a sort originated by C. A. R. Hoare. It works as follows: It places a number in its correct position in the list and then recursively uses the same scheme for the group of numbers below the correctly positioned number and the group above it. On the average, the quick sort is the most efficient sort. Let's examine the list 16, 4, 11, 9, 71, 29, 8, 13 to see how it works.

Call the first number (here, 16) *First*. We'll place it in a location such that the numbers to the right of it are greater than it and the numbers to the left of it are less than it. In other words, it will be in its correct position in the list. Do this by going forward through the list until you find a number (here, 71) greater than or equal to *First*. Then go from the back of the list to the left until you find a number (here, 13) that is less than or equal to *First*. If the subscript of the first number (71) is less than that of the second number (13), as is the case here, exchange the two numbers. The list is now

$$16, 4, 11, 9, 13, 29, 8, 71$$

Continue by preceding to the right from the position that 13 is in until you find the next number (here, 29) greater than or equal to *First*. Then go to the left from 71 until you find the next number (here, 8) less than or equal to *First*. If the subscript of the first number (29) is less than that of the second number (8), as is the case here, exchange the two numbers. The list is now

$$16, 4, 11, 9, 13, 8, 29, 71$$

Continue in this way until the subscript of the first number (29) is not greater than that of the second number (8). When this occurs, as is the case here, exchange the second number (8) with *First*. The list is now

$$8, 4, 11, 9, 13, 16, 29, 71$$

First is now in its proper position in the list. We then have to apply this technique to the numbers to the right of *First* and to the numbers to its left (this is the recursion part). These two groups are shown in brackets [8 4 11 9 13] 16 [29 71]. This technique is called *divide and conquer* since we use the same technique on different subsets. Once the subscript of the first number in a group is greater than or equal to that of the last number, the recursion for that group stops. At the end of the program, the list will be sorted. Note that you don't have to choose as *First* the first number in a group; it can be, for instance, the middle number. In Appendix B, we compute the efficiency of this sort.

17

POINTERS AND DYNAMIC STORAGE

CHAPTER OVERVIEW

As you remember from our study of arrays, the amount of memory allocated to an array is fixed when the program compiles. A method called *dynamic storage allocation* enables the computer to allocate memory locations while the program is executing. We'll use this method to produce a list of records linked to each other so that a record can either be inserted in or removed from any point in the list without disturbing all the other records. Then we'll demonstrate how to sort the records. We conclude by using dynamic allocation to implement a stack.

17.1

AN INTRODUCTION TO DYNAMIC STORAGE

When we define an array type and declare the variables to be used in a program, we determine the number of locations the computer allocates to the program. For example, in TYPE IntArray = ARRAY[1..1000] OF integer, the computer sets aside 1000 integer locations for each array of type IntArray declared. If we use more than the limit of 1000 locations in an array of that type, the computer gives us a "subscript out of bounds" message. The method we present in this chapter, on the other hand, allows us to add and delete locations for use in our program as required during execution. Because of this and since the number of these locations is not fixed, we call this process *dynamic allocation.* For multiuser systems such as those used on mainframes, the only limit to this number is the maximum number of locations the operating system can allocate to any program. For microcomputers, it's a large number allocated by the system. By contrast, since the number of locations we use, for instance, for arrays and simple variables is fixed during compilation, this type of storage is called *static allocation.*

The memory locations that can be used dynamically in a program are set aside in an area of memory called the *heap.* For our example, we will use the heap shown in Table 17.1. Each location has an internal numerical address so that the computer can refer to it. We use the word *internal* here because the numbers representing the addresses cannot be used by the Pascal programmer.

								...
100   156

TABLE 17.1. The heap is the part of memory from which the computer dynamically allocates locations while the program is executing. The numbers representing the addresses are not available to the Pascal programmer.

However, in Pascal we can instruct the computer to assign an address of an available location to a type of variable called a *pointer.* The type of pointer used for integer locations is called a *pointer to an integer location;* it is written ^integer, where the caret (^) before integer means "pointer to." Thus we may define the type IntegerPointer as TYPE IntegerPointer = ^Integer. Similarly, in TYPE RealPointer = ^Real, we would define the type Real‒Pointer as a pointer to reals. In fact, we can define a pointer type to any type we want.

The Standard Procedure new

How do we establish the fact that a pointer is a variable? In our first example, we declare Pointer1 and Pointer2 as pointer variables in

VAR Pointer1, Pointer2:IntegerPointer;

as shown in Figure 17.1*a*. However, we have not yet established any association between these variables and the available locations in the heap. How do we associate heap space with a pointer variable? We must use the standard procedure new. When we write new(Pointer1), the address of the first available location in the heap is assigned to Pointer1, as shown in Figure 17.1*a*. The amount of memory allocated to this location depends on the type being used. Since Pointer1 is a pointer to an integer location, the amount of memory space allotted is the same as for an integer. If it were a pointer to a real location, the amount of memory space allotted would be the same as for a real location.

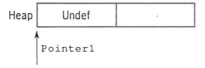

In the diagram, *Undef,* the abbreviation for Undefined, means that the contents are unpredictable since no value has been assigned to that location.

The process of associating a memory location with a pointer by using the new standard procedure is called *allocating a memory location.* In order to store a value, such as 24, in a location, we assign the value to the location indicated by the pointer. The location indicated by Pointer1 is written as Pointer1^, so we write the assignment as

Pointer1^:= 24;

The statement

writeln('Location 1 contains ', Pointer1^);

prints the value stored. Since the address of the integer location is not available to the programmer, you cannot print the value of a pointer. So, for instance, writeln(Pointer1) would cause an error.

In order to store another integer in the next available integer location, we have to associate a pointer with it, so we write new(Pointer2). The effect of this is shown in the figure:

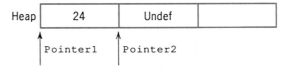

We then store an integer in the location and print it.

In order to store an integer in the next location, we decide to use Pointer1 again, so we write new(Pointer1). The effect of this is shown in the table:

Heap	24	32	Undef

Pointer2   Pointer1   HeapPtr

Pointer1 now points to the third location, that is, the contents of Pointer1 are now the address of the third location. The value, 24, stored in the first location is now lost forever! We assign a value to the third location in Pointer1 := 87 and then print it as shown in Figure 17.1*b*.

If we had not used new (Pointer1) and had just used Pointer1 := 87, we would not have taken another location from the heap, but would simply have stored 87 instead of 24 in the first location:

87	32	Undef

Pointer1   Pointer2

After executed is complete, all the information in the locations is destroyed.

TEST YOURSELF

QUESTION: Given VAR Pointer1, Pointer2: ^Integer, which of the following are incorrect?

1. Pointer1:= 3;
2. Pointer2^:= 4;
3. ^Pointer2:= 19;

ANSWER: (1) is incorrect because you cannot assign a numerical address to a pointer. (3) is incorrect because the caret should follow the pointer, not precede it.

AN INTRODUCTION TO POINTERS

```
PROGRAM Demo1 (input, output);
(* Shows how pointers work *)
TYPE IntPointer = ^Integer;
VAR Pointer1, Pointer2: IntPointer;
```

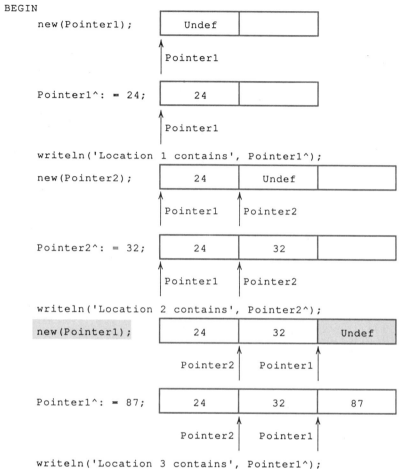

```
BEGIN
    new(Pointer1);
```
Undef

Pointer1

```
    Pointer1^: = 24;
```
24

Pointer1

```
    writeln('Location 1 contains', Pointer1^);
    new(Pointer2);
```
24   Undef

Pointer1   Pointer2

```
    Pointer2^: = 32;
```
24   32

Pointer1   Pointer2

```
    writeln('Location 2 contains', Pointer2^);
    new(Pointer1);
```
24   32   Undef

Pointer2   Pointer1

```
    Pointer1^: = 87;
```
24   32   87

Pointer2   Pointer1

```
    writeln('Location 3 contains', Pointer1^);
END.
```

FIGURE 17.1a. new(Pointer1) allocates a memory location and assigns its address to Pointer1; we refer to this location as Pointer1^. The second time new(Pointer1) is executed, a new memory location is allocated and its address is assigned to Pointer1. The original contents of Pointer1 are no longer accessible.

Location 1 contains 24
Location 2 contains 32
Location 3 contains 87

FIGURE 17.1b. Running the program of Figure 17.1a.

17.2

DETERMINING THE NUMBER OF AVAILABLE LOCATIONS

One way of determining the number of available locations of a given type is to execute new(Pointer1) in a loop a great number of times, for example,

```
FOR J: = 1 TO 1000000 DO BEGIN
    new(Pointer1);
    IF J MOD 1000 = 0 THEN
        write(' J = ',J:6)
END (* FOR J *);
```

Each time new(Pointer1) is executed, the computer moves Pointer1 to the next available location. When no more locations are left, the computer terminates the program and issues an error message such as

```
Error 203: Heap overflow error
```

The last value of J printed will give you the number of available locations truncated to the nearest 1000 for the type for which Pointer1 is an address.

17.3

ASSIGNING POINTERS TO POINTERS

In the program of Figure 17.1c, we again place an integer in the first available location, Pointer1^, but then assign Pointer1 to another pointer, Pointer2, in

```
Pointer2: = Pointer1
```

The computer interprets this as "Place the address of Pointer1 in Pointer2." In reference to our diagrams, it means "Let Pointer2 point to the same location as Pointer1," as shown in Figure 17.1c:

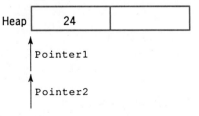

If we now assign a value to Pointer2^, such as Pointer2^: = 50, since Pointer1^ and Pointer2^ point to the same location (contain the same address), the computer places the value in the location pointed to by Pointer1, thus replacing 24.

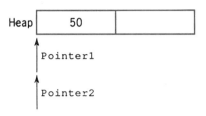

When the computer executes writeln('Location 1 now contains ', Pointer1^), since the contents of Pointer1^ are now 50, the computer prints 50, as expected. Next, the computer executes new(Pointer2) and moves Pointer2 to the next available location. When it executes Pointer2^: = 80, it stores 80 in that location.

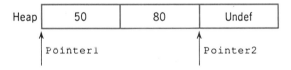

Since Pointer1 and Pointer2 now contain two different addresses, placing 80 in Pointer2 does not change the contents of Pointer1^, so writeln('Location 1 still contains ', Pointer1^) still prints the contents of the first location, namely, 50.

When new(Pointer2) is executed again, the computer moves Pointer2 to the next available location, the contents of which at this point are undefined.

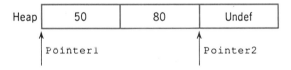

Now when the computer prints the contents of Pointer2^, it prints an unpredictable number, here 0, as shown in Figure 17.1d.

It is illegal to assign a pointer of one type to a pointer of another type. Thus given

```
TYPE IntegerPointer = ^Integer;
    RealPointer = ^Real;
VAR R: RealPointer;
    S: IntegerPointer;
```

writing R: = S causes a syntax error.

ASSIGNING POINTERS TO POINTERS

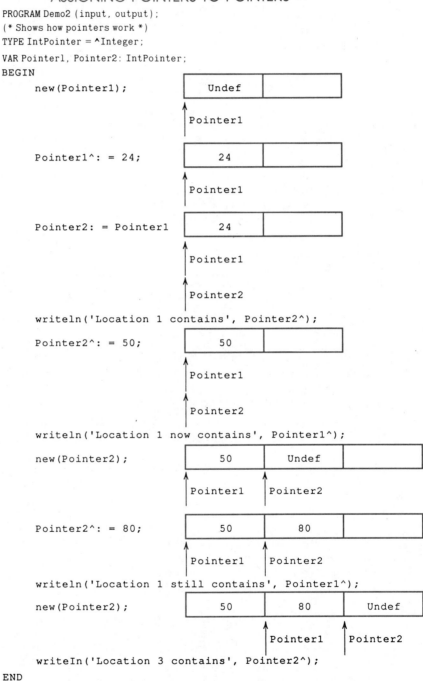

```
PROGRAM Demo2 (input, output);
(* Shows how pointers work *)
TYPE IntPointer = ^Integer;

VAR Pointer1, Pointer2: IntPointer;
BEGIN
        new(Pointer1);


        Pointer1^: = 24;



        Pointer2: = Pointer1





        writeln('Location 1 contains', Pointer2^);

        Pointer2^: = 50;




        writeln('Location 1 now contains', Pointer1^);

        new(Pointer2);



        Pointer2^: = 80;



        writeln('Location 1 still contains', Pointer1^);

        new(Pointer2);



        writeln('Location 3 contains', Pointer2^);

END
```

FIGURE 17.1c. The assignment Pointer2: = Pointer1 means that the address of Pointer1 is copied to Pointer2. So, if we place a value in Pointer2^, we place the same value in Pointer1^.

```
Location 1 contains 24
Location 1 now contains 50
Location 1 still contains 50
Location 3 contains 0
```

FIGURE 17.1d.   Running the program of Figure 17.1a. If we allocate a new location to Pointer2^ and place a value in it, we do not change the contents of Pointer1^.

17.4

PASSING PARAMETERS OF THE POINTER TYPE

Value Parameters

Passing pointers to functions and procedures can have some interesting effects. Let's explore them. Figure 17.2a shows what happens when we pass both value and variable parameters of pointer type to subprograms. In the main program we first establish a location to which Pointer1 points and then store the number 24 there. We next activate procedure One, using Pointer1 as a value parameter. As you remember, when a value parameter is used, two locations are involved—one in the main (or activating) program and one in the subprogram.

The contents of the location in the main program are copied to the location in the subprogram. Thus here, the address stored in Pointer1 is copied to Pointer3. In other words, Pointer1 and Pointer3 point to the same location. So when we write Pointer3^: = 4, it is equivalent to writing Pointer1^:= 4.

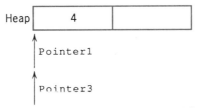

Using the same argument, note that we would get the same result if Pointer3^ were a variable parameter.

When we activate procedure Two in Two(Pointer2), we use Pointer2 as a value parameter. However, Pointer2 does not point to a location, since we have not written new(Pointer2). Therefore, when we activate procedure Two, the undefined address of Pointer2 is copied to Pointer4.

When we associate a location with the corresponding dummy parameter, Pointer4 (for instance, 1064) in new(Pointer4), the contents of Pointer2 still remain undefined

because for value parameters, values are copied only from the main program to the subprogram, and not in the opposite direction. Thus the location pointed to by Pointer4 is not also pointed to by Pointer2. Therefore, this location is local to the procedure. When Pointer4^: = 35 is executed, 35 is stored there.

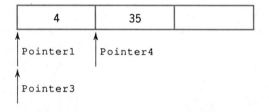

As a consequence, when we print the contents of Pointer2^ in the main program, we get the same unpredictable result that would have occurred if we had printed the contents of Pointer2^ without activating Two (here, 0). On the other hand, if we had tried to print the value of Pointer4^ in the main program, we would have gotten a syntax error, since Pointer4^ is local to Two.

Passing Pointers as Value Parameters   So far, we have seen that if a pointer (here, Pointer1) is a value parameter and has been allocated an address in the main program, its value (the address it points to) is passed to the subprogram. Since the corresponding dummy parameter (Pointer3) points to the same location, this location behaves like a variable parameter; thus Pointer1^ will contain the same value as Pointer3^ after control is returned to the main program. On the other hand, if a pointer (here, Pointer2) has not been allocated an address in the main program, and the corresponding dummy parameter (here, Pointer4) is allocated an address in the subprogram, this address behaves like a value parameter (as it should, since it is one) and cannot be passed to the main program. Consequently, Pointer2^ remains undefined.

The NIL Constant

The only constant you can assign to a pointer is the reserved word NIL. The pointer NIL does not point to any location. If the value of a pointer, for instance Pointer2, is NIL, an execution error will result if we refer to the location to which Pointer2 points—for instance, if we write Pointer2^. In a system that sets all pointer variables to NIL at the beginning of the program, the statement writeln('Location 2 contains ', Pointer2^), where Pointer2 does not yet point to a location, will produce an execution error.

Variable Parameters

When we activate procedure Three in Three(Pointer2), we use Pointer2 as a variable parameter. Thus Pointer2 and the corresponding dummy parameter, Pointer5, will be the identifiers for the same location.

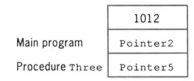

	1012
Main program	Pointer2
Procedure Three	Pointer5

Since they are pointers, they will label the same address. When we assign an address to Pointer5 by writing new(Pointer5) in the procedure, its value (the address of the location to which it points, let's say, 1012) will also be the value of Pointer2. Therefore Pointer2 and Pointer5 point to the same location.

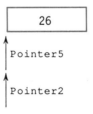

Since we assign 26 to Pointer5^ in the procedure, we can print this value in the main program, as shown in Figure 17.2b, even though we did not include new(Pointer2) there.

DATA STRUCTURE

A *data structure* describes a set of memory locations and how they are related.

POINTERS AS PARAMETERS

```pascal
PROGRAM Demo2;
(* Shows how parameters of pointer types work *)
TYPE IntegerPointer = ^Integer;

VAR Pointer1, Pointer2: IntegerPointer;
PROCEDURE One(Pointer3: IntegerPointer);
(* Stores a new constant in the location indicated by a pointer *)
BEGIN
  Pointer3^: = 4;
END (* ONE *)

PROCEDURE Two(Pointer4: IntegerPointer);
(* Creates a new location using a value parameter *)
BEGIN
  new(Pointer4);
  Pointer4^: = 35;
END (* Two *)

PROCEDURE Three(VAR Pointer5: IntegerPointer);
(* Creates a new location using a variable parameter *)
BEGIN
  new(Pointer5);
  Pointer5^: = 26
END (* Three *);
BEGIN
      new(Pointer1);

      Pointer1^: = 24;
```

24		

↑
Pointer1

```pascal
      One(Pointer1);
```

4		

↑
Pointer1

↑
Pointer3

```pascal
      writeln('Location 1 now contains', Pointer1^);
      Two(Pointer2);
```

4	35	

↑   ↑
Pointer1   Pointer4

↑
Pointer3

```pascal
      writeln('Location 2 contains', Pointer2^);
      Three(Pointer2);
```

4	35	26

↑   ↑   ↑
Pointer1   Pointer4   Pointer5

↑   ↑
Pointer3   Pointer2

```pascal
      writeln('Location 2 now contains', Pointer2^);
END.
```

FIGURE 17.2*a*. When we pass a pointer (`Pointer1`) as a value parameter to a subprogram and store a value in the location pointed to by the corresponding dummy parameter (`Pointer3^`), the same value is stored in the location pointed to by the actual parameter (`Pointer1^`).

```
Location 1 now contains 4
Location 2 contains 0
Location 2 now contains 26
```

FIGURE 17.2*b*. Running the program of Figure 17.2*a*. When we pass a pointer (`Pointer2`) as a variable parameter to a subprogram and create a new location pointed to by the corresponding dummy parameter (`Pointer5^`), the address of this new location are assigned to the actual parameter, and its contents are assigned to the location pointed to by the actual parameter.

17.5

INTRODUCTION TO LINKED LISTS

The strength of pointers is apparent when they are used to represent data structures. A dynamic data structure used instead of an array is called a *linked list.* The components of a linked list are like links in a chain; the links are called *nodes.* In the linked lists we'll study, each node contains some form of data and the address of the next node in the chain. All of this information is represented by a record divided into a *data* field and a *next address* field. An example of a linked list is shown in Table 17.2.

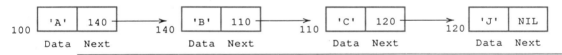

TABLE 17.2. A linked list. The numbers represent addresses of memory locations. A node consists of data (here, a letter) and the address of the next node, both of which are enclosed in this table in rectangles. The address of the first node is 100.

Note again that the numbers representing the addresses are not available to the Pascal programmer; we just show them here for pedagogic purposes.

WHILE YOU ARE READING

Two of the reasons that linked lists are useful are as follows:

1. The implementation we show here uses pointers and therefore makes use of dynamic memory. Thus we do not dimension an array.
2. Linked lists facilitate the insertion in and deletion of data from the list.

The first node in the linked list has the address 100. The data field contains 'A', and the address field contains the address of the next node, 140. The data field in this node contains 'B', and the address of the next node is 110. This process continues until the last node is reached.

How can you test for the end of the linked list? The only constant you can assign to a pointer is the reserved word NIL. You can test for NIL by writing, for instance, IF Ptr1 = NIL THEN. Thus, in order to be able to test for the end of a linked list, we assign NIL to the next address field of the last node. The pointer to the first node will be the one we use to refer to the list.

Since each node is represented by a record, the pointers will be pointers to records. We implement this, as shown in Figure 17.3a, by writing

```
TYPE Pointer = ^Node;
     Node = RECORD
       DataPart: char;
       NextAddress: Pointer
     END (* Node *);
```

The linked list is defined recursively, since the type of NextAddress in the record type Node is a pointer to the record itself. In order for this to be done, Pascal allows the definition of Pointer = ^Node to precede the definition of Node.

The program begins with new(List), where List is declared to be of type Pointer. Therefore List points to records of type Node. In other words, the location List^ is represented by a record of type Node. This means that in order to assign 'A' to the data field, we write List^.DataPart := 'A'. Similarly, the NextAddress field is referred to as List^.NextAddress.

We allocate the next node, calling its pointer Pointer1, store B in its data part, and then link the previous node (whose pointer is List) to it. To do this, we write List^.NextAddress := Pointer1. This is done for all nodes but the last one. For this node, after we assign a value to the data field, we assign NIL to the NextAddress field in Pointer3^.NextAddress := NIL. Note that you do not have to allocate a location before assigning NIL to it. Thus if P is declared a pointer, you do not have to write new(P) before writing P := NIL. If you do, you will lose the memory location allocated when New(P) is executed.

Since List^.NextAddress points to the same location as Pointer1, and Pointer1^.NextAddress points to the same location as Pointer2, then List^.NextAddress^.NextAddress points to the same location as Pointer2.

In order to print the contents of the linked list, we write the following pseudocode:

WHILE *the current address* <> NIL DO BEGIN
   Print the contents of the data field for this address;
   Assign the next address to the current address
END (* WHILE *)

This becomes procedure `Print`, where *Assign the next address to the current address* becomes `CurrentPtr:= CurrentPtr^.NextAddress`.

INTRODUCTION TO LINKED LISTS

```
PROGRAM IntroToPointers1(input, output);
(* Generates and prints a linked list *)
TYPE Pointer = ^Node;
  Node = RECORD
      DataPart: char;
      NextAddress: Pointer
    END (* Node *);
VAR List, Pointer1, Pointer2, Pointer3: Pointer;
PROCEDURE Print(CurrentPtr: Pointer);
(* Prints a linked list *)
BEGIN
  WHILE CurrentPtr <> NIL DO BEGIN
    write( CurrentPtr^.DataPart: 4);
    (* Get the next address *)
    CurrentPtr:= CurrentPtr^.NextAddress
  END (* WHILE *)
END(* Print *);
BEGIN(* main *)
  new(List);
  List^.DataPart:= 'A';
  new(Pointer1);
  Pointer1^.DataPart:= 'B';
  List^.NextAddress:= Pointer1; (* Link with previous node *)
  new(Pointer2);
  Pointer2^.DataPart:= 'C';
  Pointer1^.NextAddress:= Pointer2; (* Link with previous node *)
  new(Pointer3);
  Pointer3^.DataPart:= 'J';
  Pointer2^.NextAddress:= Pointer3; (* Link with previous node *)
  Pointer3^.NextAddress:= NIL; (* Terminate list *)
  writeln('The DataPart in the nodes is:');
  Print(List)
END.
```

FIGURE 17.3*a*.   A linked list is a data structure consisting of nodes. The pointer to each node is the pointer field of the previous node. The type for this field is a pointer (`Pointer = ^Node`) to the record representing the node. The pointer field in the last node points to NIL.

```
The DataPart in the nodes is: A B C J
```

FIGURE 17.3*b*.   Running the program of Figure 17.3*a*. When we print the linked list, we advance the pointer from node to node using `CurrentPtr:= CurrentPtr^.NextAddress`.

The statement Print(List) activates the procedure. Since the actual parameter, List, corresponds to the dummy parameter, CurrentPointer, they both point to the same location, as shown in the table for Figure 17.3a:

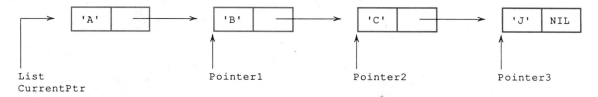

List
CurrentPtr

TABLE FOR FIGURE 17.3a.   When Print is first activated, CurrentPtr and List point to the same address, the beginning of the list.

Thus write(CurrentPtr^.DataPart: 4) prints A. Moreover, the first time CurrentPtr:= CurrentPtr^.NextAddress is executed, it is identical to CurrentPtr:= List^.Nextaddress, so CurrentPointer will point to the next node; List, however still points to the first node, since it is a value parameter:

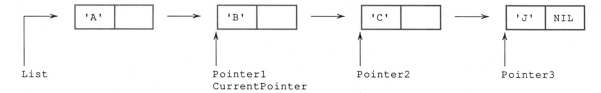

List

This process continues until the entire linked list is printed, as shown in Figure 17.3b. When the value of CurrentPtr is NIL, control is passed back to the main program. The process of running through all the nodes of a list is called *traversing the list*. It is a common practice to refer to a list by the pointer to the first node. Thus we call the linked list in this example List and can now interpret Print(List) to mean "Print the linked list that begins with the pointer List."

PROGRAMMING PITFALL

An error will result if we assign values to P^.DataPart or P^.NextAddress when the value of P is NIL.

TEST YOURSELF

QUESTION: How would you rewrite the statement part of Figure 17.3a so that you use only one pointer?

```
ANSWER:

BEGIN(* main *)
  new(List);
  List^.DataPart:= 'A';
  new(List^.NextAddress); (* Create new node linked with
  previous node *)
  List^.NextAddress^.DataPart:= 'B';
  new(List^.NextAddress^.NextAddress); (* Create new node *)
  List^.NextAddress^.NextAddress^.DataPart:= 'C';
  new(List^.NextAddress^.NextAddress^.NextAddress);
  (* Create new node *)
  List^.NextAddress^.NextAddress^.NextAddress^.DataPart:=
  'J';
  (* Terminate list *)
  List^.NextAddress^.NextAddress^.NextAddress^.
      NextAddress:= NIL;
  writeln('The DataPart in the nodes is:');
  Print(List)
END.
```

17.6

GENERATING A LINKED LIST IN A LOOP

The method used to generate a linked list in the previous program is awkward because it requires three statements per node. Using this method to generate a linked list that has for instance, 10 nodes would require 30 statements. As the next program shows, it's more efficient to generate a linked list using a FOR–DO loop. The data part in each node will contain the value of the loop control variable. The pseudocode is

> *Create the "current node" and set its address to* List;
> *Assign* List *to* CurrentPtr;
> *Store the integer 1 in its data part.*
> FOR *each successive node* DO BEGIN
> 　*Create the node that follows* CurrentPtr;
> 　*Call the newly created node* CurrentPtr;
> 　*Store the next integer in the data part;*
> END (* FOR *);
> *Terminate list;*
> *Print list.*

This becomes the Pascal code shown in Figure 17.4a. The first node is pointed to by CurrentPtr. So we translate *Create the node that follows* CurrentPtr to New(CurrentPtr^.NextAddress). Here we not only create a new node but also link it to the previous node. In order to continue this process in the loop, we must rename this newly created node. Thus we include in the pseudocode *Call the newly created node* CurrentPtr. This translates to CurrentPtr:= CurrentPtr^.NextAddress, that is, the program advances the pointer CurrentPtr by one node. The table for Figure 17.4a shows the linked list produced by the program. The integers are the contents of the data part of the record. Figure 17.4b shows the results of running the program.

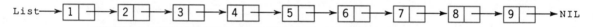

TABLE FOR FIGURE 17.4a.　Shows the linked list produced by the program. The integers are the contents of the data part of the record.

Remember, when you create a linked list using a loop, you must save the pointer to the first node; that is why we assigned this pointer to List. This enables us to use the linked list after we construct it. As an example, Print−(List) instructs the computer to begin printing using the data field of the first node. Had we not saved the pointer to the beginning of the list, the only pointer we could pass to Print would be CurrentPtr.

TEST YOURSELF

QUESTION:　What would Print(CurrentPtr) produce?

ANSWER:　It would print the information in the last node, here 9, since CurrentPtr points to the last node after the linked list is constructed.

GENERATING A LINKED LIST IN A LOOP

```pascal
PROGRAM IntroToPointers2(input, output);
(* Uses a FOR-DO loop to generate and print a linked list *)
(* Uses only two pointer variables *)
TYPE Pointer = ^Node;
    Node = RECORD
            DataPart: integer;
            NextAddress: Pointer
         END (* Node *);
VAR CurrentPtr, List: Pointer;
  J: integer;

PROCEDURE Print(CurrentPtr: Pointer);
(* Prints a linked list *)
BEGIN
    WHILE CurrentPtr <> NIL DO BEGIN
      write( CurrentPtr^.DataPart: 4);
      (* Get the next address *)
      CurrentPtr:= CurrentPtr^.NextAddress
    END (* WHILE *)
END(* Print *);

BEGIN(* main *)
  new(List);
  List^.DataPart:= 1;
  CurrentPtr:= List;
  FOR J:= 2 TO 9 DO BEGIN
    new(CurrentPtr^.NextAddress); (* Link previous node to current node *)
    CurrentPtr:= CurrentPtr^.NextAddress;(* Call present node CurrentPtr *)
    CurrentPtr^.DataPart:= J;
  END (* FOR J *);
  (* Terminate list *)
  CurrentPtr^.NextAddress:= NIL;
  writeln('The DataPart in the nodes is:');
  Print(List)
END.
```

FIGURE 17.4a. First, new(CurrentPtr^.NextAddress) creates a new node and stores its address in CurrentPtr.NextAddress. Then CurrentPtr:= CurrentPtr^.NextAddress renames the address of this newly created node.

```
The DataPart in the nodes is:
  1 2 3 4 5 6 7 8 9
```

FIGURE 17.4b. Running the program of Figure 17.4a. CurrentPtr^.NextAddress:= NIL terminates the list, so that when we traverse the list, we know when to stop.

Value Versus Variable Parameters Revisited In a procedure or function, when a pointer that is a value parameter is advanced to a new location (in Figure 17.4*a*, the next node), the corresponding actual parameter still points to the original node. If, however, the pointer is a variable parameter, the corresponding actual parameter also points to the new location.

TEST YOURSELF

QUESTION:

1. What would happen if we added another `Print(List)` to the end of the main program in Figure 17.4*a*?
2. What would happen if we did this and the formal parameter corresponding to `List` was a variable parameter?

ANSWER:

1. The program would print the linked list again, since `List` still points to the first node.
2. Because `List` is a variable parameter, it ends up pointing to the NIL node. Therefore, the second time `Print` is executed, nothing is printed.

The Linked List as an Abstract Data Concept A linked list doesn't have to be implemented by dynamic pointers; it can be implemented by an array as well. Since the concept is independent of the data structure used, we say that it can be abstracted from the data structure. In more advanced courses, a linked list is defined as a series of definitions independent of any data structure. These definitions are collectively called an *abstract data type*.

Using the WITH with Pointers By using the WITH with pointers, you can eliminate the explicit reference to the pointer. Thus `PreviousPtr^.NextAddress:= CurrentPtr;` can be written as

```
WITH PreviousPtr^ DO
    NextAddress:= CurrentPtr;
```

17.7

GENERATING A LINKED LIST USING DATA READ FROM A FILE

A linked list is more useful if it contains data read from a file. The next program shows how this is done. The top-down diagram is

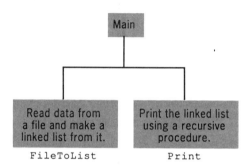

The data in the file are in the form of records for bank depositors and are in the same form as the bank file we used in Chapter 15. Now one of the fields of the record of type Node will itself be a record, so we write

```
TYPE Pointer = ^Node;
   DepRecord = RECORD
      ID, Branch, TypAcct: integer;
      Dep: real
   END; (* DepRecord *)
   Node = RECORD
        DataPart: DepRecord;
        NextAddress: Pointer
   END (* Node *);
RecordFile = FILE OF DepRecord;
```

The pseudocode for FileToList is

```
IF eof(BankFile) THEN BEGIN
  Set List to NIL;
  Write error message
  END (* THEN
ELSE BEGIN
    Create the current node and set its address to List;
    Assign List to CurrentPtr;
    WHILE NOT eof(BankFile) DO BEGIN
      read the customer record from the file;
      Store this record in the data part of the node;
      IF NOT eof THEN BEGIN (* Prevents creating an extra node *)
        Create the node that follows CurrentPointer
        Call the newly created node CurrentPointer
      END (* IF *)
    END (* WHILE *);
    Terminate list;
    Print list.
END.
```

This translates into the procedure shown in Figure 17.5*a*(I). The reason we have used a file for the data is that it saves retyping of all the data each time we test the program.

TEST YOURSELF

QUESTION: What would happen if the program doesn't test for end-of-file in the first IF and the data are such that BankFile begins with an end-of-file?

ANSWER: It creates the node for List; however, List ^. DataPart is undefined because the WHILE loop is not executed. After the WHILE loop is executed, List ^. NextAddress is set to NIL. Thus when the program prints the list, it prints unpredictable results for the contents of the first node, List ^. DataPart, and then terminates. On the other hand, if the program does test for an end-of-file and the file begins with an end-of-file, the program will not print any spurious results. It will simply print "EOF encountered."

The previous printing procedure traversed the linked list using an iterative approach (a WHILE). Let's do it now using recursion. The pseudocode is

GENERATING A LINKED LIST USING DATA READ FROM A FILE

```
TYPE Pointer = ^Node;
  DepRecord = RECORD
    ID, Branch, TypAcct: integer;
    Dep: real
    END; (* DepRecord *)
  Node = record
      DataPart: DepRecord;
      NextAddress: Pointer
    END (* Node *);
  RecordFile = FILE OF DepRecord;
PROCEDURE FileToList(VAR List: Pointer; VAR BankFile:RecordFile);
(* Copies a file to a linked list *)
VAR CurrentPtr: Pointer;
  CustomerRec:DepRecord;
BEGIN
  IF eof(BankFile) THEN
    List:= NIL
  ELSE BEGIN
    new(List);
    CurrentPtr:= List;
    WHILE NOT eof(BankFile) DO BEGIN
      read(BankFile, CustomerRec);
      WITH CustomerRec DO
        writeln(ID:4, Dep:7:2, Branch:2, TypAcct:2 );
      CurrentPtr^.DataPart:= CustomerRec;
      (* Avoids creating an extra node *)
      IF NOT eof(BankFile) then BEGIN
        new(CurrentPtr^.NextAddress);
        (* Link previous node to current node *)
        CurrentPtr:= CurrentPtr^.NextAddress;
      END (* IF *)
    END (* WHILE *);
    (* Terminate list *)
    close(BankFile);
    CurrentPtr^.NextAddress:= NIL
  END (* ELSE *)
END (* FileToList *);
```

FIGURE 17.5a(I). The procedure places each record read from a file in successive nodes of a linked list. The type definitions are also given.

```
PROCEDURE Print(CurrentPtr: Pointer);
(* Prints a linked list *)
BEGIN
  IF CurrentPtr <> NIL THEN BEGIN
    WITH CurrentPtr^.DataPart DO
      writeln(ID:4, Dep:7:2, Branch:2, TypAcct:2);
    (* Print the data part of the next address *)
    Print(CurrentPtr^.NextAddress)
  END (* IF *)
END(* Print *);
```

FIGURE 17.5a(II). Since the actual parameter is `CurrentPtr^.NextAddress` and the dummy parameter is `CurrentPtr`, each time the procedure is activated, the pointer advances one node closer to the end of the list and the data part of that node is printed.

IF *not at the end of the list* DO BEGIN
  Print the contents of the data field for the current node;
  Recursively activate the procedure using the address of the
  next node
END (* IF *)

This translates into the procedure shown in Figure 17.5a(II):

```
PROCEDURE Print(CurrentPtr: Pointer);
BEGIN
    IF CurrentPtr <> NIL THEN BEGIN
        WITH CurrentPtr^.DataPart DO
            writeln(ID:4, Dep:7:2, Branch:2, TypAcct:2);
        Print(CurrentPtr^.NextAddress)
    END (* IF *)
END(* Print *);
```

When the computer prints the results, it traverses the list and activates procedure Print for each successive node. Each time it activates Print, it places the pointer for the current node on top of a stack and prints the contents of the data part of the node. Thus if the linked list looked like

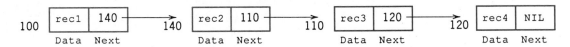

where 100 is the address of List, when the program reaches the end of the list, the stack would appear as shown in Table 17.3.

Stack

TABLE 17.3.   The stack for the pointers when the program reaches the end of the linked list. The importance of these pointers is that they refer to the records representing the nodes.

When CurrentPtr <> NIL is false, the computer returns to the previous activation of the procedure. The pointer at the top of the stack is the address (here, 120) of the node used for that activation of the procedure. If there were any statements to be executed after the recursive activation of Print, they would be executed for the record referred to by that pointer. When the computer returns to the previous activation of the procedure, the pointer at the top is removed and the pointer now at the top is the address (here, 110) of the node used for that activation of the procedure. This process continues until the main program is reached.

The main program is shown in Figure 17.5a(III), and the results of running the program are shown in Figure 17.5b.

From this discussion, it makes sense that the procedure shown in Figure 17.5c would print the linked list backward:

```
PROCEDURE PrintBackwards(CurrentPtr: Pointer);
(* Prints a linked list backward *)
BEGIN
  IF CurrentPtr <> NIL THEN BEGIN
    PrintBackwards(CurrentPtr^.NextAddress);
    WITH CurrentPtr^.DataPart DO
      writeln(ID:4, Dep:7:2, Branch:2, TypAcct:2);
  END (* IF *)
END(* PrintBackward *);
```

Here the program would traverse the linked list until it reached its end. As it returned to the previous activation of the procedure, it would use the pointer at the top of the stack for that activation to print the information in the record for that activation. Thus the last record would be printed first. This process would continue until control is returned to the main program.

TEST YOURSELF

QUESTION: How would you write a recursive procedure to reverse a linked list? If the original linked list discussed is

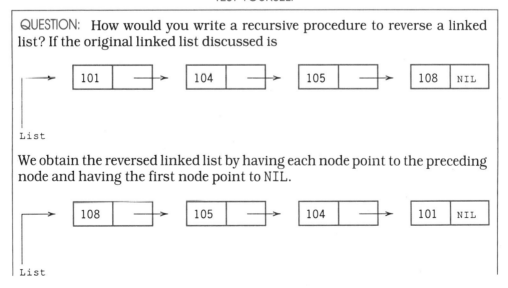

List

We obtain the reversed linked list by having each node point to the preceding node and having the first node point to NIL.

List

ANSWER:

```
PROCEDURE Reverse(Q:Pointer);
(* Recursive procedure to reverse a linked list *)
VAR P:Pointer;
BEGIN
   (* Test for list consisting of only one node with Q = NIL *)
   IF Q <> NIL THEN BEGIN
     IF Q^.Next <> NIL THEN BEGIN
     (* For all but the last node do *)
            P: = Q;
            P: = P^.Next;
            Reverse(P);
            P^.Next: = Q
        END (* IF *)
     ELSE
              List: = Q
   END (* IF Q <> NIL *)
END (* Reverse *);
```

For all but the last node, the following is done:

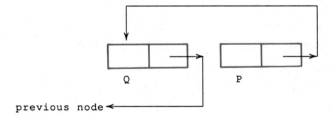

that is, the next node (P) points to the previous node (*Q*), where these pointers are stored at the top of the recursion stack for a given activation of the procedure. In the main program we write

```
P: = List;
Reverse (List);
P^.Next : = NIL
```

```
PROGRAM IntroToPointers3(input, output, RecordFile);
(* Generates and prints a linked list from data read from a file *)
(* Uses only one pointer variable *)
TYPE Pointer = ^Node;
  DepRecord = RECORD
      ID, Branch, TypAcct: integer;
      Dep: real
    END; (* DepRecord *)
  Node = record
      DataPart: DepRecord;
      NextAddress: Pointer
    END (* Node *);
  RecordFile = FILE OF DepRecord;

VAR List: Pointer;
  BankFile: RecordFile;
PROCEDURE Print(CurrentPtr: Pointer);                          {See page 737}
PROCEDURE FileToList(VAR List: Pointer; VAR BankFile:RecordFile);
                                                               {See page 737}
BEGIN (* main *)
  assign(BankFile, 'Bank1.dat');
  reset(BankFile);
  FileToList(List, BankFile);
  writeln('The DataPart in the nodes is:');
  Print(List);
END.
```

FIGURE 17.5a(III).   The main program and the headers indicating where the two procedures should be inserted when the program is run.

```
The data in the file is:
101 23.45 6 4
104 234.56 3 4
105 231.33 4 4
108 ??? 32 3 1
109 876.67 3 3
110 765.44 2 3
111 345.32 4 4
112 345.66 7 8
125 654.39 4 4
The DataPart in the nodes is:
101 23.45 6 4
104 234.56 3 4
105 231.33 4 4
108 222.32 3 4
109 876.67 3 3
110 765.44 2 3
111 345.32 4 4
112 345.66 7 8
125 654.39 4 4
```

FIGURE 17.5b.   Running the program of Figure 17.5a.

PRINTING A LINKED LIST BACKWARD

```
PROCEDURE PrintBackwards(CurrentPtr: Pointer);
(* Prints a linked list backward *)
BEGIN
  IF CurrentPtr <> NIL THEN BEGIN
    PrintBackwards(CurrentPtr^.NextAddress);
    WITH CurrentPtr^.DataPart DO
      writeln(ID:4, Dep:7:2, Branch:2, TypAcct:2);
  END (* IF *)
END(* PrintBackward *);
```

FIGURE 17.5c.   Since the procedure is recursively activated before any printing is done, the last node is the first one printed. After that is done, the procedure is completely executed for the first time; then the previous nodes are successively executed.

17.8

SOLVING A PROBLEM

In the next few sections, we will show the steps in planning a program that uses a linked list to sort records read from a file. The type of sort we will use is called the *insertion sort*. To demonstrate how it works, let's examine a linked list that has the following letters in the data fields of consecutive nodes: H, D, F, C, D, J, and A. Our goal is to create another linked list in which the data parts of consecutive nodes are sorted; that is, the data fields of consecutive nodes would be

A, C, D, D, F, H, J

We start by creating the first node in the sorted linked list and placing the first letter, H, in the data part. The pointer to this list is SortList.

We then take the remaining letters from the original list and insert them, one by one, in their proper place in the linked list SortList. For example, the second letter is placed in a node that precedes the first node:

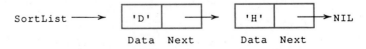

The third letter is placed in a node that is inserted between the first two nodes:

The rest of the letters are inserted in SortList in a similar way.

In the next few sections, we'll be using procedures included in previous programs. Once a procedure has been written in a previous program, we will not present it again in its entirety but will use only its heading.

BEFORE YOU BEGIN

Inserting nodes in a linked list is an ideal way of implementing the insertion sort because of the ease of connecting one node to another. Implementing this sort using an array is much more difficult.

Step I. Inserting a Node in a Linked List

Our first step in planning the program is to write a program to insert a node in a linked list. For instance, if the linked list looked like

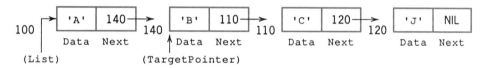

and we wanted to insert a node containing 'F' after the one containing 'B' (we call its pointer TargetPointer) and therefore before the one containing 'C' (its pointer is TargetPointer^.NextAddress), we would allocate a node (we call its pointer NextNode), place 'F' in the data part, and have the next address for this node point to node 110:

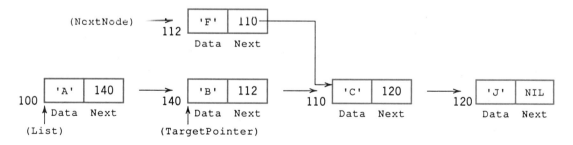

Thus we would write

```
new(NextNode);
NextNode^.DataPart:= 'F';
NextNode^.NextAddress:= TargetPointer^.NextAddress;
```

We would then make node 140 point to this newly created node:

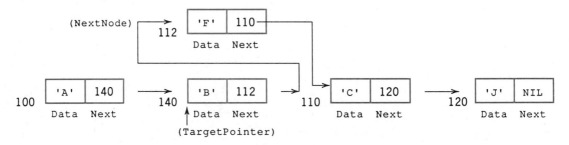

by writing `TargetPointer ^.NextAddress: = NextNode`.

We'll be using the file of bank records to create a linked list, just as we did in the previous program. The procedure that does the insertion, `Insert`, is shown in Figure 17.6a(I). We pass to this procedure two parameters: `TargetPointer` (in the next paragraph, we'll show how we'll determine its value) and the contents of a bank record to be inserted. Since the NIL pointer points to no node, we cannot insert a node after NIL, so we begin the procedure by testing whether `TargetPointer <> NIL` is true. If it is, the program inserts a node; if it is not, the program prints an error message.

Note that since our linked list is set up so that the pointer points only to the next node and not to the previous node, we can only insert a new node after our target node, not before it. To find the pointer for this target node, we must traverse the list until the ID field of the data part of the node matches the account number we type (represented by `Account`). Therefore the pseudocode is

WHILE *not at end of list and ID # has not been found* DO
Advance pointer by one node;

TEST YOURSELF

QUESTION: Why would the following translation of the preceding pseudocode be incorrect, where P is the pointer to a node?

```
WHILE (P <> NIL) AND (P^.DataPart.ID <> Account) DO
    P: = P^.NextAddress;
```

ANSWER: If the account number we type in does not match the ID field of any node, then the final value of P will be NIL. When the WHILE statement is executed for the last time, the value of P will be NIL. If your compiler does not short-circuit boolean expressions, after the computer evaluates P <> NIL and sees that it is false, it will still try to evaluate P^.DataPart.ID. Since the NIL node has no fields, this will lead to an execution error.

In order to avoid an execution error when the required ID is not part of the data part of any node (and therefore the value of P becomes NIL), we translate the WHILE into

```
Found: = False;
WHILE (NOT Found) AND (P <> NIL) DO
    IF P^.DataPart.ID <> Account THEN
        P: = P^.NextAddress
    ELSE
        Found: = True;
GetPointer: = P
```

as shown in function GetPointer; see Figure 17.6a(II). Now if the final value of P is NIL, the expression (NOT Found) AND (P <> NIL) is false; hence the computer does not evaluate P^.DataPart.ID. When the program has found a node with the required account number, then P^.DataPart.ID <> Account is false; consequently the statement P: = P^.NextAddress is not executed, and GetPointer points to the same node that the record with the required ID is in. This pointer is then passed to Insert, where it is used as the target pointer. If the required account number cannot be found, the final value of P will be NIL and thus the value of GetPointer will be NIL. We use the value of the function GetNode as an actual parameter when we activate Insert in Insert(Get-Pointer(List, Account), CustomerRec).

The top-down diagram for the program is:

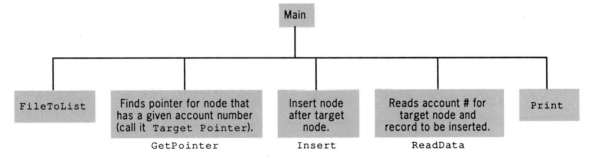

The procedure that reads the ID of the target node and the record to be inserted is shown in Figure 17.6a(III), and the main program is shown in Figure 17.6a(IV).

The results of running the program are shown in Figure 17.6b. We instruct the computer to insert the record 106 342.00 3 4 after the node (our target node) with ID 105. We have designed procedure Insert to insert a node only somewhere after the first node in the list; it will not insert one before the first node. The next program will be able to insert a node at the beginning of the list as well.

INSERTING A NODE IN A LINKED LIST

```
PROCEDURE Insert(TargetPointer: Pointer; CustomerRec:DepRecord);
(* Inserts a node after TargetPointer *)
VAR NextNode, Save: Pointer;
BEGIN
  IF TargetPointer <> NIL THEN BEGIN
      new(NextNode);
      NextNode^.DataPart:= CustomerRec;
      NextNode^.NextAddress:= TargetPointer^.NextAddress;
      TargetPointer^.NextAddress:= NextNode
    END (* THEN *)
  ELSE
      writeln('Your record cannot be found')
END (* Insert *);
```

FIGURE 17.6a(I).   The procedure inserts a node with the pointer NextNode after the node pointed to by TargetNode.

```
FUNCTION GetPointer(P: Pointer; Account:Integer): Pointer;
(* Gets the pointer for a specific record *)
VAR Found: boolean;
BEGIN
  Found:= False;
  WHILE (NOT Found) AND (P <> NIL) DO
    IF P^.DataPart.ID <> Account THEN
      P:= P^.NextAddress
    ELSE
      Found:= True;
  GetPointer:= P
END (* GetPointer *);
```

FIGURE 17.6a(II).   This function returns the pointer to the node containing the record with the required ID. If the ID is not found, the function returns NIL.

```
PROCEDURE ReadData(VAR Recordl:DepRecord; VAR Key: integer);
(* Reads record and where you wish to place it *)
BEGIN
  writeln('What record do you wish to insert');
  WITH Recordl DO
    readln(ID, Dep, Branch, TypAcct);
    writeln('What Account number do you want to insert it after');
    readln(Key)
END (* ReadData *);
```

FIGURE 17.6a(III).   The procedure reads the data for the record to be inserted.

```
PROGRAM IntroToPointers4(input, output, BankFile);
(* Generates and prints a linked list from data read from the list.
   Allows you to insert a record in the linked list *)
USES crt;
TYPE Pointer = ^Node;
   DepRecord = RECORD
        ID, Branch, TypAcct: integer;
        Dep: real
      END; (* DepRecord *)
   Node = record
        DataPart: DepRecord;
        NextAddress: Pointer
        END (* Node *);
      RecordFile = FILE OF DepRecord;
VAR List: Pointer;
   BankFile: RecordFile;
   Account: Integer;
   CustomerRec: DepRecord;
PROCEDURE Print(CurrentPtr: Pointer);                    {See page 737}
PROCEDURE FileToList(VAR List: Pointer; VAR BankFile:RecordFile);
                                                         {See page 737}
PROCEDURE Insert(TargetPointer: Pointer; CustomerRec: DepRecord);
                                                         {See page 746}
FUNCTION GetPointer(P:Pointer; Account:Integer): Pointer; {See page 746}
PROCEDURE ReadData(VAR Recordl:DepRecord; VAR Key: integer);
                                                         {See page 746}

BEGIN (* main *)
   reset(BankFile);
   FileToList(List, BankFile);
   IF List <> NIL THEN BEGIN
     writeln('The DataPart in the nodes is:');
     Print(List);
     ReadData(CustomerRec, Account);
     Insert(GetPointer(List, Account), CustomerRec);
     writeln('The DataPart of the new list is:');
     Print(List)
   END (* THEN *)
   ELSE
     writeln('Empty file encountered')
END.
```

FIGURE 17.6a(IV).   Program inserts a record after a record with a required ID. Note that we use the function GetPointer as a parameter.

```
The DataPart in the nodes is:
101 23.45 6 4
104 234.56 3 4
105 231.33 4 4
108 222.32 3 4
109 876.67 3 3
110 765.44 2 3
111 345.32 4 4
112 345.66 7 8
125 654.39 4 4
What record do you wish to insert
106 342.00 3 4
What Account number do you want to insert it after
105
The DataPart of the new list is:
101 23.45 6 4
104 234.56 3 4
105 231.33 4 4
106 342.00 3 4
108 222.32 3 4
109 876.67 3 3
110 765.44 2 3
111 345.32 4 4
112 345.66 7 8
125 654.39 4 4
```

FIGURE 17.6*b*.   Running the program of Figure 17.6*a*.

Step II. Inserting a Node in a Linked List Sorted on a Key

The next program inserts a record in its proper position in a linked list that is sorted on a key. For instance, if the ID numbers (here the key) in successive nodes of a linked list were 101, 104, 105, 108, 109, 110, 111, 112, 125, the program would insert the record with ID 114 after the node with ID 112. Thus the order of the IDs in the altered list would be 101, 104, 105, 108, 109, 110, 111, 112, 114, 125. If the ID number for a record were 100 or less, the program would place the record at the beginning of the list. What follows is a pictorial example.

If the list looked like

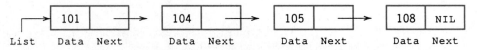

where the numbers represent the ID field, and we wanted to insert a record with an ID of 106, the program would have to traverse the list until it found an ID greater than 106 (here, the node with an ID of 108). The previous node (the one with an ID of 105) would then be the target node. In order to be able to access this previous node, we must use two pointers, where one, Follow, trails the other, Lead, by one node.

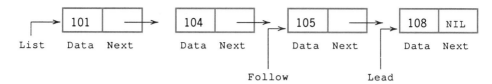

Thus when Lead points to the node containing 108, Follow points to the one containing 105. If Lead ends up pointing to the first node (the one containing 101), Follow must point to no node, so we assign it the value NIL. The pseudocode for this procedure is

> *Assign the address of* List *to* Lead;
> *Assign* NIL *to* Follow;
>> WHILE NOT *at end of list and ID # has not been found* DO BEGIN
>>> *Advance* Follow *by one node;*
>>> *Advance* Lead *by one node*
>> END (* WHILE *);
> IF *insertion must be made before the first node* THEN
>> *Place the new record at the beginning of the list*
> ELSE
>> *Insert the record after the node indicated by* Follow.

The lines *Advance* Follow *by one node* and *Advance* Lead *by one node* become in Pascal

Follow: = Lead;
Lead: = Lead^.NextAddress

First, Follow is positioned so that it points to the same node as Lead; then Lead is advanced one node. Thus they are pointing to two different nodes. Had we reversed the order of the statements, both pointers would point to the same node.

The WHILE becomes

```
Lead: = List;
Follow: = NIL;
Found: = False;
WHILE (NOT Found) AND (Lead <> NIL) DO
    IF Lead^.DataPart.ID < CustomerRec.ID THEN BEGIN
        Follow: = Lead;
        Lead: = Lead^.NextAddress
      END (* THEN *)
    ELSE
    Found: = True;
```

as shown in procedure Position; see Figure 17.7a(I). If the final value of Lead is NIL, the computer quits the WHILE loop, and the value of Follow is the address of the last node on the linked list. Consequently, in Insert(Follow, CustomerRec), the computer inserts the new node at the end of the linked list.

The process *Place the record at the beginning of the list* will be done by procedure Push; its pseudocode begins with

> *Create a new node with pointer* Temp;
> *Store the data in the node's data field;*
> *The* NextAddress *field should point to the beginning of the linked list;*

The process involved is

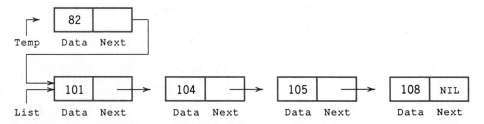

where the value of the ID in the inserted record is 82. In order for List to point to the new node, we conclude the pseudocode with *Change the address of the new node to* List. The resulting linked list is

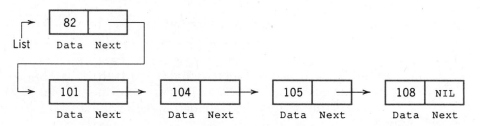

The equivalent Pascal procedure, Push, is shown in Figure 17.7a(II). Since the first node of the linked list is created in this procedure by new(Temp) and its address is assigned to List, the pointer List must be a variable parameter; otherwise, the value of List in procedure Position would be the address of the first node of the original list. We thus write PROCEDURE Push(VAR List: Pointer; CustomerRec: DepRecord). Similarly, in order for this new value of List to be returned to the main program after procedure Position activates Push, the parameter List must also be a variable parameter in the heading for Position, so we write PROCEDURE Position(VAR List: Pointer; CustomerRec: DepRecord).

Procedure ReadData now reads only the record to be inserted, since the program will now find the proper position in which to insert the new node. This procedure and the main program are shown in Figure 17.7b and the results of running the program in Figure 17.7c.

INSERTING A NODE IN A LINKED LIST SORTED ON A KEY

```
PROCEDURE Position(VAR List: Pointer; CustomerRec: DepRecord);
(* Gets pointer for record that has the largest ID less than the inserted ID;
Then inserts the record for the inserted ID in its proper position in
the linked list. Corrects for non-short-circuit boolean expressions *)
VAR Lead, Follow: Pointer;
  Found: boolean;
BEGIN
  Lead:= List;
  Follow:= NIL;
  Found:= False;
  WHILE (NOT Found) AND (Lead <> NIL) DO
    IF Lead^.DataPart.ID < CustomerRec.ID THEN BEGIN
      Follow:= Lead;
      Lead:= Lead^.NextAddress
    END (* THEN *)
  ELSE
    Found:= True;
  IF Follow = NIL THEN (* place record at front of list *)
    Push(List, CustomerRec)
  ELSE (* place record in node after Follow *)
    Insert(Follow, CustomerRec)
END (* Position *);
```

FIGURE 17.7a(I).   The procedure inserts a node in its proper place in a linked list sorted on the ID. The node is inserted after the node that has the greatest ID less than the ID of the inserted node.

```
PROCEDURE Push(VAR List: Pointer; CustomerRec: DepRecord);
(* Inserts a node at the beginning of a list *)
VAR Temp: Pointer;
BEGIN
  new(Temp);
  Temp^.DataPart:= CustomerRec;
  Temp^.NextAddress:= List;
  List:= Temp
END (* Push *);
```

FIGURE 17.7a(II).   The procedure inserts a node at the beginning of the list. It then calls the address of this node, the address of the list.

```pascal
PROGRAM IntroToPointers4(input, output, BankFile);
(* Generates and prints a linked list from data read from the list.
Inserts a record in its proper position in the linked list *)
USES crt;
TYPE Pointer = ^Node;
  DepRecord = RECORD
    ID, Branch, TypAcct: integer;
    (* AcctName: PACKED ARRAY[1..10] OF char; *)
    Dep: real
    END; (* DepRecord *)
  Node = record
       DataPart: DepRecord;
       NextAddress: Pointer
     END (* Node *);
  RecordFile = FILE OF DepRecord;
VAR List: Pointer;
  BankFile: RecordFile;
  Account:Integer;
  CustomerRec: DepRecord;
PROCEDURE Print(CurrentPtr: Pointer);                        {See page 737}
PROCEDURE FileToList(VAR List: Pointer; VAR BankFile:RecordFile);
                                                             {See page 737}
PROCEDURE Insert(TargetPointer: Pointer; CustomerRec: DepRecord);
                                                             {See page 746}
PROCEDURE Push(VAR List: Pointer; CustomerRec: DepRecord);
                                                             {See page 751}
PROCEDURE Position(VAR List: Pointer; CustomerRec: DepRecord);
                                                             {See page 751}
PROCEDURE ReadData(VAR Record1:DepRecord);
(* Reads record and where you wish to place it *)
BEGIN
  writeln('What record do you wish to insert');
  WITH Record1 DO
    readln(ID, Dep, Branch, TypAcct)
END (* ReadData *);
BEGIN (* main *)
  reset(BankFile);
  FileToList(List, BankFile);
  IF List <> THEN BEGIN
     writeln('The DataPart in the nodes is:');
     Print(List);
     ReadData(CustomerRec);
     Position(List, CustomerRec);
     writeln('The DataPart of the new list is:');
     Print(List)
   END (* THEN *)
  ELSE
    writeln('Empty file encountered')
END.
```

FIGURE 17.7b. The procedure ReadData and the main program.

```
The DataPart in the nodes is:
101 23.45 6 4
104 234.56 3 4
105 231.33 4 4
108 222.32 3 4
109 876.67 3 3
110 765.44 2 3
111 345.32 4 4
112 345.66 7 8
125 654.39 4 4
What record do you wish to insert
114 452.00 4 4
The DataPart of the new list is:
101 23.45 6 4
104 234.56 3 4
105 231.33 4 4
108 222.32 3 4
109 876.67 3 3
110 765.44 2 3
111 345.32 4 4
112 345.66 7 8
114 452.00 4 4
125 654.39 4 4
```

FIGURE 17.7c.   Running the program of Figure 17.7b.

17.9

THE PROBLEM SOLVED

Step III. Sorting a Linked List

Now that we've developed pointer procedures to perform an insertion sort on the records in a linked list, let's do the sort. We will sort the records on the ID field. The unsorted linked list, which we will call the *input list,* has ListPtr pointing to the first number; the pointer to the sorted list is SortList. The pseudo-code is

> *Copy the records from the file to linked list* ListPtr;
> *Create the first node for a sorted list with pointer* SortList;
> *Set* NextAddress *field for the first node of* SortList *to NIL;*
> *Copy data from first node of input list to new node;*
> *Advance pointer (*ListPtr*) of input list to next node;*
> WHILE *not at the end of input list* DO BEGIN
> > *Position the copy of the next node of input list in its*
> > *proper place in the sorted list;*
> > *Advance pointer of input list to next node*
> END (* WHILE *);

When we translate this into the Pascal procedure shown in Figure 17.8*a*(I), we also test whether the input list has no nodes. If it does, the program prints an appropriate message, sets SortList to NIL, and returns to the main program. The main program is shown in Figure 17.8*a*(II) and the running of the program in Figure 17.8*b*.

It is important to realize that this problem would have been exceedingly difficult to do if we had not done it in steps.

SORTING A LINKED LIST

```
PROCEDURE Sort(ListPtr: Pointer; VAR SortPtr: Pointer);
(* Sorts a linked list *)
BEGIN
  IF ListPtr <> NIL THEN BEGIN
    new(SortPtr); (Create 1st node of sorted list *)
    SortPtr^.DataPart:= ListPtr^.DataPart;
    SortPtr^.NextAddress:= NIL;
    ListPtr:= ListPtr^.NextAddress; (* Advance input list pointer *)
    WHILE ListPtr <> NIL DO BEGIN
        (* Insert node from input list in its proper place in sorted list *)
        Position(SortPtr, ListPtr^.DataPart);
        ListPtr:= ListPtr^.Next Address
      END (* WHILE *)
    END (* THEN *)
  ELSE BEGIN
      SortPtr:= NIL;
      writeln('Nonsorted list is empty')
    END (* ELSE *)
  END (* Sort *);
```

FIGURE 17.8*a*(I).   The procedure places the copy of the next node of the input list (ListPtr) in its proper place in the sorted list (SortPtr).

```
PROGRAM IntroToPointers6(input, BankFile, output);
(* Generates and prints a linked list from data read from the list. Then it
sorts the linked list *)
TYPE Pointer = ^Node;
  DepRecord = RECORD
    ID, Branch, TypAcct: integer;
    (* AcctName: PACKED ARRAY[1..10] OF char; *)
    Dep: real
    END; (* DepRecord *)
  Node = RECORD
      DataPart: DepRecord;
      NextAddress: Pointer
    END (* Node *);
  RecordFile = FILE OF DepRecord;
VAR List, SortList: Pointer;
  BankFile: RecordFile;
  Account: Integer;
  CustomerRec: DepRecord;
PROCEDURE Print(CurrentPtr: Pointer);                    {See page 737}
PROCEDURE FileToList(VAR List: Pointer; VAR BankFile:RecordFile);
                                                         {See page 737}
PROCEDURE Insert(TargetPointer: Pointer; CustomerRec: DepRecord);
                                                         {See page 746}
PROCEDURE Push(VAR List: Pointer; CustomerRec: DepRecord);    {See page 751}
PROCEDURE Position(VAR List: Pointer; CustomerRec: DepRecord); {See page 751}
PROCEDURE Sort(ListPtr: Pointer; VAR SortPtr: Pointer);      {See page 754}
BEGIN(* main *)
  reset(BankFile);
  FileToList(List, BankFile);
  IF List <> NIL THEN BEGIN
    writeln('The DataPart in the nodes is:');
    Print(List);
    Sort(List, SortList);
    writeln('The DataPart of the sorted list is:');
    Print(SortList);
  END (* THEN *)
ELSE
  writeln('Empty file encountered')
END.
```

FIGURE 17.8a(II).   The main program and the headers for all the subprograms used.

```
108 123.44 4 3
104 453.78 4 4
106 237.90 5 3
103 487.00 4 4
104 877.00 4 3
110 768.00 4 4
101 654.34 5 3
The DataPart in the nodes is:
108 123.44 4 3
104 453.78 4 4
106 237.90 5 3
103 487.00 4 4
104 877.00 4 3
110 768.00 4 4
101 654.34 5 3
The DataPart of the sorted list is:
101 654.34 5 3
103 487.00 4 4
104 877.00 4 3
104 453.78 4 4
106 237.90 5 3
108 123.44 4 3
110 768.00 4 4
```

FIGURE 17.8*b*. Running the program of Figure 17.8*a*.

17.10

STACKS

A stack is a linked list in which insertions and deletions can be made only at the beginning. Before anything is placed on the stack, the value of the pointer Stack is the NIL pointer:

$$Stack \longrightarrow NIL$$

where we use

```
TYPE Pointer = ^Node;
    Node = RECORD
        DataPart: char;
        NextAddress: Pointer
    END (* Node *);
VAR Stack: Pointer;
```

That is, we will be placing characters on the stack. When we add the node containing 'A' to it, we obtain

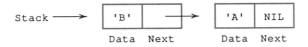

Note that after the node is added, Stack points to the new node. Thus if we add a node containing 'B' to the stack, we obtain

And if we add the node containing 'C' to that, we obtain

Since procedure Push [see Figure 17.7a(II)] inserts nodes at the beginning of a list, we'll use Push to add nodes to a stack.

If we remove a node from the stack, it must be the first node, so that Stack would become

However, all we have done is to advance the pointer, Stack, one node. The node containing 'C' is still part of the list and cannot be used as part of the heap. In order to correct this situation before we advance the Stack pointer, we must first have an auxiliary pointer (let's call it Save) point to the first node on the list:

Then by executing Stack:= Stack^.NextAddress, we advance Stack (but not Save) one node. Then, by writing dispose(Save), we can return the node containing 'C' to the heap, where dispose is a predefined function. The process of removing nodes continues until only NIL remains, that is, Stack ⟶ NIL.

The entire process is akin to stacking and removing trays, or pushing tokens into and removing them from a token holder. For that reason, this type of list is called a *push-down stack*. Also, since the *Last node In* is the *First one Out*, this type of list is called a *LIFO* list.

The action of adding a node to the stack is called *pushing down* on the stack, and the act of removing a node is called *popping* the stack. The next program will use a stack to print an input string backward.

In Figure 17.9a(I) we rewrite procedure Push (originally discussed in Figure 17.7a) so that the DataPart field is of type char; otherwise, it is the same as the version we used earlier. On the other hand, the pseudocode for popping the stack is

IF *the stack is not empty* THEN BEGIN
    Set Character *to the data part of the first node;*
    Save the stack pointer's original position by assigning it
    to the pointer Save;
    Advance the stack pointer to the next node;
    Return the node pointed to by Save *to the heap*
  END (* THEN *)
ELSE
    Print error message

Figure 17.9a(II) shows the procedure Pop, and Figure 17.9a(III) presents the main program. Its pseudocode is

Reads a string of data and places the characters on a stack
    WHILE *the stack is not empty* DO
    Print the character popped from the stack

The results of running the program are shown in Figure 17.9b. The process described here is the same one the computer uses when it translates a recursive procedure that prints a string backward (see Figure 14.1).

The Stack as an Abstract Data Concept   A stack does not have to be implemented by dynamic pointers; it can be implemented by an array as well (see exercises 14 to 21). Since the concept is independent of the data structure used, we say that it can be *abstracted* from the data structure. It is thus another example of an abstract data concept.

STACKS

```
TYPE Pointer = ^Node;
  Node = RECORD
     DataPart: char;
     NextAddress: Pointer
   END (* Node *);
PROCEDURE Push(VAR List: Pointer; Character:char);
(* Inserts a node at the beginning of a list *)
VAR Temp: Pointer;
BEGIN
  new(Temp);
  Temp^.DataPart:= Character;
  Temp^.NextAddress:= List;
  List:= Temp
END (* Push *);
```

FIGURE 17.9a(I). The procedure places characters at the beginning of the list. The pointer to the beginning of the list is renamed List.

```
PROCEDURE Pop(VAR Stack: Pointer; VAR Character: char);
(* Takes the first item from the list *)
VAR Save:Pointer;
BEGIN
  IF Stack <> NIL THEN BEGIN
     Character:= Stack^.DataPart;
     Save:= Stack;
     Stack:= Stack^.NextAddress;
     dispose(Save);
   END (* THEN *)
  ELSE
     writeln('Stack is empty');
END (* Pop *);
```

FIGURE 17.9a(II). The procedure removes the first node on the list. The following node is renamed Stack.

```
PROGRAM IntroToStacks(input, output);
(* Shows how stacks work—will print input in reverse order *)
TYPE Pointer = ^Node;
  Node = RECORD
        DataPart: char;
        NextAddress: Pointer
     END (* Node *);
VAR Stack: Pointer;
Character: char;
PROCEDURE Push(VAR List: Pointer; Character: char);
                                              {See page 759}

PROCEDURE Pop(VAR Stack: Pointer; VAR Character: char);
                                              {See page 759}

BEGIN (* Main *)
  Stack:= NIL;
  (* Place the characters on a line on a stack *)
  writeln(' Type characters on a line');
  WHILE NOT eoln DO BEGIN
    read(Character);
    Push(Stack, Character)
  END (* WHILE *);
  writeln;
  (* Pop characters off the stack *)
  writeln('The characters in reverse order are');
  WHILE Stack <> NIL DO BEGIN
    Pop(Stack, Character);
    write(Character)
  END (* WHILE *)
END.
```

FIGURE 17.9*a*(III).   The main program and the headings for the procedures. The program places incoming characters on the stack. It then removes them and prints them in the order in which they were removed. The first character placed on the stack is the last one removed.

```
Type characters on a line
ABCDEFGHIJKLMNOPQRSTUVWXYZ
The characters in reverse order are
ZYXWVUTSRQPONMLKJIHGFEDCBA
```

FIGURE 17.9*b*.   Runnning the program of Figure 17.9*a*.

CHAPTER REVIEW

Pointers
Before you can assign a value other than NIL to a location pointed to by a pointer, for example, Pointer1^:= 4, you must either

1.   allocate a location, such as execute new(Pointer1), or
2.   assign the pointer to another pointer to a location that has already been

allocated. For example, `Pointer1 := Pointer2`, where `new(Pointer2)` has already been executed.

If you want to assign `NIL` to the location, you do not have to do either of these things.

Passing Pointers to Subprograms

Value Parameters   The address of the actual parameter is assigned to the formal parameter when the subprogram is activated. If the address is changed in the subprogram, the address of the actual parameter is not changed. However, if the contents of the address are changed in the subprogram, they are also changed in the activating program, since both the actual and formal parameters point to the same location.

Variable Parameters   The address of the actual parameter is assigned to the formal parameter when the subprogram is activated. If the address is changed in the subprogram, the address of the actual parameter is also changed. Moreover, if the contents of the address are changed in the subprogram, they are also changed in the activating program.

Linked Lists

Each node in the linked list we studied was structured using the following definition:

```
TYPE Pointer = ^Node;
    Node = RECORD
        DataPart: char;
        NextAddress: Pointer
    END (* Node *);
```

If P points to a node and Q points to the next one, then we link the two by writing `P^.NextAddress := Q`.

Always end a linear linked list with the `NIL` pointer.

Stacks

A stack is a data structure in which information is added at the beginning of the list (in a process similar to pushing coins into a spring-loaded coin holder) and is removed by deleting information from the beginning of the list (in a process similar to removing coins from the coin holder).

NEW TERMS

abstract data type	linked list
data field	next address field
data structure	node
dynamic allocation	pointer
heap	popping a stack
input list	push-down stack
insertion sort	static allocation
LIFO	traversing a list

EXERCISES

1. When the value of the pointer Q is NIL, what can you not do?

2. What does the following produce?

```
VAR Q, P:^integer;
BEGIN
   new(P);
   P^: = 4;
   P: = Q;
   writeln(Q^)
END.
```

3. What does the following produce?

```
VAR P, Q, R:^integer;
BEGIN
   new(P);
   P^: = 4;
   Q: = P;
   R: = P;
   new(R);
   R^: = 5;
   writeln(Q^)
END.
```

4. Explain the difference between passing a pointer as a value or as a variable parameter.

5. What happens in procedure POP [Figure 17.9a(II)] if we exclude the IF statement and therefore do not test for the stack pointer's being NIL?

6. In procedure POP [Figure 17.9a(II)], what is the value of Character if Stack = NIL is true?

Programming Problems

7. Write a program that places each letter of the alphabet in a node of a linked list.

8. Rewrite procedure POP [Figure 17.9a(II)] as a function. What will its value be when Stack = NIL is true? Why does this not create difficulties?

9. Write a program that copies a linked list pointed to by Link1 to a list pointed to by Link2.

10. Write a program that reverses a linked list using iteration.

11. Write a program that copies a linked list such that the copied list is the reverse of the original list.

12. Write a function that returns the pointer to the last node on a list.

13. A doubly linked list is one in which each node is linked to both the next node and the previous node.

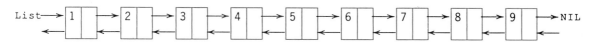

The type used is

$$TYPE\ NodePtr = {}^\wedge NodeType$$
$$NodeType = RECORD$$
$$Data:integer;$$
$$Left,\ Right:NodePtr$$
$$END$$

Given a linked list that is originally linked in one direction, write a program that forms the linkage in the other direction.

Static Pointers

Another way of implementing a linked list is by using an array defined as follows:

```
TYPE Link = 0..100;
   NodeType = RECORD
     Info:real;
     Next:Link
   END (* NodeType *);
VAR Node = ARRAY [1..100] OF NodeType;
   Avail, List, NodeNum:Link;
```

The pointers are now subscripts of NodeArray. Start by constructing a linked list of available nodes (the static analog of the available pool) in which the Next field of the first node is 2, the Next field of the second node is 3, . . . , the Next field of the 99th node is 100. The pointer to the beginning of the available list is Avail, and its value is originally 1. The guts of this is FOR NodeNum:= 1 TO 99 DO Node[Node-Num].Next:= NodeNum + 1. The value of NodeNum of 0 represents the NIL pointer, and the original value of Avail is 1. Each time a node is removed from the available list, Avail:= Node[Avail].Next. By studying the available list, we can see how dynamic pointers are allocated in the available pool.

14. Write a function called GetNode that removes a node from the available list. Note that when all the nodes have been removed, the value of Avail is 0.

15. Write a procedure that forms a linked list for integers read.

16. Write a procedure that inserts a node after node P in the list.

17. Write a procedure called ReturnNode that returns a node, P, to the available list. Hint: Node[P].Next:= Avail and Avail:= P.

18. Write a procedure that deletes the node that follows node P from the list and returns it to the available list.

19. Make several insertions to and deletions from the list, and show the makeup of the available list after each operation.

20. Using the array implementation described in exercise 14, write a procedure that pushes elements onto a stack and a function that pops the stack.

21. Using the array implementation, write a procedure that copies a linked list pointed to by List to one pointed to by ListCopy.

22. Create an available list like the one described in exercise 14, but this time, use dynamic pointers. Write the dynamic allocation equivalents of GetNode and ReturnNode. (Now the pointer will be taken from and returned to the available list you generated). The advantage of this procedure over simply using new and dispose is that in some systems when you use dispose, you cannot recover the pointer later.

23. Write a program that uses a linked list to perform a bubble sort.

24. Write a program that uses a linked list to perform a selection sort.

18

TREES AND QUEUES

CHAPTER OVERVIEW

Have you ever wondered how a program that plays tic-tac-toe was written? Most likely it was written using a data structure called a *tree*, a linked structure whose pictorial representation is two-dimensional. This chapter provides an introduction to trees and to a second data structure, the *queue*. This is a linked list in which insertions are made at the end and deletions at the beginning of the list.

18.1

AN INTRODUCTION TO TREES: TERMINOLOGY

A *tree* is a data structure consisting of linked nodes whose pictorial representation is two-dimensional. The first and highest node is called the *root*. It is linked to its descendants, which are called *children*, as shown in the following diagram, where each *O* represents a node.

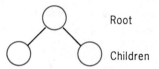

The same terminology used for families is used to describe a tree. As in a family, each child can, in turn, be a parent and have its own descendants. However, each child can have only one parent; this makes recursive traversal of a tree possible. The root is, of course, a parent.

We will discuss trees in which each parent can have at most two descendants. These trees are called *binary trees*. An example is shown in Table 18.1.

A BINARY TREE

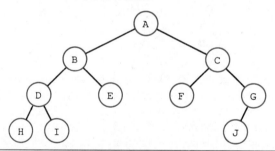

TABLE 18.1.   A binary tree. The tree consists of nodes. The top node (here, A) is called the *root*. The descendants of a node are called *children*. For instance, B and C are the children of A, and A is called the *parent*. A *leaf* is a node with no children. In a binary tree, each node has two descendants.

BEFORE YOU BEGIN

This chapter will show that trees can be used in programs that sort numbers and in ones that evaluate mathematical expressions. Trees can also be used in programs that search lists, in ones that play chess and other games, and in many other applications. So you see that a tree is a very important data structure.

A tree is normally drawn so that the data part stored in each node appears in the circle representing the node. The descendants of each node are called *subtrees*. One of the subtrees in Table 18.1 is

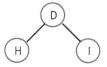

A node that has no children is called a *leaf*. Nodes H, I, E, F, and J are leaves in the tree shown in Table 18.1.

The descendant on the left is called the *left child*, and the one on the right is called the *right child*. Consequently, the following diagram applies to any part of a tree:

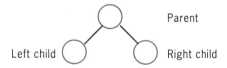

Thus each node of the tree can be defined by

```
TYPE NodePointer = ^Parent;
     Parent = RECORD
       Info: char;
       Left, Right: NodePointer
     END;
```

where Left and Right are the respective pointers to the left child and right child. Since they point to records of type Parent, the definition is recursive. This reflects the fact that each child can itself be a parent. If either of the children does not exist, the corresponding pointer is represented by NIL. Thus the Left and Right fields of a leaf are NIL.

All the nodes that are on the same horizontal line of a tree are in the same generation. Thus in Table 18.1, D, E, F, and G are all in the same generation. If the last generation of a tree has as many nodes as possible for that generation, as in

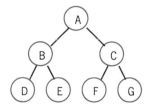

the tree is complete. The following tree, on the other hand, is not complete

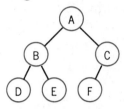

because it lacks the fourth node in the last generation.

The Tree as an Abstract Data Concept   A tree does not have to be implemented by dynamic pointers; it can be implemented by an array as well. Since the concept is independent of the data structure used, we say that it can be *abstracted* from the data structure. It is yet another example of an abstract data concept.

18.2

BUILDING A TREE

Now let's see how to build a tree. We'll place the numbers 12, 8, 7, 15, and 11 in successive nodes of the tree according to the following scheme: The number in the right child will be greater than the number in the parent, and the one in the left child will be less. We begin by placing the first number, 12, in the root. Since the next number, 8, is smaller than the root, we make it the left child (if it were bigger, it would be the right child):

All the other numbers must be compared with the root before they are placed in the proper node. Since the next number, 7, is smaller than the root, we compare it to the left child, 8. Since it is smaller than 8, we make it the left child of 8 (if it were bigger, it would be the right child):

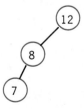

Since the next number, 15, is larger than the root, we make it the right child:

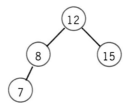

The next number, 11, is smaller than the root but larger than its left child, 8, so we make it the right child of 8. The final tree is shown in Table 18.2. What we have constructed is called a *binary search tree*. The name is derived from the fact that this tree facilitates a binary search (see Chapter 15). When we run the program, if we print the nodes of the tree in a certain order, the numbers will be sorted.

A BINARY SEARCH TREE

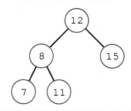

TABLE 18.2. A binary search tree. The left descendants of a node have values less than that of the parent, and the right descendants have values greater than that of the parent.

Now let's write a program that produces this tree. Figure 18.1a(I) shows function SubTree; it produces a node that has no children. Thus the pointers to the left and right children are both NIL. Table I for Figure 18.1a shows the effect of writing Root := SubTree(12); the identifier, Root, becomes the pointer to the root.

BUILDING A BINARY SEARCH NODE BY NODE

```
TYPE NodePointer = ^Parent;
     Parent = RECORD
        Info: integer;
        Left, Right: NodePointer
     END;
FUNCTION SubTree(Symbol: integer): Nodeptr;
(* Creates a tree with a node and two NIL children *)
VAR P: Nodeptr;
BEGIN
  new(P);
  P^.Info:= Symbol;
  P^.Left:= NIL;
  P^.Right:= NIL;
  SubTree:= P
END(* SubTree *);
```

FIGURE 18.1a(I).   Creates a node with two NIL children.

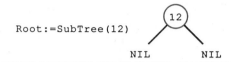

Root:=SubTree(12)

TABLE I FOR FIGURE 18.1a.   The first subtree created by the program and the statement that creates it.

Figure 18.1a(II) shows procedure LeftTree; it inserts a node as the left child for a node specified by a given pointer. If we choose Root as this pointer and write LeftTree(Root, 8), we create a node containing 8 and make this node the left child of the root, as shown in Table II for Figure 18.1a. Thus Root^.Left is no longer NIL.

Table III for Figure 18.1a shows the effect of writing LeftTree(Root − .Left, 7);. This creates a left child for the node that is itself the left child of the root and places 7 in it.

CREATING A LEFT CHILD

```
PROCEDURE LeftTree(P:Nodeptr; Symbol:integer);
(* Inserts a node as the left child for pointer P *)
BEGIN
    P^.Left:= SubTree(Symbol);
END(* LeftTree *);
```

FIGURE 18.1a(II).   Creates a subtree and links it as the left descendant of P.

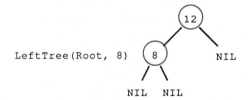

LeftTree(Root, 8)

TABLE II FOR FIGURE 18.1a.   Linking the second node (8) to the root.

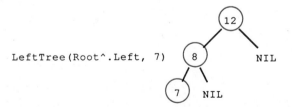

LeftTree(Root^.Left, 7)

TABLE III FOR FIGURE 18.1a.   Linking the third node (7) as the left child of (8).

Figure 18.1a(III) displays procedure RightTree; it inserts a node as the right child for a node specified by a given pointer. In Table IV for Figure 18.1a, we see the effect of writing RightTree(Root, 15). This creates a right child for the root and places 15 in it.

CREATING A RIGHT CHILD

```
PROCEDURE RightTree(P:Nodeptr; Symbol:integer);
(* Inserts a node as the right child for pointer P *)
BEGIN
   P^.Right:= SubTree(Symbol)
END(* RightTree *);
```

FIGURE 18.1a(III). Creates a subtree and links it as the right descendant of P.

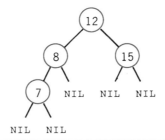

TABLE IV FOR FIGURE 18.1a. Linking the fourth node (15) as the right child of (12).

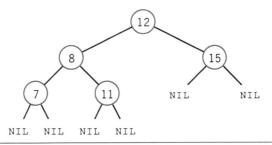

TABLE V FOR FIGURE 18.1a. Linking the fifth node (11) as the right child of (8).

Finally, Table V for Figure 18.1a shows the effect of writing RightTree-(Root^.Left, 11). This creates a right child for the node that is the left child of the root and places 11 in it.

TEST YOURSELF

QUESTION: Why docs LeftTree(Root, 8) link the node containing 8 with the root, even though the formal parameter, P, corresponding to Root is not a VAR parameter?

ANSWER: The actual parameter, Root, and the corresponding formal parameter, P, both point to the same location:

Therefore anything done in procedure LeftTree to the location to which P points is reflected in the activating program. In LeftTree, the statement P^.Left:= SubTree(Symbol) links the new subtree to P and thus to Root. So the tree so far looks like this:

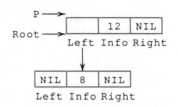

The collection of statements that generated the tree are shown in procedure Generate [see Figure 18.1a(IV)]. We declare Root as a VAR parameter in PROCEDURE Generate(VAR Root:NodePointer) so that the pointer to the root will be returned to the main program.

```
PROCEDURE Generate(VAR Root:NodePointer);
(* Builds a binary search tree with five nodes *)
BEGIN
   Root:= SubTree(12);
   LeftTree(Root, 8);
   LeftTree(Root^.Left, 7);
   RightTree(Root, 15);
   RightTree(Root^.Left, 11)
END (* Generate *);
```

FIGURE 18.1a(IV). The statements manually create a binary search tree.

Traversing the Tree

Figure 18.1a(V) displays a procedure, InTraverse, for traversing a tree, and Table VI for Figure 18.1a shows how it works. At each node of the tree, we have placed an outline of the procedure and have abbreviated InTraverse as InTra so that the many copies of the procedure can fit on the diagram.

```
PROCEDURE InTraversal( Tree:Nodeptr);
(* Prints nodes of a tree in infix order *)
BEGIN
   IF Tree <> NIL THEN BEGIN
      InTraversal(Tree^.Left);
      write( Tree^.Info:3);
      InTraversal(Tree^.Right)
   END (* IF *)
END (* InTraversal *);
```

FIGURE 18.1a(V). Prints the data in the nodes in the form LNR (left child, node, right child).

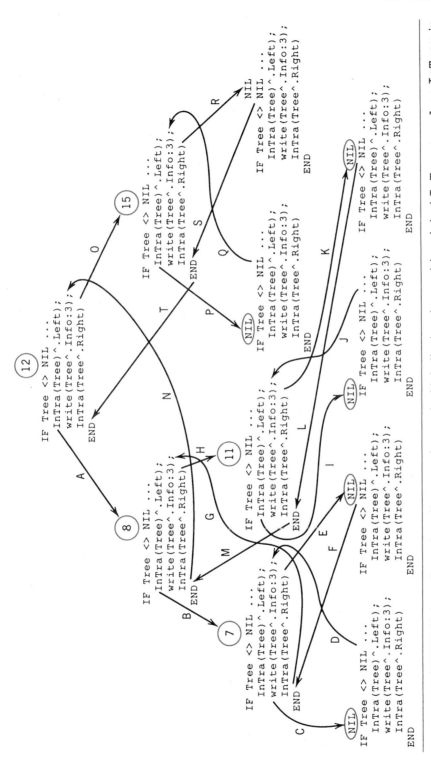

TABLE VI FOR FIGURE 18.1a. Shows how the recursion works. Note that we have abbreviated InTraversal as InTrav in order to fit the procedure into the diagram. The letters indicate the order in which the arrows should be followed. Thus A should be followed first, B second, and so forth.

From our knowledge of recursion we know that for each recursive activation of InTraverse, Pascal places the pointer to the current node on the recursion stack, and when it returns to this activation, it retrieves the pointer by popping the stack. The procedure is originally activated when InTraverse(Tree) is executed in the main program (Figure 18.1b). The pointer to the root of the tree (its Info field is 12) is then sent to the procedure. Since the pointer Tree is not NIL, InTraverse (Tree^.Left) is executed next. Thus we draw an arrow to the IF in the activation of the procedure for the left child. Since the pointer for that node (the Info field is 8) is not NIL, InTraverse(Tree^.Left) is executed next. We draw an arrow to the IF in the activation of the procedure for the next left child (its Info field is 7). Since its pointer is not NIL, InTra-verse(Tree^.Left) is executed next. So we draw an arrow to the IF in the activation of the procedure for the next left child. Since its pointer is NIL, the program backtracks to the previous activation and executes the next state-ment. We draw an arrow up to the write in the previous node. Thus the first value printed is the value in the leftmost node, 7. If a child were allowed to have more than one parent, the program could not backtrack correctly.

Next, InTraverse(Tree^.Right) is executed for the activation for the node containing 7. Since the pointer to the right child is NIL, the activation for the node containing 7 is complete and the program backtracks to the previous activation. We draw an arrow up to the write in the previous node. Thus the 8 is printed. The program next executes InTraverse(Tree^.Right), so we draw an arrow to the right child; it contains 11.

If we continue our analysis, we see that the 11 is printed. Thus the order of printing the nodes in the subtree

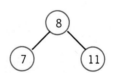

is 7, 8, 11, or left child, node, right child (abbreviated LNR). The position of the node in relation to the children here determines the name used to describe the traversal. When the node is printed between the children, the order is called *inorder*. Continuing our analysis, we see that after this subtree (the left subtree) is printed, the root is printed and then the right subtree (the node containing 15) is printed. Thus the LNR order is maintained, where *L* refers to the left subtree and *R* to the right subtree.

The LNR order in the printing reflects the fact that the printing of the *Node* is sandwiched between the recursive call InTraverse(Tree^.Left), which uses the *Left* subtree, and InTraverse(Tree^.Right), which uses the *Right* subtree. Because the tree is printed using *inorder traversal*, we call this procedure InTraversal.

The running of the program (Figure 18.1c) shows that the numbers in the nodes are printed in sorted order.

```
PROGRAM TreeGenerator(input, output);
(* Generates a binary search tree for restricted data *)
TYPE NodePointer = ^Parent;
  Parent = RECORD
    Info: integer;
    Left, Right: NodePointer
  END;
VAR Tree: NodePointer;
FUNCTION SubTree(Symbol: integer): Nodeptr;        {See page 769}
PROCEDURE LeftTree(P:Nodeptr; Symbol:integer);
                                                    {See page 770}
PROCEDURE RightTree(P:Nodeptr; Symbol:integer);
                                                    {See page 773}
PROCEDURE Generate(VAR Root:NodePointer);          {See page 774}
PROCEDURE InTraversal( Tree:Nodeptr);              {See page 774}
BEGIN (* Main *)
  Generate(Tree);
  writeln(' An inorder traversal of tree yields:');
  InTraversal(Tree)
END.
```

FIGURE 18.1*b*. The main program and the headings of the procedures used.

```
An inorder traversal of tree yields.
7 8 11 12 15
```

FIGURE 18.1*c*. Running the program of Figure 18.1*b*. We see that an inorder traversal of a binary search tree prints the values in sorted order.

TEST YOURSELF

QUESTION: Write a procedure that prints the numbers in the nodes in descending order.

ANSWER: We interchange the two recursive activations. If we rename the procedure Reverse, we obtain

```
PROCEDURE Reverse( Tree:Nodeptr);
(* Prints the nodes of a tree in reverse infix order *)
BEGIN
  IF Tree <> NIL THEN BEGIN
    Reverse(Tree^.Right);
    write( Tree^.Info:3);
    Reverse(Tree^.Left)
  END (* IF *)
END (* Reverse *);
```

There are two other ways of traversing a tree. One way, NLR, is called *preorder* (because the node precedes the children and is thus visited before them); the other, LRN, is called *postorder* because the node follows the children. In Section 18.3, we will see the significance of postorder traversal when we construct a tree for an expression.

18.3

USING A VAR PARAMETER TO CHANGE THE LINKAGE

BEFORE YOU BEGIN

In preparation for our discussion of trees, we show how to eliminate nodes from a linked list and thus change the linkage of such a list.

As shown in the table for Figure 18.2a, the next program takes a linked list consisting of nine nodes in which the data field contains the node number and removes the even-numbered nodes.

We use procedure Build, which is similar to the program of Figure 17.4a, to create a nine-node linked list. The pseudocode for the procedure used to erase the even-numbered nodes is

> *Save the pointer to the current node;*
> *Advance the pointer one node;*
> *Erase the saved node;*
> *Activate the procedure so that it erases the next node.*

This translates into the recursive procedure Erase, which activates itself when Erase(P^.Next) is executed, as shown in Figure 18.2*a*. The procedure is activated from the main program (Figure 18.2*b*) when Erase(List^.Next) is executed. Thus the pointer to the second node is sent to procedure Erase as a VAR parameter. Since the corresponding formal parameter is P, this also points to the second node. When P: = P^.Next is executed, however, P points to the third node on the list. Since P is a VAR parameter, the actual parameter, List^.Next, must now also point to the third node and no longer to the second node. Since originally P is saved in Q and dispose(Q) is executed, the second node is erased.

In general, after Erase(P^.Next) is executed, P^.Next and P^.Next^. Next label the same location. Thus every other node in the list is deleted, as shown in Figure 18.2*c*, when the program is run.

When we build a binary search tree using recursion in the next section, we will use the technique of declaring a pointer a VAR parameter.

ERASING THE EVEN-NUMBERED NODES IN A LINKED LIST

```
TYPE NodePointer = ^NodeType;
     NodeType = RECORD
        Info: integer;
        Next: NodePointer
     END;
PROCEDURE Erase(VAR P:NodePointer);
(* Erases every other node *)
VAR Q: NodePointer;
BEGIN
   IF P <> NIL THEN BEGIN
     Q: = P;
     P: = P^.Next;
     dispose(Q);
     Erase(P^.Next)
   END (* IF *)
END (* Erase *);
```

FIGURE 18.2*a*.   The procedure erases every other node of a linked list. Since the value of P is changed, P must be declared a VAR parameter.

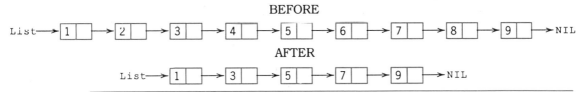

TABLE FOR FIGURE 18.2*a*.   How the linked list appears before and after the even-numbered nodes are erased.

```
PROGRAM EraseEvenNodes(input, output);
(* Generates and prints a linked list *)
(* then produces a linked list of the odd nodes *)
TYPE NodePointer = ^NodeType;
  NodeType = RECORD
    Info: integer;
    Next: NodePointer
  END;
VAR List: NodePointer;
  PROCEDURE Print(CurrentPtr: nodeptr);              {See page 737}
  (* Prints the information in the nodes *)
  PROCEDURE Build(VAR List:NodePointer);             {See Page 733}
  (* Generates a linked list of nine nodes *)
  PROCEDURE Erase(VAR P:NodePointer);                {See page 777}
  (* erases every other node *)
BEGIN (* main *)
  Build(List);
  Erase(List^.Next);
  writeln('The Info in the nodes in the new list is:');
  print(List);
END.
```

FIGURE 18.2*b*.   The main program and the heading of the procedure used.

```
The info in the nodes is:
1 2 3 4 5 6 7 8 9
The info in the nodes in the new list is:
1 3 5 7 9
```

FIGURE 18.2*c*.   Running the program of Figure 18.2*b*.

18.4

GENERATING A BINARY SEARCH TREE

BEFORE YOU BEGIN

When we form a binary search tree, one of the things we can do is to sort the numbers stored in the nodes (or sort records on a key) simply by performing an inorder traversal of the tree.

The pseudocode for creating a binary search tree by recursion is

>   IF *pointer to current node is* NIL THEN
>   *Create a new node with* NIL *descendants*
>   ELSE IF *data read* < *data in current node* THEN
>   *Activate recursively using left child*
>   ELSE
>   *Activate recursively using right child*

where the data read and the pointer to the current node are passed as parameters. This translates into procedure `InsertTree`, shown in Figure 18.3*a*(I). Procedure `BinaryTree`, which reads the data and uses `InsertTree` to place these data in the appropriate nodes of the tree, is shown in Figure 18.3*a*(II). Note that `Tree`, the pointer to the root, is originally set to NIL.

The data for the program are the same as those for Figure 18.1*a*, and the diagrams from Tables I through V for that figure also apply to this program. The first time data are read, since the value of `Tree` is originally NIL, procedure `InsertTree` creates a tree with 12 as the `Info` field for the root and NIL as the values of the left and right children. We see from

```
PROCEDURE InsertTree(VAR Tree:NodePointer; Data:integer)
```

that since `Tree` is a VAR parameter, the new pointer to the tree is passed to `BinaryTree`. Since 8, the next number read, is less than 12, the computer executes `InsertTree(Tree^.Left, Data)`. Since the value of the actual parameter, `Tree^.Left`, is NIL, the corresponding formal parameter, `Tree`, is also NIL, so the computer creates a new node with an `Info` field of 8 in the first recursive call of `InsertTree`. Since `Tree` is a VAR parameter, the new node becomes the left child of the root. Thus the fact that `Tree^.Left` and `Tree^.Right` are both actual VAR parameters enables the computer to link newly created nodes to the tree.

The main program is shown in Figure 18.3*b* and the running of the program in Figure 18.3*c*.

TEST YOURSELF

QUESTION: How does the use of the VAR parameter in the construction of a binary tree differ from its use in the preceding section when we erased even-numbered nodes from a linked list?

ANSWER: In the linked list problem, we declared the pointer to be a VAR parameter because the value of the formal parameter, P, was changed in P : — P^.Next. If it was not a VAR parameter, the original value of P would be used in the activating program. In the recursive binary search problem, we declare `Tree` as a VAR parameter so that when we create a new node in new(`Tree`), its address is passed back to the version of the procedure that activates it.

CREATING A BINARY SEARCH TREE USING RECURSION

```
TYPE NodePointer = ^Parent;
     Parent = RECORD
        info: integer;
        Left, Right: NodePointer
     END;
PROCEDURE InsertTree(VAR Tree:NodePointer; Data:integer);
(* Creates a binary search tree *)
BEGIN
  IF Tree = NIL THEN
    Tree:= SubTree(Data)
  ELSE IF Data < Tree^.Info THEN
    InsertTree(Tree^.Left, Data)
  ELSE
    InsertTree(Tree^.Right, Data)
END (* InsertTree *);
```

FIGURE 18.3*a*(I).   The procedure activates itself for each number read. When it reaches a leaf, it creates a new node. The fact that Tree is a VAR parameter means that the address of the newly created node will be passed back to the activating version of the procedure.

```
PROCEDURE BinaryTree(VAR Tree:NodePointer);
(* Reads data and activates the tree creation procedure *)
VAR Data:integer;
BEGIN
  writeln('Type your numbers on one line');
  Tree:= NIL;
  WHILE NOT eoln DO BEGIN
    read(Data);
    InsertTree(Tree, Data);
  END (* WHILE *);
  readln
END (* BinaryTree *);
```

FIGURE 18.3*a*(II).   Reads numbers and inserts them in a binary tree.

```
PROGRAM Insert(input, output);
(* Uses a recursive procedure to build a binary search tree *)
TYPE NodePointer =  Parent;
  Parent = RECORD
    info: integer;
    Left, Right: NodePointer
  END;
VAR Tree: NodePointer;
PROCEDURE InTraversal( Tree:Nodeptr);                {See page 774}
FUNCTION SubTree(Symbol: integer): Nodeptr;          {See page 769}
PROCEDURE InsertTree(VAR Tree:NodePointer; Data:integer);
                                                     {See page 780}
PROCEDURE BinaryTree(VAR Tree:NodePointer);          {See page 780}
BEGIN (* Main *)
    BinaryTree(Tree);
    writeln('An inorder traversal of the tree yields');
    InTraversal(tree)
END.
```

FIGURE 18.3b.   The main program and the headings of the subprograms used.

```
Type your numbers on one line
12 8 7 15 11
An inorder traversal of the tree yields
7 8 11 12 15
```

FIGURE 18.3c.   Running the program of Figure 18.3b.

18.5

EXPRESSION TREES

Examples of Expression Trees

An *expression tree* is a tree in whose nodes the characters used in an expression are placed so that when the tree is printed in an inorder manner, the original expression without the parentheses is obtained. Examples are shown in Table 18.3. Note that although (3 + 4) * 5 and 3 + (4 * 5) are different and produce different trees, they yield the same inorder expression.

Forming an Inorder Expression from an Expression Tree

The way one visually forms the inorder expression from a tree is as follows: Form the inorder expression from the left subtree, follow this with the node, and then form the inorder expression from the right subtree, that is, form LNR. For both subtrees, do the same, that is, form LNR. For instance, in (d) we originally get 3 + "right tree." When we evaluate the right tree, we get "right tree" − "left tree." When we evaluate "right tree" and "left tree," we get 4 * 5, and 9 + 6, respectively, obtaining the intermediate result (4 * 5) − (9 + 6). Consequently, the entire expression is 3 + 4 * 5 − 9 + 6. The program we present that builds an expression tree requires a *fully parenthesized* expression as data. We now explain how to form such an expression.

Forming a Fully Parenthesized Expression

A fully parenthesized expression is one in which

1. priority is determined only by parentheses and
2. the entire expression is placed in parentheses.

Thus (4 + (5 * 6)) is an example of a fully parenthesized expression. Its value is 34. If we wish to change the priorities, we write ((4 + 5) * 6); its value is 54.

In order to fully parenthesize the expression 4 * 5 + 6 / 7 − (8 + 9), we must first parenthesize the unparenthesized subexpressions that have operators with the highest priorities, here 4 * 5 and 6 / 7. Thus we get (4 * 5) + (6 / 7) − (8 + 9). We then have to indicate the order in which operators that have the next priority should be evaluated, here the "+" and the "−." Thus we write ((4 * 5) + (6 / 7)) − (8 + 9). Finally, we place the entire expression in parentheses, obtaining (((4 * 5) + (6 / 7)) − (8 + 9))

TEST YOURSELF

QUESTION: Fully parenthesize the following, where $ indicates exponentiation:

   a. 3 + 4 $ 5   **b.** 1 + 2 + 3 + 4 * 5   **c.** 3 + 4 * 5 − 9 * 6
   d. 3 − (4 * 5 − 9 * 6)

ANSWER:

a. (3 + (4 $ 5))	**b.** (((1 + 2) + 3) + (4 * 5))
c. ((3 + (4 * 5)) − (9 * 6))	**d.** (3 − ((4 * 5) − (9 * 6)))

EXPRESSION TREES

Expression	Tree	Inorder result
(a) 3 + 4		3 + 4
(b) (3 + 4) * 5		3 + 4 * 5
(c) 3 + (4 * 5)		3 + 4 * 5
(d) 3 + (4 * 5 – (9 + 6))		3 + 4 * 5 – 9 + 6

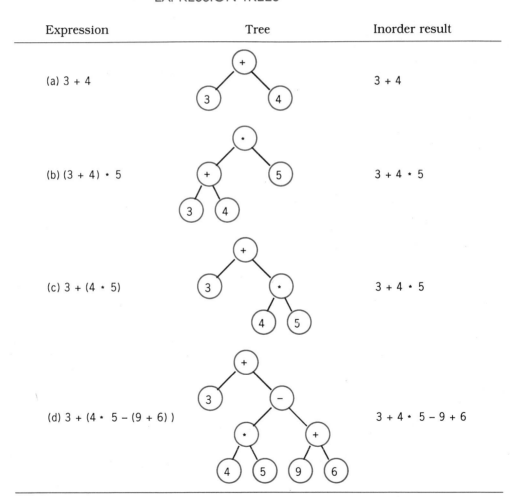

TABLE 18.3. Two different trees may produce the same inorder expression, for example (b) and (c).

18.6

BUILDING AN EXPRESSION TREE

BEFORE YOU BEGIN

Compilers use expression trees to evaluate expressions used in programs. The simplest algorithm for building an expression tree is one that reads a fully parenthesized expression.

The algorithm is as follows:

1. The first time you encounter a left parenthesis, create a node and make it the root. Call this the *current node* and place its pointer on a stack.
2. Every other time you encounter a left parenthesis, create a new node. If the current node does not have a left child, make the new node the left child; otherwise, make it the right child. Make the new node the current node and place its pointer on a stack.
3. When you encounter an operand, create a new node and assign the operand to its data field. If the current node does not have a left child, make the new node the left child; otherwise, make it the right child.
4. When you encounter an operator, pop a pointer from the stack and place the operator in the pointer's node data field.
5. Ignore right parentheses and blanks.

This becomes procedure ExpressionTree, shown in Figure 18.4a(I). It uses the following subprograms: Push, shown in Figure 18.4a(II); Pop, shown in Figure 18.4a(III); Operator, shown in Figure 18.4a(IV); Operand, shown in Figure 18.4a(V); and SubTree, which was shown in Figure 18.1a.

To see how the program works, let's analyze how it treats the expression ((3+2)*(4−5)). The caret indicates the character being processed, and P with the appropriate subscript indicates the pointer to a given node.

((3 + 2) • (4 − 5))
^

P1

P1

((3 + 2) • (4 − 5))
^

P1
P2

P2
P1

((3 + 2) • (4 − 5))
^

P1
3 P2

P2
P1

((3 + 2) • (4 − 5))
^

+ P1
3 P2

P1

((3 + 2) • (4 − 5))
^

+ P1
3 2

P1

((3 + 2) • (4 − 5))
^

•
+ P1
3 2

((3 + 2) • (4 − 5))
^

•
+   P3
3 2

P3

((3 + 2) • (4 − 5))
^

•
+
3 2 4 P3

P3

((3 + 2) • (4 − 5))
^

•
+   −
3 2 4 P3

((3 + 2) • (4 − 5))
^

•
+   −
3 2 4 5

To make our task easier, let's consider input having only single-digit operands, for example, (3*(4+5)); multiple-digit input will produce an incorrect answer. We use two types of pointers: NodePointer, the pointer to the tree, and StackPointer, the pointer to the stack. We have written the program so that it tests for the three most likely errors:

1. Too many left parentheses (then S—its type is StackPointer—will not equal NIL at the end of execution, and Code is set to TooManyLeftParens)

2. Too few left parentheses (then Tree will equal NIL at the end of execution, and Code is set to MissingLeftParens)

3. Illegal characters, for instance, A instead of 3. Then Code is set to BadToken)

where Code is a variable parameter that is passed to the main program. The main program activates procedure ActOnCode, Figure 18.4a(VI), which decides what to do, depending on the value of Code. The main program is shown in Figure 18.4b and the results of running it in Figure 18.4c.

CREATING AN EXPRESSION TREE

```
CONST Blank = ' ';
  LeftParens = ')';
TYPE NodePointer =^Parent;
       Parent = RECORD
           Info:char;
           Right, Left: NodePointer
       END;
       StackPointer = ^Stack;
       Stack = RECORD
         Info: NodePointer;
         Next:StackPointer
       END;
       Error = (OK, MissingLeftParens, TooManyLeftParens, BadToken);
PROCEDURE BinaryExpressTree(VAR Tree:NodePointer; S:StackPointer;
                              VAR Code:Error);
(* Creates a binary expression tree *)
VAR Q, P :NodePointer;
  Token: char;
  FirstNode, Valid: boolean;
PROCEDURE SetRoot(VAR Tree, P: NodePointer);
(* Sets Tree to the root node only the first time it is activated *)
BEGIN
  IF FirstNode THEN BEGIN
    FirstNode:= false;
    Tree:=P
  END (* IF *)
END (* SetRoot *);
```

```
BEGIN(* BinaryExpressTree *)
  Q:= NIL; (* Current node of tree *)
  Valid:= True;
  FirstNode:= true;
  WHILE NOT eoln AND Valid DO BEGIN
        read(Token);
      IF Token = '(' THEN BEGIN
          P:= SubTree(Token);
          SetRoot(Tree, P);
          (* Save node for operator *)
          Push(S, P);
          (* Append node as appropriate child *)
          IF Q <> NIL THEN
              IF Q^.Left = NIL THEN
                Q^.Left:= P
              ELSE
                Q^.Right:= P;
              Q:= P;
          END (* IF Token *)
      ELSE IF Operand (Token) THEN BEGIN
          P:= SubTree(Token);
          (* Append node as appropriate child *)
          IF Q^.Left = NIL THEN
            Q^.Left:= P
          ELSE
            Q^.Right:= P;
          Q:= P;
        END (* IF Operand *)
      ELSE IF Operator( Token ) THEN BEGIN
          (* Place operator in last node placed on stack *)
          Q:= Pop(S);
          IF Q <> NIL THEN
            Q^.Info:= Token
          ELSE
            Tree:= NIL
          END (* IF Operator *)
        ELSE IF (Token <> Blank) AND (Token <> LeftParens) THEN
            Valid:= False
    END (* WHILE *);
  IF Valid THEN
    IF (Tree <> NIL) AND (S = NIL) THEN
      Code:= OK
    ELSE IF Tree = NIL THEN
      Code:= MissingLeftParens
    ELSE
      Code:= TooManyLeftParens
  ELSE (* NOT Valid *)
    Code:= BadToken
END (* BinaryExpressTree *);
```

FIGURE 18.4a(I).   Creates an expression tree for a fully parenthesized expression. A "("
triggers the creation of a node, its linkage to the tree, and placement of its pointer on
a stack. An operand triggers the creation of a node with the operand and its linkage
to the tree. An operator triggers the popping of the stack and the storing of the
operator there.

```
PROCEDURE Push( VAR S:StackPointer; Pointer:NodePointer);
(* Pushes a pointer to a node onto a linked list stack *)
VAR Temp: StackPointer;
BEGIN (* Push *)
  new(Temp);
  Temp^.Info:= Pointer;
  Temp^.Next:= S;
  S:= Temp
END (* Push *);
```

FIGURE 18.4a(II).   The pointer to the node created for a "(" is placed on the stack.

```
FUNCTION Pop( VAR S: StackPointer):NodePointer;
(* Pops a pointer to a node from a linked list stack *)
VAR Save:StackPointer;
BEGIN (* Pop *)
  IF S <> NIL THEN BEGIN
    Pop:= S^.Info;
      Save:= S;
      S:= S^.Next;
      dispose(Save);
    END (* THEN *)
  ELSE BEGIN
      Pop:= NIL;
      writeln('Stack is empty')
    END (* ELSE *)
END (* Pop *);
```

FIGURE 18.4a(III).   The pointer to the node created for a "(" is popped from the stack,
and the operator is stored in the node.

```
FUNCTION Operand (Token: char): boolean;
(* Determines whether or not a token is an operand *)
BEGIN
  Operand:= Token IN ['0'..'9']
END(* Operand *);
```

FIGURE 18.4a(IV).   Determines whether the symbol read is an operand.

```
FUNCTION Operator (Token: char): boolean;
(* Determines whether or not a token is an operator *)
BEGIN
  Operator:= Token IN ['+', '-', '*', '/', '$']
End(* Operator *);
```

FIGURE 18.4a(V).   Determines whether the symbol read is an operator.

```
PROCEDURE ActOnCode(Code:Error);
(* Performs the proper action, depending on the value of Code *)
BEGIN
  CASE Code OF
    OK:  BEGIN
             write('Infix traversal of tree ');
             InTraversal(Tree)
          END (* OK *);
      MissingLeftParens: writeln('Faulty input. Missing at least one "(" ');
      TooManyLeftParens: writeln('Faulty input. Too many "("s ');
      BadToken: writeln('Bad token encountered')
    END (* CASE *)
END (* ActOn Code *);
```

FIGURE 18.4a(VI).   Performs the proper action, depending on the value of Code.

```
PROGRAM Expression(input, output);
(* Creates an expression tree and then prints infix *)
(* Stacks the pointers to operators on a linked list *)
CONST Blank = ' ';
  LeftParens = ')';
TYPE NodePointer = ^Parent;
     Parent = RECORD
          Info:char;
          Right, Left: NodePointer
       END;
     StackPointer = ^Stack;
     Stack = RECORD
        Info: NodePointer;
        Next:StackPointer
       END;
     Error = (OK, MissingLeftParens, TooManyLeftParens, BadToken);
VAR Tree: NodePointer;
  S: StackPointer;
  Code: Error;
```

`FUNCTION Pop( VAR S: StackPointer):NodePointer;`	{See page 788}
`PROCEDURE Push( VAR S:StackPointer; Pointer:NodePointer);`	{See page 788}
`FUNCTION Operand (Token: char): boolean;`	{See page 788}
`FUNCTION Operator (Token: char): boolean;`	{See page 788}
`FUNCTION SubTree(x:char): NodePointer;`	{See page 769}
`PROCEDURE InTraversal( Tree:NodePointer);`	{See page 772}
`PROCEDURE BinaryExpressTree(VAR Tree:NodePointer; S:StackPointer;` `            VAR Code:Error);`	{See page 786}
`PROCEDURE ActOnCode(Code:Error);`	{On this page}

```
BEGIN (* main *)
  S:= NIL; (* Stack *)
  writeln('Type your fully parenthesized expression and then a C.R.');
  BinaryExpressTree(Tree, S, Code);
  ActOnCode(Code)
END.
```

FIGURE 18.4b.   The main program and the headings of the subprograms used.

```
Type your fully-parenthesized expression and then a C.R.
(3+((4*5)-(9/6)))
Infix traversal of tree 3+4*5-9/6
```

FIGURE 18.4c.   Running the program of Figure 18.4b for the input typed.

18.7

EVALUATING AN EXPRESSION TREE

Postorder Traversal

We saw in Table 18.3 (b) and (c) that an inorder traversal for two different trees can give the same result, here, 3 + 4 * 5.

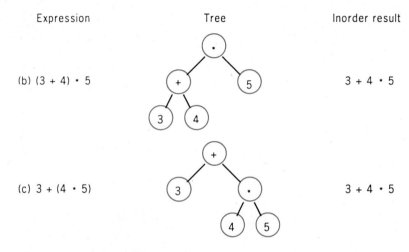

Expression	Tree	Inorder result
(b) (3 + 4) • 5		3 + 4 • 5
(c) 3 + (4 • 5)		3 + 4 • 5

A postorder traversal of the two trees, however, will give two distinct results. Since the postorder is LRN, we evaluate the left subtree, the right subtree, and then the node. LRN for the left subtree in (b) yields 34+. So LRN for the entire tree is 34+5*. Similarly, LRN for the right subtree in (c) is 45*. Therefore LRN for the entire tree is 345*+.

To write a postorder traversal recursive procedure, we must follow the order LRN, so we place the recursive activation for the left subtree and the one for the right subtree before we print the information in the node. Thus procedure PostTraversal appears as shown in Figure 18.5a(I).

```
PROCEDURE PostTraversal( Tree:NodePointer);
(* Postfix traversal of a tree *)
BEGIN
   IF Tree <> NIL THEN BEGIN
     PostTraversal(Tree^.Left);
     PostTraversal(Tree^.Right);
     write( Tree^.Info)
   END (* IF *)
END (* PostTraversal *);
```

FIGURE 18.5a(I). Prints the data in the nodes in the form LRN (left child, right child, node).

Postfix and Infix Expressions

The mathematical expressions we normally write are called *infix* expressions. An example is $3 + 4 * 5 - 9 * 6$ in part (c) of the previous question. The outcome of traversing the resulting expression tree in postorder is called a *postfix* expression. However, you can obtain the postfix expression directly from the infix one. Here's how: First, write the fully parenthesized expression. We did this in part (c) of the answer. It is $((3 + (4 * 5)) - (9 * 6))$. Then rewrite the innermost parenthesized terms so that the operator follows the operands, for example, $(4*5)$ becomes $(4\ 5*)$ and $(9*6)$ becomes $(9\ 6*)$. Thus the expression becomes $((3 + (4\ 5*)) - (9\ 6*))$, where $(4\ 5*)$ and $(9\ 6*)$ are now operands. Do the same to the terms evaluated next, first converting $(3 + (4\ 5*))$ to $3(4\ 5*) +$ until the entire expression is finally in postfix form $3(4\ 5*) + (9\ 6*) -$. Then remove the parentheses, obtaining $3\ 4\ 5\ * + \ 9\ 6\ * -$. Note that the result of traversing an expression tree in preorder (NLR) is called a *prefix* expression.

Performing the Evaluation

Usually, recursive tree subprograms follow one of the three orders, LNR, NLR, or LRN. Which one should you use to evaluate an expression tree? If you look at a simple example

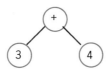

you see that you must evaluate the left subtree (here, 3) and the right subtree (here, 4) before you use the operator in the node to evaluate the expression $3 + 4$. Thus you must use LRN, that is, a postorder traversal.

Table 18.3 shows that the operands in an expression tree are found only in the leaves; the rest of the nodes contain operators. Knowing this, we write the pseudocode for recursively evaluating an expression tree as follows:

> IF *the node is a leaf* THEN
>> (* *encountered an operand* *)
>> *Return to the activating procedure the value of the operand*
>
> ELSE BEGIN (* *encountered a node with an operator* *)
>> *Traverse the left subtree until you hit a leaf and set*
>>> *Operand1 to the value of the operand in the leaf;*
>> *Traverse the right subtree until you hit a leaf and set*
>>> *Operand2 to the value of the operand in the leaf;*
>> *Using Operand1, Operand2 and the operator in the node,*
>>> *evaluate the subtree with the current node as the root*
>
> END

Note that since the two *Traverses* precede the *Using*, this is a postorder traversal. The pseudocode becomes the recursive function Evaluate, shown in Figure 18.5a(II). Since this is a function, the value of the expression is returned as the value of the function and not through an argument. Thus, in order to traverse the left subtree recursively, we write Op1:= Evaluate(P^.Left).

The function is evaluated when

1. an operand is encountered, that is, Evaluate:= ord(P^.Info) – ord('0'), or

2. the calculation involving the operators are performed, for example, '+': Evaluate:= Op1 + Op2;.

Since procedure ActOnCode activates Evaluate, we rewrite this procedure, as shown in Figure 18.5a(III). The main program is the same as the one shown in Figure 18.4b. The running of the program for different sets of data is shown in Figures 18.5b to 18.5d.

The trees for (3 + (4 $ 5)), that is, 3 + 4⁵, and ((3+4)$5), that is, (3 + 4)⁵, produce the same inorder result but different postorder results. Since Evaluate is a postorder function, it produces the correct numerical result for each tree.

If we trace the execution for (3+(4$5)), using the same technique to demonstrate recursion that we used in Table VI for Figure 18.1a, we see that Op1:= Evaluate (P^.Left) is continually evaluated down the left side of the tree

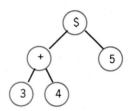

until (P^.Left= NIL) AND (P^.Right = NIL) is true. Then Evaluate and therefore Op1 are 3. Then Op2:= Evaluate(P^.Right) is executed, and the value of Op2 is 4. Next, 3 + 4 is evaluated as 7 and assigned to Evaluate. This is the value assigned to Op1 when Op1:= Evaluate(P^.Left) is evaluated for the root. The value of Op2 when Op2:= Evaluate(P^.Right) is executed is 5. Finally, 7 raised to the fifth power is assigned to Evaluate.

```
FUNCTION Evaluate(P:NodePointer):real;
(* Evaluates an expression tree; operands are stored in leaves *)
VAR Op1, Op2, Product:real;
    J:integer;
BEGIN
   IF (P^.Left= NIL) AND (P^.Right = NIL) THEN
      (* If an operand, then return its value *)
      Evaluate:= ord(P^.Info) - ord('0')
   ELSE BEGIN (* You have hit an operator *)
      Op1:= Evaluate(P^.Left);
      Op2:= Evaluate(P^.Right);
      CASE P^.Info OF
        '+': Evaluate:= Op1 + Op2;
        '-': Evaluate:= Op1 - Op2;
        '*': Evaluate:= Op1 * Op2;
        '/': Evaluate:= Op1 / Op2;
        '$': BEGIN (* Exponential *)
                Product:= 1;
                FOR J:= 1 TO round(Op2) DO
                   Product:= Product * Op1;
                Evaluate:= Product
             END
      END (* CASE *)
   END (* ELSE *)
END (* Evaluate *);
```

FIGURE 18.5a(II).   Translates the expression in the tree into a numerical value by recursively activating itself until it reaches a leaf on the tree. It then stores the value of the operand in the leaf in `Evaluate`. When it backtracks to an operator, it uses the operator's value to evaluate the subtree whose root value is the operator.

```
PROCEDURE ActOnCode(Code:Error);
(* Performs the proper action, depending on the value of Code *)
BEGIN
  CASE Code OF
    OK:   BEGIN
             write('Infix traversal of tree ');
             InTraversal(Tree);
             writeln;
             write('The postfix expression ');
             PostTraversal(Tree);
             write(' evaluated is ', Evaluate(Tree):10:2)
          END (* OK *);
    MissingLeftParens: writeln('Faulty input. Missing at least one "(" ');
    TooManyLeftParens: writeln('Faulty input. Too many "("s ');
    BadToken: writeln('Bad token encountered')
  END (* CASE *)
END (* ActOn Code *);
```

FIGURE 18.5a(III).   The original procedure, Figure 18.4a(VI), is altered so that the tree is evaluated.

```
Type your fully parenthesized expression and then a C.R.
(3+((4*5)-(9/6)))
Infix traversal of tree 3+4*5-9/6
The postfix expression 345*96/-+ evaluated is 21.50
```

FIGURE 18.5b. Running the program of Figure 18.4b using the new ActOnCode and Evaluate.

```
Type your fully parenthesized expression and then a C.R.
(3+(4$5))
Infix traversal of tree 3+4$5
The postfix expression 345$+ evaluated is 1027.00
```

FIGURE 18.5c. Running the program using a new input.

```
Type your fully parenthesized expression and then a C.R.
((3+4)$5)
Infix traversal of tree 3+4$5
The postfix expression 34+5$ evaluated is 16807.00
```

FIGURE 18.5d. Running the program using a slightly altered input.

18.8

DETERMINING THE HEIGHT OF A TREE

The height of a tree is determined by how many generations of descendants it has. Thus the height of a tree consisting of just the root is 0. The height of the tree

is 1, and the height of the tree

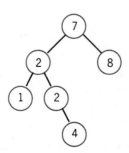

is 3. Finally, if the height of a tree with one node is 0, the height of a tree with no nodes (the pointer is NIL) is -1.

BEFORE YOU BEGIN

Certain operations require knowledge of the height of a tree. In the exercises, we ask you to write a program that displays a tree diagram on the screen. The method we outline there uses a tree's height.

This suggests the following algorithm:

The height of a tree is 1 plus the greater of the heights of its left and right subtrees.

This becomes function Height, shown in Figure 18.6a. The main program is shown in Figure 18.6b and the running of the program in Figure 18.6c.

FINDING THE HEIGHT OF A TREE

```
TYPE NodePointer = ^Parent;
     Parent = record
          info: integer;
          left, right: NodePointer
     END;
FUNCTION Height(T:NodePointer):integer;
(* Determines the height of a tree *)
FUNCTION Max(A, B:integer):integer;
BEGIN
  IF A > B THEN
    Max: = A
  ELSE
    Max: = B
END (* Max *);
BEGIN (* Height *)
  IF T = NIL THEN Height: = −1
  ELSE Height: = 1 + Max(Height(T^.Left), Height(T^.Right))
END (* Height *);
```

FIGURE 18.6a.   A tree's height is the number of generations minus one. This recursive function activates itself down a path in the tree that visits the maximum number of generations.

```
PROGRAM Insert(input, output);
(* Uses a recursive procedure to build a tree.
Creates nodes in procedure. Determines height of tree. *)
TYPE NodePointer =  Parent;
  Parent = record
       info: integer;
       left, right: NodePointer
  END;
VAR Tree: NodePointer;
  Data:integer;
PROCEDURE Intraversal( Tree:Nodeptr);            {See page 774}
FUNCTION Height(T:NodePointer):integer;          {See page 795}
PROCEDURE Insert(VAR Tree:NodePointer; Data:integer);
                                                 {See page 780}
BEGIN(* main *)
    writeln('Type your numbers on one line');
    Tree:= NIL;
    WHILE NOT eoln DO BEGIN
        read(Data);
        Insert(Tree, Data);
    END (* WHILE *);
    writeln('An inorder traversal of the tree yields: ');
    Intrav(tree);
    writeln;
    writeln('The height of the tree is ', Height(Tree) )
END.
```

FIGURE 18.6b.   The main program and the headings of the subprograms used.

```
Type your numbers on one line
15 8 23 3 28 11 9 12
An inorder traversal of the tree yields:
3 8 9 11 12 15 23 28
The height of the tree is 3
```

FIGURE 18.6c.   Running the program of Figure 18.6b.

18.9

QUEUES

In nontechnical English, a *queue* is a line of people waiting to be served. The first person on line is served first, the second one on line is served second, and so forth. A person who gets in line must stand at the end of the line. The queue is a data structure that operates the same way; the first one on the queue is the first one taken off, and new entries are placed at the end of the list.

> Queues allow us to treat processes analogous to people standing in line. For instance, programs waiting to be printed by the printer are placed in a queue.

We'll implement a queue by a linked list that has a pointer to the first node (Front) and one to the last node (Rear). For instance, a queue in which the data part of the nodes in the linked list consists of characters could be represented by:

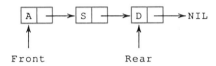

We use

```
Queue = RECORD
    Front, Rear:Pointer
END (* Queue *);
```

to define the type Queue, where Pointer is previously defined, in our case by

```
Pointer = ^Node;
Node = RECORD
    DataPart: char;
    NextAddress: Pointer
END (* Node *);
```

Adding a Node to a Queue

How do you add a node to a queue? You add it to the end of the queue and then advance Rear by one node.

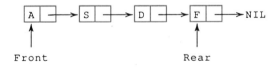

Now let's look at this process in detail. To add a node, we first create it, store the proper information in it, and have it point to NIL:

```
new(Temp);
Temp^.DataPart:= Character;
Temp^.NextAddress:= NIL;
```

Then we link this new node to the rear of the already existing queue by writing Rear^.NextAddress := Temp and advance Rear to the new end of the queue by writing Rear := Temp. If the new node is the first one on the queue, the program doesn't link the node to the rear of the queue but executes Front := Temp instead, thus pointing Front to the beginning of the queue. It must, however, still point Rear to the last node (which in this case is also the first node), so it executes Rear := Temp.

When a queue is empty, Front points to NIL, so we write the function that tests for an empty queue, as shown in Figure 18.7a(I). Using this function, we write procedure Append, which adds a node to a queue, as shown in Figure 18.7a(II).

USING QUEUES

```
TYPE Pointer = ^Node;
     Node = RECORD
            DataPart: char;
            NextAddress: Pointer
     END (* Node *);
     Queue = RECORD
          Front, Rear:Pointer
     END (* Queue *);
FUNCTION Empty(Q: Queue):boolean;
BEGIN
     Empty := Q.Front = NIL
END (* Empty *);
```

FIGURE 18.7a(I).   If the pointer to the first node points to NIL, the queue is empty.

```
PROCEDURE Append(VAR Q: Queue; Character: char);
(* Inserts a node at the end of the queue *)
VAR Temp: Pointer;
BEGIN
   new(Temp);
   Temp^.DataPart := Character;
   Temp^.NextAddress := NIL;
   WITH Q DO BEGIN
     IF Empty(Q) THEN (* Queue is empty, make Temp first node *)
        Front := Temp
     ELSE (* Add Temp to end of queue *)
        Rear^.NextAddress := Temp;
     Rear := Temp (* Rear is always Temp *)
   END (* WITH *)
END (* Append *);
```

FIGURE 18.7a(II).   A new node is placed at the front of the queue if the queue is empty. Otherwise, it is linked to the rear of the queue. The pointer Rear always points to the last node on the queue.

Removing a Node from a Queue

How do you remove a node from a queue? You remove the first node on the queue and advance `Front` by one node:

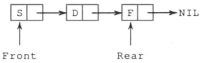

Now let's look at this process in detail. If a queue is not empty, we remove a node by

1. obtaining the character in the first node,
2. saving the pointer to this first node so that we can return it later to the heap,
3. advancing `Front` by one node, and
4. disposing of the pointer to the first node.

We thus write

```
WITH Q DO
    IF NOT Empty(Q) THEN BEGIN
        Character:= Front^.DataPart;
        Save:= Front;
        Front:= Front^.NextAddress;
        dispose(Save);
      END (* THEN *)
    ELSE
        writeln('Queue is empty')
```

as shown in Figure 18.7a(III).

```
PROCEDURE Remove(VAR Q: Queue; VAR Character: char);
(* Removes the front item from the queue *)
VAR Save:Pointer;
BEGIN
  WITH Q DO
   IF NOT Empty(Q) THEN BEGIN
     Character:= Front^.DataPart;
     Save:= Front;
     Front:= Front^.NextAddress;
     dispose(Save);
     END (* THEN *)
   ELSE
     writeln('Queue is empty')
END (* Remove *);
```

FIGURE 18.7a(III). Advances the pointer `Front` one node into the queue and then removes the first node from the queue.

QUESTION: Why is it that when the queue is empty, we don't have to set Rear to NIL in Remove?

ANSWER: In our implementation, when a queue is first formed, procedure Append points Rear and Front to the first node. For this reason, we initialize a queue by setting Front to NIL; we do not have to set Rear to NIL as well. Procedure Append sets Front to NIL in Front : = Front^.NextAddress.

The main program demonstrates the action of procedures Append and Remove to a queue. Its pseudocode is

> *Initialize the queue;*
> WHILE NOT eoln DO
>   *Read a character and place it on the queue;*
> WHILE *the queue is not empty* DO BEGIN
>   *Remove a character from the queue;*
>   *Print the altered queue*
> END (* WHILE *)

The main program is shown in Figure 18.7*b* and the results of running it in Figure 18.7*c*.

The Queue as an Abstract Data Concept   Since a queue can also be implemented by an array, the concept is independent of the data structure used. Since it can be abstracted from the data structure, it is another example of an abstract data concept.

```
PROGRAM IntroToQueues(input, output);
(* Shows how queues work, using Empty function *)
TYPE Pointer = ^Node;
   Node = RECORD
        DataPart: char;
        NextAddress: Pointer
      END (* Node *);
   Queue = RECORD
        Front, Rear:Pointer
      END (* Queue *);
VAR Character: char;
   Q:Queue;
FUNCTION Empty(Q: Queue):boolean;              {See page 799}
PROCEDURE Append(VAR Q: Queue; Character: char);
                                               {See page 800}
PROCEDURE Remove(VAR Q: Queue; VAR Character: char);
                                               {See page 800}
PROCEDURE Print(CurrentPointer: Pointer);      {See page 740}
BEGIN (* Main *)
   WITH Q DO
     Front:= NIL;
     (* Place the characters on a line on a queue *)
   writeln(' Type characters on a line');
   WHILE NOT eoln DO BEGIN
     read(Character);
     Append(Q, Character)
   END (* WHILE *);
   writeln;
   (* Remove characters from the queue *)
   writeln('The characters in line are');
   Print(Q.Front);
   writeln;
   WHILE NOT Empty(Q) DO BEGIN
     Remove(Q, Character);
     write('Remove ', Character, ' and ');
     Print(Q.Front);
     IF Empty(Q) THEN
       writeln(' nothing remains')
     ELSE
       writeln(' remains.')
   END (* WHILE *)
END.
```

FIGURE 18.7*b*. The main program and the headings of the procedures used.

```
Type characters on a line
ASDFG
The characters in line are
   A S D F G
Remove A and S D F G remains.
Remove S and D F G remains.
Remove D and F G remains.
Remove F and G remains.
Remove G and nothing remains
```

FIGURE 18.7*c*. Running the program of Figure 18.7*b*. We see how the queue appears after the front item is removed.

CHAPTER REVIEW

Trees
Terminology used for trees:

Term	Definition
Root	Top node on a tree
Leaf	A node with no children
Child	A left or right descendant of a node
Parent	A predecessor of a child
Generation	The nodes on the same horizontal level
Complete tree	One in which the last generation has every possible node
Height	The number of generations following the root
Binary tree	One in which each node has at most two descendants

A binary search tree is constructed so that the value stored in a parent is greater than the value stored in its left child but less than the one stored in its right child.

An expression tree has all the operands in the corresponding expression stored in the leaves and the operators stored in the other nodes.

The three ways of traversing a tree are

1. inorder (LNR),
2. postorder (LRN), and
3. preorder (NLR)

Queues
In an empty queue, Front points to NIL. When an item is removed from a queue, it is taken from the node to which Front points. Front is then advanced by one node. When an item is added to a queue, the newly created node follows the one to which Rear points, and then Rear is advanced by one node.

NEW TERMS

binary search tree	postfix
binary tree	postorder
child	prefix
expression tree	preorder
fully parenthesized expression	queue
infix	right child
inorder	root
leaf	subtree
left child	tree

EXERCISES

1. Why is List declared as a VAR parameter in procedure Build in Figure 18.2a?

2. Draw the binary search tree obtained from these numbers:
   23, 12, 45, 2, 6 17, 1, 3, 12.

3. Convert the following into postfix form:
   a. $(4 + 5) * (3 - 9)$
   b. $2 * 3 - (4 + (5 - 3) * 6 - 3\$2)$

4. What are the results of inorder, postorder, and preorder traversal of the following binary tree?

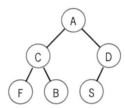

5. Draw a binary tree whose postorder traversal yields the same result as the inorder traversal of the tree in the previous program.

6. Draw the expression tree for each of the following expressions:
   a. $(4 + 5) * (3 - 9)$
   b. $2 * 3 - (4 + (5 - 3) * 6 - 3\$2)$

7. Given

```
TYPE Queue = RECORD
        Front, Rear:Pointer
     END (* Queue *);
```

   what is wrong with IF Q^.Front = NIL THEN?

Programming Exercises

8. Write a procedure to create a binary search tree using iteration and not recursion. It is similar to procedure InsertTree in Figure 18.3a, except that you must now follow one path on the tree (depending on whether the number read is less than or greater than the number in a node on the path) until the value of the pointer is NIL. You then use LeftTree or RightTree.

9. Write a program to create a binary search tree for lowercase letters of the alphabet.

10. Write a program to create a binary search tree using strings consisting of words such that an inorder traversal alphabetizes the words.

In order to test the subprograms you write in exercises 11 to 16, create a binary search tree (Figure 18.3*b*) and pass the pointer to its root to your subprogram.

11. Write a function to convert a tree into its mirror image. Use the recursive procedure with the heading PROCEDURE Switch(VAR L, R: Nodeptr). You must switch the left and right subtrees until you hit the NIL nodes. If one of the descendants is NIL, you must switch the left and right subtrees of the other descendant.

12. Write a procedure to erase a tree and return all of its nodes to the heap. Hint: You must use a postorder traversal. If you don't, you will erase a node before you get to its right child.

13. Write a recursive procedure to count the number of nodes in a tree. Use an inorder traversal, for instance, and substitute a counting statement for the printing statement.

14. Write a recursive procedure that counts the number of times, N, a given number (stored in Key) occurs in a tree. Use the heading PROCEDURE Count(VAR N:integer; Key:integer; Tree:nodeptr). Hint: See the program in exercise 3, but substitute an IF statement for the counting statement.

15. Rewrite the procedure for the previous exercise for a binary tree so that it takes advantage of the structure of a binary tree.

16. Write a procedure that counts the number of leaves in a tree.

17. Using a function, write a program to link each child to a parent in a binary tree. Use

```
FUNCTION Father(Child:NodePointer):NodePointer;
```

18. Write a program to link each child to a parent in a binary tree using PROCEDURE FatherLink(Child, Parent:NodePointer);.

19. Using a procedure, write a program to link each child to a parent in a binary tree using

```
PROCEDURE FatherLink(Child:NodePointer);
```

Bottom-Up Design

The next three exercises constitute a progression that results in a calculator that evaluates expressions according to the priority of the operators "*", "/", "−", and "+".

20. Write a program that uses a stack to evaluate a postfix expression, for example, 3 4 * 5 +, directly. The algorithm is as follows:

1. As you read the expression from left to right, push each operand on the stack (here, 3 and 4) until you encounter an operator (here, "*").

2. Pop the stack twice and perform a calculation, using the operator and the two operands popped (here, 3 * 4, or 12). Push this result (here, 12) on the stack.

We next push 5 on to the stack, and when we encounter the "+", we pop 5 and then 12 from the stack and get 5 + 12, or 17. We then push 17 onto the stack. Since there are no more data, we pop the stack and obtain 17 as the final answer. If during the program we can't pop the stack or there are data remaining on the stack at the end, then our postfix expression is wrong. Hint: Start by writing a program that processes characters in the postfix expression as they are read from the buffer. After that program works, rewrite the main program, using two procedures. The first, which has the heading

```
PROCEDURE ReadString(VAR Stream: StringArray; VAR Count:integer);
```

reads the string representing the postfix expression, places it in the array Stream, and stores the number of characters read in the string in Count. The second, which has the heading

```
PROCEDURE EvaluatePostfix(Stream:StringArray;Count:integer);
```

evaluates the expression, where StringArray is defined in String-Array = ARRAY[1..80] OF char. We will be able to use Evaluate in the final program (exercise 22), which first converts an infix expression to a postfix one and then evaluates the postfix expression.

21. Write a program to convert an infix expression string to a postfix expression string. The algorithm is as follows:

1. As you read the input string from left to right, add each operand to the output string (in 3 * 4 + 5, add 3 to the output string).

2. When you encounter the first operator (here, "*") push it on the stack.

3. Add the next operand to the output string (it is now 3 4).

4. When you encounter the next operator (here, "+"), while the operator on the stack top (here, "*") has a higher or equal precedence to this operator, pop it and add it to the output string (it is now 3 4 *). Push the operator (here, "+") onto the stack.

5. Continue this process until you read the entire input string (in our example, the output string becomes 3 4 * 5).

6. Pop the stack and add the operators to the output string until the stack is empty (the output becomes 3 4 * 5 +).

In order to make steps 2 and 4 consistent, initialize the stack with an arbitrary symbol (for instance, #) that you assign the lowest priority. Then you will be able to place the first operator encountered on the stack. (Note that the stack is empty when the present character is a "#".) The precedence of the operators should be decided in the function Precedence. Thus WHILE in step 4 begins with WHILE Precedence(Top(S), Token) DO BEGIN, where Top determines the character on top of the stack without popping it and Token represents the character just read. The conversion should be done in the procedure that has the heading

```
PROCEDURE InfixToPost(VAR Stream:StringArray; VAR Count:integer);
```

22. Combine the programs for exercises 19 and 21 so that you first convert an infix expression to a postfix one and then evaluate the postfix expression.

23. Write a program that deletes a node from a binary search tree but still maintains the inorder traversal of the tree. The node that should replace the deleted node is the one with the minimum value in the right subtree (it is called the *immediate successor*). For instance, to replace the node containing 14 in

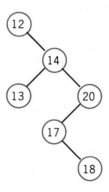

we substitute 17 for it and place 18 in 17's place

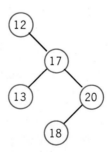

Follow these steps:

1. Write a recursive preorder procedure called Find that finds the required node and then deletes that node. Use the following pseudocode:

```
IF node <> NIL THEN
    IF node is the required one THEN
    Delete the node
ELSE BEGIN
    Find the node by searching the left subtree;
    Find the node by searching the right subtree
END
```

2. Write a procedure, DeleteNode, that deletes the required node. Use the following pseudocode:

```
IF no left child THEN
    Move the right child to the present node
ELSE IF no right child
    Move the left child to the present node
ELSE
    Replace the required node with the immediate successor.
```

The last line of the pseudocode translates into Replace(P, P^.Right), where Replace is given by

```
PROCEDURE Replace(P:NodePtr; VAR Successor:NodePtr);
VAR Temp:NodePtr;
BEGIN
    IF Successor^.Left = NIL THEN {* Find immediate
    successor *} BEGIN
        P^.Info:= Successor^.Info;
        Temp:= Successor;
        Successor:= Successor^.Right;
        Dispose(Temp)
    END (* IF *)
    ELSE Replace(P, Successor^.Left)
END (* Replace *);
```

Bottom-Up Design

The next four exercises constitute a progression resulting in a program that displays the picture of a tree on the screen. In exercises 24 to 27, use an expression tree to test your program.

24. Write a program that prints a complete tree of height $N - 1$ in which an asterisk is stored in each node. Hint: Use the following pseudocode for the recursive procedure Label that produces the tree

IF N *does not equal zero* THEN BEGIN
    Create a height 0 subtree with a blank in the node;
    Activate Label *for the left child, with N − 1;*
    Activate Label *for the right child, with N − 1*
END

25. Write a procedure that labels each node of a tree with the proper generation number. Alter the tree's definition so that Parent contains a Depth field that indicates the generation. Hint: Use the following pseudocode for the recursive procedure Label, which produces the tree

IF *the pointer to the tree does not equal* NIL THEN BEGIN
    Set Depth *to* Level *of the previous generation plus 1;*
    Label the left child;
    Label the right child
END

26. Write a program that completes a tree with subtrees whose nodes store blanks (use @s so that the printed tree can be seen). For instance, if the original tree is

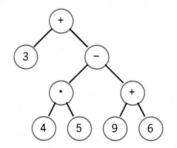

The final tree would be

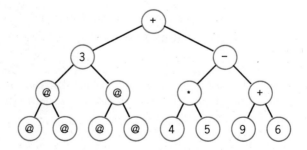

If the depth of a leaf is not the height of the tree, append blank subtrees of the proper height. Hint: In order to print the tree so that the nodes for each successive generation are printed on a new line, use the following pseudocode:

IF *the pointer to the tree does not equal* NIL THEN BEGIN
   IF *depth field equals desired level* THEN
     Print node
   ELSE BEGIN
     Search further for desired level by recursively calling
     procedure for left and right subtrees
END

Don't worry about printing the tree so that it is correctly formatted. Just print each generation on a separate line.

27. Write a program that prints the tree so that it looks like a tree. In order to do this, alter the preceding program so that after it prints an operator or operand, it prints blanks in a variable field width. This field width decreases with each generation.

28. Print the nodes of a tree using a *breadth-first* search, that is, one in which the nodes are visited according to generation. For instance, if the tree is

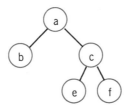

the nodes would be visited in the following order: a, b, c, e, and f. In order to do this, use a queue consisting of pointers to the nodes. Start by placing Pa, the pointer to a, on the queue. Each time you remove a pointer to a node from the queue, add the pointers to the node's left child and right child. Thus, when you remove Pa, add Pb and Pc to the queue. When you remove Pb, add two NIL pointers. If you remove a NIL pointer from the queue, since b is a leaf, don't add anything. Continue this process until the queue is empty.

29. Write a procedure that places increasing numbers in each node of a complete tree of height N. For instance, if N is 2, the tree would be

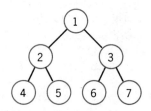

If the father contains K, then the left child contains $2K$ and the right child $2K + 1$.

30. Write a program that produces a binary search tree and places in the NodeNumber field, the node numbers indicated in the program of Exercise 29. Use the following type:

```
TYPE NodePointer = ^NodeType
     NodeType = RECORD
          NodeNumber, Data:integer;
          Left, Right:NodePointer
     END
```

31. Write a procedure that returns the number of nodes in a given generation of a tree.

32. Rewrite the program of Figure 18.4a so that it processes multiple-digit operands.

A
THE MEMORY COMPONENTS OF A MICROCOMPUTER

In a microcomputer, the part of memory into which information is written and from which it is read is called *random access memory (RAM)*. For instance, RAM is used when your program is being processed. Another part of memory is called *read-only memory (ROM)*. Storing information in ROM is an involved process and is normally done in a factory. An example of what is stored in ROM is the program that displays on the screen the characters corresponding to the ones on the keys of the keyboard. Once a program is stored in ROM, it remains there permanently; shutting off the power to the computer does not erase what is in ROM. For this reason, ROM is called *nonvolatile memory*. In contrast, RAM is called *volatile memory* because whatever is stored there is erased when the power is shut off.

A circuit miniaturized on a chip is called an *integrated circuit (IC)*. ROM and RAM are both examples of ICs.

THE RELATIVE EFFICIENCIES OF SORTING AND SEARCHING ALGORITHMS

On a given machine, the amount of time a sort or search requires depends upon the number of elements, N, to be treated and upon the number of comparisons made. The latter, of course, depends on the algorithm you use. You wouldn't want to use one algorithm to sort a large group of numbers if it required much more time than a more efficient algorithm. This appendix describes how to estimate the number of comparisons required for a given algorithm. Our estimates will only be approximate but will still enable us to distinguish between the efficiencies of the different algorithms. Let's start by estimating the number of comparisons for the bubble sort.

Bubble Sort

We'll assume that the number of elements is $N + 1$. In the worst case, the number of comparisons required to place the highest number in its proper position is N. For the second number, it's $N - 1$; for the third number, it's $N - 2$. Summing these numbers, we see that the number of comparisons needed to sort the entire array is $N + (N - 1) + (N - 2) + (N - 3) + \ldots + 1$. But this is the sum of the numbers from 1 to N. As we showed in exercise 17 of Chapter 3, the value of this sum is $N * (N + 1)/2$, or $1/2 (N^2 + N)$. For large numbers this behaves like N^2. Mathematicians state this by saying that this expression is of order N^2 [written as $O(N^2)$ and pronounced "big O of N squared"]. Let's see why it's of order N^2.

The big O approximation allows us to ignore all the constants in an expression, so we ignore the factor $1/2$. What is left is to show that N^2 and $N^2 + N$ behave the same way for large numbers. We'll do this by dividing N^2 by $N^2 + N$ and showing that for large values of N, the quotient is approximately 1. By dividing the numerator and denominator by N^2, we see that

$$N^2 / (N^2 + N) = 1/(1 + 1/N)$$

To evaluate this, it is helpful to set $1/N$ to X so that the right side of the equation becomes $1/(1 + X)$. It's important to know that for small values of X

$$1/(1 + X) = 1 - X$$

You can prove this by multiplying both sides of the equation by $(1 + X)$. The left side equals 1 and the right side equals $(1 - X) * (1 + X)$, which, when multiplied is $1 - X^2$. If N is 50, then X is 0.02 and X^2 is 0.0004; this means that $1 - X^2$ is 0.9996, which is 4 ten thousandth away from 1. So this approximation is quite good. The value of $1 - X$, on the other hand, is 0.96. If N is 1000, the value of $1 - X$ is 0.999. Thus N^2 divided by $N^2 + N$ approaches 1 for large numbers.

The fact that we assumed that there were $N + 1$ instead of N elements doesn't affect the results, since $O((N+1)^2)$ is $O(N^2 + 2N + 1)$. As you remember, we're ignoring all constants and have just shown that $N^2 + N$ behaves like N^2 for large numbers.

It turns out that the approximation of the time required for the average case (where the numbers are randomly distributed in the array) is also N^2. Let's use this result to compare the number of comparisons required to sort an array that has 200 elements versus one that has 20 elements. The 200-element array requires 200^2, or 40,000, comparisons, whereas the 20-element one requires 20^2, or 400. So a 200-element array requires 100 times more comparisons to sort than a 20-element one. We'll show that the quick sort is $O(N \log(N))$ and is thus more efficient for sorting large arrays.

Selection Sort

The estimate for the number of comparisons required in a selection sort is done the same way as for the worst case in a bubble sort. If we look at the nested loop structure

```
FOR N:=1 TO NumElements -1 DO BEGIN
    FOR Index:= N + 1 to NumElements DO
```

we see that the number of comparisons decreases each time the inner loop is executed. So the number of comparisons required is the sum of the numbers from 1 to N, and thus the sort is $O(N^2)$.

Algorithms Whose Efficiency Depends on Log(N)

First, let's review what the term *logarithm* means. *Logarithm* is another name for *exponent*. For instance, in $8 = 2^3$, the logarithm of 8 to the base 2 is 3. This is written as $\log_2 8 = 3$. Whenever an algorithm is structured so that it continuously splits the number of possibilities by one-half, the number of comparisons will depend on the log to the base 2. We'll start by analyzing the quick sort (see exercise 14 of Chapter 15).

Quick Sort

Remember that in the quick sort `First` is the subscript of the element that will eventually be placed in its proper position in the array. Let's examine the case in which the value of `First` is such that when it is in its proper position in the array, there are approximately as many numbers below it as above it. For N equal to 8, this means that there would be four numbers below `First` and four above it (of course, then there would be no room for `First`; however, we can assume that as N becomes large, the approximation that half of the numbers would be below `First` and half above it improves). Again, let's assume that as the sort proceeds, each of the two 4-number groups would be split into two 2-number groups. Since the minimum number of elements needed for a recursive call is two, the recursive call stops here. We can express this diagrammatically as follows:

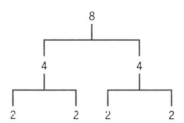

Since the number of comparisons equals the number of items in a group, the number of comparisons would be $8 + (4 + 4) + (2 + 2 + 2 + 2)$, or 24; but this is 8×3 or $8 \times \log_2 8$. The number of levels (here, three) in the diagram indicates the number of times N (here, eight) should be multiplied.

In general, if the number of elements in the original array is $N = 2^M$, then the number of levels in the diagram is M and therefore the number of comparisons is $N \times M$. However, the value of $\log_2(2^M)$ is M. This allows us to write the number of comparisons in terms of one variable, N:

$$N \times \log_2(N)$$

It's interesting to note that the worst case occurs when the array is already sorted. To estimate the number of comparisons, let's first draw the same type of diagram we drew for the previous estimate:

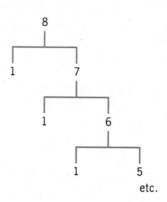

etc.

Since the procedure is not called for one element, the number of comparisons is $8 + 7 + 6 + 5 + 4 + 3 + 2$. This is our old friend, the sum of the integers. So the worst case is $O(N^2)$.

Comparing N Log(N) and N^2 Sorts

If we had 64 items to sort, a bubble or selection sort requires 64^2, or 4096, comparisons. On the other hand, a quick sort requires $64 \times \log_2(64)$ or 64×5 or 320 comparisons, 1/13th the number that the bubble or selection sort requires.

Binary Search

To estimate the number of comparisons a binary search requires, let's assume that the items are distributed in the array such that each time the range is narrowed, it is halved. If there were eight items in the list, then the first halving would produce a sublist of four; the second, a sublist of two; and the final halving, a sublist of one. Thus there would be four halvings. Remember from our discussion of the binary search that only one comparison is made each time the array is narrowed. Since $8 = 2^3$, we see that the number of comparisons (here, four) is one plus the log to the base 2 of N (here, three). This is, of course, the worst case because the program may find the required number before the final halving.

Now let's assume that the number of items in the list is $N = 2^M$. Since we can ignore constants (here, the 1 that's added) in the big O approximation, the time required to find an item in the list is $O(M)$, or $O(\log_2(N))$. The time required for a sequential or linear search, on the other hand, is $O(N)$.

MORE PASCAL STATEMENTS

There is a statement that was incorporated into the original programming languages that is also part of the Pascal syntax but is hardly ever used: the goto statement. It directs the program to go to a part of the program signified by an identifier called a *label*. An example shown in Figure C.1 is IF Switch = 1 THEN GOTO One, where One is the label.

```
PROGRAM ShowGotTo(input, output);
(* Show how labels and GOTOs work *)
LABEL One, 2, 3, Finish;
VAR Switch:integer;
BEGIN
  writeln('Type a digit between 1 and 3');
  readln(Switch);
  IF Switch = 1 THEN GOTO One;
  IF Switch = 2 THEN GOTO 2;
  IF Switch = 3 THEN GOTO 3;
  One: writeln('The input was 1'); GOTO Finish;
  2: writeln('The input was 2'); GOTO Finish;
  3: writeln('The input was 3'); GOTO Finish;
  Finish:
END.
```

FIGURE C.1.

Labels are declared in a LABEL definition and can be either unsigned integers (here, 2 and 3) or, in Turbo Pascal, identifiers (here, One and Finish) as well as unsigned integers. The LABEL definition must precede any other definition or declaration in the program.

In the statement part of the program, LABEL is followed by a ":" and then by the statement or compound statement to be executed. In our program, if GOTO Finish was omitted and One was selected, all the subsequent statements in the program would be executed.

You cannot use a GOTO to transfer into a subprogram, but you can use it to exit one.

INDEX

pas/debug/noopt   program

link/debug   program

r program

BBG) set mode screen